NORTHERN SPAIN

the collected traveler

Also in the series by Barrie Kerper

CENTRAL ITALY
The Collected Traveler

PARIS
The Collected Traveler

PROVENCE
The Collected Traveler

MOROCCO
The Collected Traveler

VENICE
The Collected Traveler

NORTHERN SPAIN

the collected traveler

AN INSPIRED
ANTHOLOGY & TRAVEL
RESOURCE

Collected by Barrie Kerper

Three Rivers Press / NEW YORK

Copyright © 2003 by Barrie Kerper
Additional credits appear on page 613.

Published by Three Rivers Press, New York, New York. Member of the
Crown Publishing Group, a division of Random House, Inc.
www.randomhouse.com

THREE RIVERS PRESS and the Tugboat design are registered trademarks
of Random House, Inc.

Printed in the United States of America

Design by Lynne Amft

Library of Congress Cataloging-in-Publication Data
Northern Spain: an inspired anthology & travel resource / collected
by Barrie Kerper—1st ed. (The collected traveler)
Includes bibliographical references.
1. Spain, Northern—Guidebooks. 2. Travelers' writings. 3. Spain,
Northern—Description and travel—Sources. I. Kerper, Barrie. II. Series.
DP285.N65   2003
914.6'11—dc21   2002044371

ISBN 0-609-80978-4

10 9 8 7 6 5 4 3 2 1

First Edition

For my mother, Phyllis, once again, who has always believed my boxes of files held something of value, and in loving memory of my father, Peter, the most inspiring person in my life, who would so much have enjoyed visiting Spain

acknowledgments

As I have tried to convey in previous editions, publishing a book requires a staggering amount of work by a dedicated team of people. Just a few of the folks at the Crown Publishing Group, with which I am so proud to be associated, who have been so dedicated, creative, and supportive include Al Adams, Alison Gross, Amy Myer, Andrea Rosen, Andy Martin, Becky Cabaza, Bette Graber, Bill Adams, Brian Belfiglio, Doug Jones, Holly Clarfield, James Perry, Jill Flaxman, Joan DeMayo, Kathy Burke, Linda Loewenthal, Maha Khalil, Patty Flynn, Philip Patrick, Rachel Kahan, Rich Romano, Stephanie Fennell, Teresa Nicholas, and Tim Mooney. Publishing friends and colleagues not part of the Random House family who also deserve thanks are Bruce Harris, Bruce Shaw, Jessica Schulte, J. P. Leventhal, and Ronni Berger. Additionally, I am grateful to Alan Mirken, who is a tireless promoter of my little series. As always, special thanks are due to the wise and seasoned art and production team of Amy Boorstein, Derek McNally, Janet Biehl, Lynne Amft, Max Werner, Robin Slutzky, Adam Korn, and Whitney Cookman. Extra special thanks are due to Mark McCauslin, who, with quiet acceptance (or possibly resignation), once again shaped a manuscript with missing text and changes galore into a readable document. I am fortunate indeed to have had the assistance of three hardworking interns, Emily Korn, Mai Bui-Duy, and Wing Mai Sang, who willingly researched and verified hundreds of facts and figures, logged many hours at the New York Public Library, and approached every assignment with zeal. *Muchas gracias* to José Guerra Cabrera, marketing manager at the Spanish Trade Commission in New York, whose enthusiasm for Spain and its cornucopia of fine food and wine is infectious. Everyone at the Tourist Office of Spain in New York has been helpful, kind, and enthusiastic on every occasion that I've visited or called, but special thanks must go to Esther Gomez in public relations, who graciously spoke with me early on in the project, searched through the archives for many of the photographs featured in this book, and patiently answered my many, many questions. I extend my heartfelt thanks to each of the individual writers, agents, and permissions representatives for various publishers and periodicals—especially Leigh Montville of The Condé Nast Publications, Daphne Ben-Ari and Julie Richards of Forbes, and David Seitz of *The New York Times*—without whose cooperation and understanding there would be nothing to publish. I remain deeply grateful to my editor, Shaye Areheart, who continues to amaze me, and Teryn Johnson, who ably assists Shaye and is equally involved in, and enthusiastic about, each of my books; to my publicist, Tim Roethgen, who works so diligently to promote the series; to Chip Gibson, without doubt one of the world's legendary leaders; and finally to my husband, Jeffrey, and our daughter, Alyssa, who is fast becoming a *ciudadana del mundo,* citizen of the world.

contents

El País Vasco

Navarra y La Rioja

¡Buen Provecho!

Mis Favoritos

NORTHERN
SPAIN
the collected traveler

Introduction

"A traveller without knowledge is a bird without wings."
—Sa'di, *Gulistan* (1258)

Some years ago my husband and I fulfilled a dream we'd had since we first met: We put all our belongings in storage and traveled around the countries bordering the Mediterranean Sea for a year. In preparation for this journey, I did what I always do in advance of a trip, which is to consult my home archives, a library of books and periodicals. I have been an obsessive clipper since I was very young, and by the time I was preparing for this extended journey, I had amassed an enormous number of articles from periodicals on various countries of the world. After a year of reading and organizing all this material, I then created a package of articles and notes for each destination and mailed them ahead to friends we'd be staying with as well as appropriate American Express offices—although we had no schedule to speak of, we knew we would spend no less than six weeks in each place.

My husband wasted no time informing me that my research efforts were perhaps a bit over the top. He shares my passion for travel (my mother-in-law told me that when he was little he would announce to the family exactly how many months, weeks, days, hours, minutes, and seconds were left before the annual summer vacation) but not necessarily for clipping. (He has accused me of being too much like the anal-retentive fisherman from an old

Saturday Night Live skit, the one where the guy neatly puts his bait, extra line, snacks, hand towels, and so on into individual sandwich bags. In my defense, I'm not *quite* that bad, although I *am* guilty of trying to improve upon pocket organizers, and I do have a wooden rack for drying rinsed plastic bags in my kitchen.)

While we were traveling that year, we would occasionally meet other Americans, and I was continually amazed at how ill-prepared some of them were. Information, in so many different forms, is in such abundance in the twenty-first century that it was nearly inconceivable to me that people had not taken advantage of the resources available to them. Some people we met didn't even seem to be having a very good time; they appeared to be ignorant of various customs and observances and were generally unimpressed with their experience because they had missed the significance of what they were seeing and doing. Therefore I was surprised again when some of these same people—and they were of varying ages with varying wallet sizes—were genuinely interested in my little packages of notes and articles. Some people even offered to *pay* me for them, and I began to think that my collected research would perhaps appeal to other travelers. I also realized that even the most well-intentioned people could be overwhelmed by the details of organizing a trip or didn't have the time to put it all together. Later friends and colleagues told me they really appreciated the packages I prepared for them, and somewhere along the line I was being referred to as a "modern day hunter-gatherer," a sort of "one-stop information source." Each book in *The Collected Traveler* series provides resources and information to travelers—people I define as inquisitive, individualistic, and indefatigable in their eagerness to explore—or informs them of where they may look further to find it.

While there is much to be said for a freewheeling approach to travel—I am not an advocate of sticking to rigid schedules—I do believe that, as with most things in life, what you get out of a trip is equal only to what you put into it. James Pope-Hennessy, in his wonderful book *Aspects of Provence,* notes that "if one is to get best value out of places visited, some skeletal knowledge of their history is necessary. . . . Sight-seeing is by no means the only object of a journey, but it is as unintelligent as it is lazy not to equip ourselves to understand the sights we see." I feel that learning about a place is part of the excitement of travel, and I wouldn't dream of venturing anywhere without first poring over a mountain of maps, books, and periodicals. I include cookbooks in my reading (some cookbooks reveal much historical detail as well as prepare you for the food and drink you will most likely encounter), and before I leave I also like to watch movies that have something to do with where I'm going. Additionally, I buy a blank journal and fill it with all sorts of notes, reminders, and entire passages from books I'm not bringing along. In other words, I completely immerse myself in my destination before I leave. It's the most enjoyable homework assignment I could ever give myself.

Every destination, new or familiar, merits some attention. I don't endorse the extreme—spending all your time in a hotel room reading books—but it most definitely pays to know something about your destination before you go. Even if you've traveled to Northern Spain before, for pleasure, you still have to do some planning to get there; and if you've traveled there before, on business, you still have to keep up with what's happening in the cities and towns where you meet clients. So the way I see it, you might as well read a little more. The reward for your efforts is that you'll acquire a deeper understanding and appreciation of the place and the people who live there, and not surprisingly, you'll have more fun.

SARRERA ENTRADA
Ikasleak eta Taldeak
Estudiantes y Grupos
017048

"Every land has its own special rhythm, and unless the traveler takes the time to learn the rhythm, he or she will remain an outsider there always."
—Juliette De Baircli Levy, English writer, b. 1937

Occasionally I meet people who are more interested in how many countries I've been to than in those I might know well or particularly like. If *well-traveled* is defined only by the number of places I've been, then I suppose I'm not. But I feel I *really know* and have *really seen* the places I've visited, which is how *I* define *well-traveled*. I travel to see how people live in other parts of the world—not to check countries off a list—and doing that requires immediately adapting to the local pace and rhythm and (hopefully) sticking around for more than a few days. Certainly any place you decide is worthy of your time and effort is worthy of more than a day, but you don't always need an indefinite period of time to immerse yourself in the local culture or establish a routine that allows you to get to know the merchants and residents of your adopted neighborhood.

One of the fastest ways to adjust to daily life in Spain, wherever you are, is to abandon whatever schedule you observe at home and eat when the Spanish eat. As Marie Louise Graff notes in her excellent book *Culture Shock!: Spain,* "You do not need to imitate *how* a Spaniard eats to be accepted, but it is advisable to eat *when* he does. Demanding an evening meal at six o'clock may encounter resistance, and you should not expect Spaniards to accept an invitation if you insist on keeping to meal times with which they are unfamiliar." Mealtimes in Spain are indeed well established, with some variation as one travels from the north of the country to Andalusia in the south. (Due to the difference in climate, people start their day earlier in Andalusia, take a longer siesta, and eat dinner later.) Besides Spain, Greece is the only other Mediterranean country that can be vexing when it comes to figuring out when to eat. My husband and I were once at an upscale campground near Epidaurus in Greece, and at 1:15 we walked over to the campground restaurant to inquire what time lunch would be served. The host said 1:30, so we decided to wait. At 1:25 it did not at all appear that the restaurant was ready to open, and no one else, not a single person, was waiting with us, so we decided to walk down to the beach and come back. At exactly 1:40 we returned, and the restaurant was completely full. The host told us that he was so sorry, but there was not a single table available. Our fellow campers—all Greeks, by the way—somehow knew, in the span of fifteen minutes, precisely when to descend upon the restaurant. Admittedly this example is somewhat extreme, but sometimes you may feel in Spain that you have arrived at a restaurant at altogether the wrong time.

After six visits to Spain, a lot of reading, and a lot of observing, I can confirm that determining when to eat is really not as complex as it may seem. In Northern Spain outdoor markets, *panaderías* (bakeries), *carnicerías* (butcher shops), and *verdulerías* (small groceries) close at one o'clock or one-thirty, so if you are planning to shop for provisions for an outdoor picnic lunch, keep this in mind as you plan the day's itinerary. Restaurants open for lunch between one and two. If you're starving, you can arrive promptly at one, but you'll probably be the first customer of the day. By two-thirty most restaurants are full or nearly so. *Tapas* bars, on the other hand, usually open by noon, and you may certainly compose an entire meal at one or more of them. You also don't have to worry about not finding a table, as *tapas* bars typically don't have many—customers stand at the bar, sometimes four and five deep. Whether you eat at a restaurant or a *tapas* bar, however, the afternoon siesta is still honored. So if you're hungry at noon, go ahead and eat, but don't assume you'll get a head start on the afternoon's activities by eating early: Nearly every business, government office, museum, or shop will be closed until about three or four P.M. As mentioned above, dinner is not typically served at six P.M., an hour entirely too early for anyone in a Mediterranean country to contemplate eating a meal. Whether you're in Galicia, Cantabria, La Rioja, or the Basque Country, the earliest the locals sit down to dinner (at home or at a restaurant) is about nine P.M. (in Madrid, ten P.M.), after the evening *paseo* (stroll). Again, *tapas* bars fill up earlier, beginning at about six-thirty or seven, but most of the patrons are just nibbling and imbibing. (Remember that dinner in Spain is usually light, as lunch is the biggest meal of the day.) Adjust your schedule, and you'll be on Spanish time, doing things when the Spaniards do them, eliminating possible disappointment and frustration.

I personally prefer this Mediterranean timetable—I grew up in a family that ate dinner later—and I believe that a big meal in the middle of the day, in combination with an evening *paseo,* is healthier than one at the end of the day. Food writer Pat Willard, in her book *Secrets of Saffron,* notes that "I will tell you this—I would live in Spain happily for the rest of my days on earth if only for the way the country eats. It is so exquisite, and so full of sense, to arise and have nothing more than a bit of toast with milky coffee or hot chocolate, knowing you will stop somewhere around eleven and have a meal that is a little more substantial, perhaps an omelette or a little sandwich made of sausage or ham. At one, it is time for a glass of wine and a tapa or two at a bar, which leads into a hearty lunch with a little more wine, after which you must retire for a small nap. Back at work for a little bit by three—or even four (for what's the hurry when twilight lingers so complaisantly?)—until the clock strikes six and it's off to find a comfortable seat at another bar for another glass of wine or a sherry, and some more tapas and talk with friends to see how the day has gone so far or to plan the evening. By the next time you look up, it's after ten o'clock and you're a little more than famished, despite the little plates of tapas that have piled up around your glass. And so you all go off down the street to a little restaurant that makes the very best cod stew, and after that, though it may be past midnight, the lights are still on in the Plaza Mayor, and music flows from an open doorway to entice you away from bed." I find nowadays that when my husband and I receive an invitation for dinner and it's for an hour before eight P.M., I am crestfallen, and the date looms ahead like a dreaded task. I would also add here that though the sun does not rise early in Northern Spain (in the late fall and winter it doesn't make an appearance until eight or eight-thirty), it is still rewarding to rise rather early. It may be difficult to convince holiday travelers who like to sleep late to roll out of bed a bit earlier, but if you sleep in every day, you will most definitely miss much of the local rhythm. By ten A.M. in Spain—and in any Mediterranean country— much has already happened, and besides, you can always look forward to a delicious afternoon nap.

About fifteen years ago the former Paris bureau chief for *The New York Times*, John Vinocur, wrote a piece for the travel section entitled "Discovering the Hidden Paris." In it he noted that the French have a word, *dépaysement*, which he translated into English as "the feeling of not being assaulted by the familiarity of things, a change in surroundings where there is no immediate point of reference." He went on to quote a French journalist who once said that "Americans don't travel to be *dépaysés*, but to find a home away from home." This is unfortunate, but too often true. These tourists can travel all around the world if they desire, but their unwillingness to adapt ensures they will never really leave home. I am of like mind with Paul Bowles, who noted in *Their Heads Are Green, Their Hands Are Blue*, "Each time I go to a place I have not seen before, I hope it will be as different as possible from the places I already know. I assume it is natural for a traveler to seek diversity, and that it is the human element which makes him most aware of difference. If people and their manner of living were alike everywhere, there would not be much point in moving from one place to another."

Similar to the *dépaysés*-phobic are those who endorse "adventure travel," words that make me cringe, as they seem to imply that unless one partakes of kayaking, mountain climbing, biking, rock climbing, or some other physical endeavor, a travel experience is somehow invalid or unadventurous. *All* travel is an adventure, and unless "adventure travel" allows for plenty of time to adapt to the local rhythm, the so-called adventure is really a physically strenuous—if memorable—outdoor achievement. Occasionally I hear a description of a biking excursion, for example, in which the participants spent the majority of each day in the same way: making biking the priority instead of working biking into the local cadence of daily life. When I ask if they joined the locals for a morning *café con leche* or an evening *aperitivo*, shopped at the outdoor *mercado,* went to a local *feria,* or people-watched in the *plaza,* the answer is invariably no. They may have had an amazing bike trip, but they did not get to know Spain—one has to get off the bike a bit more often for that—and if a biking experience alone is what they were seeking, they certainly didn't need to fly to Spain: There are plenty of challenging and beautiful places to bike in the United States.

I believe that *every* place in the world offers *something* of interest. In her magnificent book *Black Lamb and Grey Falcon*, Rebecca West recounts how in the 1930s she passed through Skopje, in what was then Yugoslavia (and is now the Republic of Macedonia), by train twice, without stopping, because friends had told her the town wasn't worth visiting. A third time through she did stop, and she met two wonderful people who became lasting friends. She wrote, "Now, when I go through a town of which I know nothing, a town which appears to be a waste land of uniform streets wholly without quality, I look on it in wonder and hope, since it may hold a Mehmed, a Militsa." I too have been richly rewarded by pausing in places (Skopje included) that first appeared quite limited.

"Travel is fatal to prejudice, bigotry, and narrow-mindedness."
—Mark Twain

"The world is a book, and those who do not travel read only a page."

—Saint Augustine

I am assuming if you've read this far that something has compelled you to pick up this book and that you feel travel is an essential part of life. I would add to Mark Twain's quote above one by Benjamin Disraeli (1804–1881): "Travel teaches toleration." People who travel with an open mind and are receptive to the ways of others cannot help but return with more tolerance for people and situations at home, at work, and in their cities and communities. James Ferguson, a nineteenth-century Scottish architect, observed this perfectly when he wrote, "Travel is more than a visitor seeing sights; it is the profound changing—the deep and permanent changing—of that visitor's perspective of the world, and of his own place in it." I find that travel also ensures I will not be quite the same person I was before I left. After a trip I typically have a lot of renewed energy and bring new perspectives to my job. At home, I ask myself how I can incorporate attributes or traits I observed while traveling into my own life and share them with my husband and daughter. I also find that I am eager to explore my own hometown more fully (when was the last time you visited your local historical society, or the best-known tourist site in your part of the country?), and in appreciation of the great kindnesses shown to me by people from other nations, I always go out of my way to help tourists who are visiting New York City—Americans or foreigners—by giving directions, explaining the subway, or sharing a favorite museum or a place to eat.

The anthologies in *The Collected Traveler* series offer a record of people's achievements and shortcomings. It may be a lofty goal to expect that they might also offer an opportunity for us to measure our own deeds and flaws as Americans, so we can realize that, despite cultural differences between us and our hosts in *any* country, we have much more in common than not. It is a sincere goal, however, and one that I hope readers and travelers will embrace.

About This Series

The Collected Traveler editions are not guidebooks in the traditional sense. In another sense, however, they *may* be considered guidebooks in that they guide readers to other sources. Each book is really the first book you should turn to when planning a trip. If you think of the individual volumes as a sort of planning package, you've got the right idea. To borrow a phrase from a reviewer who was writing about the Lonely Planet Travel Survival Kit series years ago, *The Collected Traveler* is for people who know how to get their luggage off the carousel. If you enjoy acquiring knowledge about where you're going—whether you're planning a trip independently or with a like-minded tour organization—this series is for you. If you're looking for a guide that simply informs you of exact prices, hours, and highlights, you probably won't be interested in the depth this book offers. (That is not meant to offend, merely to say you've got the wrong book.)

A few words about me may also help you determine if this series is for you. I travel somewhat frugally, not out of necessity but more because I choose to. I respect money and its value, and I'm not convinced that if I spent $600 a night on a hotel room, for example, it would represent a good value or I would have a better trip. I've been to some of the world's finest hotels, mostly to visit friends who were staying there or to have a drink in the hotel bar. With a few notable exceptions, the majority of these places seem to me all alike, conforming to a code of sameness and predictability. There's nothing about them that is particularly Spanish, Italian, French, or Turkish—you could be *anywhere*. The cheapest of the cheap accommodations don't represent good value either. I look for places to stay that are usually old, possibly historic, and have lots of charm and character. I do not mind if my room is small; I do not need a television, telephone, or hair dryer; and I most definitely do not care for an American-style buffet breakfast, which is hardly what the locals eat. I also prefer to make my own plans, send my own letters and faxes, place my own telephone calls, and make my own transportation arrangements. Not because I think I can do it better than a professional agent (whose expertise I admire) but because I enjoy it and learn a lot in the process. Finally, lest readers think I do not appreciate elegance, allow me to state that I think you'll quickly ascertain that I do indeed enjoy many of life's little luxuries, when I perceive them to be of good value to me.

This series promotes the desirability of staying longer within a smaller area. Susan Allen Toth, in one of her many wonderful books, *England as You Like It,* subscribes to the "thumbprint theory of travel": spending at least a week in one spot no larger than her thumbprint covers on a large-scale map of England. Excursions are encouraged, she goes on to explain, as long as they're only about an hour's drive away. As I have discovered in my own travels, a week spent in one place, even a spot no bigger than my thumbprint, is rarely long enough to see and enjoy it all. *The Collected Traveler* focuses on one corner of the world, the countries bordering the Mediterranean Sea. I find the Mediterranean endlessly fascinating: the sea itself is the world's largest, the region is one of the world's ancient crossroads, and as it stretches from Asia to the Atlantic, it is home to the most diverse humanity. As Paul Theroux has noted in his excellent book *The Pillars of Hercules,* "The Mediterranean, this simple almost tideless sea, the size of thirty Lake Superiors, had everything: prosperity, poverty, tourism, terrorism, several wars in progress, ethnic strife, fascists, pollution, drift nets, private islands owned by billionaires, Gypsies, seventeen countries, fifty languages, oil drilling platforms, sponge fishermen, religious fanatics, drug smuggling, fine art, and warfare. It had Christians, Muslims, Jews; it had the Druzes, who are a strange farrago of all three religions; it had heathens, Zoroastrians and Copts and Baha'is." Diversity aside, the great explorers in the service of Spain and Portugal departed from Mediterranean ports to discover much of the rest of the world, as Carlos Fuentes notes in *his* excellent book *The Buried Mirror:* "The facts remained that the Mare Nostrum, the Mediterranean, had been to all effects and purposes an Islamic lake for nearly eight hundred years, and that European expansion was severely hindered by such mastery. To find a way out, a way around, a way toward the Orient became a European obsession. It began in the Venetian republic, with Marco Polo's opening of overland trade routes to China. But soon the rise of a new Muslim power, the Ottoman Empire, once more threatened the Mediterranean; the Ottomans captured Greece and the Balkans and forced Europe and its rising merchant class to look elsewhere." And look elsewhere they did: Prince Henry of Portugal, who became known as Henry the Navigator, arranged the sailing expeditions to Madeira, the Azores, and Senegal. In 1488 the Portuguese went on to discover the Cape of Good Hope. Under Vasco da Gama, the Portuguese then added India to their itinerary in 1498. "But," Fuentes continues, "while Portugal looked east and south, it hesitated to look west over the Mare Ignotum—the Unknown Sea, the Ocean of Mystery— even when a headstrong sailor said to be of Genoese origin, cast ashore by a shipwreck near Prince Henry's castle, argued that the best way to reach the East was to sail west. The man was personally far less impressive than his work on many counts—feverish, at times uncontrolled, suspected of being a mythomaniac. But he certainly had courage and determination. His name was Cristoforo

Colombo—Christopher Columbus—Cristóbal Colón. Portugal did not listen to him. He then headed for Spain, the isolated, inward-looking country fighting its protracted war of *reconquista*, and there, in a propitious moment, offered his plan to the Catholic Monarchs. Flushed with victory after the defeat of the Moors in Granada, Ferdinand and Isabella gave Columbus the means to achieve the third great event of that crucial year of Spanish history, 1492: the discovery of America." "This sea," writes Lisa Lovatt-Smith in *Mediterranean Living*, "whose shores have hosted the main currents in civilization, creates its own homogeneous culture, endlessly absorbing newcomers and their ideas . . . and is the one I consider my own." I too consider the sea my own, even though I live thousands of miles away from it.

With the exception of my *Morocco* edition, this series focuses on individual cities and regions rather than entire countries, as readers who are not new to *The Collected Traveler* already know. I do not plan to compile a book on all of Spain, for example, since Spain is a member of two communities, European and Mediterranean. I have tried to reflect this wider world sense of community throughout this edition on Northern Spain, especially in the *Las Noticias Cotidianas biblioteca*. When I first contemplated this edition, I knew I would have to take an inclusive approach rather than a strictly geographic one. When Spaniards refer to Northern (or North, or Green) Spain, they are talking about Galicia, Asturias, Cantabria, and the País Vasco (the Basque Country). But the Camino de Santiago—a highlight of this book and one of the most famous pilgrimage routes in the world—begins in the Pyrenees and passes through Navarre, La Rioja, and Castilla y León, before ending in Galicia. It does not make any sense to exclude these other areas simply because they are not technically part of Green Spain. Additionally, due to a lack of substantial available material, I knew I would never publish individual editions on these surrounding areas, and they would therefore never be included in any of the volumes I hope to do on Spain. So this particular thumbprint is a bit bigger than I traditionally promote, but it can manageably be seen in one trip. (It would, of course, be ideal if one allowed oneself about three weeks to do so.)

Of all the regions of Spain, Northern Spain is probably the least known to North Americans. Most travelers are familiar with the Camino de Santiago, but most do not know the regions of Spain that the route passes through. Even a unit of measure such as book publishing is revealing: when I first spent some serious time in Northern Spain, in 1997, only one guidebook to this region was available in bookstores: Cadogan, a series that is published in the U.K. Now, five years later, only one other has joined Cadogan: Insight, another series that is not published in North America. A Fodor's Gold Guide entitled *Barcelona to Bilbao* was published in 2001, but to my mind it capitalizes on the popularity of two Spanish cities that in actuality have almost nothing in common: The only trait the Catalans and the Basques share is their desire for more autonomy; their language, culture, music, architecture, art, and cuisine are completely different. In 1997 my husband and I stayed at a wonderful little *alojamiento rural* (countryside lodging) in Asturias. We were the first Americans the family of Marta and Marcellino had ever met, and they insisted upon taking our picture! Since that time Northern Spain has become better known, due almost entirely to a resurgence of interest in the Camino de Santiago and the opening of the Guggenheim Bilbao. None of the stereotypical images of Spain (almost all of which derive from Andalusia) apply to Northern Spain: there are only a small handful of bullrings in the north, there is no flamenco, women are not seen with fans, the landscape is green and mountainous, there are few olive trees, temperatures never climb as high as they do in the south, and there is little if any of the Moorish architecture that so dominates in Andalusia. "When the fruit is falling in the south," Jan Morris notes in *Spain,* "the blossom is budding in the north. There are hardly any mules in the Basque country, but hundreds of thousands in Andalusia. There are hardly any bull-rings in the north-west, but every southern village has one. In Andalusia the houses are blazing white and red-tiled, in Aragon they are mud-brown and flecked with bits of straw. In Asturias they build their grain stores with tiled eaves and stilts, to keep the rain and rats out. The Basque policemen wear red berets, the men of La Mancha wear headscarves and ride about in covered wagons like Western pioneers. The churches of Valencia have blue tiled domes, the fences of Galicia are made of upright stone blocks, every part of Spain has its own traditional costume, pictured in flurries of ruffles and pleated petticoats in all the best tourist brochures." John Crow, in his essential book *Spain: The Root and the Flower*, notes an old phrase the Spaniards have, *Quien dice España dice todo* ("Who says Spain, says everything"), which is their way of stating their pride in "the infinite variety" of their land. "Other Spaniards," Crow notes, "seeking for an element of hope or of stability in their country, affirm heatedly that beneath all the regional variations Spain is one, that there is some mysterious alchemy of the land which holds it all together, some common denominator which gives the Spaniards the same character, the same aspirations, the same ideals. This wishful thinking has been going on among Spaniards for centuries, but the reality is that Spain is not a homogeneous country, with homogeneous strivings. Spain is heterogeneous at the base, and heterodoxy is her true religion." While I am extremely fond of Andalusia, intoxicatingly so, Northern Spain is a breath of fresh air, which is no secret among Spaniards, who routinely spend *their* holidays in this unique and relaxing part of their country.

Each section of this book features a selection of articles from various periodicals and an annotated bibliography relevant to its theme. (The *Información Practical* section is a bit different, as the books are incorporated into the A-to-Z listings.) The articles and books were chosen from my own files and home library, which I've maintained for over two decades. (I often feel I am the living embodiment of a comment that Samuel Johnson made in 1775, that "a man will turn over half a library to make one book.") The selected writings reflect the culture, politics, history, current social issues, religion, cuisine, and arts of the people you'll be visiting. They also represent the observations and opinions of a wide variety of novelists, travel writers, and journalists. These writers are typically authorities on all or part of Northern Spain, or all of Spain, or both; they either live there (as permanent or part-time residents) or visit there often for business or pleasure. I'm very discriminating in seeking opinions and recommendations, and I am not interested in the remarks of unobservant wanderers. Likewise, I don't ask someone who doesn't read much what he or she thinks of a particular book, and I don't ask someone who neither cooks nor travels for a restaurant recommendation. I am not implying that first-time visitors to Spain have nothing noteworthy or interesting to share—they very often do and are often very keen observers; conversely, frequent travelers are very often jaded and apt to miss the finer details that make Northern Spain the exceptional place it is. I am interested in the opinions of people who want to *know* this part of Spain, not just *see* it.

I've included numerous older articles (even though some of the specific information regarding prices, hours, and the like is no longer accurate) because they were particularly well written, thought provoking, or unique in some way, and because the authors' views stand as a valuable record of a certain time in history. Often, even with the passage of many years, you may share the same emotions and opinions of the writer, and equally as often, *plus ça change, plus c'est la même chose*. I have many, many more articles in my files than I was able to reprint here. Though there are a few pieces whose absence I very much regret, I believe the anthology you're holding is very good.

A word about the food and restaurant section, *¡Buen Provecho!*: I have great respect for restaurant reviewers, and though their work may seem glamorous—it sometimes is—it is also very hard. It's an all-consuming, full-time job, and that is why I urge you to consult the very good food and restaurant guides I recommend in the *biblioteca,* cookbooks included, especially those by Penelope Casas. Restaurant (and hotel) reviewers are, for the most part, professionals who have dined in hundreds of eating establishments (and spent hundreds of nights in hotels). They are far more capable of assessing the qualities and flaws of a place than I am—I have eaten in only about three dozen places and stayed at about fifteen hotels and can therefore only tell you about my limited experience—and likely more capable than your in-laws, who perhaps were in Northern Spain for three days and never took a meal outside of a *parador* or a Michelin-starred place in San Sebastián. I don't always agree with every opinion of a reviewer, but I am far more inclined to defer to their opinion over that of someone who is unfamiliar with Spanish food in general and the cuisine of the north in particular, for example, or to someone who doesn't dine out frequently enough to recognize what good restaurants have in common. My files are bulging with restaurant reviews, and I could have included many, many more articles; but it would be too repetitive and ultimately beside the point. I have selected a few articles that give you a feel for eating out in this part of Spain, alert you to some things to look for in selecting a truly worthwhile place versus a mediocre one, and highlight some dishes that are not commonplace in America. My files are equally bulging with hotel recommendations, but as with restaurants, I urge you to consult one or more of the great books I recommend in *Información Practical.*

The annotated bibliography, or *biblioteca,* for each section is one of the most important features of this book, and they represent my own favorite aspect of this series. One reason I do not include excerpts from books in my editions is that I am not convinced an excerpt will always lead a reader to the book in question, and I think good books deserve to be read in their entirety. Art critic John Russell wrote an essay in 1962 entitled "Pleasure in Reading," in which he stated, "Not for us today's selections, readers, digests, and anthologizings: only the Complete Edition will do." Years later in 1986 he noted in the foreword to *John Pope-Hennessy: A Bibliography* that "bibliographies make dull reading, some people say, but I have never found them so. They remind us, they prompt us, and they correct us. They double and treble as history, as biography, and as a freshet of surprises. They reveal the public self, the private self, and the buried self of the person commemorated. How should we not enjoy them, and be grateful to the devoted student who has done the compiling?" When I pick up a nonfiction book, I always turn first to the bibliography, as it is there that I learn something about the author who has done the compiling as well as about other notable books I know I will want to read.

When I read about travel in the days before transatlantic flights, I always marvel at the number of steamer trunks and the amount of baggage people were accustomed to taking. If it had been me traveling then, however, my bags would have been filled with books, not clothes. Although I travel light and seldom check bags, I have been known to fill an entire suitcase with books, secure in the knowledge that I would have them all with me for the duration of my trip. Each *biblioteca* in this book features the titles I feel are the best ones available and the most worth your time. "Best" is subjective; readers will simply have to trust me that I have been extremely thorough in deciding which books to recommend. (I have read them all, by the way, and own them all, with the exception of a few I borrowed.) If some of the lists seem long, they are, but the more I read, the more I realize there is to know, and there are an awful lot of really good books out there! I'm not suggesting you read them *all,* but I do hope you will not be content with just one. I have identified some books as *esencial*, meaning that I consider them required reading; but I sincerely believe that *all* the books I've mentioned are important, helpful, well written, or all three. I keep up with book publishing, but there are surely some books I've not seen, so if some of your favorites aren't included here, please write and tell me about them.

I have not hesitated to list out-of-print titles because some very excellent books are declared out of print (and deserve to be returned to print!) and because many, many out-of-print books can be found through individuals who specialize in out-of-print books, booksellers, libraries, and online searches. I believe the companion reading you bring along on your trip should be related in some way to where you're going. Therefore, the books listed in *Mis Favoritos* are mostly novels that feature characters or settings in Northern Spain or aspects of Spain and the Spanish.

Readers familiar with my other books may notice the absence of a section featuring personalities in this edition. The reason is simply that I have very few articles in my files about artists, writers, politicians, expatriates, or other notable residents from Northern Spain. The absence of well-known figures appears to be true for Spain in general, as Jan Morris has noted in *Spain*: "Considering the age, activity, and ability of this nation, it is surprising how few Spaniards are generally known to the world today: among monarchs, only Isabel, Ferdinand, Philip II; among fighting men only Cortés and Pizarro; among writers, Cervantes, Lope de Vega, Galdós, Federico García Lorca; among thinkers, St. Ignatius, St. Theresa, St. John of the Cross, Miguel de Unamuno and Ortega y Gasset; among composers, Vitoria and Falla; among painters, El Greco, Zurbarán, Murillo, Velázquez, Goya, Picasso, Dali, Miró; among scientists, the inventor of the autogyro; among statesmen, General Franco. It is not many, for such a nation, and the reason perhaps is that Spaniards create essentially for Spaniards. *Don Quixote*, though it obviously has its universal meanings, is essentially a book about Spain—not a vision of the world, like Shakespeare's plays." So I have included only a few biographies of some major figures in Spanish history at the end of the *Las Noticias Cotidianas* section. (I plan to add others to a separate edition on Madrid, and of course personalities unique to Cataluña, Andalusia, and so on, will be included in those editions.)

Also not included in this edition is a separate section on museums, gardens, and monuments, again due to a lack of material— Bilbao and San Sebastián aside, Northern Spain is more about the physical features of the land, nature, and cultural traditions than about must-see museums and temples of art (though there are no less than six UNESCO World Heritage Sites in Northern Spain). So books on Spanish art and architecture styles, local artists, gardens, and museum catalogs appear in *Mis Favoritos*.

Together, the articles collected and books cited will lead you on and off the beaten path, and present a reality check of sorts. Will you learn of some nontouristy things to see and do? Yes. Will you learn more about the better-known aspects of Northern Spain? Yes. The cathedral in Santiago de Compostela, *tarta de Santiago,* the Picos de Europa, Santillana del Mar, *churros y chocolate,* the tranquillity of the Asturian countryside, the beach at La Concha, *gambas a la plancha,* and a glass of Albariño are all equally representative of the region. Seeing them *all* is what makes for a memorable visit—and no one, by the way, should make you feel guilty for wanting to see some famous sites. They have become famous for a reason: they are really something to see, the Santiago cathedral and Guggenheim Bilbao included. You will have no trouble finding a multitude of other travel books offering plenty of noncontroversial viewpoints. This is my attempt at presenting a more balanced picture. Ultimately it is also a compendium of the information that I wish I'd had between two covers years ago. I admit it isn't the "perfect" book; for that, I envision a waterproof jacket and pockets inside the front and back covers, pages and pages of accompanying maps, lots of blank pages for notes, a bookmark, mileage and size conversion charts . . . in other words, something so encyclopedic, in both weight and size, that positively no one, my editor assures me, would want to read it! That said, I am exceedingly happy with *The Collected Traveler,* and I believe it will prove helpful in heightening your anticipation of your upcoming journey, your enjoyment of it while it's happening, and your remembrance of it when you're back home.

Spain has, in the last few years, suddenly become what is known as a "hot" destination in the travel industry. It repeatedly appears at or near the top of lists of most popular vacation destinations, though admittedly most of that popularity is for parts of the country other than Green Spain. But according to tourist office staff members throughout the North, the opening of the Guggenheim Bilbao has finally drawn attention to the entire northern region of Spain, and even visitors to Santiago have mentioned they would not have traveled there were it not for Frank Gehry's museum. This newly found appreciation is long overdue, to my mind, and yet in fairness it must be said that Spain's popularity is not without a few mixed blessings. As Jan Morris has noted in *Spain,* "So Times change. The Spaniard, so grave, so courteous, so passionate, so reserved, turns out to be, when given the opportunity, much like the rest of us. He will push you in the supermarket, toot his horn at the traffic lights, leave the curtains open to impress the neighbours; for he is coming to terms with the world at last, and the world is teaching him how. In the end it is bound to make the Spaniards more ordinary, as the petty squalors of industrial life overcome them too, and they lose their sense of separateness. It may be foolish to be proud and insular, but at least it makes for style. It may be wrong, even wicked, to remain a poor anachronism among the nations, but at least it kept Spain on a plane all her own, possessing what the theatre calls 'star quality,' as distinct from the Swedens and the Switzerlands as a phoenix from a pair of pigeons. Progress is sure to weaken the Spanish identity, that powerful and often baffling abstraction, and the journey over Roncesvalles will inevitably lose some of its drama."

In a way, this is the book I have most wanted to compile. The very first journey I took outside of the United States was to Spain, with my high school Spanish class, in 1975. We went to the predictable sites and cities: Madrid, Toledo, El Escorial, Granada, Córdoba, Sevilla, Málaga. I started reading James Michener's *Iberia*, finished it a few weeks after I returned, and declared that for the rest of my life I only wanted to travel in Spain, for I realized then that to really get to know a place, to truly understand it in a non-superficial way, one had to either live there or travel there again and again. It seemed to me even then, at sixteen, that it would take a lifetime of studying and traveling to grasp España. I do not pretend to have completely grasped it now, many years later; nor do I pretend to have completely grasped the other Mediterranean destinations that are featured in *The Collected Traveler*. But I am trying, by continuously reading, collecting, and traveling, and I presume readers like you are, too.

Spain will always hold a special place in my heart, if only because it *was* the first overseas country I ever visited. Though I stopped studying Spanish when I began college (I switched to French because I wanted to take advantage of a Paris Abroad program) and went on to travel to many other countries, I have never stopped thinking and dreaming about Spain. I have also found it nearly impossible, on occasion, to describe precisely what it is about Spain that is so under my skin—impossible, that is, until I read the following passage in *Eternal Spain* by Alastair Reid: "Those few who have written wisely and perceptibly about Spain from the outside—

I think of Gerald Brenan and V. S. Pritchett in particular—speak of the experience of coming on Spain as something akin to a conversion. Many people I know, from many different cultures, have taken to Spain with the same intensity, discovering there a language, a way of life, a mode of thinking, and a diurnal rhythm somehow purifying after the complexities of their own societies. Those who settled there did so with the luxury of choice; but for the native inhabitants,

their existence was a fate, a destiny, which they shouldered with an ancestral stoicism, well honed in few words, glinting with humor. Their conversations crackled with a keen sense of life and death, a dignity, an assurance. As Gerald Brenan wrote: 'As they sit at their tables outside the cafes, their eyes record as on a photographic plate the people who are passing, but on a deeper level they are listening to themselves living.' "

It may be especially difficult to convey how very wonderful Northern Spain in particular is, but I hope after reading this edition and traveling there, you will discover why the authors of the singular Cadogan guide have noted that Green Spain "offers no end of delights."

¡Buen viaje!

Informaciones Prácticas
(Practical Information)

"Spanish courtesy decrees that a negative answer to your question 'When can you come?' is unacceptable. The electrician or plumber hates to disappoint you. Perhaps he really does mean to try and squeeze a visit to your house into his already overcrowded schedule, but experience will show that you really cannot rely on his mañana. *If you are used to punctuality, this can be really frustrating. You sit at home waiting and no one appears; so you get fed up and venture out. When you come home, you find a note saying the equivalent of 'We came! Where were you?' Getting angry with the fellow in question is a waste of time. He will agree with everything you say, smile and tell you he'll come* 'mañana— seguro' *(tomorrow for sure) only to repeat the whole cycle. You simply have to learn to be extremely patient. Besides, giving way to anger or frustration will not endear you to the workman in question. If you want to make your stay in Spain a success, the first thing to get used to is* mañana.*"*

—Marie Louise Graff,
CULTURE SHOCK!: SPAIN

A–Z Informaciones Prácticas

A

Accommodations

If you arrive in any town in Northern Spain without having booked a room in advance, the local tourist office staff can assist you in finding accommodations. This assistance is more thorough and professional in the larger cities, but judging from my experience, the staff at even the smallest tourist office in the smallest *comunidad autónoma* in Spain will be happy to assist you in finding a place to stay. They may not place telephone calls for you or make reservations (especially if it's high season and they are busy), but they will tell you what choices are available, give directions, and generally help in any way they can. Unless you are traveling for an extended period of time throughout the region or throughout Spain, I don't recommend showing up without a room, especially during the summer months and especially in August, the month when *all* Europeans take their vacations. That said, Northern Spain is one of the few areas of the world where reservations are not essential in the off-season, and I have traveled there without making advance reservations for every night of my trip, with success. Still, keep in mind that many of the most wonderful lodgings are quite small, with only a few rooms, and can fill up fast during the so-named shoulder seasons, fall and spring. (During the winter months, don't be surprised if some places are closed entirely.) We all have a limited number of precious vacation days, and searching for a place to stay can be a most time-consuming and frustrating experience and certainly not what you came to Spain to do. Unless you're traveling around by train and a backpack and are going from youth hostel to youth hostel, you will probably want to carefully select the places you'll call home for a few days or longer.

Some might argue that the choice of a lodging isn't important, since we won't be spending much time in our room anyway; but I disagree. Meeting the owners of a family-run hotel or *turismo rural* property, getting to know the front desk clerk at a posh *parador,* or simply returning to a nicely kept room for an afternoon siesta are all parts of a memorable and enjoyable trip. I can find no reason *not* to devote some time to researching where you will stay—the only problem may be narrowing your choices in certain areas because of the many great available options. (Travelers seeking luxury, however, should note that this type of accommodation is not thick on the ground, so to speak, in the north, so you will have fewer choices, making your task much simpler.)

You should keep in mind that the Spanish government's star rating system for lodging establishments awards stars based on the number and range of amenities available and that it pays special attention to the availability of air conditioning, elevators, banquet rooms, hair dryers, and the like. But stars have nothing at all to do with charm or quality of hospitality. All of Spain's lodgings display a blue plaque near the entrance with a large white H (for hotel), P (for *pensión*), Hs (for *hostal*), F (*fonda*), or CH (*casa de huéspedes*) and the gold stars (from one to five) it has been awarded just beneath the letter. Generally speaking, a *pensión, fonda,* or *casa de huéspedes* is a budget accommodation. Some hotels too may be budget accommodations (if the letter R, for *residencia,* appears after an H, no meal service is offered), especially if they are one-star establishments. Again, speaking generally, most one-star establishments are equated with simple accommodations and usually offer shared bathroom facilities. Two- and three-star establishments can be bed-and-breakfast or regular hotel accommodations, usually with a private bath. Four- and five-star hotels represent the highest standards of service and can be quite luxurious or less so. You may, in your research and travels, discover places that are not classified and therefore have no rating; this is not because the tourist board has rejected them but rather because their owners have not requested to be reviewed. I have stayed in a number of places with no rating, in Spain and elsewhere around the Mediterranean, and they were all perfectly fine and clean, some even quite deserving of two or three stars. All of this is to say that you cannot depend on Spain's star rating system alone. The only amenity standing between a three-star place and one awarded four stars may be a swimming pool, or a bigger bathtub, or a ceiling fan. Penelope Casas, in her excellent book *Discovering Spain,* notes that "a small luxury hotel that lacks dining facilities may receive only four stars, and yet its prices may be super-deluxe . . . a five-star hotel that has not been renovated in twenty years and is drab, musty, and outdated may retain its original rating. You can, however, trust those hotels (there are very few of them) designated *Gran Lujo.* They take great care with every detail, and are often decorated with antiques or costly furnishings, and like to pamper their clients. Generally they are very expensive—but not all of them are." Far better is to ignore the stars and read a thorough description of a place so you know exactly what you're paying for. Following are the types of accommodations you'll find in this part of Spain:

Albergues juveniles (youth hostels) are one of the most popular choices for those seeking budget accommodations (and if it's been a while since your salad days, keep in mind that hostels are not just for the under-thirty crowd). I would take back in a minute my summer of vagabonding around Europe, meeting young people from all over the world, and feeling that my life was one endless possibility. I now prefer to share a room with my husband rather than five twentysomethings, but hosteling remains a fun and exciting experience. Younger budget travelers need no convincing that hosteling is the way to go, but older budget travelers should bear in mind that some hostels do offer individual rooms, reserved mostly for couples or small families. Do compare costs, as sometimes hostel rates are the same as those for a room in a real (albeit inexpensive) hotel, where you can reserve in advance and comfortably keep your luggage. (When hosteling, you must pack up your luggage every day, and you can't make a reservation.) Additionally, most hostels have an eleven P.M. curfew. Petty theft—of the T-shirts-stolen-off-the-clothesline variety—seems to be more prevalent than it once was, and it would be wise to sleep and shower with your money belt close at hand. There are no age limits or advance bookings, but many hostels require membership in Hostelling International, whose national head-quarters are located at 733 Fifteenth Street NW, Suite 840, Washington, DC 20005; 202-783-6161; fax: -6171; www.hiayh.org. Hours are 8:00 A.M.–5:00 P.M. Eastern Standard Time, with customer service staff available until 7:00 P.M. An HI mem-bership card is free for anyone up to his or her eighteenth birthdate. Annual fees are $25 for anyone over eighteen and $15 for those fifty-five and over. HI also publishes several guidebooks, one of which is *Europe and the Mediterranean*. Its price is either $10.95 or $13.95, depending on whether you purchase it from the main office or from one of its council affiliates around the country. (HI staff can give you the addresses and phone numbers for the affiliates nearest you.) The organization that oversees hostels in Spain is the Red Española de Albergues Juveniles (Spanish Network of Youth Hostels), and there are a number of hostels in Northern Spain. Additionally, during the summer months, student dormitory accommodations are often available in towns and cities with colleges and universities. The best resource for learning about these rooms is the local tourist office, and the staff at the North American Spanish tourist offices should be able to put you in touch with any of the local offices in Northern Spain (see the entry for Tourist Offices).

Bed and breakfast accommodations in Spain may be either simple or fancy, and they are offered in *casas rurales* or in small inns and hotels. Note that bed and breakfast establishments and *casas rurales* are not interchangeable: While *casas rurales* properties may be classified as bed and breakfasts, bed and breakfast places are often not *casas rurales* properties. The best guide, in my opinion, for seeking out B&B accommodations is *Alastair Sawday's Special Places to Stay: Spain* (Alastair Sawday Publishing, Bristol, U.K.; distributed in North America by Globe Pequot Press, Guilford, CT). I'm a big fan of this series (I've used the Paris, France, and Italy editions with great success), and it seems to me that the majority of these places do not appear in other accommodation guides. Subtitled *A Feast of Over 300 Wonderful Places All Over Mainland Spain and Its Islands,* the book actually fea-tures small hotels and inns in addition to B&Bs, so it is a worthwhile resource in both categories. Each entry is described, with two color photographs, on one page, and entries range from *casonas,* vineyard estates, farmhouses, *fincas, hostals,* and *pazos.* The Sawday authors "look for owners, homes and hotels that we like—and we are fiercely subjective in our choices. 'Special' for us is not a measure of the number of creature comforts you get but relates to many different elements that make a place 'work.' Certainly the way guests are treated comes as high on our list as the setting, the architecture and the food. We are not necessarily impressed by high star ratings. Expect this book to lead you to places that are original, individual and welcoming." It contains eighteen listings for Galicia, thirty-three for Asturias and Cantabria, and thirteen for the Basque Country, Navarre, and La Rioja. Included are also two pages of useful vocabulary, travel tips, twenty-five pages of color road maps, and a Spanish-English reservation form.

Camas (beds) are unclassified lodgings, typically offered as rooms over a bar or restaurant (or some other business) or in a regular apartment building. I have met travelers who frequent such places all the time, but I have shied away from them myself because I think the noise of a bar or restaurant would keep me from enjoying a good night's sleep, and I've read that these rooms can be downright dreary in urban locales. Also, I think that most of the time youth hostels provide equally affordable accommodations and are more lively and fun. But as another budget choice, I would definitely recommend considering these.

Camping (commonly known as *campings*) can be a viable option for those who have a car and a lot of time. The thing to understand about the European conception of camping is that it is about as different from the American as possible. Europeans do not go camping to seek a wilderness experience, and European campgrounds are designed without much privacy in mind, offering amenities ranging from hot water showers, facilities for washing clothes and dishes, electrical outlets, croissants and *café* for breakfast, and flush toilets; to tiled bathrooms with heat, swimming pools, cafés, bars, restaurants, telephones, televisions, and general stores. If you find yourself at a campground during the summer months, you may notice that entire families have literally moved in (having reserved their spaces many months in advance) and that they return every year to spend time with their friends, the way we might return every year to a ski cabin or a house at the beach. It's quite an entertaining and lively spectacle, and camping like this is not really roughing it! I have camped fairly extensively in Spain but mostly in Andalusia and along the Costa Brava, where my husband and I once stayed at a seaside campground that was nothing short of luxurious. I have an aversion to camping in the rain (ask my husband about the rainy night we spent in our tent at Lake Maggiore in Italy), so the only camping I've done in Northern Spain has been in Navarre and Andorra. For complete information about camping in Spain, readers should consult the annual *Guía Oficial de Campings* published by Turespaña and available at the Spanish tourist offices. It's been my experience that at municipal *campings* during the off-season, no one ever comes around to collect fees. The campgrounds are still open and have running water, but the thinking seems to be that it just isn't worth it to collect money from so few campers. (This will not hold true at privately run campgrounds.) If you plan to camp for even a few nights, I recommend that you join Family Campers and R'Vers (FCRV). Annual membership (valid for one year from the time you join) is $25. The FCRV is a member of the Fédération Internationale de Camping et de Caravanning (FICC) and is the only organization in America authorized to issue the International Camping Carnet for camping in

Europe. Only FCRV members are eligible to purchase the carnet—you cannot purchase it separately—and the fee is $10. The carnet is like a camping passport and provides entry into the many privately owned members-only campsites. It offers campers priority status and occasionally discounts. An additional benefit is that instead of keeping your passport overnight—which hotels and campgrounds are often required to do—the campground staff keep your carnet, allowing you to hold on to your passport. One FICC membership is good for the entire family: parents and all children under the age of eighteen. To receive an application and information, contact FCRV at 4804 Transit Road, Building 2, Depew, NY 14043; 800-245-9755; phone/fax: 716-668-6242; www.fcrv.org. ~By the way, an outstanding catalog for a most thorough selection of camping gear and accoutrements—including four pages of rainwear, good for Northern Spain, and lots of items for kids—is Campmor (P.O. Box 700-G, Saddle River, NJ 07458; 800-CAMPMOR; www.campmor.com).

Casas particulares (private houses with a room or two for paying guests) are typically unclassified lodgings. Often the owner will greet tourists at the local bus or train station and ask if anybody is looking for a room. Don't dismiss this option, especially if you are not traveling with your own car. (But if you'll be getting around with your own two feet or public transportation, do make sure you understand how far away the house is from the center of town.) Some of my best travel experiences have been spent in *casas particulares*, and a great meal or two is often part of the bargain. Prices for this type of accommodation are often the same as for a youth hostel, and there is no curfew or dormitory-style rooms.

Casas rurales or *turismo rural* (translated as agricultural tourism, the equivalent of *agriturismo* in Italy) are accommodations offered in country houses whose owners accept paying guests. These rural lodgings range from basic to almost luxurious and can be on small working farms or larger impressive estates. Readers should know in advance, however, not to expect the services of a hotel or an inn at a *casa rural*—your room may not be cleaned every day, for example—and amenities may be few, especially if you're staying on a property whose primary purpose is the daily operation of the farm. In this situation you should be prepared to tidy up yourself and enjoy getting to know your hosts. At many *casas rurales* breakfast is taken with the family, and the produce may be home-grown, jams and confections homemade, and bread home-baked. A dinner meal is sometimes offered (though there will usually be an extra minimal charge for it), and you should accept if possible. Typically this meal is quite a feast as well as a memorable experience, and if you are staying on a fairly isolated farm, there may not be any restaurants nearby anyway. There are *turismo rural* member participants in nearly all of Spain's regions, but the highest concentration of properties is in Asturias, Navarre, Aragon, Galicia, Cantabria (in both Galicia and Cantabria rural properties are more often referred to as *casas de labranza*), Andalusia, and

Catalonia. The very best source—and an excellent one at that—for these accommodations is *El Libro Verde del Turismo Rural* (The Green Guide to Rural Tourism), a complimentary 115-page directory published by the Spanish Tourist Office. This particular edition features listings for Asturias, Cantabria, the Basque Country, and Galicia and includes color photos of each property, maps, points of interest for each region, symbols representing the various characteristics and amenities, and complete contact information for each region's major tourist offices. The guide is published in Spanish, Basque, English, French, Italian, and Portuguese, and an accompanying booklet provides the *tarifas* (tariffs). You should inquire at the North American Spanish tourist offices for this absolutely *esencial* set of publications, or alternatively contact the regional tourist offices: Asturias (Dirección General de Comercio y Turismo, Plaza de España, 1 bajo, 33007 Oviedo; 985.10.64.33; fax: 985.10.64.21; www.princast.es); Cantabria (Gobierno de Cantabria, Dirección General de Turismo, P° de Pereda no. 31, 1°, 39004 Santander; 942.31.85.70; fax: 942.31.85.65; www.turismo.cantabria.org); Euskadi (Gobierno Vasco, Dpto. de Industria, Comercio y Turismo, Donostia–San Sebastián 1, 01010 Vitoria-Gasteiz; 945.01.99.84; fax: 945.01.99.31; www.euskadi.net); and Galicia (Turgalicia, Estrada Santiago—Noia, Kilometer 3–A Barcia, 15896 Santiago de Compostela; 981.54.25.00; fax: 981.53.75.88; www.turgalicia.es).

Home exchange might be an appealing option. I've read wildly enthusiastic reports from people who've swapped apartments or houses, and it's usually always an economical alternative. ~HomeLink International (Karl Costabel, P.O. Box 47747, Tampa, FL 33647; 800-638-3841 or 813-975-9825; www.homelink.org) claims to be the world's largest home exchange organization, with more than twelve thousand members, twenty-six offices around the world, and five directories published each year. ~Intervac (world headquarters: Box 12066, S-291, 12 Kristianstad, Sweden; U.S. address: 30 Corte San Fernando, Tiburon, CA 94920; 800-756-HOME; www.intervacus.com), whose name was created from the words *international* and *vacations,* was founded in 1953 in Switzerland by a group of teachers who were looking for economical means to travel. After a few exchanges, they realized this was also a great way to cultivate international friendships and understanding. Intervac services are available in fifty countries, and the company publishes five directories a year with more than twelve thousand listings. ~Trading Homes International (P.O. Box 787, Hermosa Beach, CA 90254; 800-877-TRADE; fax: 310-798-3865; www.trading-homes.com) was founded in 1991 and was a founding member, with thirteen other exchange companies, of the International Home Exchange Association. Its staff believes home exchange is "a way to give people a whole new perspective on what travel can really be like when you vacation as a local and not as a tourist." ~Seniors Home Exchange (www.seniorshomeexchange.com) is limited to members over age fifty. ~HomeExchange.com (www.homeexchange.com) is a Web-only home exchange company. Based in

Santa Barbara and founded in 1996, it features more than two thousand listings, and through the website's discussion board viewers can read of others' experiences.

A good but out-of-print book to read is *Trading Places: The Wonderful World of Vacation Home Exchanging* (Bill and Mary Barbour, Rutledge Hill Press, Nashville, TN, 1991). ~*Consumer Reports Travel Letter* presented a special report on home exchange in its November 2001 issue, noting that the number-one complaint filed by exchangers is cleanliness. Obviously different people interpret *clean* in different ways (males and females do, too), so this is something to keep in mind when making arrangements. (To request a copy, send $5 to *CRTL*, 101 Truman Avenue, Yonkers, NY 10703.)

Hostales are typically modest lodgings that are rated from one to three stars. Generally speaking, if one had to make a comparison, a two-star *hostal* is equivalent to a one-star hotel, but not always. Usually, *hostales* establishments offer rooms either with or without private bath, and are priced accordingly.

Hostales residencias (which appear on signs as HsR) are also budget accommodations but are set apart from regular *hostales* mostly because they do not offer meals. (If they do, that meal will be breakfast.)

Hotels are, of course, where most of us stay when we travel, and I feel that books exclusively about hotels are better than recommendations from general guidebooks. As with guidebooks, the right hotel book for you is the one whose author shares with you a certain sensibility or philosophy. It's important to select the right book(s) so you can make choices that best suit you and your style. I believe that you put your trust in the author of a hotel guide in the same way you put your faith in the author of a guidebook. Once you've selected the book you like, trust the author's recommendations, make your decisions, and move on to the next stage of your planning. I have never understood those people who, after they've made a reservation, seek some sort of validation for their choice—by searching the Internet, for example—for other travelers' comments and opinions. I find this to serve no good purpose and to be a poor use of one's time, and it makes me wonder why those people consulted the hotel books in the first place. Remember: *you don't know the people writing reviews on the Internet, and you have no idea if the same things that are important to you are important to them*. Authors of hotel guides carefully share their standards with you and explain the criteria they use in rating accommodations. I believe—because I read a lot of travel guidebooks and hotel guides—that most of the time authors are clear about what they look for and expect in hotel establishments, and though you might not always agree, you may at least understand how they arrived at their conclusions.

Architecture critic Paul Goldberger has written that "a good hotel is a place, a town, a city, a world unto itself, and the aura it exudes has almost nothing to do with its rooms and almost everything to do with everything else—the lobby, the bar, the restaurants, the façade, the signs, even the corridors and the elevators."

This observation applies to hotels large and small, expensive and not. Hotels like the ones Goldberger describes exist in all price categories. It is never difficult to learn of either luxury or budget places to stay; what is harder is finding distinctive and interesting places that fall in between. The following books are my favorites to use when searching for a hotel in this part of Spain:

~*Charming Small Hotel Guides: Spain* (Duncan Petersen Publishing, London / Hunter Publishing, Edison, NJ). This series features the kind of places where I most like to stay. The authors explain that some of the qualities they look for include "a calm, attractive setting in an interesting and picturesque position; a building that is either handsome or interesting or historic, or at least with a distinct character; bedrooms which are well proportioned with as much character as the public rooms below; ideally, we look for adequate space, but on a human scale: we don't go for places that rely on grandeur, or that have pretensions that could intimidate; decorations must be harmonious and in good taste, and the furnishings and facilities comfortable and well maintained. We like to see interesting antique furniture that is there because it can be used, not simply revered; the proprietors and staff need to be dedicated and thoughtful, offering a personal welcome, without being intrusive. The guest needs to feel like an individual." This guide has two types of entries: full page (for places that have nearly all the qualities listed above) and half page (for places that are still charming but don't have as many of those qualities; after all, as they note, you can't have stars on every page). Featured are thirty-eight listings across Northern Spain, in Asturias, Pontevedra, León, Cantabria, Navarra, La Rioja, Burgos, Santiago, Orense, and Vizcaya, any one of which would make a memorable night's stay.

~*Hello Spain! An Insider's Guide to Spain Hotels $40–80 a Night for Two* (Margo Classé, Wilson Publishing, Los Angeles, California). For this book and the others in her series, Classé set out to discover a selection of clean, safe, centrally located, and inexpensive places to spend the night in twenty-two Spanish cities and towns. Listings include rooms for single, double, and triple occupancies. Listings in Northern Spain are provided only for Santiago (fifteen) and Pamplona (nine), plus Madrid, of course. Classé also provides directions to each hotel, tips on making reservations, Spanish phrases for check-in, the annual schedule of holidays, festivals, and events, and "packing the unusual." I really like this book and have stayed at a few places Classé recommends. If you visit Spain frequently, or plan to, you'll want to buy this; otherwise you may want to check it out of your local library. Either way, this one-of-a-kind book is essential for identifying moderately priced accommodations. Classé notes that showing her book to the proprietor may result in a discount.

~*Hotel Gems of Spain* (compiled by Luc Quisenaerts, written by Owen Davis, D–Publications, Brussels, 1999). This is an edition in the beautiful Hotel Gems of the World series. Most of these places are to die for, with prices to match, but still,

I'd rather spend my money on one of them than on an international chain hotel. As the author notes, "By enjoying the hospitality of the people of a country for one or several nights, one can taste the history, the culture and the cuisine of such a country in a deeply personal way . . . that is why this series, and each book in itself, can be considered a valuable archive containing a piece of the wealth and beauty of a country, created by the passion of all those people who put their souls into it." Each hotel is described in four to eight pages with photos that make you want to pack your bags *inmediatamente*. Practical information—prices, contact information, and so on—is at the back of the book, along with a map. Of the thirty-two featured hotels, four are in Northern Spain (the *paradors* in León and Santiago, Landa Palace in Burgos, and San Roman de Escalante near Bilbao) and two are in Madrid (Villa Real and Santo Mauro).

~*Karen Brown's Spain: Charming Inns & Itineraries* (Clare Brown, June Brown, Karen Brown, Lorena Aburto Ramirez, and Cynthia Sauvage, Fodor's Travel Publications). My husband and I have found some of the most wonderful places to stay with the help of Karen Brown's guides. In addition to the thorough descriptions of lodgings (some of which are in castles, old mills, and buildings of historic significance), this guide includes good tips on banking, climate, clothing, driving, festivals and folklore, food and drink, telephones, and tipping. Some of the lodgings featured also happen to be member properties of the Relais & Chateaux group (see the entry below under Hotel Groups). As the authors state in the introduction, "This book is designed for the traveler looking for a guide to more than the capital city and a handful of highlights, for the visitor who wants to add a little out of the ordinary to his agenda. We do not claim to be objective reporters—that sort of treatment is available anywhere—but subjective, on-site raconteurs. We have a definite bias toward hotels with romantic ambiance, from charming stone farmhouses tucked in the mountains to sumptuous castles overlooking the sea. If you follow our itineraries (each one of which we have traveled personally) and trust in our hotel recommendations (every one of which we have visited personally), you will be assured of Spain's best lodgings while discovering the country's most intriguing destinations." They add that "sometimes we could not find an ideal hotel in an important sightseeing location where we felt we needed to have a place to recommend. In such situations we have chosen for you what we consider to be the best place to stay in the area. We try to be consistently candid and honest in our appraisals. We feel that if you know what to expect, you won't be disappointed." In Northern Spain there are seven listings for Galicia, fifteen spread out across Asturias, Cantabria, and the Basque Country, and one in La Rioja. The itineraries presented in the book are useful for planning your route in advance and deciding if you want to travel by car, but the descriptions of individual towns and sites are not detailed enough to warrant bringing the book along—this is really a before-you-go book. I find the organization of Karen Brown's guides maddeningly cumbersome: The lodgings are listed alphabetically by individual city, town, or village, but the maps are at the back of the book, so you end up constantly flipping pages back and forth to evaluate all the available choices in any given region. But the descriptions of the properties are thorough and candid, and I trust the authors that a stay at any of these places would be memorable. The listings aside, two of the features I like best about Karen Brown guides in general are the sample Reservation Request Letter (in Spanish and English so readers can construct a letter, fax, or e-mail of their own) and the list of places to stay with handicapped facilities. In conjunction with this book, readers may view the Karen Brown website (www.karenbrown.com), which provides comments from other travelers as well as updates and a direct e-mail link to most of the lodgings featured in the book. When reserving, it pays to identify oneself as a Karen Brown reader as some properties will extend a small discount. This is a great guide to consult even if you don't plan on going to other parts of Spain.

~The *Guía Oficial de Hoteles* is the official Spanish hotels bible, and it's published annually by Turespaña. Readers may consult it at the Spanish tourist offices in North America or purchase one in Spain (it's sold at bookstores and newsstands); but I have not found the guide so very helpful. Though it lists every hotel, *hostal,* and *pensión* in Spain, it informs you only of each property's star rating, rates, and facilities—in other words, there is no *description* of each place, which to me is one of the most important features of a lodging. I need to know much more about a facility besides its amenities. But the guide is useful if you're just searching for listings, or you want to learn how the Spanish government rates a property you're considering.

Hotel chains are not generally my cup of tea, either here in the United States or abroad. But some individual properties within a chain can be surprisingly unique. Some of the bigger tour operators book rooms in some of Spain's largest hotel chains, such as TRYP, Grupo Sol Meliá, and Grupo Riu.

Hotel groups often represent properties that aren't featured in other publications. Here are a few groups that feature properties in Spain—and that are also my personal favorites.

~*Estancias de España* is a group of properties—not just hotels but restaurants, too—that occupy historic buildings such as former convents, palaces, castles, country manors, estates, mills, and wine cellars. Like the Abitare la Storia (Hospitality in Historical Houses) group in Italy, Estancias properties are not government-run. "Traveling with Estancias de España," as noted in the brochure, "will afford you the opportunity not only to see and observe, but also to feel our history and art, culture, our traditions, as something live, and take part and enjoy the varied natural surroundings in the different regions of Spain." There are currently nine Estancias properties in Northern Spain, and reservations may be made directly with the inn or through the central reservations office in Madrid (Menendez Pidal 31,

28036 Madrid; 91.345.41.41; fax: 91.345.51.74; www.estancias.com). Frequent Estancias visitors may want to apply for the *privilegio* card, which offers a number of perks.

~*Paradores de Turisimo,* a government-run chain of properties, is the best-known hotel group in Spain, and I have found *paradores* to be among the finest hotels in the world (and a much better value than comparable establishments in other European countries). The Paradores chain offers unique accommodations in a variety of historic and significant properties, ranging from old monasteries and *castillos* to new and modern structures, in urban and rural settings. There are more than eighty-six *paradores* throughout Spain, and depending on how you draw the boundaries, about twenty of them are in Northern Spain, so you will have no trouble securing reservations at at least one. (You should note that summer is the busiest time of year for *paradores,* especially in Northern Spain, not surprisingly, as the weather is best then.) The summer 2001 edition of *Paradores* magazine featured an interview with Ana Isabel Marino, executive president of Paradores de Turismo (the first woman to hold this post in the seventy years of the chain's history), and she noted that "the proportion of tourists of non-Spanish nationality who visit us has reached 48 percent. What is most important is that those tourists are not preventing the Spanish from enjoying the network. Paradores is a business of the 21st century, dynamic, committed to the present and the future of Spain." Parents should be aware that the Paradores chain welcomes children, and its restaurants even offer a children's menu that is a fold-out extravaganza with games, puzzles, and a quiz. Though *paradores* are located all over Spain, some of them are geographically situated to form a natural "route." As a result visitors may explore themed routes such as the Silver Route, the Route of the Castilian Language, and the Monasteries of the Royal Places. The network makes it advantageous for travelers to follow the routes by offering special packages, including the *especial dos noches* (two-night special), the *tarjeta cinco noches* (five-night card), the *semana de ensueño* (week of enchantment), the *escapada joven* (youth escapade), and the *días dorados* (golden days, for those sixty or older). One could, with advance planning, easily arrange to stay in *paradores* across the entire length of Northern Spain without breaking the bank. In addition to providing outstanding accommodations, the *paradores* are known for offering local and regional cuisine. Visitors may request a *circuitos gastronómicos* (gastronomic tours) passport, which allows for five meals at the cost of four. (This may not apply at all properties in the chain, so inquire first.) The Paradores de Turismo office publishes a good directory, in English and Spanish, featuring descriptive information and a color photo for each *parador;* the directory is available at Spanish tourist offices in North America. Reservations may be made by contacting the *parador* directly, contacting the central reservations center (Paradores de Turismo, Requena 3, 28013 Madrid; 91.516.66.66; fax: 91.516.66.57; www.parador.es) or contacting one of the

Paradores partners in the United States: Marketing Ahead, 433 Fifth Avenue, New York, NY 10016; 800-223-1356 or 212-686-9213; fax: 212-686-0271; PTB Hotels, 19710 Ventura Boulevard, Suite 210, Woodland Hills, CA 91364; 800-634-1188 or 818-884-1984; fax: -4075; or PTB Miami, 100 North Biscayne Boulevard, Suite 604, Miami, FL 33132; 305-371-8057; fax: 305-358-7003. Those who reserve through Marketing Ahead and identify themselves as a Karen Brown reader receive a 5 percent discount (not available through a travel agent). ~A good article to read about *paradores* and their regional cuisine is "Spanish Dining Rooms Fit for King" (Penelope Casas, *The New York Times* travel section, January 13, 2002), in which the author and her husband mapped out a trip from Madrid to Galicia, stopping at ten *paradores* along the route.

~*Relais & Chateaux* is a well-known hotel group that was founded in 1954 and now has over 450 member properties, hotels, and restaurants in fifty-one countries. R&C has remained loyal to its five Cs: courtesy, charm, character, calm, and cuisine. At the time of this writing, R&C has three properties in the Basque Country, one each in Cantabria and Castilla y León, and two in Madrid. (R&C usually adds a few new members every year—some are dropped, too—so it pays to double-check on member properties periodically.) Recently the L'École des Chefs program (profiled originally in my *Paris* edition) became a member of R&C, so visitors to Spain now have the opportunity to participate in this unique restaurant experience (see Cooking Schools entry for details). The hefty (more than 600 pages) R&C guide is a good resource for discerning travelers. For a copy and more information, contact Relais & Chateaux at its North American office, 11 East 44th Street, Suite 707, New York, NY 10017; 800-735-2478 or 212-856-0115; fax: -0193; www.relaischateaux.com.

Monasteries and convents are a singular (and budget) accommodation choice. I have not seen a book exclusively devoted to monastery lodgings in Spain, but the Spanish tourist offices in North America can provide interested readers with information on the approximately 150 lodgings of this sort. (It is not required to be Christian to stay at a monastery, by the way.) You should know that staying at a convent is not the same as staying in a hotel, and you should not expect great comfort or a lot of amenities. (Few monasteries have a television or a private telephone, for example.) Rather, what you will find are simple, immaculately clean quarters, solitude, possibly a meal or two (though you need to eat when the resident monks or nuns eat), not much English spoken (a great opportunity to practice your Spanish!), a possible curfew, and possible single-sex accommodations (some convents admit only men, others only women)—and a wholly unique and untouristy experience.

Renting an apartment or villa might be a suitable choice depending on how long you'll be in the area and the number of people you're traveling with. While I very much like staying in inns and hotels, I also like the idea of renting because it can be a quick way to feel a part of the local routine—you have daily chores to accomplish just like everyone else (except that I would hardly call going to pick up provisions at the local *mercado* a chore). Though your tasks are mixed in with lots of little pleasures, sight-seeing, and trips, you often avoid the too-much-to-do rut. What to eat suddenly looms as the most important question of the day, the same question that all the local families are trying to answer. Renting therefore forces you to take an active part in the culture rather than catch a glimpse of it. A comprehensive listing of organizations that arrange short- and long-term rentals would fill a small book, and it is not my intent here to provide one. Rather, the following are some sources that have either come highly recommended or with which I have had a positive experience:

~*Barclay International Group* offers one of the world's largest and most reputable collections of apartments and villas in Europe, focusing especially on the Mediterranean destinations of Spain, Italy, France, Greece, and Portugal. When I last checked, it had no listings for villas or apartments in Northern Spain, but it is entirely possible that by the time this book is published, Barclay will have added options in the north. (I did find three wonderful apartments in Madrid.) Barclay is such a well-regarded company that I would not overlook it while researching my options. It's also a good resource for reserving extras like car rentals, sight-seeing tours, theater tickets, rail passes, cell phones, and laptop computers. Contact information: 3 School Street, Glen Cove, NY 11542; 800-845-6636 or 516-759-5100; fax: 516-609-0000; www.barclayweb.com.

~*Rentvillas.com,* an Internet company based in the United States, has sixteen years in the villa business. According to its promotional material, Rentvillas.com "is dedicated to being the most experienced, the most innovative, and the most customer-focused company in the industry." All the staff members of Rentvillas. com love to travel and make clients feel as though they're receiving their undivided attention. Not surprisingly, when last I checked, there were no properties available outside of Andalusia, the Canary and Balaeric Islands, and Catalonia; but again, it would be worthwhile to double-check with Rentvillas, as it's likely other areas of Spain will be represented in the future. To learn more about the company, you can visit its website and subscribe to its newsletter (you're able to subscribe on-line), which features missives from travelers who've rented from Rentvillas. Renters share their experiences, and Rentvillas staff offer lots of useful tips. Contact information: 700 East Main Street, Ventura, California 93001; 800-726-6702 or 805-641-1650; fax: -1630.

~When renting a property, don't forget to ask thorough questions and read the fine print. Some questions to ask include: Is there air conditioning? (air conditioning is rare, not only in Spain but throughout the Mediterranean, so inquire if there is cross-ventilation or a ceiling fan); How is the water pressure? Is hot water available at all times? Are children or pets welcome? Is there a crib for a young child?

What is the charge for use of the telephone? Are toilet paper, sheets, and blankets provided? Are there coffee filters (if there is a coffee maker)? Is there a corkscrew in the kitchen? Is there a mosquito coil? (Screens are rare in windows in Mediterranean countries, even in Northern Spain, and if you spy a mosquito coil— either the kind you light with a match or the kind that plugs into the wall—that is your clue that pesky bugs will be about after the sun goes down, and you'll be happy to have the protection.) Is there construction going on nearby? How close (or far) is the food market? (Since some of the most appealing houses in the country are in rather rural areas, you may be some distance from a main road.) In addition to these questions and a few unique to your own situation, keep in mind the following good advice from a company called Homebase Abroad, which arranges rentals exclusively in Italy: "Renting abroad is an adventure, no matter the level of house you're considering. If the myriad differences between an Italian [in this case, Spanish] home and your home, between the Italian [or Spanish] lifestyle and your lifestyle are unwelcome, you might have to conclude this is not the right trip for you and your group."

General accommodation notes to keep in mind: ~Ask for a reservation confirmation in writing. Though I may place an initial telephone call to an inn or hotel, I prefer that the final communication be by fax or hard copy of an e-mail. This allows for any language errors to be corrected and serves as an official document. While a hard copy alone does not guarantee something won't go wrong, producing one can certainly help at check-in. If you arrive at your lodging and the staff cannot honor your reservation, be polite but firm in asking for a better room elsewhere in the hotel (at the same price) or a comparable room at another lodging. (You could also push the envelope here and ask that they pay for your first night, this being their mistake and an inconvenience to you.) The hotel is obligated to find you comparable alternative lodgings—not to pay for your night someplace else—but I figure this is part of a bargaining process in arriving at a solution. You should also ask them to pay for your transportation to the other location (should this be the result), which the staff should not hesitate to do.

~When you first arrive at your hotel, ask to see your room first. This is a common practice in Europe, and it is understood that if a room is not to your liking, you may request a different one. This is also your opportunity to ask for a room upgrade; if the hotel is not fully booked (and it rarely will be during low season), you may end up with a significantly nicer room at the same rate. It never hurts to ask.

~Speaking of fully booked: If you've been told that you can't get a room, call again between four and six P.M. and double-check. This is the time of day when many establishments cancel the reservations of guests who haven't shown up.

~If a hotel you choose also has a reservations office in the United States, call both numbers. It is entirely possible that you will be quoted different rates. Also, some of the more expensive hotels offer a rate that must be prepaid in full, in advance of your trip, in U.S. dollars, but that is lower than the local rack rate.

~No matter what type of lodging you choose, *always* inquire if there is a lower rate. Reservationists—and even the owners of small inns—always hope the rate they quote will be accepted, and if you don't ask about other possibilities, they will not volunteer any. In addition, ask if there are corporate rates; special rates for seniors, students, or government and military employees; weekend rates (this usually applies only to city hotels, as business travelers will have checked out by Friday); and even special prices for newlyweds. Hotels and inns large and small all want to fill their rooms, and if you'll be staying four nights (sometimes three) or longer, you may also be able to negotiate a better rate. Most important, ask for how long the rate you're quoted is available and how many rooms at that price are left. In smaller places especially, a day can mean the difference between securing a reservation and losing it.

~Breakfast is rarely a good value taken at a hotel, especially in Spain where a Spanish breakfast typically consists of a coffee drink and a roll of some sort. Save some money—and get the same thing, often better—and join the locals at the corner *café*.

~Useful vocabulary: *almohada* (pillow); *llave* (key); *sábanas* (sheets); *manta* (blanket); *jabón* (soap); *toalla* (bath towel); *agua caliente* (hot water); *aire* (air conditioning); *calefacción* (heat); *llamada de desperatado* (wake-up call); *incluida/o* (included, as in, "Is breakfast included in the price?"); *¿Dónde podemos dejar el coche?* ("Where can we leave the car?"); *¿Tiene una habitación más tranquila?* ("Do you have a quieter room?"); *¿A partir de qué hora dan el desayuno?* ("What time do you serve breakfast?"); *¿Tendría una aspirina?* ("Do you have some aspirin?"); *¿A qué hora tenemos que dejar libre nuestra habitación?* ("What time is checkout?"); *Queremos pagar* ("We'd like to pay the bill"); *Cuánto le debemos?* ("How much do we owe you?"); *Vamos a llegar tarde* ("We'll be arriving late"); *Esperamos volver* ("We hope to return"); and *Este es un lugar maravilloso* ("This is a wonderful place").

Addresses

If you are searching for a residential or business address, note that the house number *follows* the name of the street (unlike addresses in North America, where the number precedes the street name). Also, the floor of an apartment building appears after a hyphen. So, if you see 5-3°, it refers to the third floor of building number five on such-and-such a street. (*Planta* and *piso*, by the way, are the words for "floor.") If you then see a number, 3ª for example, following the floor number, it refers to a specific office or apartment number (in this case, *tercera puerta*) on a particular floor. (*Puerta* is actually the word for "door," but in this case it refers to "apartment" or "office.")

Airfares and Airlines

We all know that not everyone pays the same price for seats on an airplane. One of the reasons for this is that seats do not hold the same value at all times of the year, month, or even day of the week. Recently I was researching some fares to Paris for a long weekend. One of my calls produced a particularly helpful representative who proceeded to detail all available fares for the entire month of September. Within that month alone there were approximately fifteen different prices, based on a seemingly endless number of variables. The best way therefore to get the best deal that accommodates your needs is to check a variety of sources and be flexible. Flexibility is, and has always been, the key to low-cost travel, and you should be prepared to slightly alter the dates of your proposed trip to take advantage of those airline seats that hold less value.

If you think all the best deals are to be found on the Internet, you're mistaken: Airlines, consolidators, and other discounters offer plenty of good fares over the telephone and through advertisements. In order to know with certainty that you've got a good deal, you need to comparison-shop, which requires checking more than one source. Many people have cornered me over the years and asked for my "secret" to finding a cheap airfare. The answer is that there is no secret, only diligent research. Price isn't the only factor in planning a trip, and if a supposedly cheap fare is offered only at times that are inconvenient for me, then it isn't cheap at all, it's outside the realm of possibility and therefore worthless. I believe that on any day of the week, the lowest fares can be found *equally* among websites, wholesalers, airlines, charters, tour operators, travel agents, and sky auctions. No website, not even Orbitz, can claim to offer all choices for all travelers, and you don't know who's offering what until you inquire.

Iberia. I like flying a country's own airline—Iberia, for example—and even though Iberia fares are usually among the highest available, its off-season fares are among the lowest, and it offers some unbeatable packages and deals throughout the year. Iberia is one of the world's oldest airlines, formally founded on June 28, 1927. Until 1939 Iberia remained a domestic airline. Its longest route, established in 1937, was from Vitoria in the Basque Country to Tétuoan in Spanish Morocco; in 1946 the airline was the first to offer service between Europe and South America; and in 1977 Iberia celebrated its fiftieth anniversary. More recently Iberia was a founding partner of the computerized European ticket reservations system, Amadeus, and in my experience over the years, Iberia has proved to be a top-notch airline in every way. (Its in-flight magazine, *Iberia Ronda,* is also quite well written and is published in both Spanish and English.) I was particularly impressed with Iberia when I traveled to Northern Spain about four weeks after the September 11 tragedy. A representative told my husband and me to arrive at the airport four hours in advance, which seemed excessive, but when we arrived, two airline armed guards escorted us to a little room away from the check-in counters. There, more security guards and dogs examined the contents of every one of our bags, which were emptied entirely and sent through the scanners one more time, empty. Everyone was very apologetic and kind, and the whole operation was carried out quite smoothly. We were grateful, and remain so, for Iberia's thorough examination. Iberia maintains three offices in the United States, in New York, Chicago, and Miami. For information and reservations, however, contact Iberia at its toll-free number, 800-772-4642, or visit its website, www.iberia-usa.com. I encourage you to consider what Iberia is offering at the time you are making your flight plans.

Research. As I think is obvious, researching airfares and airlines is essential but fairly time-consuming. If you are really determined to turn over every stone, you'll find a lot of avenues to explore in Peter Greenberg's excellent book *The Travel Detective: How to Get the Best Service and the Best Deals from Airlines, Hotels, Cruise Ships, and Car Rental Agencies* (Villard, 2001; see the General Travel entry for more details). Some "tricks" include paying split ticket fares, back-to-back ticketing, getting add-on legs for no additional cost, and buying a full-fare ticket and then returning it if you find a better deal at the last minute—these are all detailed in Greenberg's book. I find some of these tactics more time-consuming than they are worth, and I don't usually have the time to conduct an exhaustive search, but some sources I typically consult before I buy anything include 800-AIRFARE; 800-FLYCHEAP; 800-FLY4LESS; 800-6LOWAIR (just to clarify, this is the toll-free number for a firm called Air 4 Less); 800-CHEAPAIR (this is the number for American Travel Associates, a company dealing mostly with domestic flights though some international discounts are available); Orbitz (www.orbitz.com); Travelocity (www.travelocity.com); Expedia Travel (www.expedia.com); Cheap Tickets (www.cheaptickets.com); OneTravel.com; Trip.com; Flights.com; Lowestfare.com; QIXO (www.qixo.com) (pronounced KICK-so); STA Travel (Student Travel Association but plans trips for "generations X, Y and Z"; 800-777-0112 or www.statravel.com); Council Travel (known as "America's Student Travel Leader," this fifty-four-year-old company also offers good fares for adults and a host of useful stuff for students and teachers; 800-2COUNCIL or www.council-travel.com); and the travel section of *The New York Times* (my local daily newspaper), which I scan for ads of all the area agencies offering low prices. Many of these ads typically reveal the same low fares by one or two particular airlines, almost always smaller foreign lines currently trying to expand their business in the United States. (I once flew on Pakistan International Air to Paris; the PIA flight was destined for Karachi but stopped in Paris en route.) Note that the Internet sites listed here began their life as search engines for airfares only but now offer a wider range of services, including rental cars and hotel accommodations. Also, remember to consider alternative airports in your area, not just the obvious major hubs. Where I live in New York, for example, there are always different fares when I compare flights departing from Newark, New Jersey, and JFK Airport in Queens. And if you're already in Spain and want to fly somewhere else within Europe, check with Europe by Air (888-387-2479; www.europebyair.com).

Internet booking. Booking travel on the Web works best for people with simple requirements and lots of flexibility. In fact, if you can leave on really short notice, some great deals may be in store for you: a website specializing in just such spur-of-the-moment travel is LastMinuteTravel.com, which offers last-minute fares from a number of airlines, and the carriers then have the opportunity to reduce the fares if seats aren't selling. Another site is 11thhourVacations.com. With both, make sure to check their fares against the airlines' to ensure you're really getting a last-minute bargain. Participating in sky auctions (via Priceline.com or SkyAuction.com, for example) is not appealing to me personally. If you have a lot of questions, as I always do, you can't get them answered and are setting yourself up for a potential headache. I never seem to be able to find a flight scenario that works with my schedule, and I don't like the fact that I can't more finely narrow the criteria when submitting my initial bid—what *time* of day I fly is just as important as the date. The time it takes to continue submitting bids (my initial bid is never accepted) seems wasteful to me, time I could be spending getting concrete information from other sources. Additionally, I have read that the idea of submitting your own price for a ticket is illusory; in fact, the Internet firms buy discounted seats from the airlines but sell only those seats at fares above an established threshold. Bids below that level are rejected. Also, travelers seldom have control over which airlines they'll fly or which cities they'll stop in if it's a connecting flight. And most don't allow you to earn mileage points.

Paper tickets versus e-tickets. The controversy over paper tickets versus e-tickets is nearly obsolete, as most airlines' computer systems are now in synch with each other. (It was once common that if an airline has to route passengers on another flight or another carrier, holders of paper tickets are ahead of the game because airlines' computers couldn't communicate with each other. E-ticket holders had to wait in line to have their e-tickets converted into paper, and then wait in another line to be confirmed on another flight.) I still prefer old-fashioned paper, even if costs a bit more. When I have to use an e-ticket I always call the airline directly a few days after I make the reservation, and again about a week before the departure date, to make sure I am confirmed. As of this writing, American Airlines offers interline e-ticketing with Continental and United; Continental has agreements with America West, Northwest, and United; and United offers it with Air Canada, American, Continental, and Northwest.

Flights Within Europe. You may want to investigate flying to another European city first—such as London or Paris—since there are no direct flights from North America to any of the airports in Northern Spain. You'll find a greater selection of flights available, most likely to Bilbao, Santiago, and San Sebastián, and the flexibility this extra choice provides may ease some trip-planning logistics. London especially is a city filled with consolidators (known as bucket shops), and there are a number of flights from Paris too to accommodate the great number of business and vacation travelers. This said, in December 2001 a piece appeared in the travel section of *The New York Times* about how Europe's airlines are facing what is probably an inevitable outcome of September 11: the "extensive nonstop city-to-city service within the Continent and its direct service to distant former colonies may give way to an American-style hub-and-spoke system requiring many more passengers to change planes to reach their destinations." Apparently the European Union's single-market rules prohibit large government subsidies for airlines, and there soon may be only three or four major international carriers: Air France, British Airways, Lufthansa, and perhaps KLM. (This same article reported that the board of Alitalia had hinted it might cancel international flights altogether as it could not sustain its global business without major changes.) This would mean not only that there would be far fewer flights available from Paris or London to Northern Spain but also that passengers would have to fly from, say, Philadelphia to Paris, then Paris to Madrid, and then a third flight from Madrid to Bilbao or Santiago. A new European online ticket-seller, by the way, is Opodo.com (short for "opportunity to do"). Similar to Orbitz in the United States, Opodo is owned by nine European airlines (British Airways, Air France, Lufthansa, Aer Lingus, Alitalia, Austrian, Finnair, Iberia, and KLM), and the site is open to North Americans as well. Opodo, like any other Internet site, does not *always* offer the best prices or schedules, but it is one more resource to consider.

Travel agencies. Though it was perhaps inevitable that a great number of travel agencies would close due to the arrival of the Internet, do not underestimate what a quality agent can do for you. If you already have one, you know that a good travel agent is indispensable, worth his or her weight in gold. The resourceful traveler will often be able to put together a detailed trip equally as well as an average agent, but even the most resourceful and determined traveler will not be able to match the savvy of a top-notch agent. I believe that at the end of the day the Internet is a great resource tool, but it's not a human being watching over every last detail for you. The more specialized or complicated your trip is, the more reason you should employ the services of an experienced agent. To read more about exactly what a good agent is capable of, see the article "Travel Superheroes" (Wendy Perrin, *Condé Nast Traveler,* August 2002). Perrin identifies seventy travel consultants described as "better connected than the Internet, faster than a T3 line, able to book the unbookable." Of the seventy, sixty-three are members of the Virtuoso network, which specializes in leisure travel for discerning clients. Less than one percent of consultants in the Americas are accepted for membership in Virtuoso, which utilizes a worldwide network of four hundred cruise, tour, adventure, property, and ground operator partners in sixty countries. Contact Virtuoso at 800-401-4274 or www.virtuoso.com.

Consolidators. Don't be afraid of reputable consolidators, but recognize that their lower fares come with more restrictions. If your flight is canceled or delayed, you have no recourse with the airline since it didn't sell you the ticket directly, and other airlines may not honor the ticket either. (This also holds true for tickets purchased through discount Internet companies.) If you want to make any changes, you have to pay a penalty. The question to ask of a consolidator is "Do you accept credit cards?" The rule of thumb is, if it doesn't, go elsewhere; but I admit to you that on two occasions I purchased tickets with cash and had absolutely no problems. Some consolidators advertise directly to the general public, but many do not, so if you're interested in purchasing these tickets, inquire at a travel agency. (Some have long-standing relationships with certain consolidators.) There is also an organization called the U.S. Air Consolidators Association that is a consortium of consolidators. Members are firmly established with good reputations and have never filed for bankruptcy or ceased business operations. To find out more, contact the organization at 916-441-4166 or view its website at www.usaca.com. Additionally, if you are hooked on the consolidated way, you may want to get the handy Airline Consolidators Quick Reference Chart, which cross-references companies with the geographic areas of the world they specialize in. It's available from On the Go Publishing (P.O. Box 91033, Columbus, OH; fax 513-766-2002 ext. 4599; www.onthegopublishing.com) and costs about $22.

Charter flights. Reputable charter flights, too, should not be feared. I've had three good experiences on charter flights—one to Madrid—and encourage you to investigate them. The limitations are that most charters offer only coach class, and they tend to be completely full—in fact, a charter operator is legally allowed to cancel a flight up to ten days before departure if it doesn't fill enough seats. I wouldn't therefore travel with children necessarily or plan a honeymoon on a charter flight. Although I did not experience any problems on my charter flights, I understand that delays are common, and (as with consolidators) passengers have no recourse. But operators who organize charter flights are required to place passengers' payments for the flight in an escrow account, so if the flight is canceled or if the operator doesn't abide by its agreement, you receive a refund. A publication called *Jax Fax Travel Marketing Magazine* lists more than five thousand scheduled charter flights to more than a hundred destinations worldwide. Previously available only to industry folks, the general public can now subscribe. Contact Jax Fax at 48 Wellington Road, Milford, CT 06460; 800-9JAXFAX or 203-301-0255; fax: -0250; www.jaxfax.com. A single issue can be purchased for about $5 as well as a one- or two-year subscription.

Courier. Flying as a courier is no longer the amazing deal it once was, but if you're a light packer, it can still be a good deal. (Luggage is usually limited to one carry-on bag.) Couriers also can't usually reserve a seat for more than one person, although your traveling companion could purchase a ticket on the same flight. Air couriers are cogs in international commerce; they are completely legal and legitimate, and the demand for them exceeds the supply. They are a necessity simply because companies doing international business send a large number of documents overseas, and those documents can get held up in customs unless accompanied by a person. Couriers are responsible for chaperoning documents through customs and then hand-delivering them to a person waiting outside the customs area. To read a thorough account of an air courier passenger, see "Operation Courier" by Steve Hendrix, which appeared in the travel section of *The Washington Post* on December 16, 2001. Among some of the tips Hendrix shared: As a courier, you may be asked to pay a $100 refundable deposit, which you will get back after you complete your task; depending on the season and demand, you can expect to save between 30 and 60 percent on a fare, and if you are superflexible and can leave on a moment's notice, your fare may drop sharply, rapidly; typical departure cities in the United States are Washington, Boston, Chicago, Los Angeles, Miami, New York, and San Francisco, while the most most common destination cities are Amsterdam, Johannesburg, London, Paris, Bangkok, Beijing, Hong Kong, Manila, Seoul, Singapore, Tokyo, Buenos Aires, Mexico City, Montevideo, Quito, and Rio de Janeiro. Several companies arrange courier flights in the United States, but the one I'm most familiar with is Now Voyager (74 Varick Street, New York, NY 10013; 212-431-1616). To review more options, consider joining the International Association of Air Travel Couriers (P.O. Box 980, Keystone Heights, FL 32656; 352-475-1584; fax: -5326; www.courier.org). Members receive a regular bulletin with a variety of international routes being offered by air courier companies departing from several U.S. cities. Reservation phone numbers are included so you can make inquiries and schedule your trip yourself. I have seen some *incredible* bargains, and some fares were valid for several months. The website also features courier stories and back issues of *The Shoestring Traveler*.

Code-sharing. If you're making arrangements directly with an airline, ask if your flight is a "code-share." Code-sharing is complicated, to say the least. (Betsy Wade, former travel columnist for *The New York Times,* once wrote that "the general theory of relativity is not too much more complex" than the code-sharing network.) In a very small nutshell, code-sharing is an agreement between airline partners that allows them to share routes, but what it means for the consumer is that each airline sharing a code may offer a different price for the same trip or the same leg of a multistop journey. Find out which other airline(s) is in on the code, and compare prices. New in 2001 was a code-sharing agreement between Amtrak and Continental, allowing passengers who live in the East Coast cities of Philadelphia, Wilmington, Stamford, and New Haven to ride Amtrak to Newark and then transfer from the station to Continental's hub at Newark International Airport.

Flight cancellations. Airlines are not required to offer much to passengers due to flight delays or cancellations. If you have visions of free meals, hotel rooms, and flights, you may be in for a disappointment. According to the federal Department of Transportation Aviation Consumer Protection Division, "Contrary to popular belief, airlines are not required to compensate passengers whose flights are delayed or canceled. . . . Compensation is required by law only when you are 'bumped' from a flight that is oversold. Airlines almost always refuse to pay passengers for financial losses resulting from a delayed flight. If the purpose of your trip is to close a potentially lucrative business deal, to give a speech or lecture, to attend a family function, or to be present at any time-sensitive event, you might want to allow a little extra leeway and take an earlier flight. In other words, airline delays and cancellations aren't unusual, and defensive counter-planning is a good idea when time is your most important consideration." You can read the rest of the DOT's fifty-eight-page, pocket-sized brochure, *Fly Rights: A Consumer Guide to Air Travel,* by writing to the Consumer Information Center, Pueblo, CO 81009 (the charge is $1.75, which includes postage) or view it online at www.pueblo.gsa.gov/cic_text/travel/flyrights/flyrghts.htm. I found this bounty of information to be quite interesting. For those who might not know, overbooking is not illegal, "and most airlines overbook their scheduled flights to a certain extent in order to compensate for 'no-shows.'" You can read about baggage, airfares, reservations and tickets, smoking, passengers with disabilities, frequent flier programs, contract terms, health, airline safety, and complaining on the Pueblo website, too. If you *do* have a complaint you'd like to file (keeping, of course, all of the above in mind), write to the Aviation Consumer Protection Division, U.S. Department of Transportation, Room 4107, C-75, Washington, DC 20590. Each airline has its own Conditions of Carriage—known in airline lingo as "Rule 240"—which you can request from a ticket office or public relations department, but the legalese is not identical from airline to airline. From what I can tell, the airline employees who stand at the gates are the ones who have the authority to grant passengers amenities, so if you *don't* ask them for something (a seat on the next flight, a long-distance phone call, a meal, whatever), you *definitely* won't get it. It seems to me that passengers who patronize an airline frequently, or those who *politely* complain, may be first in line for any amenities.

Standby. Technically airlines no longer allow passengers to fly standby at a discount, but I've been told that seats are still occasionally sold at reduced prices for flights that aren't full. An official standby service is offered by Whole Earth Travel/Airhitch (with two U.S. offices: 2641 Broadway, 3rd floor, New York, NY 10025; 800-326-2009 or 212-864-2000; fax: -5489; and 13470 Washington Boulevard, Suite 205, Marina del Rey, California 90292; 800-834-9192; fax: 310-574-0054; www.4cheapair.com), which like a consolidator offers seats on commercial airlines that are about to be left empty. Airhitch offers very affordable flights for worldwide destinations, but you must be flexible, seeing that the company selects the date you travel based on a five-day range that you provide. The company's philosophy is akin to that of *The Collected Traveler:* "The experience of travel is a benefit that should be available to everyone. It is through travel that we each learn to accept the differences in others while realizing the similarity in our common goals. We believe travel is the best road to peace and understanding, and it's a whole lotta fun!" Airhitch also offers an option called Target Flights: You supply the dates of travel and your desired destination, plus the best quote you've obtained, and Airhitch will tell you within twenty-four hours whether it can buy a similar ticket at a cheaper price. (When I checked, this feature wasn't yet available on its website, but you can call the New York office at 800-326-2009 for details.) I've also been told that one of the best days of the year to show up at the airport without a ticket is Christmas Day. I can't personally confirm this, and it's doubtful an airline employee can either. Perhaps this is either a very well-kept secret or a myth, but if you're able to be that flexible, it would be worth trying.

Airports and Getting Around

Northern Spain is served by four airports: Bilbao, Oviedo, Santiago, and San Sebastián. Getting around and about the north from the region's airports is not problematic—there is a fairly good network of public transportation and taxi service. Getting into the Picos de Europa, however, really requires a car. As I've mentioned, travelers arriving from North America will have to fly into Madrid, and the Madrid Barajas Airport is about thirty to forty-five minutes from the city center, without traffic. The Ayuntamiento de Madrid publishes a very helpful brochure detailing taxi, bus, and Metro services from Barajas to downtown. I picked it up at the airport, but Spanish Tourist Office staff may be able to provide you with one in advance of your trip. This thorough little guide includes a Metro map, fares (including supplemental fees for a taxi), and a few tips for travelers.

In addition, a good book to consult is *Airport Transit Guide: How to Get from the Airport to the City Worldwide* (Ron Salk, editor-in-chief, Salk International Travel Premiums, Sunset Beach, California). This handy, pocket-sized paperback is indispensable for frequent business and pleasure travelers and an awfully great resource for everyone else. It has been published annually for twenty years and includes ground transportation information for 447 airports worldwide. As stated in its introduction, "In the air, others worry about getting you safely from point A to point B. But on the ground you're on your own. And unless you're returning home or being met by a welcoming committee, getting from the airport to point C may require information you don't have. That's what this book is for." The only airport in Northern Spain included in the book is Bilbao, which is really not a drawback as the other northern airports are quite small and transportation into city centers is straightforward and simple. The Bilbao airport is nine kilometers north of the city, and Salk's entry details taxi, bus, and rental car options. The Madrid

Barajas Airport is thirteen kilometers from downtown, and the entry details taxi, airport bus, and rental car information as well as parking rates. A Barajas general information telephone number to dial is 91.305.83.43. This book is a little hard to find—I used to see it frequently in bookstores but now I rarely do. I ordered mine from Magellan's mail-order catalog (800-962-4943), but you can also call Salk directly at 714-893-0812 or visit its website: www.airporttransitguide.com. The book also features a world time zones map at the back.

Altamira

The cave paintings of Altamira are one of the most popular and most significant tourist attractions of Northern Spain. They are also extremely difficult to view, as the paintings—discovered in 1879 and often referred to as the "Sistine Chapel of Stone Age Art"—are very fragile, and the number of visitors permitted to see them is severely limited. I have never attempted to visit the caves, though I would like to. Unless you are traveling with a group that has prearranged permission, you must write in advance—I've been told anywhere from three months to three years—to request permission. (The address is Centro de Investigación de Altamira, Santillana del Mar, 39330 Cantabria.) Your chances of getting permission depend upon how many other folks around the world are also requesting it. You should be consoled, however, to know that in 2001 the Cantabrian government built a visitors' center/museum (complete with an illuminated Cave of Stalactites) showing replicas of the cave paintings. Personally, unless you are a scholar, I think this is a *buena idea,* as even if you are lucky enough to visit the caves, your time down there is limited, while you can spend as long as you want at the museum and probably learn as much as if you stood in front of the originals.

B

Bargaining

Bargaining, whether for goods or for services, is perhaps less applicable to this edition of *The Collected Traveler* than others in the series. I have not encountered very many situations in Northern Spain where bargaining is readily acceptable, except at open-air (or covered) markets where individual vendors sell things like produce, fish, bread, cooking utensils, and clothing. It certainly is not the usual way of conducting business, though you may find more opportunities to bargain in southern Spain, where the milder climate lends itself to many more street vendors and outdoor markets. But because I believe that nearly every item or service is negotiable to some degree, I think it is worthwhile to be aware of the basics of bargaining and how rewarding it can be for both buyer and seller. Bargaining makes many North American visitors uncomfortable. The reasons they are uncomfortable, I've found, is that they have never taken the time to understand and appreciate the art of bargaining, and they have some of the most backward and wrong opinions, usually stemming from the idea that they're surely being taken to the cleaners. It's important to *appreciate* bargaining: it's fun, interesting, and revealing of national character. It isn't something you do in a hurry, and it's not an antagonistic game of Stratego: bargaining does incorporate strategy, but it shouldn't be a battle; the goods or services are on offer, and you do not have to purchase them.

As in my *Morocco* edition, however, I caution you against placing too much emphasis on the deal itself. There are few absolutes in the art of bargaining—each merchant is different, and the particulars of each transaction are different, and you will not be awarded a medal at the end of your visit for driving a hard bargain, especially if you have accumulated things you don't really want. More important than any of my tips that follow is that you do not lose sight of the fact that what you want is something that appeals to you in some special way that you bargain for in the accepted manner. Does it really matter, at the end of the day, that you *might* have gotten it for twenty or fifty euros less? If you end up with a purchase that you love and every time you look at it or wear it you have a warm feeling about your trip to Spain, it definitely does not matter what you paid for it. There is a difference between savvy bargaining and obsessive bargaining, and I don't know about you, but when I'm on vacation, obsessing about mercantile matters is the equivalent of postponing joy.

Here are some well-practiced and worthwhile tips that have worked well for me in Spain, Morocco, Egypt, Turkey, and France: ~Educate yourself on the items in which you're interested. If you have been able to learn what items sell for here in the States before you leave home, this is also useful information as you'll know how much (or how little) savings you are being offered. You want to avoid the risk of overpaying and purchasing items you may regret buying later, when you see things you *really* like and recognize as being of better quality—and therefore of better value—since, armed with knowledge, you can now bargain with confidence. ~Walk around the entire *mercado* first and survey the scene without purchasing a thing. It doesn't take very long to see that a lot of vendors sell identical merchandise. (I have not found Spanish markets to be very enticing for arts and crafts items; my purchases have consisted solely of food items—including jars of honey, saffron, nuts, peppers, olive oil, and vinegar—and wooden *pulpo* platters in Galicia.) Look for distinctive items, and identify those vendors you want to revisit. If prices are not marked, ask what they are for the items you're interested in, but don't linger and explain that you're just looking. What you're trying to do is ascertain the average going rate for certain items, because if you don't have any idea what the general price range is, you won't have any idea if you're paying a fair price or too much. ~If you do spy an item you're particularly interested in, try not to reveal your interest; act as nonchalant as you possibly can, and remember to be ready to start walking away. ~It's considered rude to begin serious bargaining if you're not interested in making a purchase. This doesn't mean you should refrain from asking the price on an item, but to then begin naming numbers indicates to the vendor that you're a serious customer and that a sale will likely be made. ~Politeness goes a long way. Vendors appreciate being treated with respect, and they don't at all mind answering questions from interested browsers. Strike up a conversation while you're looking at the wares; ask about the vendor's family, share pictures of yours, or ask for a recommendation of a good local restaurant. Establishing a rapport also shows that you are reasonable and are willing to make a purchase at the right (reasonable) price. ~If you don't want to be hassled by vendors as you walk through a *mercado*, make sure any previous purchases you may have made are hidden from view. To a vendor, anyone who walks through the market is a potential customer, but someone who has already spent money is even better. From a vendor's perspective, customers who have already parted with their money are interested in parting with more, if only they are shown something else they like. If you have purchased some saffron, for example, and you decline an offer to look at some more by another merchant by saying you've already bought some, you may think you're saying, "No, thank you, I've already bought some saffron and don't need any more," but the vendor will (correctly) assume that you like saffron and you're a tourist and will definitely be interested in purchasing more if he has an opportunity to show you some. I always carry a canvas tote bag for carrying whatever I've accumulated. Lots of foodstuffs (and even *pulpo* platters) fit easily into the bag, and no one but you knows they're there. ~Occasionally I feign interest in a particular item when it's a different item I *really* want. The tactic here is to begin the bargaining process and let the vendor think I'm about to make a deal. Then I pretend to get cold feet and indicate that the price is just too much for me. The vendor thinks all is lost, and at that moment I point to the item I've wanted all along, sigh, and say I'll take that one, naming the lowest price from my previous negotiation. Usually the vendor will immediately agree, as it means a done deal. ~Other times I will plead poverty and say to the vendor that I had *so* wanted to bring back a gift for my mother from "your beautiful country . . . won't you please reconsider?" This too usually works. ~If you're traveling with a companion, you can work together: one of you plays the role of the designated "bad guy," scoffing at each price quoted, while the other plays the role of the demure friend or spouse who hopes to make a purchase but really must have the approval of the "bad guy." ~If you discover a flaw in an item, point it out and use it as a bargaining chip. I do this at home as well, and I have never been unsuccessful at convincing the clerk to take some money off the price. A few times I've bought the display sample—the only one remaining in my size, for example—and wasn't charged the sales tax. ~You'll always get the best price if you pay with cash, and in fact many vendors accept only cash. I prepare an assortment of paper euros and coins in advance so I can always pull them out and indicate that it's all I have. It doesn't seem right to bargain hard for something, then agree with the vendor on a price of 100 euros, and then pay for it with a thousand-euro note. ~Remember that a deal is supposed to end with both parties satisfied. If, after much back-and-forth, you encounter a vendor who won't budge below a certain price, it's probably not posturing but a way of letting you know that anything lower will no longer be advantageous to him or her. If you feel you're stuck and have reached an impasse, try asking the vendor once more, "Is this your very best price?" If he or she has spent a considerable amount of time with you, this is the moment when it would be advantageous to compromise, or all that time will have been wasted. ~Pay attention when a merchant wraps up your purchase—a dishonest vendor may try to switch the merchandise. Though this has never happened to me, I've read a lot of letters from people who didn't know they were had until they got home. ~If you're interested in buying antiques—or making large purchases of any kind—it would be worthwhile to get a copy of the *Know Before You Go* brochure from the U.S. Customs Service. You can write for a free copy (1300 Pennsylvania Avenue NW, Washington, DC 20229) or view it online at www.customs.ustreas.gov/travel/travel.htm. Dull as it may sound, I found this document to be incredibly interesting. Of special interest here are the details on what you must declare, duty-free exemption, $200 exemption, $400 exemption, gifts, household effects, paying duty, sending goods to the United States, freight shipments, duty-free shops, and cultural artifacts and cultural property. ~As in France, you should ask questions about what you want and point to the items you're interested in, but *do not touch* the merchandise.

~Useful vocabulary: *precio fijo* (fixed price); *cajero* or *cajera* (cashier or cash register); *¿Cuál es su mejor precio?* ("What is your best price?"); *¿Es eso su mejor precio?* ("Is that your best price?").

Biking

Biking opportunities are not in short supply in Northern Spain, both for those who prefer the challenging heights of the Picos de Europa and for those whose taste runs to flatter, gentler routes. I have not seen as many bikers in the north as I've seen farther south, probably due to the climate, but a good poncho and a good attitude shouldn't deter anyone from a great biking experience. Some guidebooks offer information about local biking routes, but the Spanish Tourist Office, both in Spain and abroad, has more detailed information and maps about routes for novices and serious bikers alike. (The Spanish publisher Plaza y Janés offers the very best maps for biking and hiking; they are not sold widely outside of Spain but are found in every good bookstore and newsstand within Spain.) The presence of both the Pyrenees and the Cordillera Cantábrica make the terrain for biking in Northern Spain a bit more difficult than, say, in Andalusia, or in Tuscany and the Veneto in Italy; but gentle routes are to be found in La Rioja and Galicia and in pockets of the other northern regions. Cycling enthusiasts should know that there are few designated bike lanes in Spain, and if you're planning on carrying a bike on a train, the rule is that bikes may be brought aboard *cercanías* trains anytime after two o'clock on Friday afternoon until the last train on Sunday night. Additionally, bikes may be carried on all overnight, long-distance trains *and* on regional trains with a baggage car.

The majority of the biking-in-Spain books I've paged through tend to focus on longer, multiday bike trips as opposed to shorter circuits that take riders through the countryside for a day or a few hours. As I touched upon in the introduction, I'm not at all impressed by travelers who spend every day of their visit to Spain on a bike; in fact, they cannot rightly be referred to as travelers, but rather as bikers. Therefore I'm a bit skeptical about tour operators that arrange biking trips that don't allow for at least part of each day—or, better, several days—off the bike completely. However, some of these companies are very committed to international understanding and immersing the participants in Spanish culture, so I must embrace them as I share these views. I do admire a few tour operators, and my hope is that they will allow for more time off the bikes in future trips. I also hope that, in the meantime, participants might also share their desire for this, too, and that they will consider adding a few extra days to their journey to do some exploring without a two-wheeled vehicle. Following are some companies I'm fond of that offer quality trips:

Bike Riders Tours (P.O. Box 130254, Boston, MA 02113; 800-473-7040; www.bikeriderstours.com). Bike Riders offers tours to other places besides Spain (Canada, New England, France, Ireland, Italy, and Portugal), and some of the reasons its tours stand apart from others include the small size of each group (sixteen), accommodations in places that give a sense of the architecture and history of the region, no preset meals at restaurants, the best bikes in the business, and routes that are carefully designed to showcase the best of a region and allow riders to enjoy the day. Most routes average no more than thirty-five miles per day, though if energetic riders want to cover more ground, the staff can accommodate. Currently the company's only tour in any part of Northern Spain is "Minho & Galicia: The Pilgrim's Trail," which begins in Porto (in northern Portugal) and ends in Santiago de Compostela. The trip lasts eight days and seven nights and includes accommodations in *posadas* and *paradors,* two nights in Pontevedra, and a private walking tour of the Santiago cathedral and its old quarter. The terrain is rolling to hilly, and the journey averages twenty to forty-five miles a day.

Bravo! Adventures (690 Roosevelt Way NE, Seattle, WA 98115; 800-938-9311 or 206-463-3070; fax: -0340; www.caminotours.com). Bravo's motto is "Spain by Bike, Spain on Foot, Spain *Your* Way," and it is probably the best-known tour company to offer trips exclusively in Spain. I have seen a number of its magazine advertisements, which is how I first learned of the company. I remember that I spotted a typo in one of its ads, which initially turned me off, but I have since concluded that these folks are passionate about Spain, and, well, much as I have tried to avoid it, there are typos in my own books as well. The founders of Camino note that "Spain has always attracted a different kind of traveler—pilgrims, eccentric aristocrats, the quintessential everyman in Don Quixote, the artist and the adventurer. To all of them Spain is a fine bottle of wine to be opened, breathed in, gazed upon and then only after a certain ritual swallowed with full pleasure. We invite you to participate in those rituals and discover the snapping click of a flamenco dancer's castanets as her regal Gypsy features beckon you to be moved in the many singular moments that are Spain." Currently Camino offers a Camino de Santiago bike tour, a route that begins in Pamplona and travels west through Estella, Logroño, Santo Domingo de la Calzada, Burgos, Carrión de los Condes, León, Astorga, Villafranca del Bierzo, Sarriá, Portomarín, and Santiago de Compostela.

Bookstores

Like Spaniards (and most Europeans in general), I prefer to buy whatever goods and services I need from specialists. One-stop shopping is a nice idea in theory, but it has not been very appealing to me, as convenience seems its only virtue. Therefore I buy fish from a fishmonger, flowers from a florist, cheese from a cheese shop, and so on. And when I'm looking for travel books, I prefer to shop at travel bookstores or independent bookstores with strong travel sections. The staff in these stores are nearly always well traveled, well read, very helpful, and knowledgeable. An aspect I don't like about nationwide chain stores is that travel guides tend to be shelved separately from travel writing and related history books, implying that guidebooks are all a traveler may need or want. Stores specializing in travel take a wider view, understanding that travel incorporates many different dimensions.

Following is a list of stores in the United States that offer exceptional travel book departments. (I've also included a few stores specializing in art books and cookbooks, as some of these titles are mentioned throughout this book.) Note that all of them accept mail orders, and some publish catalogs and/or newsletters.

CALIFORNIA

Black Oak Books
1491 Shattuck Avenue, Berkeley
510-486-0698
www.blackoakbooks.com

Bon Voyage Travel Books & Maps
2069 West Bullard Avenue, Fresno
800-995-9716
www.bon-voyage-travel.com

Book Passage
51 Tamal Vista Boulevard
Corte Madera
800-999-7909 or 415-927-0960
www.bookpassage.com

The Cook's Library
8373 West Third Street, Los Angeles
323-655-3141

Distant Lands
56 South Raymond Avenue, Pasadena
800-310-3220 or 626-449-3220
www.distantlands.com

The Literate Traveller
8306 Wilshire Boulevard, Suite 591
Beverly Hills
800-850-2665 or 310-398-8781
www.literatetraveller.com
~In addition to its regular catalog, the
Literate Traveller publishes *Around
the World in 80 Mysteries.*

Pacific Travellers Supply
12 West Anapamu Street
Santa Barbara
888-PAC-TRAV or (805) 963-4438
www.pactrav.com

Rand McNally:
The Map & Travel Store
San Francisco:
595 Market Street
415-777-3131
Costa Mesa:
South Coast Plaza
714-545-9907
Los Angeles:
Century City Shopping Center
310-556-2202

Glendale:
Glendale Galleria
818-242-6277
San Diego:
Horton Plaza
619-234-3341

*Thomas Bros. Maps Store
(A Rand McNally Company)*
San Francisco:
550 Jackson Street
415-981-7520
Los Angeles:
521 W. 6th Street
213-627-4018
Irvine:
17731 Cowan
888-826-6277

The Traveler's Bookcase
8375 West Third Street, Los Angeles
800-655-0053 or 323-655-0575
www.travelbooks.com

COLORADO

Tattered Cover Book Store
2955 East First Avenue, Denver
800-833-9327 or 303-322-7727
www.tatteredcover.com

CONNECTICUT

R. J. Julia Booksellers
768 Post Road, Madison
800-74-READS or 203-245-3959
www.rjjulia.com

WASHINGTON, DC

Travel Books & Language Center
4437 Wisconsin Avenue, N.W.
800-220-2665 or 202-237-1322
bookweb.org/bookstore/travelbks/

FLORIDA

The Downtown Book Center
(for books in Spanish)
247 SE 1 St., Miami
800-599-8712 or 305-377-9941 (locally)
www.libros-direct.com

Rand McNally:
The Map & Travel Store
Palm Beach Gardens: The Gardens
561-775-7602
Tampa:
International Plaza
2223 N. West Shore Boulevard
813-348-9400

ILLINOIS

Librería Girón (for books in Spanish)
1443 W. 18th Street, Chicago
800-405-4276 or 773-847-3000 (locally)
www.gironbooks.com

Rand McNally:
The Map & Travel Store
Chicago:
150 S. Wacker Drive
312-332-2009
444 North Michigan Avenue
312-321-1751
Schaumburg:
Woodfield Mall
847-995-9606

Northbrook:
Northbrook Court
847-564-4905

The Savvy Traveller
310 South Michigan Avenue, Chicago
888-666-6200 or 312-913-9800
www.thesavvytraveller.com

MASSACHUSETTS

Brattle Book Shop
9 West Street, Boston
800-447-9595 or 617-542-0210
www.brattlebookshop.com
~Brattle's specialty is art books, but it
also stocks over 250,000 used, rare
and out-of-print books.

Globe Corner Bookstore
500 Boylston Street, Boston
800-358-6013 or 617-859-8008
www.globecorner.com

Jeffery Amherst Bookshop
55 South Pleasant Street, Amherst
413-253-3381 / fax: -7852
www.jeffbooks.com

Rand McNally:
The Map & Travel Store
Boston: 84 State Street
617-720-1125

MICHIGAN

Rand McNally:
The Map & Travel Store
Troy:
Somerset Collection
248-643-7470

MINNESOTA

Rand McNally:
The Map & Travel Store
Bloomington:
Mall of America
952-814-4401

MISSOURI

Rand McNally:
The Map & Travel Store
St. Louis: Saint Louis Galleria
314-863-3555

NEW JERSEY

Rand McNally:
The Map & Travel Store
Short Hills:
The Mall at Short Hills
973-379-1800

NEW YORK

Archivia: The Decorative Arts
Book Shop
1063 Madison Avenue, between
80th and 81st Streets, New York
212-439-9194
www.archivia.com
~Beautiful store with a beautiful
selection of decorating, garden, style,
history, and art titles, some imported
from other countries.

Bonnie Slotnick Cookbooks
163 West Tenth Street, New York
212-989-8962
~Bonnie deals almost exclusively with
out-of-print cookbooks.

The Complete Traveller
199 Madison Avenue (35th Street)
New York
212-685-9007
~In addition to a great selection of
current books, a separate room is
reserved for rare and out-of-print
travel books. Owners Harriet and
Arnold Greenberg and their superb
staff will do their very best to track
down your most obscure request.

Hacker Art Books
45 West 57th Street, New York
212-688-7600
www.hackerartbooks.com
~John Russell, former art critic of *The
New York Times,* has written of
Hacker, "For an all-round art bookstore, this one is something near to
ideal." On a recent visit to Hacker,
three students were sitting on the floor
surrounded by books and papers and
discussing Cézanne, a customer was
conversing in French with one of the
staff, another customer began talking
to me about the work of Albert
Marquet, yet another customer came
in rather breathlessly saying she just
wanted to stop by to say hello, and
another staffer was on the phone
assisting a customer—exactly the
atmosphere a good bookstore should
exude. "Know art, know life," I read
somewhere recently. To walk into
Hacker (even though one has to take
the elevator to the fifth floor) is to be
reminded of this precept intensely.
Hacker is now part of the Strand
bookstore family in New York.

Kitchen Arts & Letters
1435 Lexington Avenue, New York
212-876-5550

Lectorum Libros
(for books in Spanish)
137 West 14th Street (between 6th and
7th Avenues), New York
212-741-0220
www.lectorum.com
~Lectorum deserves special mention
as it is the oldest and largest Spanish-
language store and distributor in the
U.S., offering a huge variety of books
(everything from Latin American
literature to travel and psychology
books) and periodicals. Its specialty is
children's books, publishing over 60 of
them. Titles may be ordered online.

*The Metropolitan Museum of Art
Bookstore*
1000 Fifth Avenue (at 82nd Street)
New York
212-535-7710
www.metmuseum.org
~The Met has other outposts in New
York (including one on the
promenade at Rockefeller Center) and
around the country, but the bookstore
at the museum itself is larger and
therefore more fully stocked.
Additionally, the bookstore staff is
very knowledgeable and helpful. On
the rare occasion when the shop didn't
have a book I was looking for, staff
members were quick to recommend
other art specialty stores, not just in
New York but nationwide.

Joseph Patelson Music House
160 West 56th Street, New York
212-582-5840
www.patelson.com

*Rand McNally:
The Map & Travel Store*
New York:
150 East 52nd Street
212-758-7488

Rizzoli
31 West 57th Street
212-759-2424
~Sadly, Rizzoli formerly had a
number of stores around the country,
but in 2001 it closed all of them except
this wonderful outpost. It remains the
most perfect all-around bookstore—
with a lot of Italian imports,
naturally—I've ever known.

Strand Book Store
828 Broadway, New York
800-366-3664 or 212-473-1452
www.strandbooks.com

Strand Book Annex
95 Fulton Street, New York
212-732-6070

NORTH CAROLINA

Omni Resources
1004 South Mebane Street, Burlington
800-742-2677 or 336-227-8300
www.omnimap.com

OKLAHOMA

Traveler's Pack LTD
9427 North May Avenue
Oklahoma City
405-755-2924
www.travelerspackltd.com

OREGON

Powell's City of Books
1005 West Burnside, Portland
800-878-7323 or 503-228-4651
www.powells.com

Powell's Travel Store
701 Southwest Sixth Avenue, Portland
800-546-5025
powells.com/psection/Travel.html

PENNSYLVANIA

Franklin Maps
333 Henderson Road, King of Prussia
610-265-6277
www.franklinmaps.com
~Extraordinary selection of foreign
and domestic maps as well as books.
One journalist wrote, "What travelers
will find at the 15,000-square-foot
Franklin Map store are maps, charts,
and books covering almost every
square inch of earth and universe."

Rand McNally:
The Map & Travel Store
Philadelphia:
One Liberty Place
215-563-1101

TEXAS

Rand McNally:
The Map & Travel Store
Dallas:
NorthPark Center
214-987-9941
Houston:
Galleria I
713-960-9846

VERMONT

Adventurous Traveler Bookstore
245 South Champlain Street
Burlington
800-282-3963 or 802-860-6776
www.adventuroustraveler.com

VIRGINIA

Rand McNally:
The Map & Travel Store
McLean:
Tysons Corner Center
703-556-8688

WASHINGTON

Rand McNally:
The Map & Travel Store
Seattle:
Four Seasons Olympic Hotel
1218 4th Avenue
206-264-6277

Wide World Books & Maps
4411A Wallingford Avenue North
Seattle
888-534-3453 or 206-634-3453
www.travelbooksandmaps.com

And because some of the books I recommend are British publications, here are three excellent stores in London, all of which also fill mail orders: ~The Travel Bookshop (13–15 Blenheim Crescent, Notting Hill, W11 2EE; 44.20.7229.5260; fax: 7243.1552; www.thetravelbookshop.co.uk); ~Books for Cooks (a few doors down from The Travel Bookshop at 4 Blenheim Crescent, Notting Hill, W11 1NN; 44.20.7221.1992; fax: 7221.1517; www.booksforcooks.com); and ~Stanfords Maps, Charts, Books (12–14 Long Acre, Covent Garden, WC2E 9LP; 44.20.7730.1354, plus three other locations in and around London; Stanfords has its own dedicated phone and fax for international mail-order service: 44.20.7836.1321; fax: 7836.0189; www.stanfords.co.uk).

Additionally, I must mention my two favorite mail-order-book catalogs: *A Common Reader* and *Bas Bleu*. Both are issued monthly and offer an excellent selection of travel writing, biographies, history, cookbooks, and general fiction and nonfiction books for adults, as well as selected books for children. *ACR*'s selection is more extensive, but this does not make *Bas Bleu*'s offerings any less appealing. James Mustich Jr. is the man behind the *ACR* venture, and his reviews are of the sort that wander here and there and make you want to read every single book in the catalog. (His writing has been an inspiration to me for the annotated bibliographies in *The Collected Traveler*.) Not content simply to offer new books, Mustich even arranges to reissue out-of-print books by publishing them under his own Common Reader Editions imprint. To add your name to these catalog mailing lists, contact *A Common Reader* (141 Tompkins Avenue, Pleasantville, NY 10570; 800-832-7323; fax: 914-747-0778; www.common-reader.com) and *Bas Bleu* (515 Means Street NW, Atlanta, GA 30318; 800-433-1155 or 404-577-9463; fax: -6626; www.basbleu.com).

If your favorite bookseller can't find an out-of-print title you're looking for, try contacting Book Sense, a network of more than 1,100 independent booksellers around the country (888-BOOKSENSE or www.booksense.com), or search one of the following websites. ~Longitude (www.longitudebooks.com) is a wonderful source for travel books—which they define as comprehensively as I do, including travel narratives, art, archaeology, novels, essays, guidebooks, and so on—and maps (when you select a destination, you can view an Essential Reading list plus an accompanying map). ~American Book Exchange (www.abebooks.com) is wonderful because you purchase books directly from independent booksellers. ~ElephantBooks.com (www.elephantbooks.com) specializes in rare and collectible books. ~Alibris (www.alibris.com) offers a regular search and, if that doesn't prove fruitful, a Book Hound service, which keeps "sniffing" around for thirty days.

Buses

I have never opted to ride a bus, either between cities or within them, in Northern Spain. Certainly within city and town centers, it is seldom necessary—even in

Bilbao, San Sebastián, and Santiago—as the cities of the north are small enough for visitors to walk from end to end without public transport. Also, I am very fond of the train, and I probably would never voluntarily choose the bus unless it was my only option.

Within cities, bus stops are easy to find as they are well posted with good signs indicating routes and timetables. You may pay—with exact change—when boarding the bus, or purchase a ticket from the main bus terminal or at an *estanco* (tobacco shop; as in other European countries, nearly anything can be purchased at the corner tobacco shop, and most Spaniards buy their tickets at an *estanco*). A book of ten tickets, known as a *billetes bonabús,* may be a good idea if you think you'll use them. You need to validate your ticket by having it stamped in the machine at the front of the bus, and don't let Spain's honor system fool you: Inspectors do check for tickets, and they are not forgiving.

Somewhat oddly, there is no Spanish national bus company. Eurolines, a company operating throughout Europe, handles bus travel in Spain through its agent, Autocares Julià. There are other regional bus lines, and travelers may transfer between the regional lines and Julià, allowing for a broader network than either could offer on its own. Travelers who will be riding the bus northward from Madrid should note that Madrid has three bus stations: Estación Sur (which serves destinations throughout Spain), Terminal Auto Res (which serves points south and in Extremadura), and Terminal Continental Auto (which serves Northern Spain only).

If you're making a round-trip journey, it's always a good idea to purchase tickets for both legs; smaller villages may have only one ticket outlet, which may very well be closed at the time of your departure. ~Donosti Tour in San Sebastián offers two great bus trips for visitors, Donostia Clásica and Donostia Tecnológica. Each route lasts an hour, and the San Sebastián tourist office stocks brochures with maps that outline each one. This is actually a great way to get an overview of the city and a great value, too: you may begin and end your trip at any one of twenty-five different stops on the two routes. You may hop on and off the bus as many times as you desire throughout the course of a twenty-four-hour day, effectively receiving two tours for the price of one. The San Sebastián tourist office also stocks brochures (in English and Spanish) for Euskal Herriko (Green Services), a tour company that offers not only bus tours of San Sebastián but bike tours too, as well as other excursions farther afield, including hiking in the Basque mountains, sailing on the Cantabrian coast, visits to French Basque country, horseback riding, tuna fishing, hot air balloon rides, ice skating—just about everything. Reservations may be made through your hotel or the tourist office, or you may contact Green Services directly at 600.445.697, a line that is staffed twenty-four hours.

C

Car Rental

Though one can get to and from the major cities and towns of Northern Spain without a car, this is one part of the world where I would say it is most desirable, even essential, to have one. The Rías Baixas area of Galicia is best explored with a car, as are the Picos de Europa, the coves and towns of the Cantabrian coast, and the backroads of Navarre and La Rioja. A car isn't necessary within the individual cities and towns, such as Santiago, Oviedo, La Coruña, Bilbao, and San Sebastián, so you may not need a car for your entire trip; train and bus service, direct or with connections, is available to all of these locales. But I do recommend renting a car for at least part of a journey in the north.

My favorite feature of travel publications is the section featuring readers' letters. I have probably learned more from these letters than from any other source, and the largest number of complaints seem to be about problems encountered when renting a car. The majority of the complaints are due to false assumptions that were never clarified or questioned at the time the car was rented, and it is nearly always impossible—or at the least very difficult—to resolve a dispute with a rental car agency once you've signed the bill, returned the car, and returned home.

The most important word of advice anyone can offer you about renting a car is that no matter what you read, hear, or assume, the only word that counts is the one from your policy administrator, be it a credit card or insurance company. If you have any questions about renting a car overseas and what is and isn't covered on your existing policy (including collision damage waiver), contact your provider in advance. Request documentation in writing if necessary. It is your responsibility to learn about your coverage *before* you rent a car. I have never encountered any rental car problems, but then again I make it a habit to inspect the car, before I drive it off the lot, for any damages that could become problematic later, and I always state to the company representative, "When I return the car to you, I will not pay anything more than this amount," while pointing to the total on my receipt. This gives the representative the opportunity to say, "Oh, well, now that you mention it, there is one other possible charge . . ." which opens the door to a final discussion about what I am expected to pay. I follow the no-surprises rule: I bring up everything I can think of and ask any questions I may have at the outset. Here are some specific tips and reminders to keep in mind.

Automatic transmission. If you do not want to drive a standard transmission (stick shift) car, ask for an automatic model well in advance. Most European cars are standard, and the few automatic cars in rental company fleets go quickly.

Automobile clubs. If you'll be living in Spain for some time and will have a car, you might want to consider joining an automobile club. The best known is RACE, whose main office is in Madrid (José Abascal 10; 900.200093—note that this number may only be dialed within Spain). But short-term visitors may want to know about roadside assistance the auto clubs offer. Both Hertz and Avis offer twenty-four-hour emergency roadside assistance, and other rental firms may as well—remember to inquire when making your arrangements. Also, RACE is an international partner of American auto clubs such as AAA, so if you are a triple A member, you should qualify for free emergency roadside service (there may be certain restrictions, however, so check in advance). Emergency telephones appear every two kilometers along the *autopistas*.

Books and maps. If you'll be driving at all in the north, or from Madrid to the north, a great book to get is *Spain's Best-Loved Driving Tours: 25 Unforgettable Itineraries* (Frommer's). Five tours are of particular interest: "Navarra and Wine Country," and four tours in Green Spain: "The World of Galicia," "The Green Belt of Asturias," "Landscapes of Cantabria," and "Exploring the Basque Country." The best maps are not widely available, if at all, outside Spain. The Spanish Ministry of Transportation issues the *Mapa Oficial de Carreteras* in book form, and Campsa (the leading oil company in Spain) publishes *Guía Campsa*, a combination road map and restaurant guide. Both of these are for sale in bookstores and service stations throughout the country. With the help of the Spanish Tourist Office, you may be able to obtain one in advance of your trip by contacting a bookstore, for example, or you could arrange to have one sent to your hotel before your arrival. Michelin also publishes a spiral-bound atlas for Spain and Portugal, which is of course reliable; but just as I like to fly the airline of a country, I prefer to use maps provided by the home country.

Collision damage waiver. A point to remember about the CDW is that even if you decide to purchase it, you almost always have to pay something extra *on top of the fee you paid for the waiver* if something happens to the car, even if the something is very insignificant. So be sure to ask if there is a CDW deductible, and if so, ask what the amount is. (It could be several hundred dollars.) And if, like me, you didn't know about the *super* CDW, inquire about it, too: it translates as a waiver above and beyond the standard CDW and is a daily fee that reduces the current deductible or eliminates it entirely. Finally, there is an additional waiver for theft protection, but this one differs in that most rental car companies collect the fee from you only if indeed the car is stolen. If you didn't realize it before, you surely know by now that car rental companies have literally dozens of ways to convince you to part with your money. It's not necessarily wrong of them to concoct these avenues of revenue, but it is most definitely your responsibility as the renter to understand what you are and are not paying for.

Driver's license. You don't need an international driver's license in Spain. Save the $10 fee for driving in less developed countries, where the absence of the license could open the door for bribery to cross a border.

Driving. Driving in the fast lane on European roads can be a bit disconcerting, as any car suddenly looming up behind you is closing in at a *much* faster speed than we're accustomed to in the United States. These drivers usually have no patience for your slowness and will tailgate you and flash their lights until you get out of the way. So if you're going to pass, step on the gas and go, then return quickly to the right lane.

Gas. The price of gas in Spain—as elsewhere in Europe and other parts of the world—is high, so budget accordingly. All gas costs more on the *autopistas,* whether the pump is full or self service. Self-service pumps are common throughout Spain, but if you spy an attendant, you are supposed to wait for his assistance rather than pump the gas yourself. Some of the more modern stations, both on and off the *peaje* roads, accept credit cards as payment. Incidentally, when contemplating the price of gas, think about some of the services that are paid for with the money generated from gas prices, and the next time a senator or congressman suggests raising gas taxes in the United States, let it be known that he or she has your support! A plastic bottle of water should not cost more than a gallon of gas.

Gas stations. Gas stations offer full service on weekdays, but many stations keep the same hours as other businesses and close during the lunchtime siesta and on Sunday. Stations on the *autovías,* however, remain open continuously. At night and on weekends, there may very well not be anyone about, so plan accordingly.

Kilometers. It's helpful to begin thinking in terms of kilometers instead of miles. I jot down sample distances to use as a ready reference as I'm motoring along the minor roads (known as *carreteras comarcales* and *carreteras nacionales*) or trying to keep up on the *autopista:* 1 mile = 1.6 kilometers, so 12 kilometers = 7½ miles; 16 kilometers = 10 miles; 40 kilometers = 25 miles; 80 kilometers = 50 miles; 160 kilometers = 100 miles; 320 kilometers = 200 miles, etc.

Leasing. Consider leasing a car. Europe by Car (1 Rockefeller Plaza, New York, NY 10020; 800-223-1516 or 212-581-3040 [in New York]; 9000 Sunset Boulevard, Los Angeles, California 90069; 800-252-9401 or 323-272-0424; www.europeby-car.com) has been offering low-priced rentals and tax-free leases since 1954, and a recent Reader's Choice Awards roundup in *Condé Nast Traveler* rated it first among the top ten car rental companies for best service and rates. It truly provides one of the best values around: In addition to its good overall rates (with special rates available for students, teachers, and faculty members), it offers a tax-free, factory-direct new car vacation plan. This is such a good deal because technically the program operates more like a short-term lease, which makes the rental car exempt from European taxes. The cars are from Peugeot, Citroën, and Renault, and the prices include unlimited mileage; insurance with liability, fire, collision damage waiver, and theft; and emergency assistance twenty-four hours a day via a free phone. The only catch is that you have to pay for the car for a minimum of seventeen days—you don't have to *keep* it for seventeen days, but the price is the same if you drop it off earlier. All clients receive special discounts at selected hotels and motels (and budget hotels costing about $30 a night), as well as free parking. ~Kemwel Holiday Autos (39 Commercial Street, Portland, ME 04102; 877-820-0668; www.kemwel.com) also offers a Peugeot short-term leasing program (which they refer to as the best-kept "secret" in the business) as well as regular car rentals, chauffeur-driven cars, car-pass vouchers, and motor-home rentals, all at competitive rates. The car-pass voucher program allows you to purchase rental vouchers in three-day segments; you buy as many segments as you think you'll need, and any unused vouchers are fully refundable upon your return. (This is particularly helpful if you're not sure you need to rent a car at all or don't know how long you might need one.) I have used Kemwel on three occasions and have been very pleased. The materials one receives include charts for mileage, miles-to-kilometers, and international road signs; a handy little fold-out guide called "Travel Talk," with basic phrases in English, Italian, French, German, and Spanish; and charts for clothing sizes, kilos-to-pounds, centimeters-to-inches, gallons-to-liters, temperatures, and time differences.

Parking tickets. I've read conflicting advice on parking tickets, so I would not recommend taking a chance on getting one if you're in doubt. Rental car agencies do have your credit card number, and it seems to me they could eventually bill you for any ticket you receive and add a service charge if they're so inclined.

Rates: Remember, while you're doing your research, to compare like cars with like cars. A two-door sports car convertible cannot be compared with a four-door Sketch or Twingo. (I love the silly-sounding names of Euoropean cars.) If you're considering a variety of cars that are all unfamiliar to you, be sure to ask for a complete description, or do some advance research yourself by browsing the website of Europcar (www.europcar.com). Also, be sure to ask about all possible extra charges that may be applied to your rental, such as drop-off charges, additional driver fees, and taxes. These may vary greatly from company to company. Most of the good rental rates apply when you prepay, in U.S. dollars, in advance of your trip. Inquire about prepaid rates when you are doing your research. Hertz, for example, offers a competitive rate with its prepaid car rental voucher. The conditions are that you prepay in U.S. dollars in advance of your trip, and the voucher must be faxed to a U.S. fax number or mailed to a U.S. address. The prepaid rate does not include such things as drop-off charges, car seats, collision damage waiver, or gas, which must be paid for in local currency at the time you pick up the car.

Roads and routes. Road maps and atlases obviously employ route numbers for large and small roads (A for *autopista* and *autovía,* C for *comarcal,* and N for *nacional*). But most of the highway and road signs you'll see in Spain (and Europe in general) typically indicate cities or towns quite far away rather than road numbers. (Initially this threw me off. It reminded me of a sign I used to see years ago just outside Philadelphia for a restaurant at the New Jersey shore; the sign advertised that the restaurant was "minutes away" but was in fact two *hours* away.)

Begin thinking in terms of *direction* rather than road number, and consult your map(s) often—you'll find that it's quite a sensible way of getting around, and it forces you to be better versed in geography. The types of roads you'll encounter in Spain include the *autopistas* (or *autopistas de peaje*), toll roads that represent the Iberpistas network. Note that toll plazas are organized much the way they are in the States, with a *telepago* lane (for drivers—mostly residents—who have an electronic sticker on their windshield that automatically deducts the toll amount, like a debit card), an *automático* lane (where there are machines to pay by credit card *or* with exact change), and a *manual* lane (which have an attendant). *Autovías* are major roads but are not toll roads. They are identified by blue signs, and as they are faster than N roads but cheaper than the *peaje* roads, they're quite popular. *Carreteras nacionales* (or Red de Carreteras del Estado) make up the nationwide network of main roads and highways. They are identified by signs that display a red box with a white N inside followed by the appropriate route number. *Carreteras nacionales* featuring Roman numerals indicate roads that begin at the Puerta del Sol in Madrid. (Just as all distances in France are measured from Notre Dame in Paris, all distances in Spain are measured from the Puerta del Sol, known as kilometer zero.) Some *carreteras nacionales* are divided highways, but most are two-lane roads where the traffic moves rather slowly. They are less busy during the lunchtime hours, when even truck drivers are taking a siesta. Finally, *carreteras comarcales* are secondary roads that are identified with the letter C followed by a number. There are still other minor roads identified with an abbreviation of a province followed by a number, such as LE4151, the LE indicating the province of Lleida.

Speed limits. On the *autopistas* and *autovías*, the speed limit is 140 kilometers per hour (about 74 mph) while on regular (nontoll) main roads it's 90 kph (about 68 mph). Driving through towns and built-up areas, the limit is 50 kph (about 31 mph).

Tolls: In Spain as elsewhere in Europe, tolls are very expensive. Perhaps a sensible plan for touring the north is to drive on both toll and non-*peaje* roads. As noted above, you really can cover a lot of ground quickly on toll roads as the speed limit is nearly 80 mph, and on a day when you may need to make your way between towns that are rather far apart, the *autopista* would be worth the price.

Traffic information. Traffic updates are provided by Información de Tráfico de Carreteras, which offers a toll-free service with recorded road and traffic information. It's in Spanish only, but your hotel receptionist can call for you and translate, which may be very useful for a drive from Madrid to the north.

~Useful vocabulary: *alquiler de coches* (car rental agency); *coche de alquiler* (rental car); *gasolina* (gas); *gasóleo* (diesel gas); *sin plomo* (unleaded gas); *lleno* (fill the tank; if you don't want to fill up the tank, request an amount in euros); *ida* (one way); *cambio de sentido* (U-turn); *policía nacional* (refers to policemen in blue uniforms who preside over towns with large populations, over 30,000 or so residents;

the Basque Country, however, has its own regional police force, Ertzaintza, whose members wear red berets); *policía local* (also known as *guardia urbana* or *policía municipal;* they preside over smaller locales than the *policía nacional*); *guardia civil* (highway and border police, distinctive for their olive green uniforms; infamous for the power invested in them by Franco); *estacionamiento prohibido* (no parking); *salida* (exit); *a la derecha* (right); *a la izquierda* (left); *reducir la velocidad/más despacio* (slow down); *peaje* (toll); *peligro* (danger); *avería* (breakdown); *todo derecho* (straight ahead); *cercano* (near); *lejano* (far); *arriba* (up); *abajo* (down); *Estámos perdidos* ("We're lost"); *¿Dónde hay una gasolinera/la bomba de gasolina?* ("Where can we get some gas?"); *¿Dónde hay un taller de coches?* ("Where can we find a garage to repair our car?"); and *urgencias* (the emergency room of a hospital), a word you'll hopefully never need.

Children

"In the Basque Country," notes Beth Nelson in *Postcards from the Basque Country,* "the children reign. Pampered and protected, coddled and cosseted, indulged and adored—not spoilt—just very well loved. . . . In restaurants and bars and public places, the children are always welcome here. The street is their kingdom, you can feel their vitality. A child is a reason for pure happiness here." It is not only the Basque Country that is welcoming to kids in Spain, as even travelers who are not parents will quickly learn.

A few months before my daughter was born, I was feeling anxious that my life as a mother was going to drastically alter my ability to travel. My colleague and friend Bruce H. helped me snap out of this funk by pointing out that my husband and I would have to travel *differently* than we did before but would indeed still travel because we love it. As Bruce is both a parent and a world traveler, he advised us not to overthink the situation, because then we would find a million reasons *not* to travel. The way I see it, parents can either make the decision never to go anywhere—and thereby deprive both their children and themselves of a priceless experience—or plan an itinerary with kids in mind and take off on a new journey. I believe that children have as much to teach us as we do them, especially when traveling—their curiosity and imagination make even familiar destinations seem new.

When I first began working on this series, I could not find country-specific books devoted to traveling with children. Happily, this situation is changing, and publishers have rightly recognized this as a publishing niche to be filled (though there still is not one available for Spain). Some guidebooks—including many of those mentioned in the entry for Guidebooks—offer excellent suggestions for things to see and do with kids. Books about traveling with children in general that I've enjoyed include:

Have Kid, Will Travel: 101 Survival Strategies for Vacationing with Babies and Young Children (Claire Tristram with Lucille Tristram, Andrews McMeel Publishing, Kansas City, Missouri, 1997). Claire Tristram has visited all fifty states and thirty countries, and Lucille, her daughter, has been named "the best baby in the world" by several strangers sitting next to her on long-distance flights. Among her best words of advice: "Above all, don't let a bad moment become a bad day, and don't let a bad day become a bad week."

Travel with Your Baby: Experts Share Their Secrets for Tips with Your Under-4-Year-Old (Fodor's Travel Publications, 2001). Readers around the country contributed their real-life travel stories and tips to this small, pocket-sized edition. It has good checklists and packing lists, and I think the best overall suggestion is KTWF—Keep Them Well Fed. I have culled a lot of good ideas from this book and am now awaiting the *over-age-four* edition!

Additionally, some good tips can be gathered from a few websites. ~Merck (www.merck.com/disease/travel) offers advice for dealing with traveler's diarrhea (children under two are especially at risk) as well as jet lag, motion sickness, malaria (not a concern in Spain), and hepatitis A, plus flying tips, packing and pretravel health checklists, tips for traveling with kids, and a section for pregnant women who are traveling. ~My Lifeguard for Health (www.mylifeguardforhealth.com) has a "Traveling with Children" section that provides info on preparing a first-aid kit for family travel, tips for flying with a toddler, advice on how to handle emergencies away from home and how to help motion sickness, and tips for traveling with young kids and helping your child adjust. Perhaps best of all—if you're rather anal-retentive like me—is the emergency information form that you can print and fill out so you'll have everything you need in an emergency on one sheet. ~All About Travel Internationally with Your Kids (www.travelwithyourkids.com) may be my favorite site, even though at the moment Spain is not one of the cities or countries that founders Peter and Mari cover. (They do highlight Sweden, Norway, Moscow, London, Italy, Genoa, Brussels, Germany, Greece, Switzerland, and Rome.) The founders have two kids who were born abroad, and the family has lived abroad for about fifteen years, in six countries, and they've traveled with the kids to many more. As Peter and Mari note, "Decide how much of the trip is going to be FOR the kids and how much will be WITH the kids, though keep in mind that any trip will include a dose of each." Viewers may select a number of links, including "Eating in the Air," "Using the Toilet," "The Ear Thing," "Motion Sickness," "Diapers," "Kids Flying Alone," and "More Tips on Keeping the Kids Amused on a Long Journey." I am smitten with the advice peppered throughout this site. I was especially interested in the section covering taking pictures, some of whose tips include "Encourage kids to take pictures of things that interest them. Take photos of a Paris swingset to show friends back home ('It is sooo different you can't believe!' or 'It is just like home, can you believe?')," and "Take pictures of places that mean something just for your family: the taxi stand where you stood for forty-five minutes waiting for a ride, the restaurant in Japan where you first tasted sushi, the stranger on the street in Seoul who went out of his way to lead you to your destination when his English and your Korean made verbal directions impossible," and finally, "If you are not a good photographer, or forgot the camera, buy a postcard of the cathedral you saw and write on it, maybe marking the way 'round to that café you *should* have photographed where you drank hot chocolate after it started raining. Remembering the cathedral's architectural triumphs can fan a child's inspiration for great art; remembering the way that café smelled of burnt coffee and how good it felt to be out of the weather can build memories your family can hold as close as those wet clothes felt." Peter and Mari make you feel like you're their close friends, and they've got a wealth of practical and caring tips to share that apply equally to Spain as to Sweden.

None of the tips in all these books and websites, however, can prepare parents for a situation like the one my friend Katie found herself in. She, her husband Gary, and their one-year-old son Jack were in an airline terminal van at the Nice airport when Jack suddenly and inexplicably projectile-vomited all over everyone who was in the vicinity, on both sides of the van. After Katie and Gary hastily apologized and tried their best to clean everyone off with pieces of their own clothing, Jack repeated the performance. They did their best once again to wipe everyone off, searching desperately in their bags for *any* piece of clothing that hadn't been previously used. But by now they were also concerned that something was really wrong with Jack, as he had never done that in his short life and had not shown any signs of sickness. (As it turned out, the airport's resident doctor did detect a little sickness coming on, but everything ended up fine, except that their flight was delayed three hours.) There are just some things you can't prepare for, and some situations when you really need a sense of humor.

An observation parents will be sure to notice: In Spain (as in most other Mediterranean countries) young children stay up late at night, even in restaurants and *tapas* bars. Do not be surprised if it's midnight and there are lots of kids running around. I've never seen the children looking unhappy or tired, and it seems to make sense in a country with a tradition of an afternoon siesta. Spaniards include children in nearly every activity, so much so that I understood when I read recently that the concept of hiring a baby-sitter is relatively rare in Spain. This doesn't mean visitors can't arrange baby-sitting, but it's just another way of highlighting the widespread presence of children at a variety of venues.

Here are some general tips that have worked for me that you may want to try. *Advance planning.* ~If you really enjoy dining out in fine restaurants or hiking, it makes sense to plan a trip with other adults who also have children. This way two of the adults can have some time to themselves—perhaps for a day-long hike or a leisurely lunch at Arzak in San Sebastián—while the other two watch the kids.

Taking turns throughout the trip ensures that the adults will feel they had some relaxing, kid-free time to pursue their rarely enjoyed interests as well as quality time with the kids. Traveling with grandparents helps in this regard, too. ~Build excitement about the trip by reading your kids some appropriate books in advance, or save one or two for the airplane. A few we liked are *Getting to Know Spain and Spanish* (Barron's Educational Series) and *The Story of Ferdinand* (Munro Leaf, Viking Press); additionally, some publishers have recently added Spanish-language imprints to their lines, such as Para Niños (Random House Children's Books). Para Niños offers a selection of titles representing popular characters, such as Thomas the Tank Engine, Lilo and Stitch, Sesame Street, the Berenstain Bears, Dragon Tales, Beauty and the Beast, and Winnie the Pooh—not exactly stimulating tales about Spain, but the books are completely in Spanish, and if they help kids learn another language with interest, who cares?

~Take the kids to your favorite food store—I chose our local natural foods store—and let them select snacks for the trip. These are good not only for the airplane, but for all those times when you might need a distraction (like waiting on line, frolicking on the beach, sitting in the stroller), and if they pick out the snacks themselves, there is a much greater chance they will eat them. ~For older kids, buy an inexpensive disposable camera and let them take their own pictures. ~For kids of all ages, buy a blank journal and help them create a record of the trip. (The photos they take will go nicely in here.)

On the airplane. ~Select an overnight flight if possible. Kids are used to going to sleep at night, so you don't upset their schedule as drastically. ~Don't count on getting those roomier bulkhead seats on the plane even if you've been promised they would be yours if you check in early. Thanks to an honest airline employee, I learned recently that these premium seats—and I define them as premium for anyone traveling with children—are actually assigned first to passengers in wheelchairs and then to *passengers who paid the most for their tickets*. It's merely a false courtesy when an airline reservationist tells you that by showing up at the airport well in advance of your flight, you may be eligible for the bulkhead sets. I think this is abominable, especially since an early arrival at the airport means finding ways to entertain your children for an even longer period of time, and it seems obvious that happy children on a flight means a happier ride for everyone, including the people who paid the most for their seats. I would name the particular airline of my experience except that this measure is practiced by most if not all the airlines, so identifying only one is not accurate. If I knew a way around this, I'd tell you, but I don't, so I figure if enough of us parents make noise, perhaps the airlines will abandon this despicable practice. ~Bring along some "surprises" for the flight over. I started a pile of new books, games, and activities about a month before our departure and kept them hidden from my daughter so that she would see them for the first time on the plane. Two of the greatest books I've seen for literally hours of blissful busyness are *Best Travel Activity Book Ever!* (Rand McNally, for ages four to eight) and *The Most Incredible, Outrageous, Packed-to-the-Gills, Bulging-at-the-Seams Sticker Book You've Ever Seen* (Klutz Press, for ages four and up, winner of a Parents' Choice Award). Klutz, by the way, is my favorite publisher of unique, fun activity packages for children. Based in Palo Alto, California, Klutz celebrated its twenty-fifth anniversary in 2002. Just a few of the other items it offers that are great for traveling are the Backseat, Beadlings, Collage, and Drawing Books, and a Dream Journal for older dreamers and writers. Good bookstores carry the full line of Klutz products, but you may also want to view its website, www.klutz.com.

~My mother-in-law, Sheila, bought my daughter a tracing set of cardboard animals and colored string as an airplane activity. (The animals had holes all around tracing their shape, and you thread the string up and down through the holes until they're all filled in.) This turned out to be a great idea, even if Alyssa couldn't always follow the shape in a recognizable pattern. ~Wherever you arrive first in Spain—perhaps it will be Madrid for a day, or perhaps you'll head straight for one of the northern cities or towns—find a souvenir stand and buy one of those floaty pens—you know, the kind where Don Quixote on horseback floats back and forth—or some other kind of nifty pen so your kids can use it to write in their journals. ~When you arrive at an art museum, first buy some postcards. (This is not an original idea, but I'm expanding upon it.) If you have more than one child, tell the kids that whoever finds the most paintings or works of art first will win a special prize. (You must decide this in advance; it could be *churros y chocolate* or a toy or a boat ride in Retiro Park—whatever your budget allows—but make sure it's something they will want to compete for.) If you have one child, tell him or her to find all the artworks—there is no race—to receive a special prize. The last time I tried this was actually not in Spain but in Italy. I asked Alyssa to select five postcards from the racks in front of the Accademia, which she did with enthusiasm. Then, once we were inside, we came upon a mini-version of the bookstore about a quarter of the way through the galleries, and I saw a wooden box of colored pencils. I bought the pencils (which she loved), and she then colored on the reverse sides of the postcards. This activity enabled me to walk slowly around every room in the museum. I saw everything in a leisurely fashion, and she never once asked if we could leave.

~Strollers are both a blessing and a curse when traveling: on the one hand, when your child needs to take a nap, he or she will fall asleep quite easily in the stroller; on the other, sometimes naptime is precisely when you've reached a spot where you are forced to wake him or her. You may want to consider changing course at some point in your trip. After a few days of leaving the hotel early in the morning and not returning until late in the evening, I decided to plan our days differently, making sure we left early in the morning with not too great a distance to go—so Alyssa could walk—and returning to the hotel in time for lunch and a siesta.

In the midafternoon we would set out again, occasionally with but mostly without the stroller, making the days less physically exhausting for me and more fun for her.

~Fruit juices are sometimes unavailable in restaurants, but soda, unfortunately, almost always is. We do not keep soda in our home, so introducing Alyssa to soda has not exactly been what I consider welcome. But I feel that when traveling, a child who eats what he or she wants is a happy child, and I do not think it is productive to argue about food or drink in a restaurant. Parents all choose which battles they will wage with their children, and my own advice is that this shouldn't be one to choose. Alyssa has typically approached "new" foods with a sense of adventure, and she routinely tastes nearly everything on my plate, even if what she *really* wants is dessert. But when she wants potato chips, pizza, ice cream, or chocolate pudding, I do not deny her requests, and as a result she feels that eating out in a foreign country is great fun. *And* she understands perfectly that when we are back home, we must return to the ways of our household. I explain to her that we eat differently abroad because there is different food in different countries. (I once tried telling her that orange soda and chocolate hazelnut spread weren't available in America, but I was caught in my white lie when she spied them at the grocery store!) But you just might be able to get away with this with very young children.

Finally, for anyone who may still be wondering about the benefits of traveling with the kids, quickly find a copy of this wonderful, creative, and inspiring book: *Storybook Travels: From Eloise's New York to Harry Potter's London, Visits to 30 of the Best-Loved Landmarks in Children's Literature* (Colleen Dunn Bates and Susan Latempa, Three Rivers Press, 2002). This book will motivate anyone to help children make a connection between the books they've read (or books you suspect they may like) and the actual cities or regions of the world where they take place. As the authors note, "These actual places, so vividly imagined by young readers and so fondly remembered by adults, can become the scenes of real-life adventures. Great stories transport the reader, in his or her imagination, to another place. So why not go there for real?" Some of the books selected include *The Adventures of Pinocchio, And Now Miguel, A Bear Called Paddington, From the Mixed-Up Files of Mrs. Basil E. Frankweiler, Island of the Blue Dolphins, Paddle-to-the-Sea, The Tale of Peter Rabbit,* and *The Watsons Go to Birmingham.* No books with Spanish locales are featured, and the authors don't stray outside of North America and Europe (hopefully they will expand upon this and explore Asia, Africa, South America); nonetheless, this is one of the most fabulous books I've run across in years.

~A few handy vocabulary words: *un vaso pequeño* (a small cup or glass; this is useful in restaurants because often the cups brought for children are large cups and glasses meant for adults); *cucharita* (a teaspoon; again, this is useful in restaurants because if you don't ask, silverware brought for children will often be adult-sized;

paja (straw, or drinking straw; again, a helpful word to know for small children who can't quite grasp a glass or who find it more festive to drink from a straw).

Churrigueresque

Churrigueresque is one of two uniquely Spanish styles of architecture (the other being *plateresque*). *Plateresque* appeared first, in the sixteenth century, while *churrigueresque*—which essentially carried *plateresque* to its furthest extreme—thrived in the eighteenth. Both styles are quite extravagant and ornamental, and both have at one time or another been referred to in rather a derogatory manner, in much the same way we may consider the rococo style to be over the top. The word *churrigueresque* derives from three brothers—José, Joaquín, and Alberto—who bore the last name Churriguera. The brothers resided in Salamanca, where many of the best examples of this style can be seen. (Indeed, *churrigueresque* is often referred to as Salamanca Baroque.) Author Penelope Casas, who admittedly is known as a Spanish food authority rather than as an art historian, provides what I think is an excellent summation of this style: "it relied on Plateresque detail and Moorish influences but imposed them over the already ornate Baroque style of the late seventeenth and early eighteenth centuries. The result was an utterly wild, flamboyant look of restless motion that could hardly be carried a step further." The best examples of *churrigueresque* in Spain are not in the north, but the term is nonetheless a good one with which to be familiar.

Clothing

Though the clothing you bring on a trip is very much related to packing your suitcase, I have kept Clothing and Packing as separate entries. In general I pack light, and unless I have plans to be at fancy places, I pack double-duty items (stuff that can go from daytime to evening) in low-key colors that also mix and match so I can wear garments more than once. I also tend to bring items that aren't my favorites, figuring that if someone does snatch my suitcase or rummage through my hotel room, at least I won't lose the things I love the most. Appearance counts for a lot with Spaniards, and they—like other Europeans—tend to dress up a bit more than Americans. The Spanish also remain conservative when it comes to visiting their religious houses of worship. You will earn respect and goodwill by refraining from wearing sleeveless shirts, and short skirts and shorts, no matter how hot it is. You may find this odd in a country where topless sunbathing is permitted on the beaches, but make no mistake about it: dressing inappropriately around town and in churches is still frowned upon, especially in smaller villages.

While blue jeans are popular in Spain, I would still recommend reserving them for very casual daytime wear and the most casual of places at night. For men, suits and ties are necessary only at the finest restaurants and venues; polo shirts and khakis are always appropriate. For both men and women, it's a good idea to bring a lightweight poncho or windbreaker as well as a cotton sweater, whatever time of year you visit Northern Spain. The American obsession for color-coordinated jogging suits, complete with sneakers, is probably somewhat puzzling to Spaniards—it's not that they've never seen them before, but like the French and the Italians, they believe that jogging attire is worn *only* when engaging in that activity and is not a fashion statement. (Thankfully, I think this craze is waning among Americans.)

Although comfortable shoes are of the utmost importance, I never, ever bring sneakers—and I positively forbid my husband to bring them. And you might not bring them either once you realize that they scream "American." I prefer Arche, a line of French walking shoes and sandals for men and women, but several other lines are available (Mephisto, for example, another French line for men and women) that are also stylish *and* comfortable. I recently discovered a unique shoe line just for women: "à propos . . . conversations." I loved the shoes right away when I read they were "influenced by European women whose fashion sense does not include white athletic shoes outside of sports." All the shoes—which are soft and flexible and easily fold down to handbag or briefcase size—are limited editions and sport such names as Liquid Lemons, Peacock Punch, Linen Sands, African Sun, and Khaki Krunch. There are more than a dozen styles offered in two collections a year, and many styles are available two ways: with one solid center elastic band or two cross straps of elastic. "Like a scarf for your feet" is how they're trademarked. You can view the styles at www.conversationshoes.com or call 800-746-3724 for a catalog.

A number of mail-order catalogs offer practical clothes, shoes, packing accessories, and gadgets for travelers. I have found the clothing for women in these catalogs rather frumpy and unattractive, whereas the selections for men are significantly more appealing. But otherwise the following catalogs are all great, offering an assortment of items I rarely if ever see in retail stores:

L. L. Bean Traveler (800-221-4221; www.llbean.com). Some of the items I like best are its personal organizers, which are sized for from one to five days, come in eight cool colors, and have hooks so you can hang them up on a shower or closet rod. The catalog text notes that "the number-one way to stay organized is to spend less time searching for personal essentials," and of course the personal organizers completely fit the bill. I also like the universal packers, which are zippered cubes with mesh tops to keep clothes folded and separated, in three sizes and six colors; the lightweight microfiber luggage; the fleece poncho for women; and the chinos and polos for men.

Magellan's (800-962-4943; www.magellans.com). I particularly like the taxi wallet—you can snap it onto your belt, where it can stay hidden from view if you're wearing a blazer, sweater, or jacket over it; the arm wallet, a small nylon pouch with a zipper that fits snugly around your arm, wrist, or ankle; and the artist's watercolor set. Not for nothing is the catalog referred to as a "reference edition": it includes a country-by-country chart indicating the world's electrical and tele- phone connections, *and* it offers adapter plugs for each. And—not that women will need this in Northern Spain—Magellan's also offers Uri-Mate, disposable funnels for, well, I think you get the idea.

The Territory Ahead (888-233-9954; www.territoryahead.com). Based in Santa Barbara, The Territory Ahead is not a travel gadgets company, but it does special- ize in stylish clothing that happens to be great for traveling. I'm especially fond of its footwear and shorts offerings, and the women's items are equally as attractive as the men's.

TravelSmith (800-950-1600; www.travelsmith.com). Particular items of note include the CoolMax clothing for men and women; the microfiber raincoat for women that folds up into its own pouch; and the pack-it envelopes and cubes. I know readers may be surprised by this since I just grumbled about sneakers, but the lace-free canvas sneakers are terrific! I like them because they're stylish in a European way, weigh only twenty-two ounces, are incredibly comfy, and make locals think twice before summing the wearer up as American. Sebago makes these great sneaks, and they're available in white, khaki, and navy.

Coins

If you have leftover euros in the form of coins, you can always save them for a future trip; but perhaps a better idea is to give them to a great cause: UNICEF's Change for Good program, a partnership between UNICEF and the international airline indus- try. The program is designed to redeem normally unused foreign currency and cre- ate value by converting passengers' foreign change into life-saving materials and services for the world's neediest children. Since 1991 over $31 million has been raised through Change for Good. Thirteen airlines currently participate in the program: Aer Lingus, Air Mauritius, Alitalia, All Nippon Airways, American Airlines, Asiana Airlines, British Airways, Cathay Pacific, Crossair, Finnair, JAL, Qantas, and TWA. Flight attendants pass out small envelopes to passengers on flights back to the United States, and when you consider that approximately $72 million in inconvert- ible foreign coins and low-denomination bills are forfeited each year by interna- tional travelers, Change for Good is a remarkably wonderful idea. UNICEF notes that the average passenger carrying two dollars in foreign change, for example, could buy thirty oral rehydration packets (a life-saving mixture of salt and sugar that prevents death from dehydration) or twenty-five immunization needles, or enough high-dose vitamin A to protect thirty toddlers from blindness caused by vitamin A deficiency for one year. If you've never received an envelope on a flight and want to contribute, you may send your coins (and low-denomination bills) directly to Travelex America, Attention: Jessica Lynch, Change for Good for UNICEF, JFK Airport, Terminal 4 IAT, Jamaica, NY 11430. For more information, view the

UNICEF website at www.unicefusa.org or contact UNICEF at 333 East 38th Street, New York, NY 10016; 800-FOR-KIDS.

Communication

English speakers from North America have different ways of organizing their thoughts and expressing them from Spaniards (and from other Mediterranean and other peoples around the world). The authors of a helpful book entitled *The Hispanic Way: Aspects of Behavior, Attitudes, and Customs in the Spanish-Speaking World* (Judith Noble and Jaime Lacasa, Passport Books, Lincolnwood, IL, 1991) best explain this when they write, "Hispanics tend to be verbose and to get sidetracked, often elaborating on topics extraneous to the subject at hand." Noble and Lacasa provide diagrams indicating the differing patterns by speakers of English and speakers of Spanish. The diagram for English speakers is represented by a straight, vertical line, while that for Spanish speakers is represented by a crooked, jagged line that shoots off to the right and then just as sharply shoots left before straightening out somewhat toward the bottom. The authors go on to say that "it is not uncommon to hear phrases such as *como estaba diciende* ('as I was saying') and *volviendo a lo que decía antes* ('going back to what I was saying before'), which of course reflect the speaker's recognition of his or her digression."

Comprender

A good Spanish verb to know, as it means "to encircle, surround, include, comprise, contain," and most usefully "understand," as in *no comprendo* (I don't understand).

Consulates and Embassies

The U.S. embassy is at Serrano 75 in Madrid (34.91.587.2200; fax: 34.94.587.2303; www.embusa.es), and the Canadian embassy, also in Madrid, is located in the Goya Building, 35 Nuñez de Balboa (34.91.423.3250; fax: 34.91.423.3251; www.canada-es.org). The only U.S. consulate in Northern Spain is in La Coruña at Canton Grande 16–17 (34.981.213.233; fax: 34.981.222.808).

Cooking Schools

The best single source for cooking schools in Spain (and the entire world) is the *Shaw Guide to Cooking Schools: Cooking Schools, Courses, Vacations, Apprenticeships, and Wine Instruction Throughout the World* (ShawGuides, New York), updated annually. Both internationally famous programs and lesser-known classes are listed, and interested food lovers can also view updates to the guide at its website, www.shawguides.com. A few other good sources for classes include:

Epiculinary (321 East Washington Avenue, Lake Bluff, IL 60044; 888-380-9010 or 847-295-5363; fax: -5371; www.epiculinary.com), which was founded by Catherine Merrill, a former travel agent specializing in European and culinary vacations. Epiculinary offers twenty "distinctive cooking journeys" in Spain, Italy, and France, happily including a number of courses in Northern Spain. "Escuela de Cocina Luis Irizar" features the cuisine of the Basque Country. Irizar is a chef and cookbook author, and he teaches both amateurs and professionals at his school. This seven-day course features four cooking lessons and tastings with wine and includes visits to the Guggenheim Bilbao, Hondarribia, Biarritz, Getaria, and the Valley of Bertizarana. Accommodations are in the lovely Hotel de Londres y de Inglaterra (on La Concha, in San Sebastián), and on the final night the end of this culinary week is celebrated at a three-star Michelin restaurant. Another course, "Basque Cuisine," is a seven-day experience also based in San Sebastián. Its major difference from the previous one is that it provides the opportunity for three cooking lessons at a *sociedad gastronómica,* one of the private *txokos,* or gastronomic societies of the city (see the entry for Gastronomic Societies). This course also includes visits to Getaria, Bilbao, and the Cantabrian coastal towns of Santillana del Mar and Comillas. Finally, Epiculinary offers a "La Rioja Wine Country" trip, a three-day excursion that includes visits to the villages and towns of Haro, Laguardia, Casalareina, Santo Domingo de la Calzada, and Ezcaray; selected wineries and restaurants all around; the monasteries of Suso and Yuso; and one hands-on cooking lesson in San Sebastián at a private gastronomic society. This trip/class is particularly appealing to me because it's only a three-day commitment, for approximately $995, allowing travelers to plan an extended itinerary of their own while taking advantage of a unique food and wine journey in La Rioja.

L'École des Chefs Relais Gourmands (11 East 44th Street, Suite 707, New York, NY 10017; 877-334-6464; www.ecoledeschefs.com) is perhaps the most appealing program I've ever heard about. I first profiled L'École des Chefs in my *Paris* edition; readers may recall that this unique program—which is not a traditional cooking school but an opportunity to work in restaurant kitchens—was founded by Annie Jacquet-Bentley, a Parisian now living in the United States. She created the program after she spent time studying with some French chefs and wanted to make the experience available to others. In the spring of 2001, however, the prestigious Relais & Chateaux hotel group acquired L'École des Chefs, broadening the program to include more than a hundred Relais Gourmand restaurants in seventeen countries. Classes are mostly in two- and three-star Michelin restaurants, and although they're for nonprofessionals, applications receive an extremely thorough review. A *stage* (or length) is for either two days or five days, and apprentices may be asked to work for up to twelve hours at a time. As I edit this book, there are no L'École des Chefs restaurants in Northern Spain, but this situation is sure to change, especially since the Basque Country is so renowned for its cuisine. In the meantime I encourage interested would-be chefs to consider applying for a position at three participating restaurants in Catalonia, which is two regions over from Navarre (Aragon is in the middle): Restaurant Neichel (a Michelin two-star in Barcelona), El Raco de Can Fabes (a Michelin three-star in Sant Celoni), and Restaurant Sant Pau (a Michelin two-star in Sant Pol de Mar). To read about some first-hand L'École experiences, see "The College of Hard Cheese: Blood, Sweat and Tuna" (Andy Birsh, *Forbes FYI*, November 2001); "How Great Paris Restaurants Do It" (*Saveur* no. 35, 1999); and "Gourmet Adventurism" (*Paris Notes*, March 1999). L'École was recommended first on a list of holiday gift ideas in the December 2001 issue of *Bon Appétit*. Personally, I think it is a gift idea *par excelente,* and I wish some thoughtful person would give it to me! L'École des Chefs courses are priced at $1,100–$1,400 for two days and at $1,900–$2,600 for five days.

Correos (Post Office)

The postal system in Spain isn't entirely reliable. If you're mailing something rather important, be sure to mark it *urgente,* which means it will be treated as an express piece of mail. If you're mailing items such as books back home, you personally have to tie the box up with string, or you'll be charged for this task at the counter. (This was, and may still be, the practice in France, too, as I discovered when I was a poor student trying to send some of my treasured schoolbooks to my parents' house.) Unlike some of the older PTT offices in France, however, *correos* have no public pay phones. Lines are typically quite long at *correos,* so stamps are often easier to purchase at an *estanco* (tobacconist), which is open longer hours, too.

Corrida de Toros

Corrida is the Spanish word for "bullfight," and though bullfights are not a large part of life in Northern Spain, you may want to attend one in San Sebastián or Pamplona. I plan to provide much more detailed information about the *corrida* in later editions featuring parts of Spain where it is more prevalent; but I do want to state here that I have no patience for those who turn their noses up at bullfighting and declare it barbaric and unfair, especially if those same people eat meat. As Barnaby Conrad (author of several good books on bullfighting and an amateur matador himself) noted in *Hemingway's Spain,* "I quickly learned that although the bull had about as much chance of survival as a Swift and Armour candidate in Chicago, he did have many an opportunity to collect his opponent during the hot-blooded fifteen-minute encounter, and that most matadors were gored many, many times during their careers, sometimes fatally. And while cruel, it was not as cruel as rodeos, where the livestock is abused over and over again; or zoos, where the inhabitants are imprisoned for a lifetime; or even deer or fox hunting, where, unlike the bull, the quarry is terrified. It is certainly not to be compared to the ultimate cruelty to animals, the leg-trapping of fur-bearing creatures for the vanity of the fashionable of the world." The key point to keep in mind about the *corrida* is that it is an art form, not unlike ballet or opera. Americans typically protest that there is something wrong with the *corrida* since the identity of the winner is fixed in advance, but this is merely an indication of their lack of understanding of the *corrida*'s basic nature. "Bullfighting is not a sport, and it is therefore not a cruel sport," V. S. Pritchett wrote. A *corrida* is a drama with a plot, and this particular plot calls for the bull to die. Arguing against this outcome would be equivalent to protesting the ending of Swan Lake. It may surprise you to know that *fútbol* (soccer) is far more popular among Spaniards than the *corrida,* and that there is even an antibullfight movement in Spain—Comité Antitaurina—founded in 1986.

While the following list is not exhaustive, some very good books to consult about various aspects of the *corrida* include:

The Dangerous Summer (Ernest Hemingway, introduction by James Michener, Touchstone, 1985). This excellent book, not as well known as *Death in the Afternoon,* is Hemingway's account of a brutal season of bullfights in 1959. It has two eight-page inserts of black-and-white photos.

Death in the Afternoon (Ernest Hemingway, Scribner, 1932; first Scribner Classics hardcover edition, 1999); probably the best overall book on the subject.

Iberia (James Michener, Random House, 1968). Michener's classic devotes one chapter to Pamplona and another to "The Bulls." At the very least, his observations should be read and respected: "From that first Sunday in Valencia when I watched Lalanda, Ortega and El Estudiante fight six bulls I have been a devotee of the matadors in Spain and Mexico save Pepe Luis Vázquez the Spaniard, although strangely enough I was a good friend of the Mexican matador of that name. I have traveled with bullfighters in both countries, have read almost everything in print in both Spanish and English, plus many fine books in French, and instead of losing interest as the years passed, I have found my appetite for this art increasing."

The Last Serious Thing: A Season at the Bullfights (Bruce Schoenfeld, Simon & Schuster, 1992). Set mostly in Seville, Schoenfeld offers readers an insider's view of bullfighting's dedicated fans.

On Bullfighting (A. L. Kennedy, Yellow Jersey, 1999; Anchor Books, 2001). This beautifully written book was recommended to me by two fellows from San Francisco whom I met in my favorite store in Madrid, Antigua Casa Talavera. It was one of those recommendations that went something like "Oh! We just read the most wonderful book about bullfighting, we don't know the author's name, but she was female, and her name was British, and we don't know the title exactly though it had bullfighting in it, . . . and you must read it!" So even though that wasn't much to go on, it didn't take me long to figure out that this was the book, and I'm so happy they told me about it. Kennedy notes that "no matter what your personal opinion of the *corrida* may happen to be, these facts are inescapable: in the *corrida,* bulls and men meet fear and pain and both may die."

Passes: The Art of the Bullfight (photographs by Ricardo Sanchez, essays by José Luís Ramón and Rosa Olivares, Rizzoli, 2001). This absolutely gorgeous, horizontally shaped hardcover conveys the true elegance of bullfighting.

Covadonga

Covadonga refers both to one of the most famous battles in the history of Spain, in 722, as well as to a pilgrimage center and a beautiful corner of the Picos de Europa in Asturias. The battle, a Christian victory, is so significant because it was the first organized resistance to the Muslim advance into Spain, and over the years it has come to be a symbol of Castilian nationalism. A figure named Pelayo was the hero of this assault on the Muslims, and the shrine honoring him is in a little cave, carpeted, with a great number of burning candles. You may still see today busloads of Spaniards who've come to pay their respects and light a candle of their own. I once saw an old woman walking on her knees over to the shrine, which I don't think is a very common sight these days, but in *A Stranger in Spain,* H. V. Morton indicated that many elderly women still progressed to the shrine in that fashion. The drive up to Covadonga is breathtakingly beautiful and is worth doing even if you are behind a tour bus.

¿Cuánto cuesta?

A useful Spanish phrase meaning "What is the price?" or "How much does it cost?"

Customs

There seems to be a lot of confusion over what items can and positively cannot be brought into the United States—and on the part not only of travelers but of customs agents, too. The rules are not as confusing as they might seem, but sometimes neither customs staff nor travelers are up to date on them. Some examples of what's legal and what's not include: olive oil yes, but olives no (unless they're vacuum-packed); fruit jams and preserves yes, but fresh fruit no; hard cheeses yes, but soft, runny cheeses no; commercially canned meat yes (if the inspector can determine that the meat was cooked in the can after it was sealed), but fresh and dried meats and meat products no; nuts yes, but chestnuts and acorns no; coffee yes, but roasted beans only; dried spices yes, but not leaves; fresh and dried flowers yes, but not eucalyptus or any variety with roots. If you think all this is unnecessary bother, remember that it was quite likely a tourist who carried in the wormy fruit that brought the Mediterranean fruit fly to California in 1979. Fighting that pest has cost more than $100 million. For more details, call the U.S. Department of Agriculture's Animal and Plant Health Inspection Service at 301-734-8645 or view its website (www.aphis.usda.gov; click on "Travelers' Information").

D

Dates

Remember that, as in many other countries around the world, dates in Spain are written with the day first followed by the month and then the year, as in 9 September 1959. If you think of the elements of a date as units of measure—going from smallest (the individual day) to largest (the year)—it may be easier for you to remember if you're having trouble adjusting. If you buy airline, bus, or train tickets in Spain, be absolutely certain you are purchasing them for the correct day you want to travel as the date will be printed in the order of day, month, year (and arrival and departure times will be given using the military clock, such as 1300 hours or 1500 hours).

¡Diga! and ¡Dígame!

Literally, "Talk" or "Speak," and the command "Talk to me!" You may hear these words when someone is answering the telephone. When I first visited Spain in 1975, it was common for Spaniards to say *"¡Dígame! ¡Dígame! ¡Dígame!"*—three times—when picking up the phone because the phone system was so poor that no one would ever hear you if you said it only once. *Aló* is also common, just as *allo* is used in France.

Duende

"Soul," "spirit," "imp," and "ghost" are all pared-down definitions of this Spanish word. But do not be deceived by this seeming simplicity: *Duende* is the most essential and defining aspect of the Spanish character, the true essence of Spanishness. Like comprehending the *corrida,* comprehending *duende* is key to grasping what makes Spaniards different from everyone else. An excellent source is *In Search of Duende* (Federico García Lorca, translated by Stephen Spender and Edwin Honig, New Directions Bibelot series, 1998). Lorca often referred to *duende* as a demonic earth spirit, and this book gathers his writings about *duende* and provides a full bilingual selection of his poetry.

E

Eating Out

Like other European countries, Spain offers a variety of eating and drinking establishments for residents and visitors. Though the features that distinguish a restaurant from a *tapas* bar, for example, are usually clear, it's important to recognize the differences and to know what you should—or should not—expect from each place. (Note that some restaurants also have a *tapas* bar, and that some *tapas* bars have a separate seating area—a restaurant—with nicely set tables and a printed menu.) As Sandra Gustafson reminds us in *Cheap Eats in Spain,* "when ordering, remember where you are and stay within the limits of the chef's abilities. Do not expect gourmet fare in a self-service restaurant, and do not go to a proper restaurant and order only a small salad and glass of wine." What follows is a list of all the kinds of establishments you may encounter, a few of which are unique to Northern Spain:

Bar: An establishment that offers an assortment of alcoholic drinks and soft drinks; some also offer a small selection of *tapas* or at the very least olives. Even the smallest village in Spain will have at least one bar, which is usually frequented for the better part of a day by the local male population. Although bars in Spain are much like bars in other European countries, what *is* different are the varieties of bars and what they each specialize in (described below). You may also see something called a *bar-restaurant,* which has always struck me as funny, since a lot of restaurants also have bars. At any rate, the term simply indicates that it is more than a regular bar, though don't expect the food to be anything to write home about.

Bodega: Typically a wine bar (though usually of the old-fashioned variety, as opposed to a chic, contemporary version). Beer is also often available at *bodegas.*

Café: A small establishment that offers a wide variety of coffee drinks as well as tea, hot chocolate, sodas, and alcoholic drinks. Light fare, such as tortillas, *bocadillos,* salads, and *churros* and other pastries, is also typically available. A café always has both counter and table service, whereas a bar may have no tables at all.

Cervecería: Typically a beer bar, but wine is also usually available as well.

Chiringuito: A beachside bar, typically open only during the summer months.

Fonda: A type of inn, usually rather modest, and also serving inexpensive meals for overnight guests and those just passing through. Though *fonda, mesón, posada,* and *venta* are considered first as places to spend the night, you should keep them in mind as good-value restaurants, especially on a day when you might be driving a distance and need to stop for lunch.

Marisquería: A seafood and/or shellfish place, usually quite casual.

Mesón: A type of inn; see *fonda* entry above.

Posada: A type of inn; see *fonda* entry above.

Pub: Typically a very social place, remaining open late, and serving drinks only. Odd as it may seem to find this British institution in Spain, there are a great number of pubs in Northern Spain. Pubs are popular gathering spots for sports fans, as they almost always have a large-screen television airing local and national events (and sometimes cable feeds from the United States).

Sidrería: A bar specializing in *sidra,* the hard apple cider native to Asturias and served throughout the north, though mostly in Asturias and the Basque Country. Other drinks are usually available at a *sidrería,* as well as a limited selection of *tapas.* The first time I visited Northern Spain, I rather liked *sidra;* bartenders make quite a show of pouring it, holding the bottle high in the air above their heads and aiming at glasses on the bar or on your table. It's all very festive and fun. On recent visits, however, I concluded that I really do not like *sidra* at all; it must be drunk quickly or it loses its natural fizz, and as I am a famously slow drinker, I allow the *sidra* to warm up, and it tastes dreadful. But I do encourage every traveler to try it at least once.

Tapas bar (or *tasca*, especially in Madrid): A bar that serves a variety of drinks as well as a full array of *tapas*, little hors d'oeuvres and nibbles that one can easily make a meal of or merely sample before a more substantial dinner. In larger cities and towns, *tapas* bars are known for certain specialties or cooking styles, and it is the custom to bar-hop, spending enough time at each bar to sample a variety of *tapas*. I love *tapas* of all types, and I love them best of all in Bilbao, San Sebastián, and Madrid. It doesn't take much for me to enthuse, endlessly, about the *tapas* of Northern Spain—in my journals I have recorded in great detail every *tapa* I've ever had, sometimes accompanied by a little drawing and always by those little napkins imprinted with the name of the *tapas* bar. Of all the *tapas* I've tried in the north, there is not a single one I didn't like, but my two longstanding favorites are *boquerones* (anchovies marinated in olive oil and garlic) and the green peppers (similar to Italian *peperoncini* but longer, thinner, not as pickled, and unique to Northern Spain). The most popular drinks to wash down *tapas* are, in the north, *txakolí* (a slightly fizzy white wine, the only wine produced in the Basque Country except for the wines of the small portion of Álava designated as part of the La Rioja growing region), Albariño (young white wine from Galicia), red and white wines from La Rioja and Navarre, and beer. Every *tapas* bar has its own house brand of red and white wines. When ordering, one simply asks for *una copa* (a glass) of red or white wine; typically a variety of wines are not available, unlike in North America, where we might be offered a choice among Chardonnay, Sauvignon Blanc, Merlot, and Cabernet. The price for the house wine is very low, usually about a dollar or two. Most bars offer one or two more-expensive wines for about three or four dollars, and these are promoted with a handwritten sign posted behind the bar. Beer is ordered the same way: typically one or two house brands are available, usually lager beers. Some *tapas* bars have an assortment of liquors available, but in my experience the overwhelming majority of patrons stick to wine or beer. Wine glasses at *tapas* bars can be quite small, so even though the price can't be beat, it's easy to suddenly find you've had four or five glasses.

Taberna: A tavern that typically offers an array of *tapas* or *raciones* as well as a full bar.

Venta: A type of inn that also serves moderately priced food.

Here are some tips to keep in mind about eating in Spain:
Mealtimes. Mealtimes in the northern part of Spain follow a slightly different

rhythm than in the south, though they are generally the same. Breakfast (usually a cup of *café con leche* and a roll or pastry) is taken rather early, anywhere from six-thirty to eight, though you will find coffee and tea drinks and a variety of pastries available until late morning. At around eleven many Spaniards take a break for a snack, usually a *bocadillo* (a sandwich of sausage, ham, cheese, or a combination thereof) or a *tortilla* (a potato omelet). This meal is often referred to as *las onces,* meaning "elevenses" (as in the United Kingdom); *tomar las onces* means "to take the elevens." Though in the south of Spain *tomar las onces* almost always involves sharing a glass or two of sherry, in the north it involves sharing a glass of *aguardiente* (a clear, distilled alcoholic drink, similar to grappa in Italy or eau-de-vie in France), a word that coincidentally has eleven letters. This tradition, I believe, is not widely practiced today, at least among younger people. Beginning at about one o'clock, people start leaving their workplaces and stop in at bars for a *copa* of wine or a beer and a *tapa* or two. Lunch is served beginning at two or two-thirty and lasts until about four. In the early evening, from about six on, Spaniards may gather again and meet at a bar for some drinks and a light snack. Dinner is served beginning at around eight-thirty or nine in most of Northern Spain (though the Basques tend to eat later, between nine and eleven). If all this seems like a lot, remember that the largest meal of the day is lunch, and everything else is really just a snack.

To sit or to stand. In most other European countries, the price of food and drink differ depending on where you sit at a bar or a restaurant. But at *tapas* bars in Spain, the prices are the same whether you stand or sit at the counter or stand or sit at one of the few available tables—unless those tables happen to be outside, in which case, your drinks and nibbles can cost up to twice as much (this is more commonly, obviously, in southern Spain; as in other European countries, you can also expect to remain at your table for as long as you like). ~In Northern Spain *tapas* bars are typically very small, and customers are expected to select their own drinks and *tapas* from the counter—the bartenders rarely leave the bar, and they have what I consider to be an amazing ability to remember precisely what it was you ordered, without ever giving you a bill.

Menu of the day. Don't let the words *menú del día* necessarily turn you away from a potentially great meal. Just like the *menú turistico* in Italy and the *prix fixe* meal in France, the *menú del día* in Spain is often a good value, consisting of three preselected courses and nearly always including a carafe or half-bottle of wine. You may also encounter a *plato combinado,* another inexpensive meal option typically consisting of meat or fish with one or two vegetables and/or French fries. In my experience, a *plato combinado* is less successful than a good *menú del día,* but it is certainly filling and cheap. A *menú degustación* (tasting menu) is offered at fine restaurants and also represents a good value, consisting of about six or seven small (and delicious) courses of which the chef is particularly proud. ~Some good words of advice from *Cheap Eats in Spain* by Sandra Gustafson: "Pay close attention to the daily specials, which generally represent dishes using fresh seasonal ingredients or those the chef knows are winners" and "weekday meals are cheaper than week-end and holiday meals. Even if the *menú del día* is available on the weekend, it will usually cost you more for the exact same meal."

Credit cards. Don't expect credit cards to be accepted at bars of any type and at small restaurants and cafés. Credit is accepted, however, at nearly every large establishment, as well as those holding Michelin stars.

Nonsmoking sections. Not very many restaurants set aside a separate section for nonsmokers (and even if they did, I doubt it would be honored). But as a non-smoker, I have never been at a bar or restaurant in Spain where the smoking par-ticularly bothered me, except for the one time I ate lunch at a quick little food café in the Madrid Barajas Airport and thought I might die from the smoke.

Closed. Just as in France and Italy, most restaurants in Spain close one day of the week, and others may close either for lunch or dinner on a particular day of the week. Most close for an annual vacation (usually in the summer). Be sure to check before you set out—especially if it's a meal you've been counting on—and remem-ber that on public holidays many restaurants may be closed, for one day or several days around the holiday.

A good quote to bear in mind from time to time is the following by food writer, cookbook author, and *Saveur* editor Colman Andrews: "I believe, above all, that we ought to learn to dine, or even just sit down and eat, not with fear or with the feeling that we're doing something bad, but with the happiness born of appetite and anticipation—with, if possible, sheer, ravenous joy." Andrews penned those words for his book *Everything on the Table: Plain Talk About Food and Wine* (Bantam, 1992), but he is also quite an authority on Spanish food and wine. (His book *Catalan Cuisine* is considered a classic on the subject.) I think Andrews has the right idea about about approaching food in general, but his words are especially accurate when applied to how Spaniards, and all Mediterranean peoples really, approach their meals.

~Useful vocabulary: *a la vasca* (a dish prepared in the Basque style; other phrases indicating the same include *a la vasconia, a la vizcaína,* and *a la vascon-gada;* similarly, *a la bilbaína, a la iruñesa, a la donostiarra, a la guipúzcoana, a la tolosana,* and *a la easo.* "Whatever the name," as noted in Time-Life's *The Cooking of Spain and Portugal,* "if it is an authentic Basque dish, order it in any restaurant; you cannot really go wrong"); *¿Podría recomendar un buen restau-rante?* ("Can you recommend a good restaurant?"); *Me gustaría resevar una mesa, por favor* (I want to reserve a table, please); *Nos gustaría cenar/Queremos cenar* ("We'd like to have dinner"); *¿Podemos comer fuera?* ("May we eat outside?"); *¿Qué tienen hoy de menú?* ("What is the menu of the day?"); *¿Me trae la carta?* ("May I see the menu?"); *¿Qué recomendaría usted?* ("What do you recommend?," the waiter's favorite question, which you could ask if you eat everything);

Queremos comer algo que no tenga nada de carne ("We'd like something without meat"); *primer plato* (first course, singular and plural); *segundo plato* (main course, singular and plural); *postre/s* (dessert); *lista de vinos* (wine list); *Una ración de esto, por favor* ("A plate of that one, there, please"—useful in a *tapas* bar when you don't know what something is or you don't know the Spanish word for it; *ración*, by the way, is a common word at *tapas* bars, signifying a portion usually large enough for two people to share. Note that in the Basque Country *pintxos* [pronounced PEEN-chos] is a more common word for *tapas*, and *txikiteo* [pronounced cheek-ee-TAY-o] is the word for "going bar-hopping"); *¿Qué ingredientes tiene este plato?* ("What's in this dish?"; this question is useful if you are allergic to certain things, but obviously, if you won't be able to understand the waiter's reply, you might want to select a dish whose contents are clear to you); *La cuenta, por favor* (The check, please); *¿Está incluido el servicio?* ("Is service included?"); *error* (a mistake); *una propina* (tip); *Nos trae un cenicero, por favor* ("Please bring me an ashtray"; but smokers will probably never have to ask for one, as they are always around; *recocido* (overcooked); *no es fresco* (not fresh); *agua mineral* (mineral water, which will sometimes automatically be brought to your table; note that it isn't free, so if you don't want it, ask for *agua del grifo/agua natural*—tap water); *no pedí esto* ("This is not what I ordered"); *La vuelta es para usted* ("Please keep the change"); *Dónde están los servicios?* ("Where are the toilets?"); *El servicio está cerrado con llave* ("The toilet is closed with a key"; you're acknowledging that you need the key to open the door); finally, to show your appreciation for a fine meal, you can say *Muchas gracias, estaba muy rica la comida* ("Thank you, it was a delicious meal").

Elderly Travel

The two best-known organizations for elderly travelers are Elderhostel and Interhostel. I've listed them both here instead of under Tour Operators because I want them to stand apart from the more general travel companies.

Elderhostel (11 Avenue de Lafayette, Boston, MA 02111; 877-426-8056; fax: -2166; www.elderhostel.org) is a not-for-profit organization with more than twenty-five years of experience providing high-quality, affordable programs for adults fifty-five and over. Elderhostel has grown from programs at a handful of New England colleges to adventures at more than two thousand universities, museums, national parks, folk schools, game preserves, and historical sites in more than ninety countries around the world, including Northern Spain—when I last checked, programs were offered in Santander, Santiago, Oviedo, La Rioja, and Madrid.

Interhostel (University of New Hampshire, 6 Garrison Avenue, Durham, NH 03824; 800-733-9753; fax: 603-862-1113; www.learn.unh.edu/interhostel).

Interhostel was developed in 1980 as an international educational travel experience for active adults aged fifty and over. Its programs—more than sixty all over the world—focus on the development of knowledge and understanding of people around the world by learning first-hand about their environment and culture. Interhostel's learning vacations are sponsored by the University of New Hampshire's continuing education division in cooperation with colleges and universities abroad. At the time I was finalizing this manuscript, the only program offered in Spain was "The Pilgrim's Way," which included visits to Bilbao, Pamplona, Javier, Burgos, León, and Santiago; but new programs are added every year. In 1981 Interhostel also introduced Familyhostel, a program for children aged eight to fifteen traveling with their parents or grandparents.

F

Farmacias

As in Italy, Spanish pharmacies keep hours that are accommodating to residents and visitors alike. Every district has at least one pharmacy that is open all night and all day on Sunday. All the local pharmacies take turns being open, and the one that is open is referred to as *la farmacia de turno* or *la farmacia de guardia*. The others post a sign on their doors stating which local pharmacy is open. In the countryside your hosts will know which pharmacy in the closest town is open at night and on the weekend, and it may also be printed in the local newspaper.

Fiestas (holidays)

Holidays—both national and local—are good to know about, not only because you might want to plan a trip around them, but you might equally want to plan a trip to *avoid* them. There are a number of big fiestas of note in Spain. "The Spanish," note the authors of the Cadogan guide, "like the Italians, try to have as many as possible." National (or public) holidays include the following: New Year's Day *(Año Nuevo)*, January 1; Epiphany, January 6; Good Friday *(Viernes Santo)*, sometime in March or April; Labor Day *(Fiesta del Trabajo)*, May 1; Spain's Patron Saint Day or Feast of Saint James the Greater *(Día de Santiago Apóstol)*, July 25; Feast of the Assumption *(La Asunción)*, August 15; National Day or Columbus Day *(Día de la Hispanidad)*, October 12; All Saints' Day *(Todos los Santos)*, November 1; Constitution Day *(Día de la Constitución)*, December 6; and Christmas Day *(Navidad)*, December 25. On these dates—and sometimes on the days leading up to them or immediately following—nearly all shops, government offices, and businesses are closed, and some restaurants, too. Never assume a restaurant will be open on a holiday without calling first to confirm, and expect flights, trains, and buses to be fully booked. Madrid has some of its own holidays: Maundy (Holy)

Thursday *(Jueves Santo),* the day before Good Friday; Madrid Day *(Día de la Communidad de Madrid),* May 2; and Immaculate Conception *(La Inmaculada),* December 8. Additionally, there are three saints' days in Madrid: San Isidro (the feast of Saint Isidore the farmer—Isidore is the patron of farmers, farmworkers, ranchers, and the city of Madrid; his image is of an angel-assisted plowman and the commemoration dates from 1130); Virgen de la Paloma, August 15; and Virgen de la Almudena, November 9 (I found no entries for these last two in a nifty book, *The Birthday Book of Saints,* Villard, 2001).

Film

I'm aware that the FAA maintains that film of less than 1000-speed sent through an X-ray scanner won't harm picture developing, but my friend Peggy, a freelance photographer, maintains that multiple trips through the scanner will indeed harm film. If you pack your film in checked bags, the scanners that inspect them will be stronger than those for carry-on bags, so they should definitely be avoided. ~I always keep rolls of film—no matter what speed—accessible and hand them to the security inspectors before I walk through the scanner. (Remember to retrieve them after you pass, however!) ~If you take a lot of photos, you might want to buy some lead-lined pouches from a camera store. They're inexpensive and will protect film even in checked bags. ~Professional film (which is very sensitive and must be kept refrigerated until used and developed a day later) aside, a general guideline for us amateurs is that the higher the film speed, the faster the film—and fast film requires less light. So think about the situations in which you anticipate taking pictures, and select film accordingly. ~I happen to be very fond of black-and-white photos, so I always include a roll or two in my bag.

Frequent Flier Miles

From what I've read, the airlines seem to wish they'd never created mileage award programs. The year 2001 marked the twentieth anniversary of the frequent flier program, which was initially introduced by American Airlines. There are now fewer and fewer seats reserved for frequent fliers, and you need more and more miles to earn them. You can also earn more miles by *not* flying than ever before.

Consumer Reports Travel Letter features an annual report on frequent flier programs, and its 2002 update (in the August issue) emphasized several key points worth repeating: it's harder to accrue miles now since some airlines have lost or eliminated airline partners; upgrading remains as difficult as ever, and some airlines are requiring even more miles for upgrades; and finally, even though most airlines have announced they are no longer identifying blackout dates, this in no way translates into greater availability for frequent fliers: there are simply fewer award seats allotted during peak travel times. I found two additional factors highlighted in the

CRTL report particularly interesting: the first is that while the actual numbers of seats available for mileage award travel is apparently considered confidential information, airlines do disclose numbers reflecting the *percentage* of award seats claimed. CRTL included a chart of these percentages featuring ten carriers, which was revealing, but even more revealing was the fact that even though the data in the chart may indicate an airline has maintained, or perhaps increased, its mileage-award seat availability, the chart does not document that the total number of mileage award seats may have actually been reduced. The second factor is that airlines have been earning quite a bit of revenue—approximately $100 million a year, according to CRTL—by selling miles to travelers who fall a bit short of the necessary mileage requirements. Buying miles, to quote from the CRTL report, "can be a very epensive way to earn a free ticket." (Readers may request a copy of this excellent report by contacting *Consumer Reports Travel Letter,* 101 Truman Avenue, Yonkers, NY 10703; single copies are five dollars each.) In CRTL's 2001 report, the editors stated that at least 40 percent of frequent flier miles are earned by means other than flying. That figure had risen to 43 percent in 2002.

Call me a *pesimista,* but I believe that there is no free lunch, and while it may seem appealing to sign up for a new credit card, buy a cell phone, buy a quantity of a particular product, or shop at a certain retail establishment to earn extra miles, I think at the end of the day you are spending more money than it would cost you to purchase a discounted ticket through other means. Unless you are a true frequent flier—and, let's face it, the frequent business or pleasure traveler is exactly who the mileage award programs originally targeted—you can almost never spend enough money to make your efforts worthwhile. Even if you are spending money on goods or services that you would buy anyway, it is more than likely that just as you've accrued the number of eligible miles to fly to Spain, the airline will increase its qualifying points, ensuring that the trip remains slightly out of your reach. To my mind, the miles aren't really worth having unless you accrue upward of 500,000 or 1 million, which entitles you not only to lots of destinations worldwide but also to business and first-class upgrades and VIP treatment.

Should you happen to have enough miles and want to fly to Madrid, plan to redeem those miles about four or five months ahead, or plan to fly in the off-season. (It's also possible that airlines will reduce the miles needed for an off-season flight.) Don't immediately give up if your initial request can't be confirmed: apparently the airlines tinker with frequent flier seats every day as they monitor the demand for paying customers. If the number of paying travelers is low as the departure date approaches, more frequent flier awards may be honored.

Seats for both paying passengers and frequent fliers become available 331 days in advance of a flight, but not every airline will allow you to reserve a seat that far in advance for especially popular routes. Madrid is not as popular a destination as some others in Europe and around the Mediterranean, so technically you should be able to redeem your miles a year in advance without a snafu.

Check to see if your accrued miles have expired before you try to redeem them. All airlines have expiration dates on frequent flier miles, but they don't all strictly enforce those deadlines.

If you're desperate for miles, you can always buy some through Miles4sale.com (8235 Douglas Avenue, Dallas, Texas 75225; 866-630-8717). In addition to purchasing airline miles and upgrades for yourself, you can also buy some as a gift. The last time I checked the website, the participating airline partners were American, Continental, Delta, and Northwest. I think this is probably a more expensive way of earning miles than buying goods or services, but that's why they call it desperation.

Finally, try to reserve your valid mileage for expensive flights rather than for those that you can get for a good price anytime.

G

Gastronomic Societies

It won't take you long, when you are reading about Basque cuisine, to learn about the legendary gastronomic societies, especially noteworthy in San Sebastián, where the first one was founded in 1870. These eating clubs were established by and for men only: The only occasions during the year that women are welcome are on the eve of Assumption Day (15 August) and on Saint Sebastian's Day (20 January). While Basque women are respected and loved, their place in Basque society has traditionally not been the kitchen, which has long been considered the domain of men. Even a Basque man who wants to get a glimpse of the gathering must be invited by a member to be his guest. If he wants to join a club, he must wait for an older member to pass away and then apply for membership. I have not had the good fortune to be in the Basque Country on either Assumption Day or Saint Sebastian's Day, so I am unable to give you any sort of insider's lowdown, but there is a *great* description of a visit to one society in San Sebastián in *The Cooking of Spain and Portugal*. The editors note that "if you are introduced to Basque cooking in one of the private Basque gastronomic societies themselves, you will be served the kind of meal not to be found anywhere else in the world." Apparently, rivalry among the various gastronomic societies is not very stiff, as it is their culture as a whole of which the Basques are most proud. "Still," the editors continue, "if you happen to see a familiar dish in one of the *other* gastronomic societies, your host may remark quietly that you have already tasted that dish cooked at its best once and so need not pay too much attention. Then he will accompany you back to your hotel silently under the blue-black, glittering sky."

Greetings and Salutations

Just like the French and the Italians, Spaniards are very polite, which should be interpreted not as formal, just less casual than we are in North America. Men shake hands when greeting each other (women do, too, sometimes), and women usually always kiss each other on both cheeks. Men may also embrace each other and walk together with arms around each other's shoulders. When an introduction is made, you will notice that typically someone is referred to as the son or daughter of someone, as opposed to simply giving his or her full name. This is a way of emphasizing the family the person is from and is similar to the way one addresses mail in France, with the family name written in capital letters after the first name.

Guidebooks

Choosing which guidebooks to use can be bewildering and frustrating. I have yet to find the perfect book that offers all the features I need and want, so I consult a variety of them, gleaning tips and advice from each. Then I buy a blank journal and fill it with notes from all these books (leaving some pages blank) and end up with the perfect package for me: the journal plus two or three guidebooks I determine to be indispensable. (I don't carry them all around at the same time.) In the end, the right guidebook is the one that speaks to you. Go to the Spain section of a bookstore, and take some time to read through the various guides. If you feel the author shares a certain sensibility with you, and you think his or her credentials are respectable, then you're probably holding the right book. Recommendations from friends and colleagues are fine only if they travel in the same way you do and seek the same qualities as you in a guidebook. Also, if you discover an older guide that appeals to you, don't immediately dismiss it. Background information doesn't change—use it in combination with an updated guide to create your own perfect package. Keep in mind, too, that guidebooks within the same series are not always consistent, as they aren't always written by the same authors.

General travel: Here are some good books to consult about trip planning in general.

The New York Times Practical Traveler Handbook: An A–Z Guide to Getting There and Back (Betsy Wade, Times Books, 1994) and *Wendy Perrin's Secrets Every Smart Traveler Should Know: Condé Nast Traveler's Consumer Travel Expert Tells All* (Fodor's Travel Publications, 1997). It might seem that these two books would cover the same ground, but in fact there is very little overlap, and I refer to both of them all the time. The Practical Traveler book really is an A–Z guide, organized alphabetically, and covers such topics as airline code-sharing, customs, hotel tipping, closing up the house, and the wonderful WPA guides. Perrin's book is divided into eight sections plus an appendix, and the anecdotes featured were all previously published in the "Ombudsman" column of *Condé Nast Traveler* magazine. She covers the fine art of complaining; what to do if your luggage is damaged or pilfered; dealing with travel agents and tour operators, car rentals, shopping, cruises, and so on; and she provides the ten commandments of trouble-free travel, which I think should be given to every traveler before he or she boards the plane.

In a similar yet different vein, I highly recommend *Traveler's Tool Kit: How to Travel Absolutely Anywhere!* (Rob Sangster, Menasha Ridge Press, Birmingham, AL, 1996). "Tool kit" really is the best description of this travel bible, which addresses *everything* having to do with planning, packing, and departing. Who is this book for? Everyone, really, or at least people who are curious about the rest of the world; people who are thinking about taking their very first foreign trip; budget travelers; business travelers; people who want to travel more independently; and people who know "that life offers more than a two-week vacation once a year." It's a *great* book, with lots of great ideas, tips, and advice. I've found Sangster's checklists at the back of the book particularly helpful, and his bibliography is the most extensive I've seen aside from my own.

The Travel Detective: How to Get the Best Service and the Best Deals from Airlines, Hotels, Cruise Ships, and Car Rental Agencies (Peter Greenberg, Villard, 2001). As long as the title is, it could be even longer, as Greenberg covers—and uncovers—so very much indispensable information on all aspects of travel. If I could have, I would have excerpted nearly every entry in Greenberg's book in my own. You want to read this book. It's remarkably interesting and *esencial*.

Travel to Northern Spain. Listed below are the books I've used when planning trips to, and traveling in, Northern Spain. They appear alphabetically, not in any order of preference. I have, however, noted which features I find particularly helpful in each book, and I've indicated those which I consider to be "bring-alongs." (I use some books for very specific reasons, but don't consider them thorough enough to bring along in my suitcase.) I do not include guidebooks covering all of Spain because the sections devoted to the north in such editions are entirely too condensed; I feel it only fair to mention, however, that I do occasionally consult the *Eyewitness Guide to Spain,* for the front section of the book and the practical information section at the back; the *Blue Guide to Spain,* just because the Blue Guide is so authoritative; the *Fodor's Exploring Guide to Spain,* for the driving and walking itineraries; *Fodor's UpClose Spain,* for the variety of money-saving tips; the UpClose series is aimed at travelers on limited budgets, but not necessarily the *Let's Go* crowd; the historical background is too thin for my taste, but this series is particularly welcome because I believe this audience—intelligent travelers who want an authentic experience on a modest budget—more accurately reflects the majority of people traveling today; *Lonely Planet: Spain,* because Lonely Planet has been among my most favorite guidebook series for many years; and the *Michelin Green Guide to Spain,* because it, too, is so authoritative and is so very good at steering travelers to the most worthy historical sites.

Cadogan Guides: Northern Spain (Dana Facaros and Michael Pauls, Cadogan Guides, London; distributed in North America by Globe Pequot Press, Old Saybrook, CT). Cadogan (rhymes with *toboggan*) Guides are almost all written by the Facaros-Pauls team (they've written more than thirty now, including all of the various Spain editions), and I consider them to be of the bring-along variety. They're discriminating without being snooty, honest, witty, and interesting. The authors are not very easily impressed, so when they enthuse about something, I pay attention. I'm most especially fond of the history and culture sections in the front of each book, which reveal how perceptive the authors are and introduce readers to their style. There are lodging and dining recommendations for all budgets, and good commentary on sights famous and little known. There are the usual maps, menu vocabulary, glossary, bibliography, and list of architectural, artistic, and historical terms. This edition is among the first in the newer format for the Cadogan series. At first I was worried that my tried-and-true series had gone commercial (there's a twenty-eight-page color photo essay—in this edition by Kicca Tommasi—in the front of the book), but I'm relieved and happy to report that the photo essay is a welcome addition, and the newly designed interior of the book is perhaps easier to read. Definitely my favorite all-around guidebook. *Esencial.* ~A complementary companion to this guide is *Bilbao and the Basque Lands*, a smaller book but perfect for travelers who aren't venturing west of the Basque Country.

Discovering Spain: An Uncommon Guide (Penelope Casas, Alfred A. Knopf, 1998). Casas (for readers who may not yet know) is a cookbook author and the leading authority on Spanish cuisine in North America. (By the time you reach the end of this book, you will most definitely be aware of Penelope Casas.) Of this book, I would say that it is so *muy esencial* that if you don't have a copy, don't get on the plane. There is not a single guidebook that is better than this one. It is truly "uncommon," however, so though I rate it as indispensable, it is most useful in conjunction with other guides. Casas does not provide quite the extensive listings for hotels and restaurants as you'll find in more "common" guidebooks, and practical information is kept to a minimum. But for everything else, you simply must have this book. Casas opens with an introduction to Spain, which includes a chronology of key periods and events in Spanish history and an overview of artistic styles throughout the country. Individual chapters follow for fourteen regions of Spain, including the Balearic and Canary Islands. (Northern Spain is represented in four chapters, with La Rioja included in a chapter with Castilla y León.) Six itineraries are suggested at the end of the book, and Casas also provides a list of the *paradores* of Spain and a bibliography. Note that while I typically do not include publication dates for guidebooks since they are updated more or less annually, I did include the date for this guide (1998) as it does not need annual updating. (The book was originally published in 1992 and was revised and updated in both 1996 and 1998.) Do not let the fact that this edition is five years old deter you from seeking it out, either from a bookseller or from your local library.

Fodor's Barcelona to Bilbao (George Semler, Fodor's Travel Publications). As I noted earlier, I feel this edition was compiled to capitalize on the popularity of two Spanish cities that ultimately do not have anything in common (except for their inhabitants' desire for more autonomy) and aren't even very close geographically (although I admit I like the idea of defining them as "bookends of the Pyrenees"). But as Cadogan is the only other publisher with a volume on Bilbao, I felt I should recommend this one as well. I typically crave more information than Fodor's guides provide, but I think the entire line just keeps getting better and better every year, and I've noticed that whenever Fodor's introduces a new feature—such as color photos, a pull-out map, whatever—all the other guidebooks follow suit. I *always* read the appropriate Fodor's guide before I go, and *always* discover a handful of useful tips. Aside from the sections featuring Barcelona and the Catalan Pyrenees, this guide also includes sections on Aragon and the central Pyrenees, Bilbao and the surrounding Basque Country, Navarra, and La Rioja. I used this guide mostly for the "Smart Travel Tips" section (in the yellow pages in the front of the book) and the section immediately following it, "Destination: Barcelona to Bilbao," for its pleasures and pastimes listings, great itineraries, and the "Fodor's Choice" listings for places, churches, restaurants, lodgings, and natural resources. It's not necessary as a bring-along, but it's worth perusing in advance of your trip.

Insight Guides: Northern Spain (APA Publications, Singapore; distributed by Houghton Mifflin). I have been an enormous fan of the Insight Guides for years. When they first appeared about twenty years ago, they were the only books to provide outstanding color photographs matched with perceptive text. The guiding philosophy of the series has been to provide genuine insight into the history, culture, institutions, and people of a particular place. The editors search for writers with a firm knowledge of the place who are also experts in their fields. I do not think that the recent editions are quite as good as the older ones; but as I mentioned above, some guidebooks in a series are better than others, and coupled with the fact that there aren't many books devoted to Northern Spain in the first place, this is an *esencial* volume. The introduction (the best section, in my opinion, in *all* the books) is a series of magazine-style essays on architecture, food, markets, the people, history, the arts, and politics. Some of the essays in this edition include "Cave Painters to Columbus," "Civil War to Autonomy," "Separatism," "Cider: The Drink from Paradise," "Fishing," "The Pilgrim Route to Santiago de Compostela," "Running with the Bulls," and "Wildlife." The practical information at the back of the book is quite good (though not as thorough as in other guidebooks) and includes a variety of tips, vocabulary, and suggestions not found in the other guides. It's not necessary as a bring-along (though I admit I've traveled with my copy, since the only other guidebook I had to carry was Cadogan), but still *esencial*. ~Note that Insight also publishes a line of Pocket Guides, and one edition is devoted to Bilbao. I would certainly recommend this edition if your itinerary did not include other destinations in Northern Spain. (It's also a smaller book and therefore isn't as heavy to carry.) But if you will be traveling throughout the north, there really is no reason for a separate Insight edition on Bilbao: the city is covered well in the larger book, and the *Fodor's Barcelona to Bilbao* edition might serve short-term visitors better.

Lesbians Guide to Spain (Perez, Editorial Les Importa S.L., 2000). It may seem a shame that gay men and women have to resort to a separate guidebook, but I suppose it's no different from readers with a specific interest in, say, cooking or hiking having a separate book as well. This is the first bilingual lesbian guidebook to Spain. It's subtitled *Orange Guide for Les,* which is explained to mean "Spain is the land of the oranges and this book will take you directly to where the juice is!" That said, this guide contains more than five hundred addresses for accommodations, bars, shops, travel agencies, and professional services and associations. There are also maps. While this guide is certainly one-of-a-kind and eminently useful, I find it to be more of a companion than a solid history/guidebook. *Esencial,* however, for gay women travelers.

Let's Go: Spain and Portugal (including Morocco) (St. Martin's Press). "The World's Bestselling Budget Travel Series" is the Let's Go slogan, which is hardly debatable. Let's Go is still the bible, and if you haven't looked at a copy since your salad days, you might be surprised: Now each edition contains color maps, advertisements, and an appendix featuring a wealth of great practical information. A team of Harvard student interns still offers the same thorough coverage of places to eat and sleep and things to see and do. True to Let's Go tradition, rock-bottom budget travelers can find suggestions for places to sleep under $10 a night (sometimes it's the roof), while travelers with more means can find clean, cozy, and sometimes downright fancy accommodations. Though I don't generally recommend books on all of Spain, Let's Go does not publish individual volumes for cities and regions of Spain, and as it is positively the leading guidebook series for students and budget travelers, I didn't want to exclude it. I think the presentation of facts and history is quite substantive in Let's Go, and I would eagerly press a copy into the hands of anyone under a certain age (thirty-five) bound for Spain.

The Rough Guide to the Pyrenees (written and researched by Marc Dubin, with additional contributions by Brian Catlos and Lance Chilton, Rough Guides, London; distributed by the Penguin Group). When the Rough Guides first appeared in the early 1980s, they had limited distribution in the United States. Then the guides were sort-of-but-not-quite the British equivalent of Let's Go. I sought them out because I found the British viewpoint refreshing and felt the writers imparted more knowledge about a place than was currently available in U.S. guidebooks. Mark Ellingham was inspired to create the Rough Guides series because at the time guidebooks were all lacking in some way: They were strong on ruins and museums, for example, but short on bars, clubs, and inexpensive eating places. Or they were so conscious of the need to save money that they lost sight of things of cultural and historical significance. None of the books mentioned anything about contemporary life, politics, culture, or the people and how they lived. Now since the Rough Guides opened a New York office in the late 1990s, the series has evolved into one that is broader based but still appealing to independent-minded travelers who appreciate the Rough Guides' honest assessments and historical and political backgrounds. (These last are found in the "Contexts" section of each guide. My only complaint is that this section should appear at the beginning of each book instead of at the end.) Like its cousin Let's Go, the Rough Guide provides specifics on working and studying, gay and lesbian life, and hotels frequented both by the backpacking crowd and by those who carry luggage with their hands. I think this Pyrenees guide is outstanding, and it should receive a warm welcome from booksellers and travelers alike. (I was happy to see that I'm not alone in this opinion: *The Sunday Times* of London has called it "the best book on the Pyrenees.") Though it covers the French Pyrenees and Andorra too, it is still the very best resource for travelers who are not planning on venturing west of San Sebastián. Avalanche safety, mountain rescue phone numbers, eating and drinking, walking skills, skiing, climbing, water and food, French and Spanish national holidays and festivals, the Camino de Santiago, maps, trails, and so on are all covered, as well as the usual excellent writing and thorough detail that readers have come to expect from Rough Guides. Each edition in the Rough Guides series is dependable and informative, and this edition does not disappoint. There are maps throughout as well as eight pages of color photos. For those who are obsessed with the Internet, online updates to Rough Guides can be found at www.roughguides.com. I highly recommend this *esencial* edition as a bring-along.

Guidebooks to living in Spain. I haven't lived in Spain, so I cannot vouch personally for these titles; but if I were planning on living or working in Spain for any length of time, I would peruse each of them:

Buying a Home in Spain (David Hampshire, Survival Books, 2000).

Live & Work in Spain and Portugal (Elisabeth Roberts and Jonathan Packer, third edition, Vacation Work Publications, 2002; distributed in the United States by Seven Hills Book Distributors).

Living and Working in Spain (David Hampshire, Survival Books, 2000).

Gypsies

Gypsies are found all over Spain, but they live in much greater numbers in the south, especially in Granada. You may visit Northern Spain and never encounter any Gypsies, who have the same reputation in Spain as they do in other Mediterranean countries, which is to say not a very good one. As Jan Morris has noted, however, many of the icons that seem to us most Spanish are really Gypsy, such as bullfighting and flamenco: "Ah, the gypsies! If they are not the salt of Spain, they are the spiciest of sauces." A good book to read is *Bury Me Standing: The Gypsies and Their Journey* (Isabel Fonseca, Alfred A. Knopf, 1995; Vintage, 1996), for a thoroughly fascinating and surprising account of Gypsy life.

H

¿Habla inglés?

Do you speak English? is a question you may be asking quite often. While many people in Northern Spain are not *fluent* in English, nearly everyone knows a few words, or sometimes they will run and fetch someone who does.

Health

Staying healthy while traveling in Spain should not be a challenge, but health problems do happen. I was once very sick with diarrhea in Andalusia after drinking water from the tap, so on later trips I never drank anything but bottled water—even to brush my teeth—in Spain. But on my last two visits to Northern Spain, I drank plenty of water from the tap with no ill effects. I do, think, however, that water in the north is generally better than in the south.

A good general reference book to consult is *The Rough Guide to Travel Health* (Dr. Nick Jones, Rough Guides, distributed by the Penguin Group, 2001). In addition to an A–Z listing of diseases and health risks, it provides good coverage on being prepared (including homeopathic suggestions) as well as summaries of potential health concerns region by region around the world. Travelers with special needs—asthma, diabetes, epilepsy, HIV, disability, pregnancy, and so on—are also addressed, and a very thorough directory with a wide range of resources is found at the back of the book.

Another good overall book is *Travelers' Health: How to Stay Healthy All Over the World* (Richard Dawood, M.D. [medical editor for *Condé Nast Traveler*], foreword by Paul Theroux, Random House, 1994). This thick, six-hundred-plus-page book isn't for bringing along—it's for consulting before you go. In addition to Dr. Dawood, sixty-seven other medical experts contributed to this volume, which covers everything from insect bites, water filters, and sun effects on the skin to gynecological problems, altitude sickness, children abroad, immunizations, and diabetes. It also features essays on topics like "The Economy-Class Syndrome" and "Being an Expatriate." *The International Travel Health Guide* (Dr. Stuart Rose, Chronimed Publishing) is a book I haven't yet seen but has been recommended to me. It's apparently the only annually updated book that summarizes the most recent information on avoiding and treating illnesses. Some of the topics covered in the book are jet lag, medical care abroad, air ambulance services, travel insurance, business travel, and altitude sickness.

Travel Fit & Healthy (Fodor's FYI, Fodor's Travel Publications) is a great book with excellent suggestions for staying fit on the road. The book covers topics such as planning and packing for a healthy (business or pleasure) trip, things to do before you leave home, how to stretch and exercise en route, fitness routines at your hotel, and eating while traveling. Travel experts share a wealth of their own tips and lessons learned for avoiding the "Bermuda Triangle—fatigue, stress, and weight gain—that every traveler faces." I really love this book and have found it indispensable. (It's small, too, so you can easily take it with you.) The fitness resources section at the back includes some good websites for cycling, hiking, health clubs, and swimming pools worldwide.

Deep vein thrombosis. Not related to travel in Spain specifically but related to flying to and from is deep vein thrombosis (DVT), sometimes called coach-class thrombosis or economy-class syndrome. Visitors flying from the East Coast of the United States or Canada to Spain are probably not at great risk for DVT; even if there is a connecting flight, the total flying time is only about eight or nine hours. But travelers flying from other parts of North America may be prime candidates for this condition, in which prolonged periods of sitting in one position cause blood clots in the leg veins that can travel to the lungs and get stuck there, causing death. In the last two years, a flurry of lawsuits have been filed around the world. The suits contend that airlines have not adequately informed travelers about DVT (though some major airlines offer tips in their in-flight magazines and air video programs featuring exercises passengers can practice in their seats). Though long plane flights are not the only cause of DVT—sitting for long periods at an office desk, on a train or bus, or in a car are equally bad—it's important to remember to get up and walk up and down the plane's aisles while en route. My chiropractor tells me I should never sit for more than twenty minutes at a stretch because I have lower-back problems. Now I have another reason for getting up and moving about. Concerned travelers should contact the Aerospace Medical Association, 320 South Henry Street, Alexandria, VA 22314; 703-739-2240; www.asma.org.

Two recently introduced items might provide some relief while on a long flight and may aid in preventing DVT: Hyland's makes homeopathic tablets for leg cramps, and one of the active ingredients is quinine. The tablets are 100 percent natural and do not interact with other medications. Call 800-624-9659 for details. Two companies—Wolford America and Mediven—have introduced travel compression stockings for men and women. (There are tights for women and knee socks for men, but women have the choice of both.) Long Distance is the name Wolford is using for its stockings, but no matter the name, they are both tightest at the ankles and knees, to prompt blood flow away from the feet and toward the heart. Ask for them at department stores, travel shops, or pharmacies, and expect to pay about $21 to $45, depending on whether they're tights or knee socks.

Diabetes. Travelers with diabetes might want to refer to *The Diabetes Travel Guide* (American Diabetes Association, 2000), which is filled with good tips and info.

Disability. Disabled travelers may not already know about The Society for Accessible Travel and Hospitality (347 Fifth Avenue, Suite 610, New York, NY 10016; 212-447-7284; fax: 725-8253), a nonprofit organization that celebrated its twenty-fifth anniversary in 2001. Its website is www.sath.org, a seemingly inexhaustible resource for related information and other Internet links. Two other useful resources are Access-Able Travel Source (www.access-able.com) and the travel agency Accessible Journeys (35 West Sellers Avenue, Ridley Park, PA 19078; 800-846-4537 or 610-521-0339; fax: -6959; www.disabilitytravel.com).

Travel health websites. Some travel health websites you can consult include the National Center for Infectious Diseases' "Travelers' Health" page (www.cdc.gov/travel), part of the federal Centers for Disease Control in Atlanta. The content on the website comes from the CDC's *Yellow Book: Health Information for International Travel*. ~Travel Health Online has the very best site, in my opinion, at www.tripprep.com. It is prepared by Shoreland, a trusted resource of travel medicine practitioners around the world. When I clicked on "Spain," I found good (and fortunately not lengthy) information on vaccines and malaria (malaria, by the way, does not present risk in Spain) and other health issues (insect-borne diseases, mad cow disease, and so on) as well as reports on crime, travel, and consular information. In general, this site reports that Spain has a "high level of medical care comparable to that in other industrialized countries in Madrid, Barcelona, Majorca, and the Costa Blanca. Adequate medical care is available in the rest of the country but is not up to the standards of other industrialized countries."

Doctors. To find an English-speaking doctor, you can contact the International Association for Medical Assistance to Travellers (417 Center Street, Lewiston, NY 14092; 716-754-4883; www.iamat.org), which provides a directory of English-speaking doctors around the world. IAMAT is a nonprofit organization, and while membership is free, donations are greatly appreciated. In addition to providing the directory, IAMAT mails members material on malaria, immunizations, and so on, as well as a membership card, which entitles them to member rates should they have to pay for medical help. ~You can also always contact the closest American embassy or local U.S. military installation for a list of local physicians and their areas of expertise. Additionally, some credit cards offer assistance: American Express's Global Assist Program is available to all cardholders at no extra fee. It's a full-service program offering everything from doctor and hospital referrals to emergency cash wires, translation assistance, lost item search, legal assistance, and daily monitoring of your health condition. When abroad, you can call cardmember services at 800-528-4800; international collect at 1.336.393.1111; or the local American Express office.

Useful vocabulary: *Necesitamos un médico* ("We need a doctor"); *¿Dónde está la farmacía más cercana?* (Where is the nearest pharmacy?").

Hiking

To say there are lots of opportunities for hiking in Northern Spain is a gross understatement: Not only is this region blessed with the magnificent Picos de Europa and the Pyrenees, as well as the Camino de Santiago (which always appears on lists of Europe's top hikes), but there are also a number of lesser-known trails along the coasts of Galicia and Cantabria. Though some routes may not be gentle—the Picos are divided into three limestone massifs separated by enormous gorges, and the Pyrenees have long been considered rather impenetrable—ramblers and serious hikers alike will be rewarded in this part of Spain, whether for day hikes or longer treks. As I noted in my *Provence* edition, Friedrich Nietzsche once opined that "only those thoughts that come by walking have any value." I believe that whether one walks leisurely or hikes with a goal in mind, spending some time getting around via your own two feet makes you feel part of a place in a special way. While I would never plan a trip that had me out on hiking trails every day, setting aside some time for a ramble of any length is an especially good idea in Northern Spain, as daily life still revolves so much around the land.

My husband and I have come across families quietly tending their fields (and with no modern machinery in sight, only a donkey and metal tools) and herds of cows and sheep. This highlights an important difference between hiking in the United States and Europe as well as the entire Mediterranean basin, which is that hiking is generally not a wilderness experience there the way we know and expect it to be in North America. In Canada and the United States wide-open spaces and undeveloped land are of significant importance; but in countries like Spain, the land has been much more cultivated and lived on. Besides small villages and hamlets, transhumance—the seasonal migration of livestock, mostly sheep, and the people who tend them, from lowlands to higher pastures—also affects the land. Therefore, except in the wilder areas of the Picos and the Pyrenees, what you walk on is a well-worn *route,* not a leisurely hiking trail. The routes were obviously not created at random and often connect old paths that have existed for hundreds of years. There are very few places in Europe, now or ever, where you can backpack into completely isolated areas and not encounter roads, people, or towns. Conversely, there are few if any places in the United States where you can backpack and be assured of finding a place to sleep in a bed, plus a meal with wine or beer at the end of the day.

Spain (like other European countries) has an extensive network of mountain huts known as *refugios*. These simple huts, conveniently located along routes, are staffed by friendly folks and are typically open from mid-June to mid-September. (Some, usually those at lower elevation, remain open year-round.) Though reservations aren't always necessary, I recommend reserving in advance if possible. The Spanish tourist offices both in North America and in Spain can provide you with contact information, and some of the books listed below also include information. Most *refugios* serve breakfast and dinner, and even if you're not staying at a particular *refugio*, dinner guests are always welcome, allowing you to camp somewhere else nearby, perhaps with more privacy. Sleeping accommodations at *refugios* are not exceptionally comfortable, usually consisting of dormitory-style benches with mattresses and blankets—and no sheets. To quote from the authors of *Walking in Spain*, "check carefully how many sleepers there are to a room. Many are fine, like a high-altitude youth hostel; others, where you're one in a dormitory among thirty-five or more sweating, snoring, farting others, are less fun. Their strong point is that the guardians are almost invariably friendly and well informed. Most come back season after season and are an invaluable source of information about walks in the vicinity." These same authors note that you may also encounter unstaffed *refugios*, "the best of which can be surprisingly cosy. At the end of the day, however, they're only as clean as the last group passing through—and that can be anything from the most fastidious of fellow walkers to a herd of swine." Regardless of what condition a *refugio* is in when you arrive, I think the network is one to applaud.

Hiking books. Fortunately hiking and walking enthusiasts have a number of good resources to consult for planning where and when to hike. The only difficulty will be in choosing routes, as there are so many appealing ones! A good book to consult for hiking all over Spain is *Lonely Planet: Walking in Spain* (Miles Roddis, Nancy Frey, José Placer, Matthew Fletcher, and John Noble, Lonely Planet, 1999). Among the highlighted walks are a number in Galicia, the Pyrenees, the Cordillera Cantábrica, and along the Camino de Santiago. These are a combination of short and long hikes: the shortest is three and a half hours; the longest—the Camino Francés—is twenty-eight days. A helpful table of walks in the front of the book informs you of the duration and level of each walk in addition to the best season of the year to attempt it and special features. Notable about two of the authors—Nancy Frey and José Placer, who live in Galicia—is that they also lead month-long educational walking tours along the Camino de Santiago and are founders of On Foot in Spain (see the entry below for more details). The book features a few color photos throughout, as well as sections on flora and fauna, general facts for the walker, health and safety information, and food and drink suggestions. At the back is a language section, glossary, a map legend, and metric conversions.

Wild Spain: The Sierra Club Natural Traveler (Tim Jepson, Sierra Club Books, San Francisco, 1994). This book includes many more color photos and is an edition in the Wild Guides series (which also includes editions on France and Italy).

For the Picos, *Landscapes of Northern Spain: Picos de Europa* (Teresa Farino, Sunflower Guide) is a good edition with photos and maps. The author is a naturalist and a Spanish correspondent for *BBC Wildlife* and has lived in the Picos for many years. Farino provides one car tour, eighteen long and short walks, six easy walks, and five picnic suggestions.

For the Pyrenees, there are many good books to choose from. *Pyrenees* (another edition in the Sunflower Guide series, by Paul Jenner and Christine Smith), covers the entire mountain range in France, Spain, and Andorra. Over 250 miles of walks are featured, including the famous coast-to-coast traverse (from the Mediterranean to the Bay of Biscay) for serious walkers. The authors have lived in the Pyrenees for many years and include pilgrim routes, World War II escape routes, summit climbs, and routes that allow hikers to view some of the wildest scenery in this range as well as the habitat of marmots, vultures, and lizards. All in all there are twelve car tours, sixty-five long and short walks, and twelve picnic ideas. The accompanying map is of the pull-out variety.

Walks and Climbs in the Pyrenees (Kev Reynolds, Cicerone Press) includes, as the title suggests, not only hikes but rock climbing. Reynolds offers suggestions for walks, multiday tours, and moderate ascents of the main summits. ~A single book devoted to the coast-to-coast route is *Pyrenees High Level Route* (West Col Productions), which divides the trek up into forty-five stages with fifty-three alternatives and variations. The cool thing to note is that the author and two companions walked the route and wrote the original edition of this book in 1968, and they have since improved upon it ten times. ~Rock climbers may appreciate *Rock Climbs in the Pyrenees* (Cicerone Press, an excellent publisher of walking and adventuring guides), which details routes on the Pic du Midi d'Ossau, the canyon of Ordesa, and easier gorge descents of the Sierra Guara. ~*Trekking in the Pyrenees* (Seven Hills) details all the main trails of the 280-mile range, including the coast-to-coast hike, and its eighty maps show all the routes, distances, and points of interest. Accommodation and dining guides for all budgets are recommended, and there is a four-page section on flora of the Pyrenees. ~Readers familiar with the Grande Randonée (GR) network in France may know of the GR10, a coast-to-coast trek that is less arduous than the Pyrenean High Route because the trail remains at a lower elevation, but it is still a remarkably beautiful walk. *The Pyrenean Trail: GR10* (Cicerone Press) is the only guide I've found in English, and though the journey takes about fifty days to complete, the author has figured out a way to tackle it in sections that only take a fortnight. (That's two weeks; the author is British.) Additionally, the Cicerone Press publishes *Through the Spanish Pyrenees: GR11*, which details the Spanish counterpart to the GR10. This route is known as La Senda (the track) and was plotted by Spanish and Andorran mountain organizations.

By the way, if you have trouble finding these imported guides, I have found that the Adventurous Traveler Bookstore in Burlington, Vermont (see the Bookstores entry for contact information) regularly stocks the full line, and the staff is happy to arrange mail orders. Additionally, titles imported by Seven Hills Book Distributors may be hard to find. Seven Hills has, for nearly two decades, been a major distributor of international and small domestic presses. For further information or to request a catalog, you may view its website (www.sevenhillsbooks.com) or contact the distributor directly (1531 Tremont Street, Cincinnati, OH 45214; 800-545-2005 or 513-471-4300; fax: 888-777-7799).

Two good books to read about walking in general that I highly recommend include *The Walker Within* (by the editors of *Walking Magazine*, Lyons Press, 2001) and *Wanderlust: A History of Walking* (Rebecca Solnit, Viking, 2000).

Hiking Tour Operators

Some tour operators that offer walking and hiking trips in Northern Spain include:

Alternative Travel Group (69–71 Banbury Road, Oxford OX2 6PJ England; 44.1865.315678; www.atg-oxford.co.uk). ATG is a long-established company that offers a variety of trips in Northern Spain: "Sierras of Rioja," "Cantabria," and "Camino de Santiago." Several friends and colleagues who've attended ATG trips have raved about the quality and sincerity with which the company approaches walking. I personally was especially impressed with its winter 2001 brochure, in which the staff, addressing the September 11 tragedy, stated that "if we allow our lives to be disrupted and do not travel, the economic damage will be decisive. Terrorism will win, and we will have only ourselves to blame." I also admire that ATG has established the ATG Trust for the Environment, which aims to raise funds for conservation projects in the areas they visit. The Trust is young, and has so far completed only two projects, in Umbria: the restoration of a two-thousand-year-old path once used by pilgrims visiting the notable abbey of San Eutizio, and the restoration of two medieval wooden sculptures in Bevagna.

Bravo! Adventures (6910 Roosevelt Way N.E., PMB #428, Seattle, WA 98115; 800-938-9311 or 206-463-3070; fax: -0340; www.caminotours.com). Bravo! (detailed more thoroughly under the Biking entry) offers three hiking adventures in the north: "Walking Bilbao and the Basque Country," which includes Fuentarrabía, Urdax, Durango, and San Sebastián; "The Footsteps of St. James," which begins in Léon with an art historian and ends, eight days later, in Santiago; and a Picos de Europa journey that includes Santillana del Mar, Fuente Dé, Cangas de Onís, and Covadonga.

Breakaway Adventures (1312 18th Street N.W., Suite 401, Washington, DC 20036; 800-567-6286 or 202-293-2974; fax: -0483; www.breakaway-adventures.com). Breakaway offers cycling, walking, trekking, and barging trips in most parts of Europe, Asia, Africa, and South America. The walking trips are either guided, independent, or self-guided, and the trekking trips are fully guided walks. Currently,

Breakaway offers only one trip of any variety in Northern Spain: "Picos de Europa," an eleven-day trek that begins in Cangas de Onís (the largest town in the western Picos) and includes a visit to the Covadonga shrine. The hiking part of the journey covers the Mirador de Ordiales, El Requexon Peak, El Boquete, Cares Canyon, the tiny village of Bulnes (said to be the remotest village in Spain; no vehicles can reach it, so access is only by foot or donkey), Collado de Pandebano, Cabeza la Mesa, the village of Sotres (highest in the Picos), Horcados Rojos, Vega de Liordes, and Fuente Dé. As the Breakaway staff explains, its treks are for "those who want to enjoy the mountain ambiance in the company of like-minded travelers; for those who are committed walkers who relish the prospect of exploring off the beaten track, surmounting every pass and trekking unaided from horizon to horizon." The staff also emphasizes that "our walks are by no means the preserve of the superfit! There are trails to suit all levels of experience, many well within the capabilities of any normally fit and healthy individual." The Breakaway philosophy doesn't endorse roughing it for the sake of it, so whenever the terrain permits, vehicles, pack animals, or porters handle baggage. And as the staff notes, "if you want to get deep into the mountains you have to camp, but this can be done with style, with mess tents, tables, stools and as many creature comforts as can be mustered." Thus, accommodations on this Picos trek are offered in a mixture of small country hotels, mountain refuges, and hostels. Breakaway groups range in size from six to fifteen.

Butterfield & Robinson (70 Bond Street, Toronto, Ontario M5B 1X3; 800-678-1147 or 416-864-1354; fax: -0541; www.butterfield.com). B&R is the leader in luxury active travel around the world, specializing in biking and walking, and it offers about ninety-five trips on six continents. The best way to describe B&R is to share founder George Butterfield's own words with you: "Butterfield & Robinson creates trips around the globe for active people who want to explore great regions up close and in style. I don't know if we invented active travel, but we certainly pioneered the idea of setting your own pace, by bike or on foot, and rewarding yourself at the end of each day with a great hotel and a memorable meal . . . we create one-of-a-kind travel experiences for people who share the simple belief that has been guiding B&R for more than 35 years: you have to slow down to see the world." That introduction is from B&R's 2002 catalog, which is one of the most appealing tour operator booklets I've ever received. (It's so great, in fact, that I keep it on the shelf with my other travel books.) "Pyrénées & Bilbao" is currently the only trip B&R offers in Northern Spain; the route begins in Biarritz (in the Pays Basque) and ends in San Sebastián. Included are visits to St.-Etienne-de-Baigorry, St.-Jean-Pied-de-Port, Sare, and the Guggenheim Bilbao.

Country Walkers (P.O. Box 180, Waterbury, VT 05676; 800-464-9255; www.countrywalkers.com). "Explore the World One Step at a Time" is the motto of Country Walkers, a tour operator nearly twenty-five years old. It offers one trip, "Fabled Basque Country," in Northern Spain. The itinerary takes you through both

French and Spanish Basque country and includes the villages and towns of Sare, Burguete, Pamplona, Laguardia, and Hondarribia. The terrain is easy to moderate, and five to eight miles are covered each day, with shorter and longer options available on most days. Day three of the route is on the Camino de Santiago, and other highlights of the journey include visiting Romanesque and Gothic monasteries and private wine cellars, exploring a portion of the La Rioja wine region, walking along coastal cliffs and villages, and savoring the legendary Basque cuisine.

On Foot in Spain (Rosalía de Castro 29, 15886 Teo, La Coruña; 530.677.9770; fax: 530.677.8100; www.onfootinspain.com). On Foot is committed to offering "walking and hiking educational adventures," and each group is limited in size to between six and twelve participants. What I like best is that the joint owners/leaders (writer and cultural anthropologist Nancy Frey, Ph.D., and mountaineer José Placer) are co-authors of *Lonely Planet: Walking in Spain,* and they specialize in Northern Spain—these folks know this part of Iberia well. On Foot offers four walks, in Galicia, the Picos, the Camino, and the Basque Country and the Pyrenees. Custom-designed trips are also happily arranged. Frey and Placer explain that "traveling with us will be like traveling with a group of friends rather than with strangers. We have designed the walks (some are unique—created by us—and you won't find them on any other tour) taking into account several factors: beauty, variety of scenery, quality of trails, avoidance of main roads, and proximity to points of historical and cultural interest." Walks are rated easy, medium, and difficult, and walks of different lengths are offered most days depending on what the group wants.

Spanish Steps (P.O. Box 8653, Aspen, CO 81612; 877-787-WALK or 970-923-6859; in Spain, 617.08.15.70; www.spanishsteps.com). Though the trips arranged by Spanish Steps are unique and enticing, it's the background of the founder and guides that sold me on this company. Judy Colaneri is the owner of both Spanish Steps and Roman Roads (I'll profile the latter in an upcoming edition on Rome), and she is also a culinary-trained chef in Aspen. More important, she has walked the Camino de Santiago five times—including the Camino Francés—and knows every inch of the way. In 2002 Colaneri walked the Camino solo through Spain twice, following both the inland route and the less-traveled El Camino del Norte. She has led more than forty-five groups of pilgrims to Santiago and has studied Spanish in Barcelona, Seville, and San Miguel de Allende in Mexico. She spends eight months of the year in Europe personally guiding travelers through her favorite part of the world. Her staff includes Juan Carlos Fuentes (a native of Valladolid who has walked the Camino eight times), Lorriane Miller (who leads the Camino "Walk and Talk" journeys and has lived and worked in Spain teaching corporate executives English), and Ken Bartle (who is the photography teacher for the "Photo Spain" tour). Currently, Spanish Steps offers four trips in Northern Spain: "Camino Long Walk" (the classic tour of the Camino beginning in Roncesvalles and ending in Santiago fourteen days later; visits to historical sites with professional art historians and off-the-Camino side trips are included); "Coast and Cliffs: Camino del Norte" (twelve days of glorious hiking the coastal Camino and the Picos de Europa; the journey begins in Santillana del Mar and ends in Santiago and averages eight to ten miles a day); "Walk and Talk" (a culture and language study tour on the Camino; only twelve lucky participants hike the Camino and learn traveler's Spanish with two bilingual teachers); and "Camino Sampler" (a nine-day tour beginning on the border of Galicia and climbing to the small Celtic village of O'Cebriero; the daily hiking pace is nine to twelve miles along marked footpaths, over rolling hills, and through ancient villages; this tour guarantees the pilgrim's diploma).

Randonée Tours (100–62 Albert Street, Winnipeg, Manitoba, R3B 1E9; 800-465-6488 or 204-475-6939; fax: 204-474-1888; www.randonneetours.com). Randonnée, founded almost a dozen years ago by ecologist Ruth Marr, offers "distinctive self-guided vacations" for travelers interested in walking or cycling (and skiing, too). Randonnée was named best outfitter for self-guided walking tours by *Travel + Leisure,* and *Arthur Frommer's Budget Travel* magazine included Randonnée in its list of "World's Ten Best Hiking/Biking Tour Operators." I first profiled Randonnée in my *Provence* edition, and I have to admit it is one of my favorite companies, so much so that I'm including it in this edition even though its "Santiago de Compostela" tour doesn't set foot in Spain at all. I simply want more readers who are considering using a tour operator to know about Randonnée, even for journeys outside the scope of this book. In the event you are interested in walking one of the Camino routes in France, the Randonnée self-guided tour may be worth investigating. *Self-guided* is described as meaning "no guide, no sag wagon, and no group to hurry you along or slow you down. You have the freedom to walk independently, with support behind the scenes. Self-guided means choice, flexibility, and a tour that's just right for you. Start on any day of the week. The basics are provided and someone else lugs your bags. You are independent, but not alone. If you need emergency support, there are phone numbers to call. Self-guided is safe, affordable, and above all, enriching." The "Santiago" route covers the first two hundred kilometers of the Camino. It begins in Le Puy (one of the four main starting points for the Santiago pilgrimage) and follows the GR65, ending in Conques, stopping in St.-Privat D'Allier, Rochegude, Saugues, Le Rouget, St.-Alban-sur-Limagnole, Aumont-Aubrac, St.-Chély-D'Aubrac, St.-Côme-D'Olt (designated one of the *plus beaux villages de France*), and the Lot River Valley. Each day on this self-guided tour you "leave your luggage and head out, following the detailed Route Descriptions and supplied maps. Walk at your own pace, linger in cafés as long as you want, wander through fascinating villages, or hammer out extra kilometers." Randonnée offers other types of trips: Randonnée Plus, Short Escape, Drive & Stroll, and Partner Tours. What initially brought the company to my attention is that it offers a balance between the organized support of an escorted tour and lots of freedom and flexibility—all at affordable prices.

Hours

Spain, like its neighbors around the Mediterranean, follows the military clock, so that after twelve noon, the time of day is expressed as thirteen hundred hours (1:00 P.M.), fourteen hundred hours (2:00 P.M.), fifteen hundred hours (3:00 P.M.), and so on. Just as we do in North America, the Spaniards divide their days into four distinct phases of day and night, but their words and what they signify are a bit different from ours: *la madrugada* refers to the very early hours of the morning; *mañana* is the period just following *la madrugada* and extends up to the Spanish lunchtime, about one or two P.M.; *mediodía* refers to the middle of the afternoon, from approximately one to four; and *la tarde* refers to the late afternoon and early evening.

Opening and closing hours in Spain follow the same general pattern as in other Mediterranean countries. As I mentioned in my introduction, you should as quickly as possible embrace a schedule that allows for rather early risings, an afternoon siesta, and dinner no earlier than nine P.M. to allow for an evening *paseo*. Generally the majority of shops, businesses, and government offices are open by about 8:30 or 9:00 A.M. They close for lunch sometime between 12:30 and 1:30 and typically open again around 4:00 or 5:00. Businesses then remain open until about 7:00 or 8:00 P.M. On Saturdays, however, shops and businesses typically open at about 10:00 A.M. and close for the day at about 1:30 or 2:00. On Sundays nearly everything is closed. El Corté Ingles, the Spanish department store chain, is often open the first Sunday of every month, and a few shops open Sunday afternoon and remain open until the early evening.

Banks, however, operate on a slightly different schedule, opening from 8:00 A.M. to 2:00 P.M. and not reopening for the remainder of the day. I recommend doing bank chores first thing in the morning when there is the likeliest possibility the bank will really be open with plenty of time to make a transaction or solve a financial problem (and hopefully you won't have to stand in line too long). Banks also may be closed entirely on Saturdays, especially during the summer months. You should remember to have your passport with you when exchanging money—or performing any other transaction—at a bank.

All of this is subject to change at any time, not just in the summer. Be prepared to occasionally encounter a sign stating *cerrado hoy* (closed today) or *cerrado esta tarde* (closed this afternoon), the equivalent of our "gone fishing." These signs may be most prevalent in July and August, when nearly everyone is on vacation and therefore the time of year when opening and closing hours (and days) fluctuate the most.

Before I had spent much time in the Mediterranean, I was frustrated by how (seemingly) little I was able to accomplish in the course of a day, since I did not live in a culture where the lunch break was much longer than an hour. It's easy to lose sight of the fact that there really is plenty of time to see and do what you want by adapting to the siesta schedule. Much can still be accomplished in the hours between four and seven P.M.

I

Immigration

In 2002 Amnesty International submitted a report detailing the "frequent and wide-spread" mistreatment of foreigners, including torture, in Spain. Amnesty's report was the first to address racism in a European country, and it also expressed concern about the rise of racial profiling by the police. According to a report in *The New York Times* (April 19, 2002), Spain's economic boom in recent years and its position at one of Europe's southern frontiers has spurred an increase in immigration. The article revealed that the number of foreigners living legally in Spain has risen sharply in twenty years, with an 18 percent increase in 2000 alone, to 1.1 million. (The number was about 200,000 in 1981.) Moroccans apparently constitute the largest group, followed by Ecuadoreans. The Amnesty report noted that the rising population of immigrants has brought about "a general recognition that racism and xenophobia are at least as serious a problem in Spain as elsewhere in Europe."

Instituto Cervantes

The Instituto Cervantes promotes the teaching, study, and use of Spanish as a second language and to contribute to the advancement of the Spanish and Hispanic American cultures throughout non–Spanish-speaking countries. Created by the Spanish government in 1991, the Instituto is named after Miguel de Cervantes, author of *Don Quixote*. There are locations all around the world, including in New York City, Chicago, Albuquerque, Algeria, Egypt, Ivory Coast, Morocco, Tunisia, Jordan, Lebanon, Syria, Philippines, Austria, France, Germany, Greece, Ireland, Italy, Netherlands, Portugal, Romania, United Kingdom, Brazil, Belgium, Russia, Israel, Turkey, and Poland (more may have been added, since publication). A good selection of Spanish language classes are offered for people at different levels and for native speakers of Spanish; some branches also offer business- and medical-related classes. Those wanting to learn more than language may attend the various cultural events organized by the Instituto, which have included readings by Laura Esquivel and Carlos Fuentes and screenings of films such as *Tésis* and *Abre los Ojos,* both directed by Alejandro Amenábar. Other course offerings have covered Spanish and Hispanic American literature (a previous class, "Latin American Literature," included Gabriel García Márquez and Jorge Luis Borges, among others), wine seminars, and Spanish music history classes.

Each Instituto branch typically has an excellent library of Spanish and Hispanic American literature, resources for studying and teaching the language, music and movie titles, and reference books. The staff members are so dedicated to promoting the Spanish and Hispanic American cultures that if their individual libraries do not have what you're looking for, they'll search the catalog of Spain's national library and tell you where to find it. A valuable service the Instituto offers is a preparation course for the DELE (*Diplomas de Español como Lengua Extranjera*) certification that is issued by Spain's Ministry of Education (not every branch around the world offers this, however). The DELE certification, which tests one's ability to read, write, speak, and understand Spanish, is an "official accreditation of mastery of the Spanish language for citizens of countries in which Spanish is not the official language." The Instituto's website, www.cervantes.es/internet/acad/mar_ensena.htm, offers general information on the exam such as the locations where you can take the exam, sample test formats, and prices. Some of these wonderful opportunities are open only to those with memberships, while others are open to the general public. Membership at the student level starts at around $25 and some of the benefits include mailings about upcoming cultural events and activities, discounts at the Instituto, Spanish theaters, bookstores, and restaurants. The website is a relatively reliable source (I have found it better to call or visit the branch), and for non-Spanish speakers it can be difficult to navigate. Each Instituto branch updates its website only on what pertains to the events and courses being offered for that location (to find individual sites, open up www.cervantes.es, click on Instituto Cervantes, then Red de Centros, and finally the location you want to visit). Instituto Cervantes is an indispensable resource, and I encourage you to get involved and immerse yourself in some of the organization's wonderful offerings.

Internet Access

I'm including this here only for business travelers. If you're traveling for pleasure and feel you need to surf the Web, perhaps you should save your money and stay home. I take the view that vacations are for removing yourself from your daily grind; visiting another country is about doing *different* things, putting yourself in *unfamiliar* situations, and *removing* yourself from your daily routine. If you're dying to log on to the Internet, you're not on vacation—and obviously need to be—and you need to read *Turn It Off* (Gil Gordon, Three Rivers Press, 2001). Business travelers should know that overseas telephone services in general are not as reliable as those in the United States, ensuring that connecting to the Internet is also neither as easy nor as inexpensive. If you need to check in with the office via e-mail, consider what it will cost for a laptop, power adapter, disk and/or CD-ROM drive, plus any other related accessories, as well as how heavy it will be to carry. You may conclude that cybercafés (or Internet cafés) are more economical (and easier on your back). Fees for access to the Internet vary, but when you compare a hotel's charges for the same access—often at slower speeds—cybercafés represent good value. I found about fifty cybercafés in Northern Spain (in Burgos, Bilbao, Comillas, Gijon, La Coruña, Leon, Logroño, Oviedo, Pamplona, San Sebastián, Santiago, and Vigo) and Madrid by searching the Cybercafe Search Engine (www.cybercaptive.com), the Internet Café Guide (www.netcafeguide.com), and www.netcafes.com. Another source is *Cybercafés: A Worldwide Guide for Travelers* (cyberkath@traveltales.com, Ten Speed Press, 1989), which features a comprehensive list of the world's Internet cafés. I personally like the idea of keeping my business tasks separate from my hotel room, but those who can't stand the thought of leaving the hotel premises may be happy to know that hotels are definitely improving their Internet services. The world's major chain hotels are leading the way on this front, and some have at least one technologically savvy employee on hand to assist guests with problems. Additionally, I've noticed recently that some public telephone booths, including those at airports and in hotel lobbies, are now equipped for Internet access.

Isabella I of Spain

Isabel la Católica (the Catholic) was the wife of Ferdinand V, queen of Castile (1474–1504), and joint ruler of Aragon (1479–1504). The marriage of Isabella and Ferdinand II of Aragon in 1469 was more than just a wedding: two of the three main Christian kingdoms on the peninsula—Castile and Aragon—were merged into one. That left the third to conquer: Granada. Ferdinand agreed with Isabella's stance that if a nation was to be truly united, religious unity was essential, and thus the Spanish Inquisition was born. All non-Christians were forced to convert to Catholicism or leave the country. So the community of Muslims, Jews, and Christians that had been thriving for more than 750 years was ruthlessly destroyed. Eleven years after the Inquisition began, Granada finally fell to the Christians, and Spain was united for the first time in 800 years. Uniting a country is no small feat, but Spain under the Catholic kings became intellectually crippled, intolerant, significantly less diverse, and completely dominated by the Church. Fortunately, according to the editors of *Cool Women: The Thinking Girl's Guide to the Hippest Women in History* (Girl Press, 2002), Isabella was open-minded in other areas. She bankrolled Christopher Columbus's voyages to the New World, and "when Columbus brought Native Americans back to Spain to serve as slaves, Isabella, who fiercely opposed slavery, ordered their release." She was a patron and collector of Spanish and Flemish art and also supported the sciences. "Considered a great military genius, Isabella also planned and supervised battles and did hard time in the field, even when she was pregnant. No shrinking violet, Isabella is also said to have stood up to the Pope on a number of occasions when she disapproved of his appointments." Isabella was undoubtedly Spain's greatest queen and has been referred to as the most significant female monarch of all time.

Islam

"What makes the Spaniard unique within Western civilization? Why is Spain so different from other European countries?" asks Manuel Fernández Álvarez in a wonderful book entitled *Spain: A History in Art*. "Some people look for a simple geographic answer. But the fact is that its geography has not changed that much since the days when Spain, as so many other European lands, was but a piece in the grand imperial mosaic put together by Rome. . . . What really made the difference was the arrival in Spain of the Arabs early in the eighth century. From that moment on, Spain's development took on a distinctive character. While it is true that the Arabs also reached up into France, they were soon thrown back. In Spain it was a different story. The Moslems conquered much of the Iberian peninsula and stayed on for nearly eight centuries." Though the Muslim population in Spain is not very large (and certainly nowhere near that of neighboring France, home to both the largest Muslim and Jewish communities in Europe), it sometimes seems that the Spaniards are still haunted by Islam. It's hard to escape this feeling in the north, home to the shrine at Covadonga, but harder still when pondering the history of Spain itself. Jan Morris, in *Spain*, writes that "the timeless quality of Spanish life still feels very Muslim: at the frontier with Andorra, any hot weekend, a Spanish frontier official sits on a kitchen chair in the sunshine to examine the passports, and looks so thoroughly pasha-like, with his papers and his paunch, that you actually notice the absence of his hubble-bubble. The Spanish talent for enjoyment sometimes reminds me of the Arab countries: like the Egyptians, the Spaniards love public holidays, public gardens, picnics, lookout towers, rowing incompetently about in boats or trailing in vast family groups through scenic wonders. The deadpan face of Spanish politics sometimes evokes visions of reticent sheikhs, and the Spanish passion for sweet sticky cakes has something to it of houris, harems, and jasmine tea. Now and then the guidebook will tantalizingly observe, of some small village in the Ebro delta, perhaps, or a remote high *pueblo* of Andalusia, that its people 'still preserve certain Moorish customs'; and though the book is never more explicit, and the village, when you reach it, usually seems all too ordinary, still the phrase may suggest to you, in a properly Oriental way, hidden legacies of magic, pederasty, or high living that make the East feel pleasantly at hand."

With good reason of late, many North Americans are obsessing about Islam. I think that the obsession is overdue but is a positive step toward a better understanding and appreciation of one our world's greatest and enduring religions. It may not be surprising to learn that Islam is the second religion of France—and not by a very wide margin—due to the number of French men and women who emigrated from former Muslim colonies, but I suspect many Americans would be surprised to learn that Islam is now a major religion in the United States as well. Of all the perceptive essays and editorials that have appeared in the media over the last year or so about Islam, the following, by Thomas Cahill, author of *Pope John XXIII* (Penguin, 2002) and *The Hinges of History* series, addresses more than Islam itself and is an essential wake-up call for readers of all faiths. (In the following article, Cahill refers to Palestinian philosopher Sari Nusseibeh as an "Islamic peacemaker." Politically astute readers may recall that Nusseibeh has since offered his support of mothers of suicide bombers and female Palestinian Jihad fighters. Cahill may have chosen another philosopher for this piece if he had written it more recently, but I don't believe the inclusion of Nusseibeh detracts at all from the message Cahill is trying to impart. I sincerely hope readers will accept this essay in the spirit in which it was written.)

Once upon a time, there was a religion whose adherents thought it to be the only true one. Because their God wished everyone (or so they thought) to believe as they did, they felt justified in imposing their religion on others. Toward those who refused to bow to the "true" religion, these true believers took different tacks at different times. Sometimes, they hemmed in the infidels (as they were called) with civil disabilities, limiting their license to practice their own religion, forcing them to listen to propaganda and otherwise restricting their freedom; at other times they became more aggressive, burning holy books, smashing sacred statues and even engaging in wholesale slaughter of infidels—men, women and children—as if they were rats carrying plague.

The religion is not Islam but Christianity, whose dark history of crusades, inquisitions and pogroms lies not as far in the past as one might prefer to think.

What changed Christianity? How did Christians learn the virtue of tolerance? Centuries of bloody religious wars and persecutions finally convinced most Christians that there must be a better way to organize society, a way that did not involve quite so many burning bodies, human charnel houses and corpse-strewn battlefields.

The slow germination of this revolution in consciousness can be dated at least to the 18th century, toward the end of which a country finally emerged—America—that officially refused to play the old game of whose religion was true, and took a generously agnostic view of religious truth: you may believe what you like, and so may I, and neither can impose belief on the other.

Is there an essentially different dynamic at work in Islamic countries that keeps them from arriving at the civic virtue of tolerance? The forces of the

Enlightenment that exalted tolerance in the West were given their impetus by the European wars of the 16th and 17th centuries in which Christian was pitted against Christian—wars over points of doctrine that must have looked exceedingly abstruse, even absurd, to non-Christians, who could see only similarities between the warring systems. One might well wonder if this Enlightenment would have emerged with such vigor had the battles involved Christian against Jew—or, more exotically, against Muslim or Buddhist or Zoroastrian. Protestants and Catholics had to learn to be tolerant of one another—of different forms of Christianity—before they could learn to tolerate those whose religions were non-Christian.

In a similar way, the Muslim world is more likely to develop the virtue of tolerance as it surveys the hopelessly diverse ways in which different communities and peoples have responded to the core insights of Islam. What do Turks have in common with Taliban, or Wahhabi Muslims with Sufis? Very little, it would seem at first glance. What do Sunni Muslims have in common with Shiites? If non-Muslims can see similarities, warring Muslim factions can often see only deadly differences.

The West should not allow itself too many congratulations on its vaunted tolerance. In Northern Ireland, Catholic children are still unable to walk to school without hearing vile epithets hurled at them by foul-mouthed adults. In Britain, a Catholic may still not serve as prime minister or sit upon the storied throne of Edward the Confessor. The Vatican, for its part, first blessed tolerance as a civic virtue a scant 36 years ago—at the close of the Second Vatican Council. Prior to that time, the official Catholic position was little different from that of the mullahs of Kandahar: when we are in power, we will impose religion as we see fit.

This new Catholic blessing of tolerance—which took the form of a declaration that religious liberty is the right of every human being—was made possible chiefly because of the life and work of two uncommon human beings. The first was the courtly Jesuit theologian John Courtney Murray, who was able to reinterpret Catholic political theory to give theological primacy to freedom of conscience. Not incidentally, he was a 20th-century American, deeply in love with American political ideals.

The other was John XXIII, the pope who convoked the council with the express aim of bringing the teaching of the Catholic Church up to date. John lived his life as a man of tolerance; he hated using religion to divide people from one another. Many historians today consider him the greatest pope who ever lived, a man beloved by people of all kinds throughout the world. As he lay dying, his secretary read to him from mountains of sympathetic letters. One correspondent wrote, "Insofar as an atheist can pray, I'm praying for you." Hearing this, John, despite his pain, smiled with delight. For him, the common bond of humanity was all that was needed for profound friendship and understanding—and a little humor always helped.

Each of the great religions creates, almost from its inception, a colorful spectrum of voices that range from pacifist to terrorist. But each religion, because of its metaphorical ambiguity and intellectual subtlety, holds within it marvelous potential for development and adaptation. This development will be full of zigzags and may sometimes seem as slow as the development of the universe, but it runs—almost inevitably, it seems—from exclusivist militancy to inclusive peace.

The tolerant Islam that in the 15th and 16th centuries let the Jews of Spain, expelled by Catholic tyrants, find homes in Arab lands has not disappeared. The peace-loving Islam that in the seventh and eighth centuries protected the world's oldest portrait of Jesus from destruction by Christian iconoclasts has not been erased. These humane responses are living seeds, a little buried perhaps but capable of a great flowering.

The bloodthirsty Judaism of the Book of Joshua, in which God commands the Israelites to put all Canaanites, even children, to the sword, is hardly the Judaism of today, except perhaps at the extreme end of its spectrum—in the followers of someone like Meir Kahane or the religious fanatics who encouraged the assassination of the peacemaker Yitzhak Rabin. But in the same period as Joshua, or soon thereafter, when Gideon builds an altar in the desert to replace the altar of Baal, the god of thunder and war, he calls the new altar "Peace Is the Name of God." And the Christianity of 13th-century Europe—a time of bloody crusades and inquisitions, when Pope Boniface VIII proclaimed that complete subjection to him was "utterly necessary for the salvation of every living creature"—is very different from the Christianity of John XXIII, who wrote in his diary that "the whole world is my family."

At the extreme end of the Christian spectrum there are still intolerant bigots, as well as deranged militants who shoot up abortion clinics, but they are now far from the mainstream. And even in the 13th century, Christianity could bring forth an utterly pacifist figure like Francis of Assisi.

Over the ages, each religion learns—with many steps backward and sideways but, finally, with more steps forward—that it must find a way to live with its "heretical" offshoots and with other religions. It can't have the whole world (as Boniface VIII imagined), except in love (as John XXIII intended).

For Islam, seven centuries younger than Christianity and nearly three millennia younger than Judaism, to achieve such a relationship it needs a distinguished theoretical peacemaker like Courtney Murray and a warm-hearted, iconic peacemaker like John XXIII. If such figures emerge, they would stand on the shoulders of great theologians and saints who came before them in the rich tradition of Islam.

In fact, Islamic peacemakers are already at work. There is, for example, the Palestinian philosopher Sari Nusseibeh, who speaks repeatedly of the fruitlessness of violence and points to the irreducibly Judaic roots of Islam. Such people exist not just among the Palestinians but in countries throughout the Islamic world. At present, they may appear to be lonely voices—but not more lonely than Courtney Murray and Pope John once were.

J

Jet Lag

I have read about a number of methods to reduce jet lag that involve diet and the amount of sunlight one receives during the days leading up to departure. (An interesting article is "A Cure for Jet Lag?," *Condé Nast Traveler*, April 2000, which details new research into the use of melatonin.) Now an overwhelming number of books, regimens, and potions—both chemical and homeopathic—claim to offer jet-lag solutions. Frankly, it all seems a lot of bother to me, and I would rather spend my time in advance of a trip doing other things. I also have no incentive to try any of these so-called solutions, because I've always had success with adjusting to local time upon my arrival. If I land in the morning (I seem to usually take red-eye flights), no matter how tired I might be, I do not take a nap. I do, however, consider taking one if it is after lunch, but only then, and for no longer than one hour. On that first night, I turn in rather early—by nine or ten—to get a very full night's sleep, and I do not sleep late the next morning.

If I am fortunate enough to have a bathtub, I do not miss the opportunity to fill it with aromatic bubble bath and get in for a soothing soak. This is actually a good activity for the early afternoon, when many merchants have gone home for lunch and museums and monuments are closed for a few hours.

As an aside, I cannot resist stating my loyalty to two brands of soaking potions when traveling: Kiehl's (a New York family business since 1851, now owned by L'Oréal, with another store in San Francisco) and L'Occitane (a Provençal company with almost fifty outposts in the United States; view the company's website, www.loccitane.com, for exact store locations). Both companies offer products for men and women in plastic bottles good for traveling. From Kiehl's I like the Lavender Foaming-Relaxing Bath with Sea Salts and Aloe Vera and the Mineral Muscle Soak Foaming-Relaxing Bath with Sea Salts and Aloe Vera, while from

L'Occitane, I'm particularly fond of the restorative balm and relaxing essential oils in its Aromachologie line. Both companies happily accept mail orders. Kiehl's may be reached at 800-543-4571 and L'Occitane at 888-623-2880 or 212-696-9098.

I know all the health experts and seasoned travelers say to refrain from alcoholic drinks on the overseas flight, but I always have a glass of wine or two with my meal, and the result of all of the above is that I have never had a problem with jet lag. I do think it is wise to drink water—more than what one usually consumes—while airborne, as dehydration is a key factor in jet lag (and feeling lousy in general), and it is essential not to remain in one's seat for the entire flight. Some pundits say airline food itself is a major culprit in the effects of jet lag, and since everyone complains about it anyway, consider bringing your own meal: It will most likely be healthier, lighter, and more to your taste. You could at least bring some snacks to nibble on: Fresh and dried fruit, crackers, sliced raw vegetables, yogurt-covered nuts or raisins, even cheese and sliced meats (if eaten quickly) are all good choices and better than the typical snacks served on the plane. Finally, a toast to the good old-fashioned nap: I cannot overstate the importance, pleasure, and restorative powers of a daily afternoon nap while in Spain. Not only do most businesses and sites close for a few hours in the middle of the day anyway, but you'll feel refreshed and more alert after a brief rest. As Jane Brody noted in one of her "Personal Health" columns in *The New York Times*, naps "are far better than caffeine as a pick-me-up."

Jewish History in Spain

"To this day, Jewish history does not record a similar success story." The words of Ben Frank, author of *A Travel Guide to Jewish Europe*, are an apt reminder that Jews once made up one-third of the population of Spain and played a vital role in the history of the country. Writer Howard Sachar, in *Farewell España*, has also noted, "They number barely a million today, less than one-tenth of the world Jewish population. But long ago, on Iberian soil, they were the magisters of their people, and the leaven of Mediterranean civilization altogether." Sephardic Jews (the word *Sephardic* is derived from the Hebrew word for Spain, *Sepharad*) trace their origins back to Spain and the other Mediterranean communities where they once thrived, as opposed to Ashkenazic Jews, whose origins are in eastern and central Europe. Within Spain itself the words *conversos* and Marranos (Jews who were forcibly converted to Catholicism after 1492, when Ferdinand and Isabella forced all non-Christians to convert or leave Spain) are synonymous, each designating the same group in Jewish, Spanish, and European scholarship. Though Jewish roots are widespread in Spain, the majority of the Jewish communities flourished in Barcelona, Madrid, Toledo, and throughout Andalucía. After World War I, there were fairly large Jewish communities in Barcelona, Seville, and Madrid. In 1924 Prime Minister Primo de Rivera declared that anyone who had descended from

Sephardic families of 1492 would be recognized as Spanish citizens. In 1927 Spain offered full citizenship to all Spanish Jews, and in 1931 a new constitution offered full legal equality to Spanish Jews. Both of these gestures were later nullified by Franco, who, it has been reported, descended from a Galician *converso* family himself and therefore allowed the bombing of Guernica so that Hitler would not suspect he hailed from a Jewish family. On a happier and more humane note, a great number of Jews—it's estimated to be more than 30,000—passed safely through Spain during the early years of World War II.

Some good books to consult for further reading include Frank's *A Travel Guide to Jewish Europe,* mentioned above (Pelican Publishing Company, Gretna, LA, 2001), which highlights the historic communities of Madrid, Toledo, Barcelona, Girona, and several cities in Andalucía; *The Origins of the Inquisition in Fifteenth Century Spain* (B. Netanyahu, Random House, 1995), which must surely be the most authoritative source in print, at 1,384 pages; I daresay this book is not for the casual reader, but it is worth noting that such a comprehensive work exists; *The Jews of Spain: A History of the Sephardic Experience* (Jane S. Gerber, The Free Press, 1992); *Farewell España: The World of the Sephardim Remembered* (Howard Sachar, Alfred A. Knopf, 1994); and *The Cross and the Pear Tree: A Sephardic Journey* (Victor Perera, Alfred A. Knopf, 1995).

L

Language

Though I studied Spanish from the fourth grade through my senior year of high school and have traveled throughout Spain and Mexico, I do not speak it well, let alone fluently. This is not something I'm proud of and is actually rather embarrassing; but in my defense I suspect part of the reason I don't know the language well enough is that I was never forced to live with it—and dream in it—the way I did when I was a college student in Paris for a year. But I do know some key words and phrases in Spanish that rarely fail to bring a big smile to the faces of my hosts; I can also translate from Spanish to English when I hear it spoken—it's replying that's difficult, since I tend to reply in French! The natives of *any* country love it when visitors try to speak their language, and fortunately Spanish is relatively easy to learn. Of course, the Spanish I'm referring to is Castilian, which is considered "standard" and is technically the Spanish every Spaniard learns in school. You will encounter a great number of dialects in Northern Spain (and I'm not even including Basque), but almost everyone will recognize the Castilian variety when you speak it and will most likely be happy to converse in it as well. Occasionally, as has happened to me, you may also run across a very helpful local who really wants to point you in the right direction, and you will speak to him or her in Castilian, and he or she will reply in rapid-fire Galician, for example, and though you will have absolutely no idea what is being said, you can usually figure out the gist of it by paying attention to hands and arms.

The best language course program I've used is Living Language. There are others, certainly, but Living Language has been around longer (since 1946), the courses are continually updated and revised, and in terms of variety, practicality, and originality, I prefer it. Spanish courses are available for beginner, intermediate, and advanced levels, in both audiocassette and CD editions. ~The "Fast & Easy" course (referred to as "virtually foolproof" by the New York *Daily News*), for beginner business or leisure travelers, is a sixty-minute survival program with a cassette and pocket-sized pronunciation guide. ~The "Ultimate Course" is for serious language learners and is the equivalent of two years of college-level study. In a copublishing venture with Fodor's, Living Language also offers the pocket-sized *Spanish for Travelers,* which is a handy book/cassette reference—designed for business and leisure travelers—with words and phrases for dozens of situations, including exchanging money, using ATMs, finding a hotel room, and so on, and it also includes a two-way dictionary. ~The *All-Audio Course in Spanish* (also published by Living Language) may be better suited to readers who want to learn on the go, so to speak, as it's popular in the car, with a Walkman or Discman. Both the cassette and CD programs come with six sixty-minute recordings and a sixty-four-page listener's guide. The All-Audio course is available only at the beginner and intermediate levels. ~The Living Language *In-Flight: Spanish* course is yet another way to get some words and phrases under your belt. "Learn Before You Land" is the program's motto, and it's meant for beginner business and leisure travelers. It's a sixty-minute course, with a compact disk, featuring just enough to get by in every travel situation, including greetings and polite expressions, asking for directions, getting around, checking into a hotel, or going out on the town.

Much as I endorse the various Living Language courses, I recently discovered two other programs that I like: *At Home Abroad Spanish: Practical Phrases for Conversation* (Helen Harrison, Nigel Harrison, Passport Books) and *Get Around in Spain: The All-in-One Travel and Language Guide* (McGraw-Hill). Of the two, At Home Abroad is the better program. This Spanish edition, as the authors note, is "primarily intended for those who have some knowledge of Spanish but who may need help with additional vocabulary and expressions for specific circumstances in order to communicate and interact more effectively with Spanish speakers." The scope of each At Home Abroad volume goes well beyond that of traditional phrase books, and students living in Spain, as well as adults living and working there, will find this book particularly helpful. Independent travelers will also benefit from the sections on travel and sightseeing. ~*Get Around in Spain* is a book and cassette package that's small enough to bring with you. I find the initial section of the book—brief outlines of each region of Spain—completely worthless and written in a most elementary manner. But I have found a number of useful expressions and phrases in this little book that don't appear in other language guides or guidebooks.

Fodor's has created a nifty credit-card-sized, fold-out magnet called *Fodor's to Go: Spanish for Travelers*. You can conveniently keep it in your pocket and unobtrusively retrieve it when you need to look up a word or phrase. It is also great for pre-trip quizzing: you can keep it in your kitchen on the refrigerator at eye level and, while holding a glass of Rioja, for example, in one hand, unfold the magnet with the other and test your memory several nights a week. As this is a magnet, you have to make sure it doesn't touch your credit cards or any other data storage items.

If you prefer learning by videotape, try the three-hour, two-video course by the Standard Deviants (available through the Discovery Channel, 800-207-5775; both beginner and advanced courses are offered, and regular videocassettes are about $35 while a DVD set is about $36).

An essential book to have is *501 Spanish Verbs* (Barron's). In addition to giving really good descriptions of the various tenses, it allots a full page to each verb, showing all the tenses fully conjugated, plus the definition and a useful selection of "Words and Expressions Related to This Verb" at the bottom of each page. As if this weren't enough, there are also chapters on "Verbs Used in Idiomatic Expressions," "Verbs with Prepositions," "Verbs Used in Weather Expressions," "Thirty Practical Situations for Tourists and Popular Phrases," and "Words and Expressions for Tourists." If you're serious about learning or brushing up on Spanish, I really can't see doing it without this book.

If you fall into the category of "I'm *somewhat* serious about learning Spanish" and are more interested in learning phrases and vocabulary that go beyond the basics but are not as thorough as the Barron's bible, consider the *Jiffy Phrasebook: Spanish* (Langenscheidt, 1986). This compact volume (great for tucking into a handbag) is handy for those who have a limited Spanish vocabulary or simply want a refresher. The book is divided into chapters covering general words and phrases, train and plane travel, accommodations, banking, currency, health, and shopping, among others. Each chapter includes several useful phrases, pronunciations, and related vocabulary. A dictionary, grammar section, and an appendix with helpful information on such topics as abbreviations and weights and measures are also included. Langenscheidt also publishes the *Jiffy Travel Pack,* a phrasebook and a cassette tape package.

To help build excitement for young children coming along, there's the Living Language *Learn in the Kitchen* and *Learn Together: For the Car* series. These book/cassette kits are for children ages four to eight and include a sixty-minute bilingual tape; sixteen songs, games, and activities; a forty-eight-page illustrated activity book with color stickers; and tips for parents on how to vary the activities for repeated use. ~For newborns to age two, there is also *Baby's First Steps in*

Spanish, a book and CD set. This program is an easy introduction to understanding and nurturing a child's natural talent for learning languages, and it covers sounds, rhymes, and songs. The seventy-three-page booklet is excellent and includes resources and references for parents. Though my daughter is three—supposedly beyond the scope of this package—we still found it to be entertaining and educational.

As an aside, I would like to stress that it is never too early to begin teaching young children another language. Even my husband was pooh-poohing me when I would read to Alyssa in French, or teach her Spanish and Italian words. But she now knows more than a dozen words and phrases in French, repeatedly said *buon giorno, ciao, grazie,* and *Piazza San Marco* when she was two and a half and we were in Venice, and knows about a dozen Spanish words—simply because I repeated them over and over. *Baby's First Steps in Spanish* emphasizes the same point: "Multilingualism comes in all varieties. Monique, a French mother of two young bilingual children, was raised bilingually herself and speaks absolutely fluent French and English. But as a child she made odd comments in English, such as, 'Alas, that foolish maiden,' when a pedestrian walked in front of a taxi (a result of listening to fairy tales in English early in life). As an adult, when she speaks English, she calls corn flakes 'petals' and says the French 'euh' instead of the English 'um' when she hesitates. She also speaks proficient German and can get by in Polish. Monique's daughters, living in France, hear English primarily from their mother and French from everyone else. At age four, Lisa pointed to the doghouse and said 'chien maison,' a direct translation of the English compound word (literally 'dog house'), when the French word is actually *niche.* Now Lisa insists on speaking English with English speakers, whereas her younger sister Melina answers in French when a question is posed in English. Their father, Joel, speaks French, but learned English in adulthood and speaks it with a characteristic French accent. All of these individuals are bilingual."

For help with translating a fax, e-mail, letter, or text of any kind, try logging onto www.world.altavista.com. You input the (Spanish or other language) text you want translated and click on "Translate." It works the other way, too. I have found this particularly helpful when viewing websites that are exclusively in Spanish.

A related book for Spanish (and other language) lovers is *Le Mot Juste: A Dictionary of Classical and Foreign Words and Phrases* (Vintage Books, 1991), which includes words and phrases in classical languages, Spanish, French, German, Italian, and a smattering of other tongues around the world. It's a great reference book that I use all the time, and you may find yourself turning to it as often as I do.

Elemadrid, a Spanish language school in Madrid, offers free monthly Spanish lessons via e-mail. Interested readers may subscribe by contacting Elemadrid by e-mail (hola@elemadrid.com) or by browsing its website (www.elemadrid.com). Each lesson begins with a *palabra española del mes* (Spanish word of the month), and when I browsed, the word was *gustar* (the verb for "to like"). The authors of the lesson expand thoroughly upon the word of the month, explaining ways in which it may be used and interpreted incorrectly and offering a good selection of sentences and phrases where the word has different meanings. They also explain exceptions as well as the most common mistakes a nonnative Spanish speaker is apt to make and how to avoid them. I think this is a wonderful idea and an excellent learning tool, and I encourage readers who are at all interested in learning more than rudimentary Spanish to subscribe to Elemadrid.

Luggage

I've read of a syndrome—really—called BSA (Baggage Separation Anxiety), which you may at first be inclined to laugh at; but as reports of lost luggage have escalated in the last few years, I'm not at all surprised that fear of losing luggage is now a syndrome. (All the more reason, I say, not to check bags, and *definitely* the reason to at least pack some essentials in a carry-on bag.) Essentials, by the way, don't add up to much: It's remarkable how little one truly "needs." Recently one of my bags did not turn up when I reached my destination, and the airline representative was honest enough to tell me that when flights are full, sometimes not all the bags are loaded onto the plane—intentionally (#&!). Distressing as this is, at least it explains part of the problem and is one more reason to keep essentials with you. Even if you are the sort of traveler who cannot lighten your load, you will still probably bring a carry-on. As I write this, the standard limit for carry-on luggage is 9 by 14 by 22 inches, otherwise known as 45 linear inches to the airlines. Although not all airlines enforce this policy, it seems foolish not to comply—storage space is limited, and less baggage means more on-time schedules and better passenger safety. Some airlines have even installed sized templates at the security X-ray machines, so if your bag doesn't fit, you don't walk through. Many luggage manufacturers—including Tumi and Samsonite—have responded, turning out a variety of bags at varying prices that are meant to hold enough stuff for about three days of traveling—about the time it takes for a misrouted bag to show up, assuming it isn't lost altogether!

Before the September 11 tragedy, the biggest misunderstanding about carry-on luggage was the 22-inch bag. Some airlines would (and still will) accept these as legitimate carry-on luggage, while others did not (and still won't). I recommend the 20-inch bag, even if you have to check it, simply because it is, in the end, more practical. In the aftermath of 9/11, much of what we knew and understood about carry-on luggage applies no longer. As I edit this edition, the Federal Aviation Administration is issuing new directives on what constitutes a carry-on item; but placing calls to several airlines revealed that interpretation of these directives is really up to each individual airline. Essentially there are no universal standards among North American carriers as to what constitutes carry-on *personal items* or even a carry-on bag. Representatives I spoke with told me the list of carry-on items was subject to change daily, at the discretion of the airline.

Airlines reserve the right (and I'm glad they do) to spot-check passengers as they are passing through the gate, and decisions about the items you're carrying are made on a case-by-case basis. It may seem obvious that razor blades and pocket knives are not allowed in carry-on bags, but aerosol cans are sometimes confiscated too, as well as safety pins and cigarette lighters, and photography equipment is often examined very carefully. What women define as their tote bag or purse is open to scrutiny (a tote bag filled with clothes is usually considered not personal and therefore must be checked), though a large cosmetic case is typically considered small enough to be personal. A backpack is a carry-on personal item, but put it on wheels, and it becomes checked luggage. Computer laptop cases can also be singled out for inspection: if anything is stashed in the bag besides papers, the computer, and writing utensils, it could be seen as a candidate for checked baggage. The only way to confirm what is and isn't allowed is to call the airline you're flying with directly. Don't wait until you're at the airport to discover that you should have left an item at home. And be sure to ask about medical prescriptions, syringes, and metal items that might sound the security alarm. I have actually welcomed the limits on carry-on bags, as I have always been annoyed with people who try to sneak on more baggage than they should be carrying in the first place. In the words of Antoine de Saint-Exupéry, "He who would travel happily must travel light."

The ubiquitous—and always black—suitcase on wheels has taken a beating of late. Some travelers complain that it's too heavy to lift in and out of an overhead bin without hitting someone on the head, and trying to find one at the baggage claim is like Harry the dog trying to find his family's umbrella at the beach in the children's book *Harry by the Sea*. Plus, they've become decidedly unhip: a writer for *The Wall Street Journal* claimed that "the wheelie has become a fashion faux pas—the suitcase equivalent of a pin-striped suit on a casual Friday." I may be the lone voice in the wilderness, but the wheelie is essential for those of us with back problems. (I am extremely happy with my Dakota 20-inch wheelie, and it's forest green, by the way. The entire Dakota line is one of the better-kept secrets in the luggage world: "the hardest working bags in the business" are a division of Tumi and are equally as well made, for about half the price.) Also, I like the freedom of not having to depend on only one type of ground transportation. With a wheelie, I don't need a porter or a luggage cart, and I can choose from all forms of public (and private) transportation. If you are in a hurry or are really worried about someone else walking off with your bag, make your bags distinctive so they'll stand out on the luggage carousel. Short of buying a lemon-yellow suitcase, you could use unique luggage tags, or really go out on a limb with something called the Lock It Spot It set, which includes two locks, a large identification tag, and a thick nylon strap that you wrap all the way around your bag—in either shocking pink or bright green. It seems like a good compromise, preferable to buying that lemon-yellow bag. (For more information about Lock It Spot It, contact Christine Columbus, P.O. Box 2168, Lake Oswego, OR 97035; 800-280-4775; www.christinecolumbus.com—this is a very cool company, by the way, offering products "uniquely well-suited for the woman traveler.")

M

Madrid

I had originally included a small section on Madrid in this volume because, as I noted in the introduction, travelers from North America have to fly into Madrid first before meeting connecting flights to the north. Unfortunately, the manuscript proved to be too large, and the section had to be deleted. But rather than wait for my edition on Madrid to be published, I thought it would be helpful to mention some of the articles I was unable to include as well as some good books. Most travelers, I suspect, will only have a day or two to spare at either the beginning or end of a Northern Spain journey, unless you are planning a more extended itinerary. With such a limited schedule, therefore, you will not have much time to do more than sample the wonderful diversity of Madrid's *tascas* and restaurants, except possibly squeeze in a museum, performance, or a ramble through Retiro. One of Madrid's best pastimes is eating and drinking.

"In Madrid," note the editors of *The Cooking of Spain and Portugal* (detailed in the *¡Buen Provecho! biblioteca*), "there is a saying that the Spanish people 'eat all day and some of the night.' This is most spectacularly true of all peoples living in the central plateau and the north. Castilian appetites take second place only to those of the Basques." Though this outstanding book was published more than thirty years ago, it is still absolutely spot on, as the British would say, in its description of the five official meals that make up the daily life of a *madrileño*. The first proper meal is *desayuno* (breakfast), which is usually coffee, or sometimes chocolate, taken with a roll or a few *churros*. The second meal of the day is *las onces* (elevenses) or *almuerzo* (lunch), eaten at about eleven A.M. "By now the stomach is awake; it demands more attention and gets it—anything from grilled sausage or tomato and bread to fried squid or an omelet, depending on what province you are in and on your individual taste." Midday in Spain is from two to three, "and by 2:30 in the afternoon it is time for the *comida,* the most important meal of the day. The need for an afternoon siesta becomes evident when we consider the courses of a well-to-do Castilian's midday *comida.*" These courses may include salad ("which in Spain is served before the main course rather than after. The Spanish theory is that salad is a *pre*-fresher, not a *re*-fresher"); *entremés* (hors d'oeuvres, which may be a salad); soup; fish, meat, or game; dessert (flan, cheese, or rice pudding) or fresh fruit; and finally coffee, which is served after dessert, never with it. "At this point we have completed only three of the official meals. There are still two to go. At three or four o'clock in the afternoon life is resumed, and nobody thinks about eating again until 6:00 P.M. Even then it is still considered early to mid afternoon. This is the time of the *merienda,* the penultimate meal, which usually is just coffee and pastries—cookies, fruit tarts, cream pastries or leafy layered honeyed desserts inherited from the Moors. But in Spain if company is coming, any meal becomes a serious meal whatever the hour. The *merienda* will then include meat pies, fowl or even fish." The workday in Madrid, and almost everywhere else in Spain, ends at about seven-thirty, and *la cena* (the evening meal) is eaten between ten P.M. and midnight. *La cena* is, as has been noted earlier, a lighter meal. You may note, however, that in Madrid restaurants many people will be eating a meal equally as heavy as lunch; but those diners are more often than not hosts or guests, and it wouldn't be right for corporate executives, for example, to entertain lightly. At home, *madrileños* will eat soup and an omelet perhaps, or salad or cooked vegetables, or a small fish dish.

The articles I had to exclude from this book—and which I very much encourage you to track down—include "Tapas Bars of Madrid" (Jay Jacobs, *Gourmet,* October 1998); "Madrid's Morning Churros: Automation Creeps In" (Laurel Berger, *The New York Times,* August 15, 1993); "Talk . . . Talk . . . Talk" (Alan Riding, *Condé Nast Traveler,* October 1993); and "Feasting on Tapas Around Madrid" (Catharine Reynolds, *The New York Times,* June 11, 1995). This last article in particular—which details two *tapeos* in different neighborhoods of Madrid— is representative of the type of information a writer can provide—often not found in guidebooks—that proves to be invaluable, which is one reason why I am so keen on publishing anthologies of collected articles rather than excerpts from books. The authentic snippets revealed here are the words *una caña* and *un chato,* and here's why: if you pay close attention while you're frequenting *tascas,* you'll notice that Spaniards almost never order a beer by saying, *"una cerveza, por favor,"* and they do not ask for red wine by saying merely *"vino tinto."* Rather, they tell the bartender they'd like a *caña* (a quarter-liter-sized glass of beer) or a *chato* (a small wineglass) of either *vino tinto* (red wine) or *vino blanco* (white). A few years after this piece appeared, my husband and I were in Madrid, and we set aside two evenings for each of the *tapeos* outlined. (These are excellent routes, by the way.) At the end of one *tapeo* we decided to end the night at Cervecería Allemana (Plaza de Santa Ana, 6), especially popular with Americans but still a good place. A group of Americans was occupying most of the standing room in front of the bar, and once we elbowed our way through, the bartender probably assumed we were part of this group. But when we ordered a *caña* and a *chato,* he beamed at us and started chatting and befriended us for the hour or so we were there. Two of the Americans turned to us and asked what we had said that had so charmed the bartender, as he apparently hadn't been nearly as welcoming to them. We shared the two magic *c* words with them. I don't have any idea if they fared any better once they were in possession of this knowledge, but when I use them, I always receive a knowing look from bartenders, as opposed to a look of boredom or one bordering on disgust.

Worthy guidebooks include *Baedeker's Madrid, Hachette: A Great Weekend in Madrid, Knopf City Guides: Madrid, Louis Vuitton City Guide—European Cities VII: Madrid, Barcelona, Seville, Lisbon, Porto,* and *The Companion Guide to Madrid & Central Spain* by Alastair Boyd, which isn't a standard guidebook but rather a nearly 500-page compendium including maps, floor plans of major cathedrals, a glossary of architectural, art, and allied terms, a chronology table, suggestions for further reading, and three eight-page inserts of black-and-white photos.

Maps

Getting lost is usually a part of everyone's travels, but it isn't always a bonus. True, the surprises you may discover when lost in the mountain regions of Northern Spain are almost always greater than those discovered when you are following the beaten path. But occasionally we don't *want* to be lost, and happily there are maps (no shortage of them, actually), and I tend to have few favorites among them. In an ideal world, I think everyone should travel with a large overall map of an area as well as individual detailed maps of cities and towns. ~For driving in Northern Spain, I recommend the *Spain and Portugal Motoring Atlas* published by Michelin. This large paperback atlas, at a scale of 1:400,000, is the kind you can keep open on your lap (if you are the passenger), unlike those other cumbersome Michelin maps that you have to try to fold and unfold. Perhaps you are a better map-folder than I am, but I inevitably ruin paper maps with a thousand folds by a trip's end, so I much prefer a regular- or spiral-bound atlas that lies flat. ~For individual cities and towns, I have found that the maps offered by the local tourist offices are quite adequate and feature even the tiniest streets. They are usually more detailed than maps found in guidebooks, which typically highlight only the major roads and monuments. Two exceptions are the Baedeker and Fodor's Citypack guidebooks to Madrid, which feature very detailed maps that are separate from the books themselves and are housed in a plastic sleeve at the back.

Marketing Ahead

This organization is one that travelers to the Iberian peninsula should know about: Marketing Ahead is a representative for a quality collection of government and privately owned hotels in Spain and Portugal as well as the vintage luxury trains El Transcantabrico and Al Andalus Expreso. The company is dedicated to assisting travelers by securing all reservations and offering travel-planning advice, for both business and pleasure. Marketing Ahead is the sole North American representative for the *paradores* hotel group of Spain and *pousadas* of Portugal; so if you're planning a trip to Northern Spain and would like to stay at a number of *paradores* but simply don't have the time to make arrangements yourself, Marketing Ahead will do the legwork for you (for more information about *paradores* group, see the listing under the Accommodations entry). A number of other singular accommodations—including charming, very affordable country inns to deluxe hotels—are also represented by Marketing Ahead (request the World of Special Places brochure to review all the selections). The Al Andalus Expreso—which winds through the Andalucían towns of Granada, Ronda, Jérez, Sevilla, Cordoba, Baeza, and Úbeda—has received a fair amount of publicity in the States, understandably, as Andalucía is perennially popular with foreign visitors. But I have read very little about the Transcantábrico, which is a shame because in some ways the northern route—running from Santiago de Compostela to San Sebastian in both directions—is even more magnificent than the southern (for more details on the Transcantábrico, see the entry under the Spanish train network, RENFE).

Reservations, for both hotels and trains, must be fully paid in advance. Note that Marketing Ahead vouchers are the only proof of full payment—vouchers issued by travel agencies are not accepted by the hotels or the train lines. For information or to make reservations, contact Marketing Ahead at 433 Fifth Avenue, New York, NY 10016; 212-686-9213; fax: -0271; e-mail: mahrep@aol.com.

Mercados (Markets)

Probably due to the climate, outdoor markets are not as abundant in the north as they are in other parts of Spain. Many cities and smaller towns do, however, host weekly outdoor markets (I do not know of a daily outdoor market in northern Spain, but the enclosed daily markets in Bilbao and San Sebastián are excellent.) My husband and I love visiting *mercados,* and we often plan our itineraries around market days. Markets are great venues for soaking up local atmosphere, observing customs and conversations, eating popular street food, buying local specialties for a picnic or to stock the kitchen of a place you've rented, and searching for a unique souvenir (and don't forget to bring your camera). The *mercados* of northern Spain are not quite as enticing as the *marchés* of southern France or the *Mercato Centrale* in Florence, for example, but that's because they are not generally for tourists, so the food and goods on display represent what the local residents really need and use. The fresh fish displays are a highlight of markets in the north, and should not be missed; sometimes these are kept in an indoor facility and the *mercado* spreads out around it. Keep in mind that a *mercado* is a big event, and people come from a distance to shop and gossip. This means, however, that traffic will be heavy in and around the market as well as on the roads leading into town, and parking will be difficult. Plan accordingly, but don't let a little traffic keep you away.

Money

The best way to travel is with a combination of local cash, American Express traveler's checks (other types are not universally accepted), and credit cards. If you have
all three, you will *never* have a problem. (Note that you should not rely on wide
acceptance of credit cards, especially in the countryside.) How you divide it up
depends on how long you'll be traveling and on what day of the week you arrive.
Banks, which of course offer the best exchange rate, aren't generally open on the
weekends and, in Spain, are open only part of the day during the week. If you arrive
on a weekend and rely solely on your ATM card but encounter a problem, you
can't fix it until Monday when the banks reopen. Overseas ATMs may limit the
number of daily transactions you can make and place a ceiling on the total amount
you can withdraw. Here are some money pointers to remember.

ATM machines. ~Make sure your password is compatible with Spanish ATMs
(if you have too many digits, you'll have to change it), and if, like me, you have
memorized your password as a series of letters rather than numbers, write down
the numerical equivalent before you leave. Most European cash machines do not
display letters, and even when they do, they do not always appear in the same
sequence as we know it in the U.S. ~Call your bank and inquire about fees for with-
drawals, and ask if there is a fee for overseas transactions. (There shouldn't be, but
ask anyway.) Inquire whether you can withdraw money from both your checking
and savings accounts or only one; and ask if you can transfer money between
accounts. ~Though this is a bit anal-retentive even for me, it's possible to view in
advance the exact street locations of ATM machines in Spain online. To see where
Plus systems are, go to www.visa.com; for the Cirrus network, go to www.
mastercard.com. Once you are in, select "ATM Locator," and you'll be given an
opportunity to select a country, city, street address, and postal code (it's not essential to provide the postal code, but for best results, enter cross streets and a city). I
found over ninety locations for Bilbao alone.

Local cash. Savvy travelers always arrive with some local currency—in this
case, euros—in their possession. (I feel most comfortable with the equivalent of
about $100.) While the exchange rates and fees charged obviously vary, it is far
more important not to arrive empty-handed than to spend an inordinate amount
of time figuring out how much money you'll save—we are, after all, talking about
a very small sum of money, and it will be money well spent when you get off the
plane with the ability to quickly make your way to wherever you're going. After a
long flight, who wants to then exchange money, especially while you are looking
after luggage and/or children? The lines at exchange counters and cash machines
are very often long, and cash machines are sometimes out of order, or out of cash.
(Once I even had the admittedly unusual experience of going directly to a large
bank in a capital city only to find a posted sign stating that the bank was closed
because it had *run out of money!?*) Smart travelers arrive prepared to pay for trans-

portation, tips, snacks, personal items, and unanticipated expenses. If you're too busy to get the cash yourself, call International Currency Express and request its Currency Rush mail-order service. With two offices, in Los Angeles and Washington, D.C., the company offers excellent rates. Call 888-278-6628 and request either UPS second-day or overnight service. ~*Cajas de cambio* (money exchange) places do not offer as good a rate as banks, but they do remain open for longer hours during the day. They should really be your last resort, however, in this day and age of automatic tellers.

~Note that Visa, MasterCard, American Express, and Diners Club all charge a currency conversion fee, and have been doing so for several years. As I write this, banks that issue credit cards charge a two percent fee on purchases made abroad. Additionally, both Visa and MasterCard charge a one percent fee for converting currency. American Express and Diners Club charge a flat two percent foreign currency conversion fee. Card members may not see these conversion fees itemized on statements, but they should not assume the fees aren't being applied. Currency conversion fees seem rather outrageous and unfair to me (I'm not alone in my thinking: there are currently two lawsuits that have been filed in California over this practice), but using a credit card while overseas is still an advantageous method of payment. Credit cards provide protection to the consumer if something goes wrong with a particular purchase or vendor, walking around with large amounts of cash is never a good idea, and the difference between withdrawing money from an ATM (and paying your bank's service charge) and paying with a credit card is not enormously significant. Recently, I read that debit cards obtained through a credit union or a brokerage house are not surcharged when used overseas. When I investigated this, however, I found it was misleading. The brokerage firm of Charles Schwab was recommended as one firm that offered a debit card, so I began my research there. After browsing the company's website, I was still a bit confused about the surcharge, so I telephoned a representative, who explained to me that while Schwab does not charge an additional fee for using the debit card overseas, Visa (the provider of the card) does not waive its standard two percent fee. So, after the client pays Schwab a maintenance fee for establishing the investment account, and continues to pay Visa the two percent fee, do travelers really come out ahead? The answer, of course, is no, and I see no way of escaping surcharges completely. My husband and I established a debit card account with Merrill Lynch during the year we traveled around the Mediterranean, and it proved to be an excellent choice. I would recommend it to travelers who intend to be out of the country for a month or longer, but I do not think it makes sense to travel with a debit card for shorter periods of time.

~The euro is significant not only economically but symbolically: A single currency is believed to keep the Continent from finding reasons to go to war. In this respect, the European Union may be viewed as a model of higher authority that respects regional and ethnic identities. Euro paper notes and coins have now replaced local currencies in Austria, Belgium, Finland, France, Germany, Greece, Ireland, Italy, Luxembourg, the Netherlands, Portugal, and Spain. At this writing, the U.S. dollar and the euro are very close in value (with one dollar worth about 1.01 euros). The twelve nations that have adopted the euro make up the world's second-largest trading region with a single currency, after the United States. The biggest benefits to travelers are that we no longer have to exchange currency when we cross borders, and comparing prices is easier. Readers interested in learning more about the euro may view two informative websites: www.europa.eu.int (the site of the European Union, available in eleven languages; click on "News" and then select "The Euro") and www.ecb.int (the official euro site).

Traveler's checks. Traveler's checks should be cashed at banks, as vendors prefer not to deal with them. This is a reflection not of a dim view of traveler's checks but of the fact that vendors simply find them a bother.

Credit cards. Credit card (*tarjeta de crédito*) acceptance is vastly wider than it was even five or ten years ago, but be aware that—especially outside large cities and towns—many small inns, country restaurants and wine bars, street vendors, and shopkeepers accept only cash. *¿Aceptan tarjetas de crédito?* ("Do you accept credit cards?") is a good question to ask if you're not sure.

Refrain from wearing one of those ubiquitous waist bags, or as my friend Carl says, "Make our country proud and don't wear one of those fanny packs!" A tourist with a fanny pack is a magnet for pickpockets. I know of more people who've had valuables stolen from these ridiculous pouches than I can count. Keep large bills, credit cards, and your passport hidden from view in a money belt worn under your clothes, in a pouch that hangs from your neck, or in an interior coat or blazer pocket. My husband has had great success with a money belt worn around his leg, underneath his pants. This obviously won't work with shorts, but it's quite a good solution for long pants. The Socaroo tube sock is another good alternative: it's a cotton sock meant for joggers that also happens to be great for travelers, as it holds cash and credit cards in a small two-by-three-inch pocket. A pair of socks is about five dollars, and you may view the website (www.socaroo.com) or call 310-559-4011 for more information. ~If possible, don't keep everything in the same place, and keep a separate piece of paper with telephone numbers of companies to contact in case of emergency.

~Useful vocabulary: *monedas* (coins); *dinero* (money); *billete de banco* (bank note); *cheque de viajero* (traveler's check); *¿Dónde hay un cajero automático?* ("Where is a cash dispenser/ATM?").

Movies

Plan a meal from one or more of the cookbooks mentioned in the *¡Buen Provecho! biblioteca,* and invite some friends and family over for dinner and a movie. Though

I do not know of a single film with Northern Spain as the subject or setting, a few Spanish film suggestions include *Viridiana* and *That Obscure Object of Desire* by Luis Buñuel (readers may search the website http://us.imdb.com/sections/countries/spain for some other movies). While you're cooking, get in the mood by listening to some appropriate music: *Album Español: More Music of the Spanish Guitar* (Metropolitan Museum of Art/EMEC Distribution, Madrid), *La Sal de España—The Charm of Spain* (another Metropolitan Museum/EMEC collaboration featuring Michael Kevin Jones on cello and Agustín Maruri on guitar), and *Spanish XXth Century Guitar Music* (EMEC, Madrid, also featuring Agustín Maruri). Flamenco is from Andalusia, but if you will be taking in a performance or two in Madrid, you may be happy to know about two excellent recordings, *The Rough Guide to Flamenco* (Rough Guides) and *The Story of Flamenco* (EMI). These great choices will put you and your guests in a warm Spanish mood. (See the Music entry below for opera and works by classical musicians as well as the Celtic-inspired music of Galicia.)

Museums and Monuments

Most museums and monuments in Spain close on Mondays, but always double-check before you set off, as this is not universal. Just as in the small towns of Italy and France, many churches, castles, and other sites in Northern Spain are kept locked, and visitors must find the caretaker and request the key. Caretakers will often volunteer to open the building and show you around; a small tip is appreciated and indeed expected. Sometimes the key is kept at the local government office or, more logically, at the bar. In the north, long lines are relatively rare, except perhaps at the Guggenheim Bilbao at certain times of day.

Music

The music communities of Northern Spain are very active and would certainly be of particular interest to those who seek to take part in and explore the region's musical folklore. Ethnic musical performance is in full swing during those times of year when the natives celebrate traditional fiestas centered on antiquated pagan rites. One simply has to look at the Celtic influence in Galicia and Asturias to understand that there is in fact a very definite association between the regions and their musical traditions. In these regions, local music is perhaps most closely identified with the bagpipe.

Carlos Nuñez, one of the world's leading Uellean pipers and *gaita* (Galician pipe) players, has been a key figure in introducing Galician music to the world. He has helped re-create a traditional Galician musical atmosphere and at the same time made a huge contribution to contemporary Galician music. Nuñez is closely associated with the Chieftains, the Celtic music group, and has frequently played with them on tour. His two latest solo albums are *Os Amores Libres* (BMG/RCA Victor, 2000) and the more popular *Brotherhood of Stars* (BMG/RCA Victor, 1997), on which he recorded twelve enthralling tracks, some of which are typical of the music of Northwestern Spain. Nuñez's importance ventures beyond his wonderful manipulation of the Celtic instruments. He is helping to reintroduce the music that once imbued his home region of Galicia, while adding a distinctive flavor that's proving popular not just to Galicia but to the whole of the Western world.

The Basques likewise enjoy a native musical tradition, often attributed to Greek and Celtic influence, which is most apparent during their own fiestas and usually accompanies dancing (sometimes high energy!) in the village squares. Some notable instruments of the region are the *txistu,* a three-holed flute played with one hand and accompanied by a small drum, and the *dultzaina,* a primitive bagpipe. A growing movement of contemporary Basque music is mixing these traditional primitive instruments with instruments more popular with a younger crowd. Oskorri, a nearly thirty-year-old Basque band, has been a pioneer of folk music in the Basque tradition. Their newest album (the twenty-third in their discography) is *Ura* (Elkarlanean KD-556, 2000), which exemplifies the contemporary Basque sound and eclectic musical taste. While the albums of Oskorri may be difficult to find, one can order them through international online music stores such as www.cdroots.com. The tourist offices in San Sebastián stock a number of brochures detailing the lively seasons of orchestral music, dance, theater, comedy, and contemporary music in that city.

Thriving establishments in Northern Spain also house musical performances in the Western European tradition. Opera fans traveling to Bilbao should be sure to make reservations at the region's new opera house, Asociación Bilbaína de Amigos de la Ópera, which attracts some of the best singers in the world. Information regarding the season (September–February) can be found on the theater's website, www.abao.org. Summer is perhaps the most exciting season for classical music, with a variety of festivals that span all of Northern Spain. Festival Internacional de Santander, the oldest music festival in Spain—and one of the country's most highly acclaimed—is celebrated in Santander, which holds performances not only at its main theater, the Palacio de Festivales de Cantabria, but in churches and aesthetically significant buildings in all areas of Cantabria. The festival, which lasts from July to August, features a plethora of musical, theatrical, and dance performances and is a vital aspect of Cantabria's modern culture. More detailed information can be found at www.festival-int-santander.org. Other noteworthy summer festivals include the Festival Internacional de Música de Galicia (981.57.43.95; www.xunta.es/conselle/cultura/musica/fimg/home.htm), which lasts from June to August; the Quincena Musical de San Sebastián (943.00.31.70; www.quincena-musical.com), which lasts from early August to early September; and the Mozart Festival in La Coruña (902.43.44.43, www.festivalmozart.com), which lasts from mid-May through the end of June. Unfortunately, these last three websites are accessible only to those who understand the Galician dialect or Spanish; but staff at the Spanish tourist offices in North America should be able to provide you with additional information.

As visitors from North America to Northern Spain must pass through Madrid, readers who enjoy vocal arts may be interested to know that Madrid is a historic center for Italian opera and *zarzuela*, Spanish musical comedy that was especially popular in the 1800s and, more recently, after 1955. Madrid's premier opera house is the Teatro Royal, which opened its doors in 1850. The house is home to full seasons of opera as well as ballet and *zarzuela*. The annual season begins in September and runs through July. Reservations are highly recommended due to the theater's immense popularity (91.516.06.60). The theater's website (www.teatro-real.com) may also be browsed, though it is entirely in Spanish. The Teatro de la Zarzuela is Madrid's other major music house. Though it primarily stages *zarzuela*, it also offers Spanish opera, flamenco, and dance, including some performances for children. Reservations are suggested (91.429.71.57); the theater's website (teatrodelazarzuela.mcu.es) is accessible to English and Spanish readers and details upcoming performances and services.

Though not dedicated to opera in Spain, Fred Plotkin's *Opera 101: A Complete Guide to Learning and Loving Opera* (Hyperion, 1994) is an outstanding resource. Readers may know Plotkin for his excellent Italian cookbooks and for his food and travel writing, but in fact Plotkin has taught about opera history all over the world, written much about it, and was performance manager of the Metropolitan Opera in New York. Ann Patchett, in an article entitled "An Affair to Remember" (*Gourmet,* June 2001), nicely praises *Opera 101,* "which I later discovered is something of a bible even for sophisticated opera buffs. What Mr. Plotkin offers is basically a college course in opera." I would have to agree: Plotkin presents a history of four hundred years of opera and informs how one can become an opera cognoscente. He provides a discography; he discusses eleven operas (including two set in Spain, *Il Barbiere di Siviglia* by Rossini and *Don Carlo* by Verdi) in individual chapters; and he includes four appendixes, the last one being a complete list of opera houses around the world for travelers. (It includes eighteen listings for theaters throughout Spain, including those in Santiago, Santander, San Sebastián, Oviedo, Madrid, La Coruña, and Bilbao).

As inspiring and authoritative as Plotkin's book is, opera mavens and almost-mavens will naturally crave more. A few other titles (about which I offered more detail in my *Venice* edition) that may be of interest include *The Story of Opera* (Richard Somerset-Ward, Harry N. Abrams, 1998), *Opera as Drama: New Edition* (Joseph Kerman, University of California Press, 1988), *Ticket to the Opera: Discovering and Exploring 100 Famous Works, History, Lore and Singers with*

Recommended Recordings (Phil G. Goulding, Fawcett Books, 1999), and *History Through the Opera Glass* (George Jellinek, Pro Am Music Resources, 1993).

P

Packing

Most people, whether they travel for business or pleasure, view packing as a stressful chore. It doesn't have to be, and a great book filled with excellent suggestions and tips is *Fodor's How to Pack: Experts Share Their Secrets* (Laurel Cardone, Fodor's Travel Publications, 1997). You may think it silly to consult a book on how to pack a suitcase, but it is eminently practical and worthwhile. Cardone is a travel journalist who's on the road a lot, and she meets a lot of fellow travelers with plenty of packing wisdom to share. How to buy luggage, how to fill almost any suitcase, nearly crease-free folding, the right wardrobe for the right trip, and how to pack for the trip back home are all thoroughly covered. ~Some pointers that work for me include selecting clothing that isn't prone to wrinkling, like cotton and wool knits. When I *am* concerned about limiting wrinkles, I lay out a large plastic dry-cleaning bag, place the garment on top of it, place *another* bag on top of that, and fold the item up between the two bags. The key here is that the plastic must be layered in with the clothing; otherwise it doesn't really work. ~If I'm packing items with buttons, I button them up before I fold them; the same with zippers and snaps. ~If I'm carrying a bag with separate compartments, I use one for shoes; otherwise I put shoes at the bottom (or back) of the bag opposite the handle so they'll remain there while I'm carrying the bag. ~Transfer shampoo and lotions to plastic travel-size bottles, which can be purchased at pharmacies—and then put these inside a Ziploc bag to protect against leaks. ~Don't skimp on underwear—it's lightweight and takes up next to no room in your bag. It's never a mistake to have more than you think you need. ~Belts can be either rolled up and stuffed into shoes or fastened together along the inside edge of your suitcase. ~Ties should be rolled, not folded, and also stuffed into shoes or pockets. ~Some handy things to bring along that are often overlooked: a pocket flashlight, for looking into ill-lit corners of old buildings, for reading in bed at night (the lights are often not bright enough), or if you're staying at a hotel where the bathroom is down the hall, for navigating dark hallways at night (the light is usually on a timer and always runs out before you've made it to either end of the hallway); binoculars, for looking up at architectural details; a small travel umbrella; a penknife/corkscrew; if you're camping, plastic shoes—referred to in the United States as jellies—which the Italians and the French have been wearing on some of their rocky beaches for years—for campground showers; an empty, lightweight duffel bag, which you can fold up and pack and then use as a carry-on bag for gifts and breakable items on the way home; copies of current prescriptions in case you need to have one refilled; photocopies of your passport and airline tickets (which you should also leave with someone at home).

Paseo

The *paseo* is the evening stroll in Spain and has also historically served as a venue for young men and women to meet each other. *Everyone* turns out for the *paseo*—grandparents, babies, teenagers, and toddlers. The stroll flows a bit better on straight stretches of cobblestones, macadam, marble, or whatever, but even in large cities like Bilbao, La Coruña, and Oviedo, residents find a section of town for their walk. The most famous *paseo* in Northern Spain is probably in San Sebastián, where everyone walks along the beautiful La Concha promenade. The Spanish *paseo* is a ritual not to be missed. I have noticed that even elderly people, who may not feel up to walking, will arrange to meet their friends at a particular bench somewhere along the *paseo* route, allowing them to participate without actually walking. An essay in the wonderful book *The Walker Within* notes this popular Mediterranean ritual, "Were Americans to take up this custom, the rate of criminal violence would surely drop, for it's easier to gun down strangers than people with whom you've passed the time."

Passports

In a last-minute crisis, it *is* possible to obtain a new passport, renew an old one, or get necessary visas (not required for Spain). Some companies that can meet the challenge include: Travisa (1731 21st Street N.W., Washington, DC, 20009; 800-222-2589; www.travisa.com); Express Visa Service (18 East 41st Street, Suite 1206, New York, NY 10017; 212-679-5650; fax: -4691; www.expressvisa.com); Passport Express (800-362-8196; www.passportexpress.com); and American Passport Express (800-841-6778; www.americanpassport.com). These services are expensive (typically charging between $150 and $175), but if you're in a hurry and you don't have the time to stand on long lines that move at a snail's pace, the fee may be considered money well spent.

As in most other countries, hotel and inn proprietors are required to ask to see your passport. Details from your passport are recorded in the inn's ledger and are also shared with local authorities, which is why passports are often not returned to guests until the following day. This is not cause for alarm or mistrust; proprietors are merely following the letter of the law. If you have an imperative reason for hanging on to your passport during the first twelve to twenty-four hours of your stay, let the staff know, and they may be able to return it within an hour or so. If you are staying only one night at a particular lodging, make sure your passport is returned to you when you check out. This may seem obvious, but it does happen that both reception staff and guests forget.

Be especially mindful of the whereabouts of your passport while traveling.

According to a report in *The New York Times* in April 2001, Americans who lose their passports overseas will receive a new state-of-the-art version that will feature a computer-generated photograph of the bearer—and it will take at least a few days to process. Apparently American embassies and consulates abroad do not have the machinery to produce these newfangled passports, so all passports will now be printed at a State Department branch in Portsmouth, New Hampshire. This change is being implemented to foil terrorists and other criminals who profit from stolen passports. As the *Times* reported, "Recent court testimony has shown that members of Osama bin Laden's terrorist network have aggressively sought blank American passports." A State Department official was quoted in the article as saying that exceptions might be granted, on a case-by-case basis, for those Americans who must travel urgently, and in these instances an old-style passport may be issued. But they would be valid for a period of only about six months or a year, as opposed to ten years for a regular passport.

Periodicals

Following are some newsletters and periodicals, a few of which are not available at newsstands, that you may want to consider subscribing to in advance of your trip (or upon your return if you decide you want to keep up with goings-on in Spain):

The Art of Eating: Named "Most Nourishing Food Quarterly" by *Saveur* in 1999 and described as "one of the most respected publications in the food world" by Chef's Edition on National Public Radio, *The Art of Eating* is, in my opinion, one of the very best publications ever, of any kind. Some readers may already know about this absolutely excellent, critical, and superbly written quarterly newsletter by Edward Behr. Although not devoted to Spain, Behr is passionately interested in Mediterranean culture and cuisine. *The Art of Eating* is really *esencial* reading, so don't wait until the last minute to order back issues ($9 each, $7.50 for four or more). Further, if you really want to learn about the food traditions of North America and countries abroad, and if you care about the food you eat, you'll definitely want to subscribe to this stellar periodical. Some better cookbook and cookware stores sell individual issues of *The Art of Eating* (Kitchen Arts & Letters in New York stocks it regularly), but to receive it in your mailbox you should subscribe: Box 242, Peacham, VT 05862; 800-495-3944; www.artofeating.com. Back issues may be ordered online.

El País: Diario Independiente de la Mañana: El País is one of Spain's leading daily newspapers, and it also publishes an English edition with *The International Herald Tribune*. It's available on every newsstand and features a lot more news pertaining to Spain than does the *Tribune*.

Zingerman's News: This six-times-yearly newsletter is written by Ari Weinzweig, "guiding taste bud" of Zingerman's, the famous food emporium in Ann Arbor,

Michigan (the editors of *Saveur* have called it "a food lover's paradise" and food writer Corby Kummer wrote in *Eating Well,* "Ann Arbor? How does a midsized Midwestern university town make it onto the list of global culinary shrines?"). If you don't already know about Zingerman's, you should, and if you do already know about it and love it as much as I do, do yourself the great favor of subscribing to *Zingerman's News.* Ari's been writing it since the store opened in 1982. Reading the Zingerman's mail-order catalog is a delectable treat itself, but the newsletter is even more so, and it's developed a cultlike following among food writers and food lovers of all stripes across the United States. Ari is addictively enthusiastic about whatever foodstuff or food-related subject he's writing about, so each issue is part personal journal and part new food update. One issue in particular featured an essay entitled "Want to Improve the Enjoyment of Your Eating? Start by Buying Better Ingredients," which is an essential tenet of Spanish cooking (and of so many other Mediterranean cuisines). The essay reinforced that "the finished food you prepare will never be better than the quality of the stuff you put in," and what followed was a list of ten ingredients to buy that would immediately improve the overall quality of our meals; the list included items that any Spanish cook would insist upon: better olive oil, better bread, and better fruits and vegetables. I was pleased to see this philosophy emphasized in the April 2002 issue of *Food & Wine,* in an article entitled "The Urge to Splurge." The title at first made me bristle, until I discovered that the editors were trying to convey the same message as the folks at Zingerman's. What the editors did was select nine indulgences that are worth the cost—imported jarred tuna, dried morels, artisanal Italian pasta, king crab, Maldon sea salt, farmhouse cheddar cheese, smokehouse bacon, piquillo peppers, and imported and European-style butters—and paired them with great recipes. They also did not shy away from providing the prices both for these premium ingredients and for their pedestrian counterparts. The Zingerman's catalog, too, is typically filled with a variety of selected Spanish items, such as olive oil from Andalucía and Cataluña, sherry vinegar, almond blossom honey from Valencia, piquillo peppers from Navarra, Spanish drinking chocolate from Barcelona, and—my new favorite—rabitos chocolate-dipped figs from western Spain (you can't even believe how delicious these are). Many of you undoubtedly receive as many mail-order catalogs as I do; the arrival of the Zingerman's catalog—and the newsletter—is a special event worth celebrating. To add your name to the mailing list and/or to subscribe to the newsletter ($10 for six issues, $15 for twelve), contact Zingerman's at 422 Detroit Street, Ann Arbor, MI 48104; 888-636-8162; fax: 734-477-6988; www.zingermans.com.

Philip II

Born in 1527 in Valladolid to Emperor Carlos V and Empress Isabella of Portugal, Philip II remains one of the best-known Spanish monarchs as well as one of the most controversial (see the *Las Noticias Cotidianas biblioteca* for some good biographies). Philip is not known for anything he accomplished in Northern Spain, but his imprint is firmly fixed in and around Madrid: He set up a permanent court in Madrid in 1559 and established royal residences at Aranjuez, El Pardo, Valsaín, and El Escorial. Philip was also a great patron and lover of the arts, as witness his collection of works now in the Prado and at El Escorial. But he is mostly known for his unconditional support for the Catholic religion and its struggle to check the advance of the Protestant Reformation. Philip endorsed the Inquisition as a weapon of religious control, and the beginning of his reign saw two large autos-da-fé, one in Seville in 1558 and the other in Valladolid in 1559. Upon his father's abdication from the throne in 1556, Philip became king of all dominions subject to Spain—which included the Kingdom of Sicily, the Indies, Portugal, the Netherlands, the Ottoman Empire, and France—making Spain the greatest world power at that time. Philip is also known for the battles he waged with his subjects in the Netherlands (they rebelled against him and formed the United Provinces) and England (which had been Castile's steadfast ally for most of the previous centuries). In 1598 the conversion of Henry of Navarra to Catholicism ended Philip's claim to the French throne, and he acknowledged Henry IV as king of France by way of the Peace of Vervins. On September 13 of that year, Philip II died at El Escorial.

Photography

I would rather have one great photo of a place than a dozen mediocre shots, so I like to page through photography books for ideas and suggestions on maximizing my picture-taking efforts. Some books I've particularly enjoyed include:

Focus on Travel: Photographing Memorable Pictures of Journeys to New Places (text by Anne Millman and Allen Rokach, photographs by Allen Rokach, Abbeville Press, 1992). The authors offer much information on lenses, filters, films, and accessories (though not video cameras, for those who are fans of such items) and devote separate chapters to photographing architecture, shooting subjects in action, and taking pictures in a variety of weather conditions. The appendix covers selecting and preparing your photos after the trip, fill-in flash guidelines, a color correction chart, and a page-by-page reference to all the photos in the book.

Kodak Guide to Shooting Great Travel Pictures: How to Take Travel Pictures Like a Pro (Jeff Wignall, Fodor's Travel Publications, 1995). Unlike the other books mentioned here, which should be consulted before you go, this very handy, small paperback is good for bringing along as a reference. Six chapters present specific photographic challenges—such as city vistas, stained-glass windows, close-ups of faces, mountain scenery, motion, lights at night, and taking pictures through frames—and each is dealt with in one page with accompanying photos. This guide is meant for experienced *and* point-and-shoot photographers, and many of the images it features come from the Eastman Kodak archives, a great number of which were taken by amateurs. The final chapter is devoted to creating a travel journal.

Spirit of Place (Bob Krist, Amphoto, 2000). Hailed by *American Photo* magazine as "simply the best book on travel photography ever written," this is truly an outstanding volume for photographers of all levels. I am a big fan of Krist's work, which I've seen frequently in *Islands* magazine, and he shares some tips that I've not read elsewhere.

The Traveler's Eye: A Guide to Still and Video Travel Photography (Lisl Dennis, Clarkson Potter, 1996). Dennis, who began her career in photography at *The Boston Globe,* writes the "Traveler's Eye" column for *Outdoor Photographer.* I like her sensitive approach to travel photography and find her images and suggestions in this book inspiring. After chapters covering such topics as travel photojournalism, shooting special events, and landscape photography, she provides an especially useful chapter on technical considerations, with advice on equipment, film, packing, and the ethics of tipping.

Puente

Puente is the Spanish word for bridge, and I include it here for those occasions when the word is used to refer to an extended public holiday in Spain. If a fiesta falls on a Tuesday or Thursday, for example, Spaniards will typically extend the holiday by a day—create a "bridge"—to make a long weekend. This is useful to know if you are expecting to accomplish business, go to the bank or the post office, or call the plumber if there's a problem with the pipes at your rental property.

R

RENFE *(Red Nacional de Ferrocarriles Español)*

RENFE, the Spanish train network, offers some reduced fares to riders in addition to rail passes, but not quite the bewildering array of choices as in France, for example. A few of the discounts offered are *días azules* (blue days), a ten percent discount on specified days, which is meant to encourage the general public to travel by rail; *interrail,* a pass for those under twenty-six; and *eurodomino,* a pass for those over twenty-six. Iberrail (a Madrid-based tour operator that works mostly with travel agents and other tour companies; see its website—www.iberrail.es— for some of its offerings to individual travelers) offers good deals on rail and hotel packages throughout Spain and also markets the Transcantábrico and Al-Andalus luxury lines. No one wants to waste money, but I do not find train fares in Spain prohibitively expensive. One or two short trips may cost less at the regular fare; make sure you will get the most out of a special discount, and make sure the option you're considering isn't simply a discount for first-class travel, which you may not have wanted in the first place. In addition to different types of tickets, RENFE also offers different types of trains. TALGO and AVE are high-speed intercity lines that have the most expensive—and quickest—trains. *Largo recorrido* are long-distance trains, while *regionales y cercanías* are regional and local lines. These are slow, making every stop along the route, but they are also very inexpensive. The Basque Country has its own regional rail line, Eusko Trenbideak.

Here are a few things to remember about train travel in Spain: ~Buy tickets from the ticket office at a train station or one of the ticket machines. (I've heard the latter only accept coins.) If you purchase them from a travel agent, you'll pay a commission. ~When taking an overnight train, you may be offered either a *cochecama* (a compartment with two *camas,* or beds) or a *litera* (one of six seats in a compartment that fold down flat into a bed of sorts). I've experienced both options; if you can at all secure a *cochecama,* do so, as it is far superior to a *litera*. A supplement is charged for either, even if you have purchased a rail pass. Be sure to show the train officials proof that you paid the supplement, or they'll charge you for it on the train. ~Remember to stamp your ticket in the machines at the head of each platform. These aren't always so noticeable, so allow some extra time for finding them. Unstamped tickets usually result in a fine. ~Some rail passes may be purchased in advance from Rail Europe (the official North American representative for sixty European railroads; 877-257-2887 in the U.S., 800-361-RAIL in Canada; www.raileurope.com) and Marketing Ahead (212-686-9213; see entry under M). The Eurailpass (which must be purchased in either the United States or Canada before you leave) and the Europass (available in Europe) are valid for several time periods in Spain, Italy, France, Germany, Italy, and Switzerland and in the associated countries of Portugal, Benelux, Austria, Hungary, and Greece. ~Madrid has three train stations: Atocha, Chamartín, and Norte. TALGO trains depart from all three stations, while AVE lines head south only and depart from Atocha. ~Timetables change in May and October and are not readily available outside Spain, though the tourist office staff and travel agents should be able to provide you with them. ~El Transcantábrico is a beautiful train consisting of fourteen antique cars built between 1900 and 1930 and since restored. It runs from San Sebastián along the Cantabrian coast and ends in Santiago. This luxury line is operated by another regional railroad, Ferrocarriles de Via Estrecha (FEVE), and tickets may be purchased in the United States from Marketing Ahead. A Transcantábrico brochure at the Spanish Tourist Office was so appealing, it very nearly made me pick up the phone to book my passage. Though I haven't yet experienced the train, I think it would be an excellent way to see the coast and all the towns along the way.

~Useful vocabulary: *ida/de ida solo* (one-way ticket); *de ida y vuelta* (round trip); *andén* (platform); *vía* (track); *consigna automática* (left luggage locker); *taquilla despacho de billetes* (ticket office or window); *horario* (timetable); *de primera clase* (first class); *de segunda clase* (second class); *reservación* (a reservation); *prohibir fumar* (no smoking); *puerta* (door); *ventana* (window).

Retablos

Retablos (*retablos* in Spanish) are altarpieces decorated with painting or sculpture, and it is said that no region in the world possesses such magnificent retablos as the Iberian peninsula. The most notable examples in Spain are not in the north, but *retablos* is still a word with which you should be familiar. Readers who live in the New York City metropolitan area may know that the Metropolitan Museum of Art holds some of the finest retablos in its collection. These are displayed in the museum's medieval department in close proximity to the magnificent reja (wrought-iron screen), which was once located in the central nave of the cathedral in Valladolid. Screens like this one were used to close off the choir from the general public. The screen was a private gift from the bishop of Valladolid, and was put into place on December 7, 1763 (although painting and gilding of the screen were not finished until the following year). Visitors will not fail to be impressed by the immense size of the screen, as well as its delicate appearance, making it difficult to believe that Rafael Amezúa (the iron master from the Basque region who is believed to have fashioned the screen) could have created it on his own.

S

Los Servicios (Toilets)

Public pay toilets are not common in Spain, so you should rely upon department stores, bars, and restaurants throughout the day when you are not near your inn or hotel. At bars and restaurants, however, it is expected that patrons of *los servicios* will also be patrons of the bar at least, so plan on sitting down for a few minutes if you've had to make a stop. As I recommend in every edition in this series, never set out each day without some sheets of toilet paper in your pockets or your bag. Even toilets in some of the nicest places can be abominable, and they often do not have paper. I have always found good, soft American-style toilet paper in the bathrooms at American Express offices throughout the Mediterranean.

Single Travelers

Those traveling alone (not necessarily looking for romance) might be interested in a great book: *Traveling Solo: Advice and Ideas for More Than 250 Great Vacations* (Eleanor Berman, Globe Pequot Press, 1997). Berman offers the names of tour operators for different age groups and different types of trips and asks all the right questions in determining if a proposed vacation is right for you.

A few travel companion organizations arrange trips for single travelers who don't want to travel alone: Travel Companion Exchange (www.travelcompanions.com), Connecting: Solo Travel Network (www.cstn.org), Vacation Partners (www.vacationpartners.com), and Travel Chums (travelchums.com). While I cannot vouch personally for any of these companies, having only read about them, I understand that many travelers have had nice experiences on these trips and have met nice people. Each of the websites has a section devoted to customer feedback and one for frequently asked questions, giving you an opportunity to read testimonials. It might also be a good idea to check in with the Better Business Bureau before making a decision.

Female *and* male solo travelers should beware of revealing too many personal details about their travels. If you admit that you're traveling for an indefinite period of time, for example, the perception is that you are probably carrying a lot of money. I met an Australian man who had the bulk of his money stolen from a youth hostel safe, and he was certain it was taken by a fellow hosteler whom he had befriended (but who had disappeared by the time the discovery was made).

Slow Food

Slow Food is very much of an international movement, and though it is based in Italy (in the Piedmont region), Spain is very active, and therefore I do not think it is out of place to mention Slow Food here. Slow Food is a wonderful response to American fast food. The movement was founded in 1989 and is active in forty countries with sixty thousand members and five hundred convivia (chapters). Slow Food U.S.A. has more than five thousand members and fifty convivia. Slow Food is for food and wine enthusiasts who care about and promote traditional foodstuffs from around the world and who "share the snail's wise slowitude." (The snail, appropriately, is the organization's symbol.) As Carlo Petrini, president of Slow Food, has stated, "Food history is as important as a baroque church. Governments should recognize cultural heritage and protect traditional foods. A cheese is as worthy of preserving as a sixteenth-century building." A highlight from the organization's manifesto is "In the name of productivity, Fast Life has changed our way of being and threatens our environment and our landscapes. So Slow Food is now the only truly progressive answer."

Several programs and divisions encompass Slow Food: The Ark of Taste, a project aimed at documenting and promoting foods and beverages in danger of becoming extinct. The biennial Salone del Gusto in Turin is the largest food and wine event in the world, and its biennial Cheese in Bra (Italy) is the largest cheese show in the world. In addition there are wine conventions and tasting sessions across the United States and various food festivals around the world. Each convivium organizes educational tastings, cooking courses, trips, visits to restaurants, and lectures for its members. As for publications, in addition to the excellent *Vini d'Italia* (published in conjunction with *Gambero Rosso*), Slow Food publishes *Italian Cheese,* the first guide to traditional Italian cheeses, with 205 artisanal specialties described and documented; *Slowine,* a seventy-page magazine reporting on wine culture around the world; and an outstanding and insightful journal entitled *Slow: The International Herald of Tastes*, which is published in English, German, Italian, and French. Fraternal Tables are Slow Food funds projects in Nicaragua, Hekura (Brazil), Zlata (Bosnia), and Colfiorito in Umbria. Slow Cities are a group of towns and cities in Italy committed to improving the quality of life of their citizens, especially with regard to food issues. You can view the entire list of Slow Food programs online at www.slowfood.com.

You may also want to read two wonderful books: *Slow Food: Collected Thoughts on Taste, Tradition and the Honest Pleasures of Food* (edited by Carlo Petrini, Chelsea Green, 2001) and *The Pleasures of Slow Food: Celebrating Authentic Traditions, Flavors and Recipes* (Corby Kummer, photographs by Susie Cushner, preface by Carlo Petrini, foreword by Eric Schlosser, Chronicle Books, 2002). The first book is a collection of articles previously published in issues of *Slow*, while the second is a book of completely original material. In *The Pleasures of Slow Food*, Carlo Petrini notes that he likes the idea of this book arriving in the hands of Americans who don't yet know Slow Food. "I'd like to think they'll find resonance in the marvelous stories of individual artisans and farmers, and also in the ideas of the movement—a sort of common denominator for their own needs as gourmets, as environmentalists, as people who care about the future of the planet. It's no longer possible to separate these concerns from the concerns of other people and other places. Everything and everyone are bound up together, today more than ever." Eric Schlosser continues in the foreword by noting that the Slow Food movement "stands in direct opposition to everything that a fast-food meal represents: blandness, uniformity, conformity, the blind worship of science and technology. . . . Critics of Slow Food claim that it is elitist and effete, too expensive for ordinary people, just the latest trend among foodies and gourmands. I would use a different set of adjectives to describe the movement: necessary and long overdue. Slow Foods are mainly peasant foods—dishes and ingredients that have been prepared the same way for centuries. They are time-tested. They spring directly from regional cultures and cuisines. They are not effete. Fast food stems from an entirely different sort of mass culture and mass production. It is a recent phenomenon. Although McDonald's has been around for more than half a century, it did not begin to rely on highly processed frozen meals until the early 1970s. The centralization and industrialization of our food system has largely occurred over the past twenty years. And its huge social costs—the rise in food-borne illnesses, the advent of new pathogens such as *E. coli* 0157:H7, antibiotic resistance from the overuse of drugs in animal feed, extensive water pollution from feedlot wastes, and many others—have become apparent only recently. These costs are not reflected in the price of a burger and fries at the drive-through window. But they should be. Our fast, cheap food has proven to be much too expensive." In addition to some of the most eye-opening chapters about food ever written, Kummer provides profiles of cheese, meat, salt, shellfish, wine, fruit, and vegetable artisans as well as recipes from Slow Food member restaurants from around the world, including ten from America.

Personally, I think Slow Food may save the planet, and it is one of the more worthwhile groups to support. Interested readers may join Slow Food U.S.A. by contacting the group by snail mail (434 Broadway, 7th floor, New York, NY 10013), telephone (212-965-5640), or e-mail (info@slowfoodusa.org) or by viewing its website (www.slowfood.com). A $60 membership entitles you to a personal membership in Slow Food International, four issues of *Slow,* four newsletters of *The Snail,* two issues of *Slowine,* invitations to all Slow Food events, and discounts on Slow Food publications and merchandise. (I have to admit I'm hooked on the snail pins and the aprons.)

The Spanish Institute

The mission of the Spanish Institute, located in New York City, is "to promote greater awareness and understanding of the culture of the Spanish-speaking world." The Institute offers a full program of events and activities, including La Tertulia (a group discussion of current events and culture as a supplement for those learning Spanish), exhibitions, movies, flamenco lessons, language classes, readings, lectures (past topics have included "Democracy and Terrorism in the Basque Country: A Tragic Conflict," "Art & the Jewel" by noted art history lecturer Rosamond Bernier, and "Urban Images of the Hispanic World, 1493–1793" by Richard Kagan), and musical recitals (past performances have included "Brazilian Rhythm," "Castanets in America," and "Le Gran Tango: The Life & Music of Astor Piazzolla"). Previous art exhibitions have ranged from "Memory and Vanguardism: Eight Galician Painters," and the works of Jerónimo Jacinto Espinosa to Valentí Claverol's beautiful photographs depicting Andorran life.

The Spanish Institute also offers private language instruction for individuals or groups, tailored to their needs, and even provides a thirty-hour immersion program for students who may need to prepare for a business trip or who would like to refresh their Spanish. (Prices for private instruction for ten lessons start at around $45.) The Institute also offers translation services starting at around $63 for a 250-word minimum, $100 per hour (there is a two-hour minimum requisite); for transcripts and revisions the cost is about $60 an hour (with a two-hour minimum as well)—contact the Institute for more specifics. Group language classes are also offered that usually consist of about twelve students at convenient hours during the day. Prices for group classes start at around $410, including membership and textbook fees. For teachers and students, the Institute also has an outreach program that offers slide presentations, lectures on topics such as the arts of Spain and Mexico, the Golden Age of Spain, and contemporary art of the Dominican Republic, and tours. Membership at the student level begins at about twenty dollars, and corporate membership is also available. Some benefits include invitations to luncheons, symposia, and lectures featuring prominent business, political, and cultural leaders at a discounted rate; monthly calendar of events; invitations to special exhibition openings; discounted rates for the Salon Recital Series and exhibition catalogs; invitations to all Class Programs and other special events; and invitations to the Gold Medal Gala. The Gold Medal is awarded annually to individuals from the United States, Spain, and Latin America "in recognition of their contributions to the betterment of relations between these countries." In the past such prestigious awardees and/or attendees have included King Juan Carlos I, Queen Sofía of Spain, Oscar de la Renta, and Plácido Domingo, among others.

To find out more about services and upcoming events readers may visit the website at www.spanishinstitute.org. Unfortunately, there is only one Spanish Institute in North America in New York City (offices are located in a beautiful building at 684 Park Avenue at 68th Street, and the enthusiastic and helpful staff may be reached by phone at 212-628-0420). The staff reports that the Institute's members are from all over the United States, though obviously members who live in the New York metropolitan area would benefit most from membership.

Stendhal Syndrome

Named for the sick physical feeling that afflicted French novelist Stendhal after he visited Santa Croce in Florence, this syndrome is synonymous with being completely overwhelmed by your surroundings (my translation: seeing and doing way too much). Though it happened to Stendhal in Florence, it could just as easily have happened anywhere, and visitors who arrive with too long a list of must-sees are prime candidates. Even a relatively less traveled place—with not nearly as many attractions as Florence—like Northern Spain may cause the overambitious to expire. My advice: Organize your days, factor in how long it takes to get from place to place, and see what you want. There will be no quiz.

Studying in Spain

North Americans have quite a few study opportunities in Spain, sponsored by colleges, universities, or other educational organizations. Though the majority of these programs are available in Madrid, Barcelona, and Andalusia, there are a surprising number in Northern Spain as well. If you are a college-age student seeking a program, my advice is to select one that will allow you to stay a year or even longer. And if you have to change your major to go, do it—you won't regret it! A semester abroad is a great experience, but there is no replacement for staying a year. Alternatively, investigate attending a Spanish college or university, and remember that studying in Spain isn't limited to studying the language (courses are also offered in the fine arts, photography, painting, business, literature, and so on) or by age (plenty of programs welcome adults, and plenty of adults attend).

The guide to get to begin your research is the *Directory of Spanish Schools and Universities* (Michael Giammarella, Learning Destinations, P.O. Box 640713, Oakland Gardens, New York, 11364; 718-631-0096; fax: -0316; www.learningdestinations.com). The guide ($19.00 plus $3.00 for first-class shipping) details a variety of programs, not just language, offered throughout Spain, including courses in Bilbao, Pamplona, Vitoria, San Sebastián, Oviedo, Santiago, Vigo, La Coruña, and Burgos. When I last spoke with Giammarella, who handles all the reservations for the programs, he told me the Spanish directory itself was ever-so-slowly being updated; but he can provide a plethora of information on Spanish language programs (and others, such as cooking and flamenco) offered year-round in Spain, at all levels. Giammarella also reserves spots in a residential/family stay program, for kids aged six to seventeen, in Madrid, Salamanca, and Marbella.

Worldwide Classroom (P.O. Box 1166, Milwaukee, WI 53201; fax: 414-224-3466; www.worldwide.edu) is a great group I discovered when I was working on my *Venice* edition. Worldwide is among the largest international consortium of schools, providing information about ten thousand schools in 109 countries.

Delta Language School (Academia Delta Language School, Juan de Herrera 19, 39002 Santander, Cantabria; 942.036.886; fax: 942.216.261; www.deltalang.com) offers year-round Spanish courses, cultural activities, and carefully selected accommodations with host families as well as in hotels and apartments.

Inlingua Santander (Avenida de Pontejos 5, E-39005 Santander; 942.278.465; fax: 942.274.402; www.inlingua.com).

Iria Flavia Language Centre (Preguntoiro 9, 15704 Santiago de Compostela; 981.572.032; fax: 981.572.032; www.iriaflavia.net).

Instituto Hemingway de Español (Calle Bailen 5, 2 dcha., 48003 Bilbao; 94.416.7901 (phone and fax); www.institutohemingway.com).

The Spanish tourist offices here in North America and the offices of the Instituto Cervantes in the United States (www.cervantes.es) have numerous brochures on language and cultural programs in Spain.

T

Telephones

Spain is six hours ahead of Eastern Standard Time, seven ahead of Central Time, eight ahead of Mountain Time, and nine ahead of Pacific Standard Time. To call Spain from the U.S., dial 011 + 34 + local number. (011 is the overseas line, 34 is the country code for Spain, and the local number includes the appropriate city code.) Some city codes in Northern Spain are 944 (Bilbao), 981 (La Coruña and Santiago), 942 (Santander), 985 (Oviedo), 986 (Pontevedra), 943 (San Sebastián), 948 (Pamplona), 947 (Burgos), 987 (León), and 941 (Llaro and Logroño). When calling any city or town in Spain from the United States, it is no longer necessary to omit the initial 0. In fact, you must include it. Spanish telephone numbers generally have a total of seven digits, but do not be surprised if numbers in smaller towns have only six. To call the United States from Spain, dial 00 + 1 (the country code for the United States) + area code + number. Within Spain, to reach a Spanish operator for local assistance, dial 003. To reach an English-speaking operator, dial 025. In an emergency (the equivalent of 911 in the United States), dial 091, which is a nation-wide number. To call for an ambulance (*cruz roja*) in Madrid, dial 522.22.22. The number to dial to reach *bomberos* in case of an emergency fire is 080—but only in Madrid, Barcelona, and Seville. Telephone numbers that begin with a 6 are cell phone numbers and cost more to dial.

Phone cards. Almost all public phones in Spain no longer accept tokens. *Telefónica* is the name of the Spanish telecommunications company, and a *tarjeta telefónica* is a phone card. Phone cards, as in other countries, are now the wave of the future, and they're available in several denominations—make sure you buy one that meets your telephoning needs or you'll be wasting money. *Tarjetas telefónicas* can be purchased at *estancos* (tobacconist shops). To use a phone card, pick up the receiver and insert the card into the slot. Wait until you see the *"marque numero"* message, then dial the number. You can also place calls at *locutorios* (telephone offices), where there are individual cabins and you pay after you make the call. Inquire at the Spanish tourist office about the least expensive times of day to call.

Cell phones. I won't elaborate on my feelings about cell phone abuse here, but at least the Spanish have the excuse that their public telephone system is rather unreliable. If you feel you really must have your own cell phone, check with your service provider first to ensure that the phone is programmed to be compatible. Renting a compatible cell phone may be a better option. A few companies that offer them are Cellhire (offices in New York, Los Angeles, Dallas, and Washington, DC; 866-CH-ONLINE; www.cellhire.com); WorldCell (International Mobile Commu-nications, 801 Roeder Road, Suite 800, Silver Spring, MD 20910; 888-967-5323; fax: 301-562-1379; www.worldcell.com); and Roberts Rent-a-Phone (150 East 69th Street, New York, NY 10021; 800-964-2468 or 212-734-6344; fax: -3780; www. roberts-rent-a-phone.com). You can expect a basic rental fee to be about $40 a week, plus the cost of shipping the cell phone to you before you depart. Addition-ally, you will be charged for both outgoing and incoming calls, from about $1 to $3 a minute.

Points to keep in mind: ~Renting a cell phone is not an inexpensive option (though it may be less expensive than making calls from your hotel), and not all companies are the same when it comes to what's in the fine print. Find out in advance exactly what you're going to be charged, and ask about service fees and taxes. In 2002 a reader of *The New York Times* wrote a letter to the travel section to say that he'd found a cheaper alternative to renting cell phones: Simply buy a cell phone in Europe, where it's cheaper because there are no contracts to sign and you buy as many minutes as you'd like to use. Additionally, there are no charges for incoming calls, whether they originate next door or overseas, as long as you stay within the country. (If you leave the country, you're charged more money for incoming calls as well as a roaming fee.)

Useful vocabulary: *páginas amarillas* (yellow pages); *llamada* (telephone call); and *no cuelgue* (hold on, don't hang up).

Terrorism

It is easy to refer to the days before September 11 as "normal," especially regarding international travel. But I don't believe we should pine for those days, which really were "abnormal," as events have shown us. American travelers—and Canadians, too—must accept the fact that we are no longer immune to terrorist acts, on our own soil or on that of other nations. In an article entitled "Aftermath: Invaders; Who Hates the U.S.? Who Loves It?" (Elaine Sciolino, *The New York Times*, September 23, 2001), the writer reminded readers that nearly four decades ago, novelist Kurt Vonnegut Jr. captured the problem of the American image abroad "when he put these words into the mouth of a fictitious American ambassador who had been fired for pessimism: 'The highest possible form of treason is to say that Americans aren't loved wherever they go, whatever they do.'" We must also accept that we will probably have to pay more to travel and to help pay for the new (and expensive) security systems and programs we must now install in our airports and other public transportation centers. Additionally, I think we can count on travel taking longer than it once did (at every time during the year, not just during holidays), and we will need to practice the arts of courtesy and patience while we are all trying to figure out how to foil terrorists.

At one time planning a trip to Spain did not require making a call to the U.S. State Department, but I urge readers planning a trip to Northern Spain to first read the State Department's profile of Spain. When I recently browsed its website (travel.state.gov/travel_warnings.html), I found a surprising amount of information about where embassies are located, crime, previous episodes of violence in Spain, medical facilities and insurance, traffic safety and road conditions, and the like. Mostly due to Basque terrorist activity, Spain is included on the State Department's list of public announcements to Americans traveling abroad. (Public announcements are "a means to disseminate information about terrorist threats and other relatively short-term and/or trans-national conditions posing significant risks to the security of American travelers. They are made any time there is a perceived threat and usually have Americans as a particular target group. In the past, public announcements have been issued to deal with short-term coups, bomb threats to airlines, violence by terrorists and anniversary dates of specific terrorist events.") A public announcement is not the same as a travel warning, which is issued when the State Department decides, "based on all relevant information, to recommend that Americans avoid travel to a certain country." I mention all this not to create reasons for you to be afraid of traveling to Spain; rather, I've read that the State Department is extremely liberal in issuing travel warnings and public announcements, which is to say that it interprets *every* incident as serious. The State Department really cannot leave any stone unturned in its efforts to inform the public, so I think you should embrace a policy of "know before you go": Read up on everything, but do not allow yourself to be unnecessarily alarmed by insignificant incidents. I have found the State Department's consular information sheets particularly helpful—they're very detailed and less alarming. You may also call 202-647-6575 for information on travel warnings and public announcements.

Though some of the following tips may seem obvious, I think they are worth reflecting upon as you prepare for your trip. ~Register with the nearest embassy if it will make you feel better upon arrival. ~Pack clothes that don't make you immediately stand out from the locals. (Don't bring that really comfortable sweatshirt with the American flag emblazoned on the front, or your favorite college T-shirt.) ~Select either very expensive hotels or budget hotels. (The logic here is that moderately priced hotels tend to attract package tourists, a more obvious target.) I do want to add here, however, that I personally will not stay in expensive hotels just to feel more secure. If I choose to stay at a high-end place, it will be because I want to, not because I'm afraid to stay at a more modest place. Thinking, aware travelers are always on their toes, regardless of the threat of a terrorist attack.

A book you might want to take a look at is *The Worst-Case Scenario Survival Handbook: Travel* (Joshua Piven and David Borgenicht, Chronicle Books, San Francisco, 2001). Though it contains some humor, this little volume is really meant to be helpful, perhaps saving your life or someone else's. Some of the more threatening entries include "How to Survive an Airplane Crash," "How to Escape When Tied Up," "How to Survive a Hostage Situation," and "How to Survive a Riot." The appendix includes tips on general travel strategies, packing, flying, hotels, and travel in dangerous places, as well as a glossary of foreign emergency phrases.

In the aftermath of the horrific and senseless terrorist attacks on the World Trade Center and the Pentagon, it struck me profoundly that not only do I refuse to be made to feel like a prisoner in my own city and nation, but places in the world like Northern Spain became, in a matter of a few days, ever more precious and exceptional, more important than ever to experience at least once. I will exercise caution and plan carefully, but I will continue to fly overseas, and I hope my fellow American citizens and Canadian neighbors will reach the same conclusion: that we must not allow terrorists to win. I believe that, contrary to one's initial reaction, staying home does not make us safe. The first goal of all terrorists is to intimidate and inspire fear in people. Staying home is equal to a victory, a major one, for terrorists. If terrorist attacks are always within the realm of possibility, then so are the mundane activities of our daily existence, such as walking out the front door and picking up the morning newspaper, standing on a ladder and cleaning the leaves out of the gutter, or carrying clothes a few blocks away to the dry cleaner—each of which carries the risk of falling down and hitting our head on the sidewalk or the stone steps or the fire hydrant—not to mention drunk driving accidents, street crimes, hate crimes, heart attacks, rape, or murder.

I compile books like this because I have a deep respect for the people, the culture, and the religion of the particular place I'm immersing myself in, and I assume that my readers share this respect. I believe we are all, in a small way, promoting international understanding by reading about another place and traveling there. Gail Cornell (founder and president of the wonderful tour operator Archetours) and her staff sent me a holiday card last year with what I have found to be, in these uncertain times, a poem that is at once comforting and inspiring:

> Memory of travel
> is the stuff of our fairest dreams.
> Splendid cities. Plazas. Monuments.
> And landscapes thus pass before our eyes.
> And we enjoy the charming
> and impressive spectacles
> that we have formerly experienced.
> If we could stop again at those places
> where beauty never satiates,
> we could bear many dreary hours
> with a light heart
> and pursue life's long struggle
> with new energies.
> —Camillo Sitte, architect, 1889

Theft

Whether of the pickpocket variety or something more serious, theft can happen anywhere, in the finest neighborhood, on the bus, in a park, on a street corner. Northern Spain, unlike Barcelona and Seville, does not have a reputation for crime of any sort, not even pickpockets. (Madrid, however, requires travelers to be alert.) It bears repeating not to wear a waist pack, which is simply a neon magnet for thieves. I read about a lot of incidents that could easily have been avoided. In 1998 a lengthy piece in the travel section of *The Philadelphia Inquirer* told about a husband and wife traveling in France whose pouch containing their valuables was stolen. What made this story remarkable was that they were shocked the pouch was stolen. *I* was shocked reading their tale, because they seemed to think it was a good idea to *strap their pouch under the driver's seat of their rental car*. This couple had apparently traveled all over Europe and North America every year for twelve years, so they weren't exactly novices. I think it's amazing, however, that they hadn't been robbed earlier.

Rental cars are easily identified by their license plates and other markings that may not be obvious to you and me but that signify pay dirt to thieves. Do not leave anything, anything at all, in a rental car, even if you're parking it in a secure garage. My husband and I strictly follow one rule when we rent a car, which is that we never even put items in the trunk unless we're immediately getting in the car and driving away, as anyone watching us will then know there's something of value there. Hatchback-type cars are good to rent because you can back into spots against walls or trees, making it impossible to open the trunk.

Do not leave your passport, money, credit cards, important documents, or expensive camera equipment in your room. (Yes, American passports are very much a hot commodity.) The hotel safe? If the letters I read are any indication, leaving your belongings in a hotel safe—whether in your room or in the main office—is only slightly more reliable than leaving them out in plain view. Sometimes I hear that valuable jewelry was taken from a hotel safe, which I find baffling, as there really is only one safe place for valuable jewelry: your home. No occasion, meeting, or celebration, no matter how important or festive, requires bringing valuable jewelry. I happen to also find it ostentatious to display such wealth.

Pickpockets employ a number of tactics to prey on unaware travelers. Even if you travel often, live in a big city, and think you're savvy, professional thieves can usually pick you out immediately (and they'll also identify you as American if you're wearing the trademark sneakers and fanny pack). Beware the breastfeeding mother who begs you for money (while her other children surround you looking for a way into your pockets), the arguing couple who make a scene (while their accomplices work the crowd of onlookers), the tap on your shoulder at the baggage security checkpoint (when you turn around, someone's made off with your bags after they've passed through the X-ray machine)—anything at all that looks or feels like a setup. For a look at some common tricks, you might want to see *Traveler Beware!*, a video directed by a seventeen-year undercover cop, Kevin Coffey. This eye-opening program shows all the scams used to target business and holiday travelers. Coffey was founder of the Airport Crimes Detail and investigated literally thousands of crimes against tourists. He's been a guest on *Oprah* and *20/20* and has been featured in *The Wall Street Journal* and *USA Today*. The seventy-minute video is available from Penton Overseas (800-748-5804; www.pentonoverseas.com) and costs $14.95.

If, despite your best efforts, your valuables are stolen, go to the local police.

You'll have to fill out an official police report, but this is what helps later when you need to prove you were really robbed. Also, reporting thefts to the police alerts them that there is a persistent problem. You need to call your credit card companies (which is why you have written down these numbers in a separate place), make a trip to the American Express office if you've purchased traveler's checks, and go to the U.S. embassy to replace your passport.

Useful vocabulary: *¿Dónde está la comisaría?* ("Where is the police station?")

Tipping

Tipping in Spain is not the mystery some people perceive it to be. At many restaurants and cafés, the tip—known as *la propina*—is included in the total. You'll see this amount (usually about 15 percent) as a line item on your receipt. It is common to round the bill up, leaving anywhere from the equivalent of twenty-five cents to one dollar, but you are not obligated to do so. At *tapas* bars, leave the change; if it's a rather fancy *tapas* bar, leave the equivalent of about 5 percent of the bill. At family-run eating establishments, tips are usually not expected, but, again, if you feel the service has been especially helpful, leave an extra euro. If you stand at the counter in a café, a tip is not included in the bill, so you should leave some change. At fancy hotel bars, however, it's expected to leave more. If you receive exceptional service at any establishment, or if you want to return and be remembered, you should of course feel comfortable leaving a larger tip. Other tipping guidelines:

Taxi driver—leave the change, not more than ten percent of the total fare, and don't forget there is usually a supplement for luggage. Bathroom attendant—15 or 20 euro cents. Tour guides—about two to five euros, or a little more if they've given an exceptional or very long tour. Porter—about 50 euro cents (or more) per bag. Hotel doorman who calls you a cab—about 50 euro cents. Parking attendant who fetches your car—about 50 euro cents. Chambermaid—about two or three euros per night. Room service (if it's not already included)—about one euro. Barbers or hairdressers—about one euro depending on the cut and type of salon. Theater, movie, and bullfight usher—about one euro. For the above estimates relating to hotels, double the amounts if you're in a very expensive place. ~Be prepared to tip by putting some small change in your pocket *in advance,* before you arrive at the hotel, for example, or before you go to the theater.

Tourist (as in Being One)

Whether you travel often for business or are making a trip for the first time, let's face it: We're all tourists, and there's nothing shameful about that fact. Yes, it's true that one feels a real part of the daily grind when you blend in and are mistaken for a native; but since that's not likely to happen unless you live there, it's far better to just get on with it and have a good time.

Tourist Offices

I cannot stress adequately enough how helpful it is to contact the Tourist Office of Spain as soon as you learn you're going to Spain. Think of it as the ultimate resource: all the information you need is there, or the staff will know how to direct you elsewhere. At the New York office, I have never stumped anyone with my questions or requests, and I think readers have observed that I ask a lot of questions about a lot of little details.

A word of advice for dealing with tourist offices in general: It is not very helpful to say you're going to Northern Spain and would like "some information." Allow the staff to help you by providing them with as many details about your visit as you can: Is it your first trip? Where exactly in the north are you going? Do you need information only about hotels? The offices are stocked with mountains of material, but unless you ask for something specific, it will not automatically all be given to you. Sometimes I am amazed at what's available, at no charge—but you have to ask.

In addition to the materials mentioned within other sections of this book, a good overall publication to request is *Spain: The Official Travel Planner,* an oversize, forty-page booklet detailing travel basics—such as languages, time zones, currency, passports and visas, transportation, and communication—an overview of the regions of Spain as well as its national parks and other physical features, brief descriptions of Spain's major cities, local cuisines, sports, celebrations and festivals, handicrafts and fashion, trade fairs and conventions, travel routes around Spain (including the Camino de Santiago), regional websites, and a good map and mileage chart (previous editions of this handy guide included a detailed map, which was oddly omitted from more recent editions).

There are four tourist offices of Spain in the United States: Midwest (845 North Michigan Avenue, Suite 915-E, Chicago, IL 60611; 312-642-1992; fax: -9817), Northeast (666 Fifth Avenue, 35th floor, New York, NY 10103; 212-265-8822; fax: -8864), Southeast (1221 Brickell Avenue, Suite 1850, Miami, FL 33131; 305-358-1992; fax: -8223) and West Coast (8383 Wilshire Boulevard, Suite 956, Beverly Hills, CA 90211; 323-658-7188; fax: -1061), and one in Canada (2 Bloor Street West, Suite 3407, Toronto, ON M4W 3E2; 416-961-3131; fax: -1992). The website address is www.okspain.org.

Tour Operators

A list of full-service tour companies offering trips to Spain would fill a separate book, and it is not my intent to promote only one company or one type of trip. Frankly, while I do enthusiastically recommend the companies listed below, I'm bothered by the fact that too many tour operators today (including biking and hiking tour operators) focus on luxury meals and accommodations. A great number of people are seeking personalized service and knowledgeable guides but do not need or desire five-star elegance every step of the way. I often wonder if the luxury-oriented companies aren't missing the boat in reaching even more clients. That said, the combination of experience, insider's knowledge, and savvy guides that better tour operators offer is most definitely not found by searching the Web, for example, and organizing trips like these requires a substantial amount of research and attention to detail, which some travelers do not always have the time or inclination to do (and for which they are willing to pay a great deal). Organized tours these days now offer travelers more free time than in years past, as well as more choice in meals and excursions. The following are some companies that have appealed to me and offer an authentic experience:

Archaeological Tours (271 Madison Avenue, Suite 904, New York, NY 10016; 866-740-5130 or 212-986-3054; www.archaeologicaltrs.com). This quality company has been offering expert-led trips around the world for just shy of thirty years. Each tour features distinguished scholars who emphasize the historical, anthropological, and archaeological aspects of the areas visited. One of Archaeological's trips to Spain is the seventeen-day "Pilgrim's Road to Santiago de Compostela." This route begins in Saragossa and stops along the way at the cathedrals, monasteries, and shrines in and around Jaca, Pamplona, Burgos, León, and Oviedo. Participants also examine Celtic and Roman settlements, archaeological museums, and the fortress/palaces of the kings of Aragon and Navarre. One of the trip's highlights is a vespers Gregorian chant at the Monastery of Santo Domingo de Silo. I have recommended Archaeological in my previous editions and will continue to do so, primarily because of the noted scholars who accompany each group and because of the duration of each trip.

Archetours (260 West Broadway, Suite 2, New York, NY 10013; 800-770-3051 or 646-613-1896; fax: -1897; www.archetours.com). I first discovered Archetours (whose mottos are "World Leader in Architectural Travel Since 1995" and "Fun Tours with an Architectural Twist") at the Spanish tourist office here in New York. I was preparing for this book, and amidst all the other tour operator brochures on the shelves, the Archetours brochure caught my eye, so I picked it up and read it and knew I had found a like-minded company. The founder and president of Archetours, the personable Gail Cornell, holds a master's degree in architectural history and theory from Harvard and an MBA from Xavier University. She has designed almost all of the Archetours itineraries and led more than forty tours. As she explains in the Archetours brochure, she was determined to combine the two things she loves most in the world—travel and the study of architecture—into a career and way of life. She discovered that no other travel company was offering trips with that focus, and she was convinced that architectural travel was a niche that had yet to be filled. She left the security of a corporate career to begin this start-up operation, reasoning that there must be other people who enjoyed traipsing around the world to see architecture. She was right, and her enthusiasm is infectious.

I admit I have not traveled with Archetours on a full-length trip, but my experience with the company's services in Bilbao was top notch. Expert guides are Archetours' specialty, typically designers, architects, and art and architectural historians who accompany the small group for part or all of each trip. Daniel, our guide for the Guggenheim Bilbao, made the building and its collection come alive in a way I have never experienced before (see my enthusiastic report in the *Mis Favoritos* section). I am especially fond of Archetours because of the great number of Mediterranean destinations it specializes in. (Cornell herself is a frequent writer and speaker in classical Greek and Roman, Renaissance, and twentieth-century architecture.) "The Art and Architecture of Bilbao + Barcelona" is the one trip Archetours offers in Spain. While you surely know by now how I feel about combining Barcelona and Bilbao on the same trip, I would not hesitate to register for this one—and then I would add on two more weeks in Northern Spain! One particular feature that sets Archetours apart from nearly every other operator is the opportunity to arrange half- and full-day tours of the Guggenheim Bilbao, old Bilbao, San Sebastián, and some other sites for individuals, couples, and groups of friends who otherwise can't make the set tour dates. I think this is a wonderful offer (other tour operators, take note) as it allows independent travelers to participate in the Archetours experience without having to commit to an entire itinerary, and it provides Archetours with an additional source of revenue, not to mention the opportunity to gain new clients since travelers who enjoy their experience may very likely reserve for a trip in the future. Additionally, Archetours arranges custom trips for architectural firms, alumni and museum groups, arts organizations, and friends and families.

Cobblestone Small Group Tours (757 St. Charles Avenue, Suite 203, New Orleans, LA 70130; 800-227-7889 or 504-522-7888; fax: 525-1273; www.cobblestonetours.com). Cobblestone, founded in 1988 by Paulette Hurdlik, was the first U.S.-based agency to specialize in small group tours to the Basque homeland. Hurdlik was smitten with the Basque Country when she first visited and found that this part of southwestern France and Northern Spain was unfamiliar to most travelers. As a gesture of her affection for this region, Hurdlik developed the "Bilbao & Beyond" tour. (You may have seen this tour advertised in national magazines, as I did.) What impresses me about Cobblestone is its mission ("We distinguish ourselves by giving our guests an authentic experience") and how the staff carries it out: "We spend a minimum of two years immersing ourselves in a new region to create an itinerary of places rarely traveled. We also hand select our guides. We choose them for their knowledge, organizational skills, dynamic personalities, and English language proficiency." The "Bilbao & Beyond" trip is a thirteen-day itinerary that includes Fuenterrabía, Pamplona, San Sebastián, and Bilbao. Other trips include "Barcelona to Bilbao" (again these two cities on the same itinerary), "Wildflowers of the Pyrenees" (a thirteen-day tour of nature on both sides of the Pyrenees), and "Wine & Gastronomy" (a nine-day wine and food tour that includes three nights in San Sebastián, the city with "the best food you've never heard of," according to *Food & Wine*). More than 30 percent of Cobblestone's guests come from referrals.

Cross-Culture: Foreign Travel Programs Designed for Travelers Rather Than Tourists (52 High Point Drive, Amherst, MA 01002; 800-491-1148 or 413-256-6303; fax: 253-2303; www.crosscultureinc.com). Cross-Culture describes its trips as "group travel for people who think they don't like group travel, designed for travelers rather than tourists." In business for almost twenty years, the company has offered cultural and special interest tours and hiking programs in Europe, the Caribbean, Australia, and New Zealand. Its trips to Spain include one called "Exploring Spain: Bilboa, Salamanca & Madrid," an eleven-day itinerary that begins in Bilbao and includes visits to Santillana del Mar, the National Museum of Altamira, Burgos, Salamanca, Ávila, Segovia, and Madrid. While I'm not typically fond of an itinerary with so many stops in so few days, I very much respect Cross-Culture and do feel this is a more focused trip than, say, one that criss-crossed the entire country. (Cross-Culture offers another version of "Exploring Spain" that includes Seville, Granada, and Barcelona.) It's worth noting that Cross-Culture is one of the few—if not the only—tour company to include airfare in its prices. In an article in the travel section of *The New York Times* ("Ins & Outs of Small Groups," March 18, 2001), writer Betsy Wade singled out Cross-Country as having "more [different tours] than any other company contacted for this article."

The Wayfarers (172 Bellevue Avenue, Newport, RI 02840; 800-249-4620 or 401-849-5087; fax: -5878; www.thewayfarers.com). Founded in 1984, this operator offers walking vacations in Spain and eleven other countries. Walks are divided into four categories—Classic, Culture, Adventure, and Expeditions. The Wayfarers' walk leaders and managers are what make trips memorable. Its only Northern Spain walk is "Camino de Santiago," an Adventure walk, stopping in León, Astorga, Bierzo, Samos, Portomarin, and other towns before reaching Santiago.

If you do select a tour operator, ask a lot of questions so you get what you expect. For starters, ask if the operator employs its own staff or if it contracts with another company to run its trips. Remember, however, that standards differ around the world, and operators don't have control over every detail. For example, many beautiful old villas and inns do not have screens in the windows, and many first-class hotels don't have air conditioning. The price you pay for accommodations may not be the same as the posted rates, but you have to accept that you're paying for the convenience of someone else booking your trip. Tour operators also reserve the right to change itineraries, thus changing modes of transportation as well as hotels. If you have special needs, talk about them with the company in advance.

Trade Commission of Spain

The Trade Commission of Spain, in conjunction with the Spanish Institute of Foreign Trade (ICEX), promotes the sale of authentic Spanish food and wines, cuisine, and culture. It publishes several periodicals including *Spain Gourmetour*, *Wines from Spain*, and *Foods from Spain*, with the intention of educating retailers about trends in Spanish comestibles. *Spain Gourmetour*, the commission's main tool for information, is also very consumer friendly in its writing and presentation. Readers especially interested in the foods and wines of Spain, as well as travel information, are invited to request a complimentary issue from the Trade Commission (405 Lexington Avenue, New York, NY 10174; 212-661-4959). Like trade commissions representing other countries, the Trade Commission of Spain works primarily with journalists, chefs, teachers, retailers, and instructors; the content of its printed materials is therefore quite substantial, but quantities are also limited, and the staff has kindly asked me to emphasize that only readers with a serious interest in and passion for these topics request material. While the staff is enthusiastic about educating the general public and sharing resources about Spanish cuisine for importers and retailers, it also doesn't want to disappoint anyone. Interested readers should definitely browse the three excellent websites the Trade Commission maintains: oliveoilfromspain.com, cheesefromspain.com, and piquillopepper.com.

Travel Insurance

I have never purchased travel insurance because I have never determined that I need it, but if you think the risks to you are greater without it, it's worth considering. Ask yourself what it would cost if you needed to cancel or interrupt your trip, and how expensive it would be to replace any stolen possessions. If you have a medical condition or if a relative is ill, insurance might be a wise investment. First check to see if your existing health or homeowner's policy offers some protection. If you decide you need to purchase additional insurance, read all the fine print and make sure you understand it; compare deductibles; ask how your provider defines *pre-existing condition* and inquire if there are situations in which it would be waived; and check to see if the ceiling on medical expenses is adequate for your needs. Emergency medical insurance may be something to consider if you have a medical condition that could quickly put you at serious risk. Elderly travelers may want to consider it in any event, and they should be aware that Medicare does not cover expenses incurred outside the United States.

Travel insurance generally consists of five parts: trip cancellation or interruption coverage; trip delay coverage; emergency medical expenses during travel; emergency medical evacuation; and full-time medical and travel assistance. With a typical cancellation policy, you will be compensated for the nonrefundable deposit if the cancellation is due to a medical problem involving either yourself or a family member—essentially, for that which is uncontrollable. I have read repeatedly that it is not wise to use the insurance policy offered by a tour operator or cruise line, simply because it serves to protect the enterprise more than to benefit you or me. Therefore the best way to protect yourself from a tour operator that declares bankruptcy is to purchase travel insurance from a third-party insurer.

Predictably, there is new concern over coverage in the event of a terrorist attack after the events of September 11. Many readers may not realize that "a terrorist event" has been included in the trip cancellation or interruption clause of travel insurance policies for many years. However, most policies state that coverage only applies if the acts of terrorism occur in a foreign destination thirty days before the scheduled trip; other policies dictate only ten days before a visit. Additionally, if you've arranged a trip through a tour operator, and the operator offers an alternate trip to a different destination (where presumably there is not a threat of a terrorist attack), you are required to take that other trip or forfeit your coverage. It's worth noting again: read all the fine print, and ask a lot of questions. A quick way to compare policies and prices of travel insurance companies is to browse the website www.insuremytrip.net. Travel Guard International (1145 Clark Street, Stevens Point, WI 54481; 800-826-4919; www.travelguard.com) is one particular insurance company that has been in the spotlight since the September 11 tragedy because it has expanded its policy to cover acts of terrorism for people traveling to places where an incident has occurred within the previous twelve months.

U

Ultimo Aviso
Spanish for "last word" or more commonly "last call," as at the airport or the train station.

V

VAT (Value-Added Tax)
VAT is the tax amount that visitors to Spain (except those from EU member countries) are entitled to receive as a reimbursement. I have an entire file of conflicting information about the VAT, so even if you meet the eligibility requirements, be prepared for a potentially confusing procedure. Frankly, the procedure seems to be a lot of bother unless you are making a significant purchase, and it would be worth asking the retailer to simply not charge any tax (this worked once for me). But for those who are determined, you must: produce your passport at the time of the purchase; spend at least 90 euros at one store (but retailers are not required to partic-

ipate in the program or to match the dollar amount, so ask first); and produce receipts *and* merchandise for inspection at customs. Not all shops participate in the VAT program, but those that do are identified by a "Tax Free for Tourists" sign displayed either in the store's window or near the cash register. Note that some shops don't have the necessary *formulario* (form), and that the paperwork must be stamped by customs officials *before* you enter the United States. Problems seem to arise when the customs desk is closed, although if you'll be in any other country before you return to the States, a customs stamp from that country is also valid (if the officials are willing to validate your forms). Also, it seems customs officials are rather lax at some borders, vigilant at others.

For a 20 percent fee, a company called Global Refund will process your refund if you don't have the time—or are too intimidated—to do it yourself. Many stores in Spain are now affiliates; the refund form is known as a Shopping Cheque. Once your forms are stamped, you're able to receive a refund—in the form of cash, check, or charge card credit—right away at an ETS counter (or you can mail the forms from home). If you attempted to have your forms validated in Spain but were thwarted in your efforts, or if it has been more than three months since you applied for a refund, contact Global Refund (99 Main Street, Nyack, NY 10960; 800-566-9828; www.globalrefund.com).

W

Weather

The summer months are definitely the best time of year to visit Northern Spain—temperatures are definitely warmer, and it does rain less. The editors of Time-Life's *The Cooking of Spain and Portugal* write that "any Galician will tell you that it rains for an hour or so every day in Galicia, except perhaps in the summer. Again, rain here is not like rain in any other land. The sweeping water magnifies and sharpens the look of the countryside. The earth of Galicia is big, swollen, foggy and lush. Geologically, this is by far the oldest part of the Iberian Peninsula; Galicia bulged fresh out of the sea millions of years before any of the rest, and soon half the new earth fell back into the water and disappeared, causing the strange wonderful look of the coast. . . . Gray stone villages and country houses dot the land. From sunrise till late afternoon you see them through a low-lying, very thin mist like a veil that is bluish green, opaque and trembling over the earth. Galicia, the least known region of Spain, is perhaps the most astonishingly beautiful."

On my last trip to Northern Spain, which was in the month of October, I had to laugh when I browsed the Weather Underground website (see below). I even saved the page, which featured a five-day forecast: Today: rain; Tonight: chance of rain; Saturday: chance of rain; Saturday night: rain; Sunday: chance of rain; Sunday night: rain; Monday: rain; Monday night: rain; Tuesday: scattered clouds;

Tuesday night: scattered clouds. But it's important to keep in mind that even when it rains, it doesn't typically rain all day long or even very hard. Most days are punctuated with brilliant blue skies and sunshine, though there are certainly more of these days in the summer and early fall. Fall, in fact, may be the most beautiful time of year in Northern Spain (many places in the world are wonderful at that time of year), but each season offers its own delights. Picking the "perfect" time of year is subjective; when it's rainy and cold—and it does get quite chilly in the winter months—you don't have the pleasure of picnicking and hiking outdoors, but prices drop and you'll have little trouble securing reservations at hotels and restaurants. Go when you have the opportunity, and that will be your experience, your Spain. It's true that peak season means higher prices and more people, but if you've determined you want to be in Pamplona in July, then the cost and the crowds don't matter.

If you're a weather maven, you'll love *Fodor's World Weather Guide* (E. A. Pierce and C. G. Smith, 1998; published in 1998 in Great Britain as *The Hutchinson World Weather Guide, New Edition* by Helicon, Oxford). As frequent business and pleasure travelers know, average daily temperatures are only a small part of what you need to know about the weather. It is not helpful to learn that the average monthly temperature in Paris in April is 60 degrees without also knowing that the average number of rainy days is thirteen. This guide features weather specifics for more than two hundred countries and territories and also includes a map of the world's climate regions; humidity and wind chill charts; a centigrade and Fahrenheit conversion table; a rainfall conversion table; and a bibliography pointing interested readers to other sources.

A good website to check is www.rainorshine.com, which provides five-day forecasts for eight hundred cities around the world. Not that five-day forecasts may be predicted with 100 percent accuracy, but it's still interesting to take a look. ~weather.com allows you to explore historical data for 7,462 locations, ten-day forecasts for 77,000 locations worldwide, record lows and highs, and other useful weather-related information. ~weatherbase.com provides monthly data for perhaps fewer cities than weather.com. ~www.wunderground.com, as noted above, offers a five-day forecast along with a heat index, humidity, dewpoint, sunrise, moonrise, moonset, moon phase, and wind, as well as hurricane archive and historical conditions.

Websites

Personally, I don't find a single one of the following websites better than the Spanish Tourist Office or the appropriate book, but a few offer some good features:

www.wild-spain.com: a good resource for readers interested in outdoor activities and natural preservation as the site acts an "information service in English on nature and outdoor travel in Spain." Visitors will find news briefs on projects and other activities that affect Spain's natural environment. Past briefs have included information on volunteer summer camps in national parks (such as the Picos de Europa and the Natural Reserve of Santoña y Noja) and the National Hydrological Plan. Viewers may browse lists of related articles, photographs, reading suggestions, and a directory of organizations whose work is related to nature and outdoor travel in Spain.

www.searchiberia.com: A great general site that serves as a search engine for Spain and Portugal. This is one of the best websites I've ever browsed (I learned about the Elemadrid language school at this site). You may select from fifteen categories, including "Health and Humanities," "Arts and Entertainment," "Computers and Internet," "Society and Culture," "Regions and Cities," "Sports and Recreation," and "Travel."

www.tienda.com: "Fine Products from Spain" is this company's slogan.

Women Travelers

Whether a woman is traveling solo or not, lots of great advice is offered in *Travelers' Tales: Gutsy Women, Travel Tips and Wisdom for the Road* (Marybeth Bond, Travelers' Tales, San Francisco, distributed by O'Reilly & Associates, 1996). This packable little book is filled with dozens and dozens of useful tips for women of all ages who want to travel or who already travel a lot. Bond has traveled all over the world, much of it alone, and she shares a multitude of advice from her own journeys as well as those of other female travelers. Chapters address safety and security; health and hygiene; romance and unwelcome advances; money, bargaining, and tipping; traveling solo; mother-daughter travel; travel with children; and more. Another good book is *Travel Tips for the Sophisticated Woman* (Laura Vestanen, Xlibris, 2001), which is a more practical book than Bond's and offers great tips for all aspects of travel in Europe and North America.

The Women's Travel Club may be of interest. Founded by Phyllis Stoller, it plans numerous domestic and international trips each year and guarantees everyone a roommate. Its great list of travel safety tips was featured on NBC's *Today* as well as in *Travel + Leisure* (August 1999). Membership is $35 a year, and members receive a newsletter. Contact them at 800-480-4448; www.womenstravelclub.com.

World Heritage Sites

The list of World Heritage Sites, founded by UNESCO—the United Nations' cultural branch—encompasses 630 natural and cultural sites "of outstanding value to humanity" in 118 countries. UNESCO reports that Spain is home to more World Heritage Sites than any other country. The sites in Northern Spain are: Burgos Cathedral (added in 1984), the Altamira caves (1985), the monuments of Oviedo and the Kingdom of the Asturias (1985), the old town of Santiago de Compostela

(1985), the route of Santiago de Compostela (1993; this refers to the portion from Roncesvalles to Santiago), and the Roman walls of Lugo (2000). Readers may learn more about UNESCO and its World Heritage Sites by browsing its website: www.unesco.org/whc/heritage.htm.

World Monuments Fund

The World Monuments Fund (WMF), founded in 1965, advocates the preservation of important works of art and architecture from around the world and, through contributions, supports special conservation projects. The World Monuments Watch (WMW) program was initiated in 1996 by WMF and by founding sponsor American Express. Every two years WMF produces its *List of 100 Most Endangered Sites* to bring to public awareness the need to support special projects for these monuments. At this writing, there are nine WMF projects in Spain that have received grants, including Oviedo Cathedral (the only project in the north); but within the next few years additional Spanish projects may be added. For more information about WMF's conservation projects, or to make a donation or become a member (members enjoy lectures, gallery openings, a quarterly magazine, and special trips), contact WMF at 94 Madison Avenue, ninth floor, New York, NY 10016; 800-547-9171 or 646-424-9594; www.wmf.org.

A great book to have to learn more about the World Monuments Watch—and the fragile treasures in it—is *Vanishing Histories: 100 Endangered Sites from the World Monuments Watch* (Colin Amery with Brian Curran, Harry N. Abrams, 2002). Gorgeous color photographs of each site, whether famous or obscure, accompany the site's history and the details of its struggle for survival.

Abigail y Yo

BY CALVIN TRILLIN

editor's note

I have managed to state, *somewhere* within the text of nearly all the books in *The Collected Traveler* series, that Calvin Trillin is one of my favorite writers. Clearly, as Trillin divulges in this piece, it is never too late to begin learning another language—and it is simultaneously challenging and fun.

Me expressing what an invaluable ability it is to speak a second (or third or fourth) language will not likely be persuasive; but recently I read an essay in *The Washington Post Book World* by John Keegan, who has been referred to as our greatest living military historian. (He's the author of a good many excellent books, including *The First World War, The Face of Battle,* and *A History of Warfare*.) The essay's broad title was "The Writing Life"; *Book World* periodically invites writers to contribute a piece about the life of a writer, and at the end of Keegan's piece, he addressed what factors helped him in the art of writing. He shared that he felt he has long had an ear for the rhythm of prose, which is essential to readability. "The other great help was foreign languages. I had been taught Latin and Greek until I was sixteen and had learned French very well. Knowledge of foreign languages is the best of guides to the structure and subtleties of one's own. It is, alas, dying out in the English-speaking world, which all foreigners now want to join. The result is that English-speaking writers don't write as well as those even of the last generation did, while strange varieties of English are taking form outside its historic heartland. The absolute certainty of touch that came so naturally to Rudyard Kipling and Evelyn Waugh is probably gone forever. I deeply regret its disappearance." Though I realize Keegan is writing about literature, mostly, I think his statement may be applied to North American travelers as well.

CALVIN TRILLIN is the author of *The Tummy Trilogy* (Farrar, Straus & Giroux, 1994; Noonday Press, 1994), *Travels with Alice* (Avon, 1990), *Messages from My Father* (Farrar, Straus & Giroux, 1996; Noonday Press, 1997), *Remembering Denny* (Farrar, Straus & Giroux, 1993), *Deadline Poet* (Warner, 1995), and *Tepper Isn't Going Out* (Random House, 2001), among many others.

I suppose you could say that Abigail was living out my fantasies, if you were the sort of person who liked to rub it in. Abigail, my older daughter, had decided to spend the semester studying in Madrid. In long letters and Sunday telephone calls, she filled us in on her life in Spain: sunny afternoons at the boat pond in El Retiro Gardens, a weekend spent at the annual fiesta of a tiny village in Galicia, long discussions in the dormitory of a Spanish friend she had met in the subway and sometimes referred to as *la amiga del Metro*.

"It sounds absolutely terrific," my wife said one Sunday on the telephone, just after Abigail told us how exciting it was to be able to understand lectures in Spanish.

There was a pause in the conversation—a pause that I, in playing the role fathers have traditionally played in expensive long-distance conversations with college-age children, might have been expected to fill with "Well, okay. Fine. Good-bye." Instead, I said, "I'd like to tell you how I feel about all this, Abigail, but I don't know the Spanish word for 'envy.'"

I might have known that word. I might have known a lot of Spanish words. When I was in Spain just after college, I had the opportunity to remain in Madrid for a year to study, and I didn't take it—a decision I think about often, in the way a businessman might reflect on his decision to pass up that patch of scrubland that is now occupied by the third-largest-grossing shopping center west of the Mississippi.

I was serious about Spanish. I was never serious about French. Sure, I still exchange sour remarks with a Paris taxi-driver now and then, but my public announcement that, more or less as a matter of policy, I do not use verbs in French was widely taken as an acknowledgment that I could no longer be considered a diligent student of the language. I never made a systematic attempt at Italian, and I have simply ignored German. Spanish is my foreign language.

More to the point, Spanish is not my foreign language. In my good moments, I've been able to say what I need to say in Spanish, although not in a way that is likely to attract compliments on my grammar and syntax. In my bad moments, my attempts to speak Spanish have a lot in common with my attempts to speak Italian, which is to say that they lean heavily on gestures. I have always had trouble understanding Spanish; there have been times when a paragraph of Spanish sounded to me like one long word.

Even when I seem to be doing pretty well in speaking Spanish, I can run out of it, the way someone might run out of flour or eggs. A few years after I passed up the chance to stay in Madrid, some friends and I went to Baja California to mark an occasion I can no longer remember, and I became the group's spokesman to the owner of our motel, a Mrs. Gonzales, who spoke no English. Toward the end of a very long evening, as I listened to her complain about some excess of celebration on our part, I suddenly realized that I had run out of Spanish. It wasn't merely that I couldn't think of the Spanish words for what I wanted to say. ("I am mortified, Mrs. Gonzales, to learn that someone in our group might have behaved in a manner so inappropriate, not to say disgusting.") I couldn't think of any Spanish words at all. Desperately rummaging around in the small bin of Spanish in my mind, I could come up with nothing but the title of a Calderón play I had once read, to no lasting effect, in a Spanish-literature course.

"Mrs. Gonzales," I said, "life is a dream."

She looked impressed and, I must say, surprised. She told me that I had said something really quite profound. I shrugged. It seemed the appropriately modest response; even if it hadn't been, it would have been all I could do until I managed to borrow a cup of Spanish from a neighbor. Eventually, I came to look back on the experience as just about the only time I had been truly impressive in a foreign language.

Every few years, I work up the energy to hurl myself again at the

Spanish language, in the hope of making the breakthrough that people who learn foreign languages are always talking about. The evidence of my failures clutters the house—the Spanish-language tapes jammed in the back of a drawer, the absolutely guaranteed three-volume teach-yourself-Spanish course that falls from the highest shelf in the closet as I fumble for a suitcase I thought I might have stashed up there some years ago. It has often occurred to me that I'll never speak Spanish. People who spend a lot of time around newspapers are afflicted with the ability to imagine what is sometimes called the drop head of their obituary—an obituary large enough to call for a drop head as well as the main headline has traditionally been the principal side benefit of the trade—and the drop head I have sometimes imagined for me is "Monolingual Reporter Succumbs."

Sometimes, though, I think my Spanish breakthrough is somewhere on the next cassette. When I decided to visit Abigail in Spain this spring, I decided at the same time to give Spanish one more try. For a few weeks, I spent an hour a day speaking Spanish with a young woman from Spain who was teaching at New York University. In Spanish, I told her a lot of things about America—how the wheat got to Kansas in the nineteenth century, for instance, which is probably something that nobody in her town in Spain speaks about very often—and she told me that I did not appear to know the difference between *por* and *para*. I think I learned a lot about Spanish from her, although I continue to believe that no one truly understands the difference between *por* and *para*. I bought a new Spanish dictionary. I also bought one of those pocket computers that translate from Spanish to English and back. On the plane to Madrid, I was carrying my Spanish-English dictionary, my translating computer, a copy of *The Old Gringo* in English and of *Gringo Viejo* in Spanish, an issue of a Madrid newspaper called *El País*, and a volume that I would have to name if I happened to be among those asked by some literary journal to list their favorite books of the year—*301 Spanish Verbs*. In the interests of moderation, I had passed up *501 Spanish Verbs*, by the same author, but I felt overequipped anyway. I felt like some Wall Street hobbyist who, upon deciding he might like to do some biking around the city, immediately buys a fourteen-hundred-dollar Italian racing bike, a pair of imported leather biking gloves, three kinds of pumps, and the sort of clothing that might be seen on a competitor in the Tour de France. I was prepared. When I arrived in Spain, I intended to speak Spanish. I intended to understand Spanish. I had a fallback position, of course: Abigail speaks very good English.

"Just give me a little hint of what it's about," I said to Ginny. Abigail and I and Ginny, a fellow-student of Abigail's at the Instituto Internaçional, were in a *tapas* bar off the Plaza Mayor, eating a sort of seafood salad and a pile of tiny fried fish. We were discussing a Cervantes play called *El Retablo de las Maravillas,* which Ginny and some other American students were going to put on at the Instituto the following week. I was hoping that by having Ginny give me some idea of the plot I could avoid getting off on the wrong foot when I saw the actual performance. What I dreaded was finding myself, just before the final curtain, suddenly disabused of the notion that I had been watching a play about the early days of major-league baseball.

Abigail didn't seem concerned about being able to understand the play. Basically, Abigail could understand Spanish. It hadn't come in any blinding flash, she said. At some point, she simply realized that she had been taking in what was said by the contestants on a television game show that the family she lived with watched every Monday night—*El Precio Justo,* a two-hour Spanish version of *The Price Is Right*.

My record in attempting to understand Spanish theatrical works was not encouraging. As far as I could remember, I had last sat in the audience of a Spanish production, game but bewildered, in Vermont, where, many years ago, I spent several weeks in the summer Spanish program at Middlebury College. The Middlebury summer language programs are renowned in the field; I must be one of their rare failure stories. The summer I was there, Middlebury had half a dozen programs—each of them using a language not simply as the language of instruction but as the language that students were expected to speak in the dining hall and the dormitories and on the playing fields. The students were virtually all Americans, many of them high-school language teachers working on their master's degrees, but within days most of them had fallen into the stereotypes then identified with the countries whose languages they were studying. It was common to refer to, say, those studying French as "the French"—and to take it for granted that they would spend a lot of time criticizing one another's accents. "The Russians" were stiff-necked and basically impossible to deal with when it came to assigning hours and tables in a shared dining hall. If a great horde of people, all of them looking perfectly capable of singing loud drinking songs, burst into the local tavern together, one of the regulars was bound to mutter, in English, "Jesus, it's the Germans." I can't actually remember what "the Spanish" were noted for, but if my own experience is any guide I'm afraid it may have been indolence.

This time, though, I was serious—which was why I wanted Ginny to give me a little head start on *El Retablo de las Maravillas*. She seemed willing. "It's about some gypsies who come to a village and scare the villagers," she told me. "The villagers are kind of conformists, and the gypsies say, for instance, that all smart people can see rats on this screen. So all the villagers say they can see rats."

Ginny fell silent and began poking around in the seafood salad for one of the less suspicious-looking creatures.

"That's it?" I asked.

"Well, I don't want to give away the whole plot," she said.

I was somewhat comforted by the knowledge that when I saw *El Retablo de las Maravillas* I would have more stage Spanish under my belt. Abigail and I had decided to spend the weekend in Barcelona, and a young friend of ours who was living there, Anya Schiffrin, had promised to take us around to some of her favorite attractions—none of which, I suspect, would have made a list compiled by the bureau of tourism. I knew that on Anya's tour we'd be seeing the show at an old music hall and at the sort of night club where the entertainment is provided by the waitresses and the barman and, now and then, an inspired amateur from among the evening's clientele.

By the time we took our seats that Friday night at the music hall, a place called El Molino, I was feeling that the first two days of my latest attempt at speaking Spanish had gone pretty well. In both Madrid and Barcelona, I had used only Spanish at the hotel—I knew that virtually everyone involved spoke English, but I pretended that I was at Middlebury—and I hadn't ended up in the broom closet. I had chatted fairly easily, if briefly, with some of the venders at La Boquería, Barcelona's stupendous public market, where Abigail and I exhausted our Spanish adjectives expressing appreciation of a sandwich made by rubbing tomatoes on the inside of a toasted baguette and then loading it up with fresh anchovies. The unfortunate episode at lunch—when I spoke to the waiter, he replied to Anya—was something I had decided to accept as a small but temporary setback.

El Molino turned out to be an appropriately rococo old vaudeville house with two tiers of ornate boxes overlooking the orchestra seats. It was painted almost entirely red—what seemed to be dozens of coats, resulting in the kind of shiny finish that certain expensive decorators put on the dining-room walls of rich people in Manhattan. Although the audience sat in conventional rows of theatre seats, drinks were served, and the price of admission was folded into the price of the first drink. To accommodate the drinks, there was a narrow counter running along the backs of the seats in front of you—a menace as well as a convenience, Anya warned us, because if the man in front of you absent-mindedly put his arm around his wife's shoulders he'd be likely to put your beer right in your lap.

The show at El Molino featured chorus girls wearing a staggering array of costumes that I would describe, in general, as having too many feathers in some places and not enough in others. There were also chorus boys, although that term probably reflects insufficient respect for their age. Most of the production numbers had people in feathers moving in unison on the stage—dancing in the sense that Rex Harrison in *My Fair Lady* was singing. During feather changes, pairs of comics came out to do sketches that required nearly constant leering. The themes of the production numbers were established by ever-changing backdrops. Anya apparently noticed a puzzled look on my face when, in front of a backdrop that was difficult to identify except for a street sign that said "Via Veneto," a woman sang a song to a man while being accompanied, more or less, by eight or ten chorus girls who were dressed in something suggesting Latin-American peasant women— although I can't say I've ever actually seen a Latin-American peasant woman wearing a rug on her head. "Every day, she's heard the voice of a man, and she fell in love with him through the voice, and that's him," Anya whispered. "Why the costumes I don't know."

The audience at El Molino—certainly including our party— was enthusiastic, but I wouldn't claim that I actually followed what was being said onstage. I had the same problem the next night at the Bodega Bohemia, where the only entertainer who didn't carry drinks or wipe down the bar during the other acts was the piano player—a gray-haired old gentleman in a business suit who looked like a retired high-school principal returning to accompany the senior boys' choir, just to keep his hand in. In both places, people spoke rapidly and used a lot of slang and double-entendres. I explained to Anya that I was working, at best, with single-entendre Spanish.

Anya told us that it had taken her two or three trips to catch on to the patter at El Molino herself. Abigail reminded me that in Barcelona I had enjoyed a triumph or two in comprehending ordinary, non-leering Spanish. At lunch one day at a little seafood place in Barceloneta, the dock area, the proprietress, a jolly friend of Anya's, had told us why she avoids long trips on boats or airplanes: she believes that an accident could easily put her in the water, she can't swim, and she therefore assumes that she would be eaten by sharks. As I was telling Abigail that those precautions sounded sensible enough to me, I realized that they had been presented to us in Spanish.

I didn't feel that my Spanish had been tested on some of our stops. That had certainly been true at a dance hall Anya took us to after Bodega Bohemia—a vast place where a number of the most lavishly dressed ballroom dancers seemed to get along just as well without partners. At the event we attended on Sunday, a Sevillana festival at the Barcelona bullring, I don't think anyone could have made out all the lyrics blaring from the huge loudspeakers on the stage. In the ring, thousands of Andalusians, most of them people who had come to Catalonia for factory jobs, danced and sang and waved green-and-white Andalusian flags for seven or eight hours. Some of the participants were in the sort of clothing that Americans associate with flamenco dancers, but some of them had got into costume by wearing green jackets or green hats; looking out on the crowd, I had to shake off the impression that I had come across a horde of Boston Irish who had been taken suddenly and implausibly with a passion for melodramatic dancing.

As we drove from the Sevillana festival to our final meal in Barcelona, I told Anya how much we had enjoyed the tour.

"Oh, no!" she said. "I forgot to take you to the museum of the dead, where they let you sit in the hearses."

"Not to worry," I said. "It's always nice to save one treat for the next visit."

I understood the taxi-driver who drove us in from the Madrid airport when we returned from Barcelona. We talked about Americans and Russians. He said that Americans were more open than Russians. I thought about telling him how the Russians had behaved when they had to share the dining hall at Middlebury, even though I was quite aware that those Russians were not real Russians. When you're uncertain in a language, there's a temptation to use what you've got. The taxi-driver told me not to worry about not understanding the comics at El Molino; he said Catalans didn't talk right. The taxi-driver spoke excellent Spanish himself. It occurred to me that if I were put in charge of the government broadcasting system in Spain the first two announcers I'd try to hire would be the taxi-driver and the proprietress of the seafood restaurant in Barceloneta. She might even be willing to come to Madrid for the broadcasts, since you don't have to fly over any water to get there from Barcelona.

The conversations at the restaurant and in the taxi had been brief, of course. The real test was whether I could understand a lecture given by one of Abigail's professors. Abigail told me that the lecture in her politics class would be about the period in the late fifties when Franco's regime gradually began to change—a period that happened to coincide with my first visit to Spain. She was, I later realized, giving me a little head start. In class the next morning, I sat next to Abigail. I thought I was ready. I had spent some of the previous evening thumbing through *301 Spanish Verbs*. The professor began. He spoke beautifully clear Spanish—better, even, than the taxi-driver's. He spoke about the technocrats coming into government and about the role of Opus Dei and about the mystery that persists as to why Franco permitted the sort of economic development that he must have known would lead to an expanded middle class and demands for more freedom. I took notes.

"I understood everything," I said to Abigail at the end of the lecture.

Abigail said that she was proud of me. "I knew you could do it," she said. "Maybe you ought to come to my history class tomorrow. You could be on a roll."

I understood history, too. I was gaining confidence. I did pretty well in conversation with Abigail's *amiga del Metro* and at dinner with the family Abigail was living with. I was beginning to think that if I were staying on until the next Monday I might be ready for a crack at *El Precio Justo*. The dramatic piece at hand, though, was not *El Precio Justo* but *El Retablo de las Maravillas*. On the night before I left Spain, we took our seats in the Instituto's auditorium for the performance.

I couldn't understand it. I couldn't understand it at all. For one awful moment, I was convinced that it was being done in a language other than Spanish. When it was over, all I knew about it was that some gypsies came to a village where the peasants were rather conformist, and told the peasants that smart people would be able to see the rats on a screen.

"What was that about?" I said to Abigail at the end of the play.

"I don't know," Abigail said. "I couldn't understand it."

At first, I thought Abigail was just trying to make me feel better, but then it turned out that her friends hadn't understood it, either. Later in the evening, I talked to Abigail's history teacher—a native of Majorca who had appeared in the same play in high school—and she said she'd had some trouble understanding the play herself. That did make me feel better, although I was pretty sure that the history teacher had never been in doubt as to what language was being spoken.

The history teacher and I were speaking Spanish, of course. I decided that *El Retablo de las Maravillas* had been a special case. So was El Molino. Of course, you could argue that a lecture at the Instituto Internaçional on politics or history would also amount to a special case—if you were that sort of person. The professor, after all, has organized the material systematically, and is accustomed to speaking to foreigners, and is dealing with a subject rich in cognates. That's not the way I look at it. When I think of those lectures, what I remember is an encounter I had with a couple of American students after Abigail's history class. Abigail had suggested that I not accompany her to her history-of-art lecture ("Don't press your luck"), and I was on my way to the Metro.

"You're Abigail's father, aren't you?" one of the students said.

"We saw you in history," the other one explained. "We thought you must be really bored sitting there, unless—Do you understand Spanish?"

I hesitated for only a second. "Yes," I said. "Yes, I do."

Táboa de equivalencias

Euros	Pesetas	Euros	Pesetas
1,00	166,386*	9,00	1.497
1,50	250	10,00	1.664
2,00	333	20,00	3.328
2,50	416	25,00	4.160
3,00	499	30,00	4.992
3,50	582	40,00	6.655
4,00	666	50,00	8.319
4,50	749	60,00	9.983
5,00	832	100,00	16.639
6,00	998	200,00	33.277
7,00	1.165	400,00	66.554
8,00	1.331	500,00	83.193

(*) tipo de conversión irrevocable

Las Noticias Cotidianas— El Quiosco
(The Daily News—Points of View)

"To understand Spain it is important to remember that at least seven peoples, seven very different and conflicting cultures were mixed into one incredible medley creating the origin of the Spanish kingdoms: Iberians, Celts, Phoenicians, Carthaginians, Romans, Visigoths, and Moors. To complete the intricate mosaic, there were three religions—Christianity, Islam, and Judaism. This was the seething pot that the 'Catholic Kings,' Ferdinand and Isabella, set out to unify into the one nation of Spain."

—Manuel Canovas, SPANISH STYLE

" 'There are no other countries like Spain,' Robert Jordan said politely. 'You are right,' Fernando said. 'There is no other country in the world like Spain.' 'Hast thou ever seen any other country?' the woman asked him. 'Nay,' said Fernando. 'Nor do I wish to.' "

—Ernest Hemingway, FOR WHOM THE BELL TOLLS

Letter from Spain

By Alastair Reid

~

editor's note

Scottish writer and poet Alastair Reid lived in Spain during the 1960s and early '70s and filed a number of "Letter from Spain" missives for *The New Yorker*. I knew I wanted to include at least one of them in this edition, and after reviewing a few, I singled this one out as the best representative of a certain period in Spain: still under the (fading) regime of Franco but "newly invaded by civilization" and about ready to make sweeping changes that would, as we have witnessed, change Spain overnight.

Writer Bill Buford has described Reid as "a word magician," a compliment with which I wholeheartedly agree. Another "Letter" I was considering, dated September 17, 1962, begins with the sentence "Year in, year out, summer comes down on Spain like a great enveloping quilt, muffling not only most of the normal human activity of the country but most of the rebellious thoughts lurking in the minds of those Spaniards who have been muttering patiently for years about their situation." There is something so wonderful about that image of dry summer heat, and each of Reid's communiqués contains language equally as seductive. In that same piece from 1962, Reid noted that that particular summer saw an unsurpassed number of tourists, who had counted, as they still can today, on the predictable sun. But at the letter's end he noted that in a recent speech Franco remarked that what he wanted for Spain was "a place in the sun." Reid's Spanish friend responded to the speech by snorting, "'A place in the sun'! . . . That's easy—that's what we've always had. But that isn't enough, not anymore."

ALASTAIR REID is the author of more than twenty books of poetry and prose, including *Oases: Poems and Prose* (Canongate, 1997), *Eternal Spain* (Harry Abrams, 1991), and *Whereabouts: Notes on Being a Foreigner* (White Pine Press, 1992). He has also translated a number of works from Spanish to English, including *Extravagaria* (Pablo Neruda, Noonday Press, 2001), *Fully Empowered* (Pablo Neruda, 2001), and *A Fountain, a House of Stone: Poems* (Heberto Padilla, 1991), the last two published by Farrar, Straus & Giroux.

One dusty afternoon recently, as I was making my laborious way from Barcelona through the Pyrenees into France by a series of lurching, museum-worthy trains, I found myself in a place called Tardienta—a small gray station platform heavy with the hot afternoon and piled with crated chickens, pigeons, and amorphous bundles—with some two hours to wait for a train that only my faith in Spain told me would arrive. The station had a café of sorts, and I went in out of the blinding sun, exchanged politenesses with the company, and sat down to while away whatever time I had to; anyone who ever considers settling in Spain ought to take lessons in sheer waiting, for it is an art that Spaniards have not only mastered but triumphed over.

My companions, apart from one forlorn-looking foreigner, were principally a group of railwaymen; earlier I had seen them carrying steel railway ties that would have given pause to professional strong men, and now they were tearing into their bread and wine, playing dominoes, and laughing and insulting one another. We were all sharing wine and the shards of a conversation when the landlord suddenly drew a tattered curtain across the window and turned on an enormous television set in the corner, which until then I had not noticed. The dominoes continued at first, and only a few of the men gave any attention to the program; one by one, however, they slewed their chairs around and began to watch it, punctuating it occasionally with remarks that would most certainly suffer in translation. (Television is something I can do without at the best of times; Spanish television, however, positively gropes for the subnormal.) A few news items flickered away, and then a well-coiffed woman announcer began to tell us a few elementary facts about human anatomy, diet, and the like, which brought on a peculiarly ominous silence in the café. On the screen, a lithe young girl in a leotard appeared, bent over backward, and performed a few double-jointed stretches. The face of the matron returned. "Only half a dozen times, once a day," she assured us, wagging a finger, "and your bodies will stay strong, healthy, and vigorous." Something had to give, and it was the railwayman beside me, who stood up suddenly, knocking over his chair. I wondered if he was going to pick up the set with one hand; he could have done so with ease. But all he did was to push past me to the door, a bottle of wine clamped in his huge fist. The expression on his face would have served, I felt, as a lesson to what we call civilization.

Spain is still the most enigmatic chunk of Europe left, particularly since the rest of the Western European countries have been putting themselves in such spanking good shape that one has to look at the billboards nowadays to remind oneself which country one is in. But Spain is no longer the wasteland it was in 1947, when its frontier reopened after eleven years of isolation from the outside world; it has become the happiest European hunting ground for unprecedented numbers of tourists, hot on the trail of the sun and chasing the elusive mystique that has always surrounded everything Spanish. Under this weighty pursuit, as might be expected, the mystique has receded a bit, and along the beaten tourist track all that remains of it is a cardboard painted version. Tourist statistics stagger up and up. The Ministry of Information and Tourism cockily expects some sixteen million strangers this summer, which works out to about .5084 of a tourist to every Spaniard—an invasion on a scale that might sink weaker countries. Spanish statistics are famously idiosyncratic, but this one I choose to believe in, give or take a million. The effects of tourism on Spain have been monumental. Not only has it given the country a fat reserve of foreign currency to beef up the Spanish economy, but it has also attracted foreign companies, which, seeing the possibilities of a place where labor is still cheap and plentiful, have chosen Spain as a place to invest in and set up factories and subsidiaries—so much so that the economic soothsayers predict a real business boom in the fairly close future. This, on the surface, appears a good omen, although it will be laboriously long before its effects seep down to the dry, cracked backlands of the peninsula. Not long ago I drove through the dusty wastes of Almería, in the southeast. For miles on end there was nothing in sight but the parched, inert landscape, apparently uninhabited except that every now and again I would come on a blinding white wall on which had been scrawled in black paint *"¡Franco Franco Franco! ¡Más árboles! ¡Más agua!"*—a cry that might have come from the earth itself. Along the coasts, however, all of which have now been exotically named—Costa Brava, Costa del Sol, Costa Blanca, names of which Spaniards have their own raucously rude versions—and in the Balearic and Canary Islands, the air is heady with the smell of suntan oil; the kiosks are bursting with bullfight posters, plastic wine bottles, and the leading European daily papers; and one has to strain hard to hear Spanish spoken at all. "We are becoming a nation of waiters," one of my friends in Majorca told me. "We used to want to travel, but now, with the whole world passing under our noses, why should we bother? What surprised us at first was that foreigners would ever *want* to come to our miserable country, but, you know, they have taught us a lot. For one thing, they've taught us how backward we are, since we find that French bricklayers and English bank clerks can afford to *fly* here with their families for ten days, or even drive in their *own* cars. But perhaps the most important thing they have taught us is that, politics and economics aside, we are lucky. We are lazy in a *positive* way. Time never worries us. We have discovered that we don't need as much as the tourists, that we are happier with less. Even so, they shame us often, talking of elections and salaries. They envy us our sun and our sunniness, but we don't really envy them. That is our shame."

In one sense, tourism *is* Spain, for the process of industrialization and modernization totters along so slowly that the country could hardly dare to lean on it. Still, the economy, if not exactly in rude health, is at least out of bed and walking about, and the agricultural workers in the more backward provinces have been steadily migrating to Madrid, Barcelona, and the coast (if not out of Spain altogether), where they are able to find work, principally in construction. The excruciating problem for Spanish workers in these past thin years was not so much unemployment as semiemployment; there was just not enough work to allow them to earn a living wage. The construction that came in the wake of tourism has changed that, although hotelkeepers and property speculators live in the shadow of *la saturación,* a word they are scarcely able to bring themselves to utter. Saturation remains a specter so far, however, and the simple fact of being able to earn more money has muffled much of the people's resentment, which in 1962 seemed ready to flare out openly. The government tries to avoid trouble by making occasional concessions, by raising the minimum wage in dribs and drabs, and by keeping the stores filled with sheer *stuff*—electronic carrots that it dangles in front of the noses of the swelling middle class. (I venture to say that there are more transistor radios per ear in the peninsula than in the noisiest capitals of Christendom; the butcher I patronize keeps one playing at full volume beside a pile of his flyspecked sausages.) But under it all Spaniards and those who know Spain are uncomfortably aware that change is not far away—not just the change that comes from creeping prosperity but change in the whole fabric of the country. It dawns on them more clearly all the time that Spain is an anachronism alongside the other Western European countries, that it does not have the beginnings of representative government, that although a certain European sophistication shows in the larger cities, the *pueblo*—and for Spaniards the word *pueblo* implies not simply the small island-like villages that rise every now and again out of the dust but a whole state of mind, a shrugging Catholic fatalism, a stoical endurance—will have to undergo a complete transformation before it can ever have anything like a decisive voice of its own. The terrifying shadow of the Civil War has diminished. An entire new generation unhaunted by the memory of it has grown up. To these young people, the present regime is an old gentleman who has not much longer to live, and they are anxiously aware that the situation they will have on their hands is one for which nobody has prepared them and which cannot be expected to straggle along like an undernourished mule, paid for by the foreigners who come to goggle and bask. The mystique is still there, and it is a curious one, combining a belief in tradition, in a glorious past, and in a natural aristocracy with what V. S. Pritchett once called "the gift for discovering every day how much less of everything, material, intellectual, and spiritual, one can live on." It is easy enough, I know too well, to be awed by that sleepy zest for life boned down to its starkest, simplest essence—a seat in the sun, a pillow of appreciative silence. But the new generation is thoroughly sick of that—sick of the summer drowse, sick of the shrug and the shrinking of the mind—and eager to be European. What they are asking is not "But when?" as the generation before them did; what they are asking now is "But how? But how?"

In the texture of its ordinary life, Spain remains a monument to paradox; to live here is like being onstage in a giant drama of oppositions—a mixture of the comic and the miserable, the joyful and the disastrous, the earthy and the ludicrous. As one picks one's way through the rubble of daily life in the peninsula, one is stopped in the act of pinning down a fact or an attitude by finding in the same instant its opposite, its contradiction. Misery, yes, but often accompanied by a belly laugh; poverty, yes, but hand in hand with such generosity and nobility that one constantly has to revise one's view of the human condition. In early 1964 Spain sent ten thousand pairs of handcuffs to Cuba in exchange for cigars; in May 1965 it lost to the Republic of Ireland at soccer—an event that was taken by the people as a national disgrace. Spanish painters enjoy vast international reputations; Spanish writers founder in the doldrums of despair, too full of words to write. The island of Majorca boasts over two thousand hotels; in Old Castile there are villages without even a well—water comes in on muleback. True, one could find such contradictions anywhere if one looked for them. In Spain, however, they are the stuff of life, and hardly a day passes without their cropping up in some form or other. "Why do you stay?" says one voice. "How could you leave?" says the other. Spain itself is the only possible answer.

The year 1964 is one that will probably appear in heavy type in future Spanish history books, for then, in the month of April, a flurry of signs suddenly sprouted from every available wall and billboard bearing the simple legend "25 Años de Paz." The ubiquitous announcement that Spaniards had enjoyed twenty-five years of peace at first caused a gigantic double take among them, but once they got to thinking about it, they realized that it was at least technically true, for the Spanish Civil War did grind to an exhausted halt on April 2, 1939, and in April 1964, Generalissimo Franco celebrated his silver wedding anniversary with his country, for better for worse, for richer for poorer, in sickness and in health. While at the time there was plenty of ironic private comment on this piece of governmental self-advertisement, the country, with its indefatigable predisposition toward celebration, decided to make the best of it, and a crop of exhibitions, displays, and sporting events filled the calendar in honor of the passing of these twenty-five uneasy years. In the Basque Country and in Catalonia, the regime, with characteristic blandness, rendered the same slogan in Basque ("25 Urte Bakian") and Catalan ("25 Anys de Pau")—two languages that it had taken great pains to suppress during the years in question. The Catalans read their slogan as "*25 Anys de Por*"—a switch from "peace" to "fear" made by the smallest variation in the pitch of the vowel. The Castilians simply talked of "*25 Años de Paciencia,*" with the appropriate syllabic pause. The national reaction, however, was more rueful than angry. The twenty-five years were at least over, and even Franco's most obdurate opponents had to admit that they were something of an achievement for the little generalissimo, who, with the exception of his Portuguese neighbor Dr. Antonio de Oliveira Salazar, has proved to be the most durable of modern dictators. "You have to hand it to the little toad," they muttered, with a kind of venomous affection.

Franco, now weathering his seventy-third year, will surely become the idol of embryo historians and thesis writers, for he certainly is worth volumes of study as a touchstone for all who exercise power. It is not that he is a mastermind, or a crafty Galician, or a shrewd peasant, or an able military strategist; rather, he is someone who long ago grasped a fundamental truth for a head of state—namely, that if he never commits himself to parties or policies, either in public or in private, he will then have everyone around him reading his mind, and reading it more wishfully than accurately. A judicious silence has kept Franco where he is, and those who have always claimed to be able to read his mind are only now realizing that he may never have known it himself, or have bothered much about knowing it. Every so often, he drops a stray remark, and his interpreters carry it away like an unexploded bomb, only for it eventually to fizz out in exhausted speculation. Last year he took to reminding his people that the country was still a constitutional monarchy, over which he ruled not just as *caudillo* but also as regent. This casual hint sent monarchists of every persuasion into near-hysterics as they imagined themselves to be suddenly on the verge of a purple heyday. It is quite true that by a Law of Succession passed on July 26, 1947, Spain declared itself a monarchy with Franco as regent, and created a Regency Council to help the chief of state settle all problems arising over his successor, deeming that whoever followed in Franco's footsteps should be "a person of royal blood who fulfilled certain conditions, swore to observe the fundamental laws of the regime, and gained the approval of a two-thirds majority of the Spanish Cortes." In 1946, however, Spain had been cold-shouldered by the United Nations and by the Western powers in general and was obliged to do everything possible to look constitutionally respectable. Ever since King Alfonso XIII feebly moved out to make way for the Spanish Republic, a royal succession had seemed a kind of Technicolor dream, with no remote chance of ever being realized, but last year, with Franco looking alarmingly mortal, kings were all at once in again, and pretenders began to strut like peacocks, however hollow their pretensions.

Legally (if strict legality applies at such a lofty level), the outstanding pretender to the ghostly throne of Spain is Don Juan, the third son of Alfonso XIII, who had the dying voice of his father. At present, however, Don Juan lives amiably in Portugal, that accommodating pasture for so many exiled kings, dictators, and pretenders, and has so far kept fairly aloof in his occasional dealings with Franco. Over the past few years, his son Don Juan Carlos— who married, suitably enough, Princess Sofía of Greece and who was carefully groomed in Spain under Franco-appointed tutors— has been more in the spotlight than his father, particularly since Franco gave him a small palace on the outskirts of Madrid as a wedding present and made several conspicuous public appearances in his company. Before Juan Carlos could assume the throne, though, a few technical snags would have to be got over—his father, Don Juan, would have to renounce his claim in favor of his son, which he would probably do only after some hard bargaining; Don Juan Carlos, who is now only twenty-seven, would have to wait until he reached the statutory age of thirty laid down by the Law of Succession; and, probably most important, he would have to show himself to the Spanish people as someone with both ideas and intelligence, for he is generally regarded as a cross between a joke and an advertisement for the life of royal leisure.

The picture was further confused last year by the sudden emergence of another pretender, whose name and title sent journalists scurrying to the history books—Prince Hugo of Bourbon-Parma, who mysteriously acquired the extra name of Carlos as a prefix, to justify his claim to be the champion of the Spanish Carlists. (The Carlists, numbering about sixty thousand, are a hangover from the squabbling wars of succession that plagued Spain throughout the nineteenth century. When Ferdinand VII of Spain died, in 1833, he left only a daughter, Isabella, to succeed him. This led his brother Don Carlos to protest to the point of arms, invoking the Salic Law, which denied the right of daughters to inherit. The Carlists stood out for absolute and despotic monarchy, and Isabella, to defeat them in battle, had to yield up much of her power in the Constitution of 1837. Carlism nowadays is local to the province of Navarre and is supported by dissident Basques and Catalans out of their peculiar sense of primitive aristocracy.)

What suddenly propelled Carlos Hugo into the ring was his lightning marriage to Princess Irene of the Netherlands. The family of Bourbon-Parma is thoroughly French, and young Carlos Hugo has only recently petitioned for Spanish nationality. I remember last year in France coming across articles in the sensationalist press asking "Which of these girls will be queen of Spain?" under side-by-side photographs of Sofía and Irene. It is a question calculated to absorb readers of women's magazines but one that is just about as remote as who will be the first Miss Moon. There is no doubt but that either of the young women would be likely to decorate the hypothetical throne of Spain more substantially than her pale young consort, but to present the two of them as race horses in some ghostly royal stakes is to give way to daydreams.

In a technocratic Europe, restoring monarchs to imaginary thrones is a bit passé. Restoratism in itself means nothing—a king could be either a help or a nuisance, depending on what he does or what he is allowed to do. It is true that Spain is a constitutional anachronism, and it is just possible that a king might tide it over into a new era of political responsibility. There is also no doubt but that the profile of either pretender would lend considerably more style to Spanish stamps and coins than the froggy visage of the present chief of state, but as to the likelihood of the succession's taking place, it still rests in the implacable mandate of Franco, and of late he seems to have forgotten all about it. Indeed, toward the end of last summer the Madrid daily *Ya* went as far as to beg the chief of state in an editorial for *some* indication of his own ideas about the succession—a gesture that was symptomatic of the real puzzlement of the Spanish people. Just as I was leaving Spain in May of this year, the newsmagazine *SP* appeared on the bookstalls with the blazing legend on its cover "DESPUÉS DE FRANCO, QUÉ?" ("After Franco, what?") *Qué* indeed. Technically, Franco settled the problem of his immediate succession in 1962, when he appointed General Augustín Muñoz Grandes as his deputy; were Franco to die overnight, the supreme say-so would rest firmly in the hands of the army, with Muñoz Grandes assuming, at least temporarily, the dictatorship. Conceivably, he would yield up his supreme power to a military junta, for he, although four years younger than Franco, is in poor health, but whether he or they would attempt to bring about the royal succession is as hazardous a guess as it ever was.

There seem to be three main possibilities. Franco can make some positive declaration to ensure the royal succession, in which case he will probably hold a national referendum on the question, as he did in 1947. Or he may die without having made any explicit plans, leaving the army to go ahead independently with the restoration. Most likely, however, the restoration will quite simply never happen, which is the opinion of the harder-headed Spaniards I know. "We're in a difficult enough position now, faced with the next twenty-five years," they say. "We have literally to invent a way of governing ourselves. Why complicate things by dragging in a king?"

The restoration of the monarchy might be a useful stopgap—a breathing space in which Spain could begin to reorganize its lopsided social structure—and a king would certainly put up a better front than another hard-faced uniformed dictator. The government is fussily preoccupied these days with the face it presents to the rest of the world, and to Europe in particular, for it still dreams of being included in the well-heeled embrace of the Common Market. In fact, the only real setback that Franco suffered in his silver-jubilee year was to have his application for associate membership in the Common Market, pending since February 1962, unceremoniously turned down by the Council of Ministers in Brussels just as the "25 Years of Peace" were being trumpeted from the billboards. Associate membership would have been something of a coup for the little leader, but the united opposition of Italy and the Benelux countries quashed his application. Nevertheless, Spain's foreign trade is so much on the up that the country's application was worthy of consideration from an economic point of view—a testimonial at the least to the extent of its current prosperity. Franco's minister of information and tourism, Manuel Fraga Iribarne, has kept up an apparently endless round of speechmaking, exuding assurance as if he had no doubt that Spain needed only a few minor adjustments to turn it into a near paradise.

Although Fraga Iribarne has been studiously wooing Spanish liberals and intellectuals, he is widely distrusted by them. He has unquestionably made a few adjustments in the heavyhandedness of press censorship, but he has certainly never come near to granting the freedom of expression that he suggests is just round the corner. His touted new Press Law, which finally saw the light late in 1964, concealed under its extravagant phrasing a few minor changes in the mechanism of the censorship but none in the spirit of it, for it transferred the responsibility for published material to the editors of Spanish publications but left them subject to subsequent censorship—a risk that not many of them feel prepared to run. It is true that it is now possible to see uncut foreign films with relatively uninhibited themes in the larger cities of Spain (even though they are still, of course, subject to the Church's grading, which almost automatically prohibits good Catholics from attending any of them), but Fraga Iribarne made this choice in the interests of the impression he must make on tourists rather than out of any real concern for the enlightenment of his own people.

The happy flush that radiated from Madrid during 1964 has faded conspicuously this year in a series of fairly turbulent public manifestations. The Spanish industrial workers, sparked as they have always been by the blunt position taken by the miners in Asturias—veterans now of three years of belligerent strikes—have grown steadily more dissatisfied with the *sindicatos*, the cumbersome trade councils in which their own interests are less than adequately represented. Labor trouble is a continuing headache to Franco, and on top of it the universities—most notably the University of Madrid—began during February to hold illegal open meetings of students who, backed by the more liberal-minded of their professors, protested against the laws forbidding them freedom of assembly and allowing them to belong only to the state-controlled students' union. They held a series of meetings, as a result of which three professors were formally suspended (an action that provoked more student meetings), and ultimately they staged a full-fledged strike. In the past, the government put down similar manifestations with conspicuous brutality. This time, however, it made surprising concessions, granting the students the right to form more or less independent organizations of their own, and it has shown something of the same conciliatory spirit in dealing with outbreaks of labor unrest. All this has engendered a sudden surge of hope—or at least a subsiding of fear, for it is only a year or so since police brutality was the rule rather than the exception. (It has not, however, disappeared.)

Altogether, the atmosphere in the country during the spring of this year has been a reversal of the official benevolence and well-being of 1964, and the generalissimo has been showing signs of alarm—not personal signs, since he constantly appears in the illustrated papers hunting, Sunday-painting, playing with his grandchildren, and looking for all the world like anybody's favorite great-uncle. But publicly his alarm has shown itself most conspicuously in an extraordinary series of editorials in the newspaper *Arriba,* the official organ of the Falangist Party, of which Franco is titular head. The editorials, printed over a period of four days, suddenly and unbelievably suggested to their readers that Spain had fallen into political atrophy and that the political life of the country might be restored to health by the formation of—of all things—a legal opposition, which, given the right to suggest and criticize, would keep the government in a state of responsible alertness and help clarify the principles that Franco's "institutional stability" was based on. The paper also remarked that it considered it essential for responsible government ministers to appear from time to time before the public to explain and clarify their policies, adding that they should not hesitate to admit their mistakes. The last editorial contained the extraordinary sentence "Liberty must be granted before its absence provokes resentment and causes subversion"—a sentence that twenty years ago might have been taken more seriously and have had more meaning than now. ("If we do not make differences of opinion legal, then instead of a legalized opposition, we will have an active subversion," one Falangist leader was reported as saying in March. The Spaniards were too stunned at hearing such talk from a Falangist even to laugh, which is something for Spaniards.) There has always existed an opposition to Franco, although an illegal one, and of late the more intelligent leaders of the small and disparate opposition parties have looked as though they might be able to overcome their differences and band together under a Christian Democratic label, which would bring them considerable sympathy from the rest of Europe. Hence the *Arriba* editorials, coming at this time, more or less take the wind out of the sails of the evolving opposition, and since they obviously could never have been published without a nod from Franco, the whole and surprising campaign looks to Spaniards (who have now had twenty-six years' practice in cynicism) like another cleverly timed gambit by the generalissimo, calculated to make the opposition's aims appear identical with those of the government, and even to make opposition unnecessary.

The ripples set in motion by the *Arriba* pronouncements are still spreading bewilderment and have certainly succeeded in deflecting the unrest of early spring, which had reached a point of extreme discomfort for the regime. Characteristically, the pronouncements have been followed by the well-known *silencio oficial* that settles so often in the Spanish atmosphere, muffling protest and immobilizing activity of any kind. I had a talk a few weeks ago with an old friend of mine, a veteran opponent of the regime who has been in and out of prison, in and out of exile, to whom I have always listened but for whom I have always felt profoundly sorry. "You know, I really feel as if my time had passed," he said. "I really feel a kind of odd affinity with Franco. I'm tired. I'm too old. We lost the Civil War— that's what we could never admit and that's what Franco has been trying to teach us, brutally, since it ended. But now we're both on the losing side, he and I. We're old. We can do no more for Spain.

We need leaders, not myths; we need a present, not a past. And I think Franco sees this, too, although it doesn't appear to bother him. We've talked ourselves to death and done nothing. I don't want to oppose anymore—it has become a useless, futile gesture. I want something to *happen*. I don't even want to belong to a legal opposition. We Spaniards have nothing really to oppose except our own disastrous confusion. Take the *Arriba* editorials—they're all part of a futile game we have been playing for too long. Do they mean anything, you ask. *Hombre,* you know us better than that. You know what they are—another *camelo*!" (*Camelo* would be translatable in this context as something of a cross between a flirtation and a red herring. It is certainly the one word in Spanish that characterizes the astuteness of the regime in presenting a perpetually bland exterior to its people.)

Nevertheless, for publications that bear a blessing from above to begin bandying about words like *democracy* as something feasible in the Spanish context shows at least that the idea of an alternative to himself has occurred to Franco; apart from that, it gives the illusion of liberalization in the country. There is some, to be sure. It has dawned on the government that when some of the more than six hundred thousand Spaniards who have emigrated to countries like Switzerland, Great Britain, West Germany, and France return to their *pueblos* bursting with tales of the wonders of Western Europe ("Water coming out of things called taps, cold *and* hot"), there is going to be a good deal of awe. In these last two years, too, the Church has begun to give a good deal more attention to its social responsibilities than it ever did before, speaking out and taking a more responsible, less fatalistic stand. (The abbot of Montserrat, the monastery close to Barcelona, chose to exile himself to Italy after a series of brushes with the civil authorities.) But Spain's liberalization is illusion rather than reality, promise rather than performance; Spaniards are tasting a semifreedom in which they are less likely than before to suffer *personal* persecution but in which they are as far as ever from a revision of the whole clumsy structure of their society. And although the word *democracy* has become fashionable, even in government circles, there is still the feeling—certainly shared by me—that the Spanish character is not one that either wants to or can take the kind of responsibility implicit in a democratic system, as all Spanish history (and, most tragically, the history of the last forty years) clearly shows. For Franco to refer to Spain as "an emergent democracy" at this stage is fairly laughable, for it just about completes his hand; if one delves into his speeches—privately printed and circulated among civil authorities in a weighty volume with the title *Franco Ha Dicho* (*Franco Has Said*), which is intricately indexed to enable them easily to quote the Leader on any subject whatever—one discovers that to him Spain has been everything, short of Communist, in turn, and only a year ago was a constitutional monarchy. The fact of the matter is that it has always remained, indefinably, Spain.

It is perhaps this predicament, this self-uncertainty, that has provoked an attitude I keep coming across more and more in Spain, particularly in the cities. (One might as well say, quite simply, Madrid and Barcelona, for they are the only two cities with any profusion of thinking people, even though they think in such different ways—Madrid coolly, cynically, at an aloof remove from the underlying reality, and Barcelona bluntly, even brutally, committed to action, to creating rather than criticizing itself.) The attitude is one of impatience—impatience as much with the attitude of opposition as with the regime, and impatience above all with theory, with talk, with weary hypothesis. To the people who feel this way, opposition has become negative rather than positive; they choose to regard their country not as a political problem but as a tangible situation that they will quite shortly inherit, since, by the laws of life, the country is bound to outlive Franco and to require some fairly steady hands and clear heads. Their minds are less on gesture and protest than on facts and actualities; they have largely forsworn the endless, repetitive chess game of political speculation. As a group, they would be impossible to define (for they are not a group, and quite possibly do not know of one another's existence), but they consist mainly of specialists—sociologists, economists, architects, doctors, civil servants who work in the ministries, minor officials—all of whom have to deal with workaday matters, with technicalities, with the management and mismanagement of public funds, with plans for agrarian reform and new industrialization. They are bound together by the same attitude that lay behind the courageous protest of the students against being told what to do and what to think— the only attitude that can take Spain out of its present tangle. I come across this attitude in quite disparate friends, some of whom I have known for many years, all of whom are tired of the weight of the past and the lack of a future, and many of whom would be prepared to use the present mechanism of Spain's "institutionalism" to get the country functioning efficiently, to take it out of the shadow of its totalitarian past, and, above all, to break down, once and for all, its historical and actual isolation from the rest of Europe. "It's not a case of choosing any longer," one of my friends, an architect, said to me in Madrid. "Now we *are* Europeans. We go to congresses in London and Paris, we rub shoulders with our counterparts in these countries, we see eye to eye with them, we talk to them without feeling any different, we invite them down to stay with us—and then we have to explain away this ridiculous situation here, which we have been stuck with for so long, doing nothing more about it than signing the odd letter of protest, perhaps even spending the odd spell in prison. But now it doesn't seem grim anymore, it's grotesque! It's ludicrous! I want to build buildings I can be proud of, buildings that are a hundred times as efficient as those I have to knock out for the Ministry of Housing, but how can I explain to a French colleague that I have to do what I'm told or resign? I want to tell, not be told. I know what's wrong with Spain—at least, I know what's wrong with *my* Spain, for I see it every day. I just want to get on with what should be done, and as far as politics go, I'd be quite happy to have anybody or anything in power as long as he would say to me 'All right, get on with it!'—even if it has to be a general."

Such talk is not isolated—I hear it more and more, and coming from Spaniards, it makes uncommon sense. It does not, unfortunately, remove either Franco or the uncertainty over the succession—an uncertainty that contains the possibility of violence and the inevitability of confusion. Bright economic prospects are not sufficient to hold a country together, although in Spain's case they are certainly going to help. While I was revisiting Madrid recently, I went to call on an old gentleman of ninety-five, the grandfather of a friend of mine, with whom, in the past, I occasionally played chess. He was sitting, as dapper as ever—white-headed, in a black suit, white shirt, and black tie—in his study, and after we had been talking for a time, he waved his hand impatiently. "I suppose it would sound silly to you if I started to tell you—as I used to—about the turn of the century, when we were quite sure that we were the greatest people in the world, that we had the God-given secret of how to live, that our poetry and our painting and our conversation and our culture made us positively glow with pride." He paused, and shook his head, then went on, "Now, when I hear all of you wrangling away, tormenting this tangled present, dissecting little Paco—did you know, by the way, that just before the *movimiento* that led to the Civil War flared up, Franco was learning English with a view to going to Scotland in order to learn how to play golf? I have that on good authority, for one of his lieutenants, now dead, was an old schoolmate of mine. Let me see, where was I? Oh, yes, I was saying that when I hear you all at it, when I read the speeches, when I think a bit about what Spain has to go through now—but it will come through, mind you, it will!—I feel one thing quite clearly, and I don't mind telling it to you. I wouldn't have been anything other than a Spaniard, I wouldn't have lived anywhere but in Madrid, I wouldn't have chosen to run away from all the tragedies we've had, although, in a way, I died when the Republic did. But when I think of Spain now—and I'm not saying the world, I'm saying Spain—I'll tell you what I feel quite simply. I'm glad I'm old."

The Reign in Spain

BY JON LEE ANDERSON

∾

editor's note

Here is a more contemporary piece, dating from 1998, about that quaint yet modern institution in Spain: the monarchy, raising the question of whether Juan Carlos de Borbón y Borbón has made the monarchy essential to Spanish democracy.

JON LEE ANDERSON is a contributing editor at *The New Yorker*, where this piece originally appeared in the issue of April 27 and May 4, 1998. Anderson is also the author of *Che: A Revolutionary Life* (1997, hardcover, and 1998, paperback, both editions published by Grove Press).

The baron showed me his ancient dungeon, where a ball and chain and iron manacles are still anchored firmly in the stone wall, and then we stepped out onto one of the balconies that jut from his castle. Below was a spreading fan of carefully tended fields that belong to his family, and tiny, rock-walled plots that belong to his family's former vassals. The baron explained that for the past hundred and seventy years—ever since the abolition of *señoríos,* or feudal landholdings—the descendants of the vassals have been property owners. Yet they adhere to the tradition of primogeniture, just as he does. Each generation passes on its inheritance to the eldest son, to avoid breaking up the land. "You see?" he said smiling. "Some old traditions, the most practical ones, survive today. They are still very useful."

We went inside for drinks, and sat in armchairs in front of a log fire, in an elegant room decorated with silver-framed photographs of the baron's past and present friends—the exiled Italian King Victor Emmanuel, King Zog of Albania, Monaco's Grimaldis, Generalissimo Francisco Franco. The baron told me about his family, who received their title hundreds of years ago. In the nineteenth century they were Carlists, fierce opponents of Queen Isabel II, whose right to rule was disputed by her uncle, Don Carlos. The Carlist cause led to three bloody civil wars in the eighteenhundreds and survived as a rallying ground well into the twentieth century.

That was old history now, the baron said; his family had made their peace with the present king, Juan Carlos I, the great-greatgrandson of Isabel II. "It is thanks to Juan Carlos that we have a monarchy at all," he remarked. "And he deserves great credit for ensuring that the transition to democracy was carried out without bloodshed—in this country where we like blood so much!"

A few days later I was in Barcelona, talking to a former highranking Socialist government official in his office in a black-tinted glass tower. "This may sound ridiculous, but I am passionately loyal to the Crown," he said. "And I have a great love and respect for the king. Even if I knew something about him which I could criticize, I would never do so."

The Socialist technocrat in his office filled with modern art was in complete agreement with the old baron: Juan Carlos de Borbón y Borbón is a good thing. In 1975, when Franco died and the king assumed the throne, Spain was a backward and isolated nation that had been ruled for nearly forty years by a regime that exercised rigid censorship laws, outlawed birth control and political parties, and garrotted political prisoners to death. Today it is a socially tolerant, prosperous nation with a fully functioning democracy. "Just imagine," says Salvador Giner, a Catalonian Basque academic who is the dean of the sociology department of Barcelona University. "For forty years we had Franco, a little fascist dictator with a tasseled hat who didn't speak any foreign languages or travel anywhere. And then along came Juan Carlos. He's tall, good-looking, speaks several languages, and has a great pedigree, too—better than the queen of England, who is descended from some second-rate German princelings." To illustrate the point, Giner grabs his nose: "He's got the big Bourbon nose and"—pulling down his lower lip to make it protrude—"the Hapsburg lips."

In a series of rooms in the Prado Museum, in Madrid, there are many portraits by Goya depicting Juan Carlos's royal ancestor Carlos IV, a Bourbon who earned everlasting ignominy for surrendering Spain to Napoleon in 1808. In one of them the stout and pasty-faced king looks stiff and uncomfortable in a crimson frock coat and a powdered wig. His silk sashes and medals denote his exalted office. The effect is quite remote from that projected by Juan Carlos, who is lean and suntanned, and who sails his own boat and has a collection of motorcycles. But the facial resemblance is remarkable. There is, indeed, a "Bourbon look"—a high, sloping brow, a sweeping, fleshy nose, and a protuberant chin.

I was thinking about the Goya as I trailed Juan Carlos around during a reception in Madrid early last month. The occasion was the hundredth anniversary of the Madrid Medical Association. There had been a ceremony at which the king gave a short speech and was presented with a gold medal, and now he and his wife, Queen Sofía, were moving through the crowd, along with waiters carrying drinks and hors d'oeuvres on trays. The king and queen took separate routes, smiling and chatting. Juan Carlos has the supple body of an athlete, but I noticed that his hair is thinning and that he has acquired the slightly drooping jowls and cheeks of a man who is aging. He's now sixty.

When we were introduced, the king was disarmingly attentive. After some polite chitchat, he asked where I had learned Spanish. I told him, "In Latin America, mostly, Your Majesty, and, most recently, Cuba, which is a very interesting place. I understand that you haven't been there."

The possibility of the king's going to Cuba was a fraught subject in Madrid just then, and widely speculated on in the Spanish press. This year is the centennial of the Spanish-American War, in which Spain lost nearly all of what remained of her empire. If the king were to visit Cuba, officials of the royal household say, he would make the event a symbolic reconciliation between the two countries, just as he did with a trip in February to the Philippines, another colony lost in the war of 1898.

Spain has had a reasonably good relationship with Cuba since the early 1980s, when the Socialist Party came to power, but in 1996 the Socialists lost an election to the more conservative Partido Popular, and the new prime minister, José María Aznar, got into a war of wills with Castro, who had rejected Aznar's ambassador in Havana. Aznar then refused to nominate anyone else. In early March Castro publicly invited the king to visit him, and Aznar took this as an insult. He apparently thought Castro was attempting an end run around him.

Juan Carlos didn't respond to my remark about Cuba at first, and he turned his head away, as if to move off, but then he turned back and leaned toward me and said, confidingly, "You know, I've just sent a letter to Castro through his ambassador here. I've asked him to stop *tirándome flores*"—literally, "throwing flowers at me," a slangy expression—"flattering me, inviting me so directly to come. It creates problems. He knows that to invite me he has to go through the government here, and, first, the government has to name an ambassador. Even Felipe"—Spain's former Socialist prime minister, Felipe González—"who is not exactly *with* this government, agrees. When I saw him the other day, he said, 'Castro knows better—he shouldn't be doing that!'"

Startled as much by the king's slang as by his apparent candor, I replied that I hoped His Majesty would, after all, be able to go to Cuba. Did he think he would?

"Oh, yes," the king replied. "As soon as the government names an ambassador, *it will be fine*." These last words were spoken in clearly enunciated English.

Later, stressing that the king "should not make political declarations," one of his aides fretfully sought assurances that our chat had been off the record. She argued that if he was quoted, it would "create a diplomatic incident between Spain and Cuba." The problem didn't seem to be Cuba so much as Prime Minister Aznar, however. "There are a lot of people who wish to go to Cuba," he said curtly during a radio interview the day after the reception. The king would be able to go to Cuba when it was "his turn."

Aznar's snit and Castro's sly gesture are illuminating for what they say about the fragile nature of the relationship between even a very popular king and a democratically elected government. Although Juan Carlos is formally limited by Spain's constitution to largely symbolic public functions—ratifying laws, calling elections, accrediting ambassadors, and so forth—and despite disclaimers by members of his staff that he is "above politics," he does wield real, if difficult to quantify, political clout. The constitution identifies him as "the head of state, the symbol of its unity and permanence," and says that he will "arbitrate and moderate" its activities. This description is open to some interpretation, and the king has developed a style that seems to work quite effectively. For example, he holds daily private *audiencias* with politicians, businessmen, journalists, academics, and military officers at his residence in the Palacio de la Zarzuela, a few miles outside Madrid. The *audiencias* provide him with an occasion to dispense discreet advice and get his opinions across. John Brademas, a former congressman from Indiana who is now with the King Juan Carlos I of Spain Center at New York University, tells of having lunch with the king, and of how, when he mentioned a certain businessman's name, Juan Carlos "wrinkled his nose." It was all he had to do. "This is a king who lets one know how he feels," Brademas says.

La Zarzuela is reached via a busy highway that heads north out of the city, past the Presidential Palace. An exit just beyond a confusing new spaghetti junction of roads and overpasses leads to a gatehouse and a road that winds through a low forest of holm oaks and scrub pines, past herds of grazing deer and the occasional spotted *jabalí,* a kind of wild boar. The low-slung red brick and stone royal mansion dominates the edge of a flat ridge. Below it, tucked discreetly into the ridge, is a staff annex, which is joined to the palace by a long underground corridor lined with glass cabinets in which are displayed exquisitely crafted model boats from the king's private collection.

The head of media relations for the royal household, Asunción Valdés, has an office in the annex. Valdés speaks in chirrupy, upbeat tones and smiles a lot. Most of the administrative staff affect this style. It is as if they had adopted, collectively, the king's famously simpatico public persona as their own. "The king treats the palace gardener with the same naturalness as he does a head of state," Valdés explained brightly. "He has the gift of being able to win people over. The king gives you confidence and makes people feel comfortable around him." Valdés has had her job since 1993, when there was a big turnover of staff at the palace, after the king gave an unfortunate spate of interviews that played badly with the Spanish public. One foreign diplomat describes her job as keeping a "Verdun Line" around Juan Carlos.

"La Zarzuela can hardly be called a palace," she says. "It's really just a *big house*. The king lives here very simply. He could have chosen to live in any one of the other royal palaces, which are much larger and more luxurious, but no. Their Majesties said they wanted to live in a place with human dimensions." On the lawn outside one of the formal rooms in La Zarzuela is a brown stone sculpture by the Basque sculptor Eduardo Chillida, which, as Valdés points out, resembles a throne. She reminds me that Juan Carlos is a king who has "never worn his crown or sat on a throne." The sculpture, she says, is the closest thing to a throne he owns—"a symbolic throne."

Juan Carlos's motto is "The Crown must be earned every day," and his friends and employees are inclined to repeat the phrase with cuckoo-clock regularity. "The approval polls may be favorable, but we have to keep working," Valdés says, opening a large binder embossed with the royal seal. She examines a section labeled "Places Visited," which lists which cities every member of the royal family has gone to, and whether the visit was for social, educational, economic, cultural, or military purposes. "Here we see, for instance, that this city has not been visited very much, so we have to plan a visit soon!" she exclaims.

Juan Carlos seems to be particularly gifted at image control. "This king is no idiot," remarks Baltasar Porcel, the head of the Catalan Institute for Mediterranean Studies, who meets the King periodically at the *audiencias.* "His simplicity is very real, but it is very calculated at the same time." In keeping with his policy of creating a "modern monarchy," Juan Carlos has not isolated himself or established a royal court. This has caused resentment among some of Spain's old noble families, who were traditionally given sinecures and special access to the king. "The fact that he hasn't handed out traditional posts, like keeper of the king's food or keeper of His Majesty's hairbrush, has meant that the grandees really hate him," Joan Fontfreda Puig, a Catalan nobleman, says. "This king is more popular with the people than with the aristocracy."

Juan Carlos was not always popular or thought to be politically savvy. Indeed, at the time of his coronation, he was mocked as a dim-witted military puppet, and it was assumed that he wouldn't last long. Jokes circulated about Juan Carlos, el Breve (the Brief).

Juan Carlos's paternal grandfather, King Alfonso XIII, fled Spain ignominiously in 1931, when the Republicans took over the government. Alfonso was stripped of his citizenship, and his property was seized. In exile, first in Paris and then in Rome, he lived the life of a playboy, womanizing, gambling, and big-game hunting. His British-born wife, Queen Victoria Eugenia, who was the granddaughter of Queen Victoria, soon left him.

The republic fell in 1939, and Franco installed himself as Spain's *caudillo,* or strongman. He did not want to share power with the Bourbons, and they remained in exile. Juan Carlos, who was born in Rome in 1938, moved with his parents first to Switzerland and then to Portugal. In 1941, shortly before his death, Alfonso XIII abdicated in favor of his son, Juan Carlos's father, Don Juan.

Juan Carlos went to Spain for the first time in 1948, when he was ten. This was the result of an agreement made between Franco and his father during a meeting on Franco's yacht, which was anchored off the coast of Northern Spain. Franco proposed that Don Juan allow Juan Carlos to complete his education in Spain. He evidently felt that this would defuse a budding alliance between royalists and exiled socialists, and neutralize Don Juan, who would see Franco's invitation as opening the way to a Bourbon restoration. Don Juan accepted.

Juan Carlos spent his youth studying at special schools or cloistered in palaces where he was tutored privately and looked after by guardians, men who reported back either to Don Juan or to Franco, depending on their loyalties. He was a lackluster student, but he was good at sports and an affable, if somewhat deferred-to, classmate. Periodically, he would be summoned to the Palacio del Pardo, where Franco treated him in a grandfatherly way. At their first meeting he gave the boy a shotgun; not surprisingly, Juan Carlos's earliest memories of el Caudillo are fond ones. On holidays he visited his family in Portugal.

Don Juan and Franco met twice more to discuss the prince's future. Both times, Franco's arguments won out. Instead of studying in Belgium, as his father wished, Juan Carlos was sent to Spanish military academies. His younger brother, Alfonso, was a cadet with him, and in 1956, when they were visiting their parents in Portugal, there was a terrible accident. The boys were playing with a gun, and it went off. Alfonso was hit in the head and died immediately. Juan Carlos remained silent and withdrawn for months afterward, and has never spoken about the incident publicly.

Juan Carlos attended a university in Madrid for two years, and in 1962, when he was twenty-four, he married Princess Sofía of Greece. She was the German-Greek daughter of Paul I of Greece and Frederica of Hanover and a good match for a future king of Spain. Like Juan Carlos, Sofía was a direct descendant of Queen Victoria, and also of Kaiser Wilhelm II. They settled into La Zarzuela, which had been a royal hunting lodge. It had been badly damaged during the Civil War but was restored and outfitted by Franco especially for their use. They soon produced three children:

two girls, Elena and Cristina, in 1963 and 1965, respectively, and then, in 1968, a male heir, Felipe.

Juan Carlos had come to understand that Franco had no intention of allowing his father to take the throne. Franco dropped hints that he favored Juan Carlos as his eventual successor, but he also made sure that Juan Carlos was insecure about his future. As far back as 1952, Franco had recruited a potential alternative to Juan Carlos by inviting Alfonso de Borbón-Dampierre, his cousin, to study in Spain. Over the years, the rival cousins had each acquired a coterie of political allies who defended his cause, and friends recall that by the time Juan Carlos was in his mid-twenties, he possessed a strong sense of his dynastic heritage. He wanted to become king.

In 1972 Alfonso married Franco's granddaughter, but Juan Carlos's position had been strengthened considerably three years earlier, when Franco summoned him to El Pardo and announced his intention to name him his successor, "with the title of king." Did he accept? As Juan Carlos has told the story ever since, Franco demanded his reply immediately, and he had no opportunity to discuss things with his father.

There is an alternative version of this story, which is the case with most crucial episodes in the king's life. "That's not how it happened!" the baron who had shown me around his castle said, laughing. "He'd been demanding that Franco declare him successor for years, and when Franco did, he had to come up with an excuse to explain why he couldn't tell his father before accepting."

Three weeks after Franco made his proposal the prince stood before the Cortes, the Spanish parliament, to swear fealty to him and his regime. It was months before Don Juan agreed to speak to his son again, and according to several of Juan Carlos's closest friends, it was years before their relationship returned to normal. As Asunción Valdés describes it, "the relationship between the king and his father was something like a Shakespearean tragedy."

Don Juan did not formally withdraw his claim to the throne until 1977, more than a year after Franco died and his son was crowned. By then, Spain's new king had shown himself to be full of surprises. He fired the right-wing prime minister, Carlos Arias Navarro, and appointed a young, reformist politician named Adolfo Suárez in his place. Franco's Cortes was dissolved, and a national referendum was called to approve a law of political reform, which passed overwhelmingly. A long-standing ban on political parties was lifted, and in June 1977 Juan Carlos called for general elections. Adolfo Suárez was confirmed in office, and in 1978, when a new constitution was approved, Spain formally became a constitutional monarchy with a democratic political system.

The new constitution left Juan Carlos without the sweeping powers he had inherited from Franco, but written into it was something that for him—born in exile as the son of an uncrowned king, and as the grandson of a king who had been forced to flee his country—may well have been more important: "The Crown of Spain shall be inherited by the successors of H.M. Juan Carlos I de Borbón, the legitimate heir of the historical dynasty."

The legitimate heir is now Crown Prince Felipe, who turned thirty in January. He is tall, athletic, and poised, and he has a master's degree in international relations from Georgetown University in Washington. Recently, he began making regular public appearances and assuming some of his father's traditional duties. It has become his job to attend the inaugural ceremonies of Latin-American heads of state. In March he led a large Spanish trade delegation to Japan.

Prince Felipe is one of Europe's most eligible bachelors, and the pages of the *revistas del corazón*—gossip magazines—are full of speculation about the identity of his girlfriends and the candidates for his future bride. Most recently, he has been linked to Catherine von Hapsburg, the archduchess of Austria, but until last year the stories were all about his presumed relationship with a young American woman, Gigi Howard, whom he met when he was at Georgetown. The liaison was reportedly ended on the orders of Queen Sofía, who is said to want him to marry a daughter of one of Europe's royal houses.

News coverage of the royal family is overwhelmingly positive in Spain and doesn't normally intrude very far into their private lives. There is the occasional tabloid story about the king's alleged lovers, and off the record, mainstream Spanish journalists and even politicians friendly to Juan Carlos credit stories of a long relationship with a woman in Majorca and of shorter ones with other women. But they routinely dismiss his sexual habits as unimportant. "The business between Monica Lewinsky and Clinton wouldn't get a second reading here. In Spain that kind of thing is considered a private matter," Xavier Batalla, a writer for the Barcelona newspaper *La Vanguardia,* explains. He concedes that there is a "pact of silence in the press not to write about the king's personal things. . . . The pact of silence isn't written down. Nobody has told me anything. Maybe I know something, but I don't write it. Nobody has to tell me what to do." Batalla defends his self-censorship by dismissing "the rumorology" about the king's private life as "motivated by a political intention to damage the solidity of the monarchy."

The loyalty and peculiar defensiveness the king inspires, even from a relatively free press, stems from the circumstances of modern Spanish history. The Civil War tore Spain apart only sixty years ago. It was a brutal episode even by the standards of twentieth-century brutality. As many as a million people died. After the republic fell, Franco imposed a repressive police state in which political dissidents were tortured and beaten to death. By the early 1970s, when Juan Carlos was preparing to take the throne, there was mounting unrest and political violence. In December 1973 the Basque separatist group ETA assassinated Franco's prime minister and Juan Carlos's closest ally, Admiral Luis Carrero Blanco, in a car-bomb explosion.

Juan Carlos established himself as a bulwark against political chaos on the night of February 23, 1981, when gunwielding Civil Guard officers stormed into the Cortes, and took the entire government hostage. The leader of the attempted coup implied that the king supported them, but hours later, when Juan Carlos appeared on television wearing his uniform as the captain-general of Spain's armed forces, he called for the defense of democracy, and the attempt to overthrow the government collapsed. The king had effectively ended the era of military intervention in Spanish politics.

There are skeptics who question what went on during the seven hours between the time the Cortes was seized and the time Juan Carlos made his appearance. The official version says that he was on the phone marshaling his supporters. The skeptics say that he was on the fence. What no one calls into question is the king's extraordinary sense of what is going to work politically. As Asunción Valdés says, admiringly, "he knows where the wind blows from."

Juan Carlos's power was enhanced around this time by a reorganization of Spain's political structure. To an extent that could not have been foreseen by anyone, his early support for the limited devolution of power from Madrid to the historically distinct regions—such as Catalonia, the Basque Country, and Galicia—increased his influence. Since 1982 Spain has been divided into seventeen so-called autonomous communities. "Because of the autonomous communities, the Spanish state is very weak, and this makes the role of the monarchy very important," Charles Powell, an Anglo-Spanish historian and Spanish parliamentary aide, explains. "The king is the only genuinely national figure in a country with an unusual deficit of national symbols. There are fewer national holidays in Spain than in other European countries, and the national anthem is rarely played."

Catalonia, with its capital city of Barcelona—a traditional rival to Madrid—is the showcase for the king's relationship to the autonomous communities. Xavier Roig, a Socialist who worked as a senior aide to Pasqual Maragall, the former mayor of Barcelona, recalls that he and his colleagues tried to involve Juan Carlos in their activities when they gained power in the early 1980s. "Just imagine," he says. "We were all young then, and we came into office as leftists, but we quickly realized that to operate we had to go through the comic opera of ritualizing monarchical protocol. For example, in our internal memorandums we would write notes saying, 'I think it would be appropriate to invite H.M. the King to this activity.' The H.M. was a conscious effort, you see? We knew that we had to reinforce the role of the monarchy so as not to leave it to the right."

The head of Catalonia's autonomous government, Jordi Pujol, who seeks greater independence for Catalonia within an increasingly integrated Europe, has pursued a special relationship with the king. The idea is that Catalonia would owe fealty to the Crown as a unifying symbol, and the relationship with Spain would be more like a confederation. But, as Charles Powell points out, "if the autonomies demand a special link to the monarchy, this poses real problems for the central government."

Many Catalans believe that there was something called Operation Cristina that forged a direct link between Catalonia and the royal family. Princess Cristina, Juan Carlos's younger daughter, works in Barcelona for Fundación la Caixa, the philanthropic arm of a large bank. A Catalan close to the king denies the existence of Operation Cristina, but acknowledges that "the presence of Cristina in Barcelona is not accidental. It wasn't planned, but it's been seen to be useful."

Last October Cristina married Iñaki Urdangarín, a Basque professional handball player. "The king knows how to distribute things symbolically," Salvador Giner says. "One daughter marries a

Basque in Catalonia, the other"—Elena—"he names the duchess of Lugo, which is in Galicia. Felipe is the prince of Asturias." Baltasar Porcel adds that when the king visits Barcelona he intentionally gives his speeches partly in Catalan and partly in Spanish. "The fact that the king speaks Catalan when he's here makes it harder for the Spaniards to attack us," Porcel says.

When José María Aznar defeated Felipe González in the 1996 elections, he had to strike deals with the Catalans and the Basques in order to become prime minister, and when the haggling seemed to be going on forever, Juan Carlos got involved. "The king got on the phone," says Richard Gardner, who was the U.S. ambassador to Spain from 1993 to 1997. "He called Aznar, Pujol, and Arzallus"— the leader of the main Basque party—"and said, 'Spain cannot withstand a long period of uncertainty. Work it out. I'll be watching.'" According to Gardner, pressure from the king precipitated the deals that were struck soon afterward. In return for significant concessions, Aznar won enough votes to assume office.

When Aznar made his first official visit to the United States, in April 1997, the king again discreetly paved the way for him. A few weeks earlier, on a visit to New York, Juan Carlos had invited Gardner out to dinner. "The king took me to Plácido Domingo's restaurant," Gardner recalls. "He expressed his hope that everything possible could be done for Aznar, explaining that it was his first American visit, and that he lacked experience. He then asked— or insisted, really—that Madeleine Albright be there when Aznar came, and insisted that I write out a note, which he dictated then and there, to her. He reminded her that she was Prince Felipe's professor at Georgetown. Later, I saw Madeleine. She said, 'Oh dear, I'm supposed to go to Moscow!' But she got a later flight so that she could stay and see Aznar."

During a ceremony to inaugurate the new Juan Carlos Center at New York University, Gardner noticed that the king handed an envelope to Hillary Clinton, who had come up from Washington for the occasion. "Later on, I saw the letter," Gardner says. "In it the King asked Clinton to come two days early to the NATO summit in Madrid and go to Majorca with him. Across the top of the letter, Clinton had written 'HRC'—as the president refers to Hillary—'thinks it's a great idea. Let's do it.'"

The idea, according to Gardner, was that the Clintons would have "a little R and R" on the king's yacht, the *Fortuna*. "A week before Clinton's visit," Gardner says, "an article appeared in *ABC*"—a Spanish daily—"mentioning Clinton's sailing plans and that Aznar and his wife would also be on the boat. This was a surprise to me, so I made a call to find out." Gardner says that the White House was as surprised as he was at the news that Aznar was included on the *Fortuna* guest list. Clinton didn't want to have to engage in impromptu summitry with the Spanish prime minister. "The White House asked me to call the palace and say it would be best if Aznar didn't come."

Gardner complied, but the reaction from Viscount Fernando Almansa, the king's chief of staff, was curt. "He told me, 'It's the king's yacht and the king invites whomever he wants.' I said, 'Yes, I understand,' and went back and told the White House I thought it would be best if the matter was dropped. In the end, they all went out on the yacht for five hours—the Spanish royal family, the Clintons, Chelsea, and the Aznars. Later, in Madrid, in the President's limousine, I asked Clinton how it had gone. He said, 'Great! I had five hours with the king and the prime minister discussing what kind of world we want for our children.' I asked him, 'Who interpreted?' 'The king!' he said. So Aznar had an unprecedented five hours with Clinton, something few foreign heads of state *ever* get. And that would not have happened if not for the king."

In April 1998, when the tiff over the King's Cuba trip flared up, Prime Minister Aznar was accused of having an "inferiority complex" in the face of the king's diplomatic skills. "The king is a tough act to follow," a senior government aide says. "He is multilingual, he's known every president since J.F.K. His experience counts for a lot. Who's Aznar?"

The king's record as a promoter of Spain abroad has been particularly successful, and in early April Aznar wisely backed down on the issue of the Cuba trip and named a new ambassador, thus paving the way for the king to go to Havana. On his first trip to Latin America, in 1976, Juan Carlos was greeted by children in the streets of Bogotá yelling "Our king is back!" For most of this century, Spain was in a poor position to sell itself abroad. But its transition to democracy is widely admired by Latin-American countries that are themselves shaking off dictatorships, and its political influence in Europe through the EC and NATO makes it even more attractive to them. There has been a veritable flood of Spanish investment in the region. As much as 60 percent of Spain's private-sector foreign investment, an amount totaling some $17 billion, was poured into Latin America in the first eight months of 1997 alone, and Spanish investment in Cuba is now so visible that Cubans joke that the Spaniards have embarked on a "reconquest" of the island they lost a hundred years ago.

Spain is in much better shape economically than it was when Juan Carlos became king. In 1975, when he took office, the gross national product was about $40 billion. Today it is almost $500 billion. The stock market hit all-time highs in early April, and though afflicted with a disturbingly high unemployment rate, Spain is one of the first EC member states to have fulfilled the Maastricht guidelines for entry into the single-European-currency union.

One thing that has not changed significantly, however, is the way business is conducted in Spain. Theft of public funds, bribes, kickbacks, nepotism, and general corruption are common. One of the reasons Felipe González's Socialist Party lost the election in 1996 was that it was involved in so many scandals. Until recently, the king was not publicly tainted by this. Under the constitution, "the person of the king is inviolable and cannot be held accountable," and the Spanish press has always been very cautious in addressing any stories that might implicate him in a scandal.

The royal family's finances are the most sensitive aspect of its carefully guarded life. Politicians, royal historians, biographers, and journalists who cover the monarchy all repeat, mantralike, that "this is not a rich royal family," pointing out that the Bourbons lost their property when Alfonso XIII left Spain. During their long exile, Don Juan and his family were kept going by monthly tithes extended to them by a few noble families. Exactly what property, if any, the royal family owns today isn't publicly known. The chalet they use regularly in the Pyrenees is on loan from a ski resort, while La Zarzuela and Marivent, their summer palace in Majorca, belong to Patrimonio Nacional, a National Heritage–style organization "in the service of the Crown." The king gets a stipend of approximately $7 million a year from the state, out of which he pays some of his expenses, the salaries of his household staff, and taxes.

Traditionally, the king's financial affairs were not discussed, but that began to change in 1992, when it was discovered that Juan Carlos had "disappeared" for a few days. Prime Minister González was asked by reporters where he was, and he said he didn't know. The king turned up in Switzerland, although it appeared that he had signed a law into effect as if he'd been in Madrid. The press began to speculate furiously about the motives for his trip. "It seems he was with a woman," says Albert Montagut, the editor of the Catalonian edition of *El Mundo*. This was the first time anything negative about the king had been reported, and it opened the door to further scrutiny. "He's had to tread carefully since then," says Montagut.

What makes the king most vulnerable is his potential role as the ultimate influence peddler. Among his more ardent defenders, any suggestion that he may have engaged in unethical behavior for personal gain is angrily dismissed. Others suggest that, if he is guilty of anything, it is friendliness, and that as king he runs the risk of acquiring friends who seek benefits from their access to him. But some concede that this may not be the whole story, either. "Juan Carlos probably earns money from opening doors," a veteran palace observer acknowledges, pointing out that the practice of "putting people together for a fee" is common among European royalty.

"The money issue *is* important," Charles Powell says. "In the eighties, when a lot of people were making a fast buck, the king felt left out, and he asked people to invest money for him. One assumes that's how his friendship with Mario Conde began." Conde was the chairman of a major bank, Banesto, and an important figure in the financial world during the booming 1980s. In March he began serving a four-and-a-half-year jail sentence for embezzlement, and he has been charged with various other financial misdeeds, for which he is now standing trial. Before his fall from grace, in 1994, he was close to the palace and is rumored to have been involved in at least one moneymaking deal involving the king.

Asked about the allegations, Baltasar Porcel, who is a political commentator for newspapers and radio and who sometimes advises the king on Catalonian affairs, chooses his words carefully. "The king is a friendly man, and he has *been* the friend of Mario Conde," he says. "And if the king has been Mario Conde's friend for years, it's logical that Conde would try and accentuate the connection now that he's in trouble."

Conde seemed to be doing just that in mid-March, when he claimed that in 1989 he had paid the equivalent of $2 million to Adolfo Suárez, the former prime minister and a close ally of Juan Carlos. The money was allegedly a contribution to Suárez's party, in return for his help in resolving a bank merger. (Suárez denies this.) Conde also managed to note that he had been close to

Viscount Almansa, the king's chief of staff, for many years. Conde-watchers have interpreted his mention of Almansa as a warning shot fired across the king's bow.

What worries some of the king's allies is that Mario Conde may actually possess evidence implicating the king in shady dealings. "Conde has tapes, documents, and that kind of thing," says a well-connected businessman who has known Juan Carlos since the 1960s. "Very incriminating. It would be terrible if he decides to bring it out." But, he adds, he is guardedly confident that Conde will refrain from doing so, since he is believed to have pinned his hopes on being included in an "end-of-the-millennium grand amnesty" by the conservative government. The king, he says, is Conde's "last card," one he would use only if he felt all his hopes of freedom were lost.

"The king has these little things, these negatives, which count against him," says the baron who gave me the tour of his ancestral castle. "But to be fair, one has to take the whole picture of his life, and the way I see it, the positive far outweighs the negative." The Socialist in Barcelona who described himself as "passionately loyal" to the king agrees. "The figure of the king is the best thing we could have invented for the Spanish political system. That is why the majority of Spaniards want to protect him. . . . If he were to do his job badly, or if we had a different king, none of this would be worth anything. But as long as the king doesn't break the rules of the game, the monarchy won't break either."

The "rules" in Spain have changed utterly since the days of Juan Carlos's grandfather, and of Franco. The irony is that the king owes both his accountability and his influence to the democratic system he helped put in place. The king is no longer immune, but since the monarchy is useful and practical—like primogeniture for the baron's former vassals—he is unlikely to lose the people's support. "The monarchy is a mirror in which people can contemplate themselves," Charles Powell says. "The main reason the royal family is so popular is that it embodies the new democratic system. If you criticize the monarchy, you're questioning everything that's happened since the death of Franco. If you question the form of government, you open a Pandora's box and everything falls out of place. The monarchy has been useful. In twenty years it may not be, in which case the royal family may have to pack their bags."

Jesús Garzón: Moving Force

By Carlos Tejero

〜

editor's note

It always seems to happen this way: at the very moment I am ready to proclaim a manuscript complete, a new piece, a new writer, or a new periodical is brought to my attention. Working on this Northern Spain edition proved no exception, as at the eleventh hour I discovered the wonderful magazine *Spain Gourmetour,* published quarterly by the Spanish Trade Commission. Though, as its name indicates, the magazine is very much devoted to the cuisine and wines of Spain, it also features a number of articles pertaining to history and travel. I was so glad to come across this piece because I had been searching for a good article on transhumance, the age-old seasonal migration of livestock—and the people who tend them—between low-lying lands and adjacent mountains. Transhumance was and still is "one of the most distinctive characteristics of the Mediterranean world," according to Fernand Braudel in his masterpiece, *The Mediterranean.* Braudel notes that in the Mediterranean region in the sixteenth century, "transhumance was confined above all to the Iberian peninsula, the south of France, and Italy. In the other peninsulas, the Balkans, Anatolia, North Africa, it was submerged by the predominance of nomadism or semi-nomadism." Nomadism, to clarify, involves moving an entire community—people, animals, and even dwellings—usually for long distances, and it has never been a way of dealing with enormous flocks of sheep. Braudel informs us that geographers distinguish between at least two different kinds of transhumance. Normal transhumance involves sheep farmers and shepherds who live in the lowlands. They leave the lowlands in the summer, which is an unfavorable season for livestock on the plains. Inverse transhumance is of the kind found in Navarra in the sixteenth century (there is a photograph in Braudel's must-read book of a transhumance route on the road from Roncesvalles to Pamplona). Flocks and shepherds would come down from the highlands, the *euskari*. The lowlands served only for marketing purposes, when there was a market being held. This type of transhumance was "a frantic rush down from the mountains in winter . . . all doors were padlocked against these unwelcome visitors, and every year saw a renewal of the eternal war between shepherd and peasant." In 1938, a study was completed of all known cases of transhumance in the Mediterranean (unfortunately, I do not know if a more recent study has been attempted). All the known transhumance routes at that time were superimposed on a map of the Mediterranean region, and they measured about fifteen meters wide. The routes also bore different names in different regions, such as *cañadas* in Castile, *camis ramaders tratturi* in Italy, and *trazzere* in Sicily. In summation, Braudel writes that "transhumance implies all sorts of conditions, physical, human, and historical. In the Mediterranean, in its simplest form, it is a vertical movement from the winter pastures of the plain to the summer pastures in the hills."

In this piece we meet Spanish naturalist Jesús Garzón Heydt, whose life work has been dedicated not only to protecting native Spanish species such as the imperial eagle, black vulture, and Iberian lynx but also to reinstating the practice of transhumance. This interview was part of a feature that *Spain Gourmetour* developed entitled "21st Century Quixotes," profiles of outstanding men and women from Spain whose accomplishments transcend national borders and who, like Cervantes's hero, refuse to let mere reality prevent them from following their hearts.

CARLOS TEJERO is a journalist and has worked at ICEX since 1985.

E ven before we actually meet, I gather that Jesús Garzón is a committed conversationalist: when he arrives by taxi, I observe him engaged in several minutes of animated chat with his driver before getting out of the car. My suspicions are confirmed as soon as our interview begins. Garzón talks a lot and talks well. He communicates his passion for what he does through a torrent of talk that is nonetheless ordered and coherent, and that embraces history, anthropology, biology, economics, gastronomy—complementary disciplines that could be summed up in one word: *life*. Had he chosen to be a teacher, Garzón would have been one of those engaging, approachable figures who imbue their students with an appetite for life.

Jesús Garzón was born fifty-five years ago in Madrid but spent his early childhood partly in Cantabria and partly in Extremadura, both of which were subsequently to provide the primary scenarios for his work. His German grandfather bequeathed him a copious library, particularly strong in biology and natural history, which Jesús consumed without delay. He worked with other Spanish ecologists such as Félix Rodriguez de la Fuente, whose 1970s television series opened up the world of flora and fauna to the Spanish public, and Javier Castroviejo, one of the directors of Doñana National Park and the mainspring behind the creation of Monfragüe Natural Park (in Cáceres, southwest Spain). Last year Garzón was among the recipients of a prestigious Slow Food Award. The Slow Food organization, based in Bologna, Italy, has 65,000 members worldwide, and its aim could be summed up as championing the production of quality food and its rational consumption while according maximum respect to the environment. The practice of transhumance consists in herding livestock alternately from lowland pastures that are poor in summer but rich in the winter, to uplands that are cold and inhospitable in winter but fertile in summer. For Jesús Garzón, moving animals in this way in spring and autumn constitutes "the only efficient method of using natural resources without harming the ecosystem. . . . Transhumance was a natural, spontaneous phenomenon among wild herbivores before man came on the scene. Later, when humans began to domesticate them, they simply capitalized on those habits, driving the livestock along the same routes."

Why is transhumance so important in Spain? "Transhumance is not exclusive to Spain; it is practiced in all places where there are marked climatic differences. But what makes transhumance different in Spain from elsewhere is that it is distinguished by a specific set of laws dating back to the thirteenth century. No other country in the world has laws protective of transhumants, nor such an extensive and regulated network of livestock tracks as Spain does."

Jesús Garzón's interest in transhumance was triggered by the Rio de Janeiro Earth Summit organized by the UN in 1992. For the first time in history, representatives of all governments in the world came together to debate and agree on measures to protect biodiversity. "Until ten years ago transhumance was considered an outdated practice. But thanks to the summit, we no longer discuss whether things are modern but whether they are sustainable and viable in the long term. Practices such as transhumance, which have been sustained throughout history without damaging the environment, are viable. It was on this basis that the summit issued an appeal, subscribed to by all countries in the world, for indigenous peoples to be respected and for their knowledge to be conserved, for it is in them, and in protecting the ecosystems in which they have evolved, that mankind's future lies. Society today is very modern, but no one knows how long it's going to last."

This is the theory of sustainable development, an increasingly widespread concept: modern societies—the predominant societies of industrialized nations—are based on a finite model insofar as they threaten future generations' access to those resources that guarantee quality of life. So the nations of the world have committed themselves to protecting biodiversity. But what solutions can we, our own country, contribute? "Spain's part is to protect its livestock routes, transhumance and the popular culture related not only thereto but to the rural world as a whole, which is still very much alive and which we are still in time to preserve. Bear in mind that a large majority of Spaniards, aged between sixty and eighty, were born at a time when there was no electric light, telephones or cars. These people are the repositories of lore that connects us to our ancestors thousands of years ago, given that there was not that much difference between the resources available to them and the survival techniques they used. We cannot allow this lore to disappear— it could serve us well in the future."

For many centuries, transhumance in Spain was a vivid example of how economic progress and respect for biodiversity could be compatible. In 1273 King Alfonso X formulated the Leyes de la Mesta (Mesta Laws) to protect the interests of livestock owners and herders (who formed local associations known as *mestas,* hence the overall name). For centuries livestock farmers and herdsmen were a privileged social class. And they were by no means alone in this, for the whole of Spain developed into a world power on the strength of the wealth generated, in one way or another, by shifting five million head of cattle and sheep around the network of livestock tracks (known by different names—*cañadas, cordeles, veredas*) that crisscrossed the whole country. As domestic and foreign trade evolved, so guilds of, for example, merchants, carters, and shippers came into being. The state derived a regular, fixed income from the taxes and tolls levied on livestock farmers. Spain dominated the international wool trade—Spanish fleeces were renowned. By facilitating contact and trade among people from different regions, transhumance also influenced the linguistic unification of the country and the standardization of weights and measures.

"This whole system was thrown into chaos by the invasion of the French [during the Peninsular War 1808–1814]. Then at the end of the nineteenth century the growth of the railway accelerated the abandonment of transhumance. Little by little herds stopped using the tracks. The watering and resting places that punctuated them every ten miles were illegally appropriated by townships or private individuals." In the twentieth century roads and big public works gradually invaded and fragmented the cattle track network. Around the 1950s these problems, combined with increased road transport, caused livestock farmers to abandon transhumance on the hoof almost entirely.

"Transporting cattle and sheep by truck was soon followed by another effect: leaving herds and flocks in situ all year round, it being more convenient for farmers to bring fodder and water to the farm than to herd their animals to pasture." Transhumant herds were replaced by static ones that, though apparently in tune with the logic of progress, "triggered an ecological catastrophe. The disappearance of transhumance also meant the disappearance of great green corridors used by wildlife; wolves, which used to stalk the flocks along their tracks, became almost extinct in southern Spain, and other species such as the imperial eagle and the vulture were similarly affected; intensive grazing caused grass and tree species such as the ilex and cork oak to disappear, which in turn affected the snake and insect population and, at the end of the chain, the birds that live on them; depletion of vegetation cover allowed erosion by rain to set in, and so on and so on."

Transhumance Today

Despite this dispiriting overview, transhumance has not died out completely in Spain. Though there is still a lot of convincing to be done, public authorities have become aware of the issue thanks to fighters like Jesús Garzón, among other factors. In 1995, for example, the Spanish parliament passed a new Cattle Track Law that protects the tracks as "property in the public domain [that are] inalienable, imprescriptible and inembargable and whose primary use is reserved for the movement of cattle." Currently, a million head of cattle (some three percent of Spain's total) make use of the network "but only for short distances, taking no more than a week or ten days. Long-distance transhumance, with routes taking longer than a month, died out fifty years ago and is practiced today only by our Trashumancia y Naturaleza (Transhumance and Nature) Association in conjunction with our stockbreeder colleagues."

Jesús Garzón created the Spanish branch of the Transhumance and Nature Association—which also has branches in Switzerland and the Netherlands—in 1993, with three million borrowed sheep. Today it has its own flocks, acquired through altruistic donations by the likes of Prince Bernard of the Netherlands and Luc Hoffman, director of the Camargue Reserve in France. Its activities have gradually impinged on social awareness, largely thanks to media coverage of Garzón and his collaborators' annual invasion of central Madrid with their herds, exercising their right of way along the livestock route to Extremadura from the mountains of Cantabria or León. Trashumancia y Naturaleza came into being under the auspices of the European Natura 2000 program, "but community subsidies ran out in 1997, and since then we have received hardly any support from central or regional governments at home. All our money comes from private donations, which are not enough to cover the costs of our activities. Were we to devote ourselves exclusively to livestock, stockbreeders would make a profit, but our operation is farther-reaching than that. We breed Spanish mastiffs—the dogs traditionally used by shepherds to protect their flocks from wolves—sheep, hens, donkeys. . . . We've bought up almost the entire population of Extremaduran Retinta goats, which were in danger of extinction, so that we can regenerate the flock and ensure its excellent milk yield; we lend support vehicles and trailers to transhumant herdsmen; we lease out summer and winter pastures; we have a hand in the training of young shepherds; and we take part in national and international seminars concerned with conserving the livestock tracks. All in all, quite a gamut of fascinating activities that are difficult to carry on without institutional help."

But is transhumance an economically viable activity nowadays? How do you persuade a livestock farmer to readopt transhumance? "Economic viability is a very relative term. Intensive livestock rearing, the predominant pattern in Europe, is based on importing cheap fodder or fish meal. The only way for developed societies to produce food in an economically and ecologically viable way is to readopt solutions that are efficient in terms of energy and transport, but not at the cost of destroying the planet and the food resources of the poorest countries. Furthermore, the end products of intensive livestock rearing are of dubious quality, as shown recently by mad cow disease and the discovery of dioxins in chickens and pigs. Something can look viable in theory but turn out eventually to be a double-edged sword. I champion transhumance—extensive livestock rearing—as a major alternative approach to producing quality meat and milk, derived from virtually free-range animals, which are tantamount to free for most of their lives and which eat natural pasture and do not depend on imported fodder. It also represents a cheap alternative in terms of energy consumption—the livestock moves at a speed of two kilometers per hour—and meanwhile the animals fertilize the route as they move from one place to another, thus avoiding the organic pollution that static herds and flocks produce. Transhumance helps preserve the environment as well as being a fundamental part of our cultural heritage."

Victory at Sea, 1571—Lepanto

BY OLIVER WARNER

∾

editor's note

The Battle of Lepanto, in 1571, was a hugely significant conflict in Mediterranean—especially Spanish, Venetian, Greek, and Turkish—history. The site of this naval battle lies near the entrance to the Gulf of Corinth, known at that time as the Gulf of Lepanto. The fleet that set out to fight the Turks was primarily Spanish, with strong papal and Venetian contingents. The Christians were victorious, reasserting Spanish supremacy in the Mediterranean, and the victory was celebrated with much fanfare in Europe. But as Sir Charles Petrie, in his book *Philip II of Spain* (1963), has noted, "The battle of Lepanto did not break the back of Ottoman naval power, it did not recover Cyprus, and it did not lead to the policing of the Mediterranean by Spain. Though a tactical victory of the first order, because of the dissolution of the [Holy] League strategically it left the Sultan the victor. But morally it was decisive, for by lifting the pall of terror which had shrouded eastern and central Europe since 1453, it blazoned throughout Christendom the startling fact that the Turk was no longer invincible. Hence onward to the battle of Zenta, in 1697, when Eugene, Prince of Savoy, drove in rout the army of Sultan Mustafa II into the river Theiss, and thereby finally exorcised the Turkish threat to Europe. Though there were to be many ups and downs, never was the full prestige of Suleyman the Magnificent to be revived. His reign marks the summit of Turkish power, and it was the day of Lepanto which broke the charm upon which it rested." More recently (2000), historian Bernard Lewis, in *A Middle East Mosaic*, notes that Lepanto made very little difference to the real balance of power in southeastern Europe and the Mediterranean. "The Turkish armies remained dominant on land; the Turkish fleets were swiftly rebuilt. When the sultan expressed concern about the cost, his grand vizier replied: 'The might of our empire is such that if we wished to equip the entire fleet with silver anchors, silken rigging and satin sails, we could do it.'"

Among the Spanish wounded at Lepanto was Miguel de Cervantes, who apparently described the battle as "the most honourable and lofty occasion that past centuries have beheld." Sir Charles Petrie has noted that "both Philip and Don John [of Austria, half-brother of Philip] have been subject to criticism, chiefly civilian, for not having followed up the victory of Lepanto by an immediate attack upon Constantinople, which, according to the critics, would inevitably have been followed by the overthrow of the Ottoman Empire. The blame is usually placed upon the shoulders of the king either on the grounds of his habitual procrastination or of his jealousy of his brother."

Readers especially interested in Lepanto should note that some magnificent (and well-preserved) banners—which would have flown from the sailing ships' mastheads—are on display at the Museo de la Santa Cruz in Toledo and at the Museo Storico Navale in Venice. An excellent account of Lepanto is found in *The Decisive Battles of the Western World and Their Influence Upon History,* volume 1, by J. F. C. Fuller (Eyre & Spottiswoode, London, 1965).

OLIVER WARNER was the author of a dozen or so volumes of naval history and biography, including *Trafalgar* (Pan Books, 1966), *Great Sea Battles* (Ferndale Editions, 1981), *A Portrait of Lord Nelson* (Chatto and Windus, 1971), and *Nelson's Battles* (Pen & Sword Books, 2003).

There is scarcely a great city in Western Europe—Rome, Madrid, Vienna, Genoa, and Venice notable among them— without its proud memorials of the mighty clash at sea between Christian and Moslem forces that took place near Lepanto on October 7, 1571. It was not only a terrible encounter in itself, it was one of the most picturesque in all sea history. Painters, weavers of tapestry, carvers of trophies-of-arms, engravers of commemorative medals, and jewelers vied with one another to do honor to the Christian victory, the most extraordinary of its kind ever won.

Sea battles may be great in showing the sea commander at his most skillful or resolute; they may be tame and even indecisive as battles, yet important in their effect; or they may be both. Lepanto was great in every sense of the word. It was a milestone in the grim and protracted struggle between the Cross and the Crescent.

It was fought off the shores of Greece, at the entrance to the Gulf of Patras, and it led to a wave of renewed hope and vigor among the Christian nations. A fleet made up of the forces of the Holy League—Spain, the Papal States, and the Republic of Venice—all under the command of Don John of Austria, defeated the principal fleet of the Turks under Ali Pasha. On the victor's side, notable leaders were the Marqués de Santa Cruz, a Spaniard; Andrea Doria, leading a Genoese squadron; and Marc Antonio Colonna, who commanded the forces of Pius V. It was, in fact as in name, a company drawn from most of Catholic Europe, France excepted.

Lepanto, coming as it did after the repulse of the Turks at the siege of Malta six years earlier, made it certain that the Mediterranean would not become a Moslem lake. Henceforward no sultan would in fact exercise paramount sea power, and although this result was slow to make itself apparent, any further Moslem expansion into the Europe that they had invaded with such success would be mainly at the expense of Poland and Russia. It would be by land. By sea, Spaniards and Italians, with the example before them of the island Knights of Malta, had shown that with leadership, courage, and the help of a new weapon (in this case the heavily gunned galleass) they could withstand the ancient method of fighting solely with oared galleys, manned by slaves.

Don John of Austria, who in the year of Lepanto was not yet twenty-five—though he had already served with distinction against the Moors in Granada—was the natural son of the Emperor Charles V by Barbara Blomberg, the daughter of a wealthy Bavarian. He was thus half brother to Philip II of Spain, one of the pillars of the League; and he had long been, in name at least, the principal Spanish admiral. Fair-haired, eager for fame, Don John proved a good leader for a mixed and quarrelsome fleet.

Among the Italian forces the Venetians, led by Augustino Barbarigo and the veteran Sebastian Veniero, were smarting under the recent loss of most of Cyprus to the Turks, and they bore no love toward the Genoese, their ancient rivals at sea, led by Giovanni Andrea Doria, nephew of one of Genoa's greatest men. In Doria's squadron a Spanish volunteer was serving whose fame was destined to outshine even that of the commanders. He was Miguel de Cervantes, later to become the author of *Don Quixote*.

The League had been formed in May, 1571, through the tireless efforts of Pope Pius V. This pontiff, who held the See of Rome for only a few years (1566–72), was one of the most memorable figures in an age renowned for great men. Portraits and medals show him with a high forehead, rather sunken eyes, a strong, curved nose, and a pointed beard. He was of humble origin, and even as pope he preferred to continue the ascetic habits of a Dominican monk. His personal piety, zeal, and devotion to the Church have never been exceeded, but he had a gift for diplomacy rare in the saintly. Through his skill and patience he was able to form the first effective combination of Christian forces at a moment that was critical for Europe. His aim was twofold: to bring help to the Venetians, who were losing ground in the eastern Mediterranean, where they had long been the great traders and where they held outposts and possessions; and to prevent the power of the warlike Turk from spreading any closer to the Papal States.

Ever since the tenth century the Turks had been steadily eroding the power of the ancient Christian empire of Byzantium, with its capital at Constantinople. Checked at first by the Crusaders, they became established in Anatolia as early as 1300. Then, crossing first the Black Sea and later the Sea of Marmora into Europe, they began to advance upon the nearer territories of Christendom. The crowning humiliation came in 1453, when Mohammed II took Constantinople itself.

The Turks moved south as well as west. In 1517 Egypt was occupied by Selim I. His successor, Suleiman I, whom men called the Magnificent, extended his sway in the course of a long and splendid reign to Baghdad, to Rhodes, to Belgrade, to Budapest, and almost to the gates of Vienna, capital of the Holy Roman emperors who ruled most of Western Europe. To this day Hungarians remember the defeat of Mohács, fought less than half a century before Lepanto, as one of the saddest in their history, although much later they had their revenge on the very same field.

The Turks were united. They were bred to arms. They upheld the great cause of Islam. Only by following their example of unity and devotion, only by reviving a spiritual fire that seemed to have been damped since the Crusades, could the Christians hope to stem the tide.

If the Christians found the necessary inspiration in the noble and determined character of the Pope, they were hardly less fortunate in their tactical leader. Don John of Austria was one of those rare men who seem to have been born with a gift for war. He had been brought up in Spain, and was recognized very early by Philip II as a young man to whom responsible posts could be entrusted; and his age, his birth, and his experience against the corsairs of North Africa and the Moors in Granada all seemed to fit him to lead the great armada which the efforts of Pius V had assembled.

Don John's original rendezvous was to be at Messina. When he arrived there, he found himself in charge of more than three hundred ships, two thirds of them known as royal galleys, each with a nominal complement of one hundred soldiers in addition to the rowers who toiled at the oars.

The Spanish contingent was the largest: eighty galleys, twenty-two other vessels, and no less than twenty-one thousand fighting men. The Venetians contributed more than a hundred vessels, but most were poorly manned, and their six heavily armed galleasses were in fact the Republic's most important asset. These galleasses, which were towed into action by lighter vessels, were broader in the beam than the galley; the additional depth allowed the erection, forward, of a structure, fitted with swivel guns, that anticipated the modern armored turret.

In the galleass the usual ornamental stem of the galley was replaced by a formidable point, while lower down the solid cutwater, or prow, was effective against anything of smaller size that could not get out of the way. Sides and stern were also heavily armed, while the rowers were protected by a deck that served as a platform for the fighting men. In battle the rowers were yoked in both directions, some pulling and some pushing at the fifty-foot oars.

The Pope himself fitted out twelve galleys, hired many more, and supplied the necessary troops. No less than eighty thousand men assembled at Messina with his official blessing. Of these, some fifty thousand volunteers, impressed men, and slaves labored at the oars. The rest were soldiers. Don John, with the aid of a blackboard, explained his methods to representatives of the fighting men, gave the captains of his fleet detailed information as to how he would meet the most likely tactical contingencies, and arranged for appropriate signals.

While he was surveying and ordering his fleet, he got news that the Turks, who were believed to have massed about three hundred ships, were roving the Ionian Sea and attacking the islands therein. On September 16 the Christians put to sea, and the first precise news of the enemy came before the end of the month, when Don John anchored off Corfu. There he learned that the Turkish commander, Ali Pasha, had recently landed, burned some churches, failed to subdue the island's fortress, and had then retreated to the anchorage of Lepanto, which was far up the eighty-mile stretch of water now known as the Gulf of Corinth.

At a council of war, characterized like many such councils by acrimony and dispute, those who were for instant attack carried the day. They included Colonna, Barbarigo, Santa Cruz, and Don John himself. The season was growing late, and the differences between the Allies, never far from the surface, were increasing. Spaniards and Venetians had already come to blows, largely due to the fact that Spaniards had to be drafted into the Venetian ships to bring them up to strength.

Off Cephalonia, on October 6, a ship from Crete brought news of the fall of Famagusta, the last Venetian stronghold in Cyprus, and of the torture and death of its noble defenders. A wave of horror spread through the Allies, and an immediate advance was ordered into waters where the enemy was known to be waiting. One further item of news was not altogether cheering. It appeared that Ali Pasha had been reinforced by the ships of Uluch Ali, once a Calabrian fisherman but now the dey of Algiers and known to be a daring corsair by many in the Christian fleet.

During the night of October 6 the Turks, with a favoring wind, advanced westward toward the Christians. At dawn on October 7 the most powerful forces that had ever met at sea came within sight of one another at the entrance to the Gulf of Patras, which is west of the larger Gulf of Corinth.

Here, as at most earlier naval battles, fleets met like armies. Their formation was rigid; the commands were military; and tactics were based upon experience by land. The sailors got the ships where they were wanted, while the "generals" and their soldiers fought it out.

Before he drew up his formal line of battle, Don John gave two orders. The first was to remove the iron beaks which protruded ten or fifteen feet from the bows of certain of the fighting ships. The second was that no one should fire "until near enough to be splashed with the blood of an enemy." Both directives were wise. The battle would not be won by ramming, but by close fighting, in which the Spaniards' armor, together with their arquebuses, might prove a decisive advantage.

Barbarigo and his Venetians were placed on the left wing,

Barbarigo himself sailing as close as he dared to the inshore rocks and shoals, in the hope that his flank could not be turned. Andrea Doria was on the right wing, where papal galleys were mingled with the Genoese. In the center was the flagship of Don John, conspicuous by its high, carved poop and triple-stern lanterns, its green pennant at the forepeak, and its Holy Standard at the maintop. Near him were Veniero and Colonna. In reserve were thirty-five Spanish and Venetian galleys under Santa Cruz, ready to apply their strength where most needed.

As the fleets neared each other the six Venetian galleasses, the spearhead of the Christian attack, were towed into position. Two, in line ahead, were placed in front of each main squadron. When every preparation had been made, Don John boarded a fast vessel and sailed behind the three-mile front across which his forces extended, heartening his men and, in his turn, being cheered.

By the time Don John had returned to his own galley, the wind had changed in his favor. He was now able to see that the Turks had their fleet arrayed in the form of a huge crescent, but this was altered, almost at once, to conform to his own dispositions. There were many Christian galley slaves in the Turkish fleet. To them Ali Pasha said: "If I win the battle, I promise you your liberty. If the day is yours, then God has given it to you."

First blood was drawn by the galleasses of Don John's center. Their guns, heavier than anything the Turks possessed, did their execution at long range, sinking several Turkish galleys even before the main forces were in contact. Partly as a result of this initial setback the left and right wings of the Moslems separated from the center. Uluch Ali made a wide sweep toward the southern shore, in an attempt to outflank Andrea Doria, while Mohammed Sirocco held a similar course toward Barbarigo and the northern shore. Ali Pasha's center squadron, eluding the powerful galleasses as best it could, drove on to meet that of Don John. By midday, or shortly

after, the two flagships were locked together, crossbow and arque-
bus being exchanged for sword and scimitar, the decks slippery with
blood from close fighting. And by that time, all three squadrons
were at grips.

Against the Christian left, Sirocco's maneuver succeeded. His
knowledge of the shore line enabled him to sail even closer to it than
Barbarigo, and to surround him. The Venetian admiral was
attacked by eight Turkish galleys, and he himself was killed by an
arrow. Twice the Venetian flagship was stormed; twice it was
retaken. At last, when help came from Canale and others, Sirocco's
ship was sunk and he was thrown into the water. Although by then
badly wounded, he was rescued, only to be beheaded on the spot by
his captors.

On the Christian right the battle had at first gone equally badly.
Although Uluch Ali had not been able to outflank Andrea Doria, he
had at once doubled back to a gap that had opened in the Allied line
and had taken part of Don John's squadron in the rear. Among the
ships attacked was the *Capitana* of Malta, commanded by
Giustiniani, Prior of the Order of Saint John. The Prior fell with
five arrows in his body, and the *Capitana* was made prize. At the
most critical time Santa Cruz, seeing the Maltese in tow of the
enemy, moved to the rescue, and Uluch Ali, relinquishing his capture, made haste to retreat.

The issue was decided in the center. Here, from the first, the
virtue of Don John's order to dismantle the iron beaks had been
clear. The Turkish admiral had not done this, and though the forepeak of his flagship towered over the Christian decks, his forecastle
guns fired into the air. Those of Don John, placed at a lower level,
riddled the Turkish galley with shot just above her water line. The
armored Spanish arquebusiers soon decimated the Turkish ranks.
Not for nothing were the Spaniards reckoned the steadiest soldiers
of their time.

The climax came when Don John gave the order to board: once, twice, parties were driven back, but at last they carried the Turkish poop. There Ali Pasha, already wounded in the head, tried to buy his life with a promise of treasure. It was in vain. Even his protective talisman, the right canine tooth of Mohammed contained in a crystal ball, did not avail him. A soldier cut him down, hacked off his head, and carried it to Don John. The admiral, recoiling in horror, ordered the man to throw the grisly trophy into the sea. But the Spaniard disobeyed him and mounted it on a pike, which was then held aloft in the prow of the Turkish flagship. Consternation spread among the Moslems, and within a few moments resistance was over. The Ottoman standard, inscribed with the name of Allah twenty-nine thousand times and never before lost in battle, was lowered from the maintop. Don John was then able to turn his attention to his right wing, where all was not well.

No less than five of Doria's galleys had been stricken. On the *San Giovanni* and the *Piamontesa* virtually everyone was dead. The *Doncella* was not much better off, while in the *Florence* only the captain and seventeen seamen survived out of two hundred. The *Marquesa* was also hard pressed. It was in this ship that Cervantes was serving. He had been ill with fever before the battle, but he had risen from his sickbed and had volunteered for a place of danger. There he remained throughout the battle and received the wound that disabled his left hand for life.

Uluch Ali, whose Algerians had done most of the damage on the Christian right, retreated to the shelter of Lepanto where he learned of the death of Ali Pasha, although sixteen of his galleys turned on their pursuers and fought one of the bloodiest encounters of the entire day with Don Juan of Cardona. But as the four-hour fight came to a close, with the enemy center and right almost totally destroyed and the left in gradual retreat, Don John at last had time to survey the action as a whole and to begin to reckon his gain and loss.

Nearly eight thousand of the bravest men in Spain and Italy were dead; double that number were wounded. The Turks and Algerians lost at least three times as many killed, and some twelve thousand Christian slaves were rescued from their galleys. Never again did the Turkish sultan contrive to assemble so powerful a fleet. Christians and Turks had been roughly equal in numbers, and had fought with equal courage. Victory went to the side with better weapons and better leadership; here the galleass and the person of Don John proved decisive.

Lepanto was Don John's first and last major sea battle. He died in the Low Countries at the age of thirty-one, a man of one paramount success and many disappointments. Like the galleys he commanded, he belonged to an old order of sea warfare, one whose history went back to the days of Actium, Salamis, and beyond. The future was with sail, with the broadsides of the future ships of the line.

The "tumult and the shouting" died, the "captains and the kings" departed, the fleet dispersed, the squadrons on regular service took up new dispositions, the wounded went home to die or to be cared for; and then, slowly but surely, the news of the action spread far and wide. In the sixteenth century events took a long time to fit into a proper perspective—yet there were compensations. Great happenings made more impact than anything we hear as news today, except in the rarest circumstances. Men and women gave every episode and incident its full value, and survivors of Lepanto would tell their tales to enraptured audiences in every corner of Europe.

The cumulative impact was both astounding and permanent. The victory may be said to have begun a spirit of revival—in war, diplomacy, the arts, and architecture—which was in time to bring

Europe to the proud splendor of the flowering of the Baroque age. Vaults, cupolas, and arches, which had originated in the architecture of Imperial Rome and been modified in Byzantium, reappeared in great buildings, replacing the slender, mystical dreaminess of later Gothic buildings. There was a new, rich solidity of horizontal planes, and polychromatic exuberance in metal and marbles. All betokened renewal of belief in life, religion, art, and politics.

To be sure, Lepanto did not end Turkish power and aspiration, or even destroy Turkish sea power. More than seventy years later the Turks mounted an invasion of Crete, which was one of the main Venetian outposts. The siege began in 1645 and continued over two decades, Candia holding out against all attacks until at last attrition and hunger took their toll and the fortress fell. The Turks continued their struggle with the Holy Roman emperors of Vienna, the capital being once again endangered in 1683 and saved only by an astonishing rescue march by John Sobieski, Poland's hero-king, who rendered a unique service in the old chivalrous spirit to a fellow Christian ruler.

What Lepanto proved was that Turkish power could be contained, and that the Crescent was not invincible. It was as profound in its effects as, for instance, were the battles of Stalingrad and Midway in the last great war. It was the beginning of a long and lasting revival. Christendom had found the will and strength to push back the invader; memories of the Crusades came flooding back; and as Cervantes grew older, more mature, and more experienced, he wrote that affectionate monument to Christian chivalry, *Don Quixote*.

This piece originally appeared in the July 1963 issue of *Horizon*. Copyright © Oliver Warner 1963. Reprinted with permission.

Biblioteca

Northern Spain itself is not typically highlighted in the following Mediterranean volumes, but aspects of Spain are, so I include them here.

The Ancient Mediterranean, Michael Grant, Charles Scribner's Sons, 1969. In this scholarly work Grant reminds us that a huge proportion of our civilized heritage, "almost in its entirety, came to us from the ancient Mediterranean— from Greece and from Rome and from Israel. This fact is given too little prominence today because so many other ancient cultures, some of them from much further afield, have now been discovered. Yet it still remains true that the Mediterranean was the region from which civilisation came our way."

The First Eden: The Mediterranean World and Man, Sir David Attenborough, William Collins Sons & Co., London, 1987. The four parts of this book deal with natural history, archaeology, history, and ecology, and there is very good coverage of Mediterranean plants and animals.

The Inner Sea: The Mediterranean and Its People, Robert Fox, Knopf, 1993.

Mediterranean, photography by Mimmo Jodice, essays by George Hersey and Predrag Matvejevic, Aperture, 1995.

Mediterranean: A Cultural Landscape, Predrag Matvejevic, translated by Michael Henry Heim, University of California Press, Berkeley, 1999; previously published as *Mediteranski brevijar*, Zagreb, 1987; *Bréviaire mediterranéen*, Paris, 1992; and *Mediterraneo: Un nuovo breviario*, Milan, 1993. A beautiful, unusual book combining personal observations with history, maps, maritime details, people, and language.

The Mediterranean, Fernand Braudel, first published in France, 1949; English translation of second revised edition, HarperCollins, 1972; abridged edition, HarperCollins, 1992. Still the definitive classic. *Esencial*.

Mediterranean: From Homer to Picasso, Xavier Girard, translated by Simon Pleasance and Fronza Woods, Assouline, 2001. This recent book is perhaps in a category by itself. It's divided into five chapters—representations, narratives, figures, places, and arts—and I've been waiting for a volume just like it, filled with color and black and white illustrations and photos. As stated in the prologue, "'the Mediterranean,' wrote Bernard Pingaud in the pages of *L'Arc* in 1959, "is nothing other than the image we make of it for ourselves. The unusual thing is that we all make an image of it for ourselves, and that it is still a magnet for all those who are lucky enough to discover it one day. Herein lies a secret. It is perhaps not the secret conjured up by the "land where the orange tree blooms." It is the secret of this image itself, the secret of a dream which paradoxically contrasts abundance and drought, merriness and poverty, moderation and excess, joy and tragedy. Who can say why we need the Midi? If the Mediterranean didn't exist, we would have to invent it.'"

The Mediterranean: Lands of the Olive Tree, Culture & Civilizations, text and photographs by Alain Cheneviere, Konecky & Konecky, New York, 1997. This is that rare book that has both perceptive text and gorgeous photos.

Memory and the Mediterranean, Fernand Braudel, Alfred A. Knopf, 2001.

On the Shores of the Mediterranean, Eric Newby, Harvill Press, London, 1984; Picador, 1985. You have to travel to other places around the Mediterranean besides Spain—the former Yugoslavia, Greece, Turkey, Israel, North Africa, the Côte d'Azur, and Venice—but it's a pleasure every step of the way.

The Phoenicians, edited by Sabatino Moscati, Rizzoli, 1999. The Phoenician civilization remains mysterious, but this beautifully printed and fascinating paperback reveals a treasure trove of information in the form of essays contributed by a number of scholars. A welcome addition to Mediterranean literature.

The Pillars of Hercules: A Grand Tour of the Mediterranean, Paul Theroux, G.P. Putnam's Sons, 1995.

Playing Away: Roman Holidays and Other Mediterranean Encounters, Michael Mewshaw, Atheneum, 1988.

The Spirit of Mediterranean Places, Michel Butor, the Marlboro Press, 1986.

The Sun at Midday: Tales of a Mediterranean Family, Gini Alhadeff, Pantheon, 1997. Though Alhadeff's life was and remains partly Italian, this is a full Mediterranean memoir, beautifully written and one of my favorite books.

Mediterranean Architecture and Style

Mediterranean Color: Italy, France, Spain, Portugal, Morocco, Greece, photographs and text by Jeffrey Becom, Abbeville Press, 1990.

Mediterranean Lifestyle, photographs by Pere Planells, text by Paco Assensio, Loft Publications; distributed in the United States by Watson-Guptill, 2000.

Mediterranean Living, Lisa Lovatt-Smith, Whitney Library of Design, Watson-Guptill Publications, 1998.

Mediterranean Style, Catherine Haig, Abbeville Press, 1998; first published in Great Britain in 1997 by Conran Octopus, London.

Mediterranean Vernacular: A Vanishing Architectural Tradition, V. I. Atroshenko, Milton Grundy, Rizzoli International Publications, 1991.

Playing Away: Roman Holidays and Other Mediterranean Encounters, Michael Mewshaw, Atheneum, 1988.

Villages in the Sun: Mediterranean Community Architecture, Myron Goldfinger, Rizzoli, 1993.

The Civilization of Europe in the Renaissance, John Hale, Atheneum, 1994; first American edition, 1993. I first picked up this book because the title was so similar to Jacob Burckhardt's *The Civilization of the Renaissance in Italy.* The reviews on the back cover compared the book not only to Burckhardt's classic but also to Fernand Braudel's *The Mediterranean in the Time of Philip II.* I needed no further justification to purchase it. Featuring more than one hundred black and white illustrations, this volume covers the period from about 1450 to 1620. Some of Hale's other works, which are ideal companion volumes to this one, include *Renaissance Europe, 1480–1520* (1971); *Renaissance War Studies* (1982); *War and Society in Renaissance Europe* (1985); and *Artists and Warfare in the Renaissance* (1990).

The Decisive Battles of the Western World and Their Influence Upon History, J.F.C. Fuller, Eyre & Spottiswoode, London, volume 1: *From the Earliest Times to the Battle of Lepanto* (1954), volume 2: *From the Defeat of the Spanish Armada to the Battle of Waterloo* (1955), volume 3: *From the American Civil War to the End of the Second World War* (1956). Though I know it is incorrect to place this trilogy under the heading of "Europe," most of these decisive battles did, after all, take place in Europe, and truthfully I just haven't figured out yet how to categorize it. (Most likely I will create a separate heading for it, which it certainly deserves.) I came across it while I was reading the biography of Philip II by Sir Charles Petrie (below), in which Petrie refers to Fuller's account of the Battle of Lepanto as the single best one in print. By searching www.abebooks.com, I found the three-volume set available from a book dealer in the U.K., not surprisingly, and I'm happy to report that this is a stunning publishing achievement. Major-General Fuller was apparently the "pioneer of mechanization in the British Army" and is "known all over the world as the most fearless and penetrating of military critics." Fuller notes in the preface that "whether war is a necessary factor in the evolution of mankind may be disputed, but a fact which cannot be questioned is that, from the earliest records of man to the present age, war has been his dominant preoccupation. There has never been a period in human history altogether free from war, and seldom one of more than a generation which has not witnessed a major conflict: great wars flow and ebb almost as regularly as the tides." Not exactly an uplifting thought, but he goes on to say, "yet one thing is certain, and it is that the more we study the history of war, the more we shall be able to understand war itself, and, seeing that it is now the dominant factor, until we do understand it, how can we hope to regulate human affairs?" How, indeed. This set is worth your most determined efforts to obtain. *Esencial.*

Europe: A History, Norman Davies, Oxford University Press, 1996. In the opening line to his preface, Davies states that "this book contains little that is original," but I would disagree. From the chapter titles ("Hellas," "Roma," "Origo," "Pestis," "Renatio," "Dynamo," and so on) to the manner in which ideas and material are presented, plus the useful appendixes and notes at the end of the book, this *is* an original work, highly recommended.

Fifty Years of Europe: An Album, Jan Morris, Villard, 1997. At last count, I discovered I'd read all of Jan Morris's books except three. Hers are among the very first books I distinctly remember as being responsible for my developing wanderlust. When I saw this volume, I thought, who better to be a reader's companion on a tour of Europe on the brink of the twenty-first century? She's traveled to all of Europe's corners more than, I believe, any other contemporary writer, and one of the most appealing aspects of this book is that she often includes multiple perspectives, relating her observations to the first time she visited a place as well as more recently.

History of the Present: Essays, Sketches, and Dispatches from Europe in the 1990s, Timothy Garton Ash, Random House, 1999. The bulk of this insightful book is made up of "analytical reportages" that were originally published in *The New York Review of Books.* Ash admits that the phrase "history of the present" is not his but rather was coined by American diplomat and historian George Kennan in a review of Ash's book, *The Uses of Adversity,* in the 1980s. The phrase is the best description for what Ash has been trying to write for twenty years, combining the crafts of historian and journalist. I really like the way Ash has written this book, with a chronology for each piece and diarylike sketches inserted throughout that are drawn from his own notebooks and recollections. Among Ash's observations of Spain: "The transition to democracy in Spain after 1975 involved a conscious strategy of not looking back, not confronting or 'treating' the past. The writer Jorge Semprun speaks of 'a collective and willed amnesia.' To be sure, there was an initial explosion of interest in recent history, but there were no trials of Francoist leaders, no purges, no truth commissions. On the fiftieth anniversary of the Spanish Civil War, the prime minister, Felipe González, issued a statement saying that the war was 'no longer present and alive in the reality of the country.'"

Holy War: The Crusades and Their Impact on Today's World, Karen Armstrong, with a new preface, Anchor Books, 2002; originally published in hardcover in Great Britain by Macmillan, 1988, and subsequently published in revised editions in the United States by Doubleday, 1991 (hardcover), and Anchor Books, 1992 (paperback). Spain was not a major participant in the Crusades (France, Germany, and the Venetians were the true instigators), but Spain's Muslim, Jewish, and Christian history makes a basic knowledge of the Crusades essential toward a complete interpretation of Spain and the Spanish. Additionally, as Armstrong notes in her updated preface, "it is important for

Western people to consider these contemporary holy wars in connection with the Crusades, because they remind us of our own input, involvement and responsibilities." I think this is the single most important book of our times, and I urge you to read it and to urge friends, family, and colleagues to do so as well. Armstrong concludes her preface by stating that the Crusades show religion at its very worst. "After writing *Holy War* I was so saddened by the conflict between the three Abraham traditions that I decided to embark on the research for my book *A History of God*. [See my *Morocco* edition for details of this excellent work.] I wanted to demonstrate the strong and positive ideals and visions that Jews, Christians, and Muslims share in common. It is now over a millennium since Pope Urban II called the First Crusade in 1095, but the hatred and suspicion that this expedition unleashed still reverberates, never more so than on September 11, 2001, and during the terrible days that followed. It is tragic that our holy wars continue, but for that very reason we must strive for mutual understanding and for what in these pages I have called 'triple vision.'"

The Penguin Atlas of Ancient History (1967; reprinted 1986), *Medieval History* (1968; reprinted 1992), *Modern History—to 1815* (1973; reprinted 1986), and *Recent History—Europe Since 1815* (1982), Colin McEvedy, Penguin Books. This is a brilliant idea: a chronological sequence of maps that illustrate political and military developments, which in turn illustrate history via geography. Each individual volume is remarkably fascinating, and the four as a whole present an enlightening read. The maps appear on the right-hand pages while explanatory text accompanies them on the left-hand pages. The *Recent History* edition features Spain on the map for the year 1938 and shows the boundaries of Nationalist and Republican Spain. "The Spanish Republic," the author notes, "had come into existence in 1931, when a popular rebellion forced King Alfonso XIII to flee. The Republicans then attempted to push Spain from the eighteenth century into the twentieth in one go, a programme that alienated the church, the army and the upper classes and finally precipitated Franco's rebellion." This may be the most succinct description of how the Civil War began that I've ever read, and is really, despite many missing details, enough for the general reader and traveler to know. ~In the same series but compiled by different authors is *The Penguin Atlas of Diasporas* (Gerard Chaliand and Jean-Pierre Rageau, 1995). This edition is equally fascinating—perhaps more so, as I've not seen another volume like it—and highlights Jewish, Armenian, Gypsy, Black, Chinese, Indian, Irish, Greek, Lebanese, Palestinian, Vietnamese, and Korean migrations. The year 1492 was, obviously, a significant one in the history of Spain and the history of diasporas. Among welcome places for the expelled Jews and Muslims were the Ottoman Empire, Morocco, and the Netherlands (once it was free from Spain), though the Sephardic Jews mostly settled in the Mediterranean countries of Morocco, Tunisia, Italy, and Egypt. All of these are *esencial*.

Spain

The Buried Mirror: Reflections on Spain and the New World, Carlos Fuentes, Houghton Mifflin, 1992. Casting a wide net is at the core of *The Collected Traveler,* and considering the historic relationship between Spain and the Americas is essential to understanding Spain. In this engaging and unique book, Fuentes uses the metaphor of mirrors (inspired by mirrors found in ancient burial caches in the Americas) to explore the ways in which a national character is formed, how stereotypes evolve, and "what continuities are discovered when a human community truly understands its roots." Published on the quincentennial of Columbus's discovery of America, Fuentes offers us much to ponder and much to appreciate about the great variety of Spanish culture. The book—which is a companion volume to a Discovery/BBC television series—is profusely illustrated with color and black and white photographs and reproductions of artworks. Fuentes leaves the reader with this parting paragraph: "Today the Pyrenees have been traversed. Spain has Europe's fastest rate of growth. It offers its citizens the widest spectrum of political choice, which comes only from a mature, self-assured absence of paranoia. The danger is that as it joins the European community, Spain might become too prosperous, too comfortable, too consumerist, insufficiently self-critical—and forgetful of its other face, its Spanish American profile. Spain is in Europe, legitimately so. But it should not forget that it is also in the nations of Spanish America, 'the cubs of the Spanish lion,' as the Nicaraguan poet Rubén Darío called us. Can we be without Spain? Can Spain be without us?"

Culture Shock!: Spain: A Guide to Customs and Etiquette, Marie Louise Graff, Graphic Arts Center Publishing Co., Portland, OR, 1997. There aren't a great many books on the Spanish the way there are, for example, on the French and Italians. Fortunately, the Culture Shock! series offers a very good guide to the ways of the Spanish. Each Culture Shock! edition is authored by a different writer, and each is eminently enlightening. This Spain edition covers such topics as family and customs; language; religion and Holy Week; bureaucracy and red tape; food and drink; fiestas and *ferias;* business and working conditions; and resorts, leisure, and travel. There really is no other book quite like it, and even though it has a lot of practical information for foreigners who are living in Spain, even short-term visitors will find it indispensable. As Graff notes in the introduction, "If you are observant, you will soon learn to interpret the behaviour of a Spaniard, and as a consequence know how you should behave yourself. Manners are extremely important. Spaniards, although proud, are by nature polite and courteous. They are usually kind to foreigners. . . . 'When in Spain, do as the Spaniards do' should be your motto—within the boundaries of common sense, of course. No need to abandon your own standards and culture in order to become Spanish. You are an *extranjero* (foreigner) and will remain an *extranjero,* but 'correct behaviour' will be appreciated and, if it does not earn you total acceptance, it will at least ensure cooperative friendliness." One of the most useful tips that I think bears repeating appears under the heading "Dressing for the Occasion," in which the author emphasizes that Spaniards tend to be more formal than most other nations. It's important to remember, if you find yourself visiting a governmental department or office, to dress correctly. Graff relates a story of a friend who went to the customs office and was immediately ushered in to see the man in charge, ahead of others sitting in the waiting room. "As he was leaving he could not resist asking why he had received this preferential treatment since he had not made an appointment. The answer startled him: 'If these people do not have the courtesy to dress in a respectful manner, they can wait all day. . . .' The people considered to be disrespectfully dressed included a man wearing a pair of shorts rather than long trousers, and another wearing flip-flops instead of shoes." *Esencial.*

Eternal Spain: The Spanish Rural Landscape, photographs by Robert Frerck, text by Alastair Reid, Harry N. Abrams, 1991. This horizontal-shaped book is my favorite in the category of coffee-table photography books. The shape is important, for photos of landscapes are always best appreciated in a wide format, and these images do not disappoint: they are stunning, in fact, and though this volume features photos taken in every region of Spain, there is a chapter devoted to the northern coast (Galicia, Asturias, Cantabria, and the Basque Country) and another to the Pyrenees (Navarre, Aragon, La Rioja, and Catalonia). And of course the accompanying text by Reid makes the book that much more of a must-have volume.

The Face of Spain, Gerald Brenan, Farrar, Straus & Giroux, 1956; Ecco Press, 1995. This excellent book does not cover Northern Spain at all (Madrid and points south are its focus), but it remains a classic and unique work on Spain. Brenan lived in Andalusia when he was young, and after he was married he and his wife bought a house in Málaga, just in time to witness the country unraveling at the start of the Civil War. They went back to England, and thirteen years later they returned to Spain. Brenan notes in his introduction that "the impression that abides from my visit is of how little, after all the vicissitudes of the last thirteen years, the character of the people has changed, and this, to anyone who knew Spain before the Civil War, will be the best recommendation. To those who did not, let me say that there is something about this country and its way of life which makes a unique impression. For centuries a mixing bowl of the cultures of Europe, Asia, and North Africa, Spain today gives off a note which is unlike any other—a sharp, penetrating, *agridulce* strain, both harsh and nostalgic like that of its guitar music, which no one who has once heard will ever forget." Brenan's memoir is also a story within a story, as he relates his efforts to find the burial site of Federico García Lorca, who was shot by forces loyal to Franco in August 1936. V. S. Pritchett noted that "no writer knows Spain as well as Mr. Brenan does, and none has written about Spanish life, literature, and history so searchingly." *Esencial*.

Familiar Spanish Travels, William Dean Howells, Harper & Brothers, 1913. Readers who are passionate about Italy are no doubt familiar with the books Howells penned on Venice and other parts of that country. Those titles are classics, and this one is as well. (You'll have to search for this beautiful hardcover, with lovely illustrations and photographs, but it will be a search worth the effort.) In his foreword, "Autobiographical Approaches," Howells relates that his "passion for Spanish things" was the "ruling passion" of his boyhood. He suspects this passion began when he read *Don Quixote,* when he was ten or twelve years old. After some sixty years' delay, he arrived in Spain; and "when at last we crossed the Pyrenees and I found myself in Spain, it was with an incredulity which followed me throughout and lingered with me to the end. 'Is this truly Spain, and am I actually there?' the thing kept asking itself; and it asks itself still, in terms that fit the accomplished fact."

Hemingway's Spain, photographs by Loomis Dean, text by Barnaby Conrad, Chronicle Books, 1989. This is really an extraordinary book of photographs, if only because it focuses exclusively on the places in Spain that Hemingway loved and the Spanish pastimes he so thoroughly embraced: bullfighting, flamenco, and partying. "With Hemingway," Conrad writes, "if you didn't like Spain there wasn't much else he wanted to talk to you about." Conrad himself admits, "Long before I ever went there, I fell in love with Spain through Hemingway's writings; *Death in the Afternoon* changed my life, shaped my life, and almost cost me my life." In 1971 Conrad (an author and amateur bullfighter) and Dean (who was then *Life*'s chief photographer in Paris) were asked to narrate and shoot the first *corrida* ever shown on television via Telstar all around the world. "So Ernest Hemingway, Loomis Dean, and I have something profound in common—a deep and abiding love for Spain," Conrad writes. The photographs in this book, both in color and black and white, are simply amazing. Dean not only had the opportunity to photograph Hemingway (once for a *Life* cover) in Spain, but he traveled extensively throughout the Iberian peninsula, before and after Hemingway's final visit to Spain in 1960. Though this book will appeal to Hemingway fans, it is also for those who love Spain.

Iberia: Spanish Travels and Reflections, James A. Michener, photographs by Robert Vavra, Random House, 1968. This is the very first book I ever read about Spain, and I think it is still my favorite. It was also the first book I read by Michener, and though I went on to read a good many of his other works, few of them were quite the achievement that *Iberia* was and remains. (I do admit that Michener is probably *the* writer most responsible for my wanderlust. After I read *Iberia*, I turned to *The Drifters,* which definitely changed my life. A few years later, when my mother found my torn-and-held-together-by-duct-tape copy in my suitcase before leaving for college, she immediately confiscated it and told me I could not under any circumstances go to college with "that book" in my bag. I managed to secretly retrieve the book just before I got in the car for the drive down to Virginia, thankfully, because some of my lasting friends from college days were young men and women who had also brought "that book" to college.) If you never got around to reading *Iberia* because you thought Michener became trite and formulaic (true), put your feelings aside and pick it up—you will be extremely happy you did. Among the many, many memorable passages from this indispensable memoir is the following excerpt, which appears at the very end of the book:

Throughout this chapter I have spoken of being on a pilgrimage, and now, as I return from Finisterre to Compostela, I think it not inappropriate to speak of this pilgrimage, which was a most real thing. Walter Starkie, in his fine book *The Road to Santiago* when speaking of the four pilgrimages he made between the years 1924 and 1954, offers this cryptic sentence: "My 1954 pilgrimage bore for me a deep significance, for it marked the time of my retirement from official life, and I wished to perform religiously all the rituals, in order to prepare myself for making my examination of conscience." This statement perplexed me and I asked various people what it signified; Don Luis Morenés told me, "After the Spanish Civil War, countries like America and England were studious to send us Catholics as their representatives, and in this spirit England in 1940 sent us as their first director of the new British Institute, the fiddle-playing Irish-Catholic Starkie. He stayed in Spain during World War II, helping to organize and operate an escape route for British airmen shot down over France. That was his contribution to the grand alliance against Hitler." An English informant told me, "After the war Starkie was looked upon with diminished favor by the British but with real love by the Spanish. In 1954 he was retired from his official position, somewhat prematurely, I felt, and Spain lost one of the truest friends it ever had." It was at this impasse, when he knew nothing of his future—ultimately he landed a good university position in America—that the gypsy-loving Irishman had set out upon his final walk to Compostela.

In one sense my reason for pilgrimage was less dramatic; in another, more so. In early September, 1965, I was stricken with a sizable heart attack, and as I lay in that fitful slumber which is not sleep I thought of the good days I had known in northern Spain with Don Luis, and of the approaches to Santiago de Compostela and of how we had strained to see who would be first to spot those splendid towers rising in the moonlight, and of that portico which I had studied with affection but not carefully. And I thought then that if I ever were to leave that restricted room, which I sometimes doubted, for it seemed unlikely that I would regain sufficient strength to travel, I should like to see Compostela again.

I was lucky in that my doctor was a student of Paul Dudley White, the notable specialist of Boston, whom I had known in Russia. As a courtesy Dr. White flew down from Boston and recited his now-famous theory: "If a man with a heart attack tries to do anything at all before the passage of three months, he's an idiot; but if at the end of three months he doesn't at least try to do all he did before, he's an even greater one."

When I returned to Spain my capacity to travel and work was unknown. If I have spoken in this book with a certain regard for the trivial hill city of Teruel it is partly because it was to Teruel that I first went on my return journey, and each step I took in that pregnant place was a test to see whether I could stand the sun, whether I could climb hills, and whether my mind could focus on a specific problem for some hours. Teruel, where I had first seen the true Spain more than three decades ago . . . Teruel, where I had lived and died with the Spanish Republic . . . Teruel, which had been a magnet for years, now became important in another way, and when I discovered that I could negotiate those hilly streets I decided that I was ready for the feria at Pamplona and the long trip across northern Spain.

When I entered the cathedral of Santiago de Compostela for the last time the national celebration of which I spoke earlier was in progress. The great botafumeiro was in full swing, its massive cargo of silver and incense descending perilously toward my head as I slipped through the crowded nave to a point behind the main altar, where the organ seemed to be exploding. There I found the small and narrow flight of stairs which took me upward to a hiding point behind the great stone statue of Santiago Matamoros which occupies the center of the altar. Only the rear of his head and shoulders was visible to me, the latter encased in a metal robe encrusted with jewels, but beyond the saint I could look through the peephole in the altar and out into the vast cathedral where the censer was coming to a halt, where Father Precedo Lafuente was sitting in his red robes, where Admiral Núñez Rodríguez in white uniform was preparing to make his rededication of Spain to the apostle, and where Cardinal Quiroga Palacios waited to make his speech of acknowledgment. It was a dazzling moment, as rich in pageantry and as filled with the spirit of Spain as any that I had witnessed, and there I hid in the darkness as if an interloper with no proper role in the ceremonial except that I had completed my vow of pilgrimage and stood at last with my arm about the stone-cold shoulder of Santiago, my patron saint and Spain's.

[From *Iberia* by James A. Michener, copyright © 1968 by Random House, Inc. and renewed 1996 by James A. Michener. Used by permission of Random House, Inc.]

A Literary Companion: Spain, Jimmy Burns, John Murray Publishers, London, 1994. This is one volume in the Literary Companion series, one I like very much (some other editions feature Florence, Greece, Paris, Rome, and Venice). Though it features some excerpts from works of fiction, the overwhelming majority are nonfiction, and the selections are varied and interesting. I admit I was drawn to the book by its cover, which features a detail of one of the most magnificent paintings of all time, *El Jaleo* by John Singer Sargent (which hangs in the wonderful Isabella Stewart Gardner Museum in Boston), and I would have bought the book for the cover alone. It happens, however, that this is an absorbing anthology, and Burns is quite suited to compiling it: he was born in Madrid and spent much of his childhood in Spain, and though his career as a correspondent for the *Financial Times* of London has assigned him to Lisbon, Buenos Aires, and London, he still spends his holidays in Spain. In addition to chapters on Roman, Jewish, and Moorish Spain, the Peninsular and Carlist Wars, bullfighting, flamenco, and food and wine, a few are devoted to the north: "Across the Pyrenees" and "The Pilgrim's Way." With a twelve-page photo insert, this book is very much worth tracking down.

The Ornament of the World: How Muslims, Jews, and Christians Created a Culture of Tolerance in Medieval Spain, Maria Rosa Menocal, Little, Brown & Co., 2002. The closest this book's geographic focus lands on Northern Spain is Huesca, southeast of Pamplona and just barely in the Pyrenees. Nonetheless, it is an important recently published work and is "as wise as it is poignant," as writer Harold Bloom notes in the foreword, studying "such nostalgias, not altogether for their own sake, but also because of their current relevance. There are no Muslim Andalusians visible anywhere in the world today. The Iran of the ayatollahs and the Afghanistan of the Taliban may mark an extreme, but even Egypt is now not much of a culture of tolerance. The Israelis and Palestinians, even if they could achieve a workable peace, would still be surrounded by a Muslim world very remote from the Andalusia of Abd al-Rahman and his descendants." Menocal counters the notion of the Middle Ages as a period only of religious persecution and intellectual stagnation.

Roads to Santiago: A Modern-Day Pilgrimage Through Spain, Cees Nooteboom, translated by Ina Rilke, Harvest, 2000. When I first picked up this book, I thought it was only to be about a pilgrimage to Santiago, but in fact it is an intelligent, piercing, and sympathetic chronicle of a Dutch writer's thirty-five-year infatuation with Spain, his adopted second country. Nooteboom shares that in 1953, when he was twenty years old, he went to Italy and thought he had found everything he'd ever, unknowingly, been looking for: "The Mediterranean brilliance hit me like a bolt of lightning; the whole of human life was enacted on a single, fabulous public stage against a careless backdrop of thousands of years of sublime art. Colours, foods, markets, clothing, gestures, language: everything seemed more refined, more vivid, more vibrant than in the low-lying northern delta I come from, and I was bowled over." After that, Spain to him was a disappointment: "under the same Mediterranean sun the language struck me as harsh, the landscape as barren, everyday life as coarse. It didn't flow, it wasn't pleasant, it was obstinately ancient and out of reach, it had to be conquered. I can no longer think in those terms. Italy is still a delight, but I have the feeling—it is not possible to talk of these things without resorting to an odd, mystical terminology—that the Spanish character and the Spanish landscape correspond to what in essence I am, to conscious and unconscious things in my being, to what I am about. Spain is brutish, anarchic, egocentric, cruel. Spain is prepared to face disaster on a whim, she is chaotic, dreamy, irrational. Spain conquered the world and then did not know what to do with it, she harks back to her Medieval, Arab, Jewish and Christian past and sits there impassively like a continent that is appended to Europe and yet is not Europe, with her obdurate towns studding those limitless empty landscapes. Those who know only the beaten track do not know Spain. Those who have not roamed the labyrinthine complexity of her history do not know what they are traveling through. It is the love of a lifetime, the amazement is never-ending." Nooteboom is remarkably well traveled throughout the country, including the north and including, finally, Santiago. Outstanding and *esencial*.

Spain, Jan Morris, illustrated by Cecilia Eales, Barrie & Jenkins, London, 1964; Prentice-Hall, 1988. This beautiful hardcover edition by one of the twentieth century's best travel writers is usually a fixture on Spain bibliographies but is not always highly recommended and is definitely not given the praise I believe it deserves. *Spain* may not be quite as cohesive as many of Morris's other books, but I think it is a most interesting and valuable volume, with a notebook's worth of perceptive observations. In Morris's updated introductory note in 1988, she writes that this book portrays Spain at a turning point in its history, after Franco's thirty-five-year dictatorship. "My book is about that moment—about the Spaniards poised to rejoin the rest of us, but subject still to the mighty isolation of their past; but since such portentous historical moments recur throughout the history of Spain, perhaps it is about all Spanish moments, really." It is indeed about Spanish moments, as Morris notes near the very end of the book: "Will it work better this time? It is true that Spain always seems to be yearning for some moment of fulfilment, some chance to flower, that nowadays only democracy can allow: but though the Spaniards are eagerly seizing their new opportunities, and political liberty is all the rage, somehow democracy does not yet feel natural to the place. It will take time, in a country where autocracy has so long seemed the natural order of things— organic, hereditary, bred in the bones, as much a part of the Spanish climate as the dead heat of the Castilian summer, or that knife-edge wind beneath the ribs." With a two-page index of historical events.

Spain: The Root and the Flower, John A. Crow, Harper & Row, 1963. This book appears on every good bibliography of Spain and deserves to, as it's a classic like no other. Readers who have not yet encountered Crow will know they have picked up an exceptional book as soon as they read his dedication: "To the people of Spain whose culture has absorbed my entire professional life." Crow explains in the preface that his primary intention in writing this book has been to analyze the main currents in the ebb and flow of Spanish life, not detail long lists of royalty or wars or political changes. Therefore this work is not straight history. "History usually emphasizes political events. My purpose has been to emphasize the underlying feelings and *mores* which bring about these events." As the book was published in 1963, it's also an important record of life in Spain under Franco (who died in 1975), and the final chapters—"The Spanish Republic (1931–1939)," "Communism and Fascism in Spain," "Valley of the Fallen," and "Spain Today"—are excellent reading on their own. Spain has come a long way since 1963, yet much of its essence remains much the same: "Spain is not only a castle, it is also, for all practical purposes, an island. The country's insularity is proverbial. She belongs neither to Europe nor to Africa, but is a way station in between with qualities of each. Spain has ceased to be European by virtue of her Moorish blood. 'Africa begins at the Pyrenees,' is more than an apt phrase. It expresses succinctly the exotic, half-oriental quality which gives to the people and to the culture of Spain their most distinctive features. One must be careful to specify that the Africa here referred to is not the lower part of the Dark Continent peopled by black men. It is northern Africa, the ancient homeland of the Iberians, of the Carthaginians, a Semitic race of the Jews themselves, and of the Moors, composed of many Arabic-speaking groups. All of these ethnic and cultural groups have poured their blood and energy into the dead-end funnel that is Spain. The towering Pyrenees have sealed that funnel off from the rest of Europe more effectively than the Alps have ever sealed off Italy. Their average altitude, in fact, is higher than that of the Alps. In any case, insularity is a state of mind and a way of life; it is not merely a matter of mountains, or altitudes, or islands." *Esencial.*

Spanish Cultural Studies: An Introduction, edited by Helen Graham and Jo Labanyi, Oxford University Press, 1995. This volume, part of the Cultural

Studies series (other titles cover Italy and France), offers a variety of essays on Spanish culture from 1898 to 1992 and covers such topics as national identities, *modernismo,* the avant-garde, cultural politics of the Civil War, gender and sexuality, democracy and regional autonomy, and cultural policy. If you are a serious Hispanophile, you'll want to add it to your library. The contributors are an impressive bunch (they're all professors and lecturers and published authors in the U.K., the United States, and Spain). Black and white photographs, reproductions of posters, and artworks appear throughout the book. There's also an extensive glossary and chronology at the back, and each chapter ends with suggestions for further reading. A valuable collection.

Spanish Hours, Simon Courtauld, illustrations by Elisabeth Luard, Libri Mundi, London, 1996; revised edition 1998. This beautifully crafted memoir is a perfect mix of history, travelogue, and personal observation. I only came across it two years ago, when it was first featured in the mail-order book catalog *A Common Reader* (see the Bookstores entry in *Informaciones Prácticas*), and I immediately placed my order. Courtauld is well-traveled throughout Spain and has held various writing positions with various London newspapers. (Some chapters in the book first appeared as articles in *The Spectator* and *The Sunday Telegraph.*) As Courtauld notes in the foreword, "Madrid and Barcelona must be among the most stimulating of European cities—artistically, politically, journalistically—but they do not form part of this book. Nor do the questionable delights of the holiday resorts on the various *costas.* These are significant aspects of modern Spain; however, the characteristics of Spain and its people which I have tried to communicate are more enduring—as important decades, or centuries, ago as they are today. In Spain, as in any country, there are certain things that matter. This book is the result of an attempt to understand those hours, or moments, in Spanish life (the word *horas* covers both) which go to the heart of the country." This is the best current memoir of Spain available. *Esencial.*

The Spanish Temper, V. S. Pritchett, Alfred A. Knopf, 1955. "I write because, of all the foreign countries I have known, Spain is the one that has made the strongest impression on me. I went there first in the 1920s as a very young man and lived there for nearly two years; the effects of the experience were drastic and permanent. I might also say, without being guilty of rhetoric, that the sight of the landscape of Castile changed my life." So relates Pritchett, who was born in 1900 and died in 1997, and during the course of that long life mastered nearly every form of literature: the novel, short fiction, travel writing, biography, criticism, and memoir. *The Spanish Temper* opens with Pritchett in Biarritz en route to the Basque Country and is an excellent read from beginning to end. *The Pritchett Century* (selected and with a foreword by Oliver Pritchett,

Modern Library, 1997) is another good and obviously larger book that includes *The Spanish Temper* as well as *Marching Spain,* which he wrote in 1928. Pritchett visited Spain a number of times until 1935 and didn't expect to return; but thankfully for us he did in 1951 and 1952, and though the original Knopf edition of *The Spanish Temper* is out of print, the wise folks at the Modern Library included it in its handsome hardcover edition.

The Spanish World: Civilization and Empire, Europe and the Americas, Past and Present, edited by J. H. Elliott, Harry N. Abrams, 1991. This sadly out-of-print volume is an outstanding compilation of text and black-and-white and color illustrations. The book was published in the same year by Thames & Hudson, and either would be worth a great effort to track down.

A Stranger in Spain, H. V. Morton, Dodd, Mead & Co., 1955. Readers of my *Central Italy* and *Venice* editions know that I am quite fond of the works of H. V. Morton, and this profile of Spain is no exception. Like his numerous other travel titles, this one is a classic and deserves to be brought back into print. La Rioja, Pamplona, Burgos, San Sebastián, the Picos de Europa, Asturias, Santillana del Mar, León, and Santiago are all along Morton's route through España. (Additionally, readers spending some time in Madrid may want to read the Madrid chapters, which are excellent.) Upon Morton's arrival in Madrid, he receives a telephone call from a friend that highlights a Spanish essential: "'Welcome to Spain! Will you have dinner with me tonight? Good! Then I'll call for you round about ten.' 'About *ten?*' 'Yes, or is that a bit too early?' 'No, I'll expect you then.' And I, who regard it as one of life's greatest pleasures to be in bed at ten, groaned inwardly." Morton's final paragraph, written from Montserrat, near Barcelona, remains prescient: "Outside it is dark upon the plain, but the high peaks of the mountains are still pink. Slowly the light fades; the first star burns. I go out into the dusk, thinking that there are some places where hatred, the monstrous evil of our time, has no place."

Travelers' Tales: Spain, collected and edited by Lucy McCauley, Travelers' Tales, 1995. I hope to meet the team who created the Travelers' Tales series one day because we seem to share similar ideas about travel. Each title in this series is a great mix of carefully chosen stories in the form of book excerpts and a few extracts from periodicals, as well as tales that have not been published.

A Traveller's History of Spain, Juan Lalaguna, Interlink Publishing Group, Northampton, MA. This edition is one in a great series for which I have much enthusiasm. Each edition gives readers a compact historical overview of a place. Think of it as a mini "what you should know" guide to help you appreciate what you're seeing and reading about. At the back of this edition is a list of rulers and monarchs from the Visigoths to the present; a chronology of major events; and a good historical A to Z gazetteer. *Esencial.*

Biographies

Isabella I

Isabella of Castile: The First Renaissance Queen, Nancy Rubin, St. Martin's Press, 1992. Of the many biographies of Isabella, this is my favorite. Aside from detailing the well-known events of Isabella's life, Rubin explains more fully than I've read elsewhere the complicated waters of European politics that Isabella waded through while trying to balance more personal catastrophes. (The marriages arranged for Isabella's daughters, Juana and Catherine, produced the expected historic results, but both ended tragically.) Granted, the life of Isabel la Católica is one of history's most interesting, but this is one of those biographies I couldn't put down, which I attribute to the author's skill at writing a work that is both scholarly and engaging.

Francisco Franco

Franco: Profiles in Power, Sheelagh Ellwood, Longman, 2000. Author Ellwood is research analyst for the Iberian peninsula in the research and analysis department of the Foreign and Commonwealth Office in London. Here she presents an excellent overview of Spain's most controversial—and deeply divisive—leader. Though technically not a biography—this book is a volume in the Profiles in Power series—it nonetheless is filled with biographical material. Whatever you want to call it, I think it is the best source for a solid assessment of Franco's achievements and failures during the four decades of his rule.

Philip II

The Grand Strategy of Philip II, Geoffrey Parker, Yale University Press, 1998. Though not a strict biography, this is an engrossing work, and the author refutes previous historians' views that Philip had no "grand strategy" in overseeing his empire, which included Portugal, the Netherlands, half of Italy, Tunis, Tangier, Guinea, Angola, parts of India and the Philippines, Florida, Cuba, Brazil, Peru, the American Southwest, Mexico, and Central America. Parker believes Philip was surrounded by a strategic culture, which included a strategic inheritance from his father, Charles V, and a "messianic imperialism" that was of Philip's own making and that guided him for the rest of his life.

Philip II of Spain: A Biography, Sir Charles Petrie, W.W. Norton, 1963. Petrie—at the time this book was published, corresponding member of the Spanish Academy of History and of the Instituto Fernando el Católico of Saragossa—notes in his preface that "to write the life of Philip of Spain in six volumes would be comparatively easy, but to do so in one necessitates the omission of much that is both of interest and importance." I completely sympathize with him, as I often feel there is so much that must be omitted from my own books (or they would become the size of telephone directories). Petrie has, however, done an admirable job in condensing the life of one of Spain's most significant rulers. "By position, personality and policy," he notes, "Philip II was the giant among giants. He ruled the greatest empire since the fall of Rome." Petrie has divided the book into eleven sections, and one is devoted to the Spanish Armada, another to the revolt of the Netherlands, and another, entitled "The Shadow of the Crescent," to Spain's relations with the Ottoman Empire. When this edition appeared, it was the first new biography of Philip II in over thirty years, and though there have been editions since, I still like this one the best.

The Spanish Civil War

Fortunately for Spain enthusiasts and history buffs, a recent flurry of books has been published on the Spanish Civil War. July 17, 2001, marked the sixty-fifth anniversary of the rebellion of the Spanish army generals against the government, an action that led to the outbreak of war. Determining what the Spanish conflict was really about has preoccupied scholars and historians ever since it ended in 1939. The truth seems to be that the war was about many things; but what makes it unique is that it attracted an enormous amount of international attention. Since neither side in the conflict had the financial resources to win the war, assistance was sought from those most able to deliver it—Hitler, Mussolini, and Stalin—and for this reason alone the entire war and the issues at stake became entangled in layers of complexity, duplicity, and tragedy. In recent years much new information has been uncovered, and all the books below are well worth your attention:

A *Literary Companion: Spain,* Jimmy Burns, John Murray Publishers, London, 1994. I've recommended this wonderful book again for its very good chapter, "That Arid Square: The Civil War." The title of this chapter, by the way, is taken from a poem, "Spain," by W. H. Auden. The third stanza begins, "On that arid square, that fragment nipped off from hot Africa, soldered so crudely to inventive Europe; / On that tableland scored by rivers, / Our thoughts have bodies; the menacing shapes of our fever / Are precise and alive." At the conclusion of an excerpt from *A Moment of War* by Laurie Lee (just below), Burns comments that "Lee ended the Civil War in a cell, rejected by the very people he had come to fight alongside. His experience of the conflict is one in which heroes did not exist and where more often than not Spaniards and foreigners alike became corrupted and ideals were gradually lost."

A *Moment of War: A Memoir of the Spanish Civil War* (Laurie Lee, New Press, 1991). This is not a historical account but a personal experience—and one of the best memoirs I've ever read. It is actually the sequel to another of my favorite books, *As I Walked Out One Midsummer Morning* (Atheneum, 1969).

The Odyssey of the Abraham Lincoln Brigade: Americans in the Spanish Civil War, Peter Carroll, Stanford University Press, 1994. Not a history of the Civil War but a book detailing extraordinary oral histories, drawn from newly opened archives in Moscow, significant archives at Brandeis and Berkeley, and dozens of recollections from American veterans. For my part, I can't imagine reading about the history of the Spanish Civil War without also reading about the Abraham Lincoln Brigade (which actually is a misnomer: it was the Abraham Lincoln Battalion, itself a division of the International Brigades). Nearly three thousand Americans volunteered to join the struggle against Franco, and their efforts and dedication deserve wider recognition. Milton Wolff, last commander of the Lincoln-Washington battalion, related that "the remarkable thing was that though fully conscious of the odds against us and though suffering staggering losses in long, drawn out gruelling campaigns, we all went back to the front time after time . . . always with a belief in the possibility of victory." Author Carroll adds the Americans would not give up, in any engagement, even when faced with superior weapons and men. They repeatedly held difficult positions when conventional wisdom would have pitted them against overwhelming odds for failure. This must surely be the definitive volume on this subject, and I think it is a worthy tribute to the Americans who fought and died for the Spanish Republic.

Spain Betrayed: The Soviet Union in the Spanish Civil War, edited by Ronald Radosh, Mary Habeck, and Grigory Sevostianov, Yale University Press, 2001. A volume in Yale's Annals of Communism series, this book presents a very different view of the role of the Soviet Union in the war and provides the first full documentation of the Soviets' duplicitous and self-serving interests and activities. In a review of this important book in the *Los Angeles Times Book Review,* author Stanley Payne wrote, "All students of Soviet policy, the Spanish war and European international relations, as well as all informed readers in these fields, will be indebted to [the editors] for an unprecedented collection of material that marks something of a watershed in the history of the period. It is a book that no one interested in the Spanish Civil War can afford to be without."

The Spanish Civil War, Gabriele Ranzato, Interlink, 1999. This 124-page, five-by-seven-inch paperback is a great volume in the Interlink Illustrated Histories series. It isn't meant to be an authoritative source but I think it's an excellent volume and will serve readers and travelers who want a good overall survey well. Plus, it's a good candidate for your suitcase or your carry-on.

The Spanish Civil War, Hugh Thomas, Hamish Hamilton, London, 1977; Modern Library, 2001. I don't believe it's debatable that this "stands without rivals as the most balanced and comprehensive book on the subject" (*American Historical Review*), and I applaud the staff of the Modern Library for issuing this new paperback edition. Older editions are rather hard to find, and the less expensive paperback edition will hopefully find its way into the hands of more readers. Thomas relates in the preface that when his work was first published in 1961, it was published in Spanish by a Spanish émigré publishing house in Paris, as Madrid's Ministry of Information banned its publication in Spain. A revised edition, in 1976 after Franco's death, was finally published there, and has continued to sell in a variety of editions since then. Thomas notes that the success of his book—and those by other histo-

rians—played a part in the success of the transition to democracy after Franco. "The recovery of knowledge of why the previous democracy in Spain went wrong in the 1930s was a help in the 1970s. The recollection in tranquillity of just how horrible a failure the civil war had been helped those concerned to make a new Spain to avoid destructive rhetoric. By suggesting that the responsibility for the conflict was not easily decided, and the guilt for the most odious actions widely spread, vengeance was avoided— a fact not wholly to be expected when it is recalled how many people who had played a part in the civil war were still alive. 'Poetry,' said Shelley, 'is capable of saving us.' Cannot the same claim be made for history?" This is a thick book: minus the appendixes, bibliographic notes, and the index, it totals 930 pages. But even if you are not quite sure you want to tackle the whole thing, I recommend at least reading the initial chapter, "The Origins of the War." (I would bet that many of you will be so engrossed by this point that you'll continue on.) Thomas reminds us that the Spanish Civil War "was essentially a tragedy and interruption in the life of a European people—the one major European people, it might be gloomily remembered, that before 1936 was too poor to have a modern armament industry."

The Spanish Labyrinth: An Account of the Social and Political Background of the Civil War, Gerald Brenan, Cambridge University Press, 1943, 1960. Though this is not among the most recent books published on the Spanish Civil War, it is still one of the best, if only because Brenan is so qualified to write it.

MANANTIALES LA TOJA
HENKEL   IBERICA,S.A.
CIF A-08046799/IVA INCLUID
GRACIAS·POR SU VISITA

```
 2 X
JABON SALES           ▪700
 2 X                  @225
 JABONERAS            ▪450
COLONIA.M             ▪800
EST.4*50              ▪425
SUBTOTAL             ▪2375
TOTAL                ▪2375
CAJA                 ▪2375
EURO          14.27
13-10-2001               12:44
000452 CAJERO  D          00
```

Pazo do Souto

TURISMO RURAL
RESTAURANTE ‖   Carlos Taibo Pomb

15105 SÍSAMO - CARBALLO (A Coruña) - Telf. 981 75 60 65 - Fax: 981 75 61 91
E-mail: reservas@pazodosouto.com - http:// www.pazodosouto.com

Galicia

"*Even a few miles' travel into the countryside of Galicia shows the observant traveler the secret of this land: the granite rock which is both the glory and the curse of the region. From deep quarries, which seem to abound, the Galician digs out a gray-and-white-flecked granite which he uses for everything. A farmer wants a barn? He builds it of granite. He wants a corncrib to protect his grain from rats? He builds one of solid granite. Garages, lean-tos, small homes and large are all built of this fine stone, and nowhere else in Europe could one find so many skilled stonemasons. This sounds ridiculous, but in the fields even fences, which in other parts of the world would be built of wood, are here built of granite: long thin slabs, beautifully cut and stood on end to form stony palisades. Galicia is the granite land.*"
—James Michener, IBERIA

"*I had always believed, and continue to believe, really, that there is no more beautiful square in the world than the one in Siena. The only place that made me doubt its authority . . . is the one in Santiago de Compostela. Its poise and its youthful air prohibit you from even thinking about its venerable age; instead, it looks as if it had been built the day before by someone who had lost their sense of time.*"
—Gabriel García Márquez, "Watching the Rain in Galicia"

Spain's Coming Attraction

BY CALVIN TRILLIN

editor's note

Though he has written about a number of places around the world, Calvin Trillin has written often and passionately about Galicia, and my husband and I have come to identify him as an expert on this corner of Spain.

CALVIN TRILLIN is the author, most recently, of *Tepper Isn't Going Out* (Random House, 2001). He has been a regular contributor to *The New Yorker* for four decades and composes verse for *The Nation*.

Concerning the shellfish, I have to say that I simply had no idea. After a day or two in Galicia, the northwest corner of Spain often identified as "the bit above Portugal," I felt like some traveler who, having put off visiting Italy for many years because he has a limited interest in old churches and restored hill towns, finally shows up and realizes, for the first time, that the Italians have a way with pasta. The temptation is to ask, "Why didn't anyone tell me about this before?".

Conspiracy of silence? I wouldn't want to say. It's odd, though, that what the travel writers and brochures traditionally mention about Galicia is that it is green and that it is picturesque and that it is Celtic—not characteristics that would lead a traveler to expect a seafood paradise where a nondescript neighborhood café might have both razor clams and cuttlefish on the menu, and the bar at the airport of the best-known city, Santiago de Compostela, offers among its snacks fresh octopus. In fact, experience in some Celtic countries—Ireland, for instance—could lead you to believe that

Galicia is the sort of place where a cautious visitor might be advised to show up carrying his own lunch.

One argument against the conspiracy theory was that I had passed through "the bit above Portugal" myself twenty years or so ago without becoming aware that Galicia is to shellfish what Texas is to bragging. I can't imagine what could have been on my mind. My wife, Alice, and I had driven through rather quickly on our way to Portugal, stopping in Santiago de Compostela at the Hostal de los Reyes Católicos, which was built in the sixteenth century as a shelter and hospital for pilgrims and thirty years ago was turned into the crown jewel of the Spanish *paradors*—hotels the government has created in historic sites throughout the country. My memories of that journey are of a landscape almost shamelessly picturesque. Galician farmers have always managed to make works of art out of the necessities of farming—stone walls, for instance, and haystacks and, most of all, the simple granary. In Galicia a haystack is conical—the point finished off with a flourish, like the top of a soft ice cream cone. The granaries, or *hórreos,* are like small stone houses on stilts, with pitched tile roofs that are often adorned with a stone cross.

At the time we first drove through Galicia, the Franco regime had just appointed as tourism minister a man named Manuel Fraga Iribarne, who was said to be taking a more modern and aggressive approach to marketing Spain's attractions, and a lot of what we saw looked perfect enough to have been staged by him personally. "Ah, clever of you to place that *hórreo* in silhouette against that stand of pine trees, Fraga Iribarne," we'd find ourselves commenting as we drove along a mountain road. Passing an old woman who was dressed completely in black and pulling a cart of twigs, we might say, "Ah, back in your hardy-peasant drag, Fraga, you sly devil."

When we decided last summer to spend some time visiting

Santiago and the Galician coast—the series of inlets known as the Rías Baixas and the Rías Altas—the picture I had in my mind was of a lovely countryside that could look like the west of England or the west of Oregon. And why would someone with an oft-stated aversion to scenery go someplace with such expectations? Simple. Alice was not as enthusiastic about a trip to Spain as I was: she hates hot weather, and she says that the best paella in the world tastes remarkably like the Spanish rice served in her junior high school cafeteria. And I took advantage of the argument that has tradition-ally been used in such cases: Galicia is not much like the common vision of Spain.

There are no baking plains. There are no bullfight rings. Nobody plays flamenco guitar; in fact, some people play the *gaita*, a form of bagpipe. Some of the signs are not even in Spanish. (Galicia has its own language—*gallego,* or Galician—which sounds like a mixture of Spanish and Portuguese. A preference for it links a variety of political movements that favor more regional autonomy or even separation.) Furthermore, I told Alice, judging from what I had read about Galician fishing villages, she could presumably look forward to casting her eye on any number of scenes arranged by the master set-designer himself—Fraga Iribarne. Alice is a sucker for scenery.

Given the buildup and the memories, Alice was rather stunned by our first day on the Galician coast. We had arrived in Vigo, a city of about 250,000 people, most of whom were honking their horns. It was lunchtime, and we had found an outdoor café in the port, on a short block called Calle Pescadores. Fraga Iribarne would have shuddered at the setting. On one side of a narrow street were three or four cafés, with tables permitting the customers to stare straight into the cement back wall of a hotel that looked ugly enough from the front. There were jagged holes in the wall where pipes came through. The only thing breaking the view of the cement wall was the stand of a clothes vendor selling what looked like K-mart cast-offs.

There were four vendors of a different sort on our side of the street, just in front of the cafés—women who stood behind marble tables and shucked oysters. They acted as independent operators, bringing oysters to customers at any of the cafés. It was the café operator's responsibility to furnish the lemons. Ours did bring lemons, along with a huge spider crab and some grilled shrimp and some bread and an order of *pimientos de Padrón,* digit-size Galician peppers that are fried in olive oil and sprinkled with coarse salt and eaten whole. *Pimientos de Padrón* look like the sort of things that could clear the sinuses with a jolt, but somehow they aren't hot. You occasionally get a fiery one, but judging from our experience, I'd say the percentage is negligible; we came across only about a dozen hot peppers in a week, out of what I estimate to have been approximately 3,500 consumed.

I looked around at the view. Then I had another bite of crab, which was delicious. Then I had some more peppers. The peppers were truly wondrous. "You know," I finally said to Alice, "this place is beautiful in its own way."

The weather was perfect, I reminded Alice—it remained perfect despite all the warnings we had read about constant rain in Galicia—and there wasn't a bullfight ring in sight. On the other hand, the industrial suburbs of Vigo seemed to last halfway to Baiona, where we were staying the night in a *parador* built within the walls of a seventeenth-century fortress. And Baiona, a small town in the southwest corner of Galicia, turned out to be a crowded beach resort. It was crowded with Spanish vacationers, it's true, rather than those coastal visitors the Spanish tend to refer to in one word as drunkenglish, but still crowded. As we sat down to dinner in Baiona that evening, Alice was talking about the international perils of coastal development.

The restaurant, like virtually all Galician restaurants, simply listed the fish available for grilling—hake, sole, turbot, and monkfish—and, under the heading of *mariscos,* other sea creatures that included mussels, oysters, a tiny variety of scallops, barnacles, crawfish, three kinds of lobster, razor clams, spider crabs, ordinary crabs, octopus, squid, baby cuttlefish, clams, goose barnacles (which, I have to say, don't look like any part of a goose and would be a lot better off if they did), and two or three varieties of shrimp. Alice brightened. She is a sucker for scenery, but she also happens to be a sucker for shellfish.

There are, in fact, parts of the Galician coast that would measure up to Fraga Iribarne's standards. Looking out to sea from the fishermen's chapel near Muxía, a village in the Rías Altas, I found myself thinking that the old fox might have snuck in the night before to clear away anything that spoiled the view. The little seaside town of Corcubión presents a line of stone houses whose upper floors have been finished off with the characteristic white Galician *galería*—a sort of sun porch set out about a rocking chair's width from the facade of the building. Almost any port along the *rías* will have fishermen loading up brightly painted dories with odd-shaped *marisco* traps. There are some vast and beautiful and nearly deserted sand beaches. The old sections of Tui, the Galician city right across the river from Portugal, and Pontevedra, a provincial capital at the head of one of the *rías,* are as lovely as any I've seen in Europe. In Santiago—where pilgrims have come for one thousand years to the cathedral said to hold the relics of Saint James—the ancient buildings, graceful squares, and narrow pedestrian streets in the center of town are stunning.

But anyone who comes to the coast of Galicia expecting to see only perfect fishing villages and Romanesque squares and unspoiled mountain roads is bound to be disappointed. It's a place with a lot of urban sprawl, a place with some chintzy-looking beach development, a place where the materials used in new housing do not uplift the spirit. The postcard scenes have to be searched out. We found that we enjoyed the search—driving along narrow roads where separatists had altered letters in the road signs with spray paint to turn the town names into Galician rather than Spanish, conjuring up visions of some maniacally perfectionist schoolmarm constantly traveling country roads by night to correct any errors she finds in spelling.

Even Galicia's disappointing places had their compensations. Was O Grove, a seaside town, rather crowded and noisy? Have a *mariscada*, a mixed seafood platter, in a restaurant at the port. Did Cape Finisterre—a point that many generations of Europeans thought was literally the end of the earth—seem less dramatic than you had expected? Stop in the town of Finisterre (Fisterra in Galician), where, at one of the funky waterfront cafés that display signs announcing the availability of sardines, you can sit at an outdoor table and watch someone pull a wagon of just-caught sardines over to the man who is about to grill them right in front of you. Galicia is one of the few places I've been where you can tell travelers to eat just about anywhere, at least if they're eating seafood. When the seafood is not available fresh, it won't be on the menu, and when it's on the menu, it will be served unadorned. If there's a classically trained saucier in Galicia, I suspect he's driving a cab.

On those journeys around the coast, I always had my eyes open for signs of a fiesta. I have a weakness for fiestas, and so do the Galicians. They're noted celebrators—celebrations for patron saints and celebratory wild-pony roundups and celebrations called *romerías,* which are religious services followed by a feast. I read in a guidebook, for instance, that every June 23 and 24, at a shrine near a village called Silleda, people who feel themselves possessed by demons go through an exorcism ritual, and then everyone gathers for a feast of octopus. Alas, by the time we arrived in Galicia it was already July. That's a problem I often seem to have—not being around for the best celebrations. Hoping to catch one by chance, I laboriously translated posters and local papers—in full knowledge that, considering the precision of my Spanish, we might drive miles to what I thought was a sardine festival only to discover that the article I had read simply said that the town in question had reason to celebrate a new filtration system that would stop its drinking water from tasting of sardines.

We missed a lot of fiestas. It sometimes seemed to me that we happened to be in Galicia during the week all celebrators had agreed on as a sort of midterm break. We were there at the wrong time for the baby eel festival in Tui. We were there at the wrong time for the *romería* of Santa Marta de Ribarteme in Nieves, during which the family and friends of people who had a close brush with death the previous year march in a procession carrying coffins. But we were, in fact, in Galicia for the biggest celebration of all—the fiesta of Saint James, celebrated in Santiago de Compostela every July 25, and for days before and after.

There are any number of scheduled events in the celebration— a high mass at the cathedral with an astonishing fireworks display the previous evening in the cathedral square, concerts that range from Galician folk groups to classical quartets to rock bands, and solemn processions led by gigantic papier-mâché characters representing the variety of pilgrims who over the years have come to Santiago. But the fiesta seemed to be mainly a party in the streets. Swarms of people wandered up and down near the cathedral, stopping now and then to rest with a beer at an outdoor café or to sample the seafood displayed in restaurant windows. They were entertained by an astonishing variety of musicians—local college students in seventeenth-century costume; an impromptu combo of a trumpeter and a keyboard player; a strolling band whose outfits seemed to have been inspired by the Blues Brothers; a combination of a flutist, a guitarist, and a puppeteer whose puppet danced on the cobblestones to the music.

It was a great party, although I have to say that I still regret having missed that rare combination of exorcism and octopus feast. As I strolled through the Santiago market the day we were leaving Galicia, I couldn't help thinking of lost fiesta opportunities. The market is first-rate—a series of open-air stone buildings that were put up in this century but somehow blend in with the old buildings and narrow streets. The seafood display is, of course, magnificent. Just outside the market, women sit on stools in a line—each behind a huge basket of *pimientos de Padrón*. Padrón is only twelve miles away, and Herbón—a tiny village where, according to some connoisseurs, the *pimientos de Padrón* are even better—is just a few miles farther. Herbón actually has a *pimiento de Padrón* festival every year. We were missing it by three days. I couldn't get over that.

After a while we stopped in a nearby restaurant and had a lunch of shrimp, crab, cockles, goose barnacles, scallops, crawfish, squid, octopus, and an extra-large order of *pimientos de Padrón*. I felt a lot better.

Spain's Galicia

BY PENELOPE CASAS

⁓

editor's note

I am such an enormous fan of Spanish food authority Penelope Casas, and my files are filled with articles she has contributed to so many periodicals, that it was difficult to avoid this becoming the *Northern Spain by Penelope Casas* edition. I had to practice serious restraint when reviewing my Casas archive for this book, and even still the selections are numerous; but I believe this is only to the reader's benefit, and I think you'll agree.

PENELOPE CASAS is the author of *The Foods and Wines of Spain* (1993), *Tapas: The Little Dishes of Spain* (1985, tenth printing 1993); *¡Delicioso!: The Regional Cooking of Spain* (1996), and *Discovering Spain: An Uncommon Guide* (2001), all published by Alfred A. Knopf.

Galicia! The melodious sound of its name—pronounced *ga-'lee-thee-a*—is enough to evoke the soft breezes, silent mists, and white sands of this singular corner of northwestern Spain that I fell in love with over twenty years ago. Bordered by Portugal to the south and the Atlantic to the north and west, Galicia is a lush green land covered with chestnut trees and forests fragrant with the scent of eucalyptus. Fjordlike *rías,* or estuaries, usher the ocean inland to towns and cities, creating some of Spain's most memorable scenery. The coastline is more developed, more lively, and more open to the world than the interior, which remains overwhelmingly rural—and hauntingly beautiful.

Because of Galicia's geographic separation from the rest of Spain, the region evolved in relative isolation, allowing it to retain its own character. And Galicia's character is so distinct as to come as a great surprise to first-time visitors. Some 2,600 years ago this

264   Northern Spain

hilly country, which is not unlike Scotland, was occupied by a Celtic people called the Gallaeci, who left behind much more than just their name. In marked contrast to their fellow Spaniards, Galicians are fair-skinned, and they dance what looks like a jig to the sound of—would you believe?—bagpipes, hurdy-gurdy, harp, and laud. Men's festive costumes consist of kiltlike cropped trousers, black leggings, white shirts, and brilliant red sashes, much like traditional garb in the Highlands. True to its Celtic past, Galicia's culture has also traditionally been pervaded by fantasy, and to this day the area remains enveloped in legend and mystery. Paganism and Christianity intertwine; tales of witches stirring magic brews in misty forests mesh with accounts of miracles performed by Santiago—Saint James.

The apostle's tomb in Santiago de Compostela has been the object of religious pilgrimages since the eleventh century, and today the city of Santiago continues to be a highlight of Galicia. If your time is limited, it is the one place you will not want to miss. But a more leisurely tour might include the coastal regions north and south of Santiago as well as the interior, some of which can be seen on day trips from the city itself.

Across much of Galicia, the land has been carved into small family plots crammed with cornstalks and tall, ramrod-straight leafy greens called *grelos*. (A staple in local cooking, *grelos* are used in the hearty *caldo gallego* soup and in *lacón con grelos,* a boiled dinner of meats and vegetables.) Fields of rye and grass bend in the wind, destined to nourish the beloved honey-colored cows that robust women walk on leads to limited pasturelands.

Using the region's principal building material—granite—Galicians have erected humble homes and elegant *pazos* (manor houses), stately churches, and imposing monasteries. They have also shaped stone into unusual works of folk art that give their landscape a unique appearance. Beside countless roadways, plazas, and other significant spots stand *cruceiros,* tall granite crucifixes wrought with religious carvings. Curious *hórreos*—rectangular stone granaries on stilts, crowned by gabled roofs adorned with crosses—also dot the countryside. (The town of Combarro is a national monument because of its concentration of beautiful *hórreos.*)

As one Spanish writer has observed, "Galicians have the patience to dominate stone and give it a fine feminine skin." Certainly the sculptor José Cao Lata, who works just outside Santiago de Compostela, has patience to spare; he spends long solitary hours chipping at stone, creating huge phantasmagoric works that flow from the very depths of his fertile mind.

Food always preoccupies me in Galicia, for I know of no other place in Spain with such spectacular shellfish. I cannot get enough of it. The list of what is available seems endless: There are lobsters, spiny lobsters, *nécora* crabs, small *santiaguiño* crabs (named for the red cross on their heads, which resembles the cross of the Order of Santiago), spider crabs, tiny *quisquilla* shrimp (eaten shell and all), scallops in their shells (a rarity elsewhere in Spain), *zamburiñas* (a diminutive and highly regarded member of the scallop family), mussels, oysters, clams, cockles, razor clams, squid, cuttlefish, barnacles, *langoustines,* and octopus (which is boiled in huge cauldrons and sprinkled with oil and paprika in what is called *a feira* style). In fact, over forty varieties of shellfish can be found in Galicia.

Fish also come in dozens of varieties, including hake, sole, sardine, tuna, turbot, and cod, and the fresh and fruity white Ribeiro perfectly complements them all. Seafood—most especially shellfish—is expensive, to be sure, but Spaniards have their priorities in place: Put some *pesetas* in the gas tank, then blow everything on fine eating. During my recent trip to Galicia, I happily took my cue from them.

My journey began with a drive up Galicia's southern coast, referred to as the Rías Baixas (Lower Estuaries), where expansive white sand beaches and bays are crowded with curious wooden platforms, almost Oriental in appearance, for breeding mussels. In the busy summer town of Baiona I stopped to feast on spiny lobster at O Moscón (O is Galician dialect for "the") and to walk the town's stylish promenade and quaint back streets. I also paused for a moment's relaxation at Baiona's outstanding *parador,* one in the chain of high-quality government-owned hotels. Called the Parador Nacional Conde de Gondomar, it occupies a double-walled medieval castle situated on a promontory overlooking the blue sea.

Following the highway, I drove on to Pontevedra, where I checked into the city's wonderful manor-house Parador Nacional Casa del Barón. That night I dined on the exceptional *tapas* served in hearty portions at the congenial O Merlo restaurant.

You're not likely to read much about Pontevedra, for although it was important in Roman times as a port, the river delta beside which it sits had silted up by the eighteenth century, and the city went into a steep decline. Perhaps this is why the old quarter seems so untouched and picturesque. Few of Spain's squares can match the charm of the Plaza de la Leña (around which the Jewish quarter once thrived), and few streets can be deemed as delightful as these, paved as they are with stone and lined with arcades beneath which a market takes shape each morning.

On one side of the Plaza de la Leña stands the Museo Provinicial, housed in two adjoining eighteenth-century baronial homes. Its collections are wonderfully eclectic, albeit far from comprehensive. I was particularly fascinated by the extraordinary collection of religious objects and jewelry carved from *azabache*—jet, which is actually petrified carbon. In medieval times jet was prized for its magical powers; a piece of jet carved into the shape of a closed hand, index finger extended, was believed to protect its bearer from the evil eye, and he who carried a carving of an open hand diminished the powers of his enemy. Medieval pilgrims to

Santiago purchased such objects and returned home with them, placing jet carvings among Europe's earliest tourist souvenirs.

Pursuing the coastal route north, I headed next for a night on the paradisiacal Isla de la Toja, a beach-encircled isle that once drew Romans for its thermal springs and now attracts wealthy vacationers for its casino and sports complex. There I bought scented black Magno soap, made from the salts of the island's spa, and painted shell jewelry from country women who display their wares in big baskets. At dinner I lingered over each and every crab claw at El Crisol, just across the bridge in El Grove.

The following day, farther north in quaint Cambados (near which the highly esteemed white Albariño wines are made), I continued my seafood debauchery at the antiques-filled O Arco restaurant. And before I reached Santiago, one final seafood stop seemed necessary when I spotted the clam beds at the village of Carril and couldn't resist the thought of those famed mollusks.

Not long after the year 813, when, legend tells, a star appeared in the heavens and directed shepherds to the previously unknown tomb of Saint James, Santiago de Compostela became one of the most important sites in Christendom. (The name comes from *Campus Stellae*—"field of the star.") The tomb's significance was magnified in 844, when Saint James wondrously appeared at the Battle of Clavijo, riding a white steed and carrying a white standard with a red cross on it. Driving back the Moorish enemy, he won the battle for the Christians, earning for himself the name Matamoros, or Moor-slayer, and a permanent place in the hearts of Spaniards as their patron saint.

King Alfonso II of Asturias built a shrine over Saint James's grave that eventually developed into a Romanesque church of great beauty and then blossomed into a sumptuous Baroque cathedral. The town of Santiago de Compostela grew up around it and became, during the Middle Ages, the destination of millions of pilgrims who walked there from all parts of Europe, enduring—or often enough, succumbing to—incredible hardships.

Today Santiago retains a medieval air that can't be attributed merely to its arcaded streets and historic stone buildings. The atmosphere casts a spell over *compostelanos* and visitors as well, transporting into another era all who come in contact with the city. This is why I love to make Santiago my base in Galicia.

As with many cities, to see and feel Santiago properly you must walk around in it. The streets bustle with pedestrians, many of them students at the university, and are lined with noble homes, grand public buildings, and beautiful churches, all built from the same golden-hued Galician granite. Wrought-iron signs identify charmingly old-fashioned stores. Innumerable *tapas* bars serve Ribeiro wine in traditional white ceramic *cunca* cups; portions of big round fish or meat *empanadas;* octopus, seafood vinaigrettes, and tiny green peppers from Padrón (eating them is like Russian roulette—some are mild, others fiery); and, of course, scallops, the city's signature dish. An especially good *tapas* bar is Mesón a Charca.

The scallop, or cockleshell, has been Santiago's symbol since time immemorial. A medieval pilgrim, upon arriving in the city, would buy a scallop, eat it, and affix the shell to the brim of his hat as evidence that he had indeed reached the holy city. Eventually the scallop became associated with Santiago across much of Europe; consider the famed French dish, *coquilles Saint-Jacques,* which translates as nothing other than "scallops Saint James."

Scallops are prepared deliciously in Santiago itself. I never pass up Vilas, a classic Santiago restaurant, for the best baked scallops as well as for other fine shellfish dishes, hake prepared Galician-style (with paprika and the exceptional local potatoes), and *tarta de Santiago,* a moist almond cake that bears the familiar cross of Santiago in caramelized sugar. I also enjoy going to Don Gaiferos for similar specialties served in more elegant surroundings.

On the Plaza del Universidad your nose may lead you to the unmarked El Asesino, a tiny restaurant that has been in the same family for 115 years. Today two elderly sisters run the business, preparing their traditional dishes on a wood-burning stove, which they feed stick by stick. Ask your hotel concierge for directions.

All streets in Santiago ultimately lead to the cathedral, which stands on the Plaza del Obradoiro (also known as the Plaza de España). This is the very heart and soul of Santiago and one of the world's most splendid squares, framed by four buildings of diverse styles—the cathedral, the Colegio de San Jerónimo, the Palacio de Rajoy, and the Hostal de los Reyes Católicos—that somehow merge into a perfectly harmonious whole. It is a scene of constantly shifting activity, which I love either to plunge into or to absorb from the windows of my room at the extraordinary hotel, a *parador* that was originally built in the fifteenth century by order of Ferdinand and Isabella as an inn and hospital for pilgrims.

In the square below my window there may be crowds of tourists, some from small Spanish villages on a trip of a lifetime. Bagpipe players may blow; on the feast of Saint James, July 25, colorful festivities may be under way; even an ear-splitting rock concert might be in progress. And almost always present are *tunos,* university troubadours dressed in sixteenth-century garb, plying the crowd in attempts to make the record and tape sales needed to support their performance tours around the globe. At night they serenade the drowsing city from beneath the arches of the Palacio de Rajoy.

Santiago's grandiose cathedral is, of course, the plaza's center of attention. And what a magnificent structure it is, beginning with the Baroque eighteenth-century facade—impressive and theatrical, to be sure, but it somehow pales in comparison to the simple beauty of the twelfth-century Romanesque facade it encloses. This, named Pórtico de la Gloria, consists of three arches adorned with some two hundred figures notable for their animated expressions of joy. By tradition, every pilgrim enters the cathedral through the central portal, above which has been carved a warm, very human Christ figure. Below, Saint James the Pilgrim welcomes worshippers. The column on which he stands is touched by all arriving pilgrims; after centuries of wear, it has become deeply indented, and the shape of a hand is now clearly visible. A bevy of smiling polychromed prophets and apostles surround the saint and look benevolently down in greeting. To the left stands a rosy-cheeked, laughing Daniel.

Within the soaring cathedral, all is aglitter with gold, silver, and precious jewels accumulated over the centuries and guaranteed to strike awe in any pilgrim. Some consider it a gaudy excess, but none can deny that it is spectacular.

Exit the cathedral through the south portal to the Plaza de las Platerías, named by some accounts for the *plateresque* style of the doorway and by others for the silversmiths who traditionally worked under the plaza's arches. Jewelry stores specializing in silver and jet still occupy the plaza. Mayer, at number 2, has a particularly interesting selection.

In many ways Santiago de Compostela is an overgrown village. A visit to the daily open-air morning market, held under the arches and in the area around the Plaza de Cervantes, can't help but give one this feeling. Vendors pour in from surrounding villages, carrying produce on their heads in huge handcrafted baskets, which they set down in front of them. Their luscious fruits and vegetables glint in the morning light; farm-made cow's milk cheeses (some in the breast shape of Galician *tetilla* cheese) tilt in helter-skelter piles; huge, round unrefined wheat, corn, and rye breads, formed on top into twisted caps, compose irresistible displays; and dewy, freshly picked flowers scent the air. It is, in short, a feast of color and activity—and a taste of life from another time.

From Santiago I headed west, then north along the coast of the Rías Baixas into the less traveled regions of Galicia, the regions from which many of the city's market vendors come each day. One is obliged to drive slowly on these hilly, narrow roads that skirt *rías* and bays, but to me this is in many ways the best of Galicia, and I wouldn't miss it for the world. Near Carnota, a town that has one of Galicia's most beautiful beaches and its longest *hórreo,* I stopped to stretch my legs and for a moment watched the short, solidly built women working in the fields. Their wide-brimmed, flat-topped straw hats with black streamers looked paradoxically feminine on them. Such farm women carry on their heads everything from tall wooden *sellas* (vessels containing milk, wine, or water) to immense bundles of hay and ten-kilo sacks of potatoes.

Cabo Finisterre, a high, desolate headland jutting out into the Atlantic, divides the Rías Baixas from the Rías Altas (Upper Estuaries). As the name suggests, the point was once thought to be the end of the world, and in its rocky, rugged isolation it certainly looked that way to me.

North of Finisterre the scenery changes. The coastline becomes more dramatic and abrupt—and more treacherous, which accounts for its other name: the Costa da Morte. Near the waterfront in Camariñas, I heard bobbins clicking at a furious pace and saw María Luisa Quintana Luaces sitting where she has been stationed for at least fifteen years, making exquisite handkerchiefs and table mats. The women of this town have been engaged in lacemaking since the sixteenth century, when soldiers returning home from battle in Flanders brought with them Flemish wives who practiced this most delicate art. Signora Quintana carries on the tradition they established.

In Buño, some of whose citizens have been dedicated since Roman times to making pottery, I found no silly souvenirs but instead wonderfully rough-hewn, practical items still in everyday use in Galicia: casseroles, chestnut roasters, garlic and onion jars, and heavy wine jugs. Casa Amalia, at Santa Catalina, 35, has the best selection.

To reach La Coruña, the capital of Galicia, one must cross a narrow, sandy isthmus to the rocky islet on which it stands. Such a natural defense helped make La Coruña a key city in Spanish history, and yet it has always been upstaged by Santiago. I am fond of it just the same, for it has much to recommend it: glass-galleried houses along Avenida de la Marina on the waterfront; evocatively dark and hilly streets behind the brightly lit Plaza de María Pita; the indoor food market called Mercado de San Augustín; the Obradoiro jewelry and crafts shop at the Plazuela de los Angeles, number 7; the cozy and atmospheric Plaza de Santa Bárbara; animated Los Olmos street (bar-hoppers paradise, where I always enjoy barrel wine and octopus at Fornos); and Estrella street, with its numerous restaurants (I seek out El Rápido for the *caldo gallego* soup and grilled flounder). And one can't forget Taberna Bohemia, where late at night El Barbas (The Bearded One) delivers soulful incantations while guests' faces are intermittently illuminated by the igniting of their *queimada* (a potent drink made from a grappalike brandy called *orujo*).

A bit inland from La Coruña, I stopped in Betanzos at Edreira to enjoy nothing less than the best *tortillas* in Spain—quite a statement in a country where this potato omelet is a national dish and available just about everywhere.

Driving on, I noticed that forests were beginning to dominate the landscape and that *hórreos* were appearing less often. In Cedeira, idyllically set on a beautiful *ría,* I broke for an apéritif at the precious Taberna da Calexa and a lunch at El Náutico that included an exceptional lobster salad and an extraordinarily moist and flavorful Galician bread. El Náutico also gave me a chance to relish those highly prized *percebes* (goose barnacles).

Percebes are pried from forbidding sea-washed rocks just north of Cedeira in such tiny villages as San Andrés de Teixido, where many risk their lives in the undertaking. Others eke out a living from the pilgrims who come to worship San Andrés, guardian of fishermen. They sell primitive crafts: bread figures, childlike in design and coloring, that tell the story of the saint; naïf dolls; and unpretentious wall hangings of wood, shell, plaster, and pebbles portraying San Andrés.

You could end your exploration of Galicia here—or you could venture on. You could follow the stunning but desolate road to Cariño that hugs the rugged seaside cliffs and offers startling views of harrowing precipices (especially from the windswept Garita de Herbeira lookout). You could go on to Viveiro and the thriving Sargadelos ceramic factory, which produces starkly modern white and royal-blue chinaware and jewelry. If you time your visit to Viveiro for the first Sunday in July, you will have the opportunity to witness an exciting roundup of the wild horses seen on mountain roads. Or you could head toward the walled city of Lugo, passing through Galicia's marvelous rural interior, so serene and appealing.

One of my last stops in Galicia, in fact, was in Meira, a forgotten village in Lugo province. There Feliciano Gallego shapes blocks of wood into shoes, paints them black, and then etches into them lacy designs. He wears his pair every day, while I, back home, admire mine on their shelf and recall the comforting timelessness of that corner of Spain called Galicia.

Hotels

Hostal de los Reyes Católicos, Plaza de España, 1, Santiago de Compostela 15705; tel. 981.58.22.00

Parador Nacional Casa del Barón, Plaza de Maceda, Pontevedra 36002; tel. 986.85.58.00

Parador Nacional Conde de Gondomar, Baiona 36300; tel. 986.35.50.00

Restaurants

Don Gaiferos, Nueva, 23, Santiago de Compostela; tel. 981.58.38.94

El Asesino, Plaza de la Universidad, Santiago de Compostela; tel. 981.58.15.68

El Crisol, Hospital, 10, El Grove; tel. 986.73.00.29

El Náutico, Almirante Moreno, Cedeira; tel. 981.48.00.11

El Rápido, Estrella, 7, La Coruña; tel. 981.22.42.21

Fornos, Los Olmos, 25, La Coruña; tel. 981.22.16.75

Mesón a Charca, Calle Franco, 32, Santiago de Compostela; tel. 981.58.26.52

O Arco, Real, 14, Cambados; tel. 986.54.23.12

O Merlo, Santa Maria, 4, Pontevedra; tel. 986.84.43.43

O Moscón, Alférez Barreiro, 2, Baiona; tel. 986.35.50.08

Taberna da Calexa, Tras da Eirexa, 7, Cedeira; tel. 981.48.20.09

Vilas, Rosalía de Castro, 88, Santiago de Compostela; tel. 981.59.21.70

Ultreya el Camino de Santiago

By Abigail Seymour

～

editor's note

Olor de santidad—a smell of holiness—was the euphemism used to describe the pilgrims who came to Santiago. This is because if they arrived at the cathedral on a feast day, when the *botafumeiro,* the world's largest censer, was employed, their clothes would naturally retain the smell of the sweetly scented smoke pouring forth from this enormous candelabrum. Modern-day pilgrims may still witness the swinging of the *botafumeiro* (inquire at the Spanish Tourist Office about the dates of feast days), but it may be the journey to the cathedral itself, rather than the arrival, that is more significant. The 733-kilometer (458-mile) route from Roncesvalles to Santiago de Compostela was declared a World Heritage Site in 1993, and due to its enormous popularity in recent years, I have selected two pieces reflecting different experiences of the journey. One other piece that I regret I could not include is "On the Road to Santiago" by Robert Packard (*The New York Times,* April 27, 1997), an account of an automobile trip from Roncesvalles to Santiago. Packard was warned not to drive the camino—a friend told him, "you won't recapture the sense of the pilgrimage on foot, let alone its spirit." Though it is undoubtedly true that most people want to experience the route by walking, making the journey by car is simply another type of adventure, and may in fact be the only option available to some travelers. And besides, as Packard notes, "as if to refute the theory that it's the journey, not the arrival, that counts, Santiago, frequently enveloped in fog and drizzle, surprises one with its youthful spirits and vitality. The presence of more than 30,000 university students here, exuberantly circulating within the winner's circle of seafood and tapas bars, many as troubadors (*tunos*), helps give Santiago its contagious conviviality."

This first piece, which appeared in *Attaché,* the in-flight magazine of US Airways, originally appeared in July 1998, nearly on the brink of the new millennium. This particular issue's main feature was devoted to pilgrimages and journeys of the spirit. One contributor asked, "Is our planet so generally deprived of grace as to make pilgrimage seem the only answer?" If the numbers of pilgrims who walk the *camino* is any indication, apparently the answer is yes. For this notable issue, the editors decided to add a timeline of pilgrimages throughout history, which is reproduced (without the original illustrations) at the end of this piece. After all, though Santiago was declared a Holy City, along with Rome and Jerusalem, by Pope Alexander III in 1189, other sites and cities around the world have inspired meanderings just as meaningful.

ABIGAIL SEYMOUR, former managing editor of *Attaché,* is now a full-time photographer and writer living in North Carolina with her husband, whom she met while on a hike other than this one.

A man sleeping in the cot next to mine was snoring. He had a kerchief over his face that flapped each time he let out a breath. It was two-thirty in the morning. The other fifty or so people in the musty room of the monastery were sound asleep. I felt pale and soft and timid, among people who seemed to sleep the sound sleep of certainty.

Roncesvalles, the monastery where we were all staying in the Pyrenees, is the gateway into Spain from France on the Camino de Santiago. It was my first night on the pilgrimage; I was the only American and one of the few women in the group, as far as I could tell. Most of the people were traveling in groups of three or four, some were couples. I was alone.

Sleepless, I walked down the three flights of wooden stairs, worn in a rut down the middle. They led me to a stone entryway, the spot that in a few hours would be the start of my walk to Santiago de Compostela, five hundred miles away. There was a ring around the moon. The road faded into a gray, gauzy haze.

"Lord, hear my prayer."

The sound of my own voice, hollow and thin, startled me. I had long ago given up the idea that anyone or anything could hear me. Feeling chilled, I went back inside.

When I awoke the next morning, most of the beds were empty. My fellow pilgrims had already set out before five, before it was even light. I left two and a half hours later than they did and had the path to myself, sure that I had beaten the system. But by noon I was caught in the blazing sun with four more miles to the next refuge.

As I clumped down the mountain, trying to gauge how much my legs hurt, I came upon Burguete, a tiny whitewashed town where Hemingway stayed during the bullfight season. No sign of any fiestas, just windows shuttered against the heat and a lone bar open. Just outside of town was a series of wooden signs with just one word: *¡Ultreya!* My guidebook told me that it was a cognate of the Latin *ulter,* the same root as the English *ultra.* It was the ancient greeting exchanged by medieval pilgrims. "Beyond!" they cried to one another. "Go beyond!"

Their destination, and mine, was the cathedral in Santiago de Compostela, Spain. Inside is a marble pillar carved into a Jesse Tree, the depiction of the prophecy of Jesus' birth from the book of Isaiah: "A shoot shall come from the stump of Jesse, and a branch shall grow out of its roots." The marble tree's trunk bears an indentation in the shape of a human hand that has been worn over a millennium by millions of pilgrims. Legend says that if you put your right hand against the pillar and touch your forehead three times to the statue just below it, you will be blessed.

This act of faith is the culmination of a five-hundred-mile walk from the Spanish border with France to the spot where the remains of Apostle James were said to have been unearthed. The story goes that Saint James was beheaded in Jerusalem and his body was carried in a divinely guided boat to the western coast of Spain, where he lay undiscovered for 750 years. One night an old hermit named Pelayo saw a series of bright lights floating in the sky above a field. He began digging on the spot and discovered a well-preserved body and a note identifying the remains as Santiago—Saint James himself.

Soon after Pelayo's revelation people began walking across

Europe to venerate Saint James. At the height of the shrine's popularity in the eleventh century, more than half a million people a year walked to Santiago de Compostela. The route, which crosses the Pyrenean mountains, Navarre, and the plains of Castile and ends in the lush hills of Galicia, became an important trade road. Merchants set up shop to cater to the crowds of people pouring in, and churches and monasteries were erected to house them. "Santiago," wrote Goethe, the German philosopher, "built Europe."

The pilgrimage never died out; in fact, its popularity has surged since the Camino was named a UNESCO World Heritage Site in 1985. It remains largely unchanged since the Middle Ages, with the exception of a long, ugly stretch along a busy highway in the middle of the country. Friends of the Camino associations across Spain are working hard to divert the footpath in a safer direction without losing any of its authenticity. Pilgrim refuges have been built for modern-day seekers, providing bunk beds, cold showers, and kitchens, all staffed by former-pilgrim volunteers. During the most recent Holy Year in 1993 (when the Feast of Saint James, July 25, fell on a Sunday), 100,000 people walked, bicycled, or rode horseback the length of the Camino.

I never thought I would be one of them. I am not Spanish. I was raised a Protestant. And I am not hardy by nature. I was the sort of timid child who kept her white Keds on throughout the summer for fear of stepping on a bee. I honestly can't say for what or for whom I decided to walk to Santiago myself. All I know is that I did walk it, all the way, and that it changed me.

I was twenty-eight years old and had just gone through a divorce. I had left Manhattan with the notion of shedding my possessions and disappearing overseas. Maybe I could create myself anew, I thought, become someone more varied and textured. I came to Europe with a list of all the cities I planned to visit: Paris, Moscow, Munich, Prague, Barcelona, Athens—I never wanted to stop moving. I got a job in Madrid teaching English to business-people and lived in a small apartment in the center of the city. After a few months there, a creeping loneliness had tracked me down again, and it was time to start moving, but I didn't know where.

I spent my first Spanish Thanksgiving dinner sitting across the table from a clean-cut young American student in a bowtie. He was thin and eager and soft around the edges. I forgot his name before the end of the evening, and then forgot about him entirely. Six months later I was introduced at a party to an earthy, handsome man in faded jeans and sandals. He had long hair, an earring, and a scallop shell pendant around his neck. It took me a few minutes to recognize him without his bowtie—it was my Thanksgiving dinner companion, utterly transformed. "I have walked across Spain," Jamie told me, "along the Camino de Santiago." In those words I found what I had been looking for—whatever had changed him could change me, too.

So I set out that August for the monastery of Roncesvalles in the Pyrenees, the beginning of the walk on Spanish soil. The Camino appealed to me because I would never have to stop moving—I even thought maybe I would just stay on it forever, live on it, walking back and forth, becoming one of its eccentric fixtures, another character people would meet along the way.

That was how I ended up sleepless that first night among strangers near the border of France, ready to walk through the wilderness—Spain's and my own.

The Camino is as varied as the people who travel it. It is moody and changeable, sometimes a dripping forest path of overhanging trees and not a soul in sight, other times an exhaust-filled highway with semis whizzing by and crowds of people clogging the way. It has bridges and hills and rivers—things to cross and climb and navigate. After about a week of walking alone, I fell in with a group of people who, although we never actually declared our allegiance, remained more or less together for the rest of the trip. There were about twenty of us disbanding and re-forming each night and morning. They included Manuel, a big, lumbering, mustachioed man who worked as a cobbler in Valencia and laughed so hard at his own jokes that he would have to stop walking. He warned us that sometimes he talked and sang in his sleep, and indeed a few nights later he sat bolt upright shouting, "Chickens for sale! Chickens for sale!"

His constant companion was Sergio, a quiet vending machine salesman from the south of Spain, who revealed one night after dinner that he had been diagnosed with cancer two years before at age thirty-two. When his cancer went into remission, Sergio made a vow to walk the Camino in thanksgiving—and there he was. "*A Santiago nunca se llega, solo se va,*" he said. "You never get to Santiago, you only set out for it." Then there was Geert, a Dutch bus driver with no front teeth, who enjoyed a breakfast each morning of two yogurts and a Heineken. Christine was a doctoral candidate from Switzerland who wrote in her journal every night by flashlight.

We compared blisters and bandaged joints, pored over each other's maps, and listened wide-eyed to Camino veterans tell of what lay in store for us. We were advised to ask for Pablo in a village up ahead. The old man, they said, would give us each a perfectly whittled walking stick. I heard about Tomás, a self-proclaimed Knight Templar who lived in the mountains, carrying on the tradition of his defunct monastic order to protect the pilgrims. I heard about a fountain that spouted wine instead of water, and about a stained-glass window, made of every color in the rainbow, where the light nonetheless shone through white instead of tinted. I was urged to stop in at Molinaseca, a town so inviting that swimming pool ladders were installed on its riverbanks. I was given a scallop shell, the traditional symbol of the Camino, to wear around my neck. Its magical properties would protect me from evil.

I happened to be walking alone on the fourth day when I entered the little village of Zariquiegui, near Pamplona. Every window and door was shuttered against the midafternoon heat, but three backpacks were propped against the wall of the village church. I peered inside toward the darkened nave, and all was quiet. Light angled down through a window near the ceiling in dusty rays, and I stood with the cool wood of the door against my back as it closed. It was completely quiet—and then I heard someone take a breath. Out of the darkness near the altar came three voices singing in a cappella harmony. The hair stood up on the back of my sweaty arms. I crept into the last pew and listened. As my eyes came into focus, I saw that the singers were fellow pilgrims: two men and a woman in their twenties, wearing hiking boots, T-shirts, and shells around their necks. When they finished, I followed them back outside. They were German students who were walking to Santiago in segments, one week each year. They stopped in at every unlocked church along the way to sing.

"Why do you sing when no one else will hear you?" I asked.

"God can hear us," the woman said.

I found Pablo the whittler in the village of Ázqueta. He shyly handed me a walking stick and wouldn't take any money. The river in Molinaseca also lived up to its reputation—the water was cool and sweet, and I lingered during the hottest part of the afternoon. In the little town of Irache I actually found the fountain of wine. It turned out to be a marketing ploy on the part of a local vintner, who hooked up a tap to barrels of his house red. I never did find the miraculous stained-glass window.

In the tenth-century village of Manjarín I found Tomás the Templar. He was the only dweller left in that ghost town, living in a chaotic camp in an old, partly roofed stone house. Tomás blessed me with a steel sword on both shoulders: "*El Camino es un río*," he said. "The Camino is a river—just ride it."

I found it easier to ride as I went. Even my nationality started to fade from me like something left in the sun too long. I got browner and my Spanish improved. If anything, people thought maybe I was British or German—never American, never me.

I walked for twenty-eight days in all, from one full moon to the next, starting out with a backpack full of prissy toiletries, trendy halter tops, Band-Aids, and traveler's checks. By the time I wriggled out of my dinged-up pack for the last time, I had pared down to one change of clothes and a toothbrush.

On the last day I reached the hilltop of Monte de Gozo, where pilgrims used to dance and weep and hold each other at the first glimpse of the cathedral spires. It is now a touristy park with a view of the football stadium, a superhighway, and a rest stop. I had to ask someone to point out the spires and could barely make out three gray needles above the skyline. I wended my way through the old part of the city, still following the crude yellow arrows that had guided me that far, and suddenly rounded a corner and there it was. I looked up at the spires, and the sun shone right into my eyes. I continued on through an archway and into the grand plaza that faces the astonishing ornate facade.

Inside the cathedral the marble Jesse Tree supports an entire carved entryway. In the middle of this tall "Doorway of Glory," Santiago is seated peacefully. As I waited in line, leaning on the walking stick that Pablo had made me, it became clear that everyone up ahead followed exactly the same ritual, although slightly different from the version I was prepared for: They put their hand to the pillar, reached into a stone lion's mouth to the right, and *then* bent to tap their foreheads three times. It got to be my turn, and I did the same thing. Eyes closed, lion's mouth, forehead, tap, tap, tap.

I looked up and noticed a uniformed guard standing nearby, his eyes at a bored half-mast, arms folded across his chest. "Excuse me," I said. "What is the significance of the lion's mouth?"

He shrugged. "Nothing. Some kid reached in there this morning, and everybody who came after him's been doing it ever since."

And for all I know, they still are. I like to think so, to imagine that I was another tiny thread in this rich fabric of tradition. Are the threads mere gossamer of fact? Skeptics will tell you that the scallop shell that protected me en route was the membership badge of an ancient Venus cult. Its members dwelt in the Celtic forests and practiced rituals that Christians would find shocking. Some scholars say that the divine revelation of the tomb's location was mistranscribed by a monk with poor eyesight. They say he probably looked at an early account of Saint James' burial site whose Latin script said *Hierosolyma,* Jerusalem, and mistakenly wrote *Hispania,* Spain. There are those who try to explain away the hermit Pelayo's vision, pointing to current astronomical phenomena. I doubt that any of them have been pilgrims. On the Camino there is a much finer line between an astronomical phenomenon and a miracle.

If I was expecting something miraculous in myself, though, it had yet to happen. I didn't feel anything except tired, and sad that it was over. I said good-bye to Manuel, Sergio, Christine, Geert, and the singing Germans and returned to Madrid.

I spent several weeks going over my snapshots and watching the blisters on my feet heal and disappear. My walking stick rested in the corner of the living room. I rode the subway and taught grammar classes and wrote, but I felt as though I had been separated from a loved one. I thought about the Camino all year, wondering what winter was like in the mountains of León and how they might celebrate Easter in Santiago. You might say I was homesick, if a journey can be a home.

So when it got warm again, I went back. I worked as a volunteer at one of the Camino refuges. I cleaned toilets and kept house for more than a thousand people in two weeks. I was restless and wanted to be among them. The day before I planned to begin my second pilgrimage, I started to feel strange. I was prickly with fevered goosebumps, and everything seemed too bright and too loud.

I set out at dawn with a ringing in my right ear. By nightfall it was completely deaf. I was losing sensation in my cheek and temple, but I kept walking. León, Astorga, Ponferrada, Triacastela, mile after mile. "Beyond," I told myself. "Go beyond."

I kept walking until I couldn't stand the pain and pressure in my head. My hearing was shot, and I was angry that the one thing that had ever brought me peace—the Camino—was the very thing that was hurting me now.

Eight days away from Santiago I boarded a bus for Madrid. The doctor there told me that it was a good thing I'd come to him, since I was about eight days away from being dead—a staph infection I'd caught back at the refuge had been spreading through my ear on its way to my brain and spinal cord. Although grateful to be alive, I still felt that I had failed. When I called my Camino-mates to tell them I hadn't made it the second time, Sergio just laughed: "Don't you remember? *A Santiago nunca se llega.*"

I thought about what he said as I tried to stitch my life back together and recover from the trip. My loss of hearing took on new meaning for me—I had always thought that nothing or no one could hear me; maybe I was the one not listening. I sat in a rocking chair near the window in my apartment on Calle Huertas and finally understood the obvious: "Beyond" isn't about distance or the capacity to endure. And so I left the Camino permanently and began an altogether different journey, the search for a real home. After three years in Spain I accepted a job offer in the United States, where I am living now. My hearing is fully restored, and I try to be more open to what I hear. I have gone beyond.

I like to remember my last night in Santiago after I finished the Camino. I was lying on my back in the middle of the deserted

Plaza Obradoiro, gazing up at the cathedral. Suddenly I heard someone chattering at me from the far side of the plaza. I couldn't quite hear what she was saying, but I assumed it was along the lines of "Get up off the street, young lady!" Instead, the woman came over and sat beside me, then spun around and gestured for me to do the same.

"¡Al revés! ¡Al revés!" she commanded. "Turn around—the view is much better the other way."

The two of us lay back side by side and looked at the cathedral upside down. She was right: The spires of Santiago no longer looked rooted to the earth, but seemed to rise up out of the sky.

Galicia

Time Marches

Circa 850 B.C.: Homer's *Odyssey* isn't a tale of a pilgrimage in the conventional sense, but in later antiquity the poem is interpreted as a religious allegory about a man renouncing pleasure in favor of a sacred place of origin.

Circa 600 B.C.: The Oracle at Delphi reaches the apex of its influence. Until the advent of Christianity, the biggest names in the ancient world, including Nero, Cicero, and Aesop, travel to Delphi, which is believed to be the center of the Earth.

500 B.C.: The region around Mount Kailas in Tibet becomes a pilgrimage site. In South Asian cosmology, Mount Kailas is the *axis mundi,* and nearby Mount Meru is the center of the universe. In subsequent years Hindus, Jains, Buddhists, and followers of Tibet's Bon faith share this belief.

400 B.C.: Just prior to his death, the Buddha talks to his chief disciple, Ananda, about turning his biography into a pilgrimage. Those who want to follow the Buddha should visit his birthplace, Lumbini (modern Rummindei in Nepal); the place of his enlightenment, Bodh Gaya, India; the site of his first sermon, also known as the spot where he "set in motion the Wheel of the Dharma," now known as Sarnath; and Kushinagar, where the Buddha died of food poisoning at the age of eighty. Buddhists believe that any devout pilgrims dying en route will be "reborn in a heavenly world."

Circa 100 A.D.: Lucien, a pilgrim and essayist, describes the temple rites at Hierapolis in Phoenicia. He says that prior to entering the holy city the pilgrim shaves his head and eyebrows, sacrifices a sheep, kneels on the fleece, and puts the head on top of his own.

200s: Critics complain that Christian pilgrims will find the Holy Land filled with sin and sinners.

333: The Bordeaux Pilgrim's travelogue of a journey from France to Jerusalem is the earliest surviving pilgrimage text known.

333: Constantine builds the first Church of the Nativity over the grotto in Bethlehem where Mary is believed to have given birth. Later the church will be controlled by three main Christian groups: Roman Catholic, Greek Orthodox, and Armenian Orthodox. Thousands of pilgrims will visit the church each year. However, all is not peaceful. Controversy involving the disappearance of a silver star from the church may have contributed to the start of the Crimean War.

632: Months before his death, Muhammad leads 90,000 followers to Mecca for a farewell *hajj.*

638: The Muslims capture Jerusalem. It becomes an important destination for pilgrims because the faithful believe Muhammad stopped at the city to behold celestial glories on the *isra'*—his flight to heaven.

800: The largest Buddhist monument is built in Borobudur, Java. Said to have taken 10,000 men and a hundred years to build, the construction is a step pyramid on top of a hill.

1099: The First Crusade retakes the Holy Land, and Christian pilgrimages resume.

Middle Ages: A typical French pilgrim traveling to Jerusalem faces a round trip of 3,400 miles. At the rate of twenty-one miles a day on horseback, this works out to a twenty-three-week road trip.

1100s: Ethiopian King Lalibala orders the excavation of the town that bears his name. Envisioned as a new Jerusalem, Lalibala in modern times hosts Timkat (Epiphany) celebrations every January 12 for the country's Orthodox Christians.

1168: The Crusaders complete the Church of the Holy Sepulchre, enclosing what they believe to be the tomb of Christ. It becomes a destination for pilgrims.

Late 1100s: The word *pilegrim,* derived from the Latin *peregrinus,* meaning "stranger," appears for the first time in literature.

1200s: The Holy Land is again controlled by Muslims, and Rome becomes the primary pilgrimage destination for Christians.

1293: Marco Polo visits the tomb of Saint Thomas in India.

1300: In this Jubilee year, 2 million Christian pilgrims visit Rome and receive a complete pardon for their sins.

1300: There are an estimated 10,000 sanctuaries for pilgrims in the western portion of Christendom.

1306: Pilgrimages are time-consuming, so the devout rich begin to send proxy pilgrims. Reginald Lombard travels to Santiago de Compostela for King Edward I of England.

1392: Thomas Brygg's account of his pilgrimage to the Holy Land offers not only an itinerary but information on entrance fees and essentials like camel rentals.

1530: Christian reformers denounce pilgrimages as "childish and useless works."

1600s: Pilgrims on the Japanese island of Shikoku trek nine hundred miles in a clockwise direction in a pilgrimage honoring Buddhist saint Kobo Daishi. Along the way they pass eighty-eight Buddhist shrines and temples; each supplies a red stamp, which the pilgrims affix to their white coats.

1776: A slave-trading family builds the "Slave House" on Gorée Island in Dakar Harbor, Senegal. Now a museum, it contains residences for slave traders on its upper floor and cells for holding Africans before they pass through the "door of no return" to be shipped across the Atlantic Ocean. The island, named a UNESCO World Heritage Site, draws people of African ancestry from all over the world.

1846: Religious scholars tag the appearance of the Virgin Mary at La Salette, France, as the first of her modern visitations.

1858: The Virgin Mary appears eighteen times to the French teenager Bernadette Soubirous. In the next 125 years, Lourdes claims sixty-four miracles and eventually attracts 3 million pilgrims per year—more than either Jerusalem or Mecca.

1867: Madame Helene Petrovna Blavatsky leaves her first husband and her native Russia and begins a two-decade journey around the world. In 1875 she launches the mystical Theosophy movement in New York City.

1917: Thousands of pilgrims travel to Fatima, Portugal, and reportedly see a solar miracle. The message of the visions is said to predict the advent of World War II and the spread of communism.

1929: The British Mandate, tired of the constant infighting by competing religious groups in Jerusalem, draws up a secret memo on jurisdiction over holy places. The Associated Press reports: "Nine closely spaced pages are devoted to the Church of the Nativity, with a meticulous down-to-the-last-candlestick inventory of which sect owns what."

1943: Hollywood weighs in on the miracles of Lourdes with the film *The Song of Bernadette* starring Jennifer Jones, Charles Bickford, and Vincent Price.

1940s: Brother Roger founds the Taize community in France's Burgundy district as a place of reconciliation after World War II. Thousands make the trip to Taize every year, and its monks lead "pilgrimages of trust" to every continent.

1977: In a ritual that takes place only when the heavens are in alignment, at least 10 million Hindu pilgrims (a record number in 1977) seek salvation through immersion in the sacred Ganges River at the climax of Hinduism's holiest ritual bathing festival. The ancient festival, called the Kumbh Mela, is believed to be the largest mass gathering in the world.

1980: Kateri Tekakwitha, a Mohawk martyred in 1680, becomes the first Native American beatified by the Catholic Church. Her shrine in Auriesville, New York, draws tens of thousands in search of miracle cures each year.

1981: Six Croatian peasants claim a visit by the Virgin Mary in Medjugorje, Yugoslavia. Since then at least 11 million pilgrims have traveled to the small village.

1985: The Australian government hands back ownership of Uluru to its Aboriginal owners. Known to westerners as Ayers Rock, the mountain is a sacred site to local Aborigines and has since become the focus of spiritual pilgrimages by people from all over the world.

1986: Mormon pilgrims travel by covered wagon between Omaha and Salt Lake City in a re-creation of the journey their ancestors made with Brigham Young.

1989: On the feast day of the Virgin of Guadalupe, 3 million pilgrims gather at the basilica in Mexico City where the Virgin Mary is said to have appeared to an Indian peasant in 1531.

1993: Travel writer Alexander Frater ventures to Bodh Gaya, Buddhism's most sacred shrine, as part of a PBS documentary. While at the shrine he meets not only monks but pilgrim-oriented filmmaker Bernardo Bertolucci, in the middle of filming *Little Buddha* starring Keanu Reeves.

1993: Seventy thousand people visit the Indian Wheel, a sacred site located in the Bighorn Mountains of Wyoming. As recently as 1990, fewer than 6,000 people made the journey. Pilgrims circumambulating the wheel have worn a trench around its perimeter.

1995: Twelve pilgrims of various religious faiths start from Chimayó, New Mexico, and trace the route of the "atomic mirror" from the uranium mines where the materials for the first bombs originated, through Los Alamos to the White Sands Missile Range and Ground Zero, where the first nuclear explosion occurred fifty years before. The group then proceeds through nuclear waste dumps in Nevada, through Livermore, California, site of nuclear design labs, and across the Pacific to Hiroshima and Nagasaki. They carry gifts of healing to Nagasaki's mayor and call for the abolition of nuclear weapons.

1997: Around 95,000 people make the trek along the Camino de Santiago in Spain, following the ancient pilgrimage route to Compostela and the cathedral dedicated to Saint James. A decade before, only 3,000 to 4,000 made the journey.

1997: When a private Russian company attempts to cash in on the popularity of visits to the Holy Land by Russians, the Orthodox Church protests. Moscow's Patriarchate argues that pilgrimages are the exclusive business of the church.

1999–2000: An epic pilgrimage of peace lasting six months retraces, on horse- and camelback, the journey of the Magi. Festivals are held in cities along the route, with a twelve-day celebration in Bethlehem for 10,000.

2000: Celebration locales for the arrival of the next millennium include Rome, Palestine and Israel, and Times Square.

Santiago's Golden Legend

By Rachel Billington

editor's note

It's possible that Santiago would still be a beautiful and remarkable city even without its destination cathedral, occupying as it does a most glorious spot at the top of a hill. But without the cathedral it might not have the impressive Plaza del Obradoiro, described wonderfully by Cees Nooteboom in *Roads to Santiago:* "The impression is one of vastness, in that town square, a granite plateau bordered by granite jewels, at such altitude that you can see nothing but sky beyond. And it is *always* beautiful. Snow, night, hail, ice, moon, rain, mist, storm, sun, they all have the run of the Plaza del Obradoiro, they alter people's gestures, attitudes and gait with one stroke of their cold or heat, with the lashes of whips or the fluttering of veils, with their light or their gloom, they clear the square or fill it with people, creating an ever-changing drawing in which, as soon as you set foot on that rectangular plane, you are as much a participant as the statues dancing against the western sky, a movable element in a work of art conceived by someone else."

A note to those arriving in Santiago by car, as I did: it is maddeningly difficult to find one's way into the old part of town, let alone to the plaza. Even my husband, who is one of the best navigators on the planet, was frustrated by the lack of adequate signage, and we circled around and around the old city, with a view of the cathedral nearly always in sight, so close and yet so damn far, before we finally had to ask someone for directions. Of course, once we made the right turn, it all seemed so obvious; but truly it isn't, and if we had known in advance that it would be difficult, at least we would have been more civil to each other. Note, too, that if you are staying at the *parador,* you are permitted to enter the pedestrian-only streets and park in front of the entrance. If you're not, good luck: most of the streets are blocked to cars or are for one-way traffic in the opposite direction you want to proceed.

RACHEL BILLINGTON has written frequently about travel for a variety of publications, including *The New York Times,* where this piece first appeared. She is also the author of *Loving Attitudes* (William Morrow,

1988; hardcover; Penguin, 1989, paperback), *Occasion of Sin* (Summit, 1982), and *All Things Nice* (Black Swan, 1969), among others. Her work has appeared in previous editions of *The Collected Traveler*.

Santiago de Compostela has been a lodestar for visitors for more than a thousand years. The world's first guidebook was written in 1130 by Aymeric Picaud, a French monk, to give information to travelers on their way there. In the early Middle Ages between 500,000 and 2 million people came each year. They came, however, not for the sun or the architecture, but to visit the sacred relics of the body of Saint James.

As a center of Christian pilgrimage, Santiago rivaled Rome and the Holy Land. The Camino de Santiago, or the Way of Saint James, originated in towns all over Europe—in England, Germany, Italy, Scandinavia and, of course, France. Pilgrims set out alone, in small groups, or in large gatherings. For the most part, their paths converged in France, where the routes were organized by the Benedictines and Cistercians of Cluny and Citeaux and the Knights Templars of the Spanish Order of the Red Sword. By the time the pilgrims crossed the Pyrenees and entered Spain, they continued on two routes only—the northern coastal road, called the Asturian, and the more popular Camino Francés, or French Way. Along the latter, so much traveled over hundreds of years and still used today, were built some of the most spiritual and magnificent of Spanish buildings. Yet nothing prepares one for the wonder of Santiago de Compostela itself.

In Spain it is often impossible to separate tradition and history. But there's no doubt that a visit to this northwest corner of the Iberian peninsula is made far more exciting by some knowledge of the extraordinary events that did (or didn't) happen there. Saint James the Apostle, brother of Saint John the Evangelist, brought

Christianity to Spain and then returned to the Holy Land, where he was beheaded; his body was conveyed to Spain by his disciples in a rudderless boat that found its way to a little inland port now known as Padrón.

About fifteen miles southeast of Santiago, Padrón is a good introduction to the marvelous mysteries. If you're lucky enough to find the priest to let you in, enter the little seventeenth-century parish church of Santiago by the River Sar, which flows through the town; under the altar you can actually see the granite stone to which the apostle's boat was tied. Thus the name Padrón, taken from *piedra,* meaning "stone."

After Saint James's body reached Spain, it disappeared for eight hundred years until Pelayo, a hermit, saw a brilliant star flashing over a woodland (hence, perhaps, Compostela, from *campo de la estrella,* or "field of the star"). An ancient burial place was unearthed, and on July 25, A.D. 813, the holy remains were drawn triumphantly in an oxcart into the center of Santiago. On the busy Calle de Franco, there's a little shrine to mark the spot where the journey ended, and near the city walls, by the fine stone market, there stands the Romanesque church of San Félix de Solovia, built near the cave in which the hermit Pelayo lived; the church is notable for a twelfth-century tympanum of the Adoration of the Magi.

On the top of the Bishop's Palace, facing the great cathedral of St. James, there is a huge statue of a knight on horseback carrying a banner. Not much, you might think, to do with the James who watched with his brother at Gethsemane. But this is his reincarnation, Santiago Matamoros, the Moor-slayer, who appeared miraculously to inspire the Christians in their battles against the infidels. His banner bore an ornamental red cross, and it is still the city's symbol, marking souvenir ashtrays, key chains, and decals.

A third Saint James was created by the pilgrims themselves. He is dressed as one of them, with a wide-brimmed hat and a heavy cloak adorned with the scallop shell that was—and remains—the pilgrims' emblem. He carries a stout staff with a drinking gourd attached. This Saint James appears above the Holy Door in the cathedral's east facade, overlooking the Plaza de la Quintana.

The pilgrims usually entered the cathedral by the Puerta de Azabacheria, where the jet workers made and sold their wares. Jet and silver are still the two crafts of Santiago, and the silvermakers cluster round their own door, the Platerías, with its superbly carved Romanesque entrance and seventeenth-century clock tower.

There is an argument for never leaving the cathedral and the four great squares that surround it. The extraordinary many-layered building embraces, in its crypt, an eleventh-century barrel-vaulted church; its gigantic Gothic cloister has a dazzling filigree trellis; and its Treasury Tower recalls a Thai temple.

The eighteenth-century Baroque Obradoiro (west) facade, with its double staircase, is the most ornate. Within is an older facade, decorated with a parade of stone figures carved by Master Mateo in the twelfth century: the Door of Glory. The master carved a self-portrait on the back of the pillar on which Saint James and, above him, Christ in Glory look out into the narthex. Here Saint James and, indeed, all the more than two hundred figures, particularly the mysteriously smiling Daniel, have a warmth and gentleness that belie their granite material.

Inside, at the heart of the cathedral, yet another Saint James, resplendent in golden cloak studded with jewels, dominates the center aisle from above the main altar. Steps leading upward allow pilgrims to walk behind the statue, kiss its mantle, and embrace its shoulders. Steps leading downward uncover a small shrine where an ornate silver chest contains the bones of the saint.

Hidden from the buccaneering Sir Francis Drake in 1589, these relics were lost again for three centuries until a historian, Antonio López Ferreiro, found them in 1879. An elaborate plaque commemorating him can be seen opposite the old university buildings now housing the geography and history faculties.

The quest for Saint James leads into every corner of the city; the problem is to unravel fact from fiction. Indisputably real, because it stands four-square at the northwest corner of the cathedral in the Plaza de España, is the Hostal de los Reyes Católicos, built by Queen Isabella and King Ferdinand at the turn of the sixteenth century to house and nurse the pilgrims who were pouring into the city. Forgetting for a moment Isabella's terrible legacy of the Inquisition, her hotel/hospital is a tranquil and glorious monument to religious belief. It is built around four courtyards and displays the most beautiful hotel doorway in the world, ornamented with a profusion of carved figures, beginning with Adam and Eve. Since 1954 the *hostal* has been run as part of the Spanish national chain of *paradors*. Yet it is still a charitable foundation: each day up to ten certified pilgrims can claim three free meals a day for up to three days. These contemporary pilgrims eat with the staff, the manager explains.

It is perfectly possible to visit Santiago and see it only as another splendid European city. Its Plaza de España rivals in magnificence the shell-shaped Piazza del Campo in Siena or the Piazza San Marco in Venice. The stone-paved streets have a multitude of cafés and bars that, in term time, are thronged with some of the 47,000 students who fill the thriving University of Santiago. Yet among the tourists you will spot the pilgrims: one morning two white-haired men with backpacks entered through Mateo's Door of Glory and pressed their fingers into the holes made in the stone by their forerunners over eight centuries.

Inside the offices of the cathedral sits a representative of the secretariat whose one job is to certify the true pilgrims, those who have walked, bicycled, or ridden (on horseback) over at least fifty kilometers (about thirty miles) to get to Santiago. They bring a card stamped in the town halls along the route and sign in at a registry.

Under the heading "motives for pilgrimage," someone has written "*une promesse*" and someone else "100 percent *por Dios*" and a third "*réligieux et sportifs.*" A very *sportif* Frenchman bounds in while I am there; he has bicycled from the Rue St. Jacques in Paris, the traditional start of the route, to Santiago in ten days. The secretary tells me that the number of pilgrims has more than doubled in the past ten years.

But if Compostela is called the spiritual center of Spain, it is also the center of the strange wild country of Galicia. Down every street you can see the steep wooded mountains and lower gorse-clad hills that rise up from every river valley. Galicia has its own traditions, founded not just on Christian religions but on those of its earlier Celtic and Roman invaders. The music that is played on most street corners and in every square often features the *gaita,* a bagpipe, smaller than its Scottish cousin but indisputably the same instrument. On feast days and holy days the town is filled with students dressed in medieval costume, usually black velvet slashed with scarlet or yellow or blue. The three oldest college foundations have their own musical groups and their own positions in the town. Often they process around, making the narrow streets echo with drums and pipes.

July 25, the feast of Saint James, is the greatest fiesta day. There is a noisy fireworks display, and the Paseo de la Herradura, which covers a woody hill near the city, is used as an overspill for less spiritual celebrations. For the four days of my most recent visit, a huge fun fair rose on its slopes. In the morning the Plaza de España was filled with children holding balloons. They were joined by local dignitaries, soldiers in helmets with plumes, and a band with full choir. To the strains of the European anthem, Beethoven's "Ode to Joy," the children loosed the balloons, and up they sailed, over the stone banner of Saint James the Moor-slayer and into a clear blue sky.

Entry into the European community has not altered much in the city of Santiago. But once you leave the city to head, perhaps, eastward along the pilgrim road, anyone used to old Spain will be amazed by the new four-lane highway. Gone are the days of bone-shaking potholes. Now you can quite easily visit some of the towns and villages up to sixty miles or so from Santiago and still be back for a peaceful dinner in town. The countryside inland from Santiago is exceedingly beautiful, forests of pine and eucalyptus, smelling coolly medicinal. In the autumn the soft pinks and mauves of heather undulate across the moorlands, all against a background of rich green. (On one drive into Santiago a bee entered the car, reminding me of the old tradition that no bee or ant must be killed on the route to the city for it might contain the soul of a pilgrim forever making his way to the apostle.)

Unlike the rest of Spain, Galicia never loses its color to a long dry summer, for it rains the year round; the local people boast they have rain all but thirty days of the year. Despite this, the rocky, mountainous terrain makes it unprofitable farming land, not helped by the ancient division of land into strips and the still antiquated methods of farming. Symbols of the old ways, still in use, are the little *hórreos,* or grain barns, that stand on stilts, usually with a cross on one end of their pink tiled roofs.

About fifteen miles southeast of Santiago there is a small manor house called Pazo de Oca, which has the most romantic garden outside Ireland. Trees of camellia, avocado, yew, and ilex, rows of semi-clipped hedges, lead you by overgrown pathways to a still and shady lake. At its center a boat constructed of stone, with stone sailors at prow and stern, masquerades as an island. Its only inhabitants are a wild exuberance of hydrangea and some disdainful swans. There seems to be no record of whether pilgrims were received in this mysterious paradise, although there is a chapel within its walls.

In a small village just beyond Palas de Rei is Vilar de Donas (Place of the Ladies), a powerful Romanesque church with strong pilgrim links. It was attached to a monastery of the Knights of the Order of St. James, which was founded in 1184. There was also a hospital where great and presumably holy ladies came to tend pilgrims in need. Behind the altar the curved wall of the apse is painted with still colorful portraits of some of the ladies. They are elaborately dressed and coifed in medieval finery, and one of them, with a clever animated face, has thick loops of corn-colored plaits. The sun makes the wildflowers decorating the altar shine brightly, but deep green stains on the walls suggest that in winter it's a different story.

The Galician Spaniards are not much given to showing their feelings, which makes them seem dour at first. General Franco came from Galicia, but when he was in power he did everything possible to bring the region under the central government. It has always been one of the poorest areas of Spain, and emigration, often to the United States, has been very high. (One family called Castro ended up in Cuba.) Now Galicia has become an autonomous region of Spain, and signs are written in two languages.

The strangest example of modern development in Galicia is the village of Portomarín, where the fine Romanesque church of the Knights of St. John of Jerusalem, an important stopping-point on the Camino Francés, used to stand by the River Miño. In 1963 a dam was built, the village flooded, and the church was removed, stone by numbered stone (you can see the numbers on them still), to a higher point where a new Portomarín was constructed around it. Above the portal Christ sits in glory, surrounded by the twenty-four Elders of the Apocalypse, who seem remarkably unsurprised by their new setting.

It is tempting to continue on to the ancient Roman town of Lugo. A one-mile walk around its broad stone walls offers views of churches and countryside. In the twelfth century the city possessed five hospitals and a leper hospital for pilgrims. The sleepy old square has a thick band of shady trees on one side, beyond which yet another great Romanesque church sits in granite dignity.

Returning to Santiago along the Camino Francés, you see some of the same landmarks that the medieval pilgrims knew. Not far from where the airport stands now, a few miles outside the town, rises the hill known as Monte Gaudi, or Mountjoy, where pilgrims caught their first glimpse of Santiago and cried out, *"Mon joie! Mon joie!"* Nearer the city stands the twelfth-century Romanesque church of Santa María del Sar. It is so buttressed that from the outside it looks more like a fortification than a church. Inside, the reason is clear; the row of giant pillars down the center aisle have a severe list outward, defying gravity. It would be a somber place were it not for those crazily drunken pillars and—the day I saw it—streamers of white satin decorating the pews.

From Santa María del Sar it is only about fifteen minutes on foot to the Puerta del Camino, through which the pilgrims entered the city walls. In later years they would have seen nearby one of the loveliest small churches, Santa María del Camino, its facade decorated with a huge stone wreath of flowers. They would continue inward, washing at one of the fountains, perhaps the one in the Plaza del Toral or in the Plaza Fonseca, which faces the ancient university. At last, after many months—or even years—of traveling, of overcoming the dangers of extreme heat, cold, wet, of brigands, of sickness, perhaps of loss of faith, they would see rising up in front of them the vast spread of the cathedral. It is not difficult to imagine their relief and excitement as they realized that this was their journey's end.

Today, even for those with no religious beliefs, Santiago still sets up some indefinable longing. Sir Walter Raleigh wrote for his age:

> Give me my scallop-shell of quiet,
> My staff of faith to walk upon,

My scrip of joy, immortal diet,
My bottle of salvation,
My gown of glory, hope's true gage,
And thus I'll take my pilgrimage.

Now, modern travelers, we have a chance to wonder at the physical realities of that eternal dream. Or we can take up the pilgrim's challenge.

For Pilgrims and Sojourners

Selected Lodgings

Prices listed below are computed at a rate of 120 pesetas to $1. In most cases low season denotes the period from November 1 to March 15.

The **Hotel de los Reyes Católicos** (Plaza del Obradoiro 1; 34.981.58.22.00) has double rooms—many overlooking one of the hotel's four cloistered courtyards—for $100 (low season) and $133 (high). Though sections of the hotel are undergoing renovation (to be completed early next year), nearly 100 rooms are now available for occupancy. The hotel's subterranean restaurant serves such Galician fare as scallops with *serrano* ham, and *tarta de Santiago,* a dessert made with ground almonds. The prix-fixe dinner, with wine, is about $55 for two.

In New York reservations for Spain's *paradors,* of which the Reyes Católicos is one, can be made through **Marketing Ahead** (433 Fifth Avenue, New York 10016; 212-686-9213), which adds a surcharge of $3 a night for each double room.

The modern **Araguaney** (Calle Alfredo Brañas 5; 981.59.59.00) has a swimming pool, discothèque, and cocktail lounge. Doubles are $110 (low season) and $128 (high). The restaurant's international menu features sole *meunière* and *solomillo* (steak prepared in the Spanish style). The menu of the day, which includes wine, is about $30 for two.

The **Compostela** (Fuente de San Antonio 1; 981.58.57.00), a short walk from the old town, offers comfortable, modern accommodations. Doubles are $48 (low season) and $65 (high).

The **Suso** (Rúa del Villar 65; 981.58.66.11), in the heart of the old quarter, is small, friendly, and inexpensive. Double rooms are $18 (low season) and $24 (high).

Sustenance

Don Gaiferos (Rúa Nova 23; 981.58.38.94), regional in both décor and cuisine, specializes in fish pâtés and *estofado de carne* (a local stew). Dinner for two, with wine, costs about $85.

Vilas (Calle Rosalía de Castro 88; 981.59.10.00) and **Anexo Vilas** (Avenida de Villagarcía 21; 981.59.83.87), operated by the same family, offer such traditional dishes as scallops sautéed with ham, and *xarrete* (marinated beef hock). Desserts include *filloas* (pancakelike pastries) and *leche frita* (fried blancmange). Dinner for two, with wine, ranges from $65 to $135.

At **Alameda** (Avenida de Figueroa 15; 981.58.47.96), specialties include *empanada de salmón* (salmon pie) and fresh fish, grilled, poached, or sautéed. Menus of the day, for two, range from $30 to $40, including wine.

Reprinted by permission of Harold Ober Associates Incorporated. Copyright © 1989 by Rachel Billington. First published in *The New York Times Sophisticated Traveler,* October 1, 1989.

Cities of the Future:
Santiago de Compostela

By Leslie Camhi

~

editor's note

The September 2001 issue of *Travel + Leisure* featured an interesting article entitled "Cities of the Future." The editors noted that "by the year 2030, sixty percent of the world's population will be urbanites. That's 4.9 billion people, 2 billion more than today." Five cities, ranging in size from metropolis to megalopolis, were chosen as those shaping the twenty-first century, among them Santiago de Compostela.

Leslie Camhi is a writer and cultural critic whose essays on art, film, books, and travel appear regularly in the pages of *The New York Times*, *The Village Voice*, *Vogue*, and *Travel + Leisure*, where this piece originally appeared.

A grassy knoll beside the sleepy city of Santiago de Compostela seems an unlikely site for one of Spain's foremost architectural innovations. But there, in February, the American architect Peter Eisenman—known for his love of oblique lines and oblique theories—broke ground for the City of Culture of Galicia, a futuristic $125 million complex of six buildings. The last in a trio of ultra-contemporary edifices along Spain's northern edge (including Frank Gehry's Guggenheim Museum in Bilbao and Rafael Moneo's Kursaal Performing Arts Center in San Sebastián), Eisenman's City of Culture encapsulates the ambitions of a medieval metropolis remaking itself for a global future.

In his New York office Eisenman recently showed me models for the complex: two libraries, a history museum, a music theater, a center for new technologies, and administrative headquarters. The gently undulating, striated forms, to be clad in glass and stone, are based on Santiago's labyrinthine streets and arcaded alleys, which curve down to the city's main square, the Plaza del Obradoiro, and its great cathedral.

"When you invert it, the street plan of the old city resembles a scallop shell, the ancient symbol of Santiago," Eisenman told me. "We took that structure, put it up on the mountainside, laid a Cartesian grid over it, and warped it onto the site. We're taking the old, the sacred, and bringing it to the new, the secular."

Sacred and secular are an old couple in Santiago. This capital of Galicia, a province of Spain on the western tip of Europe, probably served as a pagan pilgrimage site long before a ninth-century hermit discovered the body of the apostle Saint James there. A holy city sprang up, where a half-million faithful soon began arriving each year via the Way of Saint James, a network of footpaths stretching across southern France and the Pyrenees. In 1994 Shirley MacLaine herself made the journey, dodging paparazzi and seeking revelation.

The Museum of Pilgrimage, which opened five years ago in a Gothic house, focuses on the cult of Saint James, but like much of Santiago it has another face. On a recent visit I made my way upstairs where, beside sculptures of the saint, Christ, and the Virgin (who wear pilgrim's clothing out of empathy for their devotees' suffering), hung self-portraits by Zhang Yuan, a Chinese performance artist whom I'd last run into at a loft party in New York. "Zhang Yuan had to abandon his country, his family, and follow a path to arrive in New York, with many sacrifices and renunciations," the museum's director, Bieito Pérez Outeiriño, explained. "So he feels like a pilgrim, too."

The scallop may be the sacred emblem of Saint James—pilgrims pinned a shell to their cloaks upon arrival—but it's also a favorite food in the *tapas* bars that line the Rúa do Franco, popular spots for the 44,000 students (almost half the city's total population) who attend Santiago's five-hundred-year-old university. The students' willingness to endure the vagaries of ancient plumbing helped keep the old city alive until EU funds contributed to a real renovation. Now they can no longer afford to live there.

So they inhabit the new city, an anonymous mass of hotels, shopping malls, and high-rises. Twice the size of the old, with ten times the population, the new city also houses the workers who provide services for Santiago's ever-widening stream of tourists. There are pizzerias and Chinese restaurants, and traces of past political conflicts—Red Square is so named because of demonstrations that erupted in the last years of the Franco dictatorship. And there's a smattering of luxury, too. Famished pilgrims may dine on local nouvelle cuisine or clothe themselves at the chic boutiques of Galician designers Adolfo Dominguez and Purificación García.

Remote from the rest of Spain, Santiago is close to the idea of Europe. In recent years Galicia's relative isolation from Madrid—reinforced by high mountains and a local dialect, Gallego—has fueled a fierce regional pride, modeled on that of the Basque country and Catalonia. Santiago was for centuries a center of cosmopolitan religious culture in a sea of underdevelopment. "Within Spain our culture can only be understood as an island," said sociologist José Pérez Vilariño. "Santiago belongs more to a European tradition than a single country."

The City of Culture project was born from this combination of ardent regionalism and transnational aspirations. It is the brainchild of Manuel Fraga Iribarne, president of the governing *xunta* of Galicia. His eight-year tenure has already seen the construction of two luminous, imposing buildings by Pritzker Prize–winner Álvaro Siza, housing the university's school of journalism and the Galician Center for Contemporary Art, on the edge of the old city. Iribarne was once minister of information under the Franco regime. But this is the new Spain; when he retires, his legacy will include these monuments to the free exchange of ideas. The City of Culture, with its state-of-the-art research center and cyborgian focus on emerging technologies, is the most expansive and inventive.

"The Guggenheim Museum in Bilbao is a magnificent building, which everyone admires, but it belongs to the past century," said Jesús Pérez Varela, the *xunta*'s minister of culture. "We want our City of Culture to belong to the new millennium."

Biblioteca

Santiago: Saint of Two Worlds, photographs by Joan Myers, essays by Marc Simmons, Donna Pierce, and Joan Myers, University of New Mexico Press, Albuquerque, 1991. As the authors note, Spain created a buffer zone of sorts across the entire southern United States, from Florida to California, to protect its silver interests in Mexico to the south. Those same parcels of land became the property of the United States in the nineteenth century, "which thereby acquired a share in Spain's historical legacy." British historian J. H. Plumb remarked in 1985 that "the United States has little sixteenth-century history," an observation that many unthinking Americans would probably accept as valid. But that century can only be dismissed as empty if one discounts the record of Spanish exploration and attempted settlement, rejecting it as foreign to America's "authentic" national history. The unreasonableness of that position has been amply demonstrated by qualified writers who, summoning reliable historical evidence, have shown that one of the oldest and most persistent threads woven into the fabric of American life is our Hispanic heritage. This is a unique project pairing text (the authors' intent was to convey some notion of Santiago's impact upon Spanish history, religion, and art) with black-and-white photos (which connect the legend of Santiago past and present, and includes images taken in New Mexico, Peru, Haiti, Mexico, Puerto Rico, and the Philippines). Santiago Matamoros (Moor-slayer) was an important saint for early Hispanic settlers who were constantly under fear of Indian attack. He appears in the art of the Americas as apostle and pilgrim, but is most often represented in the New World as a warrior-saint. Eventually he became the conqueror of Indians, too. Author Simmons notes that the academic and philosopher Américo

Castro once explained, "the history of Iberia would not have taken the path it did without the belief that the body of Santiago reposed in Galicia. American author James A. Michener echoed that thought when he remarked that to understand the inner meaning of Spain, one must travel the road that leads to the grave and shrine of St. James." This creative book is hard to find but is worth the effort for readers interested in pursuing the cult of St. James to other corners of the world.

Camino de Santiago Pilgrimage Guides

There are so very many pilgrimage guides, in so very many different languages, that it would be not only impossible to find and review them all but ultimately not very useful, I think, in helping readers distinguish between them and single out those titles that most appeal to them. So after reading and reviewing entirely too many pilgrimage guides, I selected the following books that seemed to stand apart. Each title is a little different from the others, and each offers a different viewpoint and purpose. I admit I have not yet walked any portion of the Camino, so I cannot recommend these books from personal experience; but I have walked and hiked and backpacked quite a number of times in my life, so I am keen on looking for a certain style and particular information when deciding which books would be better than others. Nearly everyone I have met who has walked at least a portion of the Camino, and nearly everyone who has contributed letters to periodicals, has recommended supplementing a guide(s) with the annually updated pilgrimage edition published by the Confraternity of Saint James.

The Camino: A Journey of the Spirit, Shirley MacLaine, Pocket Books, 2000. I admit I was skeptical about this book when it first appeared, but I include it here because there are some wonderful passages, and also because the staff at the Spanish tourist office in Santiago told me that the single reason most often mentioned by North Americans who visit there is that they read this book and it moved them to make the journey (to Santiago, not necessarily via the Camino). If a book can be this inspiring to people, then it deserves to be read. I found MacLaine's personal quest tiresome, but I enjoyed reading about her experiences on the route itself.

The Pilgrimage to Santiago, Edwin Mullins, Interlink, 2001. This paperback edition is one in Interlink's Lost and Found: Classic Travel Writing series, of which I'm very fond. Published originally in 1974, it is not quite as old or lost as some others in the series, but nonetheless I'm grateful to Interlink for returning it to print. In addition to writing this book, Mullins also wrote and presented an eighty-minute documentary film for the BBC, as well as one for French television. He first walked the Camino in the early 1970s, when the route was decidedly less trodden and sometimes impossible to find: "it was more often a question of dropping into village bars for a glass of *rioja* and enquiring politely where the old road might be. And small boys in bare feet would be dispatched to guide me through farmers' backyards and over crumbling stone walls until suddenly, half-hidden among brambles and wild roses, I'd find myself standing on a stretch of massively-paved road deeply rutted by centuries of carts and wagons." Today, of course, we can refer to this as the "Santiago phenomenon," and the route is so well marked, it's nearly impossible to get lost. Why the Camino has been embraced so eagerly by so many thousands of people interests Mullins greatly, and he ponders that walking, and especially walking a long distance, puts one in touch with a quieter, older way of life, a life that people value as our present day-to-day existence becomes more frenetic. Additionally, as Mullins notes, the pilgrimage is a walk through history, reminding us that we are walking where millions of people walked before. "All human life was once there," he writes, "treading along that long road. In fact, when I wrote this book, I wanted to call it *The Long Road to Heaven,* because to medieval pilgrims that was precisely what it was—a means of obtaining absolution, *remissio peccatorum,* the remission of sins, the promise of a passport to heaven." Mullins retraces the path from the Rue St. Jacques in Paris to Santiago, and if I were walking even a portion of this route, I wouldn't want to be without this illuminating book.

The Pilgrimage Road to Santiago: The Complete Cultural Handbook, David Gitlitz and Linda Kay Davidson, Griffin/St. Martin's Press, 2000. The subtitle defines this wonderful book even further: "Including Art, Architecture, Geology, History, Folklore, Saints' Lives, Flora and Fauna." It truly is a fascinating compendium, and is *not*—as the authors emphasize—a guide to the route; rather, it is a "handbook to the cultural contexts of the pilgrimage" (which, they note again, is what the pilgrims they met seemed to really crave). When the authors first trekked the route in 1974, they did not meet even one other pilgrim. In 1979, when they walked it again, they met exactly one other person, an elderly Frenchman who was fulfilling a promise he'd made to himself after the Second World War. The scene had changed quite dramatically by 1987 and 1993, when they met hundreds of other pilgrims, and in 1996, a Holy Year, more than 100,000 pilgrims walked the route. In addition to having extensive experience in walking the Camino, the authors are each well published on pilgrimage, medieval, and Spanish topics. Route notes and good descriptions of the towns along the way are provided, as are a map, suggestions for further reading, a time line of rulers and events, a Spanish-English glossary, an alphabetical list of artists cited, and chapters on art styles of the road and saints and religious iconography.

A Practical Guide for Pilgrims: The Road to Santiago, Millan Bravo Lozano, Editorial Everest, León, Spain, 2001. I bought this great paperback companion in Santo Domingo de la Calzada, and it is "carried out by the Centro de Estudios del Camino de Santiago" (Center for Studies into the Pilgrims' Route to Santiago). It's an extremely practical and interesting package: in addition to the book—which includes route descriptions for walkers, cyclists, and drivers, maps illustrating each stage, pilgrims' refuges and other accommodations, restaurants, gas stations, color photographs, historical pilgrims' accounts, and a list of tourist information offices on the route—there is a separate, clear plastic envelope of sorts on an elastic string that can be worn around your neck, and inside it are individual two-sided sheets for each *etapa* (stage) of the route. I think the whole thing is rather ingenious, and I would go so far as to try to obtain a copy by mail before my departure—it's available in bookstores in Madrid and in many towns along the Camino, and the Spanish tourist offices in North America should be able to help in contacting the publisher directly or a bookstore that arranges for overseas mail orders.

The Pilgrim's Guide to Santiago de Compostela, first English translation, with introduction, commentaries, and notes, William Melczer, Italica Press, New York, 1993. This is by far the most scholarly book mentioned here, and I include it for readers who are seriously interested in medieval history, and because it is unique. The author, before his death in 1995, was professor of medieval and Renaissance studies at Syracuse University. His published books and articles dealt with medieval and Renaissance art history, Christian iconography, and Christopher Columbus, and he also led the Syracuse University traveling seminar "The Medieval Pilgrimage Routes from Southern France to Santiago de Compostela: Romanesque Art in the Making." This volume presents the first complete English translation of book five of the *Liber Sancti Jacobi,* or Codex Calixtinus, from the twelfth century. Melczer states in the preface that, with regard to the actual translation, he "endeavored to produce a readable text and at the same time to preserve the outlandish idiosyncracies of the original." It will not take readers long to meet with some of these "outlandish idiosyncracies": "Should you anywhere in Spain or in Galicia eat either the fish vulgarly called *barbo* or the one those of Poitou call *alose* and the Italians *clipia,* or even the eel or the tenca, you will no doubt die shortly thereafter or at least fall sick . . . all fish and the meat of beef and pork from all of Spain and Galicia cause sickness to foreigners." A little further on, the pilgrim (who was French) reveals his distaste for nearly everyone along the Camino: "If they could, the Navarrese or the Basque would kill a Frenchman for no more than a coin," and "The Galicians, ahead of the other uncouth nations of Spain, are those who best agree in their habits with our French people; but they are irascible and contentious." About those comments in particular, Melczer notes that there must have been a rich vein of oral communication on the road. "I suspect that behind such and similar statements there is simply old-fashioned parochial, gregarious prejudice and xenophobia that, to no mean extent, lives until our own days." In addition to the Codex, Melczer addresses topics such as relics and pilgrimages, the origin of the cult of St. James, and the iconography of St. James. The book concludes with an outstanding forty-two-page hagiographical register and a thorough gazetteer, extending to the Rhine in Germany, Belgium, and the north coast of France.

The Road to Santiago, Michael Jacobs, Pallas Athene, London, 2002. This wonderful book by Jacobs—renowned as one of the leading Hispanists of his generation—is now in its third and fully revised edition. Readers may be familiar with a previous edition published by Chronicle Books, entitled *Northern Spain: The Road to Santiago de Compostela* in the Architectural Guides for Travelers series (1991). This new version, in the Pallas Passions series, is much smaller (and therefore much more portable) and includes color photos. At the back of the book is a fifteen-page practical information section, on yellow paper, that includes a glossary of architectural terms and a very good bibliography. If you're able to find only the Chronicle Books edition, you should not hesitate to buy it or check it out of the library—it remains a very good outline of the Gothic and Romanesque architectural styles to be seen in Northern Spain, and it is profusely illustrated with black-and-white photos.

The Way of St. James—Le Puy to Santiago: A Walker's Guide, Alison Raju, Cicerone Press, 2001. I like this book, which is the first single guide of the *entire* route, replacing two separate volumes previously published by the Cicerone Press. As its title suggests, this guide has walkers begin in the area of Lyon and Grenoble, and the maps recommended include the IGN 50 (Lyon, Grenoble), IGN 58 (Rodez, Mende), IGN 57 (Cahors, Montauban), IGN 63 (Tarbes, Auch), IGN 69 (Pau, Bayonne), Michelin 441 (Northwest Spain), and Michelin 442 (Northern Spain). The author also provides details of the route from Santiago to Finisterre as well as some other lesser-known Camino approaches within Spain (Seville to Astorga, for example). With photos, illustrations, a list of recommended readings, and a glossary of geological terms, this seems like a fairly complete guide; but I have heard conflicting reviews, some of which are that if one is hiking only the Spanish portion of the route, this book will be more than you need; one friend told me she consulted the book several times a day, while another said he found it not very useful at all, all of which reinforces two valid points: compare and contrast pilgrimage books carefully before deciding on one (or more) that's right for you, and do not expect to learn everything from one book; in other words, bringing along a nonpilgrimage guidebook about Northern Spain would seem to me to be essential if you want to learn about the places you're stopping en route.

~Additionally, the Spanish Tourist Office publishes some excellent material, including *The Road to Santiago* (a forty-eight-page brochure providing a good

overview with color photos and a four-panel fold-out map at the back); *Santiago de Compostela* (a forty-eight-page color brochure detailing the history of the city as well as museums, parks, gardens, cultural activities, shopping, nightlife, fiestas, eating and drinking, golf, travel itineraries, trade fairs, a city map, and a province map); *Hostels on the Santiago Pilgrim Trail in Galicia* (a really helpful package with individual cards for nine hostels along the route in Galicia; a pilgrim passport with room for stamps is also provided, as well as telephone numbers for town halls, cultural activity centers, Red Cross emergencies, the *guardia civil*, and SOS Galicia—if I were hiking the route at all in Galicia, I would be sure to get this); *Rías Gallegas* (another forty-eight-page color brochure detailing all the coastal valleys and towns of Galicia); and good fold-out brochures for individual cities and towns in Galicia, including Orense, Pontevedra, and Lugo.

~A wonderful article I was unable to include in this edition is "In Greenest Spain: An American Granddaughter Discovers Food and Family in Unexpected Galicia" by Linda Russano García (*Saveur,* No. 26). In this piece, the author warmly relates her journey to Galicia to explore her family's roots, and also provides recipes for some classic Galician dishes, including *pulpo a la feria* (fairground octopus), *caldo Gallego* (Galician meat and vegetable soup), *merluza a la cazuela* (Galician-style hake with potatoes and peas), and the very yummy *tarta de Santiago* (Santiago almond tart). Additionally, García shares some suggestions for places to stay and eat, as well as one for a special kitchen shop in Vigo that's worth a detour. View *Saveur*'s website, www.saveur.com, for more information.

Asturias y Cantabria
(Asturias and Cantabria)

"Nothing I had seen in Spain impressed me more than this glimpse of the Asturias, an unconquerable land of mountaineers, the original school of guerrilla warfare. Pelayo's commandos, who hurled rocks down upon Moorish heads and trapped armies in ravines, were the ancestors of those Asturian miners who achieved a sinister glamour in the Civil War by their utter fearlessness and their casual familiarity with explosives. The dinamitero *of those days, with a stick of dynamite in each hand, lighting the fuses from the stub of his cigarette, was the toughest of comrades."*

—H. V. Morton, A STRANGER IN SPAIN

"Spain's steep emerald-green dairy-land, Cantabria is wedged between the extraordinary Picos de Europa, the Cordillera Cantábrica and a coastline of scenic beaches . . . much of Cantabria is serenely rural, claiming to have the highest density of cows in Europe."

—Dana Facaros and Michael Pauls,
CADOGAN GUIDE: NORTHERN SPAIN

Kicking Back in the North of Spain

BY AMANDA HESSER

~

editor's note

....

The landscape of Asturias and Cantabria is "a verdant, unending feast of scenery" (to quote from a Turespaña brochure), definitely among the most scenic regions of Western Europe, and I'm not even including the magnificent Picos de Europa, constituting one of the most outstanding massifs on the Iberian peninsula. The people are friendly and generous, and the meals you'll enjoy, as described, are nothing less than spectacular.

AMANDA HESSER is a reporter for the Dining In/Dining Out section of *The New York Times* and is also the author of *The Cook and the Gardener* (W. W. Norton, 1999). She contributed this piece to the travel section of *The New York Times*.

As we traveled west from Bilbao along the northern coast of Spain, the landscape dulled. Behind us was the high drama of the Pyrenees, which we had skirted. Behind us were the elegant, well-ripened cities of San Sebastián and Bilbao. Before us lay, as far as we knew, a rural area of Spain with an ancient religious route leading to Santiago de Compostela and a climate like that of England, hardly the Spain of reputation.

Of course, my friend and I were traveling on the A6, a major highway, zipping along so that what we were taking in was like frames of film, hardly enough to comprehend and consider. About two hours west of Bilbao, in the town of Torrelavega, something happened. The highway stopped. It was as if it had been sliced off at the end like sausage, diverting speeding cars onto a much smaller, much slower road.

As it turned out, the highway ended right there, before we even got to Asturias, the region where we were headed for four days at the end of August. We swept through the seaside town of San Vicente de la Barquera, compressed into a sliver of an inlet.

The road undulated between hills and the sea, offering us tempting glimpses. But dimming ones. It was getting dark and the roads were getting smaller, eventually narrowing to a single lane. We had booked a room in a bed-and-breakfast in a converted mill, which we had found on the Internet. And we wanted to get there.

As we approached Tresgrandas, the town where our hotel was, we were in for another surprise. Tresgrandas was no town. It was barely a hamlet. And as we turned down the lane leading to our bed-and-breakfast, we were sure we had it all wrong. It was the kind of grade you find on a double black diamond ski slope, not a road, and it took us to what felt like the bottom of a well.

But there was indeed a bed-and-breakfast and an enormous, friendly, and slobbery mastiff to greet us. We settled in, had dinner, and went to bed in our small rustic room. There were more surprises in the morning.

Asturias is incongruous with much of the rest of Spain. It is green and damp and sprinkled with small farms. I sometimes felt that I was in northern California, sometimes in England or Switzerland. The region has for the most part tried to avoid the sort of development that would change the landscape, and the visitors it draws are mostly Spaniards from the south and a few British tourists.

In the area of Asturias and bits of Cantabria we were visiting, there were no great resorts to speak of, no architectural works of note by Gaudí, no wineries or great restaurants, and no well-known museums. Other than a little hiking in the national forest, we didn't have an agenda—and as we discovered, we didn't need one.

Our bed-and-breakfast was nestled in a valley of hills that rolled like the sea. A ten-minute drive north, and the land dropped off into the ocean, much as it does in Dover, from high cliffs. A ten-minute drive south, and we were in the bosom of the Picos de Europa, a mountain range that explodes from the earth like an iceberg on a calm sea. We could swim or go hiking or just take long drives down the narrow passages carved through the mountains. We did all three.

In the morning we woke to the cries of roosters and the rush of water. The roosters were out in the yard, and the water ran right beneath the hotel, as it had when it was a flour mill.

Breakfast was more than we could have wished for. The eggs were from the hens on the property, the cheese from the sheep, the jams, delicious reductions of fruits grown there in the valley. The owners, Luis Sanz and Carmen García, raised the hens, made the cheese and jams (pumpkin and orange, berry and peach) and even the *buñuelos,* a kind of *beignet,* they served us. Each day the cheeses changed and so did the jams.

Mr. Sanz and Ms. García moved to Tresgrandas to escape the pressures of city life in Madrid, where they were caterers. On their Internet site, they recount how they restored the eighteenth-century mill. We were charmed by it.

Mr. Sanz and Ms. García run their hotel with its handful of rooms well (just a few of the rooms were occupied when we were there, but weekends are booked through next February), though they come across more as idealists, determined to live close to the earth, than as hosts. Mr. Sanz, whom we saw most often, has lots of information to share, but you must work it out of him.

That first day we took a drive, a drive that began as a morning excursion and lasted all day. We headed toward the Picos de Europa, intent on driving along the Desfiladero de La Hermida, a gorge cutting through the mountains near La Hermida. Getting there took us through village after village, each its own historical collage. New houses were latched to ruins, cars yielding to heifers and goats, old women in housedresses yelling after brightly dressed children.

Before we reached the gorge, we stopped at the Hostal Covadonga, a hotel and restaurant in the center of Panes. The front porch was filled with men wearing berets and smoking cigars, their faces gray. I was the only woman there for lunch.

We ordered beers and *cocido,* a stew of white beans, leeks, blood sausage, and ham. It was as thick as mud and unbelievably good. White cottony rolls were served to soak up the sauce. We sat out on the veranda and ate quietly, listening to the music of the place—the church bells, the clapping of dominoes, and the talk of men inside the restaurant. It was tempting to linger.

Back on the road the hills rose and fell, then suddenly soared vertically all around us. These were the Picos de Europa. The road along the River Deva struggled and swerved through the gorge. At points the mountains were so steep and so close together, the day became twilight. We drove and drove; it took us all afternoon on the two-lane road to pass through the range, a distance of about thirty-five miles.

As the mountains again gave way to swells of green hills, we stopped in Carmona, a small village with nothing particular to offer other than a glimpse of the life of local farmers. We passed two men carving wooden clogs, then stopped to watch a game of *bolos Palma,* which is similar to *boulés.* There was a healthy crowd of spectators, mostly older men in berets and clogs or felt slippers, murmuring to one another as the players tossed the ball with the grace and precision of dancers.

We went hiking in the mountains another day, this time pressing by car further into the range, to Fuente Dé. Along the quiet, scenic roads, we stopped in Lebeña to see the Santa María, a tenth-century Mozarabic church, our only glimpse of the ancient pilgrims' route to Santiago de Compostela. It sits dwarfed by a rock face so magnificent and large that the church seems to cower before it. In the capitals and cornices carvings of sun and stars remain.

Just outside the church is a small food shack, run by a man who looks as if he just stumbled out of a tavern. He sells dated postcards and tour books, and local cheeses and beer. The cheeses sit under a towel in the open air with flies buzzing around. The man cut us wedges of Cabrales and a smoked sheep's milk cheese, and with his hands tore off a few pieces of baguette. Cabrales cheese is traditionally made in Asturias, but it is increasingly difficult to find made by artisan cheesemakers. These cheeses were it; they were nutty, rich, and had an aroma as potent as lilacs.

It was just the fuel we would need. At Fuente Dé the mountains do not so much rise as scream out of the ground. A gondola carries people up the 2,950-foot climb (the mountains rise 8,000 feet) in a few minutes that felt like hours, for me at least. At the top there were hikers, paragliders, and a number of people hanging out on rocks taking in the vast, majestic view of the mountain range. We hiked away from them and soon were on open steep slopes of pasture with a light wind cooling us, and carrying the songs of bells on the cows and sheep in the hills. The air was thin and clear; beyond lay a jagged, steel-colored horizon of mountains.

There are hiking trails throughout the mountain range for all skill levels. This challenging wander of a mile or so was more our speed.

Another day—which was warm and just suggestively humid as most of our days were—we drove along the coast to Santillana del Mar, a medieval town with cobblestone streets and architecture that is remarkably consistent and unchanged. A beautiful town that knows it, it is unfortunately littered with tourist shops.

That excursion was one of a few mistakes we made. We also took a drive to Comillas, a town along the coast, to see El Capricho (The Whim), a house designed by Gaudí in 1885. It is wild and beautiful like much of his work, but it is merely a shell. The interior has been converted into an expensive restaurant.

And we wasted a dinner at another ambitious restaurant in a small country village. The meal was fine, but had very little to do with Asturias or even Spanish food, for that matter.

Asturias is the kind of place where there is no artifice. The people are friendly and generous, the food is simple and satisfying, the landscape yours to admire. It reminded me of what I had read about rural France in old travel books but have yet to find there.

Our best experiences were those we had tooling around the villages near our hotel. For lunch one day we stopped at the Mesón El Paso, a truck stop along the regional coastal road, E70. When we entered, a woman turned on the lights and ambled back to the kitchen. It did not look promising. A waiter finally pulled himself from the television set in the bar and told us the fish of the day. I began with *arroz con almejas*, a dish of clams and rice in a bright green herb broth. My friend had scrambled eggs with shrimp, *pleurottes* (a mushroom), and roe. Both made us dizzy with pleasure. The shrimp were so fresh and so perfectly cooked, they popped in your mouth and were sweet as the sea. The mushrooms were nutty, the roe salty, the eggs like those from Mr. Sanz's hen.

Next we shared a *daurade*, or sea bass. It tasted, as my friend said, "as if they had stuck a frying pan out the back window and it leapt in from the sea." We recovered at the Playa de la Franca, a beach just down the road, a suggestion of Mr. Sanz. We loved it so much we decided to spend our last day there as well.

The beach is public and lies in a deep, narrow cove surrounded by high cliffs. When the tide is in, the beach is small and enclosed, but as the tide goes out, it rolls out like a great long carpet, allowing you to make your way along the shore and walk through vast tunnels carved by the sea water into the cliffs. It is a dream playground for children. And there are plenty of them, browned by the sun and gleeful. It was filled with Spanish families on vacation.

At the back of the cove are a number of rundown shacks serving food. We thought we would grab a simple bite, a sandwich and beer. Seeing a menu of fish at one of them, we were skeptical, until a man in chef's whites appeared. I thought a long day in the sun must be playing tricks on my mind. But he helped us select a live crab, lifting some from a cooler and poking them as they crept across the counter. Then he cooked it for us. We sat in our wet bathing suits and bare feet, looking out onto the beach. We had anchovies and peppers with the sweet crab, and a plate of cheeses to finish. The chef then brought us *orujo,* a local digestif.

We wore ourselves out in the waves, then took a nap before dinner. Our last of the trip, it was at Casa Poli in nearby Puertas de Vidiago. It is a *sidrería,* or restaurant where the local cider and *tapas* are served. Locals will tell you that their *sidra,* or cider, is like the cider made in Normandy. Don't believe them. It is fruity, viscous, and just a step up from vinegar.

It is so vigorously acidic that it is not even drunk straight. To drink it the traditional way, you must stand up holding the bottle above your head, then pour it behind your back into a glass held in your other hand. As the liquid falls and hits the glass—a rare occurrence—it aerates and lightens, making it more palatable. The idea is to pour just a little bit, a quarter inch or so, into the glass, then drink it quickly while it's still good. Whatever is not drunk in the first gulp is then poured into a bucket beside the table. Luckily it's cheap—cheap enough not to perplex you too much about why the Asturians haven't just fixed the flavor.

We may not have been drunk on *sidra,* but by this point we were drunk on Asturias. It is difficult in Europe to feel you are in a place that is somehow separate or undiscovered. But Asturias does feel that way. Perhaps that is why they have left the highway to the region severed the way it is—a sign that fast-paced, ambitious tourists should stop right there.

Getting There

The closest airports are in Oviedo in Asturias and Santander in Cantabria. There are also flights to Bilbao, two hours east of

Asturias. It is necessary to have a car. The best time to visit Asturias is in summer, when it's the least rainy and you can hike in the mountains and go to the beach. Fall and spring are also fine, though the Atlantic may be too chilly for swimming.

Where to Stay

El Molino de Tresgrandas (Tresgrandas, 985.41.11.91, www.molinotresgrandas.com) has eight rooms, some in the main house, some in an attached cottage. All are simply furnished, with tiled bathrooms. There are no views to speak of, but every room is filled with the music of the stream running beneath the hotel. A full breakfast with homemade jams and eggs from the henhouse costs about $5. Rooms are about $52 plus tax; the hotel is closed the first two weeks in February.

Venta de Carmona (Barrio del Palacio, Carmona, 942.72.80.57) stands like a grand villa in this small village. In fact, its eight rooms, all with bathrooms, about $46 a night, tax included, are all unpretentious, simple, and spare; the hotel is decorated with antiques and still lifes of fresh gourds.

Casas de Aldea, available at local tourist offices, is a guide to Spanish country houses that, like Venta de Carmona, have been converted into hotels.

Where to Eat

Mesón El Paso de Buelna (985.41.12.05) is a small tavern on Route N634 in Buelna, frequented by truck drivers. The small restaurant serves extraordinary fresh fish, sautéed on its skin, rice with clams, sausages, and unforgettable omelets; lunch for two is about $30.

Hostal-Restaurante Covadonga (Plaza de la Iglesia, 33570 Panes, 985.41.40.35; fax: 41.41.62) serves a vast menu of *tapas,* soups, hearty stews, and roasted meats. The three-course lunch menu is about $6.50; entrees are about $6 to $10. Open daily.

Sidrería Casa Poli (Puertas de Vidiago, 985.41.12.61) is a small cider restaurant set around a vine-draped courtyard. The lengthy menu offers everything from sliced cured ham and sautéed blood sausage to grilled sardines and blue cheese croquettes. Don't miss the cider. *Tapas* are about $2 to $4, entrees $4 to $12. Open for lunch and dinner every day except between early January and April 1, when it is open Friday to Sunday only.

Casey at the Beach

By Elena Castedo

~∽~

editor's note

I've included this wonderful piece here because it is one of the few I've found to feature the lovely and little-known coast of Asturias. In addition, it confirms the priceless and valuable experience of traveling with a child.

ELENA CASTEDO is the author of *Paradise* (Grove Press, 1990). She contributed this piece to *The Sophisticated Traveler,* a quarterly edition of *The New York Times Magazine*.

My granddaughter Casey and I are in the front seats of the bus we boarded in Oviedo, the capital of Asturias, a fertile region in northern Spain. We wind and wind around mountains so green the color needs a new name, "Asturian green," perhaps.

This serene landscape has always bred intense activism; it was here, in the eighth century, that King Pelayo launched the Reconquest

that eventually ousted the invading Moors from the Iberian peninsula. The bus driver tells me about current union unrest. (Historically
Asturias has been at the forefront of union militancy.) Although one
of my cherished hobbies is everlasting talk, my main hobby is wor-
rying, and so my thoughts are focused on whether we'll have a place
to stay in Ribadesella, the coast town to which we are headed.

I rented a beach house, called a *chalet,* seven months ago. With
Casey along, I thought an enclosed garden and a full kitchen would
work better than a hotel room. When I called the owner to ask how
much deposit he wanted, he answered, "Nothing. Just show up, pick
up the keys at the pastry shop by the beach. You can pay me before
you leave." No deposit? No contract? My American friends swore I
was going to find out the *chalet* was not available. And by July,
Spanish beach-town hotels are usually full. But I wanted to
believe—and show my granddaughter—that old Spain that
revered honor and considered your word cast in iron still existed.

My aim for this July trip was for eight-year-old Casey, who
speaks no Spanish, to encounter another language and another culture. In the process she must have a grand time. No less. Why Spain?
Because it's ancient, fascinating, and the country I lost as a toddler
when my Republican parents fled to escape Franco after the Spanish
Civil War. Why Ribadesella, a fishing town on the Bay of Biscay
where I know no one? For many reasons. It's summer, and Casey
and I love the ocean. Tradition, folklore and local pride still thrive
on Spain's northern shores, relatively unknown to foreign tourists.
Ribadesella's population is about 6,000, large enough to have all the
amenities and facilities of a town, but small enough for everybody
to know everybody, so you are always safe, even walking home at
night. Here the Sella River, site of a popular international *piragua*
(canoe) race, joins the sea. Its backdrop, the Picos de Europa mountain range, offers some of the world's most spectacular hiking, and
it is home to Tito Bustillo, a cave with prehistoric paintings often

compared with Altamira. Roman, Asturian pre-Romanesque, and Romanesque architecture abounds nearby.

Still, I wonder. Will all this be enough to keep an energetic youngster entranced for days on end? Will we have a place to stay? Our bus advances between peaks, valleys, crystalline rivers, emerald lakes, tile-roofed farmhouses, tile-roofed *hórreos*. (*Hórreos* are rat-proof granaries in which large, horizontal flat stones separate the supporting columns from the granary, so even if a rat could climb a column, it still couldn't walk upside down under the flat stone.)

We had taken the night train from Madrid to Oviedo, and our compartment with private bath had so enchanted Casey she hardly slept, or let me sleep. In the early morning we rolled our suitcases a couple of blocks to the bus station; we devoured croissants and drinks, she *zumo de melocotón* (peach juice) and I *café con leche,* before boarding this bus.

From the Ribadesella bus stop we take a taxi to Confitería Nerián, an art deco teahouse, where we are welcomed and given the keys by a smiling waitress. Our *chalet* isn't large, but has five bedrooms and baths. The master suite has a delightful sitting room, a view of the sea, and a marble-and-tile bath with a window over the garden. From the back terrace, beyond the garden, we can see a field, a canal, and a eucalyptus-covered mountain. Our street is quiet, lined with blooming bougainvillea and hydrangeas. "Cool," Casey says.

We dig for bathing suits and run to the beach, one house away. It's gorgeous, pristine, the sand just right, the water and the waves perfect for us; it has lifeguards. The shore is lined with mansions, many built by *indianos,* Spaniards who went to the New World in the nineteenth century, mostly to Cuba, amassed wealth, and came back to build large, whimsical houses. At one end of the beach, perched on top of a steep hill, the beloved Virgin de Guía, patron of fishermen and sailors, looks out to sea from La Ermita, a tiny chapel. At the other end, under the lighthouse, rocks hold abundant marine life, one of Casey's passions. A path takes us to "The Route of the Dinosaurs," with footprints of the beasts who stomped right here 150 million years ago. Hey, this is really cool! The problem is how to get Casey out of there; with little crawly crabs all over the rocks and dinosaur footprints? Good luck, Grandma.

We leave the beach for lunch. Everything we need is three or four blocks away: two pastry shops (at the top of the list of necessities), several cafés, restaurants, a bookstore, a toy store, a homemade ice cream shop, two supermarkets, a pharmacy, and the tourist office. In July all is friendly, unrushed. Downtown is at the end of a bridge that offers a panoramic view of blue mountains, green sea, and ornate turn-of-the-century buildings in pastel colors. It takes a while to cross the bridge. Casey must lean over the railing to watch the abundant and varied fish darting and swirling in the Sella River below.

That afternoon at *la plaza,* the main square, the heart of the town's life, Casey's whirling social season is launched. She is immediately accepted by the children, more than a dozen, playing there, her lack of Spanish no problem. Friendly looks and smiles, and they are all involved in vigorous chases, tag, hide-and-seek behind trees, soccer, giggling. At one end of the plaza, Cafeteria Capri has enticing outdoor tables. I sit, order coffee, and I'm soon at home among other parents and grandparents. Thereafter, incredibly well-behaved children with impeccable table manners come to play with Casey, or to pick her up or to stay for lunch or dinner and for sleep-overs. She soon knows the families of scores of townspeople, at the very least the owners of a flower shop, a bakery and a butcher shop, the hardware store, two banks, two hotels, and the main fishery. *La plaza* provides information and as much friendship as you want. Concerts and dance shows, including traditional *gaiteros,* bagpipe bands that recall the Celtic origins of Asturias, are held there often, arranged by the mayor's office. On weekends, there are lively dance bands. Children dance away, sometimes with directions from a stage in the plaza, sometimes with free-wheeling gusto, then the rest of us join in. I'm soon part of a twirling, hip-swinging group of grandparents.

Casey loves shopping for seafood downtown at Pescadería Pili, at the supermarkets and at Viveros González, a fish nursery near the bridge. In its huge pools are about thirty kinds of live sea creatures, including lobster, *centollo* (a large spider crab), *nocla* (a large crab), *nécora* (a small crab), as well as mussels, clams and eels. They can be cooked and packaged in minutes. At vegetable stands we get the makings for salads and fruit. (The first time Casey tasted the local honey-sweet green plums she devoured twenty, with unfortunate consequences.) We stop at a bread shop, which also carries home-made pastries, and assemble a meal. Asturias, cow country, pro-duces famous cheeses—Cabrales, Vidiago, Pitu, Beyos, Casey's favorite—and some local discoveries, like *cuerres*. We buy packaged desserts, including flan and *crema catalana* (créme brùlée), which are very good. Casey can't get enough Asturian milk and yogurt. The local brew is *sídra,* an alcoholic cider that Asturians will proudly "air" for you by raising the bottle up high with one arm and pouring the cider into your glass, held low with the other hand, usu-ally, but not always, with perfect aim.

After a meal at home, Casey and I like to go to a *confitería*, sit outside, have a pastry, and watch the parade of beachgoers. We also like to eat out. My favorite restaurant, El Repollu, serves traditional Asturian cuisine (the owner, nicknamed Coty, a book lover, in the dining room, his mother and sister in the kitchen). La Parrilla, noted for fish, is also good. At El Tinín, on the wharf, it's fun to sit outside and watch the water. Casey and I like the many open bars, fre-quented by men at the counter and by families, often with babies, at the tables. They serve mostly *tapas, bocadillos* (sandwiches), and drinks. Some double as restaurants at night; most have sidewalk tables. Capri is owned by my new friend Pilar de Cabo, the proud mother of nine charming and successful children. Casey becomes a fan of the local *fabada,* a stew of fava beans with sausages or clams or lobster; she loves *pulpo* (octopus) and *calamares en su tinta* (squid in its ink). She likes *merluza* (hake), *besugo* (sea bream), *pixin* (monkfish) and *lubina.* Our favorite teahouse is Chocolate, owned by Angelin and Neri, who have traveled extensively in the United States; our favorite pastry shop is Nerián; the best bread in town, and the best meringues, are from El Fornu. On the way home at night we stop at a stand for *churros,* a breakfast pastry that a cheerful blond woman makes right in front of us. La Churrería, at the wharf, offers a classic Spanish breakfast of thick hot chocolate, excellent *churros,* and the morning sun shining over the water. One morning, finishing her chocolate, Casey asks, "*Abuelita,* Grandma, why do Spaniards spend all their time sitting in outdoor cafés talking?" "I don't know, *tesoro,* treasure, but don't you love it?" "It's cool," she says.

Casey's daily ritual soon includes rides in El Litri's horsedrawn blue wagon. In the evenings, parents come to the plaza, deposit their children—some very young—in the wagon, pay about a dollar, and leave, returning an hour later to pick them up. El Litri's wagon cruises through town and along the beach with loud music, bells and honks, causing much waving and greeting among passersby. The fare includes a stop for a treat. This has been going on for nearly thirty years, without a hitch, although sometimes parents come back late, which forces El Litri to baby-sit, occasionally well into the night, but he takes it in stride. The stable is a few blocks from our chalet, and we take several horseback rides to nearby Tereñes, through wooded hills and by sea cliffs. El Litri always stops at one of two cheery bars for a *cerveza* (beer) or fruit juice.

During many spectacularly glorious sunny days Casey swims at the beach and at the magnificent pool of the Gran Hotel del Sella, but the Spanish north doesn't guarantee hot sun. As the local people say, "This green must be paid for," meaning occasional overcast skies or drizzle, which everyone pretty much ignores.

Weather notwithstanding, a young girl needs vigorous exercise. The snow-capped Picos de Europa massif, up to 8,530 feet high, offers serious hiking. The Ruta del Cares is a gorge some seven miles long that is accessible only to walkers. Provided with guidebooks and maps of more than twenty routes, we take a tame hike, but Casey's main interest, more than the shepherds' refuges, the deep gorges, and endless green and blue views, is the wild horses. We also take an exciting five-hour kayak trip down the Sella River.

Because of Casey's age, we are unable to tour Tito Bustillo and its magnificent prehistoric wall paintings, but we do go to La Cuevona, an immense cave near Ribadesella that you can drive through. Or you can explore it on foot if you are not afraid of spiders, cave creatures, and dripping water. Casey likes it a lot. Other popular outings: Centro Fauna Autóctona, in the town of Soto de Cangas, a zoo of native animals, including show-off bears, grouchy wolves, sweet vultures, and flirty owls; Puente Romano, the medieval bridge at Cangas de Onís (great fun to climb); the chapel dedicated to the Virgin in "the holy cave" in the Santuario de Covadonga, a religious site in the Picos de Europa National Park; Los Lagos de Covadonga, crystal-clear, misty lakes high in the Picos de Europa; El Conventín, an exquisite ninth-century pre-Romanesque church near the town of Villaviciosa; San Juan de Amandi, a thirteenth-century Romanesque church; and Tazones, a tiny, salty port where the young Charles V disembarked in 1517 to take possession of his kingdom.

While we are visiting Ribadesella, several traditional events take place, including the fishermen's annual homage to the Virgin de Guía. In the pink dawn, she's carried from the chapel down to the port and onto a ship for a ride on a sea filled with boats, flowers, and music. Townsfolk watch from shore. Grateful for the good time, the Virgin will see that the sea behaves and the catch stays plentiful for the next twelve months. Santa María Magdalena's treat is a flower rug the town matrons make in her honor in front of the main church.

Several days later, a *feria medieval* (medieval festival) takes over the town. Casey eats medieval food, learns how to spin yarn, weaves two baskets, diligently carves a horse's head from a stone, just as the *pedreros* decorated Romanesque churches, and enjoys the jongleurs, singers, musicians, storytellers, dancers, acrobats, jugglers, jesters, and the puppeteer. By now she's so jaded she doesn't even say "Cool!"

The last amazing surprise, right before our departure, is the Fiestas de Santiago, an all-day celebration with flower-covered floats depicting legends from the rich Asturian mythology. Although the event had been rehearsed for months, Rosi Riestra, of the Gran Hotel del Sella, succeeds in obtaining a traditional Asturian costume for Casey and then in persuading the director of one of the floats to take her aboard. From her assigned spot, Casey beams confidently, not a bit bothered by a surprise five-minute drizzle, every inch a Ribadesella girl.

The next day we take the Supra bus from Oviedo to Madrid, driving through green hills dotted with cows. Soon the colors change to earth tones as we move onto the plains of Castile, called sweet and golden by poets over the centuries.

So did Casey learn Spanish? A little. Have fun? A whole lot! Was this trip "a gift that will last a lifetime"? Only time will tell. Her last question to me when we landed in Philadelphia was revealing: "*Abuelita,* what is the next country you want me to learn about?"

Creature Comforts

High season in Ribadesella is July 15 to August 31; midseason is June 1 to July 14. Hotel room prices do not include breakfast or tax.

Gran Hotel del Sella, Ricardo Cangas 17, is on the beach (98.586.0150; fax: 98.585.7449). It was once the palace of the marchioness of Arguelles, a descendant of the orator Augustín Arguelles, who came from Ribadesella and was one of the framers, in 1812, of Spain's first liberal constitution. The hotel has 82 rooms, all with bath. In high season a double room costs about $100, in midseason about $65. There is an open-air saltwater swimming pool, a tennis court, and a public dining room. Open from April 1 to October 15.

Hotel Don Pepe, Dioniso Ruizsanchez 12, is a modern hotel, with balconies, on the beach (98.585.7881; fax: 98.585.7877). There are 52 rooms, all with bath. In high season a double room costs about $80, in midseason about $52. The hotel dining room is open to the public. Open from April 1 to September 30.

Confitería Nerian, Avelina Cerra (98.586.0787), serves snacks like pizza and hamburgers. A popular specialty is the semifrozen "Italian cake" with pine nuts and whipped cream. A light meal for two, with wine, costs about $23.

Cafeteria Capri, Gran Vía 12 (98.586.1067), has outdoor tables and serves bar food and snacks. Among the typical Spanish dishes offered are fried squid and a potato omelet. A meal for two, with wine, costs about $25.

El Repollu, Santa Marina 3 (98.586.0734), serves traditional Asturian cuisine, including white beans with clams and tuna loaf with fried potatoes. Dinner for two, with wine, is about $30.

La Parrilla, Palacio Valdés 33 (98.586.0288), offers fish dishes, including grilled monkfish and squid in its ink. Dinner for two, with wine, is about $45.

El Restaurante Tinín, Manuel Caso de la Villa 18–20 (98.586.0839), is on the wharf. Among its Asturian dishes are large white beans with sausage and octopus with potatoes. Dinner for two, with wine, costs about $25.

Chocolate, Ramón Soto 4 (98.586.1489), a teahouse, serves sandwiches and hamburgers but specializes in sweets like pancakes or pastries filled with walnuts or almonds. Tea for two, with pastries, costs about $7.

La Churrería, Sella 2 (98.586.14735), is a snack shop on the wharf. A breakfast of hot chocolate and *churros* for two costs about $5.

In Ribadesella **chalets** with from three to five bedrooms normally rent for a minimum of two weeks. In August the average price is about $3,250 for the month, or $810 for a week; in July, about $2,600 for the month, $650 for a week; in June, about $520 for the month, $130 for a week.

Two rental agents are: **Marco Cossío,** Dionisio Ruizsanchez 21, Chalet Los Mexicanos, Ribadesella (tel. and fax: 98.586.0109); **José González González,** Comercio 4–6, Office 6-A, Ribadesella (tel. and fax: 98.586.1801).

Chalets are rented without phones. A cellular phone, good for calls to Europe and the United States, can be purchased for about $100 to $200 at **Establecimientos Ramonin** (98.586.0710) or **La Tienda de Roberto** (98.586.0322), both near the Plaza Nueva.

Biblioteca

I do not own and have not been able to find any books devoted exclusively to Asturias or Cantabria. (If you discover any, please write and let me know.) That fact aside, you should make every effort to obtain a copy of an excellent fifty-one-page tourism guide published jointly by the Gobierno de Cantabria, Iberia, and España Verde. This must-have booklet, entitled *Travelling by Car Within the Cantabrian Region,* details twelve stunning routes: "Liébana and the Picos de Europa," "The Nansa Basin and the Lamason Valley," "The Western Coast," "The Cabuerniga Valley," "From Besaya to Pas: The Romantic Route," "Campoo and Valderredible: Following the Course of the River Ebro," "Around Santander: Nature and History Near the Sea," "Pas Valley, Pisuena and Miera," "The Trasmiera Coast," "Inland Trasmiera: From the Cubas Estuary to the Treto Estuary," "The Ason and Soba Valleys," and "The Eastern Coast." Maps, advisable stops, kilometers covered, estimated driving times, historical information, color photographs, and contact information for tourist information offices are all provided. I wouldn't set out without this one. *Esencial.*

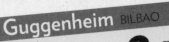

Guggenheim BILBAO

Coleccion
Permanente

3

Bilduma
Iraunkorra

Abandoibarra Etorbidea, 2 • 48001 Bilbao • Tel. 94 435 90 00

CORREOS
ESPAÑA
14 PTA

SARRERA   ENTRADA

Ikasleak eta Taldeak

Estudiantes y Grupos

017048

El País Vasco
(The Basque Country)

"*No word less describes Basques than the term* separatist, *a term they refuse to use. If they are an island, it is an island where bridges are constantly being built to the mainland. Considering how small a group the Basques are, they have made remarkable contributions to world history. In the Age of Exploration, they were the explorers who connected Europe to North America, Africa, and Asia. At the dawn of capitalism they were among the first capitalists, experimenting with tariff-free international trade and the use of competitive pricing to break monopolies. Early in the industrial revolution they became leading industrialists: shipbuilders, steelmakers, and manufacturers. Today, in the global age, even while clinging to their ancient tribal identity, they are ready for a borderless world.*"
—Mark Kurlansky, THE BASQUE HISTORY OF THE WORLD

Letter from Euzkadi

By Alastair Reid

editor's note

This is a piece that was brought to my attention by Alastair Reid himself, and I am so grateful that he did. Reid mentioned to me that this particular piece, written in 1961, was among his favorites and has stood the test of time. I very much agree, and hope you do, too.

ALASTAIR REID, introduced previously, kept Americans informed about goings-on in Spain during the critical Franco years by his regular communiqués for *The New Yorker,* where this piece first appeared.

The chances of encountering one's double in this life must be fairly slim. Nevertheless, I have begun to believe that even the most oddly shaped of us has a double—unsuspected and unsuspecting, working away quietly in some unlikely context—for I recently had the curious experience not of meeting mine but of passing an impressionable night and day in his natural habitat, in the Basque province of Vizcaya, on the northern coast of Spain. My double is a Basque sea captain who lives, between voyages, on the fringes of the town of Guernica, and I have made a tentative promise to return there when he gets back from his current voyage. I doubt if I shall go. If we confront one another, the differences between us will become obvious; as it was, in his absence, his friends all swore to our absolute duplication of one another, with much exclamation and headshaking.

I made the pilgrimage to Guernica for a concentration of reasons, after travelling about in the Basque Country, from village to village, between the mountains and the sea. The name reverberates familiarly mainly through the agency of Picasso's painting, but Picasso was only underlining the infamy of the town's complete annihilation by German bombers during the Spanish Civil War— an act of such ruthless vindictiveness that the mere mention of the name still stops conversations in Spain. But beyond that, Guernica has a much greater importance—an importance, in fact, that led to its being selected for annihilation. It was and is the symbolic capital of the Basque race, the old seat of government, where oaths were taken and laws made under its venerable oak tree, the Tree of Guernica. Here, traditionally, the elder Basque statesmen met on all matters concerning the land that Basques call Euzkadi—a mythical entity that now exists more vividly in my awareness than do many more politically established countries.

There are four Basque provinces in the north of Spain—Vizcaya, Guipúzcoa, Álava, and Navarra—which extend along the Bay of Biscay to the French border, and which, together with the three French districts of Soule, Labourde, and Basse-Navarre, form the seven provinces of Euzkadi. Although politically the Basques are Spaniards or Frenchmen (or Argentines, Venezuelans, Americans, or Australians, since they emigrate readily and always with distinction), Euzkadi is the country they continue to inhabit in the back of their minds, and while they fulfill the formalities of what they regard as their second citizenship with energy and responsibility, they look on themselves first as Basques. The respect with which they are universally regarded is a respect for those qualities of responsibility and independence, which are ruggedly Basque and which resist without difficulty all varieties of national influence.

Guernica sits squarely in a broad green valley on the River Mundaca, and to get to it I had to catch a miniature train that connected with the main line between Bilbao and San Sebastián. The train, flying through the green fields, was full of chickens in hampers and chattering passengers who waved to solitary figures working in the landscape and called to them by name. I had no ticket for this stage of the journey, which perplexed the conductor. I would have to pay six pesetas, which was fifty centimos more than if I had bought my ticket beforehand. It hurt him. Borrowing a pencil from me, he wrote out a long, patient receipt. Had I been before in Guernica? No, never, but I wanted both to visit the Tree and to see how the town had been rebuilt. Then I knew about the happenings? Yes, I did. He shook his head for a long time. I would be staying in Guernica at least overnight? Yes, indeed. He wagged his finger and went off to talk with an old man at the other end of the car, jerking his head from time to time in my direction. When he came back, he handed me a paper. This was the name of the inn where I would be most comfortable, and this was the café where I would meet the old ones of the town, those who had been there *before;* here was the proprietor's name, and here was the name of someone who would show me the Tree and the archives. I thanked him, and he apologized that he could not be there himself. The train drew in to Guernica, and he shook my hand and went off, my pencil still behind his ear.

At Guernica, the train practically emptied. Most of the people were being met—but then Spaniards scarcely ever undertake journeys of any kind without being seen off or welcomed by throngs of relatives and children. The air in Spanish airports and railroad stations throbs steadily with emotion. I took my bag and walked through the town, which had the square, cemented anonymity of all new buildings in Spain, serving their purpose but no more, unworn, unfinished, built out of an uninspired necessity but with no affection. Spain gives the impression of having been dragged unwillingly into the technological age; its heart is not there. Instead, sullenly resentful of modernity, it contrives successfully to make all instances of it seem cold, drab, and forlorn.

I found room at the inn without any difficulty—tourists in Guernica, I discovered, are mainly expatriate Basques who come in high summer to visit the Tree—and eventually made my way to the café suggested by the conductor. Conversation stopped as I entered, and the small knots of men at the bar looked at me cautiously. I nodded to them and addressed the landlord, who surprised me by speaking English—he had gone to school in England, he told me, while his father, a Basque, was first mate with an English shipping line. As time passed, I began to be aware that the men in the bar were still talking about me, but since they were speaking in the sharp, swift cadences of Basque, I could gather nothing of what they said. Just then two other men entered, and one of them, catching sight of me, came over, thumped me on the shoulders, and welcomed me back with great enthusiasm. I told him that he must be mistaking me for someone else, since I had never before been in Guernica. His face stiffened in astonishment, and at that point four or five of the other men in the bar came across quickly and surrounded us, all talking at once. One of them took me aside to explain in Spanish. "You must forgive us our rudeness in staring at you," he said, "but the truth is you resemble exactly a man who lives in this valley—but exactly!—and when you came in, we all believed you to be him, except for the fact that you are not wearing a beret and are not dressed as he would be. He is captain of a ship out of Pasajes, and we expect him home anytime now. We cannot get over the likeness." The others pressed forward to assure me that I was in every respect the double of the captain, who was called Lorenzo. I must be Basque? No. Then of Basque ancestry? I did not think so. One of the men, short, thick-shouldered, and merry-eyed, asked if I would mind helping him win a bet, to prove how absolute was the resemblance. I concurred, and he asked me to sit on a particular stool facing the door, and to remove my tie and put on his beret. A farmer from down the valley, a cousin of Lorenzo's, was due in the bar at any moment, and my friend had laid a wager with the landlord that the farmer would take me for Lorenzo within a minute of entering the café, now that I was properly dressed. I had barely sat myself down, bereted and tieless, when the door creaked open and two men came in, blinking in the light. The taller of the two looked around the bar, nodding here and there; then, catching sight of me, he started suddenly. "Lorenzo!" he called out. "But you are back too soon!" Everyone in the bar roared, and the short man rushed over to explain the wager to him. I took off the beret and put on my tie. Wryly, the landlord lined the bar with wineglasses. By now, the conversation was all conjecture over the ultimate encounter between Lorenzo and myself, which I agreed would have to take place. We were all in a high good humor.

The Basques are anything but taciturn, but while they cut swaths of talk around any subject at all—playfully, without ever seeming to take a sharp point of view—their convictions, I have found, are deep and firm, always lying under the surface and remaining for the most part unspoken. Humor runs away with them wildly. Their conversations are full of glee—extravagant exercises in preposterousness. At bottom they are the proudest and most serious people in the world, yet they are constantly making fun of their own pride. I listened one evening in St.-Jean-de-Luz to a long, straight-faced discourse proving that the mother of Yuri Gagarin was a Basque; the man who advanced the claim did so with such vehemence that he all but convinced himself, I felt. To the Basques, being born a Basque is nothing short of a miracle, yet at the same time they are free from the steady self-preoccupation that marks other small, more uncertain minor races.

That evening in Guernica became a cascade of talk, once my companions got over the impulse to goggle at me and referred to me simply as "Lorenzo." Most of the company were farmers or seafaring men, natives of Guernica, yet in one another's company the subject of the past scarcely ever came up. They had no particular reluctance to talk about it, and did so with me in the most matter-of-fact way, but among themselves it was emphatically over and gone. "Don't forget how it is with us Basques," one of them said. "We were here in our small corner of Europe before anyone else, and we're still holding on to the same bit of country—no bigger, no smaller—that we had then. By the accident of time, we're counted as Spaniards, but we still work and live here in our own way; the more they plague us from the outside, the more Basque we become." At that moment, two newcomers entered the café, and I noticed that the company switched from Spanish, which they had been speaking for my benefit, to Basque. The two men drank uncomfortably and left quickly. "Foreigners!" growled the short man. "After the Civil War, when we were rebuilding Guernica—with no help from the government—Franco thought he would water us down by shipping a lot of Andalusians up here. He should have known better—that in our own country we don't mix. He might as well have sent us Eskimos."

Guernica was destroyed on the afternoon of April 26, 1937, after the Spanish Civil War had been raging for eleven months, and nothing that General Franco did in the course of the whole war caused such universal waves of horror and alarm. At that time in history, the Basques had newly gained their independence, for which they had been pressing strongly during the dictatorship of Primo de Rivera and the years of the Spanish Republic. Progress had been slow, since first Primo de Rivera and later the Republicans were loath to give way to separatist groups, their main aim being to draw Spain together. When the Civil War did break out, however, the Republicans, to make sure of the support of the Basques, granted them autonomy, and in October 1936 the first president of the new Basque Republic, José Antonio de Aguirre, was sworn in under the Tree of Guernica. The fighting in the Basque provinces was markedly bitter; the accounts of the bombing of Guernica that I heard that evening, however, were, if anything, laconic—the memory was clear enough, but the strong feeling was suppressed and the vision cold.

"I had gone that afternoon up the valley to Amorebeita to ask my uncle, who lives there to this day, if he could lay hands on a sack or two of ground meal for me, for at that time we were just beginning to feel the food shortage," one man said. "As I was saying good-bye to him, we saw a plane with Nationalist markings circling slowly over the valley, but we thought little of it—stray planes often used to pass over to take a look at us. But as I was riding my bicycle back to Guernica, the bombers began to overtake me, flying very low. I heard some explosions, but could not believe they had anything to do with us, until I caught sight of flames in the distance. It was a Monday afternoon, and Monday, by tradition, is our market day; many people had come in to town from round about and had gone, as usual, to the *frontón* to watch a game of pelota. From behind me the planes kept coming and coming, and I could make out not only the German markings but the men in the cockpits. They drove into Guernica like buses, and by the time I reached the edge of town, pedaling furiously, the whole center was on fire from the showers of incendiary bombs they dropped. I left my bicycle and climbed the hill above our house, which already I could see was half burned. On the way I ran into my wife and two children, with a group of people who had left home at the first sign of the bombing. We knew nothing of what was happening, or why; there was little we could do but watch. I sent my wife and children to my cousin's house, across the valley. A group of us stayed, almost in a trance, scarcely feeling. The bombardment lasted barely three hours, but Guernica burned all night and well into the next day. I went at evening to see that my family was all right and then came back, to watch and wait. Most of those who escaped made their way either to Bilbao or to the houses of friends and neighbors in the countryside. There were a few of us who waited for the fires to go down, saying nothing. Next day we went back into what was left of the town. Five buildings still stood; the Tree was unharmed. I found a cellar, which I occupied for a time with four others. We got together some supplies and began to work on the ruins, with shovels. Bit by bit the people came back, and now, twenty-four years later, we have a new town. We built it ourselves, to wipe out that one day from our memory, and I suppose that if you question us now, all we will say is that the new town is more comfortable than the old one was. Once I thought I would never forget all that, but now I find it is no more than a happening in the memory."

Later, when I left the café, I walked through the moonlit town with the cousin of my double. As we passed various buildings, he would pat an occasional buttress or wall and say, "These stones were there before; I remember building on top of them," or "That house there did not burn"—as though he carried in his head a complete map of the place as it once was, stone by stone.

The next morning the short, bright-eyed man, whose name, I had discovered, was the name on my piece of paper, called early to take me to the Tree. Together we climbed a broad flight of steps to the chapel at the top of the town, which contains a small, crowded library of writings on the Basques. The original oak tree had been retired in 1860, he explained, after it had attained its legendary thousand years; its trunk is preserved there in a kind of Greek portico. We walked out into the sunlit courtyard to inspect its successor, a healthy young tree of a hundred and one, and my companion removed his beret. "We used to have trouble with tourists who wanted a leaf or piece of bark from the Tree—Basques who came back from abroad. As it is, there is a flourishing descendant of the old tree in Buenos Aires, but in autumn I generally collect a few of the fallen leaves and send them to our people abroad." We sat down on a stone bench in the sun while the little man regaled me with some of the endless mass of history and legend concerning the

Basques and which, later, in the library, I began to explore for myself. "Don't worry too much about facts," he said to me as he left me in the reading room. "There are hardly any facts about us. We say that, like a good woman, we have no history. We're as old as the Pyrenees, and we're likely to last as long, without changing very much. That's all there is to it."

I became increasingly thankful for that piece of counsel as I read my way into the morass of writings that have accumulated around the mystery of the Basques. There is little question in anyone's mind but that they are the oldest surviving race in Europe, and were in all likelihood comfortably settled in their corner before the barbarian invasions; yet they have no ascertainable history—not, at least, until the twelfth century, and even then contemporary historians complained about the haze that obscured their origins. The Basque language provides the most tangible evidence of their oddness; structurally very curious, it has no firm similarity to any other existing language and has been the main basis for the wilder suppositions that have been made about the Basques. Life in the Basque provinces, whether on the inland farms or in the fishing villages, has changed very little with time and still has a muscular, handmade tang; the songs, the tempestuous folk dances, the games, and the myths keep cropping up in spontaneous joy, with nothing of the aura of the museum. For all these reasons, ethnologists and philologists and mythologists and anthropologists have descended, and still descend, on the Basques with whoops of astonished delight and go quickly to work hacking, chiseling, and surmising. By now I have read so many improbable hypotheses on the origins and affinities of the Basque race that I have grown quite prepared to accept some of the more fanciful explanations, which, characteristically, are preferred by the Basques themselves. In an eighteenth-century pamphlet, the Abbé Lahetjuzan took pains to derive all the names in the Book of Genesis from Basque roots; the name of Eve, he explained, came from *ezbai,* a conjunction of the Basque words *ez,* meaning "no," and *bai,* meaning "yes," and standing for the dual nature of all women. The question that divides scholars is whether the Basques are in fact Iberians or whether they are directly descended from a Paleolithic race that inhabited the Pyrenees before the Iberians arrived. From what I could glean with any certainty out of the violent pro-and-con, they are now allowed to be descended from a prehistoric Pyrenean race, but modified and influenced by the Iberian invasions. Scholarly argument bases itself mostly on the discovery of ingenious linguistic parallels; freed from the onus of facts, the scholars have ranged about with abandon and, more recently, have taken to linking the Basque language with Caucasus Mountain dialects—a thesis that has a higher degree of probability than some of their earlier venturings.

Characteristically, the Basques remain utterly unperturbed by the mystery of their origins; on the contrary, they are delighted by their own inexplicability. One Sunday afternoon in San Sebastián I went with a Basque friend to the *frontón* to watch a game of *chistera*—pelota played with long, banana-shaped baskets. The game was magnificently exciting, the betting raucous, the spectators exuberant. During the intermission, we ran into a local doctor at the bar. "If you are mistaken enough to be interested," he said to me, "I have in the house a learned treatise written by a German folklorist on the forms and variations of pelota, or handball, or whatever you want to call it, proving it to be the oldest known game and full of strange implications that no Basque has ever dreamed of. This German came to see me once, but we did not get very far. He kept pressing me to tell him what I thought the game *meant,* and I told him it didn't mean anything at all; it simply *was.* Around here, as soon as we can walk we begin to hit a ball against a wall, just for the pleasure of it, and it seems to me a singularly uncomplicated fact that we have been doing so for hundreds of years. Pleasure does not alter very much, and when we get old and short of breath, we come to the *frontón* to watch others do it better. I honestly fail to see the point of his treatise—it's of no interest to us Basques, whereas the game itself is. I took him to a game or two, but he never enjoyed a single moment; instead, he kept asking me questions about the height of the wall and the shape of the *chistera*—things like that. The game is just as old as the first wall or the first ball, I told him. You may have the book, if you want it. I'm afraid it would only spoil my pleasure."

We all sat down together as the game began again, my friend and the doctor betting furiously against one another, catching the cutaway tennis balls that the bookies tossed up to them and extracting the red and blue betting slips stuffed inside. "I'll tell you one thing, though," said the doctor, leaning across to me. "The *chistera* you see the players using came about quite by accident, when someone used a fruit basket to play pelota with. Now, in the souvenir shops, you can buy *chisteras* to use once again as fruit baskets. Everything, you see, straightens out with the passing of time. I wish I had remembered to tell that to the German."

While the Basque Country forms a small, neat geographical unit fitting tidily into the right angle of the Bay of Biscay, it is no longer quite the entity it was, and the old Basque war cry *Zazpiak Bat!* (The Seven Are One!) is something of an anachronism. In the past, when France and Spain happened to be at war, the seven Basque provinces bound themselves by *traités de bonne correspondance* to remain neutral; in the course of this century, however, the diverging political paths of France and Spain have split Euzkadi in two. The unity does survive in a purely local sense; the fishermen of the Spanish Basque coast have the same preoccupations as the fishermen of the French Basque coast, and they meet and talk together as Basques, although the Frenchmen may know no Spanish and the

Spaniards no French. The Basque dialects vary slightly, but the fishing remains much the same. "We Basques have two selves," one fisherman in St.-Jean-de-Luz put it. "If you ask us suddenly what we are, we will naturally reply that we are Basques. But, over and above that, we are Frenchmen, and we have fought as Frenchmen in two wars; in a moment we can become Frenchmen, pure and simple, like slipping on another coat. It's more difficult for the Spanish Basques. While France has been a kindly mother to us, Spain has been a cruel stepmother to them, and as a result they are more belligerently Basque than we want to be. For us, there is no contradiction; we're quite happy to think of ourselves as Frenchmen."

The differences, however, go much further than that. To reach the Basque country from southern Spain, one travels north across the endless spreading plains of Castile, parched in summer, slow and indolent, without a sign of water or life. After them the small green, humped hills and, eventually, the craggy, moist Atlantic coast are a relief—the frequent *chirimiri,* the light Basque rain, falls like a benison; the towns have a good-humored bustle about them; the people are inquisitive, active, decisive, and mean business. But to make the brief journey across the frontier, at Irún, into France, although it amounts to going farther north geographically, is in fact to cross over into the laconic, easygoing air of the French Midi, where the day unwinds at a markedly slower pace under a hot, restraining sun, where work keeps stopping and starting, where the berets flop limply over the eyes. The French Basque provinces are very much of the south, and take their pulse from that, far more than from the exuberance of the Basque temperament. For this reason, they appear more theatrically Basque, and the decorative side of Basque life—the fetes and folk dances, the pageants, the pastorales, the folk singing—is staged more self-consciously in the French villages. The same things happen in Spain, but in the natural context of Basque life. As might also be expected, it is in France that one comes across the souvenir shops, the thirsty Basque-hunting tourists, and anomalies like Le Motel Basque, no less horrifying for their inevitability. The old whaling ports of St.-Jean-de-Luz and Biarritz have taken on new, luxurious, well-tailored identities, although the fishermen still fish; prosperity has dulled the sharp edge. I was chiding a French Basque I know for this one day when he stopped me short. "Don't be altogether deceived by all the paraphernalia," he said. "You'll see plenty of prosperity now on both sides of the border, and you'll probably conclude that it comes from our success at selling Basque matchboxes to the tourists. That's not all of it, by any means. Remember, for us Basques there is no border—France and Spain put it up comparatively recently, in the seventeenth century, and so gave us a new profession. Basque free trade, we call it. Why shouldn't our Spanish kin have some of the things we enjoy in France, and why shouldn't we have an occasional taste of what they have? We're all Basques, aren't we? Mutual benefit, that's what it is. We've always claimed the right to move freely across the frontier, and if it requires any ingenuity for us to take our luggage along, too—well, we have plenty."

The Basques smuggle not only with ingenuity but, more, with gusto, although I would consider it immoral to go into detail. Enough to say that among the frontier Basques smuggling is practiced with an intense devotion that makes it almost rank with the two classic activities of Basques—sheepherding and seafaring. Basques believe quite confidently that they discovered America long before Columbus but came home again to Euzkadi, not bothering to mention the discovery; at any rate, their temperament has always taken easily and naturally to the sea. They were the first fishermen who dared to put out after whales in longboats, along the Biscay coast; watchtowers still punctuate the headlands. In the eighteenth century, inclined, as usual, to be on no one's side but their own, they took lucratively to piracy and made handsome reputations as corsairs. Predictably, however, they came home with their spoils to the Basque country, married Basque girls, and settled in their native villages. Even though the coastal fishermen complain about the steady decline of the fishing, Basque seamen are still as indigenous to the sea lanes of the world as are Scottish engineers. A truck driver who gave me a lift one day told me that he signs on with a Norwegian line for a six-month voyage every two or three years, whenever he wants to buy a new truck.

As for sheepherding, the Basques are so renowned for that solitary occupation that they are nowadays in great demand, particularly in the sheep-raising regions of the United States. An average of about two hundred "alien sheepherders," as the Immigration Service has it, cross annually for a three-year stint. (They share the privilege with a rash of Basque pelota players, who spend the winter jai-alai season in Florida.) Most of the sheepherders return to the Basque Country, generally with the scantiest knowledge of English, unperturbed by the experience. Sheep, after all, are sheep the world over.

When I came to the Spanish Basque Country, it was with one very specific query in mind. After living for some time in Spain, I was well aware of how, in the twenty-fifth year of political paralysis under Generalissimo Franco, a despairing disquiet hovered not far from the surface of every conversation. In Madrid the concern has grown cynical, but I knew that among the two strongest separatist groups—the Catalans and the Basques—it still seethed with hope. "You won't have to bother with questions," said an acquaintance in Madrid. "The Basques will answer them before you have time to ask."

In our present climate of incipient internationalism, with new countries taking shape almost overnight and the large power blocs choosing up sides, the separatist tendencies of small, contrary racial groups have come to seem more and more unrealistic, if not downright comic. The Irish got in under the wire—their cause was just, and they had behind them a history of persecution and stubbornness—but the nationalist parties in Wales and Scotland, for example, have become more or less a refuge for grousers and crackpots. While I was growing up in Scotland, the clishmaclaver of aggressive nationalism rang continuously in my ears, but when I had exhausted the roles of terrorist, martyr, agitator, and cold logician, I found that, after all, it was possible to live quite fruitfully under what we used to call "the English yoke," and that the persecution we suffered was either statistically hypothetical or romantically imagined. I was at first disinclined to take Basque nationalism any more seriously, particularly since, in argument, I often surprised on the faces of my Basque friends the same wistful, faraway expression that I was well used to seeing in Scotland, and also since history shows the Basques to have been defensively, rather than aggressively, nationalistic. By now, however, I have changed my mind. One day I found, tucked into my notebook, a small card. I had no idea how it got there. On one side of it was printed the Basque national hymn and the legend *Euzkadi Es la Patria de los Vascos,* and on the other a very specific Basque Doctrine, some of the main points of which are worthy of note:

The land of the Basques is Euzkadi.

Politically, some Basques are Spanish citizens, the rest French citizens, but originally and by natural law they are neither French nor Spanish. All are, quite simply, Basque.

The French and Spanish languages have their common origin in the breakup of Latin. The true language of the Basque race is Euzkera, or Basque, utterly distinct in grammar and vocabulary from French and Spanish.

Political and social organization amongst the Basques was determined by their own laws, drawn up by and for themselves, without interference from any foreign power.

Our country has since lost its ancient right to self-government. The results have been disastrous. The purity of the language has been corrupted by Latin influence. The body and soul of the Basque race are in danger of dying out.

The remedy is for all Basques to unite in faith behind their ancient theme of GOD AND THE OLD LAWS; that is, to practice their religion faithfully and without corruption, and to reunite in recovering their ancient sovereignty, in a free confederation of the race and of a sovereign Euzkadi.

I showed the card to my friends, and they smiled mysteriously. "That will do as your passport while you are here," they said. "Only, don't show it to the *guardia civil,* or it will get you into trouble." (Basques have a sharp animosity toward the Spanish Civil Guard, whom they regard as foreign troops on their soil. By tacit agreement, no Basque ever joins them, just as few Basques ever serve as career soldiers in the Spanish army, for that would be to give official Spain a recognition that Basques withhold as far as they can.) Traditionally, all Basques subscribe to the spirit of the Basque Doctrine; to them it is part and parcel of being Basque. The Old Laws constantly invoked in all Basque documents were local *fueros,* or charters, granted in the course of the Middle Ages to particular provinces, or even to small districts, allowing them a complete local autonomy of law and custom, in exchange for which they would lend a judicious allegiance to the kings of France and Castile. The rights granted by these *fueros* were gradually formalized and codified, and the Basques put all their energies into defending them vigorously. With the French Revolution, the *fueros* of the French Basques disappeared; in Spain they lasted much longer—until after the Carlist Wars of the nineteenth century, when the Basques made the grave mistake of backing the losing side and in the wake of which they seemed to have lost all chance of ever recovering their separate privileges. Nationalism, however, is likely to survive most strongly in the face of persecution and apparent hopelessness; besides, the Basques had too long a tradition of self-esteem ever to allow themselves to subside or to blend easily into any other racial or political circumstance. This history is not peculiar to the Basques, but what interested me most was to discover how the spirit of the *fueros* stood up to the tangled present in Spain.

Generalissimo Franco came away from the agonies of the Civil War with Spain in his pocket—a narrow, dark place, where he has been content enough to let it lie, safe from fresh air. His rule has been marked by a nimble political ingenuity and, at the same time, by an extremely sharp sense of the Spanish character; he has played systematically on the insecurities and self-doubts of Spaniards in the wake of the Civil War and has kept them so much at the mercy of their own impotence that, with typical two-mindedness, they regard his implacable face on stamps and coins and in public places with explosive hatred and secret relief. Over the years, however, he has been unable to conceal a particularly vituperative hatred of the Basques; his local administration—in the province of Vizcaya in particular—has been brutally repressive. Guernica remains as vivid in his memory as it does in that of the inhabitants.

The main reason for this hatred is that if it were not for the Basques, Franco's slate would look a lot cleaner. His moral justification for the campaign that sparked the Civil War was that he was undertaking a religious crusade as Defender of the Faith; an obvious flaw in his argument was the fact that his bitterest opponents were the Basques, the most devoutly and naturally religious of all Spaniards. If he had in fact been defending the Faith, the Basques would have been likely to be the first to join him. In remaining to this day his bitterest opponents, they flaw even his self-justification.

Since the war Franco has been able to maintain an uneasy but unbroken alliance with the Spanish Church, out of a mutual need, but at the same time the Basque priests, ruthlessly and sincerely Catholic, and closely concerned with the well-being of their own people, have consistently shaken off his patronage. In May 1960 a letter signed by 342 of them was presented to the bishops of Vitoria, San Sebastián, Bilbao, and Pamplona, in the four Spanish Basque provinces. The letter was a noble document of conscience, clear, sincere, and to the point. It denounced, bitterly and outspokenly, all forms of social injustice under the Franco regime, coming down heavily on the continuing political imprisonment without trial, the repression of truth and information, and the censorship of the written word, and toward the end it added, on a characteristic note, "We also denounce, before Spaniards and before the rest of the world, the current policy in Spain, whereby, either through neglect or by downright persecution, those ethnic, social, and linguistic characteristics that God granted to the Basques are brushed aside." Franco is well versed in dealing with all forms of political opposition, but such a blunt piece of denunciation coming from priests—and especially from Basque priests—must have stung not only the general but the conscience of the Spanish Church, his uncomfortable ally.

I have listened to countless diatribes against Franco in Madrid, waiting for them to end, as they always do, in a despairing shrug of helplessness. The Basques scarcely bother to mention Franco's name; their contempt is cold, silent, final. "What if the little acorn lives to be a hundred and fifty?" they say. "We'll live longer." The present state of Spain, the Basques feel, is in no sense their fault, nor is it their doom. Being Basque allows them to remain aloof from it, especially since being Basque means to them that they are natural aristocrats, more industrious, more durable, more genuinely religious, more single-minded, less peninsular, and less easily cowed than the rest of Spain.

Nationalists are often their own worst enemies—they are wont to quarrel among themselves over the crumbs while neglecting to verify whether or not the loaf is still there. The Basques are not immune from such squabblings. Ever since Basque independence was recognized by the Republic in 1936, an official Basque government-in-exile has maintained itself, first in the United States and now in Paris, and immediately across the Spanish frontier, in St.-Jean-de-Luz and Biarritz, small clusters of exiles gather to plot, to hope, and to argue. Spanish exiles, as a rule, are like characters in an outdated play— unhappy, remote, and unnaturally wishful. For them, Spain as a reality ended with the Civil War, and they are incapable of understanding that the country has somehow emerged and gone on, however haltingly. They maintain a doubtful aristocracy of memory; beneath it, they are uneasily aware of their own historical pointlessness, and inhabit either a lost past or an improbable future. The Basque exiles with whom I spoke are in a happier position; many of them are able to live freely in France, among Basques, on the very edge of Spain. "We are much more in touch with what is going on in Bilbao and San Sebastián now than when we actually lived there," one of them told me. "As a result, we are much more respectful of the realities of the situation."

What these realities are is not so easy to discover—the Basques are argumentatively fractious and violently extreme in their political gestures. I was invited one evening in Bilbao to a meeting of "influential Basques" and climbed with some trepidation to the top floor of a crumbling old apartment building, where I found a group of about a dozen people sitting around a fire. The apartment was sumptuously furnished and looked out across the yellow, muddied waters of the Nervión River, which flows from the city to the sea. My host, a member of a prominent industrial family, took me to the window to show me the glare in the sky from the enormous ovens of the Altos Hornos steelworks, downriver. At first sight Bilbao is memorably ugly, cramped, dirty, and unplanned, but after one has spent some time in it the ugliness gives way to the feel of its sheer force, a kind of seething undercurrent of brawny vigor. Although it is less purely Basque than San Sebastián, it stands as the Goliath of the Basque provinces and gives the economic backing to all their separatist arguments. My host waved an arm at the murky river. "If we weren't Basques, we'd be Communists," he said, "because all that you see, and don't see, between Bilbao and the sea is a grotesque injustice—steelworks, shipyards, factories owned by a handful of people, their ludicrous mansions occupied a few weeks out of the year, and the workers cramped in dingy tenements, underemployed, desperate. Bilbao ought to make us feel more uncomfortable than we do, for as Basques we have always claimed to be equally endowed with nobility and humanity. But we're very much aware of the power we have, and of the fear that Franco has of us. When the time comes, we'll be ready."

The conversation I listened to was charged with high excitement and had nothing of the despairing languor I was used to in Madrid. Politically, the points of view varied to the level of anarchy, but they had in common an assured confidence—the Basque conviction of the inevitability of events, the long, patient perspective. At one point an old white-haired man sat down beside me to explain the company, his sharp chin thrusting forward as he spoke. (The prominent Basque nose is famous, but it is the hooked chin, leading forward and jerking up in emphasis, that I find distinguishes the Basques as they talk. On the medallions sold in the souvenir shops, the tilting beret, the long nose, and the curling chin of the profiles seem to be converging to a single point.) "Perhaps, if you're not used to us, you shouldn't listen too closely," said the old man. "Me, I've been a Basque nationalist all my life—only now we talk not of nationalism or separatism but of autodetermination. But it's all the same—and I'm accustomed to these escapes of steam, for we Basques have plenty of it. Among the Basques in San Sebastián you'll have found the romantics, the dreamers; here in Bilbao we are the hardheaded ones. Oh, we have Communists and Socialists and Republicans, and even a few monarchists; our politics are as mixed as you'll find anywhere in Spain. The difference is that we are Basques, and you can be sure of this—that if anything begins to happen in Spain, if there appears the least crack in the surface, we'll all become Basques at once, and we'll *take* our independence this time, firmly, with both hands. We have power, we have money, we work hard, and we have no lack of confidence. If Spain had treated us as France has treated the French Basques, we might have stayed Spaniards. But we've had our share of persecution—Franco has done everything possible to keep us from speaking our own language, for instance—and the consequences are inevitable, and not very far away. If it were not for Franco, the Basque country might be nothing more than a museum by now. Well, we're far from being moth-eaten. You'll see us independent before very long."

When we returned to the conversation, it had lost its serious edge and become more normally ludicrous. A Madrid-born architect who had settled in Bilbao was declaring himself a firm anti-Basque and was threatening to found a society for the suppression of Basques, to the delight of the others. "Living here, I've grown sick of everything Basque," he was telling them. "If I had my way, I'd ban the beret, change all the names, make it a punishable offense to speak that impossible language, forbid folk dancing and pelota, and try to get you all back to a semblance of ordinary human life. You're all blood-mad. You wouldn't marry Brigitte Bardot unless you found at least five Basques in her family tree. I wish you would get your independence, because then we could fence off the Basque country as a kind of zoo for tourists. As it is, I'll never move forward one step in Bilbao unless I change my name to Machimbarrena or Zulizarreta."

The others applauded him enthusiastically.

"The thing is, he's quite right," the old man said. "If you aren't a Basque and happen to live among us, we'll drive you mad. We have a racial superiority complex, if you like. Perhaps we are no more than relics and freaks to the outside eye, but we haven't just preserved the trappings and manners of a race; we've kept alive a whole way of being. We don't really need to write out the Basque Doctrine and the Old Laws. We know them all in our bones. It's how we are, and I can tell you that we are very far from being dead. The stupidest thing that Spain does is to tell us repeatedly that Euzkadi doesn't exist."

Now an easy humor predominated; the rest of the conversation was quick and witty and brimmed over with the restless, glancing energy that can keep a Basque talking all night without noticing it.

In a sharp essay on the Basque character, Ortega y Gasset went after this very self-confidence. "The Basque thinks that the mere fact of having been born and of being a human individual gives him all the value that it is possible for one to have in this world," he wrote. "All the superior qualities and perfections rising above the level of the elementally human are for the Basque poor, negligible excrescences. The great, the valuable in man is what is most lowly and aboriginal, the subterranean, that which keeps him tied to the earth. Since history is above all a competition and a dispute and rivalry to acquire those superfluous and superficial perfections—knowledge, art, political dominion—it is not surprising that the Basque race has taken so little interest in history."

With all due respect to Ortega, he measured the Basques against the wrong scale—and not surprisingly, because they can be measured against no scale but the one they themselves set. In truth, they are not so much nationalists or separatists as localists; they have no large, cohesive political ambitions to equal the one desire they are born with—to remain utterly local, individual, and particular. I doubt very much whether the Basque Republic, should it come to pass again, would ever bother about being represented on the international scene. As long as each village was allowed its distinctness, each individual his mannerisms, Basques would feel little need for constituent assemblies. This utter particularity is what makes them unaccountable, and can make them exasperating. They are quite happy to defy analysis, since analysis, they feel, might begin to infringe on their oddness.

The proof of all this is in that famous language, unapproachable though it is even to anyone with a good ear and a healthy grounding in the civilized languages of the world. It is pleasant to listen to as sheer sound, but there is not even a very occasional tinkle of resemblance to allow one to catch a thread of the sense; for anyone not born and bred a Basque, it remains pretty finally out of reach. Basque is almost entirely devoid of abstract terms; it is structurally agglutinative, forming concepts by an accretion of particular elements. Its few abstract nouns are all late borrowings from Latin; while it has a separate noun for every kind of tree found in the Basque provinces, the word for "tree" itself is comparatively recent. Its prevalent *k*s and *x*s and *z*s give it a bizarre look on the page; the street signs in the fishing village of Deva, enameled in both Basque and Spanish, gave me an awesome sense of the gulf between the two languages. I have waited patiently in small village inns while old men pawed through their tattered Basque-Spanish dictionaries to find a word that might put us even faintly in touch with one another, and in all my time in the Basque Country I think I have learned to say no more than nine Basque words—hardly an encouraging beginning. After a time, however, it is the surnames that first become familiar—Barandiarán, Etcheverría, Arantzazu— and the strange place names. I came one morning upon a village with the odd name of Ea, and when I stopped there for some food, it was to discover that in Basque, as happens often enough, the village had a different name entirely. Its Basque name was Ie. It is the language, finally, that leaves non-Basques forever on the outside of the mystery. A few incursions are possible, for Basque is thickly onomatopoeic (*bimbibimbaka* refers to the pealing of bells, *gili-gili* means "tickling," *irrintzi* is the noun for the neighing of horses), but beyond the physical pleasure of these words, the stranger must stay mumchance and dumbfounded.

Even so, it is not the oddness of the language, or even the careful avoidance of the abstract, that accounts for the aura of mystery that Basques seem to wear about them. Once I had stopped attempting to recognize Euzkadi either as part of France or as part of Spain, it began to seem to me like a curious nowhere, to which neither time nor judgment could ever apply. Often at evening, when the sun laid a reddish-gold light on the small deep-green fists of hills, on the tidy fields and farmyards, all beautifully touched by human hand, and when the quick, soft talk started up in the inns, I found myself wondering where on the map I could possibly be—if, indeed, I was traceable on any map at all. I began to notice, a long way off, the clop of horses, the cries of goosegirls gathering up the geese with their long hand-carved crooks, the screech of winches in the fishing villages; and the sounds, recurring and recurring, gradually began to pry me loose from all contexts other than this small nutshell of leftover life. My friends there often amused themselves by telling me wild, improbable tales of the *lamiñak,* the race of ghostly night visitors whom Basques charge with the responsibility for all strange happenings. Bit by bit I found myself easily believing every word. Even in as urbane a setting as San Sebastián, the summer capital of Spain, fringed with the international set and the shades of touring royalty (Queen Victoria visited San Sebastián in 1889 and complained to her diary that she found the tea served her by the queen regent of Spain "quite undrinkable")—even there, in the ham-hung, shell-strewn bars by the harbor, a song is likely to arise suddenly and spontaneously from a small knot of fishermen, a song so rare, so eerily remote, that it entirely obliterates the bar, the evening, and the listening ears. More than once, listening to the wailing of the weird, flutelike *tchirula,* I have shivered involuntarily. The longer I have stayed, the less like Spain it has all become; instead of the cheerful, shrugging carelessness of the Spaniards, I keep surprising a remote, ancestral look on the carved Basque faces. The next instant, however, it has disappeared, and the silence has given way to a torrent of comic preposterousness.

By now, my double, Lorenzo, has probably gone back to sea. I remember the remark of the old man in Guernica about the Pyrenees. From my window I am just able to see them, scribbled jaggedly along the skyline. At this moment they may even be alive with Basques, moving nimbly and unhampered between the two halves of Euzkadi. From here, on this hazy evening, the mountains look not only implacably durable but very, very old.

Basque Country: Spain's Unconquered Nation

BY JOHN DAVID MORLEY

❧

editor's note

Most articles about the Basques focus too much on politics and the terrorist activities of the ETA (Euskadi Ta Askatasuna, Basque Homeland and Liberty). I have long felt that this piece, written in 1991, best presents a balanced picture of the Basque people and Basque issues.

Here are three key points to keep in mind when considering the Basques. First, the ETA really isn't interested in you, the tourist. It's true that a recent car bomb in a Madrid parking garage did harm some innocent passersby, but in general, it's government officials who are targeted—successfully, unfortunately. Second, when Basques speak of their homeland, they are referring to land that is on *both* sides of the Pyrenees, in France and in Spain—it's easy to forget that there are Basques in France, as most if not all terrorist attacks occur on Spanish soil. The three provinces that make up the Pays Basque in France are Labourd, Basse-Navarre, and Soule. In Spain the País Vasco has three official Basque autonomous communities: Guipúzcoa, Vizcaya, and Álava. But the province of Navarra is also mostly Basque— Mark Kurlansky, in his excellent book *The World According to the Basques,* notes that "an old form of Basque graffiti is $4 + 3 = 1$." Finally, the Basque language ties the Basques of both Spain and France together more than any other element. A young employee at the San Sebastián tourist office told me that more Basque young people speak the language today than any genera- tion within the last one hundred years. This is significant and is really the only noteworthy change in this piece since it was written. (In 1991, as the author noted, only about a quarter of the Basque population spoke Euskera.) The young woman—who was in her twenties—at the tourist office explained to me that in 1991 students could choose whether they wanted their classes taught in Basque or Spanish; but she and her peers were not given a choice, and all their classes were in Basque. English is now not only the secondary language of instruction but is mandatory for all students. As a result, she told me, there are actually a fair number of students who do not read or speak Spanish fluently, some not very well at all. These students are of course introduced to Spanish by television, film, literature, and peri- odicals, but more often they may view television programming and read newspapers, magazines, and books in Basque. And for students who live in the more rural areas of the País Vasco, Basque may be the only language spoken at home.

After the September 11 tragedy and the Irish Republican Army's deci- sion to disarm in the fall of 2001, ETA was the "sole significant guerrilla group in Western Europe," according to a report filed by *The New York Times*. The new Europe, with a single currency, has ironically given the Basques something they've failed to achieve on their own: a borderless zone uniting Basque provinces in Spain and France. This idea of borders, or rather the lack of them, is a new one both for Europeans and foreigners. I had, in fact, initially thought to include the three provinces of the Pays Basque in this book as a nod of respect to the Basque people and as a nod to the newly united Europe *sans frontières* (without borders). H. V. Morton opined that one of the remarkable things about Spain is "the change from one region to another. Suddenly the landscape alters. You become conscious that the geological formation is different, that the vegetation is no longer the same, and that the cottages look different; and nowhere is this more noticeable than upon the boundary between Asturias and Galicia." This is very much true, and I would say that the border between Asturias and Galicia may be the most striking example of this difference in all of Spain; but there is almost no difference at all between the French and Spanish Basque border. Visitors to Fuenterrabía (or Hondarribia) and St.-Jean-de-Luz, for example, do not necessarily feel they have crossed a border. Differences do, obviously, exist as one travels farther into the Pays Basque, but there are more similarities than not. As the next book in this series will feature Southwestern France, my editor and I decided to include my articles on the Pays Basque in that upcoming edition.

In October 2001 the ETA requested a referendum that would allow French and Spanish Basques (including those of Navarre) to cast votes for or against full autonomy. At that time Prime Minister José María Aznar argued that there is no distinction between terrorists who organize attacks on the World Trade Center and those who set off car bombs. His position has been that there must be no negotiation until ETA surrenders, and as I write this, no referendum has been held. Still, the "4 + 3 = 1" equation Mark Kurlansky referred to is definitely one to watch in the years ahead.

JOHN DAVID MORLEY is a freelance writer who lives in Munich. He has lived and studied in Singapore, Malaya, West Africa, England, and Japan, and has written for *The New York Times, Vanity Fair,* and the *Asia Times,* among others. He is also the author of *Pictures from the Water Trade: Adventures of a Westerner in Japan* (Little, Brown & Co., 1985; HarperCollins, 1986).

To begin with, says Carlos, he would like me to meet a Basque writer. Carlos has taken a day off from his job in a department store to show me around his country. From Bilbao we drive up a long estuary to the small town of Algorta, overlooking the Bay of Biscay. Technically, we are in Spain. People around here, however, don't call it Spain. They call it the Basque Country.

I get my first good view of it through the kitchen window in the stone tower where Elias Amezaga, champion of Basque culture, lives not inappropriately like some kind of lighthouse keeper. On one side of Elias's bar, Carlos and I sit and listen to the stocky man in the scruffy blue-and-white sweater who on the other side is uncorking and thoughtfully sniffing bottles, as if in pursuit of some elusive essence.

Who are the Basques? No one really knows. Were they a tall, blond people with blue eyes who migrated west from the Caucasus? Or a short, dark people who gravitated north from Granada? Or a native tribe, or tribes, already indigenous to the region between the Pyrenees and the Cantabrian Mountains thousands of years ago?

Very little, says Elias self-disparagingly, when I ask him what he admires about the Basques. They are the people who always come second. They are the people it is impossible to unite. They are the people who live in a world of their own—historically, the people who could only be brought together on Sundays when they all went to church. And, yes, Basques live in the country. So those of them who live in cities aren't *real* Basques.

Elias uncorks a last bottle and pours himself a glass. Basques live in the country, he says, in houses that have wings, sufficiently far apart to leave them room to fly.

Whoever they were, they left paintings, not writings. The exuberant line drawings of animals in the caves of Santimamine, a few miles from Guernica—ancient and modern capital of the province of Vizcaya—are thirteen thousand years old. By contrast, the earliest written Basque records, dating from the late Middle Ages, are only a few hundred years old. Things got handed down by word of mouth, says Carlos. We are talking about an oral culture.

This is a bit frustrating. The Basque language is clearly ancient. It could easily have left us ancient records. When the Greek historian Strabo, writing at the time of Christ, first referred to the

Basque people—long before the Romans called them *vascones* and their legions colonized the landmass that became known as the Iberian peninsula—the Basques already appear to have spoken their language, Euskera. Not only is Euskera the only non-IndoEuropean language extant in western Europe, it is quite unlike any other language at all—a fairly sure sign of its great antiquity.

As late as a century ago, it might have made genetic sense to speak of a racially distinct Basque people. Some Basque nationalists try to claim they still are. With the migration of industrial workers from all over Spain to jobs in the Basque provinces, where they settled during the last hundred years, this view is scientifically unacceptable. One is left with a Basque people, period. So who now is *Basque*?

A teacher explains that an Euskeran term meaning "the person who has the language" defines the authentic native, but shopping around, I find standards relaxing. Joseba Goni, who runs a Basque magazine, says that anyone prepared to stand up for Basque ideals qualifies as Basque.

"Being born in the Basque Country is as much an element of being 'Basque' as speaking the language," finds Ernesto de Guerenu, dean of the Jesuit University of Deusto. "One shouldn't try to live in a museum." A majority would probably now go along with the view that anyone who lives there is Basque.

Not so fast, my friend, intervenes Carlos. *Where's "there"?* On our way to a lunch somewhere southeast of Bilbao, we are driving through an archaic landscape, the untouched rural solitude of the Arratia Valley. This is where Carlos used to come on outings as a kid. This is the valley his father left to find employment in Bilbao, and to which he returned to be buried. Carlos points out the low-walled enclosures hugging the hills as we pass.

"Never much farming here," he muses. "The mountain people of my grandfather's generation had maybe a few sheep, a cow, poultry, and an acre of maize. It was a hard living. So from the turn of the century they had two jobs—tending the livestock mornings and evenings, and working in factories during the day."

This is how life used to be for the people of Vizcaya, Guipúzcoa, and Álava—hill farmers inland or fishermen on the shore. In these three provinces of the Basque Country—granted an autonomous government by the Spanish state ten years ago—there now live two million people. For Basque nationalists, however, the notion of the historic Basque people includes half a million more in the neighboring province of Navarra, plus the two hundred thousand inhabitants of three provinces across the border in France. The three million people in these seven provinces, they claim, make up the population of the Basque Country.

All these arcane distinctions that have begun to cloud my head are momentarily scattered by the solid prospect of sitting down to lunch. Village-hopping up the valley, seven Basques minus Carlos have been drinking steadily since noon but seem not at all the worse for wear. Now, at four o'clock in a tavern in Zeberio, something to eat besides red wine now comes on the table—bread, salad, and a volcanic tureen of *alubias,* a densely flavored local dish of home-slaughtered pork with beans.

"Never refuse anything now for the sake of having it later!" advises Carlos as I eye the pot with a view to a third helping. This is probably sound advice, a Basque equivalent of *carpe diem.* What Carlos omits to mention is how much is still to come. More pork is launched at me wrapped in rice under the name *morcilla.* The trenchermen sigh and tuck in to greasy bowls of the mixed beef stew known as *callos.* Then come the puddings, liqueurs, and obligatory cigars. Whew. Lunch goes on for three hours. So does the talk, spiced with laughter, in an unceasing barrage.

As Carlos and his old school chums settle down to a game of cards, I take a stroll up the valley, beginning to grasp what Elias

Amezaga meant when he said I would have to leave the cities to find the Basque Country: sheep with bells and cows with calves. The squat stone houses with red ruined roofs. Soft, round hills with conifers turning blue as the light fades. The bark of a chainsaw where men stack firewood outside a barn. The tangled remains of last year's maize crop. And green, green the fields and mottled brown the houses dotted across the hills like little fortresses, solid in their isolation like the Basques themselves.

Leaving Bilbao and the rusty industrial shores of the estuary, I head north along the coast. In the fishing port of Bermeo, I note a *frontón,* a closed court for playing the Basque ballgame pelota, right down on the wharves, and a whale in the municipal coat-of-arms, reminder of a tradition now extinguished. Elantxobe is a fishing hamlet of not more than a hundred houses, terraced on a slope behind a sheer wall of rock to give protection from the storms coming off the Bay of Biscay. In these meager villages I am struck by the handsomeness of the churches. People here probably went hungry to build them. Turning a corner in the nondescript coastal town of Lekeitio, I find my breath taken away by the soaring, wholly unexpected grandeur of a sixteenth-century Gothic masterpiece, Santa María de Asunción.

Reluctantly veering inland, I drive south to Durango, heart of the Euskera-speaking Basque Country. On a mountain ridge I reach the border of Vizcaya and descend into the province of Guipúzcoa. Another ridge marks the boundary between this and the third Basque province, Álava. Here at last the horizon begins to widen to encompass the southern plain.

In the Basque Country the choice is between the mountains and the sea. Larger populations converge in the three main cities—Bilbao and San Sebastián along the coastal strip, Álava in the southern plain. The rest is a sparsely populated shore, empty hills inland.

The inaccessibility of the country provided its natural fortification. When the Romans colonized the Iberian peninsula, settlements grew up elsewhere. In the Middle Ages it was divided among the kingdoms of Portugal, Castilla-Léon, Aragon-Catalonia, and Navarra. The latter three were united under Ferdinand and Isabella in the late fifteenth century, initiating the idea of a Spanish Crown, though not yet of a unified Spanish nation. This would emerge under the Bourbon dynasty in the eighteenth century.

As the Romance languages developed from Latin, and the people of the Iberian peninsula began to separate as Portuguese, Catalan, and Spanish speakers, the Basque population continued to use their much older tongue, Euskera. Language and topography both set them apart.

Politically they were associated with the kingdom of Castile. The ancient customs, rights, and local privileges of the Basques—a body of laws known as *fueros*—were recognized by the Castilian crown about a thousand years ago. Hundreds of years before nationalism was invented, the history of the Basques can be described as the ebb and flow of a struggle to preserve those *fueros*—and, later, what they had come to symbolize—against the encroachment of a centralist Spanish state whose people, language, and culture were always considered alien.

In 1979, after a hundred years in limbo, the general assembly known as the *juntas generales* was opened once more in the Vizcayan capital of Guernica. The remains of a centuries-old tree, in whose shade the representatives had once come together for sessions of local government, can still be seen outside the present assembly building. It is the branching symbol of Basque rights. When the Museum of Modern Art in New York handed over Picasso's masterpiece to the Spanish government after Franco's death, the Basques must have felt it something of an irony that a home for the picture was found not here but in the capital city of the former fascist regime responsible for the destruction of Guernica that Picasso's work commemorates.

The man waiting outside the gas station for the rendezvous arranged by Carlos looks like a retired banker. His name is José Manuel Agirre. In retirement he is, but not as a former banker. He is one of the founding members of the Basque separatist organization ETA, although many simply call them terrorists.

Over coffee and cognac in a nearby restaurant I listen to Señor Agirre talk. Dapper, educated, courteous, rather *likable*, dammit, the former "terrorist" takes me painlessly through three decades of political assassination. Prompt to supply me with figures of the casualties the ETA has incurred (six hundred colleagues now in jail, three and a half thousand over time, of whom Agirre himself claims to have been the first), he declines knowledge of the casualties the ETA has caused (six hundred dead so far, who knows how many wounded).

My conversation with Señor Agirre is helpful because it gives me the measure of fanaticism. For the radical wing of the Basque nationalist movement, nothing less than independence will do. This would entail secession of not just three but all seven Basque provinces from Spain and France. I object that there is not realistically the slightest question of this happening, at least by peaceful means. No nation has ever achieved independence without the use of force, retorts Señor Agirre. Why should it be different with the Basques? The ETA is, of course, gunning for Spanish soldiers and policemen, but occasionally there are accidents, innocent bystanders. He shrugs. Such is the nature of war.

Herri Batasuna, the extreme nationalist party that shares the ETA's aim of independence, polls around 18 percent of the vote in the Basque provinces. Its supporters may not approve of how the

ETA operates, but its objectives are beyond dispute and endorsed with chilling loyalty: *They are bad boys, but they're our boys.*

Votes for Herri Batasuna are protest votes, as the party boycotts all democratic assemblies. Representation of the Basques in regional and state government is therefore left to the Basque Nationalist Party (PNV) in coalition with two smaller nationalist groups.

The Basques' list of former grievances against the Spanish state is long: charges of arrogance, or simple neglect on the part of a centralized state with no time for or interest in ethnic squabbles in its northernmost provinces; autocracy, fiscal exploitation, and police brutality; the forbidding of the use of the Basque language, even the use of Basque names at baptisms or on gravestones. Thus, when Franco died and democracy came to Spain—bringing to the Basque Country the Autonomy Statute, which assured the Basques the use of their own language, their own press, their own police, and wide fiscal autonomy—it was hoped that the ETA's murderous activities would gradually cease. But throughout the 1980s they escalated.

One of the disturbing consequences of the intrusion of violence into everyday life is that people come to *accept* it as part of everyday life. Most Basques condemn violence, but it does not seem to horrify them anymore. Or they fail to distance themselves from it convincingly. It's terrible, they say; at the same time one frequently hears the ETA described as the conscience of the Basque nation.

Francisco Díaz de Cerio, laborer, age forty-one, is shot and killed as he leaves his house in Bilbao on his way to work at seven o'clock in the morning. Married and a father of two children, the murdered man had been a member of Spain's national police, the *guardia civil*, ten years ago. For this reason he is assassinated by the ETA.

The assassination makes headlines in the local papers the day before I leave, downgrading what should have been the main item of news: the election of a new president of the Basque government. It is this fatal knack that the ETA has of diverting attention from the serious business of government to sensational crimes that understandably irritates political leaders like PNV delegate Inaki Anasagasti, spokesman for the Basque minority in the parliament in Madrid. Twenty-four hours after the killing, I speak to him at a reception in the Vizcayan provincial council in Bilbao.

The ETA's continued agitation notwithstanding, a measure of political stability has been achieved. Anasagasti sees this as one of the most important results to have emerged from a decade of Basque autonomy. When asked if thirty years of the ETA have on balance done more to help or harm the Basque cause, its chief political spokesman does not hesitate to say that the ETA is the worst thing that ever happened to the Basques.

I approach Carlos on the subject. He is sick of it. *I switch off,* he says. *ETA assassinations are a ticker tape I've gotten so used to I no longer hear it.* Interestingly, he points out that from the time the ETA stepped up its terrorism in the late 1970s, the Basque economy has been plunged in recession. Give the unemployed a job, he argues, and terrorism would end tomorrow.

The unemployment rate is dwindling after peaking in the late 1970s, but at more than 16 percent it is still high. The industrial monoculture of iron, steel, and shipbuilding that once made the region one of Spain's best performers is now the cause of its troubles. These markets have been lost to Asian competitors. And the legacy of the industrial past has been to pollute the future of the Basque Country to a degree that is worse than almost anywhere in western Europe.

"There's a connection here," agrees Francisco Letamendia, lecturer at the Bilbao campus of the University of the Basque Country (UPV). "The unemployed swell the ranks of the nationalists pressing for Basque separatism."

The outlook, statistically, might appear disheartening. Statistics, however, do not take into account the very heartening vitality of the Basque people.

By way of relaxation at their fiestas from spring through fall, Basques vie with one another to see who can lift the heaviest stone, or drive a team of oxen dragging the largest rock through open streets. With elongated baskets, bats, or their bare hands, they strike balls in the hard and fast game of pelota, sometimes risking broken fingers in the scramble across stone *frontones,* the pelota courts that almost every village is said to boast. By way of diversion, they will compete in chopping down trees, in severing logs with axes, or in rowing three miles across the open sea in old fishing boats, a sport known as trawler regattas. And the world-famous bull-running in Pamplona takes place in Navarra, of course, one of the seven historic Basque provinces.

The Basques are a very *physical* people, energetic and adventurous. The Guipúzcoa-born Juan Sebastián del Cano completed the first circumnavigation of the world five hundred years ago. Basque sailors manned the voyages of Columbus. Likely, though unproven, is their claim to have reached America as early as the Vikings. Their whalers crossed the Atlantic to operate off Newfoundland. Basque blood carried the bacillus of revolution abroad, from Simon Bolívar to Che Guevara.

"But you must remember we are not a Latin people. We do not theorize, like the Spanish. We are a practical people. We like to get on with things."

Burly, bearded Koldo San Sebastián, who could be one of those seafaring Basques himself, looks benignly across the desk where he likes to get on with things at the office of *DEIA,* one of the major Basque dailies. Behind his spectacles, his eyes sparkle.

"The source of Basque strength is still the family. Women are strong in Basque society. We like to sing, you know. Basque choirs are quite famous, not soloists, you see. Solidarity. Loyalty. Our local industries are also often family-based. Family-owned enterprises of fifty to a hundred employees, with democratic traditions, no great income differences between the owner and the workers. Maybe these Basque traditions, like the use of the Basque language, get lost in the city. But in a small country like ours, one does not need to live in the city. At work in Bilbao, I use Spanish. But at home in the country I can breathe through the Basque language."

Koldo the journalist, Laura Mintegi the Basque writer, Joseba Tobar, who teaches in Euskera—all speakers of the language tell me how it reinforces relationships and creates a community of trust and sympathy from which Spanish speakers are inevitably excluded. Yet only about a quarter of the Basque population can speak Euskera. Many thus feel the survival of the Basque nation is tied to the survival of the Basque language.

Visual evidence of the language is overwhelming, beginning with the exit signs at Bilbao airport. Signs everywhere are in Euskera and Spanish. Basque cities probably have more graffiti per square inch of wall than any in the world. Prevalence of slogans in Euskera is not an index of prevalence of the language, however, but of the hyperactive energy of Basque nationalists.

Words like *kutxa, presoak,* and *euzkadi* look down at me from hoardings all over town. There is a glut of the letters *k, x,* and *z.* I imagine the pronunciation of this archaic language to resemble a sort of throat-clearing. When I start listening to conversations in Euskera, however, I find it surprisingly mellow. No wonder. I am listening to sounds that have been casked and gone on maturing for maybe thousands of years.

Such a language is a national treasure. It is too important to be left to chance. Koldo gives me directions to the Liceo Santo Tomás, one of the most famous Euskera schools to have blossomed in the last decade, and saying good-bye to Carlos, I catch the bus to San Sebastián.

It's twenty years since I first came to this city. Not much seems to have changed. The Bay of La Concha still swings its almost perfect loop of sand. I look up from surprisingly clear green water at the empty beach, the white wide arc of the buildings along the waterfront, the nostalgic turn-of-the-century resort hotels whose former life still echoes through the arcades, the pruned trees bare on the windy promenade. The difference is that this time it's winter.

But the atmosphere is not out of season. Walking through the streets of the old town during the midafternoon lull, I can still hear the dogs scuffling on the cobbles and the canaries singing on the balconies above. Then comes a pulse, that extraordinary threshold hour in southern European cities when silent afternoons begin to throb, shopkeepers run up their shutters with a rattle, and as if this were a sign, the streets fill magically with clamorous evening life.

Here it comes. Dotted here and there over a swarm of white faces is the navy-blue Basque beret, the *chapela,* a sort of national insignia, cloth monument to the Basque identity. One used to pan down from it to kerchief, smock, and britches, but these can now be viewed in period paintings only. Worn rakishly at a paramilitary tilt or pancake style full on the crown of the head, as if dropped on the wearer with incredible skill from an upper-story window, the *chapela* worn whatever way confers unquestionable dignity. Wearers are everything one would instinctively like Basques to be: strong, solitary, proud, square-jawed, rugged—and without exception old.

Carlos, now in his late forties, tells me that his generation was the last to don the national beret in their youth. Unless they happen to belong to the local police, young men do not wear it anymore. When those aging guardians of this appreciable national symbol are gone, the Basques in Basque cities will look like everyone else in theirs. This need not matter, of course, but I have learned what store the Basques like to lay by their national symbols to keep them distinct from the Spanish.

If the Basques can afford to lose their hats, it's another matter with their language. Speaking their own language, the Basque claim to constitute a separate nation within the Spanish state seems almost self-evident. Without a language to endorse nationhood, this claim is much less persuasive.

At the entrance to the Liceo Santo Tomás, where Euskera is the sole language of instruction, hangs a map showing the seven Basque provinces according to the "current demarcations of the regions where the Basque language and its dialects are spoken." The author of this linguistic map is the philologist Prince Louis-Lucien Bonaparte. It is dated 1863.

Children run in and out to make inquiries at the reception. Outside in the playground I have heard at least some of them speaking Spanish. Crossing the threshold, they do a language switch. There's a sign at the door reminding them to do so.

Santos Sarasola, the director, ushers me into his office and runs me through the brief history of the Euskera language schools, or *ikastola*. Only thirty years or so ago they were still having to operate secretly in people's homes. Not until the Autonomy Statute did they emerge fully from the Spanish yoke. The problem facing Basque schools at the moment is a financial one. In the process of their transition from private to public status, they are not yet entitled to state funding.

Still, more than two thousand children attend the *ikastola*, some of them whose parents come from other parts of Spain. Santos is optimistic. Almost half of the children now at school-going age go or will go to Basque schools.

He doesn't believe in such a thing as a Spanish national identity.

He believes in the identity of the people making up the Spanish population. And the Basques? What about their identity?

"The Basque identity is made up of a distinct culture and language. Politically it now resides in the instrument of the Basque autonomy policy. But above all it is our *will* to be a people."

The will to be a people resides above all in the hands of the next generation. Santos takes me into a classroom where a chemistry lesson is in progress. I am shown textbooks. Formulae and symbols punctuate an ancient language on the page. All in Basque. It seems miraculous. Santos teaches me a word of Basque greeting, which I repeat as I take my leave of the class. A warm, shy murmur comes back to me from the students. There is a moment of something like breathlessness. Perhaps impossible things can happen. Perhaps, in the vision of Elias Amezaga, Basques do live in houses with wings that someday will take off and fly.

Spain's Basque Country

By Penelope Casas

editor's note

Here is a great culinary tour of the three Spanish Basque autonomous communities, Álava, Guipúzcoa, and Vizcaya.

PENELOPE CASAS, whose articles appear throughout this book, is the author of ¡Delicioso! The Regional Cooking of Spain, among others.

The Basque Country—Euskadi in the Basque tongue—is little more than a dot on the map of Spain, yet I have returned here repeatedly over the years, drawn by an appeal out of all proportion to its diminutive size. Certainly this is one of Spain's wealthiest regions, long celebrated for its exceptional food and outstanding chefs (fully one-third of Spain's top-rated restaurants are here). And scenically the Basque Country is enchanting: a stunning, rugged coastline along what is often called the Cantabrian Sea but more commonly known as the Bay of Biscay; quaint fishing villages nestled in naturally protected harbors (Basques know all too well the fury of the sea); and a lushly green interior of abrupt mountains and gently rolling hills punctuated by *baserri,* whitewashed country houses with exposed beams, gently sloped red tile roofs, and brightly colored wood balconies.

Comprising the provinces of Vizcaya, Guipúzcoa, and Álava, the Basque region is paradoxically called a "country," this in deference to its fiercely independent nature, mirroring that of France's Basque Country. In centuries past imposing mountains impeded access from the rest of the Iberian peninsula (Romans and Moors found the northern coast inhospitable and focused their attention farther south), and Basques turned to the sea for their livelihood. Even before the discovery of America, Basque fishermen sailed to the fertile fishing grounds of Newfoundland and Greenland in pursuit of whales (for their oil) and codfish, which was salted to withstand the long journey home. Today salt cod is still one of the most desirable fish in Basque cuisine.

Thus the Basque nation evolved in relative isolation, governed by representatives chosen by its own people. So strong was this tradition that in the fifteenth century, when Spain became a nation under the Catholic kings, the monarchs were obliged to respect Basque ways and to allow a certain measure of autonomy to continue, as it does today.

Basques, indeed, have a distinct ancestry, descending from a people of unknown origin. No link has ever been established, either genetically or culturally, between the Basques and other peoples of the world. One somewhat far-fetched theory proposes them to be the sole survivors of the lost continent of Atlantis, who took refuge on Spanish shores when their homeland was consumed by violent geological upheaval. Basques do, of course, speak Spanish and are gracious to visitors. Yet they cherish their native tongue, which experts have been unable to relate to other known languages; it is unwieldy, to be sure, with words like *etxekoandres* (housewives) and *eskarrikasko* (thank you) and unsuitable to modern needs, but it proudly persists. Basque sports are equally odd. Jai alai, a Basque invention, has gained worldwide acceptance, but I am at a loss to explain the attraction of events like cutting grass, hacking tree trunks, and lifting massive stones, all bona-fide sporting activities with many avid fans.

I am intrigued by the Basques' fascination with food, which goes far beyond sustenance. Indeed, it is a symbol of deep regional pride and a societal preoccupation, especially among Basque men, who in the nineteenth century established gastronomic societies that openly excluded women. (Only at off-hours have I succeeded in gaining admittance to inspect the facilities and chat with members.) These eating clubs have become fixtures of Basque life: places for men, or *tripasais,* as such food lovers are often called, to showcase their culinary talents and cook for friends in a party atmosphere that often includes performances by male choral groups known as *orfeones.*

When a passion for gastronomy took all of Spain by storm in the 1980s, the Basques were at the forefront, creating a style of cooking christened *nueva cocina vasca* (new Basque cooking) and based on regional foods prepared in previously unheard of or nearly forgotten ways. The fashion spread (many prestigious restaurants in other parts of Spain take pride in their Basque chefs and Basque cuisine), but rarely were the results as exciting or expertly achieved as in the Basque Country itself. Traditional dishes are, of course, still sentimental favorites, comfortably coexisting with even the most stylish present-day creations.

Perhaps it is the cool climate and the diversity of high-quality local ingredients that have inspired Basque chefs to greatness. Basques are firm believers in "every food in its season," and each province contributes to the success of this cuisine that melds the extraordinary seafood of the Bay of Biscay; the excellent meats, sausages, and cheeses of the mountainous interior; and the exceptional fruits and vegetables from the broad Ebro River valley in the province of Álava (Araba to the Basques). Also from Álava are the celebrated red wines of the upper limits of La Rioja (the Rioja Alta), which can be found at all fine Basque restaurants. Nevertheless, a young, dry, and fruity "green wine" called *txakoli*— the only kind the climate of the coast permits—is the ideal accompaniment to Basque fish dishes.

Salt cod, despite its reputation as survival food and the superabundance of same-day-fresh seafood, is a Basque favorite that in skilled hands becomes sublime. *Merluza* (European hake) is especially well loved here; so too spider crab *(centollo)*, seasoned and returned to its shell to become *txangurro*. And *angulas*, baby eels the size of matchsticks, captured at the mouths of rivers as they complete their incredible three-thousand-mile journey home from their place of birth in the Sargasso Sea, are a delicacy not to be missed. (Basques eat them only in season—November to March— but *angulas* freeze well and can be found elsewhere in Spain throughout the year.) Among the region's many fine vegetables are the renowned red beans of Tolosa, white asparagus, and small sweet red peppers called *pimientos del piquillo*. Thin-skinned and wood-roasted, these peppers are gastronomic stars on their own or stuffed with meat or seafood.

Often called the "region of the sauces," the Basque Country relies on four simple sauces to transform already exceptional primary ingredients into culinary wonders: green sauce *(a la vasca)*, based on garlic, white wine, and parsley, which traditionally accompanies hake; dried red pepper and onion sauce *(a la vizcaína)* and a garlic-and-oil emulsion *(al pil-pil)*, both complementing dried cod; and garlic and olive oil sauce with a touch of hot red pepper *(a la bilbaína)*, light enough for red snapper and *angulas*. Squid ink sauce, also very Basque, is specific to the classic squid dish *chipirones en su tinta*.

We approached the Basque Country from Madrid, and in the pastoral mountains of the province of Burgos we crossed into the province of Vizcaya (Bizkaia) and made our way directly to the town of Galdácano (Galdakao), not far from Bilbao, for lunch at Andra Mari. Galdácano is quite ordinary, but as we climbed into the hills to the restaurant, occupying a lovely Basque-style house next to a Romanesque church, the scenery changed suddenly. We entered an airy, inviting dining room overlooking a spectacular tableau of green hills and pine forests. "That's where we pick the *perretxiko* mushrooms featured on our menu in spring," said owner Roberto Asúa as he observed us lingering over the view.

This very first lunch, orchestrated to perfection by impeccably costumed waitresses who seemed to glide on wheels, proved to be one we would often recall with utmost pleasure. We focused on Basque specialties: salt cod and fresh anchovies in a delicate marinade; and *piquillo* red peppers, filled with spider crab over red pepper purée and accompanied by a *txakolí* wine called Txomín Etxániz. But for my companion's beef tenderloin, crusted with wild mushrooms and served over an onion compote, a red Rioja was selected. The meal concluded with well-made *canutillos*, or custard-filled pastry horns, and an assortment of local cheeses, among them the subtly smoked sheep's milk Idiazábal.

We came to Bilbao (Bilbo) as our point of departure for exploring the Basque coast, but more specifically we came here to eat. Founded in 1300 on the east bank of the Nervión River as a center of commerce, business-oriented Bilbao has had few tourist attractions, but with the opening of the lavish Guggenheim Museum Bilbao in late 1997, the city has surely expanded its cultural horizons. At any rate, I always enjoy strolling the Siete Calles, seven parallel pedestrian streets that remain from the old city and are the scene of a bustling daily market. One evening we walked from our hotel, the classically elegant López de Haro (by far my favorite here), to join the crowds of easygoing people making the rounds of *tapas* bars. Drinks in hand, these *tapas* habitués spilled out into the streets around Calle del Licenciado Poza and Alameda del Doctor Areilza.

The *tapas* at Or-Kompón are seductive, but we saved our appetites for dinner at Guría, where chef Jenaro Pildain claims the title of "codfish wizard." The compliment is far more than a catchy phrase; cod must be of irreproachable quality and freshness before it is salted, but desalting and cooking are also key, requiring extraordinary expertise. At these tasks Jenaro is peerless; in his hands dried cod becomes a dazzling and unforgettable work of art. *Bacalao cuatro gustos* allowed us to taste it in four versions, from the traditional *al pil-pil* and *a la vizcaína* preparations to Jenaro's more modern interpretations: *al Club Ranero* (with *pil-pil* and vegetable sauce) and Guría style (*pil-pil* with pimientos and spinach).

Not all of Bilbao's best restaurants are downtown. Jolastoki is some fourteen kilometers west of the city in Neguri, near the mouth of the Nervión River, where at the turn of the century Bilbao's elite built enormous gingerbread houses several stories high on proportionately small plots. Bubbly Begoña Beaskoetxea, hostess and wife of chef Sabin Arana, was in perpetual motion, attending to every guest. Begoña (named after the patron saint of Vizcaya) was quick to bring us typically *bilbaíno* dishes, beginning with the house *talo con chistorra*, a long, skinny *chorizo* sausage from the north of Spain wrapped in cornmeal flatbread. (Corn brought back from the New World found a friendly climate in northern Spain.)

Jolastoki prides itself on its seasonal menu, and on one spring visit Begoña insisted we try the early vegetables: tiny limas, incredibly sweet baby peas, and fresh white asparagus grown in the Ebro valley. There are no fewer than twenty-one kinds of wild mushrooms on the menu at different times of the year. Two Basque fish specialties—clams with rice in parsley sauce *(almejas con arroz en salsa de perejil)* and *lomos de merluza con kokotxas,* a choice cut of hake in green sauce served with its delectable "cheeks"—were superb. And, although a sweet custard and spinach tart certainly looked *nueva vasca,* Begoña informed us that spinach desserts had been part of Bilbao's cooking for as long as she could remember.

We were eager to reach San Sebastián, one of our favorite cities, but set a leisurely pace on small roads that wind around the sea so that we could fully appreciate the striking beauty of the Basque coast. At the hermitage of San Juan de Gaztelugache, situated on a rocky spike jutting out into the water, we came upon an arresting sight: a flock of white-robed nuns, here to pay homage to San Juan, cautiously descending a tortuous path before piling into a white van piloted by one of their own. By chance we were heading the same way and only just kept up with their rapid pace before we turned off at the busy port of Bermeo. Here we walked among hundreds of colorful fishing boats sparkling in the sunlight.

The Mundaca (Mundaka) River estuary forced us to detour south toward Guernica (Gernika), a town whose name has lived in infamy ever since the German bombings there during the Spanish Civil War outraged the world and provoked Picasso to paint his famous canvas. At Baserri Maitea restaurant, a pretty, whitewashed country house on an isolated hilltop just north of Guernica, in Forua, food is cooked *a la brasa* (on an open grill) in a cozy rustic dining room hung with dried corn, garlic, and dried red peppers.

As we rejoined the coast, grassy cliffs dipped abruptly to the sea, and we followed a road climbing steeply from the shore to the heights of the tiny, virtually untouched village of Elanchove (Elantxobe). Its narrow harbor (the entrance is barely wider than the boats that make port there) offers a safe haven for the town's small fishing fleet—and a splendid view from the road. There is a similarly protected port in nearby Lequeitio (Lekeitio), a town of picturesque cobbled streets that is dominated by the graceful Gothic church of Santa María de la Asunción. After a delectable meal at Kresala of simply grilled shrimp and *langoustines,* accompanied by Lequeitio's fine *txakolí,* we paused at the waterfront, mesmerized by the power of the waves crashing over the jetty.

Before long the striking El Ratón appeared, an island (now attached by landfill to the town of Getaria) so named because it resembles a crouched mouse. Getaria's native son Juan Sebastián del Cano is proudly remembered as the man who in fact completed the first circumnavigation of the globe, in 1522, after Magellan was killed en route. Today Guetaria is best known for its *asadores,* restaurants like Elkano and Talai-Pe that send their cooks into the street to entice customers with the wafting aromas of outdoor grilling.

Without doubt the city of San Sebastián, capital of Guipúzcoa (Gipuzkoa) province and known in Basque as Donostia, is a highlight of travel in the Basque Country. Within a half hour of leaving Getaria we were admiring this city—for me one of the world's most beautiful—spectacularly set like a string of pearls around a shell-shaped bay. San Sebastián was for hundreds of years a fishing village, but this all changed at the end of the last century, when Queen Isabella II was advised by her doctors to spend her summers by the sea, and she chose San Sebastián. The court and other aristocracy followed, as did her heir, future King Alfonso XII, and his wife, María Cristina. In no time the city sprouted broad boulevards, elegant shops, a waterfront promenade lined with feathery tamarind trees, and fine hotels. Both the ultra-deluxe María Cristina and the Hotel de Londres y de Inglaterra—on the waterfront and at the urban hub—are from that period.

Combining the ambiances of a beach resort and a full-fledged city, San Sebastián is a place one loves to come back to. It is particularly exciting in summer and early fall, when fiestas and festivals dominate the calendar: regattas in oar-powered boats called *traineras,* the international film festival in September, July's jazz festival, and horse-racing events. But dining places by far lead the list of attractions—nothing less than Arzak, commonly considered Spain's finest restaurant, and several more not far behind. Add to these San Sebastián's stupendous *tapas* bars, profusion of epicurean societies, and wondrous markets, and you have a city that says "food" like no other in Spain.

The subject of food brings on heated discussions in San Sebastián, such as one I joined in while dining at Arzak, the intimate and elegant restaurant that has achieved three Michelin stars. Chef and owner Juan Mari Arzak, a kind and gentle man with a cherubic face who is credited with being the originator—and still the finest interpreter—of *nueva cocina vasca,* was embroiled in an amicable debate with a childhood friend of his seated near us. The subject was *merluza,* the preferred fish in San Sebastián. "I only buy hake that has been hooked, never netted," declared Juan Mari. "*Merluza* is very fragile; if it is tossed around and bruised in a net, flavor is lost."

"But," protested his friend, "even *merluza* that is hooked must be removed immediately from the water; otherwise it will 'drown' and the taste will still be affected." If it had not been in the wee hours with the staff impatient to leave, I have no doubt the conversation would have continued until daybreak.

The following morning I joined Juan Mari for a visit to La Brecha, the city's awesome central market, housed in an immense stone building that could be mistaken for a palace. The abundance and variety of fish were astounding, and indeed some of the most expensive specimens bore signs reading *de anzuelo* (hooked). Juan Mari is a familiar figure here: Van drivers delivering produce shout greetings; he chats with egg and chicken vendors. When I accompanied him he stopped to inspect some black beans offered by a country woman. "These are the best black beans in the market," he declared. The woman beamed. He eyed some freshly shelled peas ("they sure are good-looking, aren't they?") but reproached another seller ("you should have picked them much sooner"). We proceeded up a broad exterior stairway to the second level, devoted to fish, and it was quite a sight. Hake, bass, tuna, squid, cuttlefish, *langoustine,* lobster—up to sixty varieties of fish and shellfish, all lovingly displayed and of a freshness beyond compare.

A stay in San Sebastián is of course never complete without tasting Juan Mari Arzak's latest creations. I will never forget his prawns and morels in carrot-scented olive oil accompanied by a cauliflower and almond purée and fried radish leaves. The marriage of flavors in this dish is a fine example of Arzak's culinary genius, but then again every dish emerging from Juan Mari's kitchen is a work of art. Another sublime preparation is hake with scallops in scallion vinaigrette sprinkled with squid-ink olive oil.

For a city so small, San Sebastián offers a bewildering choice of worthy dining experiences. At Akelarre, a modern chalet on Monte Igueldo that looks down upon splendid seascapes, Pedro Subijana's dishes are superb, none better than his tiny "hooked" squid, stuffed and served in ink sauce, and his *carpaccio* of scallops with green lentils. Pedro, whose father was a baker, pays particular attention to his dessert menu and is especially adept at pastries, such as frozen lemon mousse in feathery puff pastry. Casa Nicolasa, a bastion of traditional eating in San Sebastián for generations, has been some-what updated by chef José Juan Castillo, who expertly prepares Basque specialties: *revuelto de cigalas y espinacas* (soft-cooked eggs with *langoustines* and spinach); *txangurro;* and *mero con patatas panaderos* (grouper baked on a bed of thinly sliced potatoes). And at Martín Berasategui, in spacious and elegant quarters just outside the city, chef Berasategui demonstrates why he is the rising star of the Basque restaurant world with such dishes as turbot-and-mushroom-filled pasta, *txangurro* crêpes, and quail filled with *foie gras* in a mushroom vinaigrette.

Tapas bars are no less a part of eating in San Sebastián. "*Tapas* are an integral part of our cooking," explained Juan Mari, "a mini-cuisine transformed into art." And as the prime afternoon *tapas* hour approached, we headed to San Sebastián's old quarter and the port area. Here cheerfully bobbing fishing boats painted in brilliant reds, blues, and greens crowd the tiny harbor, and along the wharf casual restaurants, like Sebastián, grill fish for eager customers. The narrow streets are crammed with *tapas* bars, where the atmosphere is gregarious and the small dishes—many of them painstakingly mounted canapés—are artfully displayed and self-served on the honor system. We were overwhelmed by the selection at Portaletas, Bar La Cepa, and Casa Bartolo.

At Alotza (which, like most *tapas* bars, has a small back dining room) the ebullient owner gave us the key to the magic of the San Sebastián eating experience: "I won't deny that Juan Mari Arzak is a phenomenon and that the service and presentation in his restaurant are beyond compare. But we all shop in the same market; his fish can't possibly be better than what I serve here. My clients are tough critics who really know and appreciate quality food. It is what they are used to at home—and I must meet their expectations."

Fine weather inspired us to drive east of San Sebastián to see the remainder of this extraordinary coast. But there is nothing like returning to San Sebastián at the end of the day, unwinding at a waterfront café, and watching the crowds, dressed in their fashionable best, taking the customary evening promenade.

East of San Sebastián

Along this coast is the tiny village of Pasajes de San Juan (Pasai Donibane), hidden within a large industrial port, where Victor Hugo once lived; his house has been honored as a museum. At **Casa Camara** lobsters are kept in pots in a holding tank and brought up for clients' approval. From here the drive east along the Jaizkibel road is spectacular; it climbs into the mountains to give panoramic views of the sea, the Bidasoa River, and on a clear day the French and Spanish coasts. Fuenterrabía (Hondarribia), an ancient walled town of steep cobbled streets, is exquisitely preserved. We have often spent the night at the **Parador Nacional El Emperador** here and enjoyed dining at **Ramón Roteta**, set in an elegant villa, and at **Zuberoa**, a distinguished restaurant in a six-hundred-year-old country house just outside nearby Oyarzun (Oiartzun).

Zarauz (Zarautz), fourteen miles from San Sebastián, has become a place of pilgrimage for many Spaniards. Celebrity chef Karlos Arguiñano, whose hit television show has charmed the nation, claims a prized location in this overgrown summer town for his namesake **Karlos Arguiñano,** a small luxurious hotel in a beautifully restored stone palace, and for his popular restaurant there, with its floor-to-ceiling windows framing a glorious vista of the Bay of Biscay. Karlos keeps his food uncomplicated. "That's what brings diners back time after time," he told us. Indeed, I would return without hesitation for his *langoustine* croquettes; garlicky grilled monkfish on a bed of potato purée; or sensational lemon-glazed grilled flounder, accompanied by yet another fine *txakolí,* made here in Zarauz; and a tasting of his admirable tarts, *tortes,* and cakes.

Hotels

Karlos Arguiñano, Mendilauta 13, Zarauz; tel. 943.13.00.00; fax: 943.13.34.50

Hotel de Londres y de Inglaterra, Zubieta 2, San Sebastián; tel. 943.42.69.89; fax: 943.42.00.31

López de Haro, Obispo Orueta 2–4, Bilbao; tel. 94.423.55.00; fax: 94.423.45.00

María Cristina, Calle Oquende 1, San Sebastián; tel. 943.42.49.00; fax: 943.42.39.14

Parador Nacional El Emperador, Plaza de las Armas, Fuenterrabía; tel. 943.64.21.40; fax: 943.64.21.53

Restaurants

Lunch hours are 1:30–4 P.M., dinner 9–11:30 P.M.

Akelarre, Barrio de Igueldo, San Sebastián; tel. 943.21.20.52

Andra Mari, Elexalde 22, Galdácano; tel. 94.456.00.05

Arzak, Alto de Miracruz 21, San Sebastián; tel. 943.27.84.65

Baserri Maitea, Guernica-Forua; tel. 94.625.34.08

Casa Cámara, San Juan 79, Pasajes de San Juan; tel. 943.52.36.99

Casa Nicolasa, Aldamar 4, San Sebastián; tel. 943.42.17.62

Elkano, Herrerieta 2, Getaria; tel. 943.83.16.14

Guría, Gran Vía 66, Bilbao; tel. 94.441.05.43

Jolastoki, Avenida de los Chopos 24, Neguri; tel. 94.469.30.31

Karlos Arguiñano (see Hotels, above); tel. 943.13.00.00

Kresala, Txatxo Kaia 5, Lequeitio; tel. 94.684.02.84

Martín Berasategui, Loidi Kalea 4, Lasarte; tel. 943.36.64.71

Ramón Roteta, Villa Ainara, Calle Irún, Fuenterrabía; tel. 943.64.16.93

Sebastián, Muelle 14, San Sebastián; tel. 943.43.16.56

Talai-Pe, Puerto Viejo, Getaria; tel. 943.83.16.13

Zuberoa, Garbuno, Oyarzun; tel. 943.49.12.28

Tapas Bars

Tapas hours are usually 12–1:30 P.M. and 7–9 P.M. Reservations are not taken.

Alotza, Fermín Calbetón 7, San Sebastián

Casa Bartolo, Fermín Calbetón 38, San Sebastián

Bar La Cepa, Calle 31 de Agosto 7–9; San Sebastián

Or-Kompón, Calle del Licenciado Poza, Bilbao

Portaletas, Portu Kalea, San Sebastián

Bilbao's Cinderella Story

By Warren Hoge

∿

In a little publication I bought at the Guggenheim Bilbao bookstore, writer Francis Rambert notes that the museum, designed by Frank O. Gehry, is "a milestone in the history of contemporary architecture, as significant in its time as the Centre Pompidou in Paris or the Sydney Opera House. Emblematic of urban renewal, the titanium-clad museum symbolises the regeneration of Bilbao. No modern building has ever aroused such international enthusiasm, nor received such massive media coverage, putting the Louvre pyramid in the shade. Its success has come as a surprise: who would have imagined that one day Bilbao, then the fifty-sixth-ranking European city, would welcome this flagship of culture?" Bilbao was not only the fifty-sixth-ranking city but had been in economic decline since the 1970s. After the city's steelworks and shipyards closed, Bilbao's unemployment rate was nearly 30 percent. In 1983 the River Nervión flooded and devastated the Casco Viejo, triggering an ambitious urban plan to literally change the course of this proud Basque city. In 1989 a redevelopment plan was introduced, and it extended to the entire metropolitan area, comprising about thirty municipal districts. According to the same booklet, the redevelopment involved "demolishing and cleaning up the industrial sites along the *'ría'* [the river estuary], so as to free up areas of 'flat' land in a predominantly hilly setting." Bilbao's setting, surrounded as it is by some of the greenest hills you've ever seen, is stunning, and I've found it is insufficiently praised by visitors or by guidebook writers.

And so the Guggenheim Bilbao has indeed been welcomed, even if it has also been referred to as a "collapsed soufflé," "a cauliflower," and "a big fish at play" (see "Insider Bilbao: What You Need to Know," *Travel + Leisure,* February 1998, for more). To say the museum has also revitalized the city is a vast understatement: a survey conducted at the close of 2000 "reckons the spin-off from the museum to have been approximately 500 million dollars."

WARREN HOGE *is chief of the London bureau of* The New York Times.

Bilbao was once full of stay-away perils for the traveler. Its mood was melancholy, its skies gray, its buildings grimy, and its air foul from the blast furnaces along a stinking river that trafficked in floating objects. The gloom was deepened by the continual rain of what is statistically one of the dampest cities in Spain.

Today the only danger is dodging the aggressive street-sweeping machines that come humming and swishing around the corners of the spruced-up old town with its narrow streets and bay-windowed townhouses.

Shiny green and white sausage-shaped vehicles with exclamatory clean-up messages scripted on their sides, they symbolize the efforts the local people have made to turn their onetime eyesore of a city into a tourist attraction rivaling the more customary Spanish destinations like Madrid, Barcelona, Toledo, and the Andalusian triumvirate of Córdoba, Granada, and Seville.

It's a good thing, too, because people are coming in hordes to Bilbao, drawn by the world's most celebrated new building, the Guggenheim Museum Bilbao. It is not surprising anymore to see the standard European tour of London, Paris, and Rome include a detour to this city on the Nervión River near Spain's northern coast that has triumphantly shed its postindustrial smudge of soot.

More aware of Bilbao's old off-putting reputation than its new alluring one, my wife, stepdaughter, teenage son, and I added on a side trip to San Sebastián an hour along the coast as an enhancement to a weekend in the old Basque port. But we needn't have.

Museums and galleries have become the secular churches and cathedrals of the late twentieth century, and Bilbao today demonstrates the exhilarating truth that one of them, grandly conceived and combined with some ambitious urban planning, can restore a city's soul.

There is no sight in Europe more aesthetically stimulating these days than the Guggenheim Museum that opened here in October

1997, and not even the choruses of praise that the building has received can fully prepare you for the rush you feel at your own personal encounter with it.

It's a sight that makes people point, motion to their friends, utter "wow" sounds in all the languages that make up Bilbao's newly international street talk. It looms outsized at the end of a street of unremarkable masonry, a shimmering object that looks as if it just landed there after a trip from its own planet. With Jeff Koons's welcoming flower-bedecked *Puppy* standing benignly at its entrance, this is a friendly extraterrestrial that beckons you forward and puts an added skip in your approach.

From first glance to last lingering look, the building fulfills the promise that is bringing throngs to Bilbao. But what is less expected is the pleasure in store for your freshly educated eye once you've seen the museum and ventured out into the streets.

Bilbao's architects apparently didn't feel bound by the spirit of northern reserve that characterizes the rest of the city. A hint of the fanciful piles that crop up around the city is just four blocks away at the Plaza Moyua. It's the nineteenth-century Subdelegación de Gobierno, a Rococo concoction of red and black walls, turreted towers and fanciful facade ornamentation that looks as brash and self-indulgent next to the neighboring conventional office blocks as a dandy at a church social.

If you consider the behavior of pedestrians a telling measure of a city's personality, you will know what kind of place Bilbao is by the clutches of people at every corner waiting patiently for the light to change before they take a step forward. The residents drop this sense of civic obedience, incidentally, when they get behind the wheel. I saw several instances of cars sounding their horns angrily after barely missing a passerby, as if to say, "You won't be so lucky next time." Another tip on walking around Bilbao: Check out the sidewalks from time to time. There are lots of dogs.

A visit to the Guggenheim puts you in mind of walking. It is a building that you don't just visit but inhabit, marveling at its pillowy white interior spaces and then circling around outside to take in the play between its undulating worked titanium shell and the changing daylight. Chances are you'll wander back in the evening to see it then, too.

Even away from the museum, walking is a pastime full of rewards in Bilbao, and the broad leafy boulevard that dissects the city, the Gran Via de Don Diego López de Haro, is a good place to start collecting them. Flanked by statues at either end, the avenue is a busy commercial thoroughfare with brawny monumental buildings like the Edificío de Sota and the Palacio Foral and the whimsical Subdelegación along the way.

We strolled it our first night in successful pursuit of that just-arrived desire to fix the sense of place where you are. The grandeur of the street told us we were in a Continental city, and our destination, the Café Iruña, two blocks off the boulevard, was to set us firmly in Basque Country.

Hearty talk and laughter poured out of the *tapas* bars and cafés along the side streets leading to the Plaza San Vicente and the Iruña. A nymph with water pouring out of an amphora in her hands stands quiet sentinel over the little park while an animated group crowds around the bar of the Iruña drinking draft beer and the tart local *txakolí* aperitif wine.

The night we were there, a stirring ensemble of dancers from the south were stamping out flamenco tattoos on the small wooden stage to a wildly appreciative crowd of locals. Diners sat around tables at the base of the stage or off in curtained alcoves on a mezzanine level. Built in 1903, the café has a hint of fin-de-siècle decadence with walls and pillars covered in decorative tiles, a coffered ceiling of stucco panels, and wooden fans lazily ruffling the smoky air.

On hearing our accented Spanish, the manager José María

Gómez Valle laid out a tasting menu's selection of local hams and cheeses that upheld the Basque boast of being Spain's most revered food region—a reputation enhanced by the city's several restaurants with Michelin stars. In snatches of conversation squeezed into the brief silences between the clattering heels of the dancers. Mr. Gómez Valle said that he had many more visitors these days than he had before the museum was built and that many of them were Spaniards who until recently had considered Bilbao best avoided.

During our weekend visit, we remarked on the happy fact that so much of the tourist onslaught was Spanish and didn't therefore alter the character of the place the way a crush of foreigners might.

Midway along the Gran Via, at the Plaza Moyua, we came upon slinky glass and steel-ribbed constructions that looked like caterpillars burrowing into the pavement. They house the escalator entrances to the sleek new subway designed by Sir Norman Foster, the newly ennobled British architect who is the 1999 winner of the Pritzker Architecture Prize, widely viewed as the most prestigious in the field. Residents fondly call these additions to Bilbao's landscape "Fosteritos." The stations are attractions in themselves, brightly lighted tubes with spare high-tech platforms and staircases hung in space like javelins frozen in flight. It is design that embodies motion.

A great part of the success of Bilbao's planned renaissance is owed to the bold decision by the city's leaders to go after world-class architects like Lord Foster and Frank Gehry, the American creator of the new Guggenheim Museum. They have been aided in altering Bilbao's onetime reputation for periodic violence and public unrest by the unilateral ceasefire called last year by the Basque guerrilla group ETA. Even the old revolutionary graffiti has been washed away in the rise of civic pride.

A two-stop metro ride took us to the Casco Viejo, the old town with an area known as Siete Calles for seven criss-crossing streets that present an irresistible invitation to go exploring. Generations of artisans busied themselves creating the flourishes and designs that adorn the churches and monuments and townhouses along the shadowy streets of the Casco Viejo.

Trestlework lanterns hang from balcony corners, and second-story bowed windows, paneled in dark wood and covered by lace curtains that inevitably suggest mysteries within, hang out over the ground-floor level, almost nudging their counterparts from the other side of the street. Look up and you'll see an abundant collection of facade ornaments, weathervanes, scrolls, wreaths, coats of arms, emblems and ovals inscribed with the names of famous writers and artists who once lived in these houses.

Where the alleys spill out into open squares or onto the riverfront, edifices ranging from grand to gaudy await. The Teatro Arriaga and the Ayuntamiento, a government building, would be comfortable in a Paris square, the tilework Abando train station in a carnival arcade. The churches are austere, dark, and reverentially quiet. Many of the passageways along the river are colonnaded, framing fleeting figures darting about in the shadows on what are probably mundane daily errands, but who's to know?

Life in the old city revolves around the Plaza Nueva, an airy square ringed by fine apartments with well-tended flower boxes in their windows. There is no statuary in the square, only a broad central space and lengthy arched walkways that on Sunday mornings teem with men in the V-necked sweaters, woolen jackets, and floppy black berets favored in the Basque Country, milling about the hundreds of stands set up in front of the cafés that ring the square. This is a traditional part of Spain, and there are very few women about.

The variety of goods is typical of outdoor markets, but the content is different from that found along the Mediterranean coast of Spain. The harsh Atlantic climate governs here, and the things on offer are for people who stay inside. There are old books, magazines, collector's trinkets and pendants and pins, recordings and tapes, movie posters, stamps, coins, stones, rocks, goldfish, hamsters, pet turtles, and religious objects.

One of the most popular gathering places, the Café Bilbao, has dates on its storefront that touch on the city's descent and rebirth. "Fundado 1911," it says. "Rehabilitado 1992." The waiter who served us had pigeons flapping about his legs as he brought us our sandwiches and *txakolí*. Moments later cascading church bells sounded, and the birds swept up from the floor of the square and scattered away over the rooftops.

A lone flutist played in one corner, a raucous thrown-together band of fiddle, clarinet, trumpet, and accordion in another. More gentle music trilled on the side where hundreds of cages of canaries and parakeets and parrots were hung out for shoppers' inspection. Later that morning we went to the Plaza San Vicente to watch a staged competition held twice a year in Bilbao—a songbird contest.

As the match began, the birds' handlers spoke soothingly to their feathered charges at the edge of the grass and then hung the individual cages on numbered stakes, retreating prayerfully to the margins. Earnest men with clipboards then took their positions in the center and cocked their ears toward the thrushes as they struck up their tunes. It provided a lovely coda to a visit to Bilbao, a tough town that's found grace in the gentle touch of art.

The Museum

Guggenheim Museum Bilbao, Abandoibarra Et. 2, Bilbao; 94.435.9080. Open Tuesday to Sunday 10 A.M. to 8 P.M. (last ticket 7:30). Admission is valid for one day, allowing visitors to leave and reenter. Audio guides in English, about $4.

There is a café in the museum as well as a second cafeteria-restaurant with both outside and interior entrances. Reservations are required for the à la carte menu: 94.423.9333.

Bilbao Tourist Office (Bilbao Iniciativas Turisticas), Paseo del Arenal 1, 48005 Bilbao, 94.479.5760; fax: 94.479.5761

Lodging and Dining

Hotel Carlton, Plaza Moyua 2, 48009 Bilbao, 94.416.2200; fax: 94.416.4628. Double room about $160. About $93 on weekends.

Cafe Iruña, Jardines de Albia; 94.423.7021. Set lunch about $10; the menu changes daily. At dinner, first courses include Navarra-style bean stew ($5.70) and a selection of Iberian cured meats ($9.15). Main courses include preserved duck ($8) and steak ($13.15). Dessert, $2.30.

∽

editor's note: tours

This article originally concluded with suggestions for tour operators that featured Bilbao on northern Spain itineraries. As nearly all of the tour companies highlighted were among those I also recommend in *Informaciones Prácticas,* I decided not to repeat the listings; however, it would be a disservice not to once again mention Archetours, based in New York (see Tour Operators in *Informaciones Prácticas* for contact information). Founder and chief tour guide Gail Cornell was quoted as saying that she noticed a trend in tours to the Guggenheim Bilbao. "I see huge tour buses pulling up, herding people inside. They come in and then leave an hour and a half later; that's the whole experience." Archetours groups spend that long just looking at and admiring the museum's exterior. And Archetours groups don't call it quits after the Guggenheim: the Bilbao Museum of Fine Arts is another itinerary highlight, with its important collection of Goyas and El Grecos, as are other corners of Bilbao. As Cornell notes, it is essential to study the city and the region as a civic, architectural whole to fully understand the importance of the Guggenheim. A few tour operators recommended in the original piece include Dolmen Europe in New York (888-527-0110) and Petrabax (800-634-1188; www.petrabax.com).

Basques by the Sea

By Tom Brokaw

✧

editor's note

....

Bilbao may be the city of the moment in Northern Spain, but San
Sebastián—perhaps my favorite city in all of Spain—is no mere runner-up:
it has quietly been its lively and beautiful self, content to let neighboring
Bilbao and Biarritz steal the headlines. The following two pieces reveal the
special feel and matchless qualities of San Sebastián.

Tom Brokaw is anchor and managing editor of *NBC Nightly News*.
His typical choices for vacation destinations are those that require extra
effort to reach, like Mongolia. But San Sebastián, where he'd never been
before, was just the opposite. He told the editors of *Condé Nast Traveler*,
where this piece first appeared, that he "was seduced by everything."

E ven on a hot day San Sebastián has a certain early morning
quality. The trees seem as though their leaves were never quite
dry. The streets feel as though they had just been sprinkled."

That's Ernest Hemingway's Jake arriving in San Sebastián after
the seductress Lady Brett Ashley ran off with the bullfighter in *The
Sun Also Rises*. Jake wasn't there long before Brett summoned him
to Madrid to rescue her again from her impulses. Before he left San
Sebastián, Jake went swimming in La Concha Bay, took a nighttime
stroll around the harbor, drank cognac with a man following the
bicycle races, listened to music at an outdoor café, and commented
on the beauty of Spanish children.

Jake's brief sojourn took place seventy-five years ago, and I am
happy to report that his impressions are as fresh as the leaves on the
trees he described. However, the circumstances of my own summertime visit were not nearly so melodramatic. As a longtime fan

of jazz, and particularly of a gifted young singer named Diana Krall, I was attracted to the San Sebastián jazz festival, where she was a headliner.

My wife and I drove through the coastal mountains toward this place that the Basques call Donostia. We had little idea of it beyond the Hemingway references, guidebook descriptions of an ancient city elaborately rebuilt after a nineteenth-century fire, and its deeply rooted connection to the Basques, the proud and rebellious people of northern Spain. (San Sebastián is home to both Basque moderates and the militant underground movement, which sponsors terrorism, although that seems to be an intramural dispute with no visible effect on tourism.) Once there we were smitten by the festive Belle Epoque architecture—a delightful wedding cake of pink and white buildings, brass streetlamps, and graceful bridges over the Urumea River, which bisects the city. It is at once authentic and yet fantastic, a fairy tale for grown-ups. For a city so dependent on tourism, San Sebastián has managed to keep the conventional seaside resort tackiness to a minimum. It could serve as a model for other beach destinations, although they would be hard-pressed to duplicate the natural configuration of its shoreline. The broad, flat beaches east of the Urumea have a frontal exposure to the surf and winds of the Atlantic. To the west of the river is one of the most idyllic harbors anywhere, La Concha Bay, a shell-shaped protected sanctuary inviting swimmers and boaters alike.

San Sebastián's modern growth is along the eastern beaches, including a lively working-class and bohemian district and the handsome new Kursaal Performing Arts Center. The older city is wrapped around La Concha and set into the base of Monte Urgull, a substantial rock promontory on the harbor that is the backdrop for the city's liveliest neighborhood, Parte Vieja. The honeycomb of pavilions, *tapas* bars, and shops successfully mixes the ubiquitous T-shirt inventory with specialty items such as riding tack or cutlery.

By dusk the area is a festival of mimes, marionettes, jugglers, and magicians performing for the steady supply of polite, stylish Spaniards eating and drinking into the night.

From breakfast until late in the night, the Basque people are vigorous consumers of hearty and zesty fare, including a dazzling array of dishes drawn from the sea, such as a fish stew called *ttoro* and *kokotxas,* the treasured "cheek" of the hake, a common fish of uncommon appeal. Farmers in the surrounding mountain valleys provide lamb, ham, and vegetables, as well as an acclaimed Rioja, the region's red wine.

We wound up our San Sebastián stay with a preconcert dinner on the terrace of Akelarre at the end of Playa de Ondarreta, the secluded beach on the far western side of La Concha. The perfect punctuation to our visit was Diana Krall's interpretations of jazz divas from Sarah Vaughan to Peggy Lee on an improvised stage in the ancient courtyard of Santa María del Coro, the eighteenth-century cathedral at the foot of Monte Urgull. Appreciative Spaniards, young and old, filled the cobbled square and terraces; the surrounding walls were washed with a muted light show of burnished golds, greens, and reds. I thought again of Jake, cutting short his San Sebastián stay to go to Brett Ashley's side. I wondered, "Could she have been worth it?"

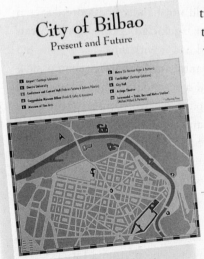

Hip to Be Square

BY RICHARD ALLEMAN

❧

RICHARD ALLEMAN is a contributing editor at *Travel + Leisure,* where this piece first appeared. He has written about travel and show business for more than twenty years for such publications as *Condé Nast Traveler, Gourmet, Buzz, Playbill,* and *In Style,* and was travel editor of *Vogue* from 1988 to 1994. Alleman is also the author of *The Movie Lover's Guide to Hollywood* and *The Movie Lover's Guide to New York* (HarperCollins) and *L.A. Man* (Warner Books). He holds an advanced degree in acting, and can sometimes be found on the stage in London or New York.

I recently suffered a minor professional *crise.* Perhaps it was battle fatigue brought on by too much time spent in the trenches of trendiness. All I knew was that after years of tracking down the newest, the latest, the hottest, and the coolest hotels, resorts, restaurants, and neighborhoods, I could not handle one more designer dinner, minimalist hotel room, or black-clad doorman with a catwalk attitude. Quite simply, I had had it with *hip.*

At the height of my disenchantment, I landed a plum assignment: Check out San Sebastián, a legendary beach town in the Basque Country of Northern Spain, where Spanish royalty summered in the nineteenth century and Hemingway characters chilled out in the 1920s. By all accounts, San Sebastián was still delightfully old-world—old-fashioned but not stodgy, stylish but not flashy, sophisticated but not pretentious. It sounded like the perfect antidote to my world-weary state.

But old habits die hard. I automatically check to see if there's a hip new hotel I should know about. Thankfully, there isn't. In fact, the town's two best places to stay have been around for ages. The grandest is the 1912 María Cristina, designed by Charles Mewes, the French architect who created the Ritz hotels in Paris and Madrid. Overlooking the Urumea River and next door to the Baroque wedding-cake Victoria Eugenia Theater, the hotel has opulent rooms and suites, a stunning marble-columned dining room, and a classy wood-paneled bar. (Despite the absence of Philippe Starck chairs, the María Cristina is still a favorite of celebs like the Rolling Stones and Robert De Niro; it's also where the A-list stays during the annual San Sebastián International Film Festival.) But it is fully booked at the time of my visit, so I drop down one star and get a room at the Hotel de Londres y de Inglaterra. Built in 1887, it's not quite as grand as the María Cristina, but it makes up for that with its stellar location on a four-mile sweep of the famed La Concha beach.

The porter opens my curtains to reveal a magnificent view of the beach and the Bay of Biscay, anchored by mountains at either end, a lumpy green island at the center. It's almost midnight by the time I unpack, but I have no interest in sleep. Instead I head down for a stroll along the elegant La Concha esplanade, with its white wrought-iron balustrade. Despite the hour, the walkway is teeming with well-dressed families, couples in love, in-line skaters, backpackers. On the beach itself, young people are having impromptu cocktail parties. Not far from the hotel I come upon a pretty park with formal gardens and wispy tamarisk trees where street musicians and poets are performing. A vintage carousel is still running, and its handsomely caparisoned camels, lions, pigs, and horses, as well as mirrored rocking carriages, are delighting children and their parents. The merry-go-round music is strangely muted, and the whole scene is surprisingly mellow, almost surreal, like a scene from a Fellini film. Hip? Hardly. *Hip* implies aggressive, hard-edged, exclusive. Judging from this brief nighttime glimpse, San Sebastián is something else entirely.

In the morning I hit the beach before exploring the town. On a summer day La Concha is a kind of upmarket Coney Island, packed with chaises, beach umbrellas, and people cheek by jowl. The sea has very small waves and the swimming is easy, but the tides are deceptively fierce and frequently soak unsuspecting sunbathers, including me. The best thing about the beach is the view of San Sebastián, its lineup of fin-de-siècle apartment buildings backed by lush mountains.

Some of the city's finest architecture lies in what is called the New Town, much of which actually dates back to the 1800s. Carefully laid out on either side of the broad Avenida de la Libertad, this compact quarter is heaven for lovers of grandiose architecture. Enchanting buildings sprout towers and turrets, domes and steeples, and gravity-defying, glassed-in miradors, balconies that command spectacular views of the town below. Styles range from columned Neoclassical to mansard-roofed French Revival to Art Nouveau—especially notable along Prim and Reyes Católicos Streets—with elaborately carved wooden doorways, stunning stained-glass panels, and unusual ceramic-tile touches. In the New Town, plazas and loggias, vest-pocket parks and gardens, constantly surprise.

If the New Town is known for its architecture, San Sebastián's old quarter, the Parte Vieja, is all about eating. Most of its tall, skinny buildings with wrought-iron balconies have a restaurant, café, or *pintxos* bar (pronounced "pinchos," it's Basque for "tapas") at street level. *Pintxos*-hopping is a major pastime here, and while certain bars are long-standing favorites, it's hard to go wrong. Before taking off on my trip, I consulted a food-critic friend who advised me not to drive myself crazy trying to dine in every good restaurant in town. "There are simply too many," she said. "You're much better off hitting the *pintxos* places in the Parte Vieja. Just check out what's displayed on the counter. If it looks good, it probably is."

I take her advice, sampling sublime smoked ham, sweet

anchovies, and an extraordinary cod omelette at Bar La Cepa. Around me waiters are pouring *txakoli,* the gutsy local white wine, in the traditional manner—holding the bottle three feet above the glass. I move on to Casa Gandarias for shrimp ceviche, ultra-light fried squid, and the best potato salad I've had since my Aunt Fanny's decades ago in my Pennsylvania Dutch hometown. Virtually everyone eats standing up, but even in these noisy, smoky, raucous surroundings, there's something serene, almost Japanese, about the beautifully presented little dishes.

Although you could happily spend a week here dining on bar food, San Sebastián has some of the finest restaurants in Spain, many of which serve innovative Basque cuisine. Realizing that I am about to move into the kind of dangerously trendy territory I'd hoped to avoid, I nonetheless book a lunch table at San Sebastián's most renowned dining room, Arzak. I'm prepared to be dazzled (read: intimidated) by its three Michelin stars, but Arzak puts me at ease with its small—just ten tables—and simple dining room. The staff of twelve works as seamlessly as a well-rehearsed *corps de ballet.* The meal is a nonstop exercise in self-indulgence.

I choose the tasting menu, which leaves me in the capable hands of the proprietor, Juan Mari Arzak. It begins with three *amuse-bouches:* a tiny potato crêpe, slivers of tender veal cheek wrapped in caramelized pineapple, and a few spoonfuls of lettuce soup with almond oil and a single clam (a classic Basque dish). Then come the appetizers: delicately fried crawfish in a pimiento and tomato purée, and squid with onion marmalade, sprinkled with toasted corn. My main dishes include smoked pompano, followed by squab with caramelized skin accompanied by a cluster of mini-asparagus. The cheese plate is a work of art, with slabs, dabs, and shavings of five local specialties. The selections become stronger as you move around the plate, the last so pungent that it burns my eyes. Dessert, if you're up for it (and you are), is a chocolate pudding with lemon sorbet on top and cassava paste on the bottom. Just when you think it's over, a tangy soup, made from a nutlike fruit called chufa, arrives with a dollop of vanilla ice cream.

After the meal I chat with Arzak, whose family has owned the house that his restaurant occupies for more than a century. His grandparents ran a tavern here; his parents, a catering operation. Arzak opened his current restaurant in the 1970's, after stints with Paul Bocuse and Pierre Troisgros. His dishes are firmly rooted in Basque culture. "We're constantly experimenting, of course, but all the products, and often the recipes, are from this region. That onion marmalade takes five hours to prepare, just as it did when my grandmother made it."

Another of San Sebastián's major-league chefs is Martín Berasategui. His is not a small family business, however, since he currently oversees six restaurants in the area, as far afield as the café at the Guggenheim Museum in Bilbao, an hour's drive away. Berasategui's most famous establishment is in Lasarte, where he can usually be found in the kitchen. It is some fifteen minutes outside San Sebastián, in a suburban villa surrounded by gardens. But after my mind-boggling lunch at Arzak, I decide to cool it and have dinner at Berasategui's vast glass-walled dining room in San Sebastián's new Kursaal Performing Arts Center.

At Restaurante Kursaal Martín Berasategui, with its blond-wood floors and beige tablecloths, I'm afraid I've finally landed in the kind of cutting-edge place I've been trying to avoid. But the views of the wonderfully flamboyant Victoria Eugenia Theater and the Kursaal Bridge—a Modernist monument whose iron-clad white pillars support gigantic Christmas-tree-ornament globes— quickly take me back to the San Sebastián I've been falling in love with. The food is also extraordinary: garlic stir-fried squid, warm lobster salad with asparagus "noodles," classic Basque hake (a white fish served in a parsley sauce). The dessert sampler is a delight: six tiny servings of such delicacies as apricot ice cream and piña colada soup.

It's the first night of the city's annual jazz festival, so after dinner I wander around the Kursaal Center and find myself surrounded by gospel singers, a Basque Dixieland orchestra, and the Barcelona Big Latin Band. In addition to the music, I am struck by the Kursaal itself. Designed by Spanish architect Rafael Moneo, it resembles two enormous Noguchi lantern lamps—especially at night, when the lights inside glow through its thick opaque-glass sheathing. San Sebastián's answer to the Frank Gehry–designed Guggenheim Bilbao, the two-year-old Kursaal has been wildly controversial. Many locals felt that their city did not need a dramatic new building to put it on the map, particularly one that jarred with its Belle Epoque essence. But as the Barcelona Big Latin Band begins blasting a salsa number, I can find no fault with this fantastic structure by the sea. If this is as close as San Sebastián comes to really being on the cutting edge, I'm not complaining.

San Sebastián is a city of festivals. Early August brings a month of classical music, called the Quincena Musical, with big concerts in the Kursaal and smaller performances in churches, convents, and plazas. But the largest and best known of the city's bashes celebrates the cinema. Now in its forty-ninth year, the 2001 San Sebastián International Film Festival kicks off September 20 and runs through the 29th. The participants are kept secret until the last moment, but last year's event brought Michael Caine, Robert De Niro, John Waters, Pedro Almodóvar (who first came into the international spotlight when his early films screened here), Morgan Freeman, Ang Lee, and artist-filmmaker Julian Schnabel (who is married to a woman from San Sebastián and has a vacation house in the area).

With little of the hype that surrounds the film orgies in Cannes, Berlin, and Venice, San Sebastián's festival is extremely popular among celebrities, who find they can explore the city without being hassled. Nonetheless, star stories abound. Orson Welles famously pigged out on *pintxos*. Claudette Colbert called San Sebastián "one of the loveliest resorts in Europe" and was particularly entranced by its fin-de-siècle lampposts (a miniature version of which is used as the festival's Donostia prize statuette). And any movie buff knows that in 1989 Bette Davis made her last public appearance here. Despite the fact that she was dying, the frail eighty-one-year-old film diva—perfectly made up and decked out in designer gowns—did all her interviews on time (chain-smoking, naturally) and managed to keep her star power operating right up to the glittering final ceremony at the Victoria Eugenia, where she was presented with the Donostia, the festival's lifetime achievement award (after the Basque name for San Sebastián). The next week she took a turn for the worse and was flown to the American Hospital in Paris, where she died.

Another star associated with San Sebastián is the legendary couturier Cristóbal Balenciaga, who was born in the Basque fishing village of Getaria, about a half-hour west of the city. Balenciaga went to Paris in 1937 and became one of the twentieth century's most acclaimed fashion designers, known for his restrained, elegant style and his fine fabrics and finishings.

With its staircases, steep cobblestoned streets, and strange tunnels, Getaria makes an idyllic day trip from San Sebastián. Both in town and down at the tiny harbor, restaurants grill fresh fish right out front. The designer's humble birthplace at No. 12 Aldamar has probably changed little in the past hundred years. Up on the town square, one storefront has an amazing display of the local hero's gowns and accessories. By 2003, however, the Balenciaga Foundation, headed by Paris designer Hubert de Givenchy, plans a permanent museum in the Getaria mansion that belonged to the local marquesa, who recognized Balenciaga's talent when he was still in his teens.

Meanwhile, San Sebastián's newest museum is dedicated to another local legend—the sculptor Eduardo Chillida, whose work can be seen at museums around the world and whose monumental steel *Comb of the Wind* rises from the rocks at the far end of the Bay of Biscay. The museum, which opened in September, is ten minutes from San Sebastián, in the mountain town of Hernani. Here a beautifully manicured hillside is studded with some forty Chillida monoliths. At the center of the property, a sixteenth-century Basque farmhouse has been redesigned by the artist to display his smaller pieces: jigsaw sculptures of marble, steel, and iron; Mayan-like stone blocks; translucent alabaster statues; and delicate hanging paper "gravitations," which are somewhere between a collage and a mobile.

"I spoke to the house," the seventy-seven-year-old sculptor says, "to see what it wanted. It needed light, so I opened it up and made it more of a cathedral than a house." Chillida encourages those who visit his "cathedral" to do something almost unheard of in an art museum: "You can touch the sculptures," he says. "Sculptures must be touched." That says a lot about the earthiness of the man and this place.

When I return from the museum to my hotel, there's a fax from my editor in New York. Seems a new designer hotel has just opened in the south of England. Could I cover it? Very hot, very hip. Fortunately, after a week of unwinding in the comforting time warp of San Sebastián, I'm almost ready to hit the trenches once again.

The Facts: San Sebastián

To reach San Sebastián, most travelers fly to the spectacular new Santiago Calatrava–designed Bilbao Airport via London, Madrid, or Paris. From there San Sebastián is about an hour away by taxi, rental car, or bus. It's also just a half-hour from the French resort of Biarritz.

Hotels

María Cristina, Calle Oquendo 1; 800-937-8461 or 943.424.900; fax: 943.423.914; doubles from about $245.

Hotel de Londres y de Inglaterra, Calle de Zubieta 2; 943.440.770; fax: 943.440.491; doubles from about $105.

Aida, Calle Iztueta 9; 943.327.800; fax: 943.326.707; doubles from about $43. An attractive nine-room pension with lots of style and ridiculously low rates.

Restaurants

Arzak, Alto de Miracruz 21; 943.278.465; dinner for two about $142.

Restaurante Kursaal Martín Berasategui, Avenida de la Zurriola 1; 943.003.163; dinner for two about $74.

Restaurante Martín Berasategui, Calle Loidi 4, Lasarte; 943.366.471; dinner for two about $130.

Kaia, Calle General Arnao 4, Getaria; 943.140.500; dinner for two about $75. Getaria's top fish place—reservations are a must.

Iribar, Calle Nagusia 34, Getaria; 943.140.406; dinner for two about $54. A good bet for freshly grilled fish.

Pintxos Bars

Bar La Cepa, Calle 31 de Agosto 7; 943.426.394; *pintxos* for two about $10.

Casa Gandarias, Calle 31 de Agosto 25; 943.428.106; *pintxos* for two about $10.

Museums

Fundación Cristóbal Balenciaga, Parque Aldamar 3, Getaria; 943.327.180.

Museo Chillida-Leku, Caserío Zabalaga, 66 Jauregui Barrio, Hernani; 943.336.006.

Museo di San Telmo, Plaza Zuloaga 1; 943.424.970. Excellent displays and installations documenting Basque and San Sebastián history, housed in a sixteenth-century Dominican convent.

Festivals

San Sebastián Jazz Festival, 943.481.179; www.jazzaldia.com.

Quincena Musical, 943.003.170; www.quincenamusical.com.

San Sebastián International Film Festival, 943.481.212; www.sansebastianfestival.ya.com.

Don't Miss

A hike up **Mount Urgull,** a mountain park at the edge of the port (it's a great way to walk off all those *pintxos*), followed by a thalassotherapy treatment at **La Perla** (Paseo de la Concha; 943.458.856), a large spa facility right on La Concha beach.

Originally published in *Travel + Leisure*, May 2001. © 2001 American Express Publishing Corporation. All rights reserved. Reprinted with permission.

Biblioteca

The Basque History of the World, Mark Kurlansky, Walker & Company, 1999. By the time you have reached the end of this book, you will know I am an enormous fan of Mark Kurlansky. (Two of his books I particularly rave about are *Cod* and *Salt,* highlighted in the *¡Buen Provecho! biblioteca*). Just as he did so successfully in those previous books, here he wonderfully weaves other stories—culinary, political, literary, and economic—into the history of the Basques. Kurlansky reminds us that the Basques are a puzzling contradiction, as they are Europe's oldest nation without ever having been a country. One of his most pertinent observations is that "the Basques are not isolationists. They never wanted to leave Europe. They only wanted to be Basque. Perhaps it is the French and the Spanish, relative newcomers, who will disappear in another 1,000 years. But the Basques will still be there, playing strange sports, speaking a language of *k*s and *x*s that no one else understands, naming their houses and facing them toward the eastern sunrise in a land of legends, on steep green mountains by a cobalt sea—still surviving, enduring by the grace of what Juan San Martín called *Euskaldun bizi nahia,* the will to live like a Basque." In unerring and exhaustive Kurlansky style, this book is positively *esencial*. If you only have time to read one, this is it.

Boundaries: The Making of France and Spain in the Pyrenees, Peter Sahlins, University of California Press, 1989. Though it has an academic title and is published by an academic press, this book is not dull or heavy going. It's really quite brilliant and thought-provoking, and as it addresses national identity, it's also quite apropos to our times. Sahlins relates that the Pyrenees border between France and Spain was set, if arbitrarily, as long ago as 1659. Over the next two centuries the border became solidly fixed. Sahlins deftly examines how the valley of Cerdanya (which lies in both Spain and France) in particular was perceived by both governments and how they defined jurisdiction over people versus territory. Within the context of the Pyrenees, Sahlins's book is nothing less than a microcosmic study of the modern nation-state as well as the nature of national identity. Highly recommended.

Postcards from the Basque Country: A Journey of Enchantment and Imagination, Beth Nelson, Stewart, Tabori & Chang, 1999. This hard-to-categorize hardcover book is lovely, unique, quirky, offbeat, and very personal. It's not a work of fiction, however; rather, the author introduces the reader to the Pays Basque (mostly) through pages of her diary, which are filled with musings on travel, the Basques, and her own life. Each page is an individual collage, filled with paper ephemera such as stamps, old postcards, maps, timetables, and photos cut out of magazines. "From Biarritz to Bilbao, the Bay of Biscay is the heart of a Basque," Nelson notes. And about travel, she writes, "you don't really long for another country, you long for something in yourself that you don't have or haven't been able to find." I'm fond of this little book, and it's a nice souvenir (and a great gift, too).

Tratuak: Bilboko Alde Zaharreko Saltegiak (Dealings: Shops in the Old Quarter of Bilbao), Museo Arqueológico, Etnográfico e Histórico Vasco, 2001. Published to accompany an exhibit of the same name, this nicely printed paperback catalog is published in Basque, Spanish, and English and is thoroughly engrossing. I thought it rather serendipitous to discover that an exhibition was mounted on this subject because as I was walking from my hotel in the Casco Viejo to the Museo Vasco, I was struck by how appealing the shop windows were, and how beautiful the architectural details were. Truly, I've never been in any city—Paris, Milan, and Rome included—where the shop windows were so stylish. Amaia Basterretxea, directress of the Museo Vasco, notes in the catalog that the aim of the exhibit was "not to look at the history of trade in the area but instead to look at how traditional shopping coexists with the new concept being gradually imposed, which commonly involves franchise. There are today fewer of those shops in which the owners offer personalized, familiar attention, shops that were known more for their personnel than for their products," an observation that is all too familiar in the United States. But for the residents of the Casco Viejo, it must be all relative, because nearly every shop I frequented seemed to be family owned, with the staff personally greeting every person who walked in the door, doling out kisses and hugs to some. Basterretxea continues, "Today shops seek to attract the client via an image, one in which we participate as mere spectators and in which the shop window and its composition are of as much moment as the stock itself, if not more." The book features a chapter on "Shop Signs in the City: Fragments of a History" and includes color photographs of shop windows, goods for sale, promotional material, and an archive of photos of businesses in Bilbao dating from the 1890s. Though this exhibit is long over, a visit to the Museo Vasco is recommended, and so is this book. It's also one of the very few books at the museum with any English text.

~Euskadi—Basque Country with Pleasure: Everything Worth Seeing, Visiting and Knowing is a publication (in English) of the Basque tourism department. It's unusual to come across such a thorough, well written, and useful tourism publication. It's really more of a magazine, with good maps, historical outlines of the region and individual cities, a calendar of special events, and nature highlights. I especially like the lists of nature preserves, twenty-six fabulous beaches on the Bay of Biscay, reservoirs, and western valleys, as well as suggested itineraries. There are also eight pages of practical information. Hotels and restaurants are not included in the magazine, but with an accompanying guidebook you need nothing else to introduce you to the beautiful and varied region of the Basques.

Request a copy from any of the Spanish tourist offices in North America or from the Basque tourism website (www.basquecountrytourism.net), or pick up a copy at any local tourist office when you arrive.

The Basque Series

Readers truly interested in the Basques simply must get to know the Basque Series, published by the University of Nevada Press in Reno. If you are curious, as I initially was, about why this series—with over forty titles—is based in Nevada, it is because great numbers of Basques have emigrated to Nevada, New Mexico, California, Arizona, Utah, Idaho, Oregon, Washington, Wyoming, and Colorado. An entire ethnographic display at the Museo Vasco in Bilbao is devoted to this theme. Robert Laxalt relates in *The Land of My Fathers: A Son's Return to the Basque Country* that when he and his wife were living in St.-Jean-Pied-de-Port, his cousins lived on the Street of the Americans. They were puzzled by this because they thought they were the only Americans in the village, but they soon learned that the villas on that street were built in the 1920s and 1930s by Basques who had lived in the United States and worked as sheepherders for as long as ten or twenty years in the mountains and deserts of the American West. "The Basques who had come back with money and built their villas consorted mainly with each other in the bistros and on village feast days, sharing mutual experiences in towns named Reno, Fresno, San Francisco, Los Angeles, among others."

And so the University of Nevada Press is a perfect home for these wonderful books, and I encourage anyone interested in learning more to read at least a few of the titles in this series. They publish an eighteen-page catalog showcasing the series (readers may request one by contacting the university at Mail Stop 166, Reno, NV 89557-0076; 877-682-6657; www.nvbooks.nevada.edu). There are too many titles to list here, but the selection is quite remarkable. Just a few titles representing the full range of the list include *Chorizos in an Iron Skillet: Memories and Recipes from an American Basque Daughter; Basque Dance; A Travel Guide to Basque America: Families, Feasts & Festivals* (this would be particularly great, I think, for immersing yourself in the Basque culture before and after a trip); *The Basque Poetic Tradition;* several dictionaries (Basque to English and the reverse); *The Basque Diaspora; The Guernica Generation: Basque Refugee Children of the Spanish Civil War; The Basques, the Catalans, and Spain;* several bilingual children's books; and the complete works of Robert Laxalt, who passed away in 2001. I think it is fair to say you won't find a better selection of Basque fiction and nonfiction—published in English—anywhere.

I have not read every title, but of those I have, I especially love *A Book of the Basques* (Rodney Gallop) and *The Land of My Fathers: A Son's Return to the Basque Country* (with photographs by Joyce Laxalt) and *Sweet Promised Land,* both by Robert Laxalt. In *The Land of My Fathers,* Laxalt alternates traditional Basque maxims and beliefs with recent stories and events that illustrate the old tales. Among them are:

~"My cousin Eliza claims that the Basques have a masochistic nature. When it is time to work, the Basques approach it as though it were a flagellation. It is as if they are punishing themselves. Eliza feels that the Basques want to sweat and toil in the old way. *By the sweat of your brow,* she claims the Bible says. If you are working for someone, you must give it your all, or it will not be money honestly earned. But I know they are not punishing themselves. For them, work is a cleansing. The Basques derive pleasure from it. They emerge from work as if stepping out of a bath. There are smiles on their faces when a laborious task is done. When it is time to play—be it at jai alai, handball, or the running of the bulls—they will play as hard as they worked. They will think of nothing else."

~"I learned then what I always suspected. The Basques are not vindictive, but neither are they a forgiving people."

~"The Basques don't have much use for those who don't do their duty or fulfill their obligation to family. These ne'er-do-wells are relegated to inscrutable silence and oblivion."

~"Among the Basques, to ask for a written contract implies a lack of trust. A man's word is a thousand times stronger because it commits his honor. The written law is intended to bring order to society, but the Basques already possess that with unwritten tradition."

ESPAÑA 20+5

CABALLO CORREOS

F.N.M.T. 1989

SANTA IGLESIA CATEDRAL
SANTO DOMINGO DE LA CALZADA
LA RIOJA

•

Agradecemos su aportación de 300 Pts. para
mantenimiento de personal, iluminación y limpieza.
Y esperamos que la visita le haya resultado grata.

VISITA A LA IGLESIA, CLAUSTRO Y DEFENSAS

23619

Oficina de Información Turística
Santo Domingo de la Calzada (La Rioja)

La Rioja
TE DEJARÁ HUELLA
Gobierno de La Rioja

PARA BIL

BARCELONA

PONGA N

correos
ESPAÑA 100
F.N.M.T.

Navarra y La Rioja
(Navarre and La Rioja)

"To go eastward from Navarre to Catalonia is to move from a primitive country of stolid, hardheaded, jota-dancing peasants to a province of maritime wealth and thrifty, business-minded entrepreneurs . . . Pamplona, picturesque capital of Navarre, lies in a magnificent setting at the foot of the Pyrenees. Only twenty-eight miles to the north is the famous pass of Roncesvalles where Roland and Charlemagne's rear guard made their legendary stand against the Spaniards. It is Alpine scenery all the way: pine trees, wild roses, cascades of water, and lonely peaks."
—John Crow, SPAIN: THE ROOT AND THE FLOWER

"Crossing the Sierra de Cantabria south of Vitoria, you enter the dry, southern Mediterranean climate so friendly to the Tempranillo grape. There's nothing subtle about this change; from the Herrera mountain pass, the road quickly plunges almost 5,000 feet to the wine-growing flatlands. Just before descending, you can survey this scene from the impressive gray peaks of the 'Rioja Balcony'—looking down at Laguardia, Logroño, Haro, and all the Rioja wine towns."
—FODOR'S UPCLOSE: SPAIN

Pamplona in July:
¡Viva San Fermín!

By Penelope Casas

∽

editor's note

The province of Navarra is bordered by the French Pyrenees along its northern edge and extends to the River Ebro in the south. It is quite beautiful, especially in the mountainous north (H. V. Morton wrote that "the road from Pamplona to Roncesvalles is twenty-eight miles of Switzerland"), and its capital city—and undoubtedly its most famous—is Pamplona.

I did try once to go to Pamplona for San Fermín, but as a why-call-ahead? type of college student, I naturally had no place to stay. (In more recent years I have had the pleasure of visiting Pamplona—*not* during the fiesta—and found it quite charming.) Here's one of my favorite San Fermín accounts, one of the few that doesn't dwell on drunken debauchery. Though it was written twenty years ago, in 1983, the fiesta of San Fermín still "lives on undiminished," as the writer noted then.

It's worth reminding North Americans interested in running with the bulls that the experience does not come without risk. In 1995 a twenty-two-year-old American was killed at San Fermín when he was knocked down by one bull and then gored by another. At that time *The New York Times* reported that officials in Pamplona said tourists too often arrive with little or no knowledge of the dangers of running with the bulls, insufficient training, too little sleep, and too much alcohol. There are, on average, about ten to twelve injuries each year during the celebration, and of those injured, most are foreigners, the largest proportion of them American. An American government official was quoted as saying that Americans seem to be the nationality "with the most problems" at the festival and that "Europeans and Spaniards see the running as a show or spectacle like bullfights and leave the performance to the professionals. Americans come here with the image of *The Sun Also Rises* and just don't realize how dangerous it is and how easy it is to trip up." (The young American who died was the first foreigner to die at San Fermín and the thirteenth to die there since 1924.)

Penelope Casas, introduced previously, received the 1983 Spanish National Prize of Gastronomy for her book *The Foods and Wines of Spain*.

It is exactly noon on July 6, and Pamplona is relatively quiet but alive with expectation. An enormous crowd has squeezed into the small square facing the Ayuntamiento, Pamplona's city hall, and can hardly suppress its excitement. The mayor appears on a balcony and declares, "Fellow citizens, ¡Viva San Fermín!" then once again in Basque, "¡Gora San Fermín!"

A rocket fires and Pamplona explodes with delirious merriment, as if a charge of electricity had suddenly jolted the town. And the week-long madness of San Fermín, so vividly related in Hemingway's Sun Also Rises, has begun.

"I can't believe it's 1983 and we're in Pamplona for the running of the bulls," says an American friend who is visiting San Fermín for the first time, for surely the fiesta is an anachronism, completely out of step with life in the 1980s, and a custom that should have disappeared with Hemingway's Lost Generation. But the truth is quite the contrary. The fiesta of San Fermín lives on undiminished and is, if anything, more vigorous than ever.

Eighty-year-old Gerónimo Echagüe, a native of Pamplona whom everyone knows simply as "Gerónimo," has run the bulls every day of the fiesta since 1914 and lives his life in anticipation of the following year's sanfermines (an informal way of referring to the fiesta). Mr. Echagüe is less than five feet tall and considerably less fragile than his slightness implies; his hair is only touched with gray.

"When July arrives, my blood boils," Mr. Echagüe says. "It's been like this since that day decades ago when I met the great torero El Gallo. He rumpled my hair and said, 'Hi, kid.' That's when the mania struck me.

"Oh, yes, I have been injured many times and have spent months on end in the hospital," Mr. Echagüe continues, "but even as a child I loved danger. God has watched over me. Today I am master of Pamplona and one day my life story will appear. I'll call it 'The Tragic and Bloody Memoirs of San Fermín's Best Runner.'"

For Mr. Echagüe and the people of Pamplona *los sanfermines* is much more than the running of the bulls, the phenomenon that most excites tourists, writers, and photographers. It is a fiesta that neither began nor ended with Hemingway and for many Pamploneses is a deeply felt religious event.

Although the origins of the fiesta as it is celebrated today are somewhat cloudy, it seems that several centuries ago there were three separate events—a regional fair, a bullfight festival, and a religious holiday—that gradually merged into one. Perhaps this helps to explain why San Fermín is such an odd mixture of religion and secularism, of solemnity and joyfulness.

San Fermín is the patron saint of Pamplona, capital city of the northern province of Navarra in the Basque Country. The saint's image, accompanied by a solemn group consisting of the bishop and church and city officials, is paraded through the streets of the city to applause and cheers. San Fermín is worshipped in the chapel bearing his name all during the holiday week, and each morning a small statue of the saint is put at the place where the bulls begin to run. Participants heartily sing to the saint, punctuating their words by gesticulating vigorously with rolled newspapers (carried to wave at bulls that get too close) and practically demanding that the saint deliver them from danger. This is not an awe-inspiring saint but a friendly figure, to whom Pamploneses turn throughout the year for help and comfort.

It was fifty-seven years ago that Ernest Hemingway introduced the rest of the world to this fiesta, exciting thousands of foreigners to test their machismo against the bulls, and Hemingway remains a powerful presence in Pamplona. A street, the Paseo de Hemingway, is named for him; a huge bust of the writer stands in front of the bullring, and at the cafés and restaurants he frequented Pamploneses and visitors still reminisce about the days when the great writer held court. To this day many young and middle-aged men still try to emulate him, sometimes in physical appearance but more often in testing their prowess by running the bulls, even though those who knew Hemingway insist that he never participated in the morning runs.

Curiously, the influx of so many foreigners has little effect on the overwhelmingly local nature of the fiesta of San Fermín. On the afternoon of July 6 the town of Pamplona takes to the streets and casts aside everyday clothes for what has become the uniform of the fiesta—white shirt and pants, a long, red, fringed sash knotted low at the waist and a small red scarf rakishly tied around the neck. Although sneakers are the most common footgear, many still wear the traditional white espadrilles laced with red. Children—even infants in strollers—echo their parents' dress with the most charming results. Nor are animals and city statuary excluded; they, too, sport red scarfs.

Cafés and bars, especially around the Plaza del Castillo (the center of festivities), are crowded and lively, as they are continuously for the duration of San Fermín. Dozens of local bands circulate through the streets playing the typical *riau riau* music of Navarra. The beat is lively and infectious and few can resist the temptation to get up and dance. Suddenly the plaza is a mass of bobbing heads with hands held high. As one band passes, followed in Pied Piper fashion by those still dancing, another arrives, and the dancing continues. You will probably never walk down any street in Pamplona at any hour for these eight days and not see someone dancing.

In between bands a parade of giants (each is sort of a one-person float) and "big heads" (papier-mâché heads on people) gracefully twirls through the streets, to the accompaniment of rat-tat-tat drums and the haunting sound of the oboelike *chistu*, a local instrument. The giants are as tall as the balconies of the houses and elegantly clothed in brightly colored velvets and brocades. They too become a common sight as the week progresses.

The first day of the fiesta is also a time to touch base with old friends (most visitors to Pamplona have been to the town many times before), to cast off all worldly cares, and to prepare the body and mind for the week to come. Few sleep much the first night; the streets pulse until dawn, and even those lucky enough to have hotel rooms cannot escape the din below their windows. But who cares to sleep? Morning brings the first running of the bulls, and the anticipation keeps weary bodies from rest. San Fermín is an endurance test and a time to perfect the art of catnapping. A full night's sleep is out of the question for the next week.

At six-forty-five A.M. on July 7, the day of San Fermín (it has only been an hour or two since the city settled down for the night) the people are rudely awakened by crisply dressed marching bands playing invigorating reveille. Nobody minds, for this is the alarm clock that signals the approaching *encierro,* or the running of the bulls.

We roll out of bed, hastily dress in San Fermín garb, and head toward the cobbled street, Calle Estafeta, where the bulls will run. Storefronts are boarded, barricades in place across side streets, and revelry in full swing, as police good-naturedly clear the street. Anyone obviously intoxicated is removed, as are all women; both groups are expressly forbidden to participate. (Some feminists had appeared on television the night before, protesting this gross curtailment of their rights.)

Pamplona's police chief, formally dressed in a brass-buttoned uniform and immaculate white gloves, and the city's socialist mayor—in shirtsleeves—make their way along the route, and once they are satisfied that all is in order, a rocket is fired to warn of the bull's release. Even before the rocket sounds, an enormous group of runners has already begun to sprint up the street and is resoundingly jeered by the crowd.

There is no danger at this time, but most will return home claiming to have run the bulls. A smaller group soon approaches, running with more urgency, but still some distance from the bulls.

Then the real runners appear, dashing faster than they ever thought possible, for the bulls are right on their heels. It is now a matter of life and death.

Six huge bulls, bred for fighting and accompanied by steers who point the way, finally come into sight. They are determinedly staring straight ahead and intent on staying together. This is unknown territory, and they are just as scared as the runners.

In a flash this amazing scene has passed, and first-time visitors soon realize that they have absorbed little of what has just happened. They are anxious for the next day's run, to sort out all the pieces of what could be the beginning of a lifelong fascination with San Fermín.

If all goes well, the run ends within two or three minutes with the bulls safely in their corrals behind the bullring, and the firing of another rocket to indicate that the run is over. If this signal fails to come quickly, trouble has occurred along the route. (A good runner listens for the rockets and keeps track of the number of bulls that have passed.) Usually the run transpires without serious injuries, but if a bull becomes separated from the herd, he strikes out in fear at anything around him. Such was the case on the second day when a native of Pamplona and a young lawyer from Boston were caught by the horns of Caracolito, a bull that would fight bravely that afternoon. (Both men, after several days in the hospital, recovered.)

Attention shifts to the cafés of the Plaza del Castillo, where the morning events are excitedly discussed over big cups of strong coffee. Runners show up, clutching their rolled newspapers like badges of courage; relief from the early morning tension is palpable. American aficionados like to gather at the Cafe Txoko, and they hasten to offer their congratulations to such well-known American runners as Matt Carney, who was written about by James Michener in *Iberia;* Joe Distler, a teacher of English literature and proprietor of the Riverrun restaurant in TriBeCa; and white-haired and heavily bearded Jim Corbett, returning to San Fermín after open-heart surgery. ("Where else are you going to be in July?")

Although there are events in Pamplona to keep one going day and night, midday is the best time to catch up on lost sleep. Then back to the cafés or better still to the dozens of bars and taverns along Calle Estafeta for a lunch consisting of *tapas,* a Spanish specialty that might include typical Pamplona dishes like shrimp dipped in batter and deep-fried or simply grilled, *chistorra* (sausage), *pinchos* (combination appetizers served on toothpicks), croquettes, fried squid, and fresh anchovies.

There is a relative lull in activity until the excitement starts to build as the six-thirty P.M. bullfight approaches. The bands of *las peñas,* clubs from Pamplona and elsewhere in Navarra that prepare all year for the week of insanity in San Fermín, pass through the Plaza del Castillo playing what has become the familiar rousing *riau riau* music, and in their wake thousands enthusiastically proceed to the nearby bullring. The San Fermín fiesta can be appreciated and enjoyed on many levels, but it is clear after a day or two in Pamplona that this holiday is primarily the Festival of the Bull and that this noble creature is the basis for the fiesta's tremendous vitality and worldwide appeal.

For years controversy has raged over bullfighting, and it will probably never abate. Anyone attending a *corrida de toros* should do so with an open mind and an understanding of the event. In Pamplona, of course, the bullfight is just another aspect of the general madness of San Fermín—it is very Spanish to juxtapose gaiety and the threat of tragedy in a single fiesta—and watching the public at the bullring is a show in itself.

The stands pulsate with exuberant dancing, ear-splitting music, lusty singing, and rhythmic swaying. Bags of flour shower on the crowd, cooled by sudden spritzes of champagne and seltzer, and huge picnic baskets of food and drink are happily consumed during the death-defying spectacle. Remains of food and drink rain on the unfortunate *torero* or *picador* who fails to live up to expectations.

The Calle Estafeta is a crush of people for the rest of the evening. Such crowds seem oppressive at first, but it soon becomes apparent that everyone is under control and there is little to fear. (The city's rules read: "The young of Pamplona express their joy in many ways, but always within the restraints of proper behavior and respect for others. Some foreigners who do not know our customs mistake these good times for libertinism, and if they do, they will be severely punished.") By midnight many bands make their way to the Plaza del Ayuntamiento where hundreds dance themselves into a frenzy until the wee hours of the morning.

For eight full days the events of San Fermín are repeated. Exhaustion, of course, settles in by the end of the week, mixed with the sadness that San Fermín must end and the routine of everyday life return. The last evening, July 14, is one of lament. Many of the cheerful white costumes are changed to somber black ones, and the haunting song *"Pobre de Mi"* ("Poor Me") is sung in dirgelike measures.

By the next morning San Fermín has vanished into thin air—no more crowds, no more merriment—but participants are already making their plans for the following year. They send postcards to friends or organize parties on key dates of the year—January 1, February 2, March 3, April 4, May 5 and June 6—only to reunite once more on that magical date, July 7, when Pamplona once more explodes with joy—as it has done unfailingly for centuries.

La Rioja

BY PETER TODD MITCHELL

❧

editor's note

Though this article was written in 1987, it remains my favorite piece on
La Rioja. I think it provides an excellent overview of the history, beauty, and
food and wine (of course) of the region. It was in this piece that I first learned
of the village of Laguardia, one of my favorites in all of Spain. As I did not
receive confirmation that this piece would be featured here until the eleventh
hour, I was unable to check if all of the hotels and restaurants mentioned are
still in operation. Travelers will have to investigate on their own, though I
can confirm that the outstanding restaurant Marixa, in Laguardia, is happily still thriving (and worth a detour).

PETER TODD MITCHELL lived in Spain and wrote frequently about
Spanish—and other destinations—for many years for *Gourmet,* where this
piece first appeared.

The Ebro is Spain's greatest and most legendary river. It tumbles
from its source in the crags of Cantabria, where the peasants
call it "the mountain renegade," for it steals their water and rushes
with it across the entire country until, with a majestic sweep, it
empties into a wide delta on the Mediterranean. Its tributaries are
many; and one of them, the Rio Oja, gave its name to a territory
so lush and fertile that it has been dubbed Spain's Garden of Eden.
In the Middle Ages this verdant strip was crossed by Europe's most
thriving route of pilgrimage, the road to Santiago, and the multi-
tudes on their way to the shrine of Saint James further assured
prosperity.

The area known as La Rioja bestrides the Ebro and includes
stretches often disparate in culture: from the Rioja Alta in the green

hills of the north, where the best of the wine is produced, down to the Rioja Baja, where the waters open out onto the wide plain that leads to Aragon. There the river feeds the fields that produce fruit and vegetables for much of Spain. Happily for the traveler there is an excellent *parador* at each end: one at Santo Domingo de la Calzada, not all that far from Burgos; and another near the Aragonese border, in the ancient Roman town of Calahorra. Between these two well run stations is a multitude of sights, souvenirs of a medieval past long predating the arrival of vintners from Bordeaux to perfect the wines that have made Rioja a household name. The modern pilgrim can enrich his journey with the best of these wines and delicious regional food as well.

The Parador Nacional Santo Domingo de la Calzada greeted us on our first night, as it does many who drive up from Madrid. The little town around it has been sheltering travelers since the eleventh century. A *calzada* is a causeway, and the one here was of prime importance; transferred by King Sancho to the southern bank of the Ebro so that it would pass through his territories, it was the main pilgrim route to Santiago. Santo Domingo was a hermit who felt compassion for the pilgrims as he watched them struggling to ford the Rivers Oja and Navarrete and then continue their trek with scant refuge or safety. Because he was a builder, first of roads, then of bridges, and finally of hostels, he was able to do something about this. At the start he had to beg funds for his work from princes, but soon they realized that his interests bore some relation to their own, and his projects were handsomely endowed. His largest hospice was here and was much expanded in later centuries, finally to become a *parador*, which explains the imposing Gothic halls of the interior.

Across from the *parador* is the cathedral, one of the earliest Gothic churches in Spain and filled with carvings related to the miracles of Santo Domingo. One of them has been commemorated for us not in stone but "live." The story behind this concerns a boy who, stopping here en route to Santiago with his family, was hanged for theft. He had rejected the advances of the innkeeper's daughter, and she had cleverly slipped a piece of silver into his knapsack and then denounced him as a thief to the authorities as he was leaving town. His parents returned from Santiago to find their son still on the gibbet, not dead at all and demanding justice, while the judge was about to tuck into a double roast—a cock and a hen. He said that the boy's story sounded about as likely as his dinner's standing up on the plate to crow, which it then did. The boy was thus cut down and released, and an elaborate cage was put in the cathedral to house a cock and a hen (which are now rotated every fortnight to save wear and tear). From then on every pilgrim left here with a feather in his hat.

The Santo Domingo *parador* is particularly well run, with a good kitchen and rooms that are comfortable—in the back quiet and in the front overlooking the cathedral square with all its comings and goings. The number of rooms is limited, however, so one should reserve ahead, particularly as Santo Domingo is a unique vantage point from which to visit the sights of the Alta Ebro, and the wine capital of Haro is across the river but only half an hour away.

It goes without saying that the wines both at the *parador* and in Haro's varied restaurants are choice, but one soon realizes, by a glance at the menus or a quick stroll for window-shopping, that grapevines form only part of La Rioja's wealth. The vegetables and fruits are of such high quality that the region thrives on their export: tinned, preserved in glass jars, or fresh. More than once when my friends have been loading their cars with cases of Rioja wine they have thought me demented to be hoarding jars of amber peaches; succulent crimson peppers; green beans marinated in garlic; and jams of cherry, apricot, or plum. But I have the privilege of keeping house in Spain, and these provisions last me the winter through.

This horn of plenty empties, too, into the local cuisine, which winds like the Ebro through four popular traditions: those of Navarre, Castile, Aragon, and the Basque Country—with a fifth influence, that of the Arab occupation, in the realm of sweets (such as the favorite, *rosquillas,* light doughnuts flavored with anise). *A la riojana* usually means that the area's sumptuous red peppers play some part, with either chops, roasts, or chicken. Artichokes are used with lamb, and beans are used not only in variations on the French cassoulet but also to accompany quail, as in *codornices con pochas,* one of the best dishes of the *parador.* On our first evening we supped lightly, for en route we had lunched heartily on roast lamb at Casa Florencio in Aranda del Duero. Because ninety-five percent of the asparagus exported from Spain hails from La Rioja, we decided to begin with a token portion. We followed this with *huevos a la riojana* (eggs scrambled with tomatoes and decked out with fried triangles of bread and thinly sliced local sausage) and plump strawberries for dessert. For wine we chose a red Tondonia of López de Heredia, even though the house wine is excellent.

The next morning we set out to visit Haro, the bustling capital of Rioja Alta. Along the roads leading to Haro one sees the main reason for the town's wealth, the surrounding vineyards, many with familiar names heavily posted and often with *bodegas* inviting the traveler to sample vintages by the glass. The older part of town leads up to the church of Santo Tomás, with a splendid chiseled Renaissance portal in the style known as *plateresque* (like the work of a silversmith), and the many seigneurial residences around it bear testimony on their facades to the noble houses of Haro: the Paternina, the Bezara, the De la Cruz. Right below is the Plaza de la Paz, a charming square with a bandstand, cafés, and store windows that tempt one with both wines and the best of the local preserves (my favorite is Juan Gonzalez Muga at number 5). At Calle Santo Tomás 3 is one of the town's two best restaurants, rather forbiddingly called Beethoven II, a name that belies its good roster of dishes *a la riojana* in an attractive setting. Near the Plaza de la Paz, at Calle Lucrecia Arana 17, is Terete, a restaurant so famous that it needs no decor at all—and in fact has none. There's a flight of battered stairs, checkered tablecloths, and efficient service from elderly ladies, and that's it. But its *cordero lechal* (milk-fed baby lamb) is considered the best around, and people flock from afar to partake of it. There are few trimmings. A meal begins with a small spate of *tapas: morcilla,* the Spanish answer to *rillettes; alubias con chorizo,* a sampling of beans with sausage in a Riojan version of cassoulet; and *picadillo,* a spicy concoction based on marinated pork and potatoes. The lamb itself is roasted to perfection in wood-burning ovens. The wine of the house is red, and a creamy *tarta mantecada* (butter cake) ends one's feast.

Of all the places that one can visit from Santo Domingo, my favorite is San Millán de la Cogolla, with its two monasteries, Suso and Yuso, set in the same idyllic valley. Suso, the older of the two, is perched in a grove of pines, and only the church remains: a fascinating combination of Visigothic and Mozarabic, which survived the Moorish occupation. The stone sarcophagus of the saint is a masterpiece of sculpture, his mourners on it including a dog on a leash—and quite appropriately, as Saint Millán was a shepherd whose miracles brought pilgrims from all over La Rioja. Some of his deeds bordered on folklore (such as stolen horses remaining paralyzed till set free). Soon he joined Saint James of Compostela as a fellow *matamoro* (killer of Moors), and in more than one battle they were seen riding together through the sky on their white chargers.

Saint Millán is immortalized in the poems of Gonzalo de Berceo, born in the village that announces this valley and raised at Suso, where he became the first poet of renown to write in Castilian. He used the language to suit his odes, and the lyric beat of his ballads was to appeal to many a poet of our time. For subject matter he had material aplenty, for he lived in an epic age when Spain, on the brink of a Saracen world, was waging its own Crusade at home, and when a pilgrimage to Compostela was equal in the eyes of the Church to one to Jerusalem. The Galician shrine became a holy city for Christians soon after the remains of Saint James (Santiago) were found in a field lighted by blazing stars (Compostela). The wars against the Arab invaders were to last for centuries, often taking a terrible turn, particularly when fanatic Muslim sects declared a jihad and destroyed everything in their path including Compostela itself, which was leveled in the tenth century by the Córdoban leader al-Mansūr. It was rebuilt, and its pilgrims always stopped off in San Millán to pay their respects to the second *matamoro*.

In the valley below, the monastery of Yuso, a larger sanctuary, was soon established and became the "Escorial de La Rioja," as the medieval buildings were swallowed up by an immense Herreresque structure with cloisters and Baroque interiors. Yuso's background of mountains and fir trees reminds one of the great abbeys of Austria, and thanks in part to its prodigious libraries it became an elitist center of learning from which the Castilian language emerged in its finest form. Many who might have been equal in the eyes of God were not up to the standards of Yuso; Santo Domingo de la Calzada was turned away for his lack of literacy. Still among Yuso's treasures is the wondrously carved late Byzantine ivory casket that held the remains of Saint Millán and worked miracles of healing for sundry supplicants.

Many an illustrious scholar complained of the icy halls of Yuso in winter, but the cold seemed far away in the sunshine that warmed our road to Nájera, where in the early Middle Ages the kings of Navarra held court. The hills and fields around Nájera are now laden with grapevines and lie tranquil; but if one were to close one's eyes, the ring of battle and the thunder of cavalry charges might still be heard, for many a victory was paid for here with heavy cost. The earliest was the legendary Battle of Clavijo, fought against the emir of Córdoba in 845, when Santiago first descended from the heavens on his white steed, bearing a flag with a bloodred cross, and slew sixty thousand infidels with his own sword. In 1367 came the Battle of Nájera, won by King Pedro the Cruel (aided by the Black Prince and an English army) and lost by the king's very Christian brother, Henry of Trastámara, pretender to the throne.

Here the wars between the nobles and the royal houses of Navarra, Castile, León, and Aragon had raged for centuries and would continue on until Ferdinand married Isabella and they united Spain. If the castles seen on these heights are in ruins and if the wines produced on their lands are not château-bottled, it is thanks to the determination of that royal couple to make themselves secure against a rebellious aristocracy. Long before Louix XIV met the same problem by building Versailles, the Spanish monarchs were leveling castles and settling their nobles in whatever the capital was at the time—Toledo, Valladolid, or Madrid—where they were allowed palaces galore but fortified towers nevermore.

Nájera has retained its calm, its old mansions, and the trees along the banks of the Najerilla. Its church of Santa María la Real has been a magnet for travelers ever since it was founded in the eleventh century by King García IV. The king was pursuing a partridge in open country and followed the bird into a cave, where he found it nestling at the feet of a statue of the Virgin. As in many other miraculous instances, the image had most likely been hidden centuries before to escape Saracen raids; and here it was soon to have plenty of company, for around the entrance to the cave was built a pantheon of nobles of Navarra, guarded by two formidable soldiers in stone. It is reached by way of a splendid Flamboyant Gothic cloister and a spacious church that harbors later tombs, including the dukes of Nájera and the counts of Haro. The most eloquent is that of Doña Blanca, a Navarrese queen. The cliff that shelters the cave cuts right into the old part of town, which is a delight for strolling, with plenty of cafés where one can cool off with a glass of wine and *tapas* before pushing on to Logroño.

The road to Logroño passes by Navarrete, a large village that can be a severe test for those whose fear of overweight baggage on planes wars with their love of unusual ceramics. This has always been the center for a kind of white glazed ware on which the sparkle of the white has been offset by the reddish clay of the base, much in the style that Picasso was to use years later; and stands that sell it line the road. The town itself, an old one, is dominated by an enormous church, the Asunción, where the sacristan will throw light on a glorious *retablo* at the main altar and some of the best grillwork that I have seen.

I had been told more than once by Spanish friends that Logroño, the capital of La Rioja and its largest city, was a prosperous business center and of small interest otherwise. I had been told wrong and was first enlightened by the peerless Walter Starkie in his book *The Road to Santiago*. The famed turreted bridge built by Santo Domingo no longer crosses the Ebro, but the old quarter of Logroño rises from the riverbank with a flourish of church steeples and retains the same silhouette that the town had when it served as gateway from Navarra to Castile. The two streets through which the pilgrims streamed on their way to Burgos are still there, as are the four major churches where they worshipped. These churches can be visited in chronological order, the oldest facade being that of San Bartolomé, with its remarkable Gothic sculptures. Nearby is the cathedral, Santa María la Redonda, its two Baroque towers somehow blending in with its Gothic architecture; and not far away is the finest tower of all, the spire on Santa María del Palacio, which many find unequaled in Spain. For Baroque one must visit the colossal statue of Saint James on his charger over the door of his own church, Santiago, on the Rúa Vieja.

These old streets, tall and narrow, have remained medieval and are lined, as they always have been, with *tabernas;* and so the pavements literally reek of wine. In the midst of this Rabelaisian background rises the palace built by the marquis of Covarrubias in the eighteenth century, a spacious town house the lower floors of which have been turned into Logroño's most opulent restaurant. La Merced (Marqués de San Nicholás 109) is decorated with considerable imagination, its rooms varying from the more intimate ones near the entrance to the airy, pale green salon, surely once a patio, where we chose to lunch. Here immaculately attired waiters function in a world of plush, marble, and potted palms that is in distinct contrast to what is going on in the world right outside; and there were enough brass burners for the flambéed dishes being served around me to bring back distant memories of the Pump Room in Chicago.

A perusal of the menu (accompanied by chilled glasses of La Ina and crisp shrimp croquettes) showed us that one could either opt for international cuisine (smoked salmon and Chateaubriand with béarnaise) or, as we did, take advantage of both the regional dishes and the time of year: fresh peas *salteados* (cooked with diced cubes of local ham), scrambled eggs with wild mushrooms and chopped green baby garlic, stuffed peppers *a la riojana,* or hake in a sauce of peppers. We started with a *menestra de verduras,* in which a host of vegetables play a part—some boiled, some fried—including green beans, cauliflower, leeks, peas, artichoke hearts, and carrots; and an order of stuffed artichokes au gratin. Our baked salmon was accompanied by tender green asparagus, and we finished with another celebration of the season, sumptuous raspberry tarts. A white Marqués de Cáceres accompanied the meal—as did a certain amount of scrutiny of the other diners on my part.

At some tables the ladies would easily have passed as stylish enough for Madrid's Calle de Serrano and the men wore discreet tailored suits. At others the entire family, including in-laws, had obviously come in from the country, the men retaining their head-gear (jockey caps with sunshades) and the women in rural attire. All received the same courteous service, but they surely received more or less the same bill, too. La Merced is by no means cheap, and the lands around Logroño must be far from poor to keep the restaurant as full as it was. It would be a good idea to reserve (tel: 22.11.66) before the palace's weighty doors are flung open at one-thirty for lunch.

The Calle de La Merced leads up to the more modern areas of Logroño, passing by the very worthwhile art museum, the Museo de La Rioja, where the contents of disused convents and churches—*retablos,* sculpture, and some fine paintings—are expertly displayed in an eighteenth-century mansion. The Merced also leads up to the Calle del Peso, which runs alongside the central market and offers plenty of restaurants *not* in palaces. The best of these are El Fogón at number 6 and an agreeable Art Nouveau nook, Cachetero Comidas, a bit farther on. The main square of Logroño is a spacious plaza called the Espolón, with fountains and promenades and faced by a colonnade enlivened by the better cafés, where one can enjoy an apéritif. For those who wish to spend the night in town, I found the Hotel Los Bracos on a treelined street to be the most gracious and remarkably quiet.

We decided to cross the Ebro and head about 20 kilometers northwest to spend the night at Laguardia, which we had been told is one of the most perfect medieval hill towns around. It is situated in the southern corner of Álava, a region that extends up into the Basque Country but is known here as La Rioja Alavesa. Laguardia could be a twin to Cordes in France or Volterra in Tuscany when it comes to its position, surging quite suddenly from its plain and still surrounded by gates and walls. Upon entering—on foot only—one finds a world of squares, streets, churches, and fountains that has not changed for centuries. It is ideal for wandering, which we did, taking in the churches of Santa María de los Reyes, with one of Europe's few remaining polychrome portals, and of San Juan, Romanesque and built into the city walls. By the time we had finished lingering over our wine under the arcades of the main square, we discovered that the hotel that we were counting on no longer existed and the only one extant, the Marixa, was full. The people of Álava are notorious for their courtesy, however, and after practically turning Laguardia upside down to find us a room, they located a hostel in the hills where we were able to make a reservation.

Before heading off to our hotel, we dined at the Marixa on outstandingly good food. Javier Santamaria, the proprietor and chef, obviously has more than a nodding acquaintance with French cuisine; thus, although our meal was *riojana*, it was far more sophisticated than we had expected as we settled into his sparely decorated blue-and-white dining room overlooking the valley below. As a *tapa* we sampled the flavorsome pork pâté, and for entrées we chose a tangy *salpicón de mariscos* (vinaigrette of seafood with a whiff of Galicia) and an order of *pencas* (the white stalks of Swiss chard) with slices of ham and cheese and a cream sauce that was both rich and subtle. Perfect roast lamb, basted with a sauce of white wine and garlic, served as our main course; and to accompany it I asked for some potatoes *a la riojana*, cooked with oil, vinegar, garlic, and pepper and usually served as a *tapa*. The word *tapa* supposedly derives from the verb *tapar,* which means "to stop or hold back" (one's appetite in this case), but I see no reason why *tapas* shouldn't enhance a meal rather than just delay it. For dessert we indulged in a deliriously good specialty of the Marixa: *melocotones rellenos,* peaches filled with an ice of vanilla, chopped nuts, and orange liqueur and served with a creamy caramel topping laced with orange juice. Our wine was a superlative red Solar de Samaniego '78, chosen in part to honor the local literary celebrity Félix María Samaniego, the *fabulista* who was born here and whose fables were the Spanish answer to Lafontaine's.

Our hostel turned out to be an isolated country hotel on the road to Vitoria, set in the shadow of the Sierra de Cantabria at a point where the lower slopes of the mountains are littered with dolmens of the Iron Age. One would think that a river and a few miles would make scarce difference in climate and character, but a change could be felt even before the clear skies of the early evening had been obscured by a heavy mist that rolled through the valley at night. This was the very weather that once favored the witches who plagued these mountains since time immemorial. At one point their number so grew that Philip II sent the Holy Inquisition to wipe them out; but they survived its stakes and torments and prevailed long enough to surface in the paintings of Goya. There one sees them dancing around bonfires on the Eve of Saint John, with a goat-headed Satan as their guest of honor.

The following morning the haze slowly lifted, and we were able to set off for some of the towns that might greet travelers who come into La Rioja from the north. The nearest, Viana, was another fortified citadel, suspended in air on a small plateau, and I insisted on circling all the way to the top to visit the tomb of that falcon of the Renaissance Cesare Borgia, brother to Lucrezia, perpetrator of a thousand crimes, and the model for Machiavelli's *The Prince*. Viana does him proud, as he lies clearly marked in a place of honor in front of the cathedral. The Borgias were of course Spanish, but to die here fighting a local count made a sad end for a leader of men who aimed to master all of Italy. Viana turned out to be more than worthwhile for its own sake, being a methodically planned town of the fifteenth century just like Ferrara, where Lucrezia reigned as duchess.

Our favorite town of this region north of Logroño is Estella, which is definitely within the borders of Navarra; but in these lands, if you walk more than a few leagues in any direction, you can find yourself in another province. Estella, with its myriad monuments, is compressed into a rocky opening along the River Ega, so that its churches, palaces, and plazas are either crowded alongside the rushing torrent or perched like toys on the dizzying heights above it. The day on which we passed through was a Navarrese holiday, and the entire population was dressed in white with red sashes and the cafés along the Ega were mobbed. We lunched well on fish at Rochas, Príncipe de Viana 16, and turned south to rejoin our river, the Ebro.

By the time we reached it at Calahorra, the river had emerged into the agricultural lowlands that lead it to Aragon, a landscape not unlike parts of the American West, with rocky hills, mustard and rust in color, presiding over a plain verdant with orchards. Its crops are exported from Calahorra, the capital of Rioja Baja and already populous in the days of the Romans, who made it one of the most thriving cities on the road from Tarragona to Cantabria. Statues to Roman consuls, Quintilian and Prudentius among them, line the esplanade that leads to the Parador Nacional Marco Fabio Quintiliano, which turned out to be modern, spacious, and air-conditioned, a combination that can serve one well when the wind is blowing from the southeast. Our rooms looked over the valley, so the calm was complete; and a light dinner of gazpacho, grilled trout, and sangría made with red Paternina was proof enough of a well-run kitchen.

An evening of comfort gave us the energy to set out the next morning on a festive road of Baroque art, beginning here in Calahorra. The old town is an enclave unto itself, quite separate from the section around the *parador,* and the cathedral is on its edge, right off the main road to Saragossa. It is not to be passed by.

One wonders where the wealth came from to turn its lofty Gothic interior into such a treasure trove of statuary, *retablos,* and paintings. The element of luck has surely played a part, for the cathedral has escaped the hurricanes of destruction brought on by Bonaparte, the Carlist Wars, and the Spanish Civil War. As we were leaving, the doors of the sacristy opened and a procession issued forth of choirboys in white followed by the archbishop and an entourage of prelates in red. The mirrors and gold of the chapels reflected banks of candles, and the organ was being played at a volume majestic enough to finish off the first act of *Tosca.*

As one heads south, leaving behind the stony structures—Romanesque or Gothic—of the road to Santiago, one enters an exuberant world more akin to Mexico or Peru. White interiors burst with Baroque angels and contain that same realm of gold, plaster, and tropical polychrome that was to be transported to the Americas by the style known as *churrigueresque.* No church better displays this style than San Miguel Arcángel in Alfaro, where a sober brick exterior belies the exuberance of color and carving that awaits one inside. Alfaro was our last town in La Rioja, but we followed the Ebro on its course through other provinces, leading to such unexpected wonders as the fascinating medieval city of Tudela and the dreamlike monastery of Veruela. In Aragon the terrain becomes parched, and, seeing the farmers trying to deal with a dour providence, one realizes how great has been La Rioja's fortune: to be a land that has always flourished with such ease. It was only a final act of bounty that sent the vintners down from a Bordeaux that had been devastated by phylloxera to establish fresh fields for new vineyards. But that is another story.

Hostelries

Hotel Los Bracos, Bretón de los Herreros 29, Logroño, La Rioja; 22.66.08.

Parador Nacional Marco Fabio Quintiliano, Calahorra, La Rioja; 13.03.58.

Parador Nacional Santo Domingo de la Calzada, Santo Domingo de la Calzada, La Rioja; 34.03.00.

Restaurants

Casa Florencio, Arias de Miranda 14, Aranda de Duero, Burgos.

Beethoven II, Calle Santo Tomás 3, Haro, La Rioja.

Cachetero Comidas, Calle Laurel 3, Logroño, La Rioja.

El Fogón, Calle del Peso 6, Logroño, La Rioja.

Terete, Calle Lucrecia Arana 17, Haro, La Rioja.

La Merced, Marqués de San Nicolás 109, Logroño, La Rioja.

Marixa, Sancho Abarca 8, La Guardia, La Rioja.

Rochas, Principe de Viana 16, Estella, Navarre.

The *Next* Reign in Spain

By Bruce Schoenfeld

~

editor's note

Most articles written about La Rioja digress immediately or eventually into a numbing recitation of wine labels, points and ratings, and wine industry lingo. While the outstanding wines of La Rioja certainly do deserve to be rated as among the best in the world, and do dominate daily life in this part of Spain, I believe travelers deserve to read pieces that offer more depth, like this one.

BRUCE SCHOENFELD is an Emmy Award-winning television writer who contributes frequently to *Wine Spectator, Saveur, The New York Times Magazine, Outside,* and *Gourmet,* where this piece originally appeared. He is also the author of *The Last Serious Thing: A Season at the Bullfights* (Simon & Schuster, 1992) and is currently working on a book featuring former tennis player Althea Gibson (to be published by HarperCollins).

The Rioja region looks like something a fourth-grader would draw. Improbable towns are perched precariously on top of hills that jut from the gentle landscape; around them are fertile flatlands, laid out in Crayola purples and browns. To the north, a series of mountain ranges buttresses the Rioja from the sea. To the south, a mesa seems to stretch all the way to Madrid. This is farming country, and people here eat and drink what they farm. There are no Michelin stars in the Rioja, no celebrity chefs with television shows, yet its unadorned cuisine is among the best in Spain, and its wines have been internationally famous for more than a century. It is the part of Spain where bullfight aficionados pay attention to the bulls, not the matadors who try to tame them with a performer's art, and that same emphasis on raw materials has carried over to its cuisine. Seasonal vegetables, free-range lamb, and fish trucked in from the Bay of Biscay, an hour north, are the star attractions here. The best a chef can do is stay out of the way.

But the Rioja is changing. Frank Gehry's Guggenheim Museum transformed Bilbao from Spain's Pittsburgh into one of Europe's top attractions. The new headquarters he has designed for Marqués de Riscal, in Elciego, looks like a giant titanium butterfly, or perhaps a flamenco dancer in midtwirl. The Rioja has never seen anything like it. The word is that Martín Berasategui, with his three Michelin stars in the Basque Country, will run a restaurant inside it. And Santiago Calatrava, whose Milwaukee Art Museum addition is America's edifice of the moment, has designed a winery for Bodegas Ysios, a new project of the winemaking giant Bodegas & Bebidas. The tourists are coming, as well as restaurants that cater to them and chefs eager to win stars. So are more of the international-style wines that most Rioja wineries have recently started turning out with Robert Parker's palate, not respect for tradition, in mind. I figured I had better eat the delightfully simple meals of the Rioja and drink its fragrant and elegant wines while I still could.

Not long ago I joined Maria José López de Heredia and her sister, Mercedes, at Terete, a restaurant in Haro that dates to 1877. Both in their early thirties, these women represent the generational change that is sweeping through the Rioja as the old chefs and winemakers and grape growers who came of age in the Franco years cede their businesses to their sons and daughters. The López de Heredias are one of Spain's most traditional wine-producing families, and they have been eating at Terete for generations. Maria José loves this kind of unpretentious restaurant, but she also loves the high-concept gastronomy of the Basque Country and Catalonia.

"I go to Arzak with my family," she says, referencing Spain's most exalted restaurant, one of the few to have earned three Michelin stars. "And they criticize it."

"I don't like Arzak," Mercedes says from across the table. Mercedes is elegant and feminine, almost cartoonlike in her Spanishness. She would have been at home in Hemingway's Spain, discussing the merits of bullfighters like Manolete and sipping a traditional Rioja. She isn't at home at Arzak, a true temple of modern gastronomy.

Mercedes wears hoop earrings and a chartreuse suit and a perfectly painted face, a look straight out of an Almodóvar movie. Maria José dresses in jeans and work boots, like the law student she was for five years in Bilbao. Together with their two brothers, they help run the R. López de Heredia Viña Tondonia winery for their father, Pedro. To me, they represent both halves of the Rioja's coming generation.

Maria José is the international face of the winery, traveling to Norway, the Netherlands, Japan. Mercedes, who recently got a degree in winemaking, continues to learn the craft from her father. She monitors sales figures, sources wood for the barrels, and does the payroll, looking immaculate all the while. They both supervise the harvest each year, dressed in the blue zip-up overalls trash collectors or astronauts might wear. One brother, Julio César, manages the vineyard land, and another, Rafael, does marketing. It's a true family business, the scale of which you hardly see anymore in the Spanish wine industry.

Our conversation is interrupted by the arrival of a *menestra* of carrots, artichoke hearts, mushrooms, and green beans that have been coated in a flour and egg batter and fried to just the beginning of crispness. There's some olive oil involved, and perhaps lamb stock in the sauce, but I have no time to inquire. Our waitress, whose great-grandfather founded Terete, drops off the food and is gone without a word. No unnecessary pleasantries. In this part of the world, that's typical, too.

La Rioja is Spain's oldest and most renowned wine region. Until lately, Riojas weren't made to appeal beyond the Spanish border. They've always had more oak than ripe fruit, more balance than power. They have been available around the world, but wherever you were when you pulled the cork on a Marqués de Riscal or a López de Heredia or a Muga, it tasted like Spain. Suddenly, though, highly extracted, fruit-driven wines designed for the American palate are emerging from this region.

These new wines, nearly all of them made by established wineries, are sold for high prices in double-thick bottles. Many are well crafted, but most of them lack the singular personality of a great Rioja. Riscal's Barón de Chirel was the first of them. It was made in the late 1980s as a means of restoring the winery's reputation, which had flagged when quality slipped. Imitations from other wineries now fill the shelves of El Corte Inglés, the national department store. The odd Latinate names of many of these wines— Gaudium, Aurus—announce their novelty to the Spanish public.

"Many of these wineries are owned by corporations," Mercedes says. "They have shareholders and bank loans, and they have to keep selling their product. We own our winery, we own our land, and we have loyal customers. We make wines the way we want to, we age them as long as we want to, and we don't care about what anyone else is doing."

"I personally think that what Riscal has done with the wine and the winery is good marketing," Maria José says. "I congratulate them. But should we all do that? No. There's still, in Spain, the search for authenticity. There are people who want those deep, dark wines that taste like Cabernet, but there are also enough people who want wines made in the old style."

She takes a sip of what anyone would consider an authentic wine, a López de Heredia 1942 Viña Bosconia Gran Reserva. The López de Heredia style has always been to strive for elegance and balance, mature traits in life and in wine, though that means sacrificing the immediate kick of ripe red fruit that so many wineries covet. As a result, López de Heredia wines don't get exalted reviews, but they drink well just about forever.

I wonder about the future of some of the new-style wines, built sleek like sports cars. Will they ultimately become the standard in the Rioja? What will happen to the cuisine here, and to places like Terete, when the flashy restaurants open? Will anyone still want *menestra* or a simple lamb chop? I look at Mercedes, with her eyeliner perfectly applied, and then at Maria José, a traditionalist in the denim clothing of a modernist. It occurs to me that these two women constitute my last line of defense.

Although some wineries here own vineyard land and others don't, nearly all of them buy grapes from several of the hundreds of small, independent farmers scattered throughout the region. That's because the Rioja has so many microclimates and other meteorological curiosities that a superb harvest in one place can mean disaster a few miles away. Most major Rioja wineries are owned by conglomerates and must produce millions of bottles annually. Too much is at stake to rely on a few plots of land in a single part of the region. López de Heredia is the exception. The family owns all of its vineyard land, just as it seasons its own wooden barrels, handcrafted from American oak, and still vinifies wine the traditional way, fermenting in huge wooden tanks and fining with egg whites.

The López de Heredia winery was founded in 1877. The structure itself, which looks vaguely Swiss, seems lopsided. An Art Nouveau tower, trimmed in fire-engine red, pokes out from a wing like one of those early examples of skyscrapers you see in architecture textbooks. But the family loves it. The offices, done up in frosted glass and wrought iron, feature swinging saloon doors that seem transported from the Wild West. The cellar is filled with thousands of old bottles slumbering behind cobwebs—the sisters call it The Cemetery. Here Mercedes and Maria José open three vintages of Gran Reserva: the 1968, 1964, and 1954 of their Viña Tondonia and Viña Bosconia red wines. Some show better than others, but the freshness is uniformly remarkable. Most Bordeaux would be dead and gone at a similar age.

The red Tondonias are bottled in the broad-shouldered bottles of Bordeaux. They age in oak for a year longer than a Bosconia does, and they're not quite as soft and smooth as the Bosconias when they're young. Bosconias, sold in slope-shouldered bottles like those from Burgundy, have a greater concentration of Tempranillo, a grape that has a slightly higher level of alcohol and has always been Rioja's most prominent. They show sweet, dusty fruit in their youth and an ethereal elegance as they age. The '68 Bosconia, in particular, has the refinement and power of a glorious old Gevrey-Chambertin, though it's undeniably a Rioja. All the wines are classic Riojas, in fact, made from classic Rioja grapes like Tempranillo, Garnacha, Mazuelo, and Graciano. Some of the new-wave releases include a surreptitious dollop of Cabernet Sauvignon, the great grape of Bordeaux and Napa. "I like Cabernet," Maria José insists. "There's a place for those wines. It just isn't here."

When I first met Maria José, years ago, she informed me that the wine-drinking world was divided into Tondonians and Bosconians. This seemed absurd, since the majority of the world has no idea that Tondonias and Bosconias even exist. Lately, though, I've come to see what she means. It's a philosophical division. Tondonians are literalists, traditionalists, math majors, Yankees fans. They see the world in clear-eyed fashion, and they gravitate toward the sure thing. That's Mercedes. Bosconians like Maria José are dreamers, aesthetes, Red Sox fans, perhaps even closet revolutionaries. They seek out the undiscovered, the subtle, the mysterious.

"Do you remember that conversation?" I ask Maria José a few hours later, but she can't hear me over the whine of the car engine. She's driving down a narrow road in the purple darkness, going far too fast in a 1968 Mini Cooper about the size of a pedal boat. "Nobody wants to drive with me," she says. I understand why. Maria José reacts to red lights and stop signs the way a fighting bull does to a pink cape.

Our destination is Ezcaray, a village of houses clumped together in the Spanish style, and the restaurant Echaurren. It's immaculate, with velvet curtains and hardwood floors—sort of an updated version of Arzak. Marisa Paniego and her son, Francis, preside over the kitchen—rather, two kitchens. In one, Marisa cooks traditional Rioja food with uncommon flair. In the other, Francis transposes the traditional into a medley of tiny dishes that are so evolved as to be almost unrecognizable. He'll be cooking for us tonight. "One must renovate the tradition and maintain it at the same time," he tells us before the meal.

We eat a parfait of pig's ear, drizzled with balsamic vinegar from Modena and accompanied by tiny bits of duck liver. Alongside is a ceramic spoon filled with lamb's fingers sitting in a rich sauce tasting of olives. We have ravioli stuffed with veal cheek and suffused in vanilla oil. As the dinner progresses, Mercedes becomes increasingly agitated. "Who would want this?" she whispers.

I haven't the heart to tell her that, indeed, much of the world wants exactly this. Such food is coming to the Rioja whether Mercedes wants it or not. Francis is merely the advance guard.

The next afternoon we gather to celebrate Mercedes's thirty-first birthday at López de Aguileta, in Labastida, which is as traditional as Rioja restaurants get. Luis Aguileta and his wife, Esperanza Perez, run an *asador*, a restaurant built around an oven and decorated like someone's comfortable dining room, in this small town in the Basque part of the Rioja. Ten wooden tables are set on a tiled floor, and the menu is simple—six fish and five meat entrées. Aguileta has cooked in Madrid, Barcelona, and Marbella. He returned to the Rioja in 1992 to open a restaurant in a nineteenth-century house five minutes from his birthplace. He serves us grilled sausage and Patanegra ham. Then leeks in white vinegar, shrimp croquettes, and peppers from Guernica sautéed in hot oil. Mercedes is exultant. "This is Spanish cuisine," she says, resplendent in her black top and a silver necklace. "At Arzak they give you anchovies in chocolate. I will never eat anchovies in chocolate."

Her two brothers are here, and her parents, and Maria José, and they've brought López de Heredia wines from recent vintages. We eat sea bream grilled with garlic and parsley and a bit of red pepper, and then slices of beef, cooked rare and salted perfectly. "I always say, 'Honey was not meant for the mouth of a donkey,'" Maria José says, repeating a Spanish proverb. In many ways she's as sophisticated as anyone I know, but her comment rings true. The charm of the López de Heredia wines, like the charm of the Rioja region, lies in a lack of artifice.

Nevertheless, I'm determined to experiment. Toward the end of the meal I order several of the new-style Riojas from the wine list, since even the most traditional restaurants carry them these days. I want Pedro López de Heredia, the patriarch of the family and the man responsible for the continued philosophy of the winery, to try one. I pour a glass and set it in front of him. He swirls it and sniffs it, looks at it from one angle and then another, moves it to the right side of his plate and then the left. Like a child determined not to eat his vegetables, he does everything but put it to his lips. Finally, he takes a sip, then another. I ask his opinion, but he offers platitudes.

I know there are strong opinions running through his head, percolating around a wisdom that has mitigated the difficulties of several dozen vintages, but I can't get at them. He's hiding behind a genial, almost courtly, demeanor.

When we leave the restaurant, Pedro asks me to ride with him. On the way back to the winery, we make an unannounced detour to his vineyards. We drive up one row and down another. Like a guide on a tourist bus, Pedro announces to me which grapes are grown where, and what each patch of soil contributes to the finished wine. It dawns on me that this is his way of saying that a great wine is made in the vineyard, not the winery. Modern winemaking techniques can smooth out rough edges, but only the land can impart true character. What did he think of the wine I'd given him at lunch? I have my answer.

That evening, from a watchtower in the walls of old Laguardia, I look out on the Castilian plain. Before me is Calatrava's Ysios winery, undulating like an ocean wave, its silver panels glinting in the setting sun. It is a remarkable building, breathtaking in its ultra-modern splendor. Still, I'm feeling wistful, and not just because of the quiet dusk. Honey wasn't meant for the mouths of donkeys, and an area so genuine isn't made for such frippery as world-famous architecture and television chefs.

Standing there, high above the Spanish landscape, I recall that 1968 Bosconia I'd tasted at The Cemetery, then tasted again during one of my meals here. It had ripe cherry fruit and an enveloping elegance, and it promised another forty years of life. It was the conceptual opposite of the meals of tiny appetizers that will be all the rage here any day. The armies of the night are coming, I see clearly, with their made-to-order wines and *amuse-bouches* and vertical appetizers that look like Gehry designs. It is only a matter of time. For now, I have the taste of Bosconia on my tongue. As darkness falls, its finish lingers on.

It's fortunate for wine drinkers that the efficiency consultants haven't yet discovered the *bodegas* of Spain's Rioja region. Only businesses run with some archaic notion of responsibility—and the cash flow to sit on hundreds of thousands of dollars' worth of unsold inventory—would harvest grapes each year, bottle wines, and then not release those wines for years and even decades.

That's exactly what many traditional Rioja wineries do, especially with their oak-aged Reservas and Gran Reservas from outstanding vintages. Bodegas Montecillo finally let go of its 1970 Gran Reserva in the 1990s, while the vintage of López de Heredia's Viña Bosconia Gran Reserva available in stores is the soft and elegant 1981, a wine already two decades old. That's taking the notion of selling no wine before its time almost to absurdity.

Those who liked their wines young and bold and tannic traditionally had little choice in the Rioja. Lately, though, that has started to change. As a reaction to the success that once obscure Spanish regions such as Priorato and Ribera del Duero have enjoyed with bigger, international-style wines, many of the more ambitious Rioja wineries have started producing similar new-wave bottlings, in addition to their regular lines.

These wines, many of which aren't aged in the *bodega* long enough even to be classified as Reservas under the rules of the Rioja appellation, tend to taste much more like what the rest of the world is drinking. That can be good and bad. The best of them—beginning with Marqués de Riscal's Barón de Chirel, a complete, complex wine that doesn't sacrifice its sense of place—are good enough to stand beside the world's better Cabernet Sauvignons in depth and flavor profile. (Indeed, the Barón de Chirel is a blend of Rioja's traditional Tempranillo grape and Cabernet, making it the Spanish equivalent of Italy's super-Tuscans.)

Viña Artadi is different. The entire winery is devoted to tannic, ageable, but fruit-driven wines more reminiscent of Spain's Ribera del Duero region than of the Rioja. Try the 1998 Pagos Viejos Reserva, or the immense and concentrated 1998 Viña El Pisón, wines that can stand up to anything, including the most elaborately constructed meal.

Yet if you're eating the traditional cuisine of the Rioja—roasted lamb, seasonal vegetables, and the fleshy white fish of the Bay of Biscay—the more nuanced style of a traditional Rioja is probably a better fit. The wines of Muga, from the simple Crianza up to the ethereal Prado Enea, are invariably well made and delicious. So is La Rioja Alta's Viña Ardanza Reserva. The 1993 (the 1995 was released as we went to press) isn't as delightfully fragrant as the 1989 and 1990, but the oak and tannins do a balletic balancing act with a core of sweet fruit.

It's among the oldest wines you're likely to find on the shelves of your wine shop, but young for a Reserva-level Rioja. You can drink it now, or pay your $30 and age it yourself.

This piece originally appeared in the February 2002 issue of *Gourmet*. Copyright © 2002 by Bruce Schoenfeld. Reprinted with permission of the author.

¡Buen Provecho!
(The Cuisine and Restaurants of Northern Spain)

"The designation of the entire northern coast of Spain as a gastronomic entity is admittedly broad; each of its four regions was shaped by diverse historical and cultural influences and has a distinctive appearance as well. Even when it comes to food there are significant differences, but a common thread is a keen interest in fine food and an emphasis on seafood, typically prepared in a sauce."

—Penelope Casas, *¡DELICIOSO! THE REGIONAL COOKING OF SPAIN*

"The three most frequently asked questions in the Pays Basque: What did you have for lunch yesterday? What are you having for lunch today? What are you thinking of having for lunch tomorrow?"

—Beth Nelson, *POSTCARDS FROM THE BASQUE COUNTRY: A JOURNEY OF ENCHANTMENT AND IMAGINATION*

Eating in Spain

BY TOM BURNS

editor's note

Spain Gourmetour, the premier publication of the Spanish Institute for
Foreign Trade, featured an excellent series throughout 2000 entitled "Eating
in Spain," which addressed culinary customs in Spain. This piece represents
part two of the series, and though it doesn't exclusively focus on the north,
the author emphasizes a truth prevalent throughout Spain: Spaniards wholeheartedly enjoy their food, routinely turning a meal into a festive party.

TOM BURNS has been a foreign correspondent in Spain for more than
twenty years. He is also the author of *Hispanomanía,* a critical account of
the romantic view of Spain as interpreted by American and British authors.

When we got to the restaurant, after two in the afternoon, there
was no one there save for the waiters. This surprised me
because there had been a lot of doubtful humming—"We might just
be able to squeeze you in, sir," and other remarks in the same vein—
when I had made the booking earlier in the day. Reservations and
exact timings were essential because the restaurant was not just
popular but, more importantly, because it almost exclusively served
paella in all its myriad manifestations; rice, as we all know, cannot
be kept waiting, and you choose your *paella* when you make your
booking.

The restaurant, which had been warmly recommended by local
friends, was on the edge of the Albufera, the large inland lagoon
and complex of rice paddy fields that lies close to Valencia, and we
had been having an extraordinary ecological trip, boating around
among the herons and egrets that nest in the lagoon's rushes, before
lunch. We had hurried back from the bird-watching mini-cruise for

the lunchtime appointment, only to find the restaurant as empty and silent as the Albufera's fabulous expanse of water. Then it turned out that we had been too punctual and were merely the first to arrive. The place was indeed fully booked. Within minutes the restaurant was filled to overflowing and the waiters were hovering around the tables balancing the *paellas* aloft as if they were flying saucers.

What struck us with the force of a thunderclap was the sudden noise. Once the hordes of diners had descended, you could hardly hear yourself speak. So we started shouting to one another, which was what everyone else was doing.

There were a few tables for two (the four of us were crammed into one of them), and most tables were occupied by groups of anything up to twelve. Some all-male groups looked to be formed by office workers who had sped out of Valencia for a long midweek lunch that was thinly disguised as a business meeting. Other tables were occupied by entire families—it was the start of the vacation season—and presided over by the family patriarch who was inviting children and grandchildren to a regular treat. And between mouthfuls of *paella*, they were all screaming at the top of their lungs.

Astonished by the decibel level, my wife came up with the theory that the *valencianos* were all partially deaf because the tens of thousands of fireworks that they let off year after year during their spectacular Fallas festival in March necessarily caused serious damage to their eardrums. "They are genetically noisy because every generation is blasted by more and more firecrackers and hears a little bit less," she informed our party. A second theory was that our fellow diners were merely enjoying themselves.

The counterargument insisted that, as naturally exuberant, impatient and expressive people, the Spaniards, in this case the effervescent *valencianos* in the restaurant, were having a ball. They were not in the least bit bothered about letting everybody else know what a good time they were having. On every table half a dozen people seemed intent on telling their neighbors some funny story or other that absolutely everybody simply had to hear immediately. Since they were all telling their supposedly fascinating ribald tales at the same time, they had to shout to make themselves heard.

The Fallas-induced deafness theory, attractive though it was, was eventually knocked down as we adjusted to the hullabaloo and more or less agreed, shouting of course, on the "everybody is just enjoying themselves" explanation. The winning argument was that every popular and well-run restaurant in Spain is, as a rule, extremely noisy, although, in deference to my wife, it was acknowledged that this particular eatery on the banks of the Albufera lagoon earned the prize for being noisier than any other we could remember anywhere else in Spain. So far so good. But that was clearly not the end of it.

Once we had settled the issue of the shouting diners, it struck me that there was a follow-up to the whole debate: there is something special about Spaniards and their approach to eating in the company of family and friends.

An old adage has it that "an Englishman eats to live and a Frenchman lives to eat." A Spaniard certainly belongs to the second category but there is more to it than that. A Spaniard not only lives to eat but thoroughly enjoys himself doing so. Eating in Spain is an entirely social and festive occasion. Food brings people together, large families and also all the friends, which goes toward creating a huge extended family; eating and partying are one and the same thing in Spain. It is as if America's Thanksgiving and Fourth of July were held at the same time, every weekend all year round.

Paella can be top notch, as it was in this particular Albufera restaurant, which was so enthusiastically patronized by discriminating albeit noisy *valencianos*. Quite rightly, Valencia claims this extraordinary rice dish as its heirloom. But *paella* is also standard fare across wide stretches of Spain where people invariably gather to eat together. Spanish men who declare themselves to be incapable of frying an egg take particular pride in their *paella* expertise. Go to any picnicking area outside a Spanish town, where the local authorities lay on stone built grills, firewood, and trash cans for the weekenders, and you will find the male of the family stacking up his *paella* ingredients—chicken, pork, rabbit, seafood, assorted vegetables, beans, and anything else he intends to put into the *paella* pan—and carefully measuring the exact quantities of stock and rice.

As the embers start to glow, the *paella* pan is joyfully placed on the grill and a celebration centered on food gets under way. It is *de rigueur* to applaud the cook when the rice has soaked up all the stock and nestles amid the *paella*'s other ingredients. The Basques are legendary for their serious knowledge and love of food, and they lend a lot of festive ritual to their eating. Spain is a country with an outdoor lifestyle, and the Basques are masters of the long al fresco lunch around a grill, around a *parrilla,* in a culinary celebration that is known as a *parrillada*. This is a feast that makes conventional barbecues in the backyard seem like a potato chips and peanuts aperitif given by a skinflint. The Basques are at it every weekend when the weather is good, and they are acting out an ancestral prac- tice because the *parrillada* is the direct descendant of the beachside charcoal fires on which local fishermen grilled the catch that they were unable to sell and of the roast lamb-on-a-spit that the local shepherds perfected to keep body and soul together as they watched their flocks high above the Basque Country's verdant valleys.

Prime fare in a *parrillada* is an outsize veal chop called a *chuletón*—that sometimes has been previously marinated in olive oil, parsley, and garlic—and which would certainly satisfy at least two hungry and normal mortals. A normal chop is a mere *chuleta,* and most Basques don't rate it. The *chuletón* gurgles and sizzles in the center of the grill while on the edges of the grill, or *parrilla,* onions, peppers, tomatoes, and other vegetables cook more gently, along with whole heads of garlic. Potatoes are nowadays wrapped in tinfoil (modernity has its uses) and buried among the embers. The garlic, when suitably softened, is pried out of its skin and either spread on bread or directly onto the *chuletóns.*

A lot of other top local produce can be, and is, slapped onto the *parrilla*—lamb cutlets, blue fish, especially sardines, spicy sausages, spare ribs, kidneys, and the rest—and all is accompanied by lashings of wine. A first-time attendant at the *parrillada* festivities that countless countryside restaurants stage in the Basque Country, and indeed right across Northern Spain, will, of course, be amazed by the deafening sound of happy people having a good time.

Catalonia also takes pride in communal barbecues that seem to have existed since around the time that fire was invented. Marinated chicken and particularly rabbit take the honors here, in place of the massive chops that the Basques invariably feed on, and vegetables rather than mere accompaniments form whole dishes in themselves. The green onion, an underrated vegetable in most places, is something of a star among Catalans, who call it a *calçot*. The new green onions are celebrated in spring with the *calçotada,* one of Catalonia's most endearing get-togethers among families and friends. The *calçots* are blackened on the grill, peeled to reveal once more their whiteness and, juicy and still hot, dipped into Catalonia's famed sauces. Catalans are brilliant sauce makers, and the best salsas are the pungent *alioli,* made by blending garlic and oil, and the pepper-based *romesco*. People then suck and chew (bibs are provided) and, between one *calçot* and the next one, generally party away.

Thinking about such eating habits, what one ends up with is a naturally exuberant, impatient, and expressive people who, at the slightest opportunity, gather in a large circle round a campfire (or crowd a restaurant) to noisily swap stories and jokes in an intensely convivial atmosphere in which food is actively enjoyed.

It strikes me that this is a throwback to more pastoral, stress-free times and that the celebratory essence of the occasion is as relevant now, and as obvious, as it was then. *Paella* picnickers, *parrillada* protagonists, and those who keep the *calçots* company mingle and wander around among an ever-widening circle of festive eaters, and this indulgent reversion to rustic habits does have, thankfully, a modern urban projection—the *tapa* tradition.

The way in which groups of people prop up bars to consume their food and the manner in which they walk about from *tapa* bar to *tapa* bar (each will have its specialties), nibbling, drinking, and endlessly chatting, is authentically Spanish.

Tapa food in its infinite variety is delicious. Few things are more satisfying in the food department than to spear one tasty morsel sizzling on its platter after another with a toothpick or a small fork or, better still, to pick the delicacy directly with your fingers. But even better is the sheer enjoyment that is conjured up in a good *tapa* crawl. What happens is that you start off with a group of convivial friends and the group gets bigger and bigger as it moves around from one bar to another and the night wears on. It is yet another example of the all-embracing Spanish eating ritual, festive and unifying.

This piece originally appeared in the September–December 2000 issue of *Spain Gourmetour: Food, Wine & Travel Magazine*. Reprinted with permission.

Pig Heaven It Is!

By Gully Wells

editor's note

Admittedly, this piece, which details the most perfect meal of the writer's entire life, was not enjoyed in Northern Spain. But I like this piece so much, and it represents so well the revered status of two Spanish culinary classics, that I could not resist including it in this edition. (Besides, the author thoughtfully provides the names of three restaurants in Bilbao where *jamon ibérico de Joselito* and Vega Sicilia Unico may be joyfully consumed.)

GULLY WELLS is a features editor of *Condé Nast Traveler,* where this piece first appeared in the April 2000 issue. She writes often about Mediterranean destinations, and her work has appeared in previous editions of *The Collected Traveler.*

Once, many years ago, in an old house overlooking Toledo, I ate the perfect meal. It was wintertime, the sky was the color of slate, and there might even have been snow in the air. The town was deserted, creating the illusion that the cathedral, the synagogue which had once been a mosque, El Greco's house, and every single one of the narrow, intricate cobbled streets were mine and mine alone. I spent the morning wandering around. By the time I got back to the house, it must have been early afternoon, and I was cold, damp, and very hungry. Time for lunch.

A fire snapped, and then roared—yellow flames shooting up the chimney—in the massive fireplace in the kitchen, but nobody seemed to be doing any cooking. Instead, one of my Spanish friends went to the larder and returned with an entire haunch of ham, covered in mottled, pale gray mold, its long, elegant shank ending in a surprisingly delicate black hoof. Another friend disappeared into the cavernous, cryptlike wine cellar, deep below the private chapel, and emerged with four, maybe five, bottles of red wine. And somebody else found the bread that the housekeeper had baked that morning. That was it.

The wine was opened and poured into heavy glass tumblers, the ham sliced and arranged on a big plate, the bread put in a basket, and then we sat down at the long oak table in front of the fire. I don't think we even bothered to set the table. In fact, I know we didn't. We picked up the rosy, translucent slices of ham, shot through like marble with veins of fat, and ate them with our fingers. We broke the bread with our hands, and we sipped the wine slowly, but not too slowly, rolling it around in our mouths so that the taste of the grapes mingled with the sweet perfume of the ham. I may have been young, and possibly naïve, but I had traveled a bit and had even eaten Parma ham in Parma and drunk Margaux in Margaux. Yet I had never, ever experienced *anything* as sublime as this particular ham and this particular wine. They seemed to inhabit that imaginary stratosphere where Mozart is your piano teacher, Michelangelo your house painter, Jefferson your dinner companion, and Coco Chanel your neighborhood dressmaker.

Finally, after a few more greedy mouthfuls, I said what, until then, I'd only been thinking, which was quite simple: "This is the best ham and the best wine I have ever had in my entire life." My friends looked not the least bit surprised, shrugged their shoulders, and said, *"Claro,"* which translates as: "But of course it is, you foolish young American. What else would you expect from *jamón ibérico de Joselito* and a Vega Sicilia Unico 1973?" So began my first lesson in how two families in Spain painstakingly produce, predominantly for the domestic market, in exactly the same way they have been doing it for more than a century, and in strictly limited quantities, the wine and ham that surely must be served at the very best restaurants in heaven.

Over the years I tried many times, whenever I was in Spain, to recreate this meal. Sometimes I would find *jamón ibérico de Joselito* on a restaurant menu, but then I'd look at the wine list and the Vega Sicilia Unico would be missing; or I'd be at a friend's house in Madrid, where, as a special treat, the wine would be produced, but inexplicably, they would serve it with something other than *jamón*. And even though any Spaniard who cares about such things will tell you that, *"Claro,"* Vega Sicilia and *jamón Joselito* are obviously supreme in their respective fields, nobody was ever able to explain to me precisely *why* this is so. What makes this ham and this wine different from all others? How are they produced, and where and by whom? In the end, my curiosity—and greed—triumphed, and last fall I made a pilgrimage to Spain to discover the answers to all of these questions. And also, I have to confess, to see if my perfect meal was as magical in reality as it remained in my memory.

Vega Sicilia Unico is a wine that inspires legends. So expensive is it (about $250 per bottle in New York wineshops), and so few bottles are produced each year (between forty thousand and a hundred thousand) and so few consumed outside Spain, that even the most passionate wine connoisseur has probably tasted it less often than she would wish. I'd heard a rumor that Prince Charles had wanted to serve it at his wedding but couldn't, because there simply was not enough available that year; somebody else had told me that there were often years when none was produced at all, because the owners would rather skip a year or two than release a less than perfect wine. And if having royal blood doesn't do the trick, don't think mere money will: there are just over three thousand regular buyers and two thousand waiting patiently for the privilege of being allowed to write that check. Each time I mentioned Vega Sicilia, I seemed to hear another story—some true, some not, but all of them adding to the aura surrounding this mythic wine.

With all of these legends swirling around in my head, I drove north from Madrid toward the Duero River to visit the Ribera del Duero, the valley where some of Spain's best wines are made. Less well known and less productive than the Rioja in terms of volume, the area is becoming increasingly popular among wine aficionados. I went to Valbuena de Duero by way of Segovia, where I stopped to admire the Roman aqueduct (still in perfect working order) and to have lunch at the Restaurante El Duque (boiling hot garlic soup and pitifully small but entirely irresistible roast suckling pig). I arrived at the *bodega* as the very first grapes of the season were being picked and moved into the vats. It seemed as though the Grape Gods were with me that day.

Pablo Álvarez, whose family bought Vega Sicilia in 1982, was standing on the steps of the *bodega* dressed like a perfect English country gentleman with the slightly mournful face of an El Greco, smoking a Marlboro and waiting to show me just how these very ordinary-looking grapes were transformed into anything but ordinary grape juice. "Remember," he said as we walked toward the vineyards at the back of the *bodega,* "that every great wine comes from a difficult place. Here we have an extreme climate. At twenty-six hundred feet above sea level, we get very hot summers and freezing winters with a frequent risk of hail. Our soil is not the best, and with only eight hundred vines per acre and only five hundred acres under vine, our yield is low."

We were a long way—geographically and philosophically—from California, with its heavenly climate, rich soil (they pack in between twenty-four hundred and four thousand vines per acre), armies of enologists, high-tech production methods, and gigantic aluminum vats. Suddenly the sky turned thunderously dark, and a few drops of rain fell (not so good for grapes that are about to be picked) as Pablo led me into a shed where an elderly gentleman was busy toasting over an open fire the oak barrels in which the wine is aged. Most great wines are bottle aged, but Vega Sicilia derives its unique character in part from these handmade oak *barriques*. After two fermentation periods, the wine is transferred to oak barrels, where it sits, aging gracefully, for six or seven years (for Unico; for Valbuena it's two and a half years).

We emerged from the shed and walked across the yard. "There's the wood for the barrels," Pablo said, pointing to a neatly piled stack of planks. "We let it age for three or four years before making the barrels." Next he waved in the general direction of the nearest vines. "These typically last up to sixty years. After that we remove them, let the soil rest for four years, replant, and leave the new vines for twelve years before we pick a single grape. A plant is like a person, it needs to mature." I nodded my head (what woman approaching her late forties wouldn't agree with the profound wisdom of Pablo's statement?) and slowly, very slowly, began to understand how important a role *time* plays in the alchemy of Vega Sicilia.

After looking at the vaulted hall where the barrels were stacked, and admiring the elegant Italian lamps made of aluminum disks covered in pure gold leaf (a wine like this raises the interior decorating bar, too), we walked back to Pablo's office, where a bottle of Vega Sicilia Unico stood in the middle of his desk. It would not be released until next year, so it didn't yet have a label, but I like to think that even blindfolded I would have recognized this wine. Pablo poured us each a glass. I took one sip, and without even trying I was back in the kitchen in Toledo.

Of course, all ham starts with a pig, but a truly great ham starts with a happy pig. I was standing in the dappled sunlight at one of the *fincas*, or farms, that the Joselito brothers own near Zafra in Extremadura, that tough and uncompromising region in southwestern Spain, staring at some extraordinarily happy-looking pigs. Some were lolling about in mud, like fat ladies at the Golden Door, and others were rooting around, stuffing their mouths full of acorns, like fat ladies at Le Cirque 2000. And all of them had the same elegant little black hooves, which seemed too small to support their massive bodies, like fat ladies squeezed into Manolo Blahnik stilettos.

Juan Fernández Palanco, who is one of the mainstays of Cárnicas Joselito, was sitting in the shade of a holm oak, giving me a tutorial on the Ibérico breed of pig. Descended from the Mediterranean wild boar, with a distinctive gray coat, these pigs are native to the Iberian peninsula and must *never* be confused with Serrano pigs, their larger, whiter, and far less cultivated cousins, which were introduced into Spain from northern Europe in the 1950s. A mere five percent of the cured ham produced in Spain comes from Ibérico pigs, and only some of those feast on a diet of acorns, like the Joselito fat ladies, for the last three or four months of their short but happy lives.

These particular pigs, Juan told me, were born on a farm near Córdoba in Andalusia and were then brought to the *finca* at about three months. They would spend almost a year roaming about the estate, eating grass, roots, bulbs, and acorns in what is called the *montanera* phase of their lives. Whereas most producers slaughter their pigs at eleven or twelve months, Joselito waits until they are at least eighteen months old before sending them to what in Spanish is rather quaintly called the *sacrificio*. After which the next stage— the curing—begins three hundred miles away, in a town called Guijuelo.

José Gómez Martín, the younger of the two Joselito brothers, shook my hand as I walked into his office, a room on the first floor of Cárnicas Joselito headquarters. His hands were as soft as the skin on a suckling pig's bottom. The table that dominated the room was suitably long—big enough for a board meeting—and on the walls, where you might expect to see portraits of the founding fathers of the company, were framed photographs of . . . some very handsome and contented-looking Iberian pigs. José gestured to them, beaming, as if he were showing me his own children, and we both agreed that they were, without a doubt, the happiest and most beautiful pigs on God's earth.

In the long process of creating the supreme *jamón Joselito,* if Extremadura contributes the oak trees that produce the acorns that give the pigs their distinctive flavor, then Guijuelo, one of Spain's less alluring towns, contributes the climate. For ham to cure absolutely naturally in the air, it is essential that it hang in a place with exceptionally dry, cold winters, very hot summers, and a wide range of humidity throughout the year. There seemed to be something ironic about the fact that the smooth perfection of both Vega Sicilia and *jamón Joselito* depend upon climates that are harsh in the extreme. Although there was probably some moral in that paradox, it was not one that I was ever able to figure out.

The curing process begins with sea salt—not just any sea salt but extra-coarse salt from a tiny village called Torrevieja, on the Mediterranean coast near Alicante. As José explained to me, the hams are piled up, with salt in between each layer, and are left for ten days, during which time they are "turned" three or four times. Next, the salt is rinsed off with cold water, and the ham is skinned and then hung upstairs to "settle" for about a year. The pigs are always led to the *sacrificio* at the start of winter, so that the first hanging period takes place during the dry, cold months, when the wind sweeps in off the sierra and through the open windows, creating the perfect temperature and conditions for the curing process.

José gave me a white coat, just in case the *jamones* decided to drip on me, and we took the elevator to the fourth floor. As we stepped out, I looked down a vast room (called the *secadero*), as long and wide as the nave of a medium-size cathedral, and saw thousands of hams dangling from hooks in the ceiling. Both walls of the "cathedral" were lined with screened windows that had shutters that could be closed the minute rain threatened to blow in.

After about a year on the upper floors, the hams are moved to the *bodega* in the basement, where they finish curing. José and I got back in the elevator and descended to the much darker, less breezy, and slightly warmer basement, where the hams begin to grow the *penicillium,* the soft gray mold that I remembered from the ham in Toledo, which coats the outside and gives the meat its bouquet and complexity of flavor. As the hams age, the *penicillium* gets darker until, after another year in the *bodega,* they are ready to be shipped.

All of the great restaurants in Spain, the gourmet stores, and the Casa Real, as King Juan Carlos's household is known, put in their orders way ahead of time, and tags are then attached to the hams they have reserved. I asked José about exports, and he shrugged his shoulders. "We sell about ninety percent of our *jamón* here," he said, "and we export a small amount to a few European shops and restaurants. But since we make only sixty thousand hams a year, which are all sold immediately, and since we don't want to increase production, exports are not a priority." And what about America? I asked. "The FDA makes it too complicated. They are worse than the EU." José smiled and shrugged again, and we walked out into the street and back to his house for lunch—a *copita* of wine and a slice or two of *jamón.*

The haunch of ham sat at one end of the long wooden table, and a single bottle of Vega Sicilia Unico Reserva Especial stood at the other. José built a fire, the flames swooshed up, and he poured the wine into two tumblers before starting to carve, carefully placing the slices of ham on a white plate between us. That was it. We picked up the ham with our fingers, we sipped the wine, and I marveled, for the second time in my life, at the total simplicity of true perfection.

Jamón y Vino

You could spend quite a bit of time running around Spain trying to match up the perfect wine and the perfect ham. One option is to go to a good wine store and buy a bottle of Vega Sicilia Unico, then go to a gourmet food store and get half a kilo of *jamón ibérico de Joselito,* and then find the perfect companion and head out to the perfect field (in spring or summer). Or book a table at one of the following restaurants, where a bottle of Unico costs between $75 and $130, depending on the vintage (the Unico Reserva Especial runs closer to $200). Should the *jamón Joselito* not be available, make sure they have another fine *jamón ibérico.* Several good brands are produced in the same time-honored way used by Cárnicas Joselito. The price of a plate of ham should be between $10 and $18.

Barcelona
Orotava: 93.487.73.74
Via Veneto: 93.200.72.44

Bilbao
La Viña del Ensanche: 94.415.5615
Restaurante Extebarri: 94.658.3042
Victor Montes Restaurant: 94.415.7067

Madrid
Casa Lucio: 91.365.32.52
Jockey: 91.319.24.35
Viridinia: 91.523.44.78

Seville
Casa Robles: 95.456.32.72
La Alquería de Hacienda Benazuza: 95.570.33.44
Taberna del Alabardero: 95.456.06.37

From the Saffron Fields of Spain

BY SALLY SCHNEIDER

∾

editor's note

The saffron fields of Spain are nowhere near the north; rather, they lie in the province of Aragon and in the Castile–La Mancha region, near Madrid. But saffron is so much a part of Spanish cuisine, no matter where one might be in Spain, and it is the defining ingredient in some of the Mediterranean's greatest dishes, that I couldn't imagine this book without a major piece about saffron.

SALLY SCHNEIDER is a consulting editor and frequent contributor to *Saveur*, where this piece first appeared. She is also the author of *A New Way to Cook* (Artisan, 2001) and *The Art of Low-Calorie Cooking* (Stewart, Tabori & Chang, 1990, hardcover; 1994, paperback), among others.

Damp cold seeped into my boots, chilling me to the bone. Around me workers bundled up in old clothes crept across the field, bent nearly double as they deftly plucked small flowers from seven-inch-high plants. A bitterly cold night was giving way to day, the landscape changing from the dreamlike monochrome of first light to a tableau in brilliant colors—the deep green of distant hills, the royal blue of the brightening sky, the rich purple of the blossoms. But as welcome as it seemed, the approaching dawn lent some urgency to the work at hand: saffron must be picked before the sun's warmth wilts the day's new blossoms.

I had been taken to this field, in the Aragon region of northeastern Spain, by veteran saffron farmer Indalecio Gómez to witness the harvest of this precious commodity—a process unchanged for centuries. For two to three weeks each October, the saffron harvest consumes the lives of Spanish growers and their families—

Spain has long been an important producer of the spice—as they race to strip their small fields.

Gómez held one of the blossoms in his hand. The fall-flowering saffron crocus *(Crocus sativus)* is as delicate as the spring crocus, to which it is closely related. Six lilac-colored petals form a goblet shape on its thin stem. Gómez gently opened the petals to show me the treasure inside—three crimson, threadlike stigmas in the center of the blossom that will be transformed into the costliest spice in the world.

As I watched the pickers moving across the field, baskets hooked to their belts, I had the strange feeling of being in another time. A man driving a horse-drawn wagon waved as he rattled down the lane. It might have been the nineteenth century.

This was not my first visit to the saffron fields of Spain. I fell under saffron's spell half a dozen years ago. It was then, while staying with a friend in the Spanish wine region of Rioja, that I met my friend's mother, María Gómez. The Gómez family has cultivated saffron for many generations in the town of Bañon, 75 miles south of Saragossa in the Aragonese province of Teruel, and she talked about the spice, and about the traditions of its harvesting and processing, with such passion that I knew I had to see it for myself. Since then I've traveled repeatedly through Spain's main saffron-producing provinces, from Teruel in the northeast, to Cuenca, Albacete, and Ciudad Real in the Castilla–La Mancha region, in central Spain.

On one occasion I watched the *monda*—in which the damp red stigmas are painstakingly hand-stripped from the flowers—in the sleepy La Mancha town of Barrax. There, inside a former restaurant, three generations of mothers and daughters were sitting at a flower-covered table, their hands moving in a blur. On the floor around them were thousands of petals. The room was filled with a subtle, exquisite aroma recalling freesia and vanilla, an aroma giving no hint of the complex flavor of the spice itself, which is at once floral and pleasantly bitter, reminiscent of tobacco, hay, and cedar, with nuances of pepper, citrus seed, and menthol.

A handsome and somewhat fierce-looking woman in her seventies, dressed entirely in black, talked tenderly to her teenage granddaughter as she worked. With one hand she picked up a flower and separated the petals; with the other, she stripped the threads from the yellow style to which they were attached. (She took care not to include the styles themselves, which would diminish the saffron's value.) The threads were then tossed onto a tin plate, and the spent flower dropped to the floor. The old woman stripped each blossom in less than four seconds. An experienced picker, she could strip about 1,100 flowers in an hour, producing about a quarter of an ounce of saffron; a day's work would yield two to three ounces of the spice, an amount worth as much as $850 on the retail market.

"How long will you work today?" I asked the women, who talked and sang songs as they labored. They laughed shyly, shrugging and pointing to several baskets of flowers still waiting in the corner. "Till it's done," said one. "Till it's done."

There is no machine that can strip the saffron flowers, just as there is no mechanical way to speed their harvest. Hardworking hands must process about 70,000 flowers to obtain a pound of finished saffron. Hence the spice's astronomical price—roughly $450 a pound wholesale and as much as $4,500 retail for saffron of the highest quality. For first-time buyers of saffron in the supermarket, knowing this might lessen the shock of paying about $5 for half a gram, the yield of about eighty hand-picked flowers.

Saffron is almost as old as civilization, and its influence on culinary history has been vast and almost mythic. It was apparently first cultivated in Persia and Asia Minor in ancient times and is praised in the Bible's Song of Solomon, in Homer's *Iliad*, in Virgil's poems, in the *Papyrus Ebers* (an important ancient Egyptian medical text), and in the first-century cookbook of Apicius. Saffron was introduced to Spain by the Moors in the tenth century. (Its name derives from an Arabic word of unknown origin, *za'faran*.)

During the Middle Ages, the use of saffron in cooking spread throughout Europe. Saffron is the defining ingredient in some of the Continent's most celebrated dishes—Spain's *paella*, the *bouillabaisse* of Provence, *risotto milanese*—and is essential to the cuisines of India, Morocco, and Iran. It has also been coveted throughout history as a dye, a perfume, and a medicine.

As with any expensive commodity, saffron has inspired fraud. Unscrupulous merchants have coated it with molasses, honey, or wax to add weight. Faux saffron has been devised from red-dyed cornsilk, fine shreds of red wood, and the petals of safflower, arnica, and marigold. Brick powder, metal oxides, and lead powders have been used to mimic ground saffron, as has turmeric. In addition, importers say that inferior-grade saffron is often passed off as the highest quality, due in part to blatant deception by some unethical Spanish exporters.

Though some sources estimate that as much as 60 percent of the world's saffron is produced in Spain, the Spanish government now puts the figure at 15 to 20 percent. The rest comes from Iran, India, and Morocco, with some small-scale production in Crete, France, Turkey, Italy, and elsewhere. But at least 90 percent of the saffron sold in America is Spanish.

The La Mancha region, a vast, spare plateau beginning about 35 miles south of Madrid, is said to produce the best saffron of all. Here the landscape resembles an eccentric mix of the American West and poetic Spanish farmland. The region's windmill-dotted fields and its vineyards and olive groves evoke the legend of Don Quixote; its arid plains and low mesas are straight out of a Louis L'Amour novel. The saffron fields emanate from scruffy *manchego* farming villages like Membrilla, La Solana, San Pedro, Barrax, and Munera. A festival honoring the saffron rose, as the flower is known locally, is held in the village of Consuegra around the last Sunday in October. Otherwise the harvest is a quiet affair, often going unnoticed by the casual traveler.

It was not in La Mancha but in Aragon, in Bañon, that I really saw saffron up close—thanks to María Gómez and Indalecio Gómez, who is María's brother. The siblings share a direct and unaffected manner. María Gómez, strong and compact, wears the plain dress and cardigan sweater typical of the country women you see in local markets all over Spain. Indalecio Gómez is a robust, balding man, his face weathered from years of working outdoors. Gómez is wise in the ways of his world, knowing things like where to find the delicious *seta de cardo* mushrooms that were invisible to my eye, and how to rid the saffron fields of rodents with a bellowslike contraption that forces smoke into their burrows.

When I asked how long the family had been in Bañon, Gómez replied simply, "Forever"—with a sweeping gesture to indicate centuries past. This ancient village, which looks like a Cubist painting, all ochre and terra-cotta rectangles, predates the Moors.

No farmer in this region grows just saffron. Gómez cultivates grains and raises pigs on his farm and planted saffron crocuses to provide extra income. A farmer will tend a plot of saffron only as large as he and his family can harvest. One hectare (about two and a half acres) will yield from 6 to 12 pounds of saffron (depending on irrigation) and might require 15 or 20 people to harvest. Some saffron fields are as small as an eighth of an acre.

Once the long labor of stripping the flowers is finished, the threads must be carefully and quickly dried to develop their flavor and to remove moisture, which can cause the saffron to rot. If this is done incorrectly, hundreds of dollars in saffron can be destroyed in an instant. The wet threads are placed in a drum-shaped sieve over a heat source, most often the embers of a wood fire, and watched carefully. Farmers often develop their own refinements, like the ingenious one Gómez has devised: He dries his saffron by leaving the sieve overnight on the floor of his house, on tiles heated by a "Roman oven," a wood-fired furnace built into the foundation. In another household I saw saffron placed in a metal plate on a burner over a low flame on the kitchen's small gas stove. On the next burner simmered a stew of shrimp, clams, garlic, and tomatoes.

The threads will lose about 80 percent of their weight in the drying process. Five pounds of fresh stigmas will yield one pound dried, for which a successful farmer will receive 41,000 to 50,000 pesetas (between $340 and $415). To weigh the saffron, most farmers still use homemade scales—roughly crafted tin plates hanging from iron chains attached to a crude crosspiece. Weights are made of hand-forged iron, often stamped with the family crest or another personal symbol.

Farmers are paid in cash or scrip. In the latter case, an agent issues a farmer a receipt that can be redeemed at the local bank. The informality of this arrangement is indicative of the degree of trust that exists between the buyers, the growers, and the banks.

Not all farmers necessarily sell their saffron as soon as it is harvested. It can be kept for years if stored in an airtight vessel away from light and moisture. Some stash it away for emergencies, or until they can get a better price. "It is like having a savings account," María Gómez explained to me, adding that parents often leave saffron to their children in their wills. One woman, seemingly of little means, surprised the town by leaving her children more than 30 pounds of saffron, accumulated over the years. Farmers often hide saffron among their good clothes, which are then permeated with its aroma. The churches are filled with the smell of saffron when everyone wears his Sunday best.

Saffron production in Spain has declined by 50 percent over the last two decades—though it seems to have stabilized in La Mancha. As the cost of living has risen in Spain, some farmers, especially the younger ones, consider it too much hard work for too little profit. And farmers face increasing competition from other saffron-producing countries, especially Iran and India, where labor costs are lower.

To illustrate the frustrations a saffron farmer can encounter, Indalecio Gómez took me early one morning to meet Manuel Martín Villalba. Villalba, who has been cultivating saffron for three decades, was picking flowers with his son Juan José in his field on the outskirts of the Aragonese village of Monreal del Campo. He was clearly disheartened as he gestured sadly at the field dotted sparsely with saffron flowers. This would be his last harvest. He could earn only half of what he made twenty-five years ago, he said, due to competition from La Mancha and to severe weather, which had stunted his plants.

He pulled one up by the roots. "Normally," he said, "a mature plant like this would be large and have three to five flowers. This year all the plants were small, with only one flower growing out of each root system. We had no rain in March, when it is critical. Then there were months of drought, followed by hard rains all fall. We knew it would be a disaster."

Despite the hardships of the saffron farmer's life, Villalba obviously regretted that this was his final harvest. He spoke of the pleasure he had taken through the years in a way of life that has been handed down from father to son for generations. He had hoped to pass it on to his own son.

We helped Villalba pick the remaining flowers in the field. He poured them into a cardboard box, which he gave to me. "You will have some Teruel saffron to take home to America," he said.

Later, we stripped the blossoms in María Gómez's tiny dining room. Her brother's wife, Esperanza Zorraquino, her hands thickly callused from farm work, nimbly stripped five flowers to my one.

The Saffron Trade

One of Spain's largest saffron exporters is Safinter, based in an elegant old villa in a wealthy residential district of Barcelona. Though the company now cultivates its own saffron, the bulk of its supply still comes from independent farmers. Each batch of saffron that arrives at Safinter is analyzed to assure that it meets strict standards. The highest government quality designation is Mancha (not necessarily from La Mancha), sometimes labeled as Mancha Superior or Mancha Selecta. This saffron is characterized by long, flexible stigmas and a deep red color, with no more than four percent other flower parts. The Rio and Sierra grades have more yellow styles, a slightly paler color, and less aroma.

Saffron actually from La Mancha enjoys a particularly high reputation. This may have to do with its consistency and wide availability. Whether it has a better flavor than other Spanish saffrons, or than top-quality saffron from Iran or India, is debatable. As American importer Buddy Born, who buys almost exclusively in La Mancha, puts it, "Like wine, saffron will be different from year to year and from one place to another. And taste in saffron is a very subjective thing."

Saffron is sold as whole threads or in powder form. Threads are preferable, since you can see what you're getting. Use your senses to examine the saffron: look for long threads, about three-quarters of an inch, and a bright or deep red color, with few yellow styles. Smell the saffron and taste it if possible. Pure dried saffron is very aromatic and tastes pleasingly bitter yet floral. A stigma placed on the tongue should never taste sweet. Ground saffron may be adulterated and often has less flavor.

Markets—even Indian ones—typically sell only Spanish saffron, both because of its quality and because it is widely available. The manager of one Indian market told me that he takes Spanish saffron back to India when he visits. Iranian saffron has been favorably compared with Spanish, but because of the trade embargo against Iran, it cannot be sold legally in the United States. Nevertheless, it is openly available in Iranian markets in this country. It has shorter threads and can have an excellent flavor. The best Iranian saffron comes from the Mashhad region. There is a saying in Iran that you must not eat too much saffron because it will make you laugh so hard that you could laugh yourself to death.

The Guide: Saffron Country

The province of Teruel, in the region of Aragon, is the age-old saffron center of Spain. Production there is on the wane, however, and you're more likely to see harvesting in the flat, prairielike landscapes of La Mancha, in late October. The town of Membrilla, for instance, is virtually surrounded by saffron fields. (Drive off the main road down side streets to the edge of town.) Processing takes place in private houses. To get a close look, try expressing your interest to the locals, keeping in mind that you're far more likely to be invited home in La Mancha than in more reserved Aragon.

Where to Stay

There are no better bases for exploring in Aragon and La Mancha than its *paradores,* or national inns. Their range of style is great: some are romantic, occupying restored monasteries or castles; others are modern and cold. All have restaurants serving good food based on local traditions. To book any of the six listed here, call Marketing Ahead (800-223-1356), the official representative of the Paradores de Turismo de España. (*Parador* rates include buffet breakfast.)

Parador de Almagro, *Ronda de San Francisco 31, Almagro (26.86.01.00; fax: 26.86.01.50). Rates: about $143.* A charmer, with 55 rooms, in a former sixteenth-century convent, complete with period-style furnishings.

Parador de Cuenca, *Paseo Hoz del Huécar, Cuenca (69.23.23.20; fax: 69.23.25.34). Rates: about $166.* Another reconstructed sixteenth-century convent in one of Spain's most dramatic cities, where houses cling to steep cliffs on the side of a deep ravine. This new *parador*, with 62 rooms, sits across the ravine from the houses, providing a stunning view.

Parador de La Mancha, *Carretera nacional 301, kilometer 251, Albacete (67.50.93.43; fax: 67.22.60.92). Rates: about $115.* A pleasant 70-room inn in the style of a *manchego* farmhouse, with furnishings to match, in the heart of the saffron-harvesting area near San Pedro.

Parador de Manzanares, *Carretera nacional Madrid–Cádiz, kilometer 175, Manzanares (26.61.04.00; fax: 26.61.09.35). Rates: about $97.* A modern, very plainly furnished inn with 50 rooms. But nearby Membrillo is the perfect place to see the saffron harvest, in the fields at the edge of town.

Parador de Teruel, *Carretera de Zaragoza–Teruel (78.60.18.00; fax: 78.60.86.12). Rates: about $112.* A modern building, but built in the classic stone style of the region. There are 60 rooms. A good base for exploring Teruel.

Parador Marqués de Villena, *Avenida Amigos de los Castillos 3, Alarcón (69.33.13.50; fax: 69.33.11.07). Rates: about $156.* An authentic castle, built as a fortress by the Moors, it is one of the most stunning inns in the whole *parador* system, with only 13 double rooms.

Hotel Albarracín, *Calle Azagra, Albarracín (tel. and fax: 78.71.00.11). Rates: about $104.* Even though the hotel, located in a historic building, is rather simple, staying here might be a better bet than lodging at the *parador* in Teruel. Albarracín is a charming town, with easy access to the surrounding mountains, an area of beautiful, almost unearthly terrain.

Posada de San José, *Julián Romero 4, Cuenca (69.21.13.00; fax: 69.23.03.65). Rates: about $58–$65.* A charmingly attractive inn filled with antiques, located in one of the famous "hanging houses" on the cliffs of Cuenca. The rooms are comfortable but small, and the view is memorable.

Where to Eat

Teruel has no great restaurants, but look for *chuletas de cordero* (baby lamb chops) and the delicious local ham on the menus at simple establishments, or sample local *tapas.* In La Mancha, the following places are recommended *(dinner with drinks, tax, and tip:* Expensive—Over $40; Moderate—$20–$40; Inexpensive—Under $20):

Fonda Santiago, *Contreras 4, El Bonillo (67.37.00.17). Dinner: Moderate.* Great for grilled sausages and stewed vegetables with game.

Mesón Casas Colgadas, *Canónigos, Cuenca (69.22.35.09). Dinner: Moderate.* A superb setting in one of two side-by-side hanging houses dating to the sixteenth century. (The other one is the Spanish Museum of Abstract Art.) *Sopa manchega* (garlic soup), lamb chops, and game are the specialties.

Mesón El Corregidor, *Plaza Fray Fernando Fernández de Córdoba 2, Almagro (26.86.06.48). Dinner: Expensive.* Regional cooking. The house specialty: *berenjenas de Almagro* (marinated baby eggplants).

Nuestro Bar, *Alcalde Conangla 102, Albacete (67.22.72.15). Dinner: Expensive.* A casual setting with typical *manchego* country furnishings and excellent regional cuisine.

Fiesta de la Rosa Del Azafrán. Held in Consuegra, this is the best of the La Mancha region's saffron festivals, with folkloric events and a saffron-stripping contest. For more information, call the Spanish tourist offices in North America.

Museo Monográfico del Azafrán, *Plaza Mayor 10, Monreal del Campo (78.86.32.36).* Displays on the history, uses (including medicinal), and conservation of saffron around the world.

This piece originally appeared in the May–June 1995 issue of *Saveur.*
Copyright © by Sally Schneider. Reprinted with permission of the author.

The Riches of Spain: Its Cheese

By Frank J. Prial

~

editor's note

In the last five years or so, Spanish cheeses—especially those from the north—have remained solidly at the top of my favorites list, and happily, as noted in the following two pieces (one an introduction to the cheeses of Northern Spain, the other a report on their growing availability), they have become easier and easier to find in supermarkets and specialty shops alike, along with traditional Spanish accompaniments such as *membrillo* (quince paste) and fig and date wheels with almonds.

FRANK J. PRIAL is the wine columnist for *The New York Times*. He is also the author of *Wine Talk* (Times Books, 1978) and *The Companion to Wine,* which he coauthored with Rosemary George and Michael Edwards (Prentice-Hall, 1992).

Since Elena Arzak took over the kitchen at the family's Michelin three-star restaurant here from her father, there have naturally been a few changes. But one tradition remains the same at Arzak: a dedication to fine Spanish cheese.

Charles de Gaulle once remarked on the difficulty of governing a country with some 240 different kinds of cheese. By that standard, Spain's leaders have little to complain about since their country has only about a hundred.

It's probably an exaggeration, but Arzak's cheese cart seemed to have most of them. At a dinner there recently, Ms. Arzak saved us the trouble of having to choose; she simply served four of the most renowned.

We had *queso de cabra de Vizcaya,* a goat's milk cheese with mineral nuances in its flavor from Vizcaya province, where Bilbao is located. We had *Idiazábal ahumado,* a sharp, nutty-tasting, and almost buttery smoked sheep's milk cheese from a village south of here, on the road to Navarra. And we had *Cabrales con manzana,* a sharp blue cheese from Asturias that she blends with a compote of apples from the same region.

If that weren't indulgence enough, we also had *torta del Casar,* a soft young sheep's milk cheese from Extremadura that at its peak, at this time of year, is soft and runny enough to eat with a spoon like a French Vacherin.

The cheeses were served with the ceremony and sensibly small portions of a fine restaurant, and they were nicely matched with a 1990 Gran Reserva from Chivite. But I encountered the same reverence at little *tapas* bars and in country stores. Whether served with beer or the best sherry, on fine china or a toothpick, cheese in Spain is as essential as bread itself.

A two-week ramble through Northern Spain served as a delightful primer to a little-known but spectacular part of Europe and a treasure trove of fine cheeses that are finally beginning to be appreciated in the United States.

Northern Spain is sometimes called Green Spain, because its forests, lush valleys, and snow-capped peaks belie the tourist image of oranges, flamenco, and sun-baked villages. The region produces more than half of all Spain's best cheeses.

Two mountain ranges, the Pyrenees and the Cantabrian *cordillera,* which stretch from the Mediterranean to the Atlantic, protect and nurture a culture more like Switzerland's than southern Europe's. The massif of the Picos de Europa, in the center of the *cordillera,* has been called Spain's National Park of Cheeses because some twenty varieties are produced from the milk of the sheep, goats, and cows that graze, often side by side, on its slopes.

Driving from one town to another, from the mountains to the seaside and back to the mountains, we picked up the habit of stopping in late morning for *tapas*. Lunch in Spain, like dinner, is notoriously late in the day. No midday meal begins at midday; two P.M. is more the norm, and many restaurants are still busy serving lunch at four.

This means the long morning hours are best broken up with a few *tapas,* the delightful appetizers that are an integral part of Spanish life. Here in San Sebastián, which is Spain's unofficial capital of gastronomy, there are dozens of *tapas* bars, many of them clustered in the old part of the city between the harbor and the Central Market.

Cheese, usually Manchego, is an important *tapa,* served in small slices bathed in olive oil and in chunks on toothpicks, alone or paired with *serrano* ham or *chorizo.* We soon learned to plunge into the noisy crowd at the bar, pick out what we wanted, and back away, returning later to pay up. It's on the honor system, so you must save your toothpicks or little plates to keep count.

Beer is the best drink with cheese *tapas,* although in Guernica we had good cider and in Logroño's *tapas* bars we drank simple red wine. Here in Basque Country, *txakolí* (pronounced choc-o-LI), the local white wine, goes well with both cheese and the seemingly endless array of seafood *tapas* on offer—octopus, hake, small crabs, anchovies, and more.

As with fine wines, the names of the best Spanish cheeses are controlled by the government to prevent the proliferation of cheap imitations. There are twelve *denominación de origen* cheeses in Spain, almost all of them from the north. Two of the four we had at Arzak, the Cabrales and the Idiazábal. The Manchego of the *tapas* bars is another.

Cabrales comes from Asturias, which nestles between Galicia and Cantabria along Spain's northern coast. The coastline is alternately rocky and sandy and is battered by strong winds and rain in winter. The interior, mountainous and rugged, is the source of the region's best cheeses.

Cabrales resembles Roquefort but is creamier, its veining a deeper blue and the flavor less salty. Both are usually aged in caves for three to six months.

Idiazábal is from northwest Navarra and the Basque Country. The name comes from a Basque village, where it is supposed to have originated. Traditionally, the cheese was made by Basque shepherds from the milk of Latxa sheep in communal shepherds' huts high in the Pyrenees, where all summer and into the fall they absorbed fireplace smoke. Today the cheeses are smoked over hardwood.

Not all Idiazábal is smoked, but all of it is made from unpasteurized sheep's milk. The raw milk is what gives Idiazábal its buttery texture and rich nutty taste. Smoking Idiazábal adds a delicious dark aftertaste.

The *queso de cabra de Vizcaya* is a firm but spreadable goat's milk cheese from a region that specializes in sheep's milk cheeses. To me, it tasted a bit chalky but very flavorful.

One of Elena Arzak's favorites—and now one of mine—the *torta del Casar,* comes from Extremadura and is made from unpasteurized sheep's milk. The texture is creamy, so much so that the cheese can be scooped from the rind with a spoon, and the flavor is rich and nutty.

One of the best cheese stories I came across in Spain—the cheese is pretty good, too—concerns Garrotxa (pronounced ga-RO-cha) from the town of the same name in the Mediterranean part of the Pyrenees. About twenty years ago a small cooperative of goat farmers in that town decided to bring back a cheese that had been made in their region a hundred years earlier but had all but disappeared. The farmers were part of a "neorural" movement of young people who had decided to quit professional careers and return to the land.

Farmhouse-style cheeses, made from goat's, sheep's, and cow's milk, are a favorite project of the group. Garrotxa is one of these cheeses. It is soft and buttery, and is usually covered with a natural mold induced by the humid climate in the high pastures.

A reason in itself to return to these mountains.

A New Appetite in America

By Florence Fabricant

～

FLORENCE FABRICANT writes about food for a variety of periodicals and is the editor of the Food Notes column for the Dining In/Dining Out section of *The New York Times,* where this article appeared on May 10, 2000.

Cheeses from Spain were once a rarity in American shops. Now, even supermarkets are selling mild ivory Manchego, and the more powerful Cabrales and Mahón are becoming easier to find, too.

But leaving it at that would be like representing Italy only with Parmesan, pecorino, and fontina. Or just being able to buy Brie, Roquefort, and Montrachet from France.

Like those countries, Spain produces scores of distinctive cheeses. But in Spain many are still made in tiny batches, sometimes on farms with just a single herd of sheep or goats. These mom-and-pop producers make just enough to supply their villages.

"Most of them are very local, just farmers who made traditional cheeses for their area," said José Guerra, the marketing manager for Foods from Spain in New York, a government trade group. In fact, Mr. Guerra said, until recently you couldn't even find these regional cheeses in Madrid.

It seems something of a miracle that over the last few years so many of these assertive, richly nutty cheeses have begun making their way to America, thanks in part to the Spanish government's promotion and also because of the growing interest among cheese connoisseurs here. More than 1.5 million pounds of Spanish cheese were imported last year, up from just over 650,000 pounds in 1995, according to the United States Commerce Department. But even now, some varieties, like the smoky Idiazábal, are available only sporadically.

They are worth seeking out—in some respects, even more than many of the imported French varieties. Many of the best traditional French cheeses are made from unpasteurized milk and are aged less than sixty days, so they don't comply with U.S. government regulations. (Many Bries and Camemberts are modified for export and made with pasteurized milk.) But with Spanish cheese it's possible to sample the best here: though most are made from unpasteurized milk, a great many traditional Spanish cheeses have always been aged more than sixty days.

"French cheeses have become more compromised by industrialization and demand," said Max McCalman, the cheese expert at Picholine in Manhattan. "Now is a good time to get Spanish cheese, before it is industrialized."

More Spanish cheeses are made from sheep's milk or goat's milk than from cow's milk. Many are made from a mixture of the three, which varies depending on the season. Though many people may think of sharp pecorino as typical of sheep's milk cheeses, in Spain they vary from buttery to strongly assertive.

"Spanish cheeses are more artisanal and look less factory-made," said Kevin Tyldesley, the cheese buyer at Gramercy Tavern. "But there's a lot less diversity of style. For example, I haven't come across really soft, soft cheeses like Camemberts or triple creams from France."

Gramercy Tavern is on a growing list of restaurants serving Spanish cheese. Picholine, Hell's Kitchen, and Acquario also buy them, as do places that serve Spanish food, including Solera, Plácido Domingo's, Meigas, and Bolo. Most of the time they're on the cheese tray or the *tapas* menu, although Bolo routinely makes salads with Cabrales, Spain's great blue cheese, and Hell's Kitchen uses Manchego and Idiazábal in its quesadillas.

The best way to begin a love affair with Spanish cheese is to taste. Visit a good cheese shop—one that is well stocked and has a high turnover—and ask for sample slivers of three or four. Then buy two to take home and nibble with some cured ham or olives at cocktail time, the way the Spaniards do. Or serve them with fresh or dried fruit, or a drizzle of honey at the end of dinner. Some cheese shops sell *membrillo,* winy Spanish quince paste, which often accompanies wedges of cheese for dessert.

Manchego, Spain's most popular cheese, is good for novices. For one thing, the cheese has eye appeal: dark rinds of the thick cylinders are beautifully patterned with close crosshatching from the molds in which they are made. Manchego is a sheep's milk cheese usually aged three months to a year, during which time its pale off-white interior gradually deepens to ivory. It has a relatively mild flavor, especially when young, and hints of walnuts as it ages. Chunks of aged manchego are delicious steeped for an hour or so in fruity olive oil. Two other cheeses, Zamorano and Castellano, are similar to Manchego, and many people prefer their somewhat more complex flavor.

Ibérico, unlike the others, is a factory-made cheese that has less character than the traditional varieties; cheese exporters expected it would have more appeal and began promoting it about nine years ago, Mr. Guerra said.

Mahón, a cow's milk cheese from the island of Minorca, with an orange rind, has the kind of nuttiness with buttery overtones you might associate with aged Monterey Jack and is good used just the same way.

Roncal, a classic firm-textured sheep's milk cheese from Navarra, in Northern Spain, has been made for more than a thousand years and was the first of about a dozen cheeses to be given an official appellation, or *denominación de origen*. A deep ivory cheese with saltiness tempered with a touch of sweet, it is excellent when used like Parmigiano-Reggiano.

Torta del Casar is an aromatic satiny sheep's milk cheese that can become as fluently lush and full flavored as Vacherin.

Idiazábal, a smoked sheep's milk cheese from the Basque Country, has a pale interior and firm, supple texture similar to provolone. "The smoked flavor is well balanced and doesn't have a plastic quality of many smoked cheeses," Mr. Tyldesley said. Try it in a stuffing for baked chicken breasts, or in a grilled portobello mushroom sandwich.

Another intriguing smoked cheese is San Simón, which is almost egg shaped and resembles scamorza, the Italian smoked mozzarella. *Tetilla*, the mildest and among the least distinctive-tasting of Spanish cheeses, is cow's milk cheese similar to San Simón, but not smoked.

Garroxta (pronounced ga-RO-cha), from Catalonia, is a goat's milk cheese with a sturdy gray rind, a white interior, and delightfully herbal overtones. It is less crumbly than French or American goat cheeses, and though it has a certain sharpness, it doesn't have a strong goaty flavor.

Queso de Murcia al Vino, or Drunken Goat, is becoming one of the most popular Spanish cheeses in the United States. It is a smooth, mild white goat cheese with a faintly winy aroma.

Cabrales, Spain's famous blue-veined cheese from Asturias, can be difficult to find in good condition. In some American shops, it is too strong and almost gummy—the result of inconsistent temperature or humidity. The cheese should be on the soft side with clearly defined veining, a grassy aroma, and a pungent, complex, but not overly salty flavor.

Picón, made in the neighboring province of Cantabria, is almost identical. If the Cabrales doesn't pass muster, try the Picón.

Spanish cooks make relatively little use of cheese. *Paella,* for example, is not routinely dusted with grated cheese the way Italian *risotto* is.

"Many Italian cheeses are used in cooking," Mr. McCalman said, "whereas in Spain, cheese is a food, often consumed as an appetizer course." Steak with a creamy sauce of Cabrales is a rare example of a Spanish dish made with cheese.

But Spanish cheeses make excellent substitutes for Italian, French, or American ones in many dishes, especially when the ingredients owe allegiance to Spain.

I shredded Roncal over asparagus for baking, much the way Parmigiano-Reggiano is used in northern Italy. Thin shavings of mild young Manchego glazed individual pizzas made with a saffron-scented dough, roasted red peppers, and *chorizo.* And little nuggets of Idiazábal folded in at the last minute imparted a subtle smokiness to a rice pilaf colored and seasoned with fresh herbs and garlic.

After just a little experimenting, I could see Manchego, Garroxta and Idiazábal becoming as essential in my kitchen as Parmesan, Gruyère, and cheddar.

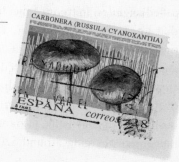

¡Buen Provecho!   485

In Pursuit of Angulas

By Bruce Schoenfeld

❧

editor's note

Of all the culinary delights unique to Northern Spain, *angulas* are perhaps the most distinctive. They are also rare, only available in season (October to February), and are almost impossible to find outside of the Basque Country. But a dish of *angulas,* as the author notes, is an unforgettable food experience, so readers who are also serious foodies will not regret planning their trip to coincide with the season.

BRUCE SCHOENFELD, introduced earlier, is a frequent contributor to *Saveur,* where this piece first appeared. He is also the author of *The Last Serious Thing: A Season at the Bullfights* (Simon & Schuster, 1992).

I had drunk so much good Rioja immediately prior to trying *angulas* for the first time, a decade ago in the Basque Country, that I hardly noticed how much they looked like small gray worms. The wine was a 1964 Viña Tondonia, plucked from the cellars at Urepel, a San Sebastián restaurant renowned for its fish. It was nearly four o'clock in the afternoon, late for lunch even by Spanish standards, and I had been imbibing since noon. As a result, I mindlessly plowed through the bowl of baby eels (full-grown eels are called *anguilas*) in front of me. It was only later, after I sobered up, that I gave them any thought. Then I recalled a subtle yet distinctive flavor—almost but not quite overpowered by generous amounts of garlic and dried red pepper—and a tactile pleasure in chewing and swallowing the pliant, silky strands. For the duration of my trip, I made sure to experience the sensation repeatedly, seriously depleting my bank account in the process. At the time restaurants were charging around $20 per serving, which seemed a bit steep. Unfortunately, dwindling supplies of this Basque delicacy have since sent prices even higher. But for *angula* aficionados, it seems that no price is too high; they're just happy to find them.

The *angula* season is short, running only from late October to February, and it is quite difficult to find fresh, good-quality *angulas* outside the Basque region any time of year. Surely one reason for their scarcity is the epic journey the eels make to get to Spain: leaving their spawning ground in the Sargasso Sea, between Bermuda and Puerto Rico, these tiny, transparent elvers—little more than three inches long and as thin as a blade of grass when they arrive at their destination—travel about three years and some three thousand miles to reach the muddy rivers of Northern Spain. They are scooped from the water in large nets by fishermen called *anguleros* and are dealt with in one of three ways: sold immediately while still alive; submerged and killed in water laced with nicotine (which purges them), then washed and blanched in salted water to turn them opaque; or transferred to freshwater nurseries *(viveros)* for eight to ten days to fatten before they're killed. (Because their spines darken during this period, eels sent to nurseries are called *angulas de lomo negro,* or black *angulas.* These are slightly more expensive, and some say more flavorful, than their more common, paler counterparts.) Depending on the quality, availability, and the time of year—their prices increase as the season progresses—raw *angulas* go for $70–$170 a pound wholesale, while blanched elvers, sold loose or in plastic packages, generally cost a little more. *Angulas* are also available frozen, but they pale in comparison.

According to legend, the Basque people originated on the lost continent of Atlantis, eventually migrating to northern Iberia—to the mountainous region straddling the border of present-day Spain and France. Basque culture is famously elusive and insular. The difficult Basque language, Euskera, peppered with rough consonants like *k, x,* and *z,* bears little relation to French or Spanish or any other known language (though it unaccountably shares some structural attributes with Finnish). Basques mark their holidays with odd spectacles: tossing animals from apartment windows, racing bulls through city streets. But the food they eat, and their obsession with it, offers a window into their culture. Basque cuisine, which features rare ingredients and complicated preparations, is one of the world's most evolved and celebrated. In fact, San Sebastián, a city of just 177,000 inhabitants, boasts a total of seven Michelin stars; if nearby suburbs such as Oiartzun and Lasarte are included, the number reaches twelve.

Against this gastronomic landscape, full of innovative chefs, *angulas* are one of the few dishes typically cooked in a uniform style—in this case, *a la bilbaína*. This traditional Basque method, named after the city of Bilbao, capital of the Basque province of Vizcaya (Biscay), involves lightly cooking sliced garlic and dried red pepper in olive oil in an earthenware vessel called a *cazuela,* then adding and quickly sautéing the *angulas.*

Five years ago I spent a week in San Sebastián consuming the intricate fare prepared by the city's best chefs. But what I enjoyed the most were not the hake cheeks in green sauce or the pigeon in phyllo dough; it was those unaccountably alluring baby eels, always eaten with a flat wooden fork (which helps bring the slippery creatures safely to the mouth, doesn't impart a metallic taste, and won't get so hot in the sizzling oil that it risks burning the diner). "We're a traditional society," says Ramón Roteta, whose elegant eponymous restaurant in Hondarribia is famous for its eels. "*Angulas* reflect that tradition." (Top restaurants in Barcelona, Madrid, and beyond include *angulas* on their menus, but you're not likely to find any worth eating on the American side of the Atlantic.) It's generally agreed that the best *angulas* come from Aguinaga, a tiny and unprepossessing Basque town in the Guipúzcoa province on the Rio Oria that is home to three eel-processing plants. On moonless nights (*angulas* travel only in the dark), *anguleros* walk along the river's edge holding lanterns to lure the elvers into their nets. The fishermen return to the plants at daybreak carrying plastic pails filled with the night's catch. The yield is seldom as large as it used to be: in 1998—admittedly a particularly bad year for eels—just 3,200 pounds of *angulas* were fished in Northern Spain, compared with about 27,000 pounds in 1977. But whether the decline is due to unusually wet weather, overfishing, some natural cycle, or side effects from pollution in the North Atlantic is uncertain.

What is clear is that demand for *angulas* far exceeds supply. In fact, the genuine item has become so scarce that some Basques now buy imitation *angulas,* called *gulas,* made from *surimi*—processed fish—at the bargain price of about $12 a pound. But many others gladly sacrifice a new tie or a car tune-up for a taste of the real thing. Several times I've spent $600 on a week's worth of bullfight tickets, and I once laid out $90 for a small but satisfying order of exalted lobsterlike *cigalas* (crayfish), but I don't generally share the Spanish penchant for pursuing passions at any cost. So when I book a table at Zuberoa, my favorite restaurant in Spain, on my final afternoon on a recent visit to San Sebastián, I tell myself I'm doing so merely for a light lunch; in other words, *angulas* won't be on *my* menu. But Hilario Arbelaitz, the chef and co-owner, who buys from a local supplier and can still get top-quality *angulas*—for a price (last year he was charging $40 for a 5½-ounce serving)—tells me that he is worried about the future: "It's the start of a bad trend," he says of the declining catch. So I convince myself that I had better eat the delicacy while I still can. The *angulas* arrive sizzling in a *cazuela,* as usual, and with one bite that subtle but unmistakable taste is back—a taste as singular as the Basques themselves.

Albariño: A Wine of the Sea

By Gerald Asher

❧

editor's note

Spanish wines are currently holding the top spot on my favorite wines list. This statement does, however, require a bit of an explanation: readers of my *Paris* edition may recall how much I love French wine; in that book, I wrote, "in comparison with like wines from other countries, French wine is almost always, over 95 percent of the time, better." I still believe this is true, but what I mean to say about Spanish wines is that I have not traveled in any other country where the wines were so consistently good, sometimes amazing. In other words, I have had plenty of great bottles and glasses in France and Italy, for example, but I have also been served extremely mediocre ones, for the same price as a significantly better, good-quality everyday wine in Spain. Unfortunately, many of the memorable wines in Spain never make it out of the country, let alone to North America. But fans of Spanish wines are growing, and Spanish wine production is changing rapidly. I am keeping my fingers crossed that Spanish wines will grow in popularity and earn the respect they so deserve on this side of the Atlantic.

One wine in particular that I am crazy for is Albariño, a wonderful young white wine from the Rías Baixas in Galicia that thankfully has recently developed a following in North America. In much the same way that a Muscadet from the Loire valley is the perfect wine for shellfish, Albariño is positively the *only* wine to drink with any dish from the sea served in Northern Spain (unless you are in the Basque Country, whose few vineyards produce only one wine of note, *txakoli,* the only proper accompaniment to that region's seafood *tapas* and entrées). Albariño is also a terrific beginning to *any* meal, whetting one's appetite subtly for the *golosinas* (tidbits) ahead. Particularly upon my last return trip from Northern Spain, I found I was craving Albariño incessantly and was pleased to discover that the respected wine shop Zachy's, in Scarsdale, New York (16 East Parkway, Scarsdale, New York 10583; 800-723-0241; www.zachys.com), carries a good selection. (Zachy's ships nationwide, by the way, if you have trouble finding Albariño where you live.) You may, by now, think I am exaggerating ridiculously about an inexpensive white wine, but the following two pieces attest to the unsung glories of Albariño.

GERALD ASHER has been writing about wine for *Gourmet*—where this piece first appeared—for many years. He is also the author of *On Wine* (Random House, 1986), *The Pleasures of Wine* (2002), and *Vineyard Tales* (1996), both published by Chronicle Books. Among the numerous honors he's received are the 1998 James Beard Award for articles on wines and spirits, and the 1974 Merite Agricole, an award for services rendered to agriculture, and one that is rarely given to foreigners.

Has a totally unfamiliar white wine ever given us such a jolt? Such pleasure? Albariño, from Rías Baixas in northwest Spain, is still no more than an eddy in a puddle compared to the ocean of Chardonnay we consume every year. But in the United States sales of this seductively aromatic wine have bounded from just 2,000 cases in 1992 to more than 30,000 in 2000. If production could have supported it, sales would have risen even faster.

In Spain the wines from this small corner of Galicia have won praise on all sides—they are now on the list of every serious restaurant from Seville to San Sebastián—and for at least the past decade, they have had a place at the royal table.

Albariño is actually part of a much larger secret. In summer, when northern Europe invades Spain's Mediterranean beaches, the Spanish themselves disappear to Galicia, a private green refuge tucked between Portugal's northern border and the Atlantic. Santiago de Compostela, the region's capital, ranks with Rome and Jerusalem as a place of pilgrimage for the world's Catholics, of course. But for most Americans it's usually just a stop on a wider European tour. Having paid their respects to the cathedral—its altar ablaze with gold and silver—and allowed themselves to be beguiled for a day or two by the medieval charm of narrow, winding streets that open abruptly onto vast plazas of an austere splendor, they are on their way. Rarely do they venture the short distance to the coast, with its countless bays and inlets—the *rías*—or discover, farther inland, the rivers that long ago carved out deep canyons in Galicia's ancient mountains (now mostly protected as natural parks), or walk in woods where paths are banked with creamy rock-roses and clearings edged with beds of tiny scarlet wild strawberries.

Galicia is hardly the Spain of popular imagination: of strumming guitars, stamping heels, and carnations between the teeth. The Moors never established themselves here, so Galicia dances in slippers to the Celtic drum and bagpipe, and its pilgrims walk in sneakers and parkas (but still with cockleshells pinned to their hats) on roads punctuated by tall crucifixes directing them to the tomb of Saint James. For curious travelers there are mysterious cave drawings and prehistoric dolmens, feudal castles and Romanesque churches, Roman bridges (still in daily use) and monasteries built near remote passes where pilgrims in centuries past could find a night's shelter and protection from brigands unimpressed by their piety. Elsewhere are sober, seventeenth-century stone *pazos*—manor houses presiding over villages that still live on what they can wrest from a wild land and an even wilder sea. Like Brittany and the west coast of Ireland, Galicia is a place of sudden storms and drowned fishermen, of lighthouses, ghost stories, wee folk, and things that go bump in the night.

Above all, however, it's a place where one eats and drinks well. There are mussel and oyster beds in the *rías*, and every village up and down the coast has its own line of fishing boats. Only Japan consumes more fish per capita than Spain, and in this region, which boasts two of Europe's most important fishing ports—Vigo and La Coruña—meat is rarely more than a footnote on the menu. Even the scruffiest of the bars and taverns that line Santiago's twisting Rúa do Franco serve just-caught fish of unimaginable variety cooked with a confidence that would put any restaurant in Paris or New York on the defensive.

No one knows when the vine was introduced to this part of Spain. It can be assumed that the Romans, who settled in the area two thousand years ago to mine the hills near Orense for precious metals, would have provided for themselves somehow. The first reliable record we have that links past to present, however, is of vineyards planted in the twelfth century by Cistercian monks at Armenteira, in the Salnés Valley near the fishing port of Cambados. (According to local legend, Albariño is descended from cuttings of Riesling brought from Kloster Eberbach in the Rheingau by some of these Cistercians. It's a pretty story, but recent DNA research has shown beyond a doubt that there is no such connection; the variety's origin is, therefore, still a matter of speculation.)

More vines were planted later on lands granted to the monastery of Santa María de Oia, forty or so miles south within the sharp angle formed by the estuary of the Miño—the river that establishes the frontier with Portugal—and the Atlantic. From these early beginnings evolved the vineyards of Val do Salnés to the north and those of O Rosal and Condado do Tea to the south. (A fourth defined zone roughly midway between them, Soutomaior, was created recently, but it produces such a small quantity of wine that, commercially, it has had no impact as yet.)

There are all kinds of shadings and subtleties to be explored—with wine there always are—but an explanation of the differences between Salnés on the one hand and Rosal and Condado on the other is enough to illustrate most of what one needs to know about Albariño. The vineyards of Salnés form an open bowl facing west to the ocean. From the terrace of the Martín Códax winery on Burgans Hill, above Cambados, there is a limitless view of the bay and the Atlantic beyond. The individual shelves and terraces of vines face this way and that to catch the sun, but all are exposed to whatever blows in from the sea. The vineyards of Rosal and Condado also turn about, to accommodate the rise and fall of a terrain shaped by the streams and rivulets that feed the Miño, but their broad direction is always to the south, to the river. Rosal is affected by the ocean less directly, and Condado—because it is farther upstream—even less. Their vineyards are drier and warmer than those of Salnés; they get less rain and have more hours of sun.

There are other differences, too. Vines in Salnés are grown on a fairly homogenous granitic sand, while those of Rosal and Condado also contend with crumbled schist, clay, and the rolled pebbles typical of any place where the water's flow has shifted. These differences of soil and prevailing weather do not make any one zone better than the others (though you can be sure that's not the way the growers see it), but they do impose distinct and varied characteristics on their wines. A Salnés Albariño is bolder than one from either Rosal or Condado. It has good acidity and a pungent aroma and flavor (some say of pineapple), and it gives a powerful, fleshy impression. Its focus is intensely varietal. Rosal wines—and to an even greater degree those from Condado—are more graceful and more supple. Their flavor steals across the palate and lingers there. If a Salnés wine tends to express the varietal more than the site, a Rosal or Condado wine does the opposite.

The official revival of Rías Baixas (pronounced REE-as BUY-zhas) had its start in 1980, when the local board of control recognized the distinct qualities of the Albariño wines produced in Galicia with a new *denominación de origen*. The ruling was rewritten by the Spanish legislature in 1988 to conform to European Economic Community standards that required the primary definition of an appellation to be geographic rather than varietal. The redrafted regulations formally established four zones and listed Albariño, Loureiro, Treixadura, and Caíño Blanco as the main vine varieties recommended to be grown within their boundaries.

Any Rías Baixas wine labeled Albariño is made from that variety alone, and a Salnés wine is almost always one hundred percent

Albariño. The other recommended grape varieties do not grow as well in that valley: conditions are too extreme. But that isn't the case for either Rosal or Condado, where Loureiro and Treixadura in particular have always contributed to the style of the wines. In fact, regulations require, for example, that a wine labeled Rías Baixas–O Rosal must have at least a little Loureiro to enhance its natural fragrance, and one sold as Rías Baixas–Condado do Tea is understood to have the benefit of Treixadura's finesse and structure. Using other varieties in this way reinforces long-standing distinctions among the zones of Rías Baixas, but Albariño now predominates in more than 90 percent of the vineyards, and most producers offer Rías Baixas only as an Albariño varietal wine.

The aroma and bite for which Albariño is celebrated owe much to the cooling proximity of the ocean and to the stress-free growth guaranteed by ample spring rain. In Spain, at least, these are conditions unique to the Rías Baixas. Ground humidity brings potential problems, of course, even though Albariño has a thick skin. As protection from rot, the vines are trained over high, horizontal pergolas. The hefty granite pillars used are not the most elegant supports, but they fit in with the local custom of scattering vines about in handkerchief-size plots like untidy afterthoughts. A vineyard is sometimes no more than an arbor attached to the side of a house, an arrangement of granite and wire in an awkward bend of the road, or a backyard shared with a patch of turnips or cabbages. For years, most families in Rías Baixas have had vines to make wine only for their own consumption. It was a crop grown for the household—like peppers, corn, and potatoes—that sometimes provided a surplus that could be sold.

Ironically, it was a crisis in the fishing industry that sparked Albariño's resurgence. New restrictions on fishing in European waters in the mid-1980s hit small ports like Cambados, Baiona, and La Guardia badly. The big factory ships of Vigo and La Coruña could go in search of new fishing grounds; boats from the smaller villages have a limited range, though, so these communities had to find a way to supplement what was earned from the sea. Shopkeepers, schoolteachers, and particularly the fishermen themselves—everyone with a few vines—moved from making wine for their own consumption to expanding their production and selling it. From the five hundred acres of vines existing in Rías Baixas in 1986, the acreage is now close to six thousand.

The Martín Códax winery, one of the first to come onto the scene in Salnés, was founded in 1986, funded by a group of small growers who knew they could achieve more together than if each tried to make and market wine on his own. With modern equipment—good presses, refrigeration for cool fermentation, easy-to-clean stainless-steel tanks—they were able to reveal Albariño's forgotten qualities. "And who is Martín Códax?" I asked Pablo Buján, the firm's sales manager. "The prime mover of the project? The partner with the biggest holding?"

"He was a thirteenth-century Galician poet and troubadour from this very place," Buján replied. "He drank a lot of wine."

The thirsty Códax would doubtless be pleased to know that the winery named for him is probably the most successful in Rías Baixas, producing almost 1.5 million bottles of wine in a normal year. To understand the difficulty of this feat, one must remember that the grapes are grown by more than two hundred partners who together own nearly four hundred acres of vines divided over twelve hundred separate plots.

Over the years land in Galicia has been divided and divided again through successive inheritance. Vineyard plots on the terraced hillsides got smaller and smaller, and in the end those at a distance from the villages were hardly worth the effort needed to cultivate them. In the 1940s and 1950s, under General Franco, most were given over to stands of eucalyptus trees to provide pulp for a paper mill in Pontevedra. In the rain their drooping leaves and peeling bark lend a wistful melancholy to the landscape. But where the trees have been cleared, the original terracing can still be seen.

"Our natural trees are oak and chestnut. Eucalyptus trees give a poor return and are bad for the soil," says Javier Luca de Tena, director of Granja Fillaboa, with a dismissive wave of the hand. Angel Suárez, manager of the Lagar de Cervera (now owned by the Rioja Alta winery), endured several years of painstaking negotiations with disparate owners to put together enough land to restore a rational, workable vineyard. Often a single row of trees belongs to one family, and the next one, to another. Each of four brothers will cling to his clump of half a dozen eucalyptus trees when their entire holding, taken together, makes up a block no bigger than a kitchen garden.

A program encouraging owners to swap land in order to build up the size of individual holdings has not been a great success. Apparently, the smaller the patch, the greater its mystical importance to someone unwilling to part with it. To put together an economically viable vineyard, therefore, takes a great deal of forbearance and much money. (One doesn't buy land in Galicia, one bribes the owner to part with it.)

Another Rioja winery, Bodegas Lan, now owns Santiago Ruiz in O Rosal, a small producer of such prestige in Spain that it could afford to dispense with marketing a varietal Albariño, despite the demand, and concentrate on producing a Rías Baixas–O Rosal, a superb wine in which Albariño's exuberance is tempered by Loureiro to just the right degree. La Val, another producer in Rosal, also makes, along with its particularly delicious varietal Albariño, an exquisite wine made from Loureiro and Albariño—reversing the proportions used by Santiago Ruiz.

I was not surprised when José Luis Méndez, son of the owner of Morgadío, told me that his family was trying to think of a way in which Loureiro could be brought back into the vineyard. The producers' dilemma is that they would all like to offer the more stylish wine that a proportion of Loureiro can give, but they don't want to give up the right to the magic name Albariño on the label. Both in Spain and in the United States, it gives instant recognition. While in Galicia recently, I lunched with Angel Suárez at a restaurant near the old fishing harbor of La Guardia. We chatted over a bottle of his 1998 Albariño and a dish of assorted fish—hake, turbot, and monkfish—simmered with potatoes and served in a sauce of garlic and *pimentón,* a very small pepper, dried over a slow wood fire and ground to a fine powder. It has a hauntingly smoky, sweet-sharp taste, and no Extremaduran or Galician kitchen is ever without it.

I enjoyed the wine, but Suárez said 1998 had been a difficult year for Rías Baixas. Spring came early: the vines sent out tender shoots in February, but the weather then turned very cold, with a predictable effect. Hailstorms in April did further damage, and rain in June meant that the fruit set poorly. As a result, the crop was barely 40 percent of the previous year's and never did reach the level of quality hoped for.

"A red wine region copes with this kind of difficulty more easily," he said. "Red wine is usually aged for a year or two, and differences of crop size from one year to another can be blurred, at least, by delaying or bringing forward the release date. Albariño is best when bottled and consumed young. We have no stocks to fall back on. Production is increasing a little every year, but at present, even when the crop is of a good size—almost seventeen million kilos of good quality grapes in 2001 as opposed to half that in 2000—it seems there is never quite enough to meet demand."

He poured the last of the 1998 into my glass, leaving none for himself.

Though all Galicians speak and write Castilian—the Spanish of Salamanca, Toledo, and Madrid—they traditionally use Gallego, a Spanish that is close to Portuguese in vocabulary, spelling, and pronunciation. Rías Baixas would be Rías Bajas in Castilian. Town names can be found with Castilian or Gallego spellings depending on which map one is consulting. O Rosal is the same place as El Rosal, Tui is Tuy, and Salvaterra is not a misspelling of Salvatierra. In every instance, both versions are correct and the regulations specifically embrace and protect both Castilian and Gallego names for everything.

An Albariño Shopping List

All prices are approximate.

Val do Salnés:
Martín Códax Albariño 1998, $13
Burgans Albariño 1998, $11

O Rosal:
Lagar de Cervera Albariño 1998, $17
La Val Albariño 1998, $15

Condado do Tea:
Fillaboa Albariño 1998, $15
Morgadío Albariño 1998, $19

Souvenir Wines

By David Shaw

∽

DAVID SHAW is the media critic for *The Los Angeles Times,* and contributes frequently to *Food & Wine,* where this first appeared.

We had driven almost two hours from our small hotel in the French Pyrenees, all the way across the mountains to the Spanish border, through the resort town of Roses and along a winding, bumpy one-lane mountain road. The only visible sign of civilization came in the form of bulldog heads stenciled on some roadside rocks. We were on our way to El Bulli (The Bulldog), a much-praised restaurant that food critics everywhere have described as "the most interesting in the world today." Once seated, I began studying the wine list and realized I'd made a big mistake.

I'd recently fallen in love with Spanish red wines and had prepared for our trip by reading up on and tasting as many of them as I could find. Unfortunately, it hadn't occurred to me to do the same with Spanish whites. And as it turned out, El Bulli, located near the Mediterranean Sea, specializes in seafood, notably shellfish.

Now, I'm not a white-wine-with-fish, red-wine-with-meat kind of guy. In fact, I like red wine with almost everything. However, I do think the acidity of white wine generally makes it a better companion to shellfish than almost any red. I confessed my ignorance and my preference to the sommelier and threw myself on his mercy. He recommended Albariño, a wine made in the Rías Baixas region of Galicia, the windy, rainy, westernmost part of Spain. In particular, he said, we should order the Albariño from a producer named Granbazán.

The choice was superb, perfect with each of our four dishes, which included shrimp, clams, mussels, and cuttlefish. The wine wasn't quite as flinty as a Muscadet, nor as rich as my favorite Chablis; instead, it had just the right amount of fruit, acidity, and body to both complement and emphasize the flavors of the shellfish. And it was very reasonably priced—a mere $28—a fact that's especially noteworthy in a Michelin three-star restaurant.

We tried several other Albariños during our time in Spain but didn't find any we liked as well as the Granbazán. So on our last day in Barcelona I went to a wine store near our hotel and bought two bottles, one for my wife and me, and one for the family we were traveling with. (I would have bought a case, but I didn't want to carry it and figured I'd have no problem finding the wine at home. That was my second mistake.)

I decided to track down the Granbazán a few days after our return to Los Angeles. I began calling the wine merchants I regularly deal with. None had ever heard of my wine. I phoned a few stores in San Francisco and even three or four shops in New York. The answer was the same. So I expanded my search to include a few local restaurateurs, two prominent sommeliers, several wine distributors, an importer, and even two wine writers. Still no luck.

While I was on the hunt, I was also reading up on Albariño. The forerunner of the Albariño vine, I learned, was most likely brought to Spain in the Middle Ages by German pilgrims visiting the shrine of Santiago de Compostela. The wine ultimately became one of the most highly regarded in Europe. But it began to fall from favor in the 1960s and 1970s, thanks in part to a decline in the local fishing industry and a subsequent economic downturn. It didn't help that the Albariño grape is tough to grow, with a skin so thick that relatively little juice can be extracted, resulting in low yields and low profits—a risky combination in a weak economy. By the mid-1980s only five Albariño makers survived, and production had shriveled to five hundred acres. But with an improved economy, full-scale production resumed in the 1990s. Today Albariño is grown on more than six thousand acres and made by more than fifty different wineries, about twenty of which ship to the United States. Just not Granbazán. Or so it seemed.

In the meantime I wasn't just reading about Albariño, I was also tasting as much of it as I could find. I bought Albariños from the producers Morgadío and Lusco, from Martín Códax, Santiago Ruíz, Fillaboa, and Burgans. I drank the wines both with and without food, together and separately. My verdicts remained fairly consistent: they were all fine, but none was as good as the Granbazán (although I thought the Morgadío was definitely the best of the alternatives).

It wasn't until I was several weeks into this seemingly fruitless search that I had a small epiphany of sorts. I decided to start all over, at the most obvious place of all. I opened the telephone book and looked up "Spain." I started with the Spanish Commercial Office. They connected me to a man who, they said, "helps us with all the Spanish wines that come into this country." In turn, that man gave me the number of a small importer of Spanish wines, named José Bargo, based in Edgewater, New Jersey. Bargo? Bingo!

A week later, Granbazán in hand, I walked into my favorite local fish restaurant and ordered a dozen oysters. It was like visiting an old friend. Yes, I was in downtown Los Angeles, with a view decidedly not that of the Mediterranean. But with the Granbazán in my glass, it was almost as if I were in Spain once more.

Albariño All-Stars

As with most modestly priced white wines, Albariño is generally best consumed young, so I'd recommend looking for the most recent vintage in your local wine shop. A few of the better Albariños, such as the Granbazán and the Morgadío, seem to benefit from an extra year of bottle age. All prices are approximate.

Burgans ($10). Relatively light but with a crisp taste and clear, citruslike acidity. It's an interesting alternative to Muscadet as an accompaniment to oysters.

Granbazán ($19). The richest and yet most nuanced of all the Albariños I've tasted.

Lusco ($22). One of the more full-bodied Albariños I tried, yet still possessed of the wine's characteristically flinty edge, which manages to cut through the iodine flavor often evident in shellfish.

Martín Códax ($12). Surprisingly firm and well structured, especially for a wine in this very reasonable price category.

Morgadío ($20). While many Albariños are said to smell of pears and almonds, this one really does. It's also full-bodied, with more complexity than one generally finds in most Albariños.

In Spain, a Mild Red Pepper
Is Hot

By Penelope Casas

~

editor's note

If, after reading this piece, you find it hard to believe there can be such a difference between *pimienta* and *pimiento,* or that the red and green bell peppers cultivated in North America are *completely* different from their Spanish cousins, trust me—and the author: they absolutely are, and you'll discover this for yourself not only by trying them in restaurant dishes but by visiting markets in the Basque Country and Navarra. The first sign that something's different is the size of Spanish peppers—they're much larger, and the red ones give off a wonderful rich smell wholly unlike any red bell pepper I've encountered, even at the farmer's market.

Penelope Casas, introduced earlier in this book, is the leading Spanish food authority in North America.

In Spain's galaxy of foods, a red pepper called *pimiento del piquillo de Lodosa*—no more than four inches long and narrowing to a "peak" (thus the name *piquillo*)—has recently achieved star status. Sold in jars and cans, the peppers are so exceptional that even the finest restaurants in Spain, which otherwise deem preserved vegetables of any kind unfit for their tables, will use nothing but *pimientos del piquillo de Lodosa* for some of their finest dishes. The *pimientos del piquillo de Lodosa* are so carefully processed that it is hard to distinguish them from those just picked and freshly prepared. And Spanish restaurateurs based outside Spain, when visiting home, are known to fill suitcases with Lodosa peppers, finding certain dishes impossible to execute without them.

Success, naturally, spawns imitation and even downright deception. Therefore the *pimientos del piquillo* of eight small towns—Lodosa, Andosilla, Cárcar, Mendavia, Sartaguda, San Adrián, Azagra and Lerín, all in the region of Navarra close to the northern bank of the broad Ebro River—have been granted their very own appellation of origin: Pimientos del Piquillo de Lodosa, an honor similar to that accorded the fine Rioja wines produced nearby. Take the same pepper seeds, plant them elsewhere, and the results are decidedly inferior.

The best way to appreciate the subtle flavor and fine consistency of a *pimiento del piquillo* is to eat it in the traditional way: lightly sautéed in an earthenware casserole with olive oil, garlic and salt. *Piquillo* peppers also impart their color and flavor to a variety of dishes. They may be combined with garlic, olive oil, and vinegar into a simple salad and are wonderful accompaniments to grilled meats. Some restaurants are more inventive; Arzak, in San Sebastián, sautées them with plums to accompany *langoustines*. *Piquillos* lend themselves elegantly to stuffing, and most chefs choose to fill them either with meat, fish, or shellfish. Often finished with a puréed red pepper sauce, the stuffed peppers are quickly heated in the oven or run under the broiler right before serving.

In the regional cuisines of Navarra, La Rioja, Aragon, and the Basque Country, ordinary red peppers are integral ingredients of such peasant dishes as *bacalao al ajo arriero* and *a la vizcaína*—two versions of dried cod with red peppers—and of stewed lamb, pork, or chicken, prepared Chilindrón style or *a la riojana*. But *pimientos del piquillo de Lodosa* are strictly reserved for a culinary elite that prizes these peppers above all others, seeks them out no matter what the obstacles, and is willing to pay the higher price for the excellence that the Lodosa label assures.

Spaniards have been inordinately fond of all kinds of peppers ever since Columbus found this native American vegetable in the

New World, where it had been cultivated for thousands of years. The bite that peppers gave to Indian foods resembled that of the Far Eastern black pepper prized by Europeans. And since Columbus believed he had indeed found a westerly route to the East, he assumed he was tasting the same pepper and called the new spice *pimienta,* the Spanish word for black pepper.

Today these two unrelated products are distinguished in the Spanish language by the difference of one vowel: *pimienta* is "true" pepper—*Piper nigrum* and other varieties of the *Piper* genus—and *pimiento,* a word introduced in 1495, refers to the red or green table vegetable of the entirely distinct Capsicum genus (another permutation of the word, *pimentón,* means powdered red pepper, or paprika).

Peppers were enthusiastically incorporated into regional cooking, and in the space of a century could be found in almost every European cuisine. Today they are present—for some tastes to excess—in a wide array of Spanish *tapas* and main courses. Red peppers are generally preferred to green (red peppers are ripened green peppers), and mild peppers please Spanish palates more than hot varieties; Spain's cooking has never been based on spicy foods. But of the dozen or so varieties of peppers that are grown in Spain, *pimientos del piquillo de Lodosa* from Navarra, often called *manjar de reyes* (food of kings) and *oro rojo* (red gold), are synonymous with the best.

Navarra is a region of geographic variety, from the Pyrenees in the north where a myriad of rivers rush toward the Ebro, to the rich agricultural lands of the Ebro valley to the south. Navarre's rivers are well stocked with trout, and the area produces an excellent cheese called Roncal and outstanding vegetables—especially peppers and white asparagus—grown in the area north of the Ebro called La Mejana, a gentle microclimate of fertile crumbly soil. Navarrese claim they can select their vegetables from all others in blind tastings, and in fact I have little difficulty distinguishing Lodosa *pimientos del piquillo* from all competitors.

The Lodosa peppers are brilliantly red, have a profoundly woody aroma, and are intensely flavorsome and just slightly piquant with a subtle taste that is never harsh or bitter. They are exceptionally thin and fine textured—not at all fleshy—but have body and hold their shape even when cooked. Such attributes are a result of plant selection by local growers over many decades, and *pimientos del piquillo de Lodosa* are further enhanced by the strict rules imposed by the Regulatory Council of the Denomination of Origin.

After harvesting, the peppers are washed and as quickly as possible roasted over a wood-burning fire or charcoal embers. Extreme care is taken to keep the peppers intact. They are cored, seeded, and—as mandated by the council—meticulously skinned by hand with the aid of cloths or small knives and never rinsed during this process. The peppers are then bottled or canned—also by hand—and sterilized. No water, brine, or seasoning of any kind, all of which can damage their delicate taste, is permitted. The ingredients label on an authentic Lodosa product simply cites "peppers in their own liquid."

The demand for Lodosa peppers inevitably outstrips the supply. "Our peppers are all spoken for before the harvest is even completed," says José Luis Mañu, chief of the Lodosa regulatory council. The bottled peppers make their way to stores by Christmas—many El Corte Inglés department stores sell them, as do specialty shops like Mantequerías Germán Navas in Madrid—and the supply often runs out by summer.

Some companies outside the Lodosa region, seeking to take advantage of Lodosa's good name, give their products the look of quality with attractive upscale packaging and labels reading "artisan product" and "wood roasted." (While genuine Lodosa peppers command, for example, $6 to $8 for the 10-ounce jar, other peppers sell at less than a third of that.)

And although in October visitors to the Ebro region are greeted by colorful strings of peppers hung from whitewashed village walls, drying in the bright sunlight, and village women at their doorsteps roasting peppers on grills, such peppers cannot claim to be Lodosa peppers. Nor can those sold at the bustling red pepper market, Mercado de Lobete, just over the border in La Rioja. Lodosa *piquillos* never reach there; they have all been quickly and quietly sold to Spain's top restaurants and gourmet shops.

Where to Dine on the Peppers

Dishes made with *pimientos del piquillo de Lodosa* are usually served in the best restaurants. Here are some that feature the peppers; prices listed are for an average dinner for two people (in 1992), not including wine.

Madrid

In Madrid many top restaurants, especially those with Basque chefs, rely on Lodosa peppers. Among them:

Senorío de Bertiz, *Comandante Zorita 6, 91.533.27.57; $120.* The peppers are served stuffed with hake and shrimp and covered with a sauce that is a purée of *pimientos,* vegetables, and fish stock.

El Cenador del Prado, *Prado 4, 91.429.15.61; $130.*

Navarra

In Navarra, where Lodosa is situated, the peppers are served in many fine restaurants. Among them:

Josetxo, *Plaza 1 Príncipe de Viana, Pamplona,* 948.22.20.97; $120. The peppers are served stuffed with either hake, codfish, crab, or meat or are baked in garlic or fried.

Tubal, *Plaza de Navarra 2, Tafalla,* 948.70.08.52; $90. The peppers are served, among other ways, stuffed with baby squid, or in rabbit with snails and *pimiento del piquillo.*

Atalaya, *Dabán 11, Peralta,* 948.75.01.52; $90.

Europa, *Espoz y Mina 11, Pamplona,* 948.22.18.00; $100.

Maher, *Ribera 19, Cintruénigo,* 948.81.11.50; $90.

Basque Country

Pimientos del piquillo are essential to new Basque cuisine. Restaurants serving them include:

Arzak, *Alto de Miracruz 21, San Sebastián,* 943.28.55.93; $130. The peppers are served with a local fish called *karbarroka* in a light *pimiento* cream sauce. Also on the menu is *langoustines* with plum and pimiento.

Akelarre, *Paseo del Padre Orcolaga 56, Barrio-Igueldo, San Sebastián,* 943.21.20.52; $140.

Karlos Arguiñano, *Mendilauta 13, Zarauz,* 943.13.00.00; $140.

Spanish Highs

ANYA VON BREMZEN

~

editor's note

I was so happy when this article appeared, because it is one of the very few to rave about the cuisine of Asturias, where a handful of chefs are staging a culinary revolution.

ANYA VON BREMZEN is a contributing editor at *Travel + Leisure*, where this piece first appeared.

I was having lunch in a windswept fishing village in the middle of nowhere. Laundry snapped furiously in the breeze while seagulls circled over gaggles of fishermen tending their nets by tatty white houses. Viavélez—population 80—is so insignificant that even the most detailed maps fail to acknowledge it. And two years ago the chilly Cantabrian Sea nearly washed away Taberna Viavélez Puerto, the restaurant where I was eating a meal that, in L.A. or London, would have critics leaping with excitement. I took a slow slurp of tea-and-chocolate soup, then broke the gossamer band of bitter chocolate encircling a tart tomato *gelée* and Szechwan pepper ice cream. It was the sharpest dessert I'd tasted all year. And this wasn't even the best restaurant I'd discovered on my trip to Asturias, the misty and remote region east of Galicia in Northern Spain.

Having roamed Spain for almost a decade to report on its astounding gastronomic developments, I've stopped being surprised at the edgy inventiveness that flourishes in unlikely places. But Asturias? Spain's answer to the Scottish Highlands, this is where Spanish lovers of *agriturismo* come to hike in the Picos de Europa, Europe's last great mountain wilderness, go whitewater rafting, and explore the cliffs and beaches on the two-hundred-mile coast. The population is *puro y duro* and so is the food: mountain cheeses like the smelly blue Cabrales, dense *charcutería,* never-ending beans. The regional masterpiece is *fabada,* the Asturian cousin of cassoulet, and the local tipple is *sidra,* a diabolically acidic apple brew consumed in dim taverns called *chigres. Sidra* is poured at arm's length into wide-bottomed glasses; you swallow your aerated inch, splash the rest onto the sawdust-covered floor, and start over. The average Asturian male consumes about ten liters of the stuff a day. Napa Valley this isn't.

And yet. Madrid restaurant critics had whispered to me about a quartet of Asturian chefs who were cooking up a *revolución conceptual* among the pig farms, cornfields, and shepherds. I packed my bags.

First on my list was the village of Arriondas, at the foot of the Picos de Europa. Why this drowsy *pueblo* is home to not one but two Michelin-starred avant-garde restaurants is anyone's guess. Queasy after the previous night's intake of *sidra,* I walked into El Corral del Indianu and found it unexpectedly sleek—thick stone walls painted an electric Bermuda blue, white tablecloths set with Modernist tableware. José Antonio Campo Viejo, the chef-owner, has raven hair and an impenetrable mountain accent. I tasted his soup. One just-cooked clam floated in an iridescent purée of peas, releasing sweet-briny perfumes of the sea into the concentrated sweetness of early summer. It was heartbreakingly lovely. By the third course, I felt a rush of adrenaline: *I've discovered a genius!*

Whereas Ferran Adrìa, the guru whose Catalonian restaurant kicked off Spain's culinary revolution, operates in an abstract realm akin to theoretical physics, Campo Viejo constantly references the local vernacular: exploring its nuances of smokiness, rendering unctuous sausage-and-bean combos into crisp counterpoints, blurring boundaries between sea and woods, sweet and savory, high and low, liquid and solid.

Dusted in coarse cornmeal—an allusion to chicken feed—a little hunk of foie gras masqueraded as blood sausage in a pool of musky, hyperreduced garbanzo broth; next to it was a chicken "bonbon" with a molten *foie* filling. *Pote asturiano,* a wintry extravaganza of cabbage and pig parts that normally cries out for Mylanta, was deconstructed into a Fabergé-pretty assemblage of porcine ravioli and quivery sausage mousses suspended in a diaphanous young cabbage purée.

This is food where each detail could be a star dish in itself—like the nuggets of lamb sweetbreads glazed with Pedro Jiménez (a raisiny sherry) accessorizing bream from the River Sella, in a play of sweet flesh against crisp skin. The pig in two textures was a study in altered states, the flesh "melted" in the oven to a smooth creaminess, the skin brittle—a savory crème brûlée from the fourth dimension. For dessert, Campo Viejo unveiled his latest experiment: a zany marriage of sweet peas and foie gras.

Save for a few master classes with Adrìa, Campo Viejo is entirely self-taught.

Before my second dinner in town, at Casa Marcial, I drove up to see the nearby mountain lakes. The serpentine road threaded beside plunging ravines and lookouts onto Kodak-moment alpine panoramas. El Casín, my lunch grail, turned out to be an idyllic shed with a view of glacial Lake Enol cupped by stony primordial hills. Cowbells provided a Steve Reichean sound track to my meal of wild boar *chorizo* and baby goat, roasted until the meat fell apart into succulent shreds. When a monster cow approached and fixed its gaze on my wedge of pungent Cabrales, I fled.

Casa Marcial, run by Campo Viejo's drinking buddy Nacho Manzano, is in an old farmhouse on a hill overlooking rolling foothills that are swathed in an eye-popping green. More green awaited me inside: an iced cucumber soup poured around a green pepper sorbet swirled with green olive oil. I went on to a silken-fleshed river salmon in a pool of melon gazpacho, and a backyard chicken braised a deep mahogany brown, its gizzards folded into one big *raviolo*. In retrospect this was a fine meal. But after the bravura at Corral, Manzano's style felt a bit green.

My next restaurant, El Cabroncín, took me from the Picos to a weird suburb of Oviedo (the region's industrial capital, with a medieval core) that made the Jersey Turnpike look almost lyrical. My taxi driver—I would never have found the place if I'd been driving—circled around a car dealership and a cosmetics factory, then finally located the proper dirt road and deposited me in a suddenly pastoral patch by a stone house and a *hórreo*, one of those raised wooden granaries that are to Asturias what covered bridges are to Vermont. Before long I was sipping Quercus—a new bubbly from boutique *cava*-producer Agustí Torelló—and admiring a tableau of clams, *berberechos* (Cantabrian mini-clams), and *percebes* (Galician goose barnacles) arranged on a delicate fennel purée.

A fragrant sauté of wild mushrooms came next, crowned by a Day-Glo–orange egg yolk in a crunchy *serrano* ham basket. It was exactly the kind of smart neorustic dish I wanted to eat here, beneath old wooden beams supporting a pitched farmhouse roof. Gilding the lily was a glass of elegant '96 Roda I Rioja Reserva recommended by Pepe Vega, Asturias's star sommelier. Pedro Martino, the practically teenage chef, makes a mean salmon in *sidra*, but his true calling is meat—whether it's an *ibérico* pig, as spoon-tender as good Memphis barbecue, or Castilian baby lamb shoulder, cooked to the same jammy softness and paired with tiny rare lamb chops. I adored the wooden box holding shot glasses of iced herbal infusions; the funky dessert wine from the Canary Islands; the cool sophistication of apple cannoli in a bittersweet licorice sauce. I also liked the ridiculously low bill.

I didn't particularly like the idea of driving a hundred miles to the Galician border for lunch. On second thought, a slow trip to nowhere would be an excuse to explore Asturias's little-visited northwestern coast, gorge on fresh-off-the-boat seafood, and sleep at a *casona de indianos,* one of the extravagant turn-of-the-century mansions that appear like fantastic white elephants all over the region. Built by *indianos*—Asturians who returned home with fortunes made in Latin America—some are being converted into inns.

I found such a *casona,* Villa La Argentina, in the old whaling town of Luarca, and ate pristine shellfish at the restaurant Sport. The following day I went on to Viavélez for lunch at Taberna Viavélez Puerto (where our story began). I was the only guest. Paco Ron, the chef-owner, greeted me on a terrace tented in billowy fabric. Ron has lived and cooked in Madrid, Barcelona, and San Sebastián. He appeared disheveled and disillusioned. His food was quietly dazzling.

First came a martini glass filled with frozen goat cheese foam that melted into the warm ethereal sweetness of beet mousse underneath. An egg yolk stuffed with smoky salt cod peeped from a bowl of asparagus soup. A cardamom-scented sauce of sweet corn and a reduction of blackberries flirted with the dark, chocolate notes of squab. Once a year Ron prepares a banquet for the town's fishermen; they reward him year-round with their prize catch, such as the hake that he served with a silky potato emulsion and peppery young turnip greens sprinkled with sea salt. The dish was the essence of purity and refinement.

That night, in the Art Nouveau guest room of Palacete Peñalba (designed by a disciple of Gaudí), I tossed and turned in my bed, dissecting Ron's lunch. How can one actually stuff a poached egg yolk? Or produce ravioli out of cabbage—each the size of a bean!— that burst with a complex bacony reduction? And above all, how can anyone make a living cooking virtuoso Michelin-starred food in a windswept fishing village in the middle of nowhere?

Picos de Europa. Base yourself at the **Parador de Cangas de Onís** (Villanueva; 98.584.94.02; fax: 98.584.95.20; doubles from about $93). Taste *sidra, chorizos,* and cheeses at the bucolic **El Bodegón del Dobra** (Carretera Cangas de Onís, Punto Pontón, kilometer 150; 98.584.91.95). Have lunch at **El Casín** (Lake Enol; 98.592.29.27; $25 for two) and dinner at **El Corral del Indianu** (14 Avenida de Europa, Arriondas; 98.584.10.72; tasting menu for two $72) and **Casa Marcial** (La Salgar; 98.584.09.91; tasting menu for two $69).

Oviedo. Stay at the lavish **Hotel de la Reconquista** (Calle Gil de Jaz; 98.524.11.00; fax: 98.526.63.80; doubles from $168). Dine at **El Cabroncín** (Carretera Paredes N1, Lugones; 98.526.63.80; tasting menu for two $42). Consider visiting Gijón, the world's greatest repository of faded Art Nouveau architecture.

Northwestern Coast. Drive to Luarca for dinner at **Sport** (8 Calle Rivero; 98.564.1078; $45 for two) and overnight at **Villa La Argentina** (Villar de Luarca; 98.564.01.02; fax: 98.564.09.73; doubles from $45). Drive west for lunch at **Taberna Viavélez Puerto** (Viavélez; 98.547.80.95; tasting menu for two $69), and end the day with seafood *paella* at **Marisquería Peñalba** (Figueras del Mar; 98.563.61.66; dinner for two $40). Sleep at **Palacete Peñalba** (Figueras del Mar; 98.563.61.25; fax: 98.563.62.47; doubles from $56).

Pride of Plate

BY GULLY WELLS

❧

editor's note

"Basque cooking," as noted in *The Cooking of Spain and Portugal*, "seems to come out of nowhere, a part of the earth, a thing in itself . . . paradoxically, Basque cooking is not foreign or alien to other Spanish palates. Its distinction is not in its strangeness, for, unlike the language and the many unique Basque traits, Basque food is not removed from the rest of the Peninsula by history or custom. Falling as it does within the Spanish zone of sauces, the Basque kitchen is not the most individual of the Spanish kitchens. It is merely the best." I provide this excerpt as an explanation of sorts as to why I have included the following pieces about the cuisine of Bilbao, San Sebastián, and some other, smaller towns of the Basque Country.

GULLY WELLS, introduced previously in this section, is a features editor of *Condé Nast Traveler,* where this piece first appeared.

On my first day in Bilbao, my guide to the Basque Country, José Luis Iturrieta, a Sacramentino monk turned journalist and fanatical gastronome, told me a joke. A visitor from Navarra arrives in Bilbao and heads for the newly unveiled Guggenheim. Clearly overcome by Frank Gehry's genius, he gazes up in speechless admiration at its sparkling silver exterior. Finally, he is able to utter a few words: "My God! If that's the can, then the asparagus must be *incredible!*"

In just one short sentence "El Guggen" (which many Basques regard as an expensive American folly stuffed with trash left over from the New York branch) is put down, while food (in this case the enormous white phallic asparagus that the Basques inexplicably favor over all other varieties) is quite properly elevated to a position in the firmament next to God's right hand.

I was familiar with the controversy swirling around the Guggenheim, having run into a journalist from Pamplona a few weeks before who spat out the words "cultural imperialism" as he roundly condemned the entire project. What I wasn't quite prepared for was the passionate and everlasting love affair between the Basques and their food. It is not simply that any restaurant anywhere in Spain with aspirations to greatness will always have several Basque dishes on its menu or a Basque chef in the kitchen—or, if they are blessed, both. It has much more to do with a deep cultural tradition that regards the quality of the cuisine as something almost sacred. It is part of being Basque.

For Pedro Subijana, a chef from San Sebastián, this makes perfect sense: "It is only logical that we should defend our national identity, of which we are so proud, through some part of our culture." Housewives will shop daily in one of the open markets for the very best—and most expensive—delicacies, while their husbands will join one of the famous gastronomic societies, where they go not just to eat and discuss food but to actually cook it. And both sexes will happily spend hours deconstructing the subtler aspects of the *bacalao al pil-pil* they had for dinner last night, comparing it to the *ródaballo al txakolí con pimientos* they cooked last week, and then moving on to the even more challenging question of how to make the next day's dinner *truly* memorable. The love and enthusiasm never flag. It's almost as if they were talking about their own children.

The three Basque provinces—Vizcaya, Guipúzcoa, and Álava—occupy a region in the northern part of Spain, extending from the coastline of the Bay of Biscay to the Pyrenees. And so it is the sea and the mountains that are the inspiration for the very best Basque dishes. The misty green hills produce tender lamb, wild mushrooms, and game, while the homesteads, or *caseríos,* where the farmers work and live, contribute handmade cheeses, homegrown fruit and vegetables, and fresh herbs from their kitchen gardens. Traditionally the Basques have been farmers and fishermen, and even though most people's way of life obviously changed profoundly with industrialization, what they ate did not. The sea still provides the hake, bonito, sea bream, turbot, tuna, squid, and—above all—the beloved salt cod, or *bacalao,* that forms the backbone of so many meals. All fishermen, as well as any self-respecting cook, swear that they can tell at a glance the difference between a fish caught on a line and one trapped in a net.

"First the mountains, then the sea, and last of all we'll see how a chef of genius combines them both in *la nueva cocina vasca,*" said José Luis, who had deftly defined the contours of our gastronomic pilgrimage through the Basque Country. All I had to do was follow in his footsteps, look, listen, and above all, eat.

It was dusk, and raining, when we arrived at the tiny hamlet of Axpe, just south of Bilbao. "*Chirimiri,*" José Luis said, looking up at the fine mist falling on the steep green hills, and so began my first lesson in the charming onomatopoeic byways of the Basque language. The pealing of bells is *bimbibimbaka,* and my favorite salt cod dish of all time, *bacalao al pil-pil,* gets its name from the noise that the bubbling oil makes as the sauce cooks. The origins of this impenetrable language, with its strange surplus of the letters *t, x, z,* and *k,* are, as they say, lost in the *chirimiri* of time. Nobody knows for sure where the Basque people came from, and according to Alastair Reid, a longtime aficionado of this part of Spain, the Basques are positively "delighted by their own inexplicability." It sets them further apart from Spain—which, for many Basques, is just what they want.

Etxebarri, the restaurant that José Luis was taking me to, occupies one side of a small square at the bottom of a hill. Downstairs it looks like a simple bar where locals hang out, watch *fútbol* on TV, and drink *sidra*, pressed from apples grown in nearby orchards. But as I quickly discovered, this is just a cunning front for the sublimely sophisticated food served in the upstairs dining room. There may have been menus, but I never saw one. Instead, we were presented with an ice-cold bottle of *txakolí,* the slightly fizzy white wine that is produced only in the Basque Country, and shown a basket of wild mushrooms that still smelled of the woods where they had been picked that afternoon. We sipped the wine, and moments later the mushrooms reemerged from the kitchen, barely cooked in olive oil, garlic, parsley, and their own mysterious primeval juices. Next came a platter of rose-pink *jamón ibérico Joselito,* the sweetest, most velvety ham imaginable, made from pigs that had spent their short but charmed lives snuffling around under oak trees, gobbling up as many acorns as they possibly could. Whether it was nurture or nature that produced their exquisite taste, I could not tell you, but just one mouthful made me moan in a way that I felt was somehow inappropriate in front of a man who had, after all, once been a servant of God.

From the hills we next swooped down to the sea. Some barely cooked *almejas* (clams) *a la plancha* appeared, grilled for what must have been a split second or two and (in deference to my companion's former line of business?) described by the waiter as being in the style of Saint Laurence, who, as all good Catholics will remember, was said to have been martyred on a metal grid over a bed of red-hot coals. It was at this point that I began to worry about what would come next. How could I possibly eat any more?

Easily, I'm afraid, was the answer. We went back up into the hills and were offered *chuletas,* baby lamb chops, again quickly grilled over a wood fire so that they were still blushing inside. After the meat came the obligatory Spanish palate-cleanser course of Ducados cigarettes, and then it was time for dessert: ice cream made from fresh, slightly tart sheep's cheese and served with blackberries, followed by a brilliantly contradictory apple crisp that managed to be both hot and cold and smooth and crunchy all at the same time.

It must have been after midnight when we emerged into the cold, starry night and I saw the stone church across the tiny square and beside it the huge wall, or *frontón,* where the national game of pelota is played. I understood instantly that in this small space were contained the three fundamentals of Basque life: food, religion, and pelota. What more could a man possibly need?

The talk at lunch the next day in a small seafront restaurant named Kaia in Getaria was of . . . fish, of course. We sat beside the window overlooking the water, and as the sky clouded over, the pretty blue waves were abruptly transformed into a rough and slightly threatening cauldron of dark gray bubbling soup, reminding us that it was the sea which had given life to these fishing villages for more than a thousand years, and it was the sea which still held the trump card and could claim those lives whenever it chose to. Ernesto Chueca, whose family produces the region's best *txakolí* (so good that the king of Spain practically bought up the whole of last year's vintage for his daughter's wedding), was trying to demonstrate precisely where on a fish's anatomy *kokotxas* come from. He leaned his head way back and then ran his fingers along the underside of his chin.

"In English they translate it as 'cheeks,' which is not right, but whatever you call them, these are the most delicate and delicious part of the *merluza* [hake]." As if on cue, the waitress appeared with a dish of these delicacies, bathed in a slightly gelatinous *salsa verde,* which went down as easily as Ernesto's *txakolí.* Next came fresh anchovies in olive oil, which bore no relation to their oversalted cousins, then some sparkling *gambas a la plancha,* followed by the freshest sole I've ever tasted, lightly brushed with oil (traditionally, a chicken feather is used), sea salt, and lemon and then grilled *a la donostiarra,* over a wood fire, for no more than a minute or two. "You know they're ready when you can snap the head off," Ernesto said as he mimed the snapping of the sole's head with his fat fingers. The conversation drifted like a dragnet, from the economics of fishing and how fewer and fewer fishermen have their own small boats, to what color lure to use to catch the very youngest and sweetest *chipirones* (squid), and then it swung around, with mounting outrage, to the cost of *angulas,* those minuscule baby eels that Hemingway described as "tiny as bean sprouts" and that are the greatest of all Basque delicacies. At the market in San Sebastián, I'd seen baskets of these translucent silver creatures, with their pinprick black eyes, and wondered why they were the only fish without a price tag.

The answer turned out to be the classic "If you have to ask, then you most certainly can't afford them." *Angulas* have always been expensive, but in the last few years, as José Luis explained, the cost has become a bad joke—they are now about 15,000 pesetas per pound, which is more than $100—on account of the Japanese, who will happily pay any price for them. And the worst part is that the Japanese don't even *eat* them. Instead, they release them into their rice paddies to devour the bacteria, like some kind of miracle detergent, and then let them grow big and fat before harvesting them. José Luis shrugged his shoulders, as if to say, how could you expect any non-Basque to begin to understand *angulas.*

At first it might seem strange that the cod, that native of the ice-cold North Atlantic, should have played such a central role in Basque cuisine. According to Mark Kurlansky—who wrote the definitive book on cod, *Cod: A Biography of the Fish That Changed the World*—during the Middle Ages, when Europeans ate whale, it was the Basque fishermen who sailed as far as North America in search of this valuable commodity. Along the way they discovered that if cod were salted, it could last long enough to keep the men going on these extended fishing trips.

By about the year 1000 the Basques were exporting salt cod, or *bacalao*, all over Europe and had developed such a taste for it that, even after refrigeration, most Basques still prefer salt cod over fresh cod. (And in fact, there is not even a word in Spanish for fresh cod. They call it "fresh" *bacalao*.)

The cod industry was helped along by the Catholic Church, which strictly regulated the number of meatless days in the year. Eating flesh was believed to stimulate thoughts of other kinds of flesh, while fish was a "cold" food that would keep men's minds on less incendiary matters on holy days. Old habits die hard, and *bacalao* is now firmly entrenched in the Basque national food psyche. Go shopping in any market, and you'll always find a *casa de bacalao* nearby, where all different cuts are sold, from the extravagantly priced *kokotxas* down to the cheaper tail and side cuts.

On our last day together, José Luis promised to introduce me to a man who was, in his opinion, one of the very best, and certainly one of the most innovative, chefs in the whole Basque Country. In the mid-1970s, when France was going crazy for nouvelle cuisine, a number of Basque chefs felt the same winds of change blowing over the Pyrenees. Which makes perfect sense, since Basque food has always favored the freshest and best raw materials, prepared relatively simply. Some of the most original cooks were working in San Sebastián, only a few miles from the French border, and it is here that Martín Berasategui recently opened his own restaurant. He had a classical training and can obviously cook all the traditional dishes, but he has chosen to challenge himself and delight his customers by taking off on his own trajectory. He knows the rules, which is why he's allowed to break them.

The dining room at Martín Berasategui looks out over gentle hills and a neatly planted *potager*. There is a huge stone fireplace, chandeliers, and a pretty antique sideboard: The feeling is of *haut bourgeois* comfort. It is the kind of place where affluent San Sebastián businessmen bring their most favored clients during the day and their wives or mistresses in the evening. The decor may be subdued and a little stuffy, but the food is anything but. There are riffs on traditional Basque dishes like *bacalao*, but here the cod is transformed into a delicate crème and served with an infusion of transparent, almost colorless tomato *jus*. Peasanty eels are combined in a *millefeuille* with aristocratic *foie gras* and a tart green apple sauce, and oysters are poached in *agua de mar*, literally "seawater," a mysterious and subtle sauce that suggests the briny depths of the ocean and for which Martín refused to divulge the recipe. Maybe it did contain real seawater. Who knows?

It was starting to get dark, and we were only halfway through our nine-course menu. Just as I was about to admit defeat, some new extraordinary dish would be put before me, and there was nothing I could do but try it. And once tasted, like some irresistible drug, it was impossible not to finish. Sparkling superfresh bonito was grilled in the classic, simple Basque style, but the ragout of *chipirones* that followed was complex in the extreme, and the whole dish was suffused with truffle oil. Martín next gave us grilled baby lamb *chuletas* and, in a nod to the New World, had created a crème from fresh corn and orange and walnuts. José Luis raised his glass to me—it happened to be an Artadi Crianza 1994 from a tiny medieval village called Laguardia—and, without speaking, we toasted the brilliance of the food before us.

When the chocolate mousse arrived, I couldn't help myself. A sigh of deep pleasure, an audible intake of breath, and I quickly looked across at José Luis, who, if he heard me, was too polite to acknowledge it. His eyes were closed, he was smiling, and an expression of beatific ecstasy was slowly spreading across his face.

Basque Bets

Although the very best Basque food is probably found on its home ground, there are still some stellar Basque restaurants in the rest of Spain, most notably in Madrid. In the United States, try Marichu, in New York.

Restaurants

In Spain

Andra Mari, Barrio Elexalde 22, Galdakao-Bizkaia (94.456.00.05; prix fixe, about $33 and $52).

Bodegón Alejandro, Calle Fermín Calbetón 4, San Sebastián (943.42.71.58; entrées, about $7–$15).

Etxebarri, Plaza San Juan 1, Axpe-Marzana, Axtondo-Bizkaia (94.658.30.42; entrées, $4–$26).

Gorrotxa, Alameda Urquijo 30, Galería, Bilbao (94.443.49.37; entrées, about $12–$20).

Kaia, General Arnao 10, Getaria (943.14.05.00; prix fixe, about $35).

Martín Berasategui, Loidi Kalea 4, Lasarte (943.36.64.71; entrées, about $13–$22; prix fixe, $60).

Ordago, Sancho Dávila 15, Madrid (91.356.71.85; entrées, about $14–$17).

In the United States

Marichu, 342 East 46th Street, New York City (212-370-1866; entrées, $12–$24).

Hotels

López de Haro, Obispo Orueta 4, Bilbao (94.423.55.00; doubles, $178).

Mendi Goikoa, Barrio San Juan 33, Axpe, Valle de Atxondo (94.682.08.33; doubles, $86).

María Cristina, Calle Oquendo 1, San Sebastián (94.342.49.00; doubles, $187–$214).

Reading

The Basque Table, by Teresa Barrenechea; published by Harvard Common Press, $23.

Brave New Basque

By Anya von Bremzen

༄

ANYA VON BREMZEN, who appears never to tire of Northern Spain, contributed this piece to the quarterly food magazine *Williams-Sonoma Taste*. (Note that the chef Ferran Adrià referred to in this piece is not in San Sebastián but in Catalunya, where he made headlines—and earned three Michelin stars—for his restaurant El Bulli; his newer venture is Roses, in a small village on the Costa Brava.)

It's almost impossible not to fall head over heels for the Basque city of San Sebastián, the achingly elegant former seaside retreat of Spanish nobility. With its pearly sands and a wide promenade framed by Belle Epoque finery, the shell-shaped La Concha is easily the world's loveliest bay. The brooding Old Quarter lights up after dark with the bustle of an all-night local pub crawl known as *poteo*. And there are grande-dame hotels like María Cristina and leisurely side trips to charmed fishing villages and interior hills so green that Ireland seems drab in comparison.

But even if San Sebastián were an industrial park, I'd return again and again for the food—from exquisitely confected *tapas* washed down with the fiercely local white called *txakolí* to the sublime sorcery of the city's avant-garde chefs, from epic steaks of countryside cider houses to the sweetest of baby squid flash-grilled at waterside shacks. A city studded with Michelin stars, San Sebastián is where food lovers from Madrid and Seville escape for illicit weekends of unending gluttony, and where French snobs from neighboring Biarritz—even clued-in Parisians—come to marvel reluctantly at the culinary couture so much cheaper and more original than their own.

The Catalan chef-guru Ferran Adrià of El Bullí in Roses may be grabbing the headlines, but Spain would never be the millennial mecca for progressive cuisine without San Sebastián chefs like Pedro Subijana and Juan Mari Arzak. Back in the 1970s, they turned Spanish gastronomy on its head, coining a style known as *nueva cocina vasca*, or new Basque cuisine, a culinary idiom inspired by local traditions coupled with nouvelle cuisine concepts borrowed from France. Soon Basque chefs were revolutionizing haute kitchens all over the country, and Spain never looked back. And while Catalonia does have its share of wondrous food, I've never eaten as consistently well in Barcelona as I did on my recent visit to San Sebastián.

The New Wave

The first stop on my eating itinerary was Martín Berasategui's eponymous restaurant, nestled in the lap of low hills in the posh suburb of Lasarte. The hollow outside, with its meticulously arranged *potager* and its riot of hydrangeas, was so deliciously lush that I hardly noticed the rather staid Relais Châteaux–style dining room. Then the food came.

Rafael García Santos, Spain's premier restaurant critic, once described Berasategui's degustation menu as *"espectáculo gastronómico colosal."* He wasn't kidding. San Sebastián's most-talked-about chef tossed off one virtuoso course after another, barely letting me catch my breath between six *amuse-gueules*—tiny soups, herbal granitas—and a dollhouse's worth of minidesserts. Somehow I managed to register the astounding precision of his signature napoleon of smoked eel, *foie gras,* and caramelized apple; the simple Mediterranean poetry of his anchovies with a marmalade of wood-roasted peppers; the beauty of his *gêlée* of sea urchin and scallops with a warm fennel broth. Berasategui appeared as I was finishing a scoop of apple sorbet afloat in a sweet soup of just-picked baby peas. He greeted me with a vigorous handshake, delivered a tirade on the art of food presentation, then zoomed off "to teach Basque cooking to little Basque schoolchildren."

Berasategui's interest in pedagogy is central to his vision: in addition to running his two-Michelin-starred restaurant, he mentors a group of young chefs with whom he shares a restaurant empire poised to challenge the supremacy of Adrià. "Ferran's cuisine, it's like—boom!!!—*Muy conceptual,"* explains Berasategui's fresh-faced protégé, Andoni Luis Aduriz, the brilliant chef de cuisine at Mugaritz restaurant. "Ours is ingredient-driven, simple on the surface but extremely complex underneath."

Set in the hills just outside town, Mugaritz can be reached by a highway from San Sebastián in a matter of minutes, but Aduriz instructed me to take the rambling bucolic back road. Eventually it brought me to his twenty-first-century Basque *caserió,* or homestead, a chic-rustic barn with terra-cotta floors and haystacks visible from the huge windows. Not exactly the kind of place I expected to encounter a futuristic bonbon of spiced pear, olive oil, and granita of Idiazábal (Basque ewe's cheese) or an undulating white plate holding a stunning white slab of turbot in a sweet-bitter broth strewn with slivers of candied pomelo. I couldn't help thinking what a sensation this food would cause in New York or Los Angeles.

Besides Aduriz and Bixente Arrieta, who heads the Guggenheim restaurant in Bilbao, Berasategui's disciples include the shy twenty-three-year-old Erika Medina. Berasategui put Medina in charge of the sleekly minimalist restaurant Kursaal, at the city's showcase performing arts center of the same name, conceived by architect Rafael Moneo as a pair of tilted translucent cubes. Medina's confident neoclassical style shines in her toothsome squid rice flourished with parsley oil and her *bacalao* (salt cod) in a garlic emulsion updated with a delicate ragout of *txangurro*, the prized local spider crab. Dessert? A typical Berasategui assortment of glasses, spoons, and cups holding whimsies like apricot sorbet and a runny chocolate mousse with mint foam.

The Old Guard

Energized by the young generation, the fathers of *nueva cocina vasca* are cooking like never before. I knew this the minute I tasted—make that heard—the appetizer at Akelarre, chef Pedro Subijana's two-Michelin-starred panoramic *chalet* on Mount Igueldo over the Bay of Biscay. "Watch out for a surprise," the waitress winked, leaving me with a blood-sausage fritter set on a plain-looking apple purée. Suddenly, the purée started making funny little noises, as if tiny firecrackers were exploding inside. But even the crackling fritter was upstaged by dessert, a cunning trompe l'oeil of a poached egg consisting of a yolk-like candied kumquat peeking from coconut soup.

And in between? There was an ethereal tempura of prawn perched on an oddly delicious yogurt and peanut mousse; medallions of veal tongue, brined for three days until the meat achieved an impossible softness; and the ubiquitous Basque *chiprón* (baby squid) on a savory rice pudding under a gossamer sheet of caramelized squid ink.

Another bastion of haute cuisine, Arzak has been open for more than twenty-five years, but the ebullient Juan Mari Arzak doesn't need an injection of energy with his daughter Elena Arzak Espina at the helm. Although the restaurant cultivates a refreshing informality for an establishment with three Michelin stars, the food is anything but laid-back. Inspired by the Basque landscape of haystacks in the fields, Elena arranges *cigalas* on crisp mounds of rice noodles, ringed by a delicate sauce gently enriched by *foie gras*. Her memories of village women grilling leeks on the beach translate into sea bass bathed in black broth infused with the evocative flavor of leek ash. My dessert was a smoked—smoked!—chocolate mousse. Anywhere else this would be the meal of a lifetime. In San Sebastián it was just another good dinner.

Cider, Steaks, and Salt Cod

Of course Basque cooking isn't all postmodern pyrotechnics. To get a taste of the traditional cuisine, I went to Illumbe, a cider house in the apple-rich village of Usúrbil, where rough-hewn walls and long wooden tables set the stage for rounds of fresh cider accompanied by simple but serious food. Illumbe turned out to be the domain of José Angel Aguinaga, cider-maker, meat connoisseur, and hunter extraordinaire. When Aguinaga isn't chasing wild pigeons, he supervises the aging and grilling of his thick *chuletones,* or T-bone steaks. The meat is butchered from Galician cows that supposedly have better pedigree than the Spanish royal family.

While the *chuletones* sizzled on the grill, we tasted the cider straight out of the vat. "A good Basque cider," Aguinaga explained, "contains about twenty carefully chosen apple varieties—sweet, sour, even bitter!" Then it was *bacalao* three ways—in a garlicky soup with the melodious name *zurrukutuna;* in an overplump tortilla, or omelet; and *al pil-pil.*

After this extraordinary meal, I set off on a bright coastal road for the picturesque village of Getaria, looking for a seafood experience to compare. Here, tucked away on a narrow balconied street, Kaia could pass for any other bourgeois fish house with dull nautical decor and windows framing boats in the small fishing port below. But make no mistake: Kaia is a mecca for Spanish seafood worshipers and counts chefs like Berasategui among its faithful.

Taking cues from lunching bankers, I ordered a few silky fat anchovies and a plate of *kokotxas,* the pricey glands from the underchin of a fish called hake. The glands are a delicacy venerated by the Basques. Lightly battered and fried just long enough to seal in the succulence, they tasted almost like oysters, only meatier. My next dish, Kaia's grilled *langoustines,* inspired the French chef Michel Bras to pronounce it the best seafood he had ever encountered. Chances are that he thought the same about the grilled *rodaballo* (turbot), especially if he washed it down with the crisp *txakolí* produced by the restaurant's owners. Toasting their just-arrived fish, a loud Madrid family at the next table raved, "*¡Estupendo, fenomenal!*" My sentiments exactly.

In and Around San Sebastián

Where to Stay

María Cristina sparkles with fin-de-siècle glamour. Calle Oquendo 1; San Sebastián; 943.424.900

Where to Eat

Akelarre, Paseo del Padre Orcolaga 56, San Sebastián, 943.212.052

Arzak, Alto de Miracruz 21, San Sebastián, 943.285.593

Illumbe, Barrio Txoko Alde, Usúrbil, 943.371.649

Kaia, General Arnao 10, Getaria, 943.140.500

Kursaal, Zurriola 1, San Sebastián, 943.003.162

Martín Berasategui, Loidi 4, Lasarte, 943.366.471

Mugaritz, Otzazulueta Baserria, Aldrua aldea 20, 943.542.555

Do the *Tapas* Crawl

Chiquiteo, the Basque answer to the Spanish *tapeo,* or *tapas* crawl, reaches its zenith in San Sebastián's Old Quarter. At **Astelana** (Iñigo 1; 943.426.275), fishermen lunch on the city's definitive *bacalao* canapés and croquettes and *tortilla de ropa vieja.* The tiny **Goiz Argi** (Fermín Calbetón 4; 943.425.204) packs them in with its butterflied anchovies, shrimp brochettes and canapés of fish mousse. Rustic **La Cepa** (31 de Agosto 7; 943.426.394) is the source for garlicky mushroom sauté and *jamón Joselito,* the world's greatest cured ham, while the upmarket **Borda Berri** (Fermín Calbetón 12; 943.425.638) trades in warm *foie gras* toast and sea urchin mousse. Run by Alex Montiel, the disciple of chef Ferran Adrià, **La Cuchara de San Telmo** (31 de Agosto 28; 943.420.840) ups the ante with *tapas*-size dishes of green ravioli topped with bacon and shrimp and crisped veal lips with apples.

Biblioteca

Mediterranean Cookbooks and Food (Spain is well represented in all of these titles)

A Book of Mediterranean Food, Elizabeth David, Penguin, 1988.

Cod: A Biography of the Fish That Changed the World, Mark Kurlansky, Walker Publishing Co., 1997. The first single-subject book I read about a culinary ingredient was *Peppers: A Story of Hot Pursuits* by Amal Naj (Alfred A. Knopf, 1992), and I discovered I was crazy for this type of book. So years later, when I discovered *Cod,* I knew I would love it, and indeed I did. I couldn't stop talking about it, in fact, just as I hadn't been able to stop talking about all the wonderful things I learned about peppers. The fascinating story of cod crisscrosses the globe from Newfoundland, New England, the Basque coast of Spain, Brazil, West Africa, and Scandinavia, but the Mediterranean is never very far from the thread. Kurlansky notes that "from the Middle Ages to the present, the most demanding cod market has always been the Mediterranean. These countries experienced a huge population growth in the nineteenth century: Spain's population almost doubled, and Portugal's more than doubled. Many ports grew into large urban centers, including Bilbao, Porto, Lisbon, Genoa, and Naples. Barcelona in 1900 had a population of almost one million people—most of them passionate *bacalao* consumers." Especially in the Basque Country but all across the north, cod is a major component in the cuisine, and there really is not a restaurant or *tapas* bar that does not offer cod, in some form, on its menu. In the chapter "The Fish That Spoke Basque," Kurlansky reminds us that "the most highly developed salt cod cuisine in the world is that of the Spanish Basque provinces." Fresh or dried salt cod is a ubiquitous Mediterranean staple (except in the Muslim countries), making an appearance in such dishes as *bacalao a la vizcaína* (Basque Country), *sonhos de bacalhau* (Portugal), salted cod croquettes (Italy), *brandade de morue* (France), and *taramosalata* (Greece), among others. (Kurlansky provides recipes for each.) *Esencial.*

The Feast of the Olive, Maggie Blyth Klein, Aris Books (Addison-Wesley), 1983; revised and updated edition, Chronicle Books, 1994.

From Tapas to Meze, Joanna Weir, Crown, 1994.

Invitation to Mediterranean Cooking: 150 Vegetarian and Seafood Recipes, Claudia Roden, Rizzoli, 1997.

Mediterranean: The Beautiful Cookbook, Joyce Goldstein, Collins (produced by Welden Owen), 1994.

Mediterranean Cookery, Claudia Roden, Alfred A. Knopf, 1987.

Mediterranean Cooking, Paula Wolfert, HarperCollins, 1994.

The Mediterranean Diet Cookbook, Nancy Harmon Jenkins, Bantam Books, 1994.

A Mediterranean Feast: The Story of the Birth of the Celebrated Cuisines of the Mediterranean: Food of the Sun: A Culinary Tour of Sun-Drenched Shores with Evocative Dishes from Southern Europe, Jacqueline Clark and Joanna Farrow, Lorenz Books, 2001. Though there are a few common recipes in this volume, a great number of them do not appear in other Mediterranean cookbooks, and the ones I've tried have been really delicious. Not many Northern Spain recipes are featured (though there is one for Galician broth), but a number of southern Spanish dishes are, including *churros,* gazpacho, and zarzuela (named after the Spanish musical comedy).

Mediterranean, From the Merchants of Venice to the Barbary Corsairs, Clifford A. Wright, William Morrow, 1999. An outstanding and exhaustively researched book. If you want to read only one book on Mediterranean cuisine, this is the one. Wright explains that "I wrote this book in an attempt to extend one man's—Fernand Braudel's—vision, love, and scholarship, and I augmented it with my own research and love of Mediterranean food, in the hope of providing a guide to the Mediterranean that has not been attempted before. The weaving of history and gastronomy in *A Mediterranean Feast* was meant to reveal the culinary structure of the Mediterranean—its rugged contours, oppressive reality and blue delight—through the eyes of geographers, travelers, historians, and cooks, what Braudel means by 'total history.' Braudel's writings were an attempt to seek out the 'constant' of Mediterranean history, the structures and recurrent patterns of everyday life that provide the reference grid. For myself, and this book, the constant is the food of the Mediterranean, its cuisine and recipes."

The Mediterranean Kitchen, Joyce Goldstein, William Morrow & Co., 1989. A unique feature of this wonderful book is that Goldstein indicates how, by changing only an ingredient or two, recipes can go from being Spanish, say, to French, Portuguese, or Moroccan, which illustrates the core ingredients that all the countries in the region share and also allows for more mileage out of nearly every recipe.

Mediterranean Light, Martha Rose Shulman, Bantam, 1989.

The Mediterranean Pantry: Creating and Using Condiments and Seasonings, Aglaia Kremezi, photographs by Martin Brigdale, Artisan, 1994. This is an excellent resource for home cooks who want to have a kitchen full of Mediterranean preserves, flavored oils and vinegars, liqueurs, and spice and herb mixtures at the ready. In addition to recipes for these essential staples, there are seventy recipes for dishes that feature them, including some from Spain.

Mostly Mediterranean, Paula Wolfert, Penguin, 1988.

¡Buen Provecho! 533

Olives, Anchovies, and Capers: The Secret Ingredients of the Mediterranean Table, Georgeanne Brennan, photographs by Leigh Beisch, Chronicle Books, 2001. As Brennan notes, some of the Mediterranean's most humble snacks and dishes deliver a sense of gustatory well-being completely out of proportion to their simplicity because "the traditional uses of three preserved ingredients, olives, anchovies, and capers, give the food an endless variation of character and depth." In addition to recipes (a few I particularly liked include Anchovies and Lemon on Black Olive Bread, Anchovy Stuffed Eggs, and Pan-Seared Salmon with Capers and Green Peppercorns), Brennan provides information on the cultivation and preservation of olives and capers (and a good brine recipe for salt-curing olives) and on the fishing for and preservation of anchovies.

Olives: The Life and Love of a Noble Fruit, Mort Rosenblum, North Point Press, 1996. One chapter in this excellent book, "Olive Heaven," is devoted to Spanish olive oil, especially the delicious Núñez de Prado of Andalusia. As readers know by now, olive trees are not prevalent in the north of Spain; but as food writer María José Sevilla told Mort Rosenblum, "In Spain, everything is cooked in olive oil." Spain is the world's largest producer of olive oil, producing more than Italy and Greece combined. Much of Spain's export surplus leaves the country in bulk with no producer's label, destined mostly for Italy. A man named Juan Vincente Gomez Moya, who heads an organization called Asoliva, explained to Rosenblum that among consumers, Spanish oil is woefully underrated. "We make the best oil anywhere, but people don't know it. Spain is the great unknown." He had a simple explanation: the big market is the United States, and Americans have associated olive oil with Italy for generations. Italians are better at elegant labels and marketing. Half the sales are to restaurants and the food industry, which Gomez says are dominated by Italian-Americans. Supermarkets absorb much of the rest, and buyers stock what they know. For myself, about four or five years ago I began buying Spanish olive oil almost exclusively after hearing that it was of such good quality and less expensive than its Italian competitors. One brand in particular that I enjoy is Unió. Núñez de Prado is pricier, so I use it sparingly. If you cannot find Spanish oils where you live, both The Spanish Table (206-682-2827; www.tablespan.com) and Zingerman's (888-636-8162; www.zingermans.com) feature a variety of quality Spanish oils in their mail-order catalogs.

Salt: A World History, Mark Kurlansky, Walker & Co., 2002. Here's another fascinating volume from Kurlansky, this time the single subject being one humans and animals cannot survive without. Kurlansky reminds us early on in this book that "salt is so common, so easy to obtain, and so inexpensive that we have forgotten that from the beginning of civilization until about a hundred years ago, salt was one of the most sought-after commodities in human history." (Note that the low cost of salt does not apply to today's designer salts, such as *fleur de sel,* which is handmade and somewhat labor intensive and is "traditional in a world increasingly hungry for a sense of artisans.") One thing I love about books like this is the wealth of trivia one discovers: under Kurlansky's microscope, no stone is left unturned, and you feel like you've just read a long version of *Ripley's Believe It or Not.* I usually walk around for weeks asking "Did you know . . . ?" questions of anyone who will listen, and then I reel off all the amazing things there are to know about cod or salt. For example, did you know that salt makes ice cream freeze, removes rust, seals cracks, cleans bamboo furniture, kills poison ivy, and treats dyspepsia, sprains, sore throats, and earaches? (As an aside, readers interested in more myriad uses for salt should get a copy of the nifty *Solve It with Salt: 110 Surprising and Ingenious Household Uses for Table Salt,* Patty Moosbrugger, Three Rivers Press, 1998.) Besides practical uses, salt is believed by Muslims and Jews to ward off the evil eye, and bringing bread and salt to a new home is a Jewish tradition dating back to the Middle Ages. "In Christianity, salt is associated not only with longevity and permanence but, by extension, with truth and wisdom. The Catholic Church dispenses not only holy water but holy salt, *Sal Sapientia,* the Salt of Wisdom." As the title indicates, this is a worldwide story, but it's very much a Mediterranean story, too. Kurlansky writes that "the entire coast of the Mediterranean was studded with saltworks, some small local operations, others big commercial enterprises such as the ones in Constantinople and the Crimea. The ancient Mediterranean saltworks that had been started by the Phoenicians, like power itself, passed from Romans to Byzantines to Muslims. The saltworks that the Romans had praised remained the most valued. Egyptian salt from Alexandria was highly appreciated, especially their *fleur de sel,* the light crystals skimmed off the surface of the water. Salt from Egypt, Trapani, Cyprus, and Crete all had great standing because they had been mentioned by Pliny in Roman times." Finally, as in *Cod,* Kurlansky warns of what can happen to a seemingly endless resource due to greed and short-sightedness. The lovely French coastal village of Collioure, where artists such as Matisse spent many happy days, once had eight hundred anchovy fishermen; now it has none. I was humbled when I learned that the La Baleine sea salt I've been buying for years is owned by Morton's; and I was surprised to learn that most of the salt mined today is destined for de-icing roads in cold-weather places around the world. *Esencial.*

Secrets of Saffron: The Vagabond Life of the World's Most Seductive Spice, Pat Willard, Beacon Press, Boston, 2001. I'm a nut for single-subject food books— as you've probably ascertained from my descriptions of *Cod* and *Salt*—so I was thrilled to discover this wonderful and fascinating little book on saffron, that quintessential Spanish ingredient. Willard has uncovered a wealth of facts and figures on saffron. One that most impressed me was that Nuremberg, by the mid-1400s, had become the main marketplace for goods coming into central Europe from the Mediterranean. I guess I hadn't considered it before, but the city is situated at the crossroads of the major trade routes and is surrounded by a superior network of rivers and bridges. In 1358 the city passed the *Safranschou* law, which was "to govern the inspection and quality of saffron. On any given day, there were at least seven different varieties of imported saffron for sale in the city's market—French, Spanish, Sicilian, Cretan, Austrian, Greek, and Turkish—all with their own subtle differences in taste and potency." I never knew before I read this book that saffron also once thrived in England (in Norfolk, Suffolk, and the coastal area of Essex), Switzerland (in Basel), and Lancaster County, Pennsylvania (a small amount still does, actually, and makes it as far as the Reading Terminal Market in Philadelphia). Sadly, when Willard visited the town of Consuegra, in La Mancha, there was only one saffron farmer; this in an area that was once brimming with saffron. "It is the simple truth," she writes, "that as Spain has grown away from the shadow of Franco's regime and become one of the more prosperous of the European communities, production of saffron has slipped—the work is too demanding, as always too hard. France has once more begun to export a crop, but it is a small amount—a boutique crop at best—while only a small part of the potent and heady Kashmiri harvest manages to pierce through the decades-long combat lines between India and Pakistan. These days the scandal in the saffron world concerns the rising production from Iran—the rebirth of the old Persian crocus fields, cared for and tended by the religious faithful who break their backs in long hours of picking, happy with the early pennies they receive for their labor since it is done for the Almighty in Paradise." I loved this book so much I read it in one day (it's only 216 pages), and I think my favorite part appears in the next-to-last chapter, when Willard finally finds the answer to the question that has haunted her since her trip to Consuegra: why has she had such an absorbing obsession with saffron? She discovers "at last, what this tiny flower has always embodied and through the ages shared with the world—that so little is needed to turn life into a sumptuous feast." This is a beautifully written book, and Willard also includes a handful of recipes (I admit I haven't yet tried any, but the saffron crème brulée is calling my name) as well as tips on buying, storing, cooking with, and growing saffron (also how to use it as a dye). *Esencial.*

Culinary Classics

Cooking with Daniel Boulud, preface by Pierre Franey, photographs by Todd France, Random House, 1993. If this were merely a good cookbook with good recipes, I would not single it out for special mention; but the fact is that this is an extremely outstanding cookbook with incredible recipes, and a feature that any Spanish (or Mediterranean) cook will appreciate and admire are the "Seasonal Markets Lists" found at the end of the book. If there was ever a more inspiring way to emphasize cooking foods in their proper season, I haven't found it. Our supermarkets make it easy to forget that foods do still have seasons in which they grow and thrive and are harvested. (Just because supermarkets sell asparagus and plastic tomatoes in January doesn't mean they're in season—they're only inferior, tasteless, and flown in from somewhere else.) There are also *great* recipes interspersed between the seasonal food lists, my favorite part of this incomparable volume. Daniel Boulud is one of the world's greatest chefs, but he is very down to earth, not at all high-falutin'. To my mind, this cookbook is among the best ever published.

The Physiology of Taste or Meditations on Transcendental Gastronomy, Jean Anthelme Brillat-Savarin, translated by M.F.K. Fisher and with illustrations by Wayne Thiebaud, Counterpoint (by arrangement with The Arion Press), 1994, distributed by Publishers Group West; original translation copyright 1949, The George Macy Companies, Inc.

Spanish Cuisine

The Cooking of Spain and Portugal, Peter Feibleman and the editors of Time-Life Books, Time Inc., 1969. The Foods of the World series was an extraordinary publishing feat. Each hardcover edition was an amazing collaborative effort, the likes of which we'll probably never see again. (Not only did each book bring together a group of relevant food authorities and creative publishing professionals, but a separate, spiral-bound recipe booklet accompanied each volume.) I am one of those people—and I am not alone—who is nuts for this series, recognizing it quite rightly as the superlative set it is. I once had a tug-of-war contest at the Strand bookstore here in New York with another customer who reached for the *French Provincial Cooking* volume at the same time I did—but I refused to let go, and it's now in my kitchen. In this volume Feibleman notes that "for those who love Spanish and Portuguese cooking, there is something here that is more solid, sturdier and at the same time brighter and more wholly satisfying than the cooking of any other people. We who have learned to love it never seem to want to forget it; we come from all classes, from all places, with all tastes . . . in fact, we seem to have in common only that which we are unable to give any valid reasons for our preference in terms that really mean anything to anybody else." I think that perhaps the best summation of Spanish cuisine and its place in the daily lives of Spaniards is also found in the pages of this wonderful book. The editors set the stage for this somewhat rambling but ultimately accurate portrayal by beginning, "somewhere in the peninsula of land called Iberia that protrudes into the Mediterranean, the Bay of Biscay and Atlantic waters, a train is leaving a railway station." One of the passengers on this train is a peasant woman who is sitting in a third-class carriage. The woman is sitting on one of two hard wooden benches, each of which bears four other people. "She holds a big black satchel, and inside it she carries a thick, golden, cold potato omelet; three or four *bocadillos*, or hard-roll sandwiches of thick, cooked veal; several small loaves of crusty bread; a yellow chunk of pungent sheep or goat's cheese; some juicy, ripe oranges and apples; and a bottle of light, dry red wine. As the train pulls out into open country and the day wears on, the woman opens the swollen satchel and begins to take out food for her husband and two hungry children. But before she serves them, she turns to the other people sharing the compartment and asks each one individually whether he or she will share the meal. Each person will answer formally by saying no, and then by expressing a wish that the food may benefit both the woman and her family. Undiscouraged, the peasant woman continues to offer a small veal *bocadillo*, perhaps a wedge of the rich, country omelet, or some wine and cheese to each of them—until she herself is convinced that the strangers have enough to eat or are honestly not hungry. Only then will she hand some food to her own family and slowly eat with them as the carriage bounces and rattles through the rocky land." As it happens, another passenger on this train is a young duchess, who is sitting in a first-class carriage, who "makes certain that her companions and employees have been attended to by the waiter. Then she orders for herself a meal of broiled Mediterranean sole followed by crisp roast partridge with small browned onions, sliced carrots and new potatoes, and finally coffee. While she eats, the duchess keeps an eye on her companions to make sure no one is lacking anything. Like the peasant woman, she eats slowly, watchfully, with a certain pride in the knowledge of her own individuality combined with a deep-grained sense of responsibility for others. Neither woman, noble or peasant, would think of eating without first seeing that those around her were already fed. These two women would respect each other if they met, for each would recognize in the other certain traits and characteristics—just as both would look down rather critically on women of the newly burgeoning middle classes of Spain and Portugal who may eat without regard for anyone else, and whose lack of formal manners may leave a great deal to be desired." One chapter in this book, "Hearty Land Dishes and Fine Seafood," is devoted to Asturias and Galicia (and includes recipes for these provinces' most famous dishes, *fabada asturiana, caldo gallego,* and *merluza a la gallega*), and another, "A Winning Way with Sauces," is devoted to Navarra and the Basque Country. *Culinaria Spain,* edited by Marion Trutter, Konemann Verlagsgesellschaft,

Cologne, Germany, 1998. This large, nearly five-hundred-page hardcover book is an edition in the Konemann Culinaria series, which I very much like. It covers every corner of Spain (including the Canary Islands) and features individual chapters on the cooking of the Basque Country, Asturias, Cantabria, Galicia, and Castilla y León. Among books that feature authentic recipes and color photographs of the landscapes and food traditions of Spain, this is the best one.

¡Delicioso!: The Regional Cooking of Spain, Penelope Casas, Alfred A. Knopf, 1996. Unlike her *Foods and Wines* book noted below, Casas has organized this volume by regions of Spain. Visitors to Northern Spain will want to read "Spain: The Country of Tapas," "Northern Coastal Spain: Region of the Sauces," and "Northeastern Interior Spain: Region of the Peppers." And in case you were wondering why so many dishes are served in terra-cotta vessels, Casas reveals that "Spanish chefs prefer cooking with earthenware, the most ancient kind of cooking utensil known to man, but they have a hard time explaining why. 'The food just tastes better,' they are likely to say. Emeterio, owner and cook of Tres Coronas de Silos restaurant across from the Santo Domingo de Silos monastery (an architectural gem of the Romanesque period), who serves his outstanding garlic soup in earthenware bowls, gave me an equally vague explanation: 'A bowl made of earthenware is essential to this soup; earthenware gives flavor.' Tradition and low cost account in part for finding earthenware in all sizes and shapes in every Spanish home and in every restaurant kitchen, no mater how trendy it may be (a famous Velázquez painting, *Old Woman Frying an Egg*, shows an egg being cooked over an open fire in an earthenware bowl). But there are other somewhat ineffable reasons why chefs will not part with their *cazuelas*—wide, shallow, primitively made casseroles that are the most common shape for cooking. Perhaps the food really does taste better, if only in a Proustian sense, for the cooking vessel recalls home, hearth, and mother in the kitchen. I learned long ago, however, that earthenware also has practical properties that make it exceptional." (You'll have to read the book to find out what these properties are.) *¡Delicioso!* is not, by the way, repetitive of Casas's first book; *both* volumes are *esencial* in a well-stocked kitchen or in the kitchen of anyone wanting to learn more about the diversity of Spanish cuisine.

The Foods & Wines of Spain, Penelope Casas, Alfred A. Knopf, 1979; eighth printing, 1993. "Over the years, as I traveled to every region of Spain and delved into lesser-known regional cooking, my admiration for Spanish cooking became even greater. I am constantly amazed, however, to find how little the world knows about Spanish cuisine and how it has become confused with the cooking of the rest of the Spanish-speaking world. In Spain the food is not hot and spicy, as many assume it to be, nor does it include *tamales, tacos, enchiladas, frijoles,* or anything even vaguely resembling these traditional Latin American dishes." Though Casas wrote those words in her preface more than twenty years ago, I find that they are still, sadly, true. I cannot understand why there aren't more authentic Spanish restaurants in North America, though it's true that there are more good *tapas* bars—and a handful of very good Spanish restaurants—than there were a decade ago. In any event, if you are interested in reading about and/or cooking Spanish food, you need this book above all others. It's organized by course—*tapas, ensaladas, sopas y potajes, mariscos, carnes, panes, postres,* and so on—and ends with a chapter devoted to the wines of Spain. Positively the definitive book on Spanish cuisine; there is no substitute. *Esencial.* (By the way, I have taken care to note the number of printings for this book—as well as others by Casas—because I learned from her editor's office that each time a book is scheduled to be reprinted, Casas updates the text, often adding significant amounts of new information and finds while deleting or changing other entries. This is not typical in book publishing; an author may be given an opportunity to correct a glaring error before another printing, but adding material or updating text is not a common practice. You may happily be assured, then, that if you borrow or buy a Casas book in its most recent printing, the information has been updated since its original publication.)

Music and Food of Spain, Sharon O'Connor, Menus and Music Productions, Inc., Piedmont, California, 1993. This book and compact disk package is part of a wonderfully creative series entitled "Menus and Music," perfectly suited to *The Collected Traveler.* I hope I have the pleasure to meet O'Connor one day, as she obviously shares my belief in immersing oneself in another culture. She writes in the introduction to this Spain edition that "a meal should engage all of the senses. Taste, of course, is primary, but aroma, color, texture, and of course sound should be a part of the enjoyment. I hope this volume of 'Menus and Music' will help you create and enjoy a great Spanish dinner!" Each edition in the series features a book of recipes accompanied by a CD of appropriate music selections. For Spain, O'Connor gathered recipes from Relais and Chateaux inns and restaurants of Spain (featured restaurants in the north include Arzak in San Sebastiàn and Landa Palace in Burgos) as well as fine Spanish restaurants in the United States. The CD features an hour of classical Spanish guitar music and three Catalan folk songs for cello and guitar, all performed by guitarist Marc Teicholz and cellist O'Connor—yes, she's also a cellist! Among the Spanish composers whose work is featured are Albéniz, Falla, Granados, Tárrega, and Turina, and two of the selections include "Asturianna" and "Asturias." "The guitar," notes O'Connor, "is deeply Spanish," and "although Spanish food is quite regional, the country is united in its love of the guitar." At the back of the book are helpful conversion charts, a list of restaurant contributors, and mail-order sources for special ingredients and equipment. I am crazy for this edition and this entire series (other volumes include *Italian Intermezzo, Bistro, Dining and the Opera in Manhattan,* and *Afternoon Tea Serenade;* call 800-444-9515 for more information or view the website, www.menusandmusic.com), and hope you will be, too.

My Kitchen in Spain: 235 Authentic Regional Recipes, Janet Mendel, HarperCollins, 2002. I am a little embarrassed to admit that I discovered Janet Mendel only a year ago. I don't know how it is possible that someone who has lived in Andalucía for more than thirty years and written five other Spanish cookbooks escaped my attention for so long, but somehow she did. My guess is that most bookstores do not have enough space to devote to Spanish cooking, and many book buyers do not perceive Spanish cooking as "important" as French or Italian, so what little space there is is devoted to the works of Penelope Casas (and I do not mean this as a negative), coffee table books, and perhaps some volumes on Spanish wines. In addition to this, until fairly recently Mendel's books were available only in Europe. Therefore, customers are not likely to have discovered her books unless they learned about them through word of mouth. The five other books by Mendel include *Cooking in Spain, The Best of Spanish Cooking, Traditional Spanish Cooking, Shopping for Food and Wine in Spain,* and *Tapas and More Great Dishes from Spain.* I have read that *Traditional Spanish Cooking* (Garnet, 1997) is an excellent book, and I wish I had a copy. It's proven to be a bit difficult to find, and as I haven't yet seen it or read it, I cannot recommend it with authority (though I'm inclined to say that if you see a copy, you should snatch it up). You shouldn't have any trouble finding *My Kitchen in Spain,* however, in libraries or bookstores. In this volume, Mendel observes that "in spite of enormous changes in life, it is surprising how little the cooking in village homes has changed." She notes, "I continue to be astonished at the variety and richness of Spanish cooking. Spain has fabulous cheeses, hams, sausages, breads, pastries, rice dishes beyond paella, wonderful seafood and great artistry in its preparation, superb fruits and vegetables, and the world's best olive oil. There are dishes to suit every taste—light and fresh fare, hearty and soul-satisfying." I especially enjoyed reading Mendel's opening chapter, "How I Came to Live in Spain" (she arrived in 1966 with her husband, both reporters who had left their newspaper jobs in Chicago to live for a year in Spain) as well as "The Village, Then and Now," which describes the village she lives in above the Costa del Sol. Mendel has truly witnessed some major historical events in Spain, as well as the transformation of a rather sleepy coastline into one of the world's most popular playgrounds. Some of the recipes from Northern Spain include Galician-style octopus, *fabada Asturiana, caldo Gallego,* red beans Basque style, and Galician mussel stew, among others. Mendel also provides informative essays throughout the book on such topics as olive oil, Christmas in Spain, salt cod, cheeses, legumes, and cured Serrano ham. She also provides five sources for Spanish foods and cooking equipment. This is not a book I would define as definitive; rather, it is a personal yet comprehensive overview of both classic and contemporary Spanish cuisine, one that would be welcome and well-used in any kitchen.

Spanish Cuisine: The Gourmet's Companion, Matt A. Casado, John Wiley & Sons, 1997. What really sold me on this book—which I unfortunately did not discover until after I had returned from my last trip to Spain—is that the author, a Spanish- and American-trained hotel and food service manager—is the author of *The Food and Beverage Service Manual* and *Conversational Spanish for Hospitality Managers and Supervisors* (both also published by Wiley). A combination restaurant companion and culinary reference, this extremely useful book provides an overview of classical Spanish cooking (and a little bit about Portugal) as well as regional highlights. The various glossaries are significantly more thorough than those in *World Food: Spain* (see below) and include a complete dictionary of Spanish dishes, ingredients for hundreds of dishes organized by course, a Spanish-English glossary of cooking terms, regional cooking styles and preparations, and descriptions of Spanish wines and liqueurs.

Tapas: The Little Dishes of Spain, Penelope Casas, Alfred A. Knopf, 1985; tenth printing, 1993. Similar to her *Food and Wines* book above, I think this is the definite book on Spanish *tapas.* I've made so many recipes from this book that came out so perfectly that I've lost count. It is a great answer for the question, which book should I cook from? When your friends or colleagues are coming over for a little *feria,* recipes from this book are sure to be a huge hit. *Esencial.*

To the Heart of Spain: Food and Wine Adventures Beyond the Pyrenees, Ann and Larry Walker, Berkeley Hills Books, California, 1997. This wonderfully written paperback is "not quite a cookbook or a wine book, nor is it a travel guide. It is, instead, a little of all three, with a smattering of history and culture to boot." The authors have written six other food and wine books featuring Spain and Latin America (two of them, I'm sorry to say, I haven't read yet: *The Pleasures of the Canary Islands* and *A Season in Spain*), and their passion for Spain is abundantly evident in this volume. I knew I was going to love it from reading the preface, in which the authors write, "What this book is really about is Spain. Spanish days and Spanish nights . . . One of the great attractions of Spain for the modern traveler is the feeling that something a little out of the ordinary might happen at any time. This is because Spain is not quite Europe, not quite Africa, but altogether something else. In Spain, the unexpected is only a step or two away." Individual chapters focusing on northern regions include "Rioja and Navarre," "Basque Country," "Celtic Spain," which covers Galicia,

Asturias, and Cantabria. There is a good and lengthy recipe section at the end of the book. *Esencial*.

World Food: Spain, Richard Sterling, Lonely Planet, 2000. This little pocket-sized edition is decidedly more hip than *Spanish Cuisine*, discussed above, and it's jam-packed with color photos and a variety of tidbits of food-related information. Unlike *Spanish Cuisine*, I have traveled with this volume, so it's been wear-tested, so to speak—I found myself unable to stop referring to it. The author can be simultaneously humorous and wise, as he is here when addressing vegetarians: "Dead pig is a vegetable. Many Spanish cooks will attest to this. You specifically ordered your dish 'without meat' and incredulously watch the straight-faced waiter defend those surprise bits of mystery flesh with 'that's not meat, it's ham.' The visiting vegetarian must pack a small stash of vitamins and a big sense of humour. It's not to say you can't enjoy a wide variety of Spanish delicacies, but if you find devouring any of God's creatures repulsive, you'll need to be diligent. A strategy for the transient herbivore might be to map out all the vegetarian restaurants and stick to that route. This would be about as typically Spanish as pursuing a route of Hare Krishna temples. You can do it, but where's the Spain in it?" A small complaint about the useful phrases given: nowhere is it expressed how to say, "I'd like to make a reservation, please." Seems like an obviously simple phrase to figure out, but it would still be incredibly helpful if the phrase were given, so that if, like me, you're calling from Cantabria to try to make a reservation at Arzak, say, in San Sebastián, you can at least begin the conversation with the proper words. (I ended up saying something like "I'm telephoning from Cantabria for a table for two, please.") Either this or *Spanish Cuisine* is *esencial*.

Basque Cuisine

The Basque Kitchen: Tempting Food from the Pyrenees, Gerald Hirigoyen with Cameron Hirigoyen, photographs by Chris Shorten, HarperCollins, 1999. There aren't many Basque cookbooks available in North America, in English, so if you're eager to start cooking from one, this is it. The Basques, as you'll discover, have an enormous respect for food, equal to the French—"To know how to eat is enough" is an old Basque phrase. In addition to the full range of recipes, from appetizers and salads to sweets (and the ones I've tried are outstanding), Hirigoyen also provides a "Notes on Ingredients" section, a culinary guide to the Basque Country, and mail-order sources for Basque foods and related items (most helpful).

The Basque Table: Passionate Home Cooking from One of Europe's Great Regional Cuisines, Teresa Barrenechea with Mary Goodbody, Harvard Common Press, 1998. Barrenechea is chef and owner of the widely acclaimed

Marichu restaurants in New York City and the New York suburb of Bronxville, in Westchester County. According to the Spanish Tourist Office, Marichu serves the most authentic Spanish food in the U.S., a statement with which I might have to agree. Though I've never met Barranechea personally, it seems to me that the adjective that best describes her is *passionate*—as in passionate about Basque cooking and culture. In the introduction to this excellent cookbook, Barranechea states that Basques believe their food is the best in the world. "After traveling all over Spain and abroad and falling in love with other cuisines, I have come to the conclusion that Basque cooking justly deserves its reputation as being among the best." Certainly anyone who has spent even a short time in the País Vasco knows this to be true, and those who have not yet visited the Basque region will quickly arrive at the same conclusion. "I do not know of any other place in the world where cooking is as revered an art, and as dominant in the national consciousness, as it is in the Spanish Basque country," Barranechea continues. "Not even across the border, on the French side, can this collective culinary fanaticism be found. It is one of the most important and distinctive traits of our culture. For Basques, food is a major topic of conversation—with the taxi driver, with fellow bus passengers, with friends lying on the beach. Listen to a conversation between Basques, and most likely you will hear what they had for dinner the previous night, what they will have for lunch that same day, or where you can get this or the other unusual ingredient. We Basques happily live for our next meal!" In addition to all the recipes for pinchos, first and main courses, and desserts, there is a section called "Basque Basics"—my favorite—which offers fifteen basic sauces and flavorings that every good Basque cook worth his or her salt relies on "to turn a good meal into a spectacular one, a simple dish into a memorable one." A most inspiring cookbook, also with some interesting highlighted text boxes about *sidrerías*, traditional Basque dances, sports, men's gastronomic clubs, baby eels, etc.

Life and Food in the Basque Country, María José Sevilla, New Amsterdam Books, Lanham, Maryland, 1989. Though this book contains recipes, it is more a valuable history and testament to food traditions held sacred by the Basques. Chapters include "Market Day at Ordicia," "The Caserío," "The Life of a Fisherman," "The Cider and Wine Houses," and "The Gastronomic Societies." Sevilla shares a good summation about Basque cooking by the chef Pedro Subijana, who says, "It would be very difficult to define this cuisine precisely. It has its roots in the cooking of the people and it is true to its culinary traditions and practice. There are slight variations between the cooking of the different provinces of Guipúzcoa, Vizcaya, Álava and Navarra, but they all pride themselves on using local produce in season. Basque cuisine has several different sources of inspiration, ranging from peasant dishes to the cuisine of the bourgeoisie; it is alive and constantly evolving, without losing its uniqueness and identity; it is very close to the heart of all Basques." Additionally, Sevilla explains that the portraits related in this book depict the inhabitants of southern Basque Country. Of French-Basque cooking, she says its main characteristic "is that it is an inland cuisine, relying on the fruits of the soil, with a bias towards dishes using meat, together with maize, the cereal which came to revolutionize the life of the Nation when it arrived from the Americas; these are the twin pillars on which depends its success. This is an obvious contrast to Spanish-Basque cuisine, which, although it also incorporates inland dishes, is at its most characteristic when it creates delicious dishes using the fruits of the sea." *Esencial*.

Restaurant Guides

Eating and Drinking in Spain: A Menu Reader and Restaurant Guide, Andy Herbach and Michael Dillon, Open Road Publishing, Cold Spring Harbor, NY, second revised edition 2002. This is one book in a series (other editions feature Italy, Paris, and France) that I *love*. It's a small paperback that fits easily in a pocket, so you won't look like a nerd in a restaurant as you look up a word. More important, it's *really* thorough: seventy-eight pages of Spanish menu words and methods and styles of cooking that, as we all know, are what trip people up the most, such as *aliñada* (marinated or seasoned with salad dressing), *arroz a la emperatriz* (rice with apricots, raisins, truffles, milk, and Cointreau), *arroz en caldero* (rice with red peppers and seafood), *ensalada valenciana* (salad with lettuce, potatoes, and oranges), *garrapiñadas* (glazed), or *merluza a la Gallega* (cod with potatoes and paprika, from Galicia). Plus, these guys are funny: in the margins, they've made such notations as "I'll pass" (next to the entry for *raspas de anchoas,* deep-fried backbones of anchovies), *"No me gusta!"* (next to *sesos*, brains), and "You don't want to mix these two up!" (next to entries for *panceta,* bacon/pork belly, and *pancita,* tripe). A Spanish pronunciation guide is included, as well as an English-to-Spanish glossary of food words and related phrases; there are a number of Central and South American dishes featured, too. The authors also provide the names for some of their favorite places to eat in Spain, including three listings for Bilbao, four for Pamplona, four for San Sebastián, and three for Santiago, plus three suggestions for shops selling Spanish food and wine specialties. I especially applaud the authors' mission statement: We want people to eat in restaurants that don't provide English menus. "We love the United States, but we want foreign when we're on foreign soil. Nothing against fast food, but when we're in Spain, we want it to look Spanish. Golden arches don't belong on the Plaza Mayor. As we see it, a menu in English is the first step in the Americanization of the restaurants of the world. And once a place isn't foreign, what's the point of going there?" I wouldn't go to Spain without this in my bag: *Esencial*.

Gourmetour Guía Gastronómica y Turística de España, Grupo Editorial Club de Gourmets/Club G., S.A., Graficas Marte, Rapygraf, S.L. This exceptionally well-organized, annually updated book (in Spanish only) is a comprehensive guide to Spanish foods and culture. It strays well beyond other food books as, in addition to reviews of restaurants and bars, there are reviews for hotels; places of interest (such as museums, beaches, parks, picturesque places); shopping; and regional specialties. It is, in fact, one of the best books of its kind that I've ever seen. Some of its other great features are the detailed maps throughout the book, a mileage chart, gastronomical dictionary, wine chart, and a thorough index of restaurants, hotels, and cities. Perhaps best of all is a section outlining each region of Spain, with specifics on climate, topography, and history. Following this is a brief overview of the distinguishing features of each region's gastronomy, and includes local specialties and typical ingredients. I absolutely love this book, and urge readers who, like me, have a keen interest in Spanish cooking and culture to buy a copy as soon as you arrive in Spain (it is not available in North America, unfortunately). Alternatively, I feel certain a good concierge or the owners of a small inn would be happy to obtain a copy for you upon your arrival. I do not have a good command of Spanish, but it truly isn't difficult to decipher the highlights of the text. *Esencial*.

Lo Mejor de la Gastronomía, Rafael García Santos, Unigraf, S.L. Here is another annually updated book—also in Spanish, also only available in Spain—covering Spain's gastronomy. Author Santos is wholly dedicated to preserving the culinary arts of Spain, and his passion is reflected in the detailed descriptions of foods, cooks, wines, and products. The book is organized thematically: "The Best Cooks," "The Best Pork," "The Best Andalusian Tapas Bars," "The Best Red Wines," "The Best Products" are just a few of about thirty themes. Within each of these sections are the establishment's address, business hours, telephone number, price, and rating. As a quick reference, the *"índice geográfico"* lists the regions, city or town, and the establishments reviewed. At the beginning of the book is a chart listing each theme, numerical ratings, and the establishments that fall under those ratings. I like how color coding is used to list the specialties of cities and towns. *Lo Mejor de la Gastronomía* is an excellent resource for food enthusiasts and for those who desire a good, overall guide to Spanish gastronomy. Travelers who prefer more of a straightforward restaurant guide may select the *Gourmetour* edition; for true Spanish gastronomes, however, I recommend purchasing both of these books. This one's *esencial*, too.

Michelin Red Guide: Spain and Portugal. The exhaustive Red Guide is without doubt the one that is most familiar to North Americans. Michelin reviewers will steer travelers in the right direction, and as this guide (in Spanish only) can easily be found in bookstores and libraries, it's a great resource to consult in advance of a trip (it's a rather chunky hardcover, so it's not a good candidate for bringing along unless you think you'll really be using it a lot; I do know some folks who would never leave home without the appropriate Michelin Red Guide, and they never complain about its weight). Though I am a big fan of the Red Guide, I do think the two Spanish guides listed just above are even better choices (note that they're even heavier, however, than the Red Guide). I personally recommend consulting Michelin thoroughly before your departure, and then purchasing at least one of the other Spanish guides in Madrid or one of the northern cities.

~*La Librería Gastronómica* is not a restaurant guide but something a bit more unique: it's a gastronomy catalog featuring more than sixty works from around the world, and thus in a number of different languages in addition to Spanish. Interested readers may request a free catalog by mail (Ausiàs March, 25, 08010 Barcelona, Spain), telephone (933.18.20.82), fax (933.02.50.83), or e-mail (libreriagastronomica@montagud.com). Visit the website for more information (www.libreriagastronomica.com).

Of Related Interest

The Cheese Plate, Max McCalman and David Gibbons, photographs by Susan Salinger, Clarkson Potter, 2002. I love the *Cheese Primer* (see below), and can't really imagine a more perfect book about cheese; but when *The Cheese Plate* was published, I realized that the *Cheese Primer* could, in fact, be complemented with a book that featured color photographs and even more information on creating cheese courses. McCalman is America's first maître fromager (cheese sommelier), and he helped to create the successful cheese programs at the celebrated restaurants Picholine and Artisanal in New York. Though he is a nut for so many of the world's finest cheeses, McCalman has said that "the first cheeses that really spoke to me were Spanish; even many of the *quesos* produced by small factory cheese makers in Spain are of artisanal quality." He included thirteen cheeses from Spain (six from Northern Spain) on his list of favorites in this book. As McCalman notes, Green Spain has a much wetter, cooler climate than the rest of the country, and therefore there are more lush pastures, picturesque mountain valleys . . . and more cows. "Ancient traditions in these bucolic settings have produced a marvelous array of cheeses, particularly in Asturias. This is the heartland of Spanish cheese, home to a disproportionate number of the country's world-class artisanal cheeses." A beautiful, practical book.

Cheese Primer, Steven Jenkins, Workman Publishing Co., 1996. Though it is not exclusively about Spanish cheeses, they do figure large in this excellent cheese bible. (I had the great pleasure of meeting Jenkins last year at a benefit in New

York, and he *loves* Spanish cheeses.) Jenkins, the first American to be awarded France's Chevalier du Taste-Fromage, created and/or revitalized the cheese counters at such New York food emporiums as Dean & DeLuca and Fairway. In addition to presenting the cheeses of Spain (one chapter covers the northern coast of Spain and another is devoted to the cheeses of the Pyrenees) and twelve other regions of the world, he explains how cheese is made, the basics of butterfat, and the seasons that are best for making and eating cheese. (Yes, most cheeses have a season, which is determined by the pasturage vegetation that cows, goats, and sheep have been eating at the time of milking.) Jenkins also offers great suggestions for buying and serving cheese and for creating cheese plates at home. And for travelers, he provides the names of cheeses—most never exported—to look for in various regions. This is the most comprehensive book on cheese I've ever seen and is an *esencial* addition to any food lover's library.

The Joy of Coffee: The Essential Guide to Buying, Brewing, and Enjoying, Corby Kummer, 1995, hardcover; 1999, paperback, both Chapters Publishing, Shelburne, VT. A comment I hear often from people who visit Spain, Italy, and France is that the coffee is so much better there. In my opinion it's not the coffee that's better but the quality of the dairy products used. Coffee, after all, doesn't grow in the Mediterranean, and roasters and vendors can buy excellent beans as easily as anybody else around the world. If you're a coffee drinker, you can judge for yourself, and I've included this book here for those who want to know more about the elixir they love. There are other coffee books on the shelves, but I find this to be the best volume on coffee ever published. Kummer, a well-known food journalist, is a senior editor of *The Atlantic Monthly* and has also contributed to *Martha Stewart Living, New York, Food & Wine,* and other periodicals. He covers coffee plantations, cupping, roasting, grinding, storing (the best place, if you drink it every day, is not in the freezer, as many people mistakenly believe), and brewing, plus separate chapters on espresso, caffeine versus decaf, and a country-by-country guide. There are also recipes for baked goods that pair particularly well with coffee. (I've made almost all of them and can vouch that they are especially yummy.)

About Spanish Wine

A Traveller's Wine Guide to Spain, Desmond Begg, foreword by María Isabel Mijares y García-Pelayo, photographs by Francesco Venturi, Interlink Books, Massachusetts, 1998. Not quite as detailed and in-depth as the *Wine Roads* book just below, this is still a most worthy traveling companion for those who don't desire more than a general background. There are individual chapters on Navarra, La Rioja, and Galicia, as well as maps, a description of the Spanish wine label, tips on driving in Spain and for visiting a *bodega,* a reference section (on the blue pages at the back of the book), and color photographs throughout. At 144 pages, this is also a lightweight bring-along.

The Wine Roads of Spain, Marc and Kim Millon, HarperCollins, 1993. Despite its 1993 copyright, this is still the best single book on the wines of Spain, and in addition to individual chapters featuring Galicia, Castilla y León, Navarra and the Basque Country, and La Rioja, there are descriptive travel itineraries for visitors, addresses of vintners who welcome visitors, recommended hotels and restaurants, notes on regional gastronomy, photographs and maps, and lists of professional wine organizations and wine museums. *Esencial.*

Good Books About Wine in General

Great Wines Made Simple: Straight Talk from a Master Sommelier, Andrea Immer, Broadway Books, 2000. Spain is included as part of a larger chapter, but Immer notes that "Spain is *the* wine source for the millennium—offering value, tradition, and innovation all rolled up into good-tasting vino with soul." Immer's more recent book, a companion volume of sorts, is *Andrea Immer's Wine Buying Guide for Everyone* (Broadway Books, 2002). For this refreshingly honest little guide (it's approximately the same shape as the Zagat guides), Immer surveyed wine professionals and ordinary consumers to identify the most popular and available wines on the market. The result is a compilation of more than four hundred top wines that are available around the country in stores and restaurants. No vintage bottles are listed; these are current, ready-to-drink wines (an Immer insight: "Ninety-five percent of the quality wines on the market are meant to be consumed within one to three years of the harvest (the vintage date on the label), while they they are young, fresh, and in good condition. Most wines do not get better with age, so why wait?"). Among the Northern Spain wines featured are red and white selections from La Rioja, one red from Navarra, and Martín Codax Albariño. I am an especially big fan of Immer, notably due to her observation that the American wine publications lack "someone with a little authoritative perspective validating the average person's taste and budget." It seems to me that American vintners have collectively decided to ignore the concept of everyday wine and concentrate instead on wines that average $15–20 a bottle. They clearly don't understand (or don't care to) that in order to create a nation of wine drinkers, the industry must continually raise new generations of wine drinkers. I mean no disrespect to American vintners, in any particular state; but this is an important concept to touch upon and is essential to understanding much of the culture in Spain and elsewhere. Creating pricey boutique wines is an exciting, creative challenge for vintners, but in wine-drinking countries, consumers drink wine every day, at least with one meal and more often with two. Wines, therefore, must be priced accordingly. Readers who have visited Spain previously (or France and Italy) may have noticed that the vast majority of wines available for sale—whether at a *supermercado* or a small specialty shop—are priced under $10, many under $5. At bars, a glass of wine is priced between $1.50 and $4, and even at many restaurants, a good bottle of wine is about $10. People who live amid vineyards simply take a plastic jug to a vintner and have it filled with the local red or white; when my brother and sister-in-law visited Provence, they enjoyed a red wine one evening at an inn where they were staying. When they asked about it, the *patron* told them it was from the vineyard down the road, so the next day they set out to buy a few bottles. The price? Three bucks a bottle. To this day, they maintain it was among the best wines they've ever had. While it's possible to find a few American wines under $10 a bottle, I personally have found them undrinkable (you know, the kind that give you a headache before you've finished one glass). Dear readers, if you have found a favorite, everyday American wine under $10 a bottle, please write and let me know about it; and if, like me, you haven't, be vocal and let the vintners of our nation know that we will support their efforts in making quality, inexpensive wines we can drink every day. Finally, read Andrea Immer's book for some great, affordable wine recommendations! In 1997 Immer, one of only ten women in the world to qualify as a master sommelier, was named Best Sommelier in America.

Jancis Robinson's Wine Course, BBC Books, London, 1995.

Making Sense of Wine, Matt Kramer, Quill (an imprint of William Morrow), 1989.

The Oxford Companion to Wine, edited by Jancis Robinson, A. Dinsmoor Webb, and Richard E. Smart, Getty Center for Education in the Arts, 1999.

Pairing Wine and Food: A Handbook for All Cuisines, Linda Johnson-Bell, Burford Books, 1999.

Tasting Pleasure: Confessions of a Wine Lover, Jancis Robinson, Viking, 1997. Spain and some Spanish wines are featured in a few of the twenty-four essays. In one chapter, Robinson notes that "although I'm ready to be seduced by whatever comes along from Spain's extremely active winemakers, I am currently most excited by the slightly austere but definitely noble white wines of Galicia in the far northwest."

Vineyard Tales: Reflections on Wine, Gerald Asher, Chronicle Books, 1996. Of the twenty-nine essays, only one—"Ribera del Duero: A New Star for Old Castile"—is devoted to Spain; but the entire book is a delight to read.

The Wine Bible, Karen MacNeil, Workman Publishing Co., 2001. If it isn't yet obvious, I love books that have "bible" in the title, so I was eager for this book's publication. Author MacNeil is director of the wine program at the

Culinary Institute of America in Napa Valley, California, and has written about wine for a number of periodicals, including *The New York Times, Food & Wine, Saveur,* and *Wine Spectator*. This accomplishment may indeed represent, as vintner Robert Mondavi attests, "the most complete wine book ever." In addition to a sixty-two-page chapter devoted to Spain, MacNeil covers the rest of the wine-growing world and also provides individual glossaries of wine terms for Spain, France, Italy, Portugal, Germany, Austria, Hungary, and Greece; the 1855 classification of Bordeaux chart; and a thorough bibliography. I do have a quibble with her spelling of "Galegos," the word referring to the people of Galicia. I have only seen it spelled this way once before, and the commonly accepted spelling is "Gallegos." It's a small quibble, though. This is an outstanding book, profusely illustrated, packed with history, recommended labels, and even some tips for visitors (in the Spain chapter, MacNeil suggests six bodegas to visit in La Rioja, and even offers her choice for the best seaside tavern in Spain: Tasca Xeito, 19 rua Dr. Fernández Albor, La Guardia, Galicia; 986.61.04.74).

The World Atlas of Wine, Hugh Johnson and Jancis Robinson, Mitchell Beazley, London, 2001. Fifteen pages are devoted to the wine regions of Spain.

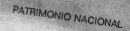

PATRIMONIO NACIONAL

PALACIO DE ORIENTE

VISITA A LOS SALONES DE REPRESENTACION OFICIAL
GALERIA DE TAPICES Y REAL CAPILLA

PTAS. 30,00

ESPAÑA
CORREOS
5 PTAS.

Consejo Internacional de Museos

ESPAÑA
CORREOS

COD 120 PTS

Mis Favoritos
(Good Things, Favorite Places)

"To let the threat of a shower or two keep you away would
be to miss out on the best preserved and most idiosyncratic
corners of old Europe, a place that has kept a sense of place
in the face of creeping homogeneity, one full of unexpected
pleasures: a Roman bridge over a brook, the fishmarket in A
Coruña, a tableland in northern Castile abruptly cut away
by a canyon filled with eagles, a spontaneous party that lasts
until dawn in an outdoor sidrería, old women herding their
cows home by twilight, the walls of stained glass in León, a
Basque tug-of-war match, and a sunset at Finisterre, the end
of the world."

—Dana Facaros and Michael Pauls,
CADOGAN GUIDE: NORTHERN SPAIN

Chillida-Leku:
A Sculptor's Place

By Sonia Ortega

∽

editor's note

Eduardo Chillida is arguably the most famous artist, in any medium, to hail from Northern Spain. The relationship between his sculpture and the Basque region is so remarkably complete that you cannot view one without the other.

I had read very little about the Chillida-Leku Museum, but Daniel, my expert guide at the Guggenheim Bilbao, enthusiastically raved about it. I think even readers who are not fans of contemporary sculpture will agree that this a beautiful, off-the-beaten-path spot.

Sonia Ortega is a journalist and has been coordinator of *Spain Gourmetour,* where this piece first appeared, since its first issue.

Hernani is a little town some 10 kilometers (6 miles) from San Sebastián, in the Basque Country, Northern Spain. This is where sculptor Eduardo Chillida settled in 1951 after spending three years in France, a period when he produced his first sculptures, in plaster. His house in Hernani stood opposite a forge, and it was there, almost by accident, that he first became aware of the plastic potential of iron and where he first worked the tough but malleable material now so characteristic of his work.

Today, the town is also the site of Chillida-Leku, the sixteenth-century house and grounds that constitute the combined sculpture park and museum where both the man and his work have found their rightful place in the world. Chillida explains it thus: "I strongly believe that we all come from somewhere, and I think this is of vital importance. The ideal situation would be for us to have our roots in one place but for our branches to extend worldwide, so that we recognize the value of the ideas of other cultures. Anywhere at all can be an ideal place as long as it suits you, and here in the Basque Country is where I feel myself to be in my proper place." He could hardly state his credo more clearly. The Basque word *leku* means "place" or "space," so the museum that houses the work of this universally relevant Basque sculptor translates as "Chillida's Place" or "Chillida's Space." Chillida-Leku is Chillida's vision made real, an environment in which artworks, landscape, and architecture fuse together as naturally as the materials of his imposing iron and steel sculptures.

Its focus is Zabalaga, a sixteenth-century country house that the Chillida family bought as a ruin and has since restored sympathetically. It took twelve years to convert the ruined stone and timber house they bought in 1983 into what we see today. Architect Joaquín Montero and Chillida worked together on the project whose intention was not to restore the house to its original function but rather to treat it as a sculpture in itself, emptying the interior and letting in space and light. Working slowly and using only artisan methods, they have exposed its mighty oak beams completely, creating the effect of the timbers of a vast ship or a gigantic tree. This is more than just an art exhibition area: it is another of Chillida's "sculptural spaces," in the same category as his *Elogio de horizonte* in Gijón, and his proposed project to hollow out Tindaya Mountain on the island of Fuerteventura. The house and park contain works that Chillida himself has chosen to retain over the years with a view to exhibiting them eventually in his home territory. In the course of seventeen years, more than forty large-scale sculptures, mostly iron and granite pieces (some of them enormous—*Looking Light I,* for example), have been installed in the museum's 12 hectares (30 acres) of splendidly wooded grounds. Some of them will stay at Chillida-Leku only long enough to acquire a weathered patina before being transferred to the locations for which they were specifically created, though the majority are permanently positioned.

The interior of the old house contains a hundred or so small- and large-scale pieces ranging from his first works in plaster and early pieces in iron, through works in alabaster, granite, steel, and terra cotta, to drawings and *gravitaciones*—collages on paper or felt in which images are superimposed so that they acquire volume. The exhibits on the main, lower floor are illuminated by natural light that floods in through a huge window, filling the space and gilding the rough stone walls hung with the contrasting textures of felt *gravitaciones*. The exhibits on this floor are medium- and large-scale pieces representative of the last twenty years of the sculptor's work.

A fine wooden staircase leads to the upper floor, which is divided into three rooms. The first of these, organized chronologically, contains the plaster sculptures—*Forma y Torso (Form and Torso)*—made in Paris between 1948 and 1951, and the iron pieces cast in Hernani after Chillida's return from France. This is when we start to recognize the Chillida we know, working in metal. All these works are accompanied by contemporary drawings.

The next room contains projects for public pieces, some of them subsequently realized on a monumental scale and others that never came to fruition. They attest to Chillida's ongoing commitment to public sculpture. Alongside the projects are several alabaster sculptures dating from the 1960s, a large terra-cotta and oxidized copper mural, and a series of quintessentially Chillidan drawings of hands. Still on the upper floor, a glass door leads to a section designated *El Chillida Más Íntimo* (The More Intimate Chillida). Here we find the more delicate works—smaller-scale terra-cottas that have served as maquettes for various granite sculptures, and paper *gravitaciones* in which we see Chillida incorporating volume into drawing for the first time, combining line with built-up layers and cutouts.

The exterior appearance of the house has been kept faithful to the original, including its coat of arms. It gives immediately onto a vast meadow (it comes as no surprise to learn that Zabalaga means "wide field" in Basque), while higher ground behind is wooded with beeches, oaks, magnolias, poplars, and chestnut trees. Sculptures have been excitingly placed throughout the grounds, some out in the open, others in little clearings among the trees, their location seeming completely natural, as if they had grown where they stand, art and nature in a symbiotic relationship that is a key characteristic of Chillida's work.

Chillida-Leku is run by the Chillida family with Kosme de Barañano (director of Valencia's IVAM—see *Spain Gourmetour* no. 48) as artistic consultant. Its facilities include a comprehensive library on Eduardo Chillida (to be expanded to include a newspaper and periodical archive), an archive, and a film auditorium. The films shown provide an opportunity to see the artist at work and to appreciate his range: from the sheer strength required to work in iron to the delicacy of his "more intimate" *gravitaciones*. One includes a sequence based on a phrase written on paper by Chillida that states: "One line can unite the world; one line can divide it. Drawing is beautiful and awesome." Above all, it is the beauty that comes across at Chillida-Leku.

Fagollaga: Choice Cuisine

A little road leading out of Hernani follows the course of the River Oria through the town's industrial outskirts and into the wooded countryside beyond. Just before a bend in the road stands an unpretentious, white-fronted country house: this is Fagollaga (a Basque name meaning "place of many beech trees"), which Isaac Salaberría's great-grandmother established as a restaurant where she served traditional popular Basque cuisine back in 1904. Some of her classics, beautifully executed, are still on her great-grandson's menu today.

Excellent though they are, however, these are not the chief gastronomic attraction at Fagollaga: the cuisine that typifies it today is characterized by its imaginative approach and technical skill, fine ingredients being allowed to speak for themselves in a quest for very specific, pure, pronounced flavors.

Still only thirty, Isaac Salaberría is considered one of the most talented new-generation chefs—he was chosen Cook of the Year by *Lo Mejor de la Gastronomía* restaurant guide in 1999. He is already famous for his way of "deconstructing" dishes, serving sauces separately, often in little ladles, so that it is up to the diner whether to follow the house suggestions or decide for himself what to combine with what. His *salmonete con crema de almendra tierna y jugo de regaliz y azafrán* (red mullet with fresh almond cream and licorice and saffron sauce) and *foie gras a la plancha sobre jugo de pollo escabechado, puré de maíz y sorbete de piña* (grilled foie gras with *jus* of soused chicken, creamed sweet corn, and pineapple sorbet) convey the spirit of this approach.

More traditional flavors emerge in a supremely delicate and aromatic *charlota de patas de cerdo* (charlotte of pig's trotters, potato slices, herbs, and sesame) and the delicious marriage of fresh pasta and spider crab meat in *lasagna de txangurro*. The same creativity shows in desserts such as *jugo de pera con ensalada de tomate y helado cremoso de yogur* (pear juice with a salad of tomato and yogurt ice cream) or *crema de arroz con leche con gelée de fresas, cava y ruibarbo con sorbete de cacao* (creamed rice pudding with strawberry, cava, and rhubarb gelée and cocoa sorbet). There's a lot of artistry in the food at **Restaurante Fagollaga**—the perfect place to eat after a visit to Chillida-Leku: Carretera de Goizueta, 20120 Hernani, Guipúzcoa; 943.550.031.

Eduardo Chillida—Languages: English, Spanish. This is the main page of the site on Eduardo Chillida and covers the essential points of his biography and his most emblematic works. It is also the site for Chillida-Leku.
www.eduardo-chillida.com/en_ie_museo

Art Forum—Language: Spanish. One of the sections on this site is "Cátedra," in which writers of prestige discuss the work of a specific artist. This is the address for the article on Chillida-Leku.
www.forodearte.com/catedra/chillidaleku

Hispanart—Language: Spanish. Hispanart is a portal on art comprising both general sections and others that center on a specific subject and artist. One of these special sections is devoted to Chillida-Leku and is structured as a guide to the different parts of the museum.
www.hispanart.com/Chillida

Regional Council of Guipúzcoa—Languages: English, French, Spanish. This page within the regional council's site gives comprehensive information on tourism in the province with suggestions for routes and visits, as well as links to town council sites.
www.gipuzkoa.net/turismo

Rural Tourism in the Basque Country—Languages: English, Spanish. This page gives information on accommodations in Basque farmhouses with prices.
www.encomix.es/nekazal

Mis Favoritos

Granted it's quite personal, but this is my list—in no particular order and subject to change on any day of the week—of some favorite things to see, do, and buy in Northern Spain. I am mindful that singling out "bests" and "favorites" inevitably means that something I very much like will be forgotten. So I emphasize that this is by no means a definitive list; rather, it contains some wonderful things that I am happy to share with you in the hope that you might also enjoy them, and that you will reciprocate by sharing your discoveries with me.

A word about shopping: I am not much into acquiring things, so as a general rule shopping is not one of my favorite pastimes; but I do enjoy buying gifts for other people, especially when I'm traveling. To borrow a quote from a great little book called *The Fearless Shopper: How to Get the Best Deals on the Planet* (Kathy Borrus, Travelers Tales, 2000), shopping is "about exploring culture and preserving memory—the sights, sounds, smells, tastes, tempo, and touch of a place." Most of what I purchase therefore—even for myself—falls into the culinary category, because for me food and drink are inextricably linked to a place. Food and drink can be extended, of course, to pottery, for which I have a particular weakness. Though inferior ingredients and carelessly prepared food can never be masked by a beautifully set table, a delicious meal is even better when it is served in vessels, on dishes, and with utensils unique to its origins. Every time I open the little glass jar of saffron, the tin of roasted *piquillo* peppers, or the container of *pimentón* in my pantry, I am instantly transported back to the shops where I bought them, and I remember as if I were there yesterday the delicious meals I had in Northern Spain prepared with these key ingredients; each time I serve Spanish olives in the small ceramic bowl with a separate compartment for the pits, I think of the lovely sea-side town of Santillana del Mar where I found it; and when I set my table with the beautiful ceramic plates from Talavera, there is no doubt that, for an evening, my family and friends and I are in Spain. To quote again from Kathy Borrus, "I am surrounded—not by things but history and culture and memory." I have found that even the *supermercados* of Spain sell beautifully packaged items of yummy stuff that in the U.S. is hard to find or expensive or both.

A word about stores: business hours being what they are in Spain, you might want to adopt my motto, "When in doubt, buy it now." I learned years ago that the likelihood of being able to retrace my steps past a particular merchant *when it was open* was slim. If you spy some yummy marinated Manchego, some *jamón serrano,* some local pottery, a painting, a Basque beret, a hard-to-find-at-home Rioja wine, or *anything* that has your name all over it, *vaya* (go) and get it, for Miguel's sake. One has regrets only for the roads not taken—or in this case, the object not purchased! It bears repeating that, in general, most shops are open from about nine-thirty in the morning to about one-thirty in the afternoon, at which time merchants close for lunch and reopen anywhere from four to six P.M. Typically, shops will then remain open until about seven-thirty or eight. This applies only to Tuesday through Friday. Some shops do not open until the afternoon on Monday, and nearly all retail businesses are closed entirely on Sunday. Saturday is the tricky day of the week: most stores are open only until lunchtime, not to reopen again until Monday. During the summer months many establishments close for a longer period during the afternoon and stay open later in the evening.

Galicia

~Parador Hostal de los Reyes Católicos (plaza del Obradoiro 1, 15705 Santiago de Compostela; 981.58.22.00; fax: 981.56.30.94;

Santiago@parador.es). You already know of my preference for the Paradores chain of hotels, and this one, just diagonal from the cathedral in the main plaza of Santiago, is widely regarded as the grandest and most famous of them all. (I would say that the *parador* in Granada, in the gardens of the Alhambra, is the runner-up.) The staff of the Santiago *parador* have a reputation among travel writers as being a bit frosty, and I would agree that I have received a warmer welcome at all the other *paradores* I've visited; but in fairness, this *parador* receives a lot of walk-in traffic off the plaza, and it must be difficult at times to distinguish between actual guests and gawkers. The service I received there, while perfunctory, was accommodating and swift. Soon after I checked into my lovely room, overlooking one of the beautiful and peaceful courtyards, I discovered there was only one set of towels, and before I could even request another set for my husband, there was a knock at the door, and a maid was delivering a large pile of towels, washcloths, and a robe. The *hostal* actually has four beautiful courtyards, and it seems to me that it would be impossible to receive anything but a quiet room, unless one were facing the plaza, which can be quite noisy even though no motor vehicles are allowed into the plaza itself. (There are, however, a few parking spots for guests of the *parador* just in front of the main entrance; after you retrieve your bags and check in, an attendant moves your car to a secure, off-the-plaza parking space, and when you depart, he will bring your car around to the front again.) The dining room at this *parador* is especially impressive, and a meal here is memorable. So is a stay, and if you are considering a hotel splurge, this is it. (I use the word *splurge* somewhat exaggeratedly, as accommodations this nice in France or Italy, for example, would cost three or four times as much.)

~Restaurante El Asesino (plaza Universidad 16, Santiago de Compostela). I never have learned why this wonderful little place is named "The Assassin," but the restaurant's business card features a drawing of a chef chasing a chicken with a knife. Anyway, El Asesino was founded in 1873 and remains my favorite restaurant in Santiago. It's quite casual—although you may see large families file in dressed in finery—but the food is excellent, and if you sit in the front room, you have a view into the kitchen. For a lunchtime meal my husband and I once shared an enormous repast of *navajas, pulpo, merluza* with potatoes, peas, and red pepper, *pimientos de Padrón, queso y membrillo,* and a bottle of Pazo de Villarei Albariño, and the tab came to just over $40. The wine was the equivalent of only $10. While you can still find places like this—places that serve plentiful, seasonal, and well-prepared meals at good-value prices—in the countryside of France and Italy, for example, they are not as numerous as in Spain.

~O Beiro Vinoteca (rua Raina 3, Santiago de Compostela; 981.58.13.70; www.obeiro.com). This warm and inviting little place is both a wine shop, where visitors may taste before buying, and a small restaurant (upstairs), with a menu of local and regional cheeses, *chorizo,* ham, olives, and light food to accompany the wines and ports. This is a great place to visit if you are curious about Spanish wines and want to try some. The restaurant offers the largest selection of wines by the glass that I've encountered in Northern Spain, and all are reasonably priced. The staff in the shop is especially knowledgeable and friendly and can assist you in shipping bottles home.

~Café Jacobus (three locations in Santiago de Compostela). Jacobus is a coffee shop/bar chain, not the type of establishment I ordinarily prefer; but I went to all three of the locations in Santiago and *really* liked them. The quality and variety of coffees, breakfast breads and pastries, teas, hot chocolate, ice creams, beers, and wine are excellent, and the atmosphere is quite nice, too.

~A Tafona (Calle Preguntoiro 20, Santiago de Compostela). This small bakery makes a number of irresistible breads and cakes (including a delicious morning bun filled with cream) but also sells a few local specialties, such as jars of hazelnuts in honey, which I can confirm are outstanding over a bowl of vanilla ice cream.

~*Tarta de Santiago*, eaten just about anywhere in Santiago de Compostela. This incredibly yummy, moist almond cake—found in nearly every shop and restaurant in the city—is fabulous, and it doesn't spoil quickly: some shops sell the cake with an expiration date stamped on the box, which seems to be approximately three weeks from the day of purchase. I sampled the *tarta* often and really did not find one to be better than another. I also brought one home (I carefully packed it in my carry-on bag) and enjoyed it with friends, serving it with whipped cream on the side.

~The Spanish tourist office in Santiago de Compostela (Rúa de Vilar 43; 98.158.40.81). In addition to the fact that the staff are amazingly friendly, helpful, thorough (they dutifully speak to every-one who walks in and keep a record of where visitors are from and what brought them to Santiago), and multilingual (in rapid-fire suc-cession I listened to one representative speak to six visitors in as many languages), there are some truly attractive Santiago souvenirs to buy here, better than I saw in any shop. Santiago was honored with the title of European City of Culture in 2000 (a booklet of related activities—in English, Galician, and Spanish—is an impres-sive 135 pages; the staff may still have a few copies left it you'd like to see one), and there is a great line of corresponding celebratory stuff like cool pens; T-shirts, polo shirts, and sweatshirts in a range of sizes and colors; baseball caps; ashtrays and key chains; coffee mugs; bookmarks; pins, and more, all bearing the Santiago star emblem. There are also some good-quality color posters and some good books about the city and the cathedral. Truly, I've never been in a tourist office, anywhere, with items this irresistible.

~Pazo de Oca (just over the province line in Pontevedra, only 25 kilometers from Santiago). An eighteenth-century country estate,

Pazo de Oca is one of those attractions that receives no more than the requisite few lines in guidebooks. I'm not certain why, because it's one of the most beautiful, out-of-the-way villas I've ever visited; but I would include Pazo de Oca on a list of top five things to see in Galicia. I suppose it's not better known among foreigners because it *is* rather a detour, and the route is not exactly well marked once you exit off the main road—you are decidedly off the bus-coach tour when visiting Pazo de Oca. There is no printed material about the rambling estate, and you cannot visit the pretty stone villa itself, only the magnificent grounds. All I was able to learn about the property is that it once belonged to the duchess of Alba (whose portrait was painted by Goya) and that it still remains in the family. The helpful staff at the Santiago tourist office told me they did not have any information about the estate and that there are no books published about it; so I apologize for not being able to share more details with you, but it is perhaps enough for you to know that the drive to Pazo de Oca is definitely worth the journey. My husband and I did not see a single non-Spaniard when we were there, which only made it feel more like a well-kept secret. The grounds are astonishing and vast, with orchards, fountains, ponds, sweet-smelling vines and bushes, and enormous old trees. Unfortunately, picnicking is not allowed, so plan your visit accordingly. Check with the Santiago tourist office first about the hours the grounds can be visited, as no public telephone number is available.

~Pazo do Souto (15105 Sisamo, Carballo, La Coruña; 981.75.60.65; fax: 981.75.61.91; www.pazodosouto.com). This lovely property is a member of the *turismo rural* association of Galicia; I read about it in *Alistair Sawday's Special Places to Stay: Spain* (see the Accommodations entry in *Informaciones Prácticas*). Proprietor Carlos Taibo Pombo is a warm and friendly host, and his stone house and inn—dating from 1672—is beautiful and inviting. If I translated the history of the property correctly, it seems that as a young boy, Carlos used to come to this building when it was literally in ruins as it served as the village schoolhouse. Every day they worried that the roof might cave in. Carlos was bright and did well in his studies and emigrated to Switzerland. He worked hard, saved his money, and returned to the village to buy the ruins of Souto and converted it into his family home and an inn. Today he works in the flower-exporting business, and as you gaze out upon the countryside around the property, you'll discover why this part of Spain is especially conducive to cultivating flowers. As in most European country inns, there are no screens in the windows, but those plug-in devices that keep mosquitos away have been thoughtfully provided on the night tables. There is a large and comfy bar and restaurant downstairs with a huge fireplace and a television, and a good breakfast is offered as well as dinner. (The restaurant is well known and is quite good, and unless you are planning on driving into La Coruña or somewhere else for the evening, it's a good idea to have dinner at Souto, as it really is out in the country, with nothing else around.) Carlos and his family will organize local trips by horse, mountain bike, tandem bike *(bicicleta carrera)*, and four-wheeler, with a guide. They also have information about Acquavision Galicia, local boat trips. In a little room off of the reception area is a display of locally produced items, such as baskets, ceramics, and food products that are appealing and make wonderful gifts. There is also a large room upstairs with games, books, couches, and tables for relaxing, reading, and socializing. Pazo do Souto is not far from either Santiago or La Coruña and offers a peaceful opportunity to experience the Galician countryside. Highly recommended.

~La Coruña. The capital city of Galicia is quite overlooked by foreigners, but it shouldn't be, as it's an extremely pleasant place to spend a day (and part of the evening, too, for the *tapas* bar scene is just as lively here as elsewhere). The city's location, jutting out into the Atlantic, is beautiful, and its roots date back to the Celts and Romans. The Torre de Hercules (Tower of Hercules) is the world's only functioning Roman lighthouse and was built in the second century (and restored in the eighteenth). It was from here that the Spanish Armada set sail in 1588. My most lasting memories of La Coruña include its animated plaza, the Romanesque church of Santa María del Campo and its little *campo* in the *ciudad vieja,* and the enclosed glass galleries of the grand beautiful white houses along the Avenida de la Marina. (A glass gallery, by the way, is known as a *mirador,* the same word you'll see often in mountainous areas to designate a spot that offers a pretty vista or vantage point.)

~Casa do Arco (Calle Real 1, 15117 Laxe; 981.706.904; portozas@valem.com), Galicia. Casa do Arco is a small hotel, *mesón,* and restaurant, recommended by Carlos Pombo of Pazo do Souto (above), located in the pretty little seaside town of Laxe. The lunch my husband and I enjoyed here made us completely forget the rainy day outside. Jeff declared the *pulpo con cachelos* (octopus with spicy potatoes and pork) one of the best dishes he'd ever had, and the *parrillada de verdures* (thinly sliced and grilled endive, zucchini, eggplant, tomatoes, asparagus, and trumpet mushrooms sprinkled with big crystals of salt) were definitely the single best grilled vegetables I've ever encountered. (Nowadays I can barely stand to eat the cliché and ubiquitous grilled vegetables in the States, so inferior are they.) We shared the *arroz Costa da Morte,* a *dos raciones* dish of broccoli rape and shellfish, which was to die for. By the time we had finished, the sun had come out, which is often the way it is in Galicia.

~Isla A Toxa (La Toja, in Castilian), the Gran Hotel de La Toja, and the soaps, lotions, and colognes of the Manantiales de La Toja. Talk about a place where there are few North Americans! It's true that there are other corners of Northern Spain where you can really lose yourself and not hear a word of English, but to my mind, none of them are as beautiful and relaxing as La Toja. I suspect that part of the reason the island is so little visited by non-Spaniards is that it's just that much farther to reach, in the same way that Nassau, in the Bahamas, is visited by more vacationers than, say, Eleuthera or Harbour Island, because it's the end of the line—there are no more legs of the journey to endure. I do not mean to suggest that getting to La Toja is especially long or difficult; it's just that it *is* an island, and the pleasures of the mainland and the town of O Grove are often enough to keep visitors from wandering across the bridge over the Arosa estuary. The Gran Hotel de La Toja is one of Spain's grand old hotels, and even if time limits prevent you from staying a night there, the hotel's bar and restaurant are quite good and enjoyable. Adjacent to the hotel is a lovely garden and *malecón* (seaside walkway, like a boardwalk) to stroll around, and at the far end of the garden is a beautiful little chapel entirely covered with white scallop shells. You cannot ascertain from a distance that shells make up its exterior, but as when approaching an Impressionist painting, you slowly begin to see each shell's outline. Unfortunately, a few of the shells have not escaped some universal lovers' graffiti, but otherwise they are unmarred. The interior of the chapel is pretty, too, especially if it's a sunny day to illuminate the stained glass windows. Just across from the chapel is a small white, rather nondescript building that I at first thought was a snack bar, as there were so many people coming and going. I then realized it was a shop, selling the beauty products of the spa (dating from at least 1905) for which La Toja is famous. Penelope Casas, in *Discovering Spain,* expresses her fondness for the Magno soap produced here, which is actually black and made with the health-giving salts of the spa; it smells *wonderful,* the color notwithstanding. In addition to this great soap, there is a full line of related products for both men and women. I have become particularly fond of the *agua de colonia* and may have to soon write to the Gran Hotel to see if someone would be kind enough to arrange to send me some more! None of the items are very expensive (certainly they're less expensive than soaps and lotions in Provence, for example), and there are lots of items nicely packaged for gifts. The Gran Hotel La Toja is considered a luxury hotel, but it offers a number of special vacation packages that are a very good value. Both the six days/six nights and three days/three nights Vacaciones de Salud La Toja packages offer seven spa options for guests, including antistress, "*bebe* and Mama," sauna treatments, mineral baths, massage, and so on. The hotel is mentioned in most guidebooks, but usually only the telephone and fax numbers are given; view its website at www.latojagranhotel.com or contact the hotel at 36991 Isla de La Toja, Pontevedra; 986.73.00.25; fax: 986.73.00.26; info@latojagranhotel.com.

~*Pimientos de Padrón,* anywhere in Galicia. It's true that you never can tell how fiery a Padron pepper will be until you taste it, but I am addicted to them, no matter how strongly they may be searing the inside of my mouth. The truth is, the peppers are hardly ever that hot, and usually there are only a few in a batch that are. Calvin Trillin wrote a wonderful piece about *pimientos de Padrón* for *Gourmet* (November 1999) that I was unable to include in this book, in which he readily admits that he has a tendency to go on and on about these scrumptious peppers. "They are on a list I keep in my head of the victuals that, despite being my favorite dishes in one part of the world or another, rarely seem to be served outside their territory of origin—a list I sometimes refer to as the Register of Frustration and Deprivation." Trillin also notes that 30 percent of the *pimiento* crop is consumed in Galicia, while the entire remaining portion is distributed throughout Spain, which is why you'll never find these *pimientos* anywhere else. Further, since the peppers are harvested in Galicia only in the summertime, if you find them on a menu in Madrid, say, in January, they are not from

Padron but rather are from southern Spain or possibly North Africa. (Happily for those of you who may have missed this piece by Trillin, it will appear in an upcoming collection of his writings.)

~O Merlo and the city of Pontevedra. The restaurant O Merlo is recommended in *Discovering Spain* by Penelope Casas, and that was reason enough for my husband and I to drive there from Santiago for lunch. It was more than worth it: O Merlo is a wonderful little restaurant, and if you are standing at the bar, even for only a few minutes, it won't take long for you to notice the collection of more than ten thousand—really—key chains hung on every square inch of wood beam on the ceiling. But besides this identifying feature, the menu is outstanding, and O Merlo has been honored with an award in 1989 from La Sociedad Gastronómica Garbanzo de la Plata. (There is a framed letter testifying to this, and Casas was president at the time.) We thoroughly enjoyed *chipirones quisados* (stewed squid), *pimientos de Padrón* (our batch was fiery here), *gambas a la plancha,* and *pimientos del Bierzo con anchoas* (a platter of wonderfully flavorful red peppers marinated in olive oil and fresh anchovies, our favorite dish). It was obvious that the other customers were as pleased with their dishes as we were (all the tables were filled, by the way), and the service was courteous and efficient. After our meal we walked around the pedestrian zone of Pontevedra, where, as Casas notes in her book, the sun is nearly always shining.

~*Hórreos,* ubiquitous in Galicia and Asturias, but especially those in the coastal town of Combarro (near Pontevedra), which has been designated a national monument due to its unusually numerous constructions. *Hórreos*—which by now you know are stone granaries that are raised off the ground to keep rodents and rain out—can be ordinary or quite beautiful, and I have probably taken a ridiculous number of photos of them; the display of *hórreos* in Combarro really impressed me.

~The small, not-very-absorbent napkins at *tapas* bars, ubiquitous throughout Spain. I love these little napkins that bear the name of the bar (usually) or at least the phrase *Gracias por su Visita*. They're easy to collect if you're trying to keep a record of all the bars you frequent. What I probably will never become accustomed to is that one is supposed to crumple up the napkin and throw it on the floor after it is completely soiled. Typically, there is a metal bar running the length of the counter for visitors to rest a foot on for balance while standing up. The area between the bar and the counter is where these little napkins pile up, and as someone who would never litter and is very conscious about recycling, it is always hard, when I first arrive in Spain, to get the hang of this. But after a few days I am crumpling and tossing with the best of them, and oddly, there is something rather satisfying about the act, and anyway, when in Rome . . .

Asturias

~La Casona de Pío (Riofrio 3, Cudillero; 985.59.15.19). Another recommendation from Alistair Sawday's wonderful book, this little gem bills itself as *"un pequeño rincón del paraíso asturiano"* (a small corner of paradise in Asturias). *Gem* refers to the inn itself, its famous and outstanding restaurant, and to the town of Cudillero, which lies at the bottom of a beautiful winding road on the coast. The village of Cudillero is built around a port and climbs up the mountainside with green hills all around. Readers might be reminded of Italy's Cinque Terre villages, but Cudillero is about a thousand times less fashionable, less expensive, and less popular. La Casona de Pío is definitely the best place to stay in the village and is also one of the nicest places I've ever stayed in Spain. It's a simple inn, built of the local gray stone, and each room is tastefully decorated and comfortable. A meal at the restaurant is a must, even if you do not plan on staying the night. My husband and I had a lunch there that we consider among the top ten we've ever had. It began with *fabada con calamares* (the beans were so buttery and so big it could have been lunch all by itself), *pimientos rellenos con mariscos* (pimentos stuffed with shellfish), *sopa de mariscos, salad de Pío* (lettuce, tuna, tomatoes, beets, carrots, bean sprouts, black and green olives, onions, hard-boiled egg, and cheese), a bottle of Martín Códax Albariño, and *arroz con leche* with a crispy crust. When we entered the dining room—at what we felt was the right time, one forty-five—we were the only diners there apart from one other couple. But within an hour every table was taken, and it appeared that some customers were locals and others had driven a distance to eat there. After our siesta we hiked up the footpath to the top of the village, a fairly steep and strenuous walk, and the views were gorgeous. The front desk staff at the *casona* are very kind, and though not everyone speaks English, it is not hard to make yourself understood, and they can assist you with most anything. An assortment of historic photos of Cudillero hangs on the walls of the little lounge area, and there are some interesting books (in Spanish) to look at—I especially liked *Atlas Aereo de Asturias, Diccionario Histórico de Asturias,* and *Diccionario Geográfico de Asturias,* which is a huge book with photographs and text for each entry in the region. It doesn't take long to walk all around the village during the evening *paseo,* and you can stop in at the San Remo or half a dozen other places for a drink—but I should warn wine drinkers that the only good wine in town is at Casona de Pío and Mesón el Faro; stick to *sidra* or *orujo* everyplace else.

~Hiking around the Mirador del Fitu. On one side of the ridge the view is of green, green hills, cows, and typical Asturian stone houses. On the other, flat fields of crops eventually reach the blue sea.

~La Casona de Mestas (Mestas de Ponga, 33557 Mestas; 98.584.30.55; fax: 98.584.30.92). La Casona is a modernized hotel in an old stone building right in the heart of the Picos, about halfway between Cangas de Onís and San Juan de Beleno. The restaurant, with floor-to-ceiling glass windows on two sides, features *cocina asturiana,* and the hotel is famous for its thermal baths. There are fourteen rooms, each with private bath, and guests may partake in hiking, horseback riding, and biking nearby. La Casona is not a fancy place—it's furnished simply without much charm and is moderately priced; but it's quiet and in a tranquil setting and is one of the few places to stay deep in the Picos.

~Cangas de Onís. Cangas is one of the larger towns in this part of Asturias and is a nice place to come to shop in some of the small stores, eat and drink in the bars and restaurants, and walk by the medieval stone bridge (from which now hangs a huge cross) over the River Sella. Cangas was the first capital of reconquered Spain; carved on one of the pillars of the Capilla de Santa Cruz is a cross over a crescent moon, symbolizing the Christian victory over Islam.

~Desfiladero de los Beyos gorge, Picos de Europa. The *desfiladero* is a dramatic and beautiful drive that takes one from the Picos to the edge of Castilla y León or vice versa. According to the Cadogan guide, the six-kilometer route is "the narrowest motorable gorge in Europe."

~La Casona de Villanueva (33590 Villanueva de Colombres; 98.541.25.90; fax: 98.541.25.14). The description of La Casona in *Alastair Sawday's Special Places to Stay: Spain* captivated me right away, especially the phrase "a truly exceptional place to stay." My husband and I quite agree, and I would rearrange an itinerary any number of times for the opportunity to stay here. (That said, I was completely unable to rearrange my plans on my last visit to Northern Spain, which was planned for this book, and I remain disappointed, as I am longing to return there.) La Casona, an eighteenth-century stone farmhouse, is one of the loveliest inns I've ever visited. Every corner of the building, from the entrance hall to the dining and guest rooms, is beautifully decorated with antiques and artwork and fresh flowers. Though I loved our room, I equally enjoyed sitting outside in the enclosed garden—which overflows with roses, flowering vines, and fish ponds and is also home to a vegetable garden—in complete country silence. The La Casona brochure I have states there are eight rooms while the Sawday book quotes six; whatever the number, I advise you to secure a reservation in advance as there is no place as nice as this for miles around. (The double room with the sitting room is especially grand, though it costs a bit extra.) La Casona has been awarded a two-star rating but has enough charm and beauty for three. Breakfast is good and often includes homemade preserves; dinner, with produce from the garden and delicious wine, is available upon request. Villanueva is convenient to the Picos, though we stopped here on our way *out* of the mountains, ready for the pleasures of La Franca beach (about five minutes away), some fishing villages, and nearby Romanesque churches. Highly recommended.

~Tortilla, anywhere in Spain, but especially with a roasted green pepper on top, most often encountered in the north.

Cantabria

~El Capricho, Comillas. Another wild *modernista* work by Antoni Gaudí, El Capricho was designed and built for Antonio López, marquis of Comillas, whose son married the daughter of Joan Guell of Barcelona. (Readers who have visited that Catalan city will recognize the name from the Parc Guell.) The building is a fantasy mansion with a tower that seems to be a combination lighthouse/minaret. The building is constructed mostly of brick with a traditional ceramic tile roof, and from a distance you can just make out bands of green ceramic tiles running around the width. As you approach the building, however, you discover that these bands are glazed green and gold ceramic tiles featuring brilliant sunflowers. El Capricho really is something to see, and I can't get enough of those sunflowers! The building is no longer a private residence and is now a rather mediocre restaurant, I've read.

~Santillana del Mar. "The most beautiful village in Spain" is how Jean-Paul Sartre described this not-really-by-the-seaside little town. (The sea is nearby, in Suances, about 5 kilometers by car, but usually *del mar* attached to a name signifies that it really is "by the sea.") It's difficult to disagree with Sartre, as Santillana is truly beautiful; but there are a lot of beautiful villages in Spain, and I'm not certain I would put it at the top of the list. But it is absolutely worth visiting (though it can get very crowded when the tour buses arrive), and the Parador Gil Blas is a fabulous place to stay. What I love most about Santillana is its cobblestone street, *Calle de las Lindas,* made smooth after many years of feet, hooves, and wooden carts.

~The beach at Laredo. While it will never equal the superlative La Concha beach in San Sebastián, the long, wide beach in the town of Laredo is quite nice. The sand is soft and white, there is a nice boardwalk with benches and showers to rinse off your feet, and there are plenty of restaurants, cafés, and hotels nearby. The drive down the hill into Laredo—with beautiful, sweeping views over the sea—may be what I like best about this Cantabrian town, and I think the old town itself is really a great place to spend some time. True, other than the Iglesia de la Asunción cathedral there aren't a lot of cultural sites to see, but culture isn't usually why one visits a beach resort. True, also, that the development around the curve of the beach isn't attractive, but the beach itself sure is, and even in October there are plenty of sunny days when it's warm enough to don a bathing suit or at least shorts and a T-shirt.

Castilla y León

~The city of León. A corruption of the Roman *legio* (legion) and capital of Christian Spain in 914, León is one of the least-publicized cities in Spain, at least in English. It remains, however, a logical city to stop in while en route to Santiago, as well as a logical city from which to begin a tour of Northern Spain. (It's about a four-and-a-half-hour drive from Madrid.) My husband and I are really fond of León, as it's one of those not-too-big cities of historical significance with some unsung gems, similar to Avignon, Segovia, and Ravenna. León's three major sights are all related to the Camino and its pilgrims. The cathedral (La Pulchra Leonina—Belle of León) has 125 stained-glass windows and is home to the tomb of King Ordono II, who moved the capital of Christian Spain from Oviedo to León; the Hostal San Marcos was originally the pilgrims' hospice and is today one of the most magnificent *paradors* in the chain; and the Basilica de San Isidoro is the Romanesque church where the remains of San Isidoro were brought from Arab-occupied Seville and put in an urn, which was an attraction for the pilgrims. The brass scallop shells embedded in the stone walkways next to the fortified walls of the old quarter mark the route to Santiago. The basilica was built into the side of the city walls in 1063. Twenty-three kings and queens of Spain were once buried in the adjoining Panteón de los Reyes, which has been proclaimed the Sistine Chapel of Romanesque art and was the first building in Spain to be decorated with scenes from the New Testament; the tombs were destroyed by the French during the Peninsular War. The Casa de los Botines is an early building (1891) by Catalan architect Antoni Gaudí, in the Plaza de Santo Domingo. The *tapas* bar scene at night in the Barrio Humedo is an unsung gem. It is worth stopping at the *hostal* even if you do not plan to spend the night. My husband and I, when we were in León for our ten-year wedding anniversary, stupidly did not make a reservation at this *parador,* deciding instead to stay at a pleasant enough place—Hotel Paris—in the old quarter's pedestrian zone. It wasn't until the next morning, when we went to the *hostal* for breakfast, that we realized we'd made a mistake: the building is an outstanding architectural splendor, and the monastery portion is one of the best examples of the *plateresque* style in all of Spain. León is very much worth including on your itinerary.

~The city of Burgos, chosen as capital of the kingdom of Castilla y León in the eleventh century by Ferdinand I. Besides its justifiably famous Arch of Santa María, its cathedral (along with León and Toledo, Burgos boasts one of Spain's great Gothic cathedrals), the statue of El Cid, and its *plaza mayor*, what I love best about Burgos is its *paseo* along the Paseo del Espolón. Also, Burgos is reportedly the town in Spain where the most pure Castilian Spanish is spoken. I understood nearly every single word spoken to me in Burgos (not that I could answer, necessarily), and I haven't been enrolled in a Spanish language class since the twelfth grade. Truly, I found it remarkable, and if you have studied Spanish for even a short while, you will probably understand much more in Burgos than anywhere else in Spain.

The Basque Country

~Guggenheim Bilbao. Positively nothing you've seen in photographs or video clips can adequately prepare you for the Guggenheim's outpost in Bilbao—the museum is truly one of those monuments that exceed expectations. The sight of it from a distance *will* be instantly recognizable, of course, but as you approach the amazing structure and then when you are standing right in front of it, you will realize that all those photographs you've seen do not do it justice. The Guggenheim Bilbao is awesome, brilliantly conceived, and "an astonishing icon of the modern age," according to one of the museum's booklets. My advice to visitors (and this is never mentioned in all the glowing articles about the museum) is to engage the services of a guide. If you are already familiar with contemporary art, you will recognize and appreciate the individual styles of the artists in the Guggenheim Bilbao's collection (including Jenny Holzer, Jim Dine, Eduardo Chillida, Sol LeWitt, and Richard Serra); but if the work of contemporary artists leaves you perplexed and wondering what all the fuss is about, you will be glad to be accompanied by a knowledgeable guide. In addition to the museum's permanent collection and special exhibitions, the building itself is at least—if not more—interesting, and while walking around the exterior by yourself is rewarding, it is ten times more so when you are with someone who can fully explain the architectural elements, the unusual political and cultural partnership that enabled the project to move forward, and the ways in which the museum relates to the city of Bilbao. The museum offers free guided tours and audio guides and will also arrange private tours.

Alternatively, you may want to consider contacting Daniel Eguskiza, who is one of the great guides employed by the tour operator Archetours (see the entry for Tour Operators in *Informaciones Prácticas*). Daniel, who holds an advanced degree in modern art, enthuses about—and explains the theories of—the works of every artist. He is a big fan of the work of Frank Gehry and of his native city, and I would personally rearrange my trip to accommodate Daniel's schedule for the opportunity to meet him and share in his knowledge of the museum. (He also knows quite a bit about Bilbao's history and current cultural scene and could probably be persuaded to conduct an extended tour of the city itself.) Daniel may be reached by his cellular phone (60.781.69.57) or by writing to him at Hermano Benjamin 2-3 B, 48.950 Erandio, Spain.

An aside about the Guggenheim's three gift shops: I found an exceptionally nice selection of books and related items in them. In particular, I was most fond of the Guggenheim Bilbao spiral-bound notebooks in unusual shapes; museum pens, pencils, and erasers; T-shirts, tins of crayons, key chains, and little notepads bearing the adorable Jeff Koons *Puppy* logo for children; and a wide variety of books about the museum at every price range.

Browse the museum's website (www.guggenheim-bilbao.es/ingles) for more information.

~Librería Cámara (Euskalduna 6, 48008 Bilbao; 94.422.19.45; lib.camara@tsai.es). Not only is this the leading multilanguage bookstore in Bilbao, it's one of the best bookstores I've had the pleasure of visiting anywhere. There's a great selection of periodicals, too, in English, French, Italian, German, and Spanish. The store specializes in the categories of antiquity, architecture, film, decoration, photography, military history, music, travel, and Basque history. I discovered a wonderful series entitled Patrimonio Historico de Bizkaia, which is a set of small books—actually more like brochures—with individual sheets on every monument and historical site in the Basque region. Unfortunately, it is available only in Basque. I also found a series of hiking and topographical guides for the Pyrenees and other alpine areas in Northern Spain, published by Editorial Alpina. Each guide has a pull-out map at the back, and they are in Spanish. (Better than just Basque!) Also, I saw two great books in Spanish—*La Arquitectura del País Vasco* and *Las Casas Vascas*—filled with lots of black and white photographs that looked very interesting. Cámara is closed on Saturday afternoons after one-thirty.

~*Tapas* bars of the Casco Viejo, Bilbao. The *tapas* scene in the Casco Viejo is extremely lively and tons of fun. Like San Sebastián's Parte Vieja (see entry on page 584 for more details), this old quarter of the city is a pedestrian zone, so walking around from bar to bar is a pleasure. (It helps if one is staying in the quarter, because if you find yourself a bit tipsy after a while, you don't have far to go.) Some places I particularly like include Inma, Café Bar Bilbao (where I especially enjoyed green olives, anchovies, and green pepper on a toothpick), Los Fueros (where the specialty of the house is small *langoustines* rolled in sea salt and grilled—yum), Berton, and my favorite of them all—my second favorite in all of Spain—Casa Victor Montés (plaza Nueva 8). Montés is a cut above all the other *tapas* bars and also has a separate area, across from the gleaming bar, with tables for more serious eating. I would even say that if one had extremely limited time in Bilbao and could visit only *one tapas* bar (which would be a great shame), it should be Montés.

~Iturrienea Ostatua (Santa María Kalea 14, 48005 Bilbao; 944.161.500; fax: 944.158.929). This quirky little hotel is conveniently located in the Casco Viejo and is quite a charming place. After you push the buzzer at street level, you enter the building and have to climb a flight of stairs to the gardenlike lobby, where there is also a small breakfast nook. The staff is friendly, and everyone seems to speak English, and they are very helpful in assisting visitors with tips on Bilbao. The majority of the rooms—if not all of them—do not have windows to the outside, so it can seem a little claustrophobic. When I stayed here, it was an unexpected visit, and I was offered the only room available, which had a window that opened into an inner sitting room. I didn't mind (though my husband did), as I knew I was going to be so busy outside that I would probably only spend a total of six hours there. As the hotel was so full, I did not have the opportunity to see other rooms, but interested readers who desire windows should inquire if there are any rooms facing onto the street. For the charm, the moderate price, and the location, this is a great place, but note that it's quite popular, so plan accordingly.

~Guetaria (Colón de Larreategui 12, 48001 Bilbao; 94.423.25.27). Daniel, the Guggenheim Bilbao guide I mentioned above, took my husband and me to this wonderful restaurant known for its grilled fish and meats (and for a waiter who was honored as Bilbao's best in 2001). The restaurant is larger than it appears because it wraps around to the right, just past the large grill. This beautiful back room is quiet and rather elegant, but one does not need fancy dress to dine here—it's the sort of place where business colleagues might gather side by side with tourists from the museum, which is about a ten-minute walk away. Our waiter amply demonstrated his skill in helping us choose the best local specialties of the house, dessert included, as well as a bottle of *txakolí*. An excellent moderate to moderately expensive choice in downtown Bilbao.

~Museo Vasco (La Cruz 4, Bilbao). I'm a big fan of quality ethnographic museums, and this one, in the heart of the Casco Viejo, is among the best. The museum itself is actually built around a beautiful old Jesuit cloister and, somewhat confusingly, runs smack against the Cathedral de Santiago. (You'll find the cathedral before you find the museum, most likely.) It's unfortunate that the accompanying signage is almost all in Basque and that the staff (at least those I encountered) does not speak a word of English. I undoubtedly missed much, but ethnographic displays are fairly self-explanatory. Every aspect of Basque life is featured here: cheese-making, sheep-herding, typical clothing, ship-building, the Civil War, basketry, fishing, costumes worn at festivals, weaving, ceramics, emigration to America—it's all here, and the museum was blessedly free of crowds when I visited. (I'm told it is never very crowded.) I loved the old etchings of San Sebastián, and the wooden tools, sheep bells, and display of a typical street scene. Some books are available for sale downstairs by the receptionist desk, but nearly every single one is in Basque. There are also a few nice gift items fashioned after objects in the museum's collection or based upon traditional Basque items.

~The sacred oak tree of Guernica. When, on that fateful Monday, 26 April 1937, a weekly market day, the Nazis sent their Luftwaffe planes to bomb the little town of Guernica beyond all recognition, more than a thousand people were killed—but not the sacred oak tree. This is no ordinary tree, dear reader, even though it did eventually die about twenty years ago. A new oak sapling was planted right next to the original, which is good, I think, because that original tree is enormously significant, and you can't very well expect people to continue making pilgrimages to a dead stump forever. If you somehow missed the significance, ponder this excerpt from Robert Laxalt's excellent little book, *The Land of My Fathers:* "The prisons of Spain, and the graveyards, were, in 1961, filled with those Basques who refused to abandon either their language or their sacred *fueros*, the rights of man that Spanish monarchs for six centuries had promised to uphold. Even King Ferdinand V and Isabella after him had gone to the province of Viscaya in 1476 and paid homage—under the spreading branches of the Tree of Gernika— to Basque rights. The emotions that the Tree evokes from pilgrims are strong. For the Basques, the Tree of Gernika represents *order in life, strength, endurance, immoveability, dignity, loyalty to heritage, defiance to tyranny*—all the sources of inner renewal most vital to survival as an individual and as a race." Guernica itself might not be worthy of a detour if not for the tree.

~Vitoria-Gasteiz. Vitoria is the capital both of the Basque Autonomous Community and of the province of Álava and is another town often overlooked by visitors crossing the region. Its old quarter—*la parte vieja*—is gorgeous and is filled with beautiful medieval and Renaissance buildings. "A city of unexpected delights" is how the authors of the Cadogan guide describe Vitoria, with which I agree. It is better known, however, for its balanced development, pedestrian areas, parks (forty), and gardens (80,000 trees and bushes), and it boasts one of the highest standards of living in Europe.

~Every square foot of San Sebastián (Donostia in the Basque language), which Penelope Casas has described as "one of the most beautiful cities in the world." Among my favorite attributes of this lovely city are the Alderdi-Eder gardens, with their feathery tamarind trees; the La Concha beach; the big white lampposts along the La Concha waterfront promenade; the Kursaal Center for the Performing Arts; the Plaza de la Constitución (which once was a bullfighting ring, hence the numbers posted above the different balconies, which would have been rented out as boxes); the facade of Iglesia de Santa María; the grounds of the Palacio de Miramar; *Peine de los Vientos* (the *Windcomb Ensemble* sculpture by Eduardo Chillida); the Plaza de Guipúzcoa, with its pretty garden in the center and shopping arcades all around; the María Cristina bridge (which looks like it could belong in Paris); and walking, walking, walking . . . up the footpath around Monte Urgull, along the River Urumea, and with the *donostiarras* for the evening *paseo* along the La Concha and Ondarreta promenades.

~Museo de San Telmo (Plaza de Ignacio Zuloaga 1, 20003 San Sebastián; 943.42.49.70). In August of 1813, during the War of Independence (see entry below for Calle 31 de Agosto), the church of the convent of San Telmo was devastated and plundered: all its decorative elements—paintings, carvings, altarpieces—were stolen, leaving the walls completely empty. In 1929, when it was decided to restore the church and remake the building into a museum, the painter Ignacio Zuloaga suggested that the walls be painted with motifs commemorating significant historical events and activities of the Basque people. Catalan painter José María Sert was selected for this task. (In 1899 Sert had moved to Paris, where he met Misia Natanson, who was friendly with a number of prominent painters in Paris at that time and who would later become his wife; Sert is probably best known in the United States for his decorative work in Rockefeller Center in New York, completed in 1930.) Sert's eleven canvases here at San Telmo are among the most dramatic and unique I've ever seen, and they represent the full range of themes in the life and history of Guipúzcoa (one of the three administrative regions of the Basque Country), a nation of ironworkers, saints, merchants, sailors, fishermen, shipbuilders, freedom, wisdom, legends, and *fueros*. An additional canvas is the altar of the people, which covers the areas of the old church apse. While the Sert canvases are definitely the highlight of this museum, the other exhibits—which also document the history, traditional activities, deeds, and beliefs of the people of Guipúzkoa—are worth seeing, too; though the accompanying text is not in English.

~Leaning over the white filigree railing along the La Concha promenade in San Sebastián and watching the waves crash into the sea wall . . . and then walking over to the Parte Vieja for *tapas*!

~The *tapas* bars of the Parte Vieja, San Sebastián. Before I visited San Sebastián for the first time, I had read repeatedly that food was taken more seriously here than anywhere else in Spain, and that the *tapas* bars would literally take your breath away. It was an understatement. I have attempted to describe to friends, colleagues, and family members how amazing and outstanding the *tapas* bars of San Sebastián are, but I fail every time. After all, one friend asked, what's so great about a bar that serves food? Well, the answer is that the *tapas* are like nothing you've seen anywhere else in Spain. They glisten like jewels on the bar counters, delicately and carefully prepared, perfect creations that you almost can't bear to eat. They are moderately priced, and so is the beer and wine, so that two people can settle in at the counter and eat and drink famously and not spend more than $25 or $30. And this is the Parte Vieja, a pedestrian zone, where you can wander at will, going from place to fabulous place. The atmosphere is just so much fun, and the attention to detail is so impressive, that there are really few places I would rather be than at one of my favorite bars in San Sebastián: Bar Borda Berri (Calle Fermín Calbeton 12; 943.42.56.38), Bar Eibartarra (Calle Fermín Calbeton 24; 943.42.04.42), Beti-Jai (Calle Fermín Calbeton 22; 943.42.77.37; specializing in shellfish and seafood, but I've also had wonderful creations such as artichoke, white asparagus, and green olive on a toothpick, and if you want Spanish *jamón,* they'll slice it up special for you), and Casa Bartolo (Calle Fermín Calbeton 38; 943.42.17.43). The first time my husband I stopped into the Bartolo, there were twin brothers behind the bar. On my last visit the twins were nowhere in sight, but the *tapas* were still excellent. Don't, however, try moving the napkin container on the bar, or you will receive a rather nasty look from the fellow behind the bar, and he will pick it up and move it back to precisely where it was before you thoughtlessly moved it. On occasion, I have wandered away from the Parte Vieja for *tapas* and have especially enjoyed Iturrioz (San Martín 30; 943.428.316).

~Calle 31 de Agosto, San Sebastián. I am always intrigued by street names, as they signify much about a city's history. This particular street is in the Parte Vieja, which has been destroyed twelve times by fire since the thirteenth century. (Structures here were initially built of wood and only later of stone.) The last and most dramatic of these fires took place on August 31, 1813, during the War of Independence. San Sebastián was under siege by Napoleonic soldiers when it was attacked by Anglo-Portuguese allied troops. What was meant to be an act to liberate the city sadly turned into terrible pillaging and burning that razed the entire city to the ground, with the exception of two churches and a row of houses, a stretch that has been known since then as Calle 31 de Agosto.

~Hotel Niza (Zubieta 56, 20007 San Sebastián; 943.42.66.63; fax: 943.44.12.51; www.hotelniza.com). For a follow-up trip to San Sebastián, I wanted to stay in a different hotel than on my previous visit. The Niza was mentioned in only one guidebook I consulted, which I felt was either a good sign or a bad one. I decided to try it, especially since it was located directly on the La Concha promenade and thus couldn't possibly be a poor choice. It turned out that not only was I right, but this lovely hotel exceeded my hopes. I don't have any idea why it isn't featured in more guidebooks. The Niza— a three-star, moderate to moderately expensive hotel—is one of the nicest and most stylish places I've ever stayed, and I will happily book a room there on my next visit to San Sebastián. Its location, at the end of a row of hotels along the promenade, is perfect, as visitors may reach the promenade either by walking out the front door and turning right or heading out the back entrance of the hotel's bar/restaurant/coffee shop. The pretty lobby area is a comfortable place to relax, and the old-fashioned elevator is one of my favorite features of the hotel. (Remember to close the door completely or it won't function properly.) There are eighteen rooms *a la playa* (facing the beach), seventeen facing the *calle* (street), and six interior single rooms. I had a *playa* room with a most magnificent view, which I would suggest you request, though the *calle* rooms have beautiful enclosed glass balconies. (I believe these also keep street noise to a minimum.) From the Niza's location on La Concha, it's about a fifteen-to-twenty-minute leisurely walk to the Parte Vieja and a ten-minute stroll to Plaza de Guipúzkoa. Highly recommended.

~La Flor y Nata (Calle San Martín 48; 943.46.95.95), San Sebastián. This inviting little *pastelería* offers an outstanding assortment of morning pastries and lunchtime snacks, and table service is friendly and quick. There are also nicely packaged treats for gift giving.

~Museo Producto Artesanal del País Vasco (Santiago Auzoa s/n. 20750, Zumaia, Guipúzkoa; 943.86.25.12). I have actually never been to this museum, which features artisanal products of the Basque Country, but I picked up a brochure about it (in Basque, Spanish, and French) at the Museo Vasco in Bilbao, and it looked so intriguing I decided to mention it here as I have not read about it elsewhere. Zumaia is 52 kilometers from Bilbao, 78 from Vitoria, and 100 from Pamplona.

~The drive from San Sebastián to Pamplona. I compile a list of great drives, and this route is among my favorite in the world. It is just so beautiful that I could never forget it; it is blissfully free of carloads of tourists; and at the end of it, of course, you are in the pleasant town of Pamplona, and hopefully it isn't San Fermín, because otherwise you won't see much of it or learn why it is the Gateway of Spain (or, in the 730s, Gateway to France, as Abd al-Rahman used it in reverse until the North African Muslims—and their dream of Europe—were defeated at Poitiers).

Navarra and La Rioja

~*Monumento a los Fueros* (Plaza del Castillo), Pamplona. I suppose another visitor could look at this monument and think it nothing special; but I feel it is so symbolic of Navarra, and also of a unique feature in Spanish history, that it really *is* something special. The bronze statue is actually an allegory of Navarra, holding a copy of the Ley Foral (Fueros Law), and was built in 1893 when the powers that were in Madrid tried to rescind some of the *fueros*. The broken chains symbolize freedom, as they represent the chains taken from the Moorish king Miramolin's tent at the Battle of Las Navas de Tolosa in 1212. (The real chains, by the way, are kept in Roncesvalles, along with the emerald the king wore in his turban.) The chains are also featured on Navarra's coat of arms.

~The *Rutas del Vino de La Rioja* brochure published by the La Rioja tourist office. This great, four-language (Spanish, English, French, and German) fold-out map highlights three wine routes: the *ruta de la vina alegre* (route of the happy wine), *vina amable* (friendly wine), and *vina recia* (hearty wine) throughout La Rioja. Not every single winery in the region is featured on these routes, but those vintners producing *crianza* wines who wanted to be featured in this brochure are included. Also included is information about the excellent Estación Enológica y Museo del Vino in Haro, grape varieties unique to the region, the *vendimia* (annual grape harvest), a vintage chart, and production and aging notes differentiating between *crianza* (wines at least three years old that have been aged at least one year in oak casks), *reserva* (select wines that have been aged for a total of three years in the cask and in the bottle, of which at least one year was in the cask), and *gran reserva* (wines of the best vintages that have aged at least two years in the cask and three in the bottle). This is a great map companion to have before setting out on a driving tour. Inquire at the North American Spanish tourist offices about availability, or view the *gobierno de La Rioja* website: www.larioja.com/turismo.

~The village of Laguardia, La Rioja. Not to be confused with La Guardia on the coast of Galicia near the Portuguese border, Laguardia is a tiny medieval village surrounded by vineyards and low-lying hills. Technically, it belongs to the Álava province of the Basque Country, but it is also a part of the La Rioja wine-growing area of Spain. My husband and I hadn't planned on stopping here on our first visit to Northern Spain, and we hadn't even read about it, but it was recommended to us by Marcellino, our host at a small country farm named La Quintana in Asturias. Marcellino said it was his favorite village in La Rioja, and so without a hotel reservation, in the early fall, we made our way there, and we are so glad we did. Place it where you will, it doesn't really matter—to this day I dream about one of the very best meals I've ever had at Laguardia's most famous restaurant, Marixa (Sancho Abarca 8; 941.60.01.65). Without doubt the most delicious stuffed red pepper with cod is found here, and though one could certainly get carried away at Marixa and spend a lot of money, the restaurant is really moderately priced, and you can eat splendidly and not spend a king's ransom. As wonderful as Marixa is, it is the village of Laguardia itself that is memorable. When we visited, there was some sort of music festival going on in the main plaza. (I'm sorry to say the tourist office was closed the entire time we were there, and so I never found out exactly what was going on, and no one we met spoke English.) But the little festival was wonderful, with different people of all ages playing a wide variety of classical instruments, and the villagers clapping enthusiastically after each performance. Every generation was out on the plaza that evening—babies, toddlers, teenagers, parents, and grandparents—and almost everyone was drinking wine. I thought to myself that the whole scene, so warm, wholesome, and community-oriented, would never happen in the States, simply because people were drinking wine. We have a lot to learn from our European friends about quality of life, and Laguardia is a good place to start.

~The cathedral and *parador* of Santo Domingo de la Calzada, La Rioja. The walled village of Santo Domingo de la Calzada, just a few miles from Haro, grew up along the pilgrimage route to Santiago de Compostela. The story goes that a young man, who was born in 1019 as Viloria de Rioja, attempted to heed the call of his vocation by applying for admission to two local monasteries, but for whatever reason he was denied. Seeing that the pilgrims en route to Santiago were in great need of basic amenities in the area, he took it upon himself to build a road (25 kilometers long), a bridge (with twenty-five spans), and a hospice (that offered lodgings as well as medical care for the pilgrims and is now the *parador*). The town took the name of its founder, Saint Dominic of the Road, after his death. Visitors to Santo Domingo will read of the amusing (and possibly apocryphal) story known as the miracle of the cock and hen. (There is a version in every guidebook as well as on pages 423–24 of this book, and though each is slightly different, they all explain the famous line *Santo Domingo de la Calzada, que canto la gallina después de asada*), but what I will say is that there really is a *gallinero* inside the cathedral, which is just adjacent to the *parador*. Inside it are a live cock and hen, who are sometimes asleep and sometimes very much not, and I don't care if the story is or isn't true: I love that there is a cathedral in Spain that is also home to a chicken coop—"the most superb hen-coop on earth," according to H. V. Morton. (Both the cock and hen are always white, by the way, and are donated and changed every month.) The *parador* is one of my favorites in all of Spain: the great room opposite the reception desk is absolutely stunning, with great Gothic stone arches and pillars, and the staff is particularly welcoming and helpful. There is another sitting room, past the dining room, with lots of big comfy chairs and couches. The small bar, which also serves light dishes and *tapas,* is just to the right of the main entrance and is a lively place to enjoy a drink in the afternoon or evening, when locals often arrive to meet friends.

~El Rincón de Emilio (P. Bonifacio Gil 7, 26250 Santo Domingo de la Calzada, La Rioja; 941.34.09.90). My husband and I enjoyed yet another amazing meal here at El Rincón, a restaurant mentioned in most of the guidebooks. I find myself desperate for adjectives to describe this meal—every meal, really—in Northern Spain: I am simply running out of superlatives, and my Roget's Thesaurus is no longer helpful. The chef at this unassuming place, representing La Rioja, was a finalist in the sixth annual Spanish Cooking Championships. We came for lunch one chilly wet day and were quickly warmed with *sopa de casa* (which was onion) and a bottle of Viña Real. A *menestra verdura,* lamb leg with salad, stuffed *pimientos* with seafood, and *arroz con leche* followed, all of which may not sound particularly extraordinary, but it was. And once again, when we arrived, we joined three other tables of diners; when we left, the place was full, reminding me, as if I needed to be, that *se come bien* (one eats well) in Spain.

~The wine town of Haro, La Rioja. I am immensely fond of Haro, wine capital of La Rioja (and just a few minutes' drive from the wonderful *parador* in Santo Domingo de la Calzada). Though not as pretty as nearby Briones—often referred to as a perfectly preserved Renaissance town—Haro feels more like a serious wine town, and nothing beats walking around the *herradura* (horseshoe), a loop in the old quarter around the Plaza de la Paz. All the taverns and wine shops are clustered here, and you can spend many happy hours walking from place to place, sampling wine and *tapas* and perhaps arranging to have some wine shipped home. I like all the bars in Haro and do not have a favorite; but a *vinoteca* and shop I particularly like that seems to really stand out is Isabel Gutierrez Ortíz (plaza de la Paz 5; 941.30.30.17; seleccionvinos@wanadoo.es). Not only are there hundreds of individual bottles of wine but all kinds of boxed assortments that are great for gifts or as a treat for yourself. (Some of them are designed to be taken on the plane.) The *vinoteca* part of the store allows visitors to taste a wide variety of red and white Riojas. The wonderful selection of peaches, peppers, onions, asparagus, sauces, and condiments packed in glass jars is irresistible; they can also be packaged with wine—and some of the shop's beautiful wine accessories—to create a unique *recuerdo* (souvenir) of La Rioja.

Madrid

~Museo del Prado. The Prado's permanent collection is outstanding, and though it's quite large and extensive, it's quite a bit less intimidating than the Louvre, for example, so that visitors who allot at least two hours there will see a large majority of the works. I am especially fond of the still life paintings of fruits, vegetables, cheeses, and Spanish pottery by Luis Egidio Meléndez; the large historical paintings—such as *Defensa de Cadiz*—in the circular dome at the north entrance by Felix Castelo; the vast range of works by Goya; the large canvases by Velásquez; and the large and magnificent collection of Italian paintings of the Renaissance (including works by Fra Angelico, Mantegna, Botticelli, Rafael, Correggio, Parmigianino (notably *Sagrada Familia con angeles*), Bellini, Tintoretto, and Titian (especially *Ofrenda a Venus, La bacanal de los Andrios,* and his portraits of Carlos V and Philip II). The museum's cafeteria provides a nice opportunity to sit down and relax with a *café cortado* or something more substantial (but remember, the difference between the smoking and nonsmoking sections is negligible), and the various book and gift shops, which are somewhat tucked away periodically throughout the museum, offer some unique items that are great for gift-giving as well as good-quality postcards and a number of museum publications in English.

~Museo Thyssen-Bornemisza (Paseo del Prado 8). Though this remarkably thorough collection represents nearly every period of art (everything from thirteenth-century Italian primitives to twentieth-century modern pieces), it is especially renowned for its avant-garde works, of which Madrid really did not have much until the museum opened in 1992. The enormous collection—more than nine hundred paintings, sculptures, and tapestries—is owned by Baron Hans Heinrich Thyssen-Bornemisza, whose fifth wife, Carmen Cervera, known as Tita, is Spanish. (Technically the baron still owns the works, as they were "on loan" to Madrid for ten years, and as I write this, the official transfer and purchase have not yet been confirmed.) Aside from Queen Elizabeth II's, the baron owns what may well be the greatest private holding of art in the world. The collection had previously been housed at the baron's Villa Favorita on Lake Lugano in Switzerland, and its move to Madrid has allowed the works to be displayed in a much larger and more appropriate space, and many more people now have the opportunity to see them. A few of my favorites among the more modern works are the canvases *Metropolis* by George Grosz and *La calle Saint-Honoré después del mediodía* by Camille Pissarro. There is also one of the finest Canalettos I've ever seen, *Vista de la Plaza San Marcos en Venecia.*

~After the Parte Vieja section of San Sebastián, the *tapas* bar scene in Madrid is my favorite in Spain, and in fact, if someone forced me to select one *tapas* bar that is my absolute favorite, I would say La Trucha (Nuñez de Arce 6) near plaza de Santa Ana in

Madrid. (My second favorite is Victor Montés in Bilbao). I don't want to repeat all the great places recommended in Catharine Reynolds's article, but I do want to say something additional about a few of them as well as mention a few others. Los Gabrieles (Calle Echegaray 17; 94.429.62.61) is certainly one of the most beautiful bars I've ever visited, and I would never miss stopping in there on a visit to Madrid. The various rooms guarantee that visits never become routine, and there are occasionally *martes flamencos* (Tuesday night flamenco performances). La Casa del Abuelo (Victoria 12; 94.522.59.15) pours a red house wine that is shockingly sweet, almost as sweet as Manischewitz. This was, and remains, a surprise to me, and the proprietor is prouder than proud to serve it—bottles bear the bar's name, so I believe it is made especially for him. The first time I tried it, I thought that perhaps I was judging the combination of the shrimp (which are delicious) and the sweet red wine too harshly, that perhaps it was a favorite flavor combination of *madrileños;* but on repeated visits I have concluded that I don't like it at all. However, it is a must-try combo, and the glasses are small, thankfully.

~Antigua Casa Talavera (Isabel La Católica 2; 91.547.34.17). I first read of this *"primera casa en cerámica Española"* in *Discovering Spain* by Penelope Casas, but since then I'm happy to say that it has been recommended in a number of guidebooks and articles. And it deserves to be. If, like me, you are a nut for ceramic pottery, you will not find a better store in all of Spain—in fact, the kind and sweet couple who run the shop offer pieces from almost every corner of the country—and you will surely feel you are in *paraíso* when you see the selection. Pottery from Northern Spain is largely absent from this shop, so if you are attracted to the styles you see in the north, you should definitely purchase them there; but for just about everything else, you will find an ample selection of complete dinner plate sets, candle holders, tiles, large platters, bowls of all sizes, small dishes for olives, nuts, and condiments, pitchers, and rare and antique pieces. There is one catch: the owners do not accept credit cards, so come prepared with cash. (The first time I visited, I didn't know about the cash-only policy, but it was agreed that I would return the next day with cash in hand, and they kindly held my purchases until my return.) On my second visit I happened to visit the store when two American visitors from San Francisco were there, and it turned out that none of us had quite enough cash to pay for our purchases. We all walked down toward the Gran Via to a bank's cash machine, but I still could not extract enough money to pay for everything. When we returned, all of our purchases had been prepared for airplane carry-on transport, and when I explained that I still did not have enough money to pay for everything, they called the bank, and I was permitted to pay the balance on a credit card. (You should note, however, that this was an exception, and while I'm sure it has been offered before and since, you should not count on it.) The owners also do not arrange shipping, but they do put interested visitors in touch with a company they have been recommending for years, Belmar Shipping (Flor Alta 2, just behind Gran Via 54; 91.521.68.91). Belmar may be a good company for you to know about in any event, as it handles international packing and shipping for parcels, baggage, merchandise, and furniture by sea, air, and train. It also offers insurance and can inform you of export regulations and conditions. As I have mentioned previously, if you see some items at Antigua Casa Talavera that you feel you must have, do not assume they will be there forever—buy them. The pattern I started collecting on my first visit was practically unavailable when I returned two years later, and I had to go forward with a mix-and-match selection, which was fine, but still . . . The shop is on a side street off the Gran Via and is easily reached by the plaza Santo Domingo metro stop. The store closes at about one-thirty on Saturday and is closed on Sunday.

~Restaurante El Sena (Isabel La Católica 11, 91.547.10.37). There I was, just up the street at Antigua Casa Talavera, finalizing my purchases on a Saturday afternoon just before closing. My husband, who has an unusually perfect sense of direction, arrived at the front door, having found his way by memory of a visit two years prior. (He remembered neither the street nor the name of the shop.) At two o'clock we were hungry, and the owners directed us to this wonderful restaurant a few doors away on the opposite side of the street. It is the kind of place that positively no tourists frequent, unless they heard about it the same way we did. For the equivalent of about $25, we ate like royalty and thoroughly enjoyed the "usual" dishes of *ensalada mixta, menestra de verduras, pollo asado con patatas,* and *paella valenciana.* We were made to feel like family, and so were the other diners. I'm still not sure why the restaurant is named after the Seine in Paris, but there was no French accent—spoken or in the food—here, just typical Spanish care and execution.

~Hotel Arosa (calle de la Salud 21; 91.532.16.00; fax: 91.531.31.27). The three most famous hotel addresses in Madrid are the Ritz, the Wellington, and the Palace, and while they are indeed grand (and expensive) with much to recommend them, certainly a few other addresses represent a better value. One of them is the Arosa, which I had read about in several hotel guidebooks. The hotel, actually a four-star Best Western property, is definitely not a mediocre choice. Occupying the upper floors above the outstanding bookstore, Casa del Libro, on the Gran Vía, the Arosa is bright and airy and furnished in a modern, minimal style. Rooms are rather large, and the hotel's location is excellent—*cerca de todo* (close to everything, as noted on the hotel's stationery), within walking distance of many of Madrid's worthiest museums and monuments. In addition to the usual perks of direct-dial telephones, hair dryers, minibar, national and international television channels, radio, and laundry (except Saturday and Sunday), the Arosa offers sight-seeing services, a florist, fax and telegram services, a hair stylist, meeting rooms, computer connections, mobile phone and car rental, airport shuttle service, and the ability to view the current status of your bill on the hotel information screen on the TV set. The newfangled key cards, besides opening room doors, also turn the lights on and off, which can be annoying, so make sure that you request two cards if you are sharing a double room (or one of you will be in the dark). There is, importantly, a parking garage. (Drivers have to make a sort of loop to arrive at the hotel's entrance on calle de la Salud, a one-way street; you pass the Casa del Libro and the hotel on your right as you're making your way along the Gran Via; turn right onto the next street that isn't one-way in the wrong direction, and then turn right again onto calle de la Salud; the hotel entrance is on your left side. The staff will handle parking your car.) If you're looking for number 21 as you're driving along the Gran Via, keep an eye out for the hotel's peach-colored facade above the Casa del Libro's dark green window awnings. The Arosa's staff is very helpful and friendly, and the second-floor bar and restaurant—which shares the floor with reception—is a nice place to eat, drink, meet friends, or read and relax. The airport shuttle operates from about six-fifteen A.M. to six-fifteen P.M., once every hour at a quarter past the hour, and the trip takes about twenty-five to forty-five minutes, depending on traffic. The Arosa is an excellent Madrid hotel choice, and I'm looking forward to my next stay there.

~Hotel Carlos V (Maestro Victoria 5, 28013; 91.531.4100; fax: 91.531.3761). The Carlos V is another Best Western property, this one a three-star classically decorated place on a pedestrian walkway just a few minutes' walk from the Puerta del Sol. The Carlos V is in an ideal location, perhaps even better than the Arosa's. The fact that I am recommending two Best Western properties in the same city may seem rather odd, but the truth is that both of these hotels are great, have a fair amount of character, are a cut above a lot of other places in the same category, and are in locations that can't be beat. (Also, I knew in advance that the Carlos V was a Best Western hotel, but I did not know the Arosa was until I arrived.) The Carlos V is recommended in a number of guidebooks and is popular among North Americans, but I didn't find this so noticeable except in the coffee shop/restaurant, at breakfast time. (I usually take breakfast outside of my hotel anyway, but I was determined to do so here, because whenever I walked by the lounge in the morning, it seemed as if I were in an American hotel.) There are more than sixty rooms at the Carlos V (which was fully renovated in 1996), and they are all inviting and carpeted; some have small terraces—you might want to request one of them when reserving. Besides its convenient location, there is public parking next door to the hotel and a shuttle service to and from the airport. Highly recommended.

~The Goya frescoes of Ermita de San Antonio de la Florida (Glorieta San Antonio de la Florida 5 or Paseo de la Florida; 91.542.07.22). I would not recommend a visit to San Antonio de la Florida to every visitor to Madrid with limited time, but I would definitely alert Goya fans to this wonderful little gem. The fresco on the dome of the church is my favorite work of art in Madrid and is among my top favorites in the world. I first read of it in an article entitled "What's Doing in Madrid" that Penelope Casas wrote for the travel section of *The New York Times*. She raved about the frescoes, and since then I have seen it mentioned in some (though not all) guidebooks. The church was built during the reign of Carlos IV, and the present structure stands on the site of two previous ones. (The church takes its name from the pastureland of la Florida, on which the first original church was built.) The church was declared a national monument in 1905, and one of the oldest traditions in Madrid—the festivities honoring Saint Anthony in this neighborhood along the Manzanares River—has long taken place here; since

1929 they have been held every June 13. In just four months Goya painted the cupola with an immense fresco depicting a diverse crowd of eighteenth-century onlookers staring in amazement at a man miraculously rising from his grave. This man had been murdered and is now bearing witness to the innocence of Saint Anthony's father, who was unjustly charged with the crime. It is extremely difficult for me to describe how unique this fresco is; Goya painted a railing around the dome (that viewers at first think is real), and standing on the floor looking up into the center of the dome is a surreal and beautiful experience. Art critics consider the fresco to be among Goya's finest works, and Goya's tomb is housed in the chapel here. (His remains were brought from Bordeaux, where he died in exile in 1828.) The Ermita is not in the city center but is within walking distance (about ten minutes) from the Jardines del Palacio Reál and the Estación del Norte (Príncipe Pio). *Esencial* for Goya enthusiasts, even at the exclusion of visiting the Prado. The Ermita is open from about ten to two and four to eight Tuesday through Friday (closed on Monday), and from ten to two on Saturday and Sunday.

~Aldeasa (airport shops in Barcelona, Bilbao, Jerez, Madrid, Santiago, Seville, and Valencia). An airport shop is hardly the sort of place I would recommend, as "duty free" is not generally a concept that excites me, and I don't generally enjoy buying souvenirs at airports. But not all airport stores are like the different shops that make up Aldeasa. In the Madrid Barajas Airport there are several outposts of Aldeasa, and one in particular offers a range of unique and interesting items from a number of Spanish museums. Another shop offers a nice assortment of Spanish food specialties—such as olives in jars and in vacuum-packed pouches, *turrón,* saffron in little glass jars, nuts, chocolates, *pimentón*—all great for gift-giving. So if you only just found the rhythm of Spain at the end of your trip and are about to leave for home empty-handed, make a concerted effort to arrive at the airport early enough to browse Aldeasa.

~The Spanish Table: Food, Wine and Tableware in the Traditions of Iberia (1427 Western Avenue, Seattle, Washington, 98101; 206-682-2827; fax: -2814; 109 North Guadalupe Street, Santa Fe, NM 87501; 505-986-0243; 1814 San Pablo Avenue, Berkeley, California, 94702; 510-548-1383; fax: -1370; www.tablespan.com). If you return home and realize that you so regret not buying those Spanish culinary objects of your desire, worry not: The Spanish Table will probably have what you wished you purchased. If you are passionate about Spain or simply love Spanish food and wine, you need to know about The Spanish Table. Though I have not (yet) had the pleasure of visiting either the Seattle or the Berkeley store, this wonderful Spanish food emporium is precisely the type of "immersion" shop I love, offering an exhausting range of foodstuffs, cookware, cookbooks, maps and guidebooks, music from Spain, Portugal, and former Spanish colonies, and Spanish and Portuguese wine. A list of items unique to Northern Spain include Galician wood *pulpo* platters, Albariño wines, Asturian *sidra* and *fabada*, Navarran white asparagus, a variety of Basque Idiazábal cheese, red and green *piquillo* peppers, Galician-English and Basque-English dictionaries, a *queimada* bowl, and a compact disk featuring a vocalist from San Sebastián. The Spanish Table also carries an extensive selection of *cazuelas* (clay pots with and without lids) and *ollas podridas* (clay pots traditionally used for cooking beans). Though these pots are not associated exclusively with the cuisine of the north, they are wonderfully versatile and adapt well to other types of cuisine, too. (A *cazuela,* by the way, can also be used as a festive drinking vessel! My friend Louise D. once hosted a *cazuela* party. She and her housemates mixed up a huge batch of potent brew, and guests were requested to bring their own *cazuela* from which to drink this alcoholic melange. Not everyone knew exactly what a *cazuela* was—word went around that it was a type of bowl—and among the containers brought were stainless steel mixing bowls, plastic beach pails with matching shovels, European beer steins, saucepans, and gravy boats, so you can imagine how quickly the party became festive.) While some of these specialty items may be found in North America's other grand food shops, The Spanish Table is devoted exclusively to Spain and the Iberian peninsula, and it approaches the Spanish culinary arts in the same way a travel bookshop approaches travel, with a wider view of related disciplines. A number of great recipes are included with the Spanish Table's catalog—I've particularly enjoyed the Marinated Manchego, and the *Piquillo*-Romesco and Artichoke Heart and Manchego Cheese spreads. I can't resist ordering items for myself, but gift certificates are also available for Spain enthusiasts.

Biblioteca

Fiction and Poetry

Bernard Atxaga
> *Obabakoak,* translated by Margaret Jull Costa, Pantheon, 1992. This novel won Spain's National Prize for Literature and is one of only several hundred books, in four centuries, to be written in Basque. The title translates as "The People and Things of Obaba [a Basque village]."
> *Two Brothers,* translated by Margaret Jull Costa, The Harvill Press, London; distributed in the United States by Farrar, Straus & Giroux, 2002.

Pío Baroja
Ernest Hemingway, after being awarded the Nobel Prize in 1956, visited Baroja when he was literally on his deathbed and told him the prize rightfully belonged to him. Unfortunately for those of us who do not read Spanish, the vast majority of Baroja's works have not been translated. This title, however, is widely considered to be one of his best—it was originally published in 1909 and is set in the Basque Country: *Zalacaín the Adventurer: The History of the Good Fortune and Wanderings of Martín Zalacaín of Urbia* (Lost Coast Press, 1997).

Rosalía de Castro

Rosalía de Castro (1837–1885) is Galicia's most famous poet and writer, and fortunately a number of her works have been translated into English (see titles below). I'm told that her tomb, near Santiago, is still a much-visited shrine (I have not been myself), and as John Crow notes in his book *Spain: The Root and the Flower,* Castro praised her native Galicia in a prologue to one of her books: "Lakes, cascades, torrents, flowering *vegas,* valleys, mountains, skies sometimes blue and serene as those of Italy, melancholy and clouded horizons, although always beautiful like those of Switzerland; tranquil and serene streams and shores, tempestuous capes that terrify and amaze by their gigantic and dull fury . . . immense seas . . . what more shall I say? There is no pen that can enumerate so many charms. The earth is covered in all seasons of the year with green grasses, herbs and flowers; the mountains are clad with pine trees, with oaks and with *salgueiros;* the gentle winds touch them lightly the fountains and torrents gush forth to crystalline spray summer and winter, now through the smiling field, now in the deep and shadowy glens . . . Galicia is always a garden where sweet aromas, freshness and poetry are inhaled with every breath of air."

Between the Maternal Aegis and the Abyss: Woman as Symbol in the Poetry of Rosalía de Castro, Michelle Geoffrion-Vinci, Fairleigh Dickinson University Press, 2002.

Daughter of the Sea, Rosalía de Castro, translated by Kathleen N. March, Peter Lang Publishing, 1995.

Poems (Women Writers in Translation series), State University of New York, 1991. Rosalía de Castro is included in this anthology.

The Poetics of Rosalía de Castro's Negra Sombra, Joanna Courteau, Edwin Mellen Press, 1995. This is volume twenty-three in the Hispanic Literature series.

The Radical Insufficiency of Human Life: The Poetry of Rosalie de Castro and J. A. Silva, Aileen Dever, McFarland & Co., 2000. This unique book is the first comparison of the poetry of Castro and José Asunción Silva, a Colombian poet as equally unappreciated in his lifetime (1865–1896) as Castro. Author Dever uses the ideas of three twentieth-century Spanish thinkers—José Ortega y Gasset, Xavier Zubiri, and Pedro Lan Entralgo—and applies the concept of radical insufficiency as a method of comparing the poets' work. I was, and remain, completely unfamiliar with Silva, I'm sorry to say, but this appears to me to be a truly interesting book that I plan to delve into at a later date. The poets did not know each other and most likely did not even know of the other's existence, yet their works share remarkably similar characteristics.

Rosalía de Castro and the Galician Revival, Shelly Stevens, Tamesis Books, 1987.

Miguel de Cervantes

Don Quixote, several editions available, in both hardcover and paperback.

Ernest Hemingway

For Whom the Bell Tolls, Scribner, 1940, 1995. Scribner has recently issued beautiful hardback editions of a number of Hemingway's other works, including *For Whom the Bell Tolls, The Sun Also Rises,* and *Death in the Afternoon* (nonfiction).

Federico García Lorca

Though Lorca (1898–1936) did not hail from the north, his work reveals so much about the Spanish character in general that any one of his books would make fine companion reading.

Collected Poems: A Bilingual Edition, Farrar, Straus & Giroux, 2002.
Three Plays: Blood Wedding, Yerma, and the House of Bernarda Alba, Noonday Press, 1993.

Joanna Trollope

A Spanish Lover, Random House, 1993. One of my favorite passages from this novel is related in a conversation between Frances, the main character, from London, and Luis, her new lover: "'In the thirties, when my father was a young man, Spain was a symbol, for the whole world, of divided beliefs. You were right to call our Civil War fearful, of course it was, it was about hope and despair. You English now have no good word to say for Franco, to you he is a fascist monster. To me he was indeed a despot, and I believe that tyranny is a second-rate ideology, but he was not a monster. After the fall of France, Frances, in the last World War, when I was a child and you were not yet born, he refused to ally himself with Hitler. He saved Spain from the Nazis and he would not let them close the Mediterranean, so the rest of Europe owes something to him for that at least. Of course, this is a terrible place, but it is not evil in its terror, it is tragic.' Frances looked at him. 'Why are you telling me all this? Why did you bring me here and lecture me like this?' He took both her hands. He leaned toward her, and his eyes shone as they had shone at her across the café table in Granada. "Because you must understand, Frances, about Spain, about the Spanish. I have shown you charming things, pretty things, ancient things, curious things. You have been in my hotel, and its garden, you have seen a little of Granada, you have smiled at some of the people who work for me, but that is not enough. It isn't enough to see the sunshine, it isn't even enough to see the magnificence, you have to see too how melancholy Spain is, how stubborn, and proud and full of violent conflicts of opinion. You have to *understand.*'"

Miguel de Unamuno

Unamuno (1864–1936) was recognized in his lifetime as one of Europe's most influential and outstanding writers and is still held in high regard today. He was Basque and was once described by *The New York Times* as "the incarnation of his country, one whose consciousness was a Spanish consciousness, made in Spain." In addition to writing novels, Unamuno was known also as a philosopher, poet, dramatist, existentialist, and political thinker.

Niebla, Lectorum, 1999.

San Manuel Bueno, Martir, Elliot's Books, 1998.

Three Exemplary Novels, translated by Angel Flores, Grove Press, 1987. This book is not as well known as *Tragic Sense of Life* (below) but is considered to be Unamuno's finest literary achievement. The stories—each a tragedy—include "Two Mothers," "The Marquis of Lumbria," and "Nothing Less Than a Man."

Tragic Sense of Life, translated by J. Crawford Flitch, Dover, 1990; Peter Smith, 1954. This is Unamuno's most famous work.

General Art and Architecture Reference

Angels A to Z: A Who's Who of the Heavenly Host, Matthew Bunson, Crown, 1996. This is *not* just another angel book. It's a fascinating and useful reference you'll be glad to have. From *abaddon* to *zutu'el* and with numerous black and white reproductions of major and minor artworks, this is really a great resource for looking at art. In his foreword Bunson gives several reasons for the popularity of angels and says "Finally, and perhaps most important, throughout history one thought has proven powerfully constant and nearly universally accepted by Jewish writers, Christian saints, Muslim scholars, and followers of the New Age: The angel is one of the most beautiful expressions of the concern of God for all of his creations, an idea beautifully expressed by Tobias Palmer in *An Angel in My House:* 'The very presence of an angel is a communication. Even when an angel crosses our path in silence, God has said to us, "I am here. I am present in your life."'"

The Artist in His Studio, Alexander Liberman, Random House, 1988. This hard-to-categorize book is a splendid record of Liberman's visits to a number of artists—thirty-one of them, nearly all of whom were French or worked in France—in the 1940s after the war. Liberman felt compelled to personally meet these artists and take photos in their studios because he feared that if he didn't, the remarkable flowering of painting and sculpture that the first half of the twentieth century had witnessed would leave no trace. No doubt he was also moved to do so by World War II's annihilation and destruction. Though the majority of the artists featured are French, Spaniards included are Picasso, Miró, and Dali. A unique and special book, filled with color and black and white photographs and the text of Liberman's conversations with each artist.

Churches, Judith Dupre, introduction by Mario Botta, HarperCollins, 2001. Though this brilliantly conceived book features churches all over the world, the chapter entitled "The Early Christian Church" includes the cathedral in Santiago. The cover of *Churches* is actually two folding panels that you open as if you were opening the doors to a church and they invited you to step inside. Dupre is also the author of two other favorite books of mine, *Skyscrapers* and *Bridges* (both published by Black Dog & Leventhal), but this one may be her most impressive project to date. (I hope more are in the works!) Note that this is not a "Christian" work; it's for anyone who's interested in architecture, art, travel, photography, or religion.

From Abacus to Zeus: A Handbook of Art History, James Smith Pierce, Prentice-Hall, 1977. Pierce has keyed the A–Z entries in this useful guide to the second edition of H. W. Janson's *History of Art*, which I mention only to illustrate that this is an extremely thorough and indispensable reference. Entries are presented A–Z within five chapters: "Art Terms, Processes, and Principles"; "Gods, Heroes, and Monsters"; "Christian Subjects"; "Saints and Their Attributes"; and "Christian Signs and Symbols."

Greatest Works of Art of Western Civilization, Thomas Hoving, Artisan, 1997. Hoving, former director of the Metropolitan Museum of Art, has here selected works of art "that had bowled me over visually and emotionally, the ones that after years I could describe down to the tiniest details, as if standing in front of them. These are the ones that changed my life, the ones I believe to be the pinnacles of quality, elegance, strength, the best mankind has created, the hallmarks of unalloyed genius." Among Hoving's eclectic selections are four works by Spaniards (*The Third of May, 1808* by Goya, *The Persistence of Memory* by Dalí, *Les Demoiselles d'Avignon* by Picasso, and *Las Meninas* by Velázquez) and two that hang in Spanish museums (*The Garden of Delights* by Bosch—in the Prado—and *The Burial of Count Orgaz* by El Greco, in the Church of Santo Tomé in Toledo). Hoving also describes Velázquez as "not only a genius but perhaps one of the top five who ever lived—but he was also one of the most accomplished curators and connoisseurs in history. Many of the finest Italian paintings in the Prado were acquired by Velázquez in 1649 and 1650 on a trip to Italy, where the Spanish king Philip IV sent him to buy art for the royal collection. He almost didn't return, or at least that's what Philip began to think after Velázquez kept delaying his homecoming." The order in which the works appear in this book are "a fantasy order," not alphabetically by artist, precisely the way Hoving would prefer to see them again, "shock after beautiful shock."

History of Art, H. W. Janson, Anthony F. Janson, 6th rev. ed., Harry N. Abrams, 2001. Still enormous (and now slipcased), still a classic, and still a fixture on college and university campuses.

The Illustrated Age of Fable: The Classic Retelling of Greek and Roman Myths Accompanied by the World's Greatest Paintings, Thomas Bulfinch, foreword by Erika Langmuir OBE, Stewart, Tabori & Chang, 1998. Someone was really thinking when he or she came up with this brilliant idea for a book. Three paintings featured are in the Prado's collection (*Venus and Adonis* by Titian, *The Colossus* by Goya, and *The Crossing of the Styx* by Joachim Patenier) and two from the Museo Thyssen-Bornemisza (*The Death of Hyacinth* by Giambattista Tiepolo and *The Argonauts Leaving Colchis* by Ercole de'Roberti). This is an essential book to have. As Bulfinch noted in his original book, first published in 1855, "our book is not for the learned, nor for the theologian, nor for the philosopher, but for the reader of English literature, of either sex, who wishes to comprehend the allusions so frequently made by public speakers, lecturers, essayists, and poets, and those which occur in polite conversation." Bulfinch was aware, as Langmuir notes in her foreword, that many less privileged men and women felt excluded from what he called "cultivated society." Langmuir adds, "His book was designed as much to remove a social barrier as to inform and delight."

The Oxford Companion to Christian Art and Architecture: The Key to Western Art's Most Potent Symbolism, Peter and Linda Murray, Oxford University Press, 1998. A thorough reference guide with color plates; general background to the Old and New Testaments and Christian beliefs; a glossary of architectural terms; and a detailed bibliography.

The Story of Art, E. H. Gombrich, 16th ed., Phaidon Press Limited, London, sixteenth edition, 1995. Although Sir Ernst Gombrich has authored numerous volumes on art, this is the one that established his reputation. To quote from the jacket, "*The Story of Art* is one of the most famous and popular books on art ever published. For 45 years it has remained unrivalled as an introduction to the whole subject." Though a comprehensive book, Spanish artists and those who worked in Spain are well represented.

The Panorama of the Renaissance, Margaret Aston, Thames and Hudson and Harry Abrams, 1996. I was late in learning about this book, having only discovered it by chance while combing the shelves at Hacker Art Books in New York (see Bookstores in *Información Practical* for contact information). But better late than never: this is the book on the Renaissance I'd always wished someone to do. Aston has had the ingenious idea of presenting the entire epoch of the Renaissance with more than a thousand illustrations spanning the whole of Europe. Thus we see what is happening in Belgium, for example, at the same time as in Spain and Italy, and in all areas: art, science, exploration, war, personalities, religion, daily life, fashion, architecture, eroticism, royalty, music, women, great cities, banking and business, and philosophy. The reference section at the back includes a biographical dictionary, timelines of Renaissance history and culture, a map, a glossary, and a gazetteer of museums and galleries with collections of Renaissance art. Spain and its personalities and rulers are included, as well as artworks from the Prado. This sixty-three-page section alone is worth the price of the book. *Esencial*.

Paper Museum: Writings About Paintings, Mostly, Andrew Graham-Dixon, Alfred A. Knopf, 1996; originally published in Great Britain by HarperCollins, 1996. Graham-Dixon, at the time his book was published, was art critic for *The Independent* in London (he may still be); thus, as he notes, "nearly all the pieces in this book were written between nine o'clock in the morning and six o'clock in the evening, on Mondays." Though the vast majority of the sixty-one essays do not focus on Spanish artists, a few do feature Velázquez, Goya, Miró, Picabia, and Picasso. A number of other books also gather previously published art essays, but this one is among my most favorite. Graham-Dixon has, according to the publisher's descriptive text on the jacket, "the rare and extraordinary power to make us feel as if we were present at the creation of great art, so that these paintings come alive in our mind's eye."

The Voices of Silence, André Malraux, translated by Stuart Gilbert, Doubleday, 1953. This wonderful book has long been among my favorite art volumes. Malraux's text, accompanied by a plethora of black and white photos, covers a diverse range of artworks, including the lady of Elche and El Greco, among other Spanish names. He opines that "one of the reasons why the artist's way of seeing differs so greatly from that of the ordinary man is that it has been conditioned, from the start, by the paintings and statues he has seen; by the world of art. It is a revealing fact that, when explaining how his vocation came to him, every great artist traces it back to the emotion he experienced at his contact with some specific work of art: a writer to the reading of a poem or a novel (or perhaps a visit to the theater); a musician to a concert he attended; a painter to a painting he once saw. Never do we hear of a man who, out of the blue so to speak, feels a compulsion to 'express' some scene or startling incident." Out of print but worth tracking down; I frequently see editions in used bookstores.

Who's Who in the Bible, Peter Calvocoressi, Penguin Books, 1987, 1999. This volume features more than 130 artworks—in both black and white and color— and is devoted exclusively to the people in the Bible. With biographies of more than 450 characters (some famous, others less so, others just ordinarily famous "whose names are familiar even when what they did is ill remembered," and the rest completely unfamous) from the Old and New Testaments and the Apocrypha, curious readers can find out the defining qualities of people from the Bible and learn how they have inspired artists, musicians, and literature through the ages. With six genealogical charts, six maps, and a glossary, this is an indispensable monastic companion (paperback, too, if you want to pack it).

Spanish Art and Architecture

Much of the architecture of Northern Spain is pre-Romanesque and Romanesque, and less is Gothic, so I am recommending a few good survey books that feature some of the better-known monuments in the north.

Journey into Romanesque: A Traveler's Guide to Romanesque Monuments in Europe, George Nebolsine, Putnam, 1969. An out-of-print but good book, by a past president of the American Romanesque Society. This one is unmatched by any other contemporary publication as Nebolsine also provides directions on how to reach all these monuments. (Granted they are less valuable now, but it's a great idea for a book.) With twenty maps and hundreds of photographs.

Romanesque Art in Europe, edited by Gustav Künstler, New York Graphic Society, Greenwich, CT, 1968. This beautiful out-of-print work is actually a compilation from six volumes published between 1955 and 1968 by Schroll Verlag of Vienna. It remains my favorite volume, and I urge readers who are fans of the Romanesque to search for a copy. The section devoted to Spain opens with the lines, "It is undeniable that Romanesque art is richest, most varied, and of the highest artistic quality in France. And yet there seems to be no end to the quantity and variety of Romanesque art in northern Spain; nowhere else is the impact of Islam on Christendom quite so apparent." The chapter continues with a map of the pilgrimage route to Santiago and features black-and-white photos of the Monasteriro de San Salvador, Iglesia del Santo Sepulcro, and Iglesia de San Román in Navarra; Colegiata de San Isidro in León; and the cathedral in Santiago.

The Romanesque: Towns, Cathedrals and Monasteries, Xavier Barral I Altet, Taschen, 1998. This edition in the wonderful Taschen World Architecture series is filled with color photos and good detail on southern and northern Romanesque monuments. (Buildings throughout Spain are included in the southern Romanesque section.) There are more than forty titles in Taschen's World Architecture series, and if you haven't discovered any of them yet, I encourage you to do so. Individual editions are published in seven categories: *The Ancient World, The Medieval World, The Pre-Columbian, Islamic Masterpieces, The Splendours of Asia, Stylistic Developments from 1400,* and *The Modern Age.* I'm especially fond of this series because the books are rather authoritative (but not overwhelmingly so) while still being very accessible for the interested but not scholarly reader. This Romanesque edition includes a good glossary of terms, and a number of monuments throughout Northern Spain are highlighted.

Spain: A History in Art, Bradley Smith, introductions by Manuel Fernández Álvarez and Marquis de Lozoya, Simon & Schuster, 1966. "Perhaps more than that of any other country, the art of Spain reflects the character of its people, as well as its history." And so this beautiful survey—a "visual-textual history of Spain"—begins, taking readers from the cave paintings of Altamira to the lady of Elche, the Segovia aqueduct, Romanesque art along the pilgrims' road to Santiago, Moorish architecture, the cathedrals of Mexico and South America, the monastery of El Escorial, the paintings of Goya, the architecture of Antoni Gaudí, the films of Luis Buñuel, the operas of Manuel de Falla, and the paintings of Juan Gris, Salvador Dalí, Joaquín Sorolla, and Pablo Picasso. If this book were published today, the color reproductions would be of finer quality; but this is a small quibble, as this is an excellent volume bound in a soft, red velvet cover. It is sadly out of print but very much worth a search.

The Story of Architecture, Patrick Nuttgens, Phaidon, 1983, 1997. Romanesque architecture is featured in one chapter, but I really like this book for the following passage: "Whether we are aware of it or not, architecture is part of everybody's personal history. The chances are that it is in a building that we are born, make love, and die; that we work and play and learn and teach and worship; that we think and make things; that we sell and buy, organize, negotiate affairs of state, try criminals, invent things, care for others. Most of us wake up in a building in the morning, go to another building or series of buildings to pass our day, and return to a building to sleep at night."

Single Artist Books and Museum Catalogs

The following definitive volumes (some are comprehensive catalogs that accompanied museum exhibitions) are worth a special effort to track down. Some of them are *catalogues raisonnés,* or they represent an artist's work in Northern Spain. Artists who are not from or did not work in the north are not included here, so readers will not find books about Picasso, Dalí, Gris, Sorolla, or Miró. I have, however, included Goya and Velázquez, as these two painters are so well represented in the collection of the Prado in Madrid.

Eduardo Chillida

Chillida, photography by David Finn, text by Giovanni Carandente, translated by Richard-Lewis Rees, Könemann, 1999; originally published by Ediciones Poligrafa, S.A., Barcelona; and *Chillida,* Peter Selz, James Sweeney, Harry N. Abrams, 1986. Chillida is the Basque region's most famous sculptor, and these are both beautifully produced volumes that showcase the full range of his work.

Chillida: 1948–1998, Museo Nacional Centro de Arte Reina Sofía and Aldesea, 2000. This book accompanied the exhibition of the same name in October 2000.

Frank Gehry

Frank Gehry: Architect, Jean-Louis Cohen, Guggenheim/Harry N. Abrams, 2001; and *Frank O. Gehry: The Complete Works,* Francesco Dal Co, Monacelli Press, 2001. While Gehry is not Spanish (he hails originally from Toronto), his name is now closely associated with the Guggenheim Bilbao, and both of these excellent surveys feature the architect's monumental museum there.

Francisco Goya

Francisco Goya y Lucientes, 1746–1828, Janis Tomlinson, Phaidon, 1994. Phaidon has long been among the premier art book publishers, and this volume on Goya is one of the most definitive.

Goya, Fred Licht, Abbeville, 2001. Licht is the author of several highly regarded books on Goya, including *Goya: The Origins of the Modern Temper in Art,* which was honored with the College Art Association's Charles Rufus Morey Book Award in 1983. He is also the curator of the Peggy Guggenheim Collection in Venice.

Diego Velázquez

Cambridge Companion to Velázquez, edited by Suzanne L. Stratton-Pruitt, Cambridge University Press, 2002. An excellent source, including much more historical information than most other books as well as a chapter on Velázquez contemporary Calderon de la Barca.

Diego Velázquez, Dieter Beaujean, Könemann, 2000. Like the Taschen paperback edition below, this is a good introductory survey (in paperback at an affordable price), including definitions of general art terms and a fairly thorough summary of the works of Velázquez.

Velázquez, Antonio Domínguez Ortiz, Alfonso Pérez Sánchez, Julián Gállejo, The Metropolitan Museum of Art, 1989. This is the catalog that accompanied an exhibit here and remains one of the leading publications on Velázquez. The book is extremely detailed and features thorough commentary on individual paintings, excellent historical, political, and cultural background, and loads of painting details.

Velázquez, Norbert Wolf, Taschen, 1999. This is a good-quality paperback edition, priced at about eleven dollars, for those interested in learning something about Velázquez but not so interested that they're willing to spend a lot on a serious, coffee table tome.

Velázquez: Painter of Painters, José López-Rey, Taschen, 1996. An authoritative volume with good detail of the works featured as well as historical background, style summaries, biographical information, and analysis of technique.

Jardines (Gardens)

The Garden Lover's Guide to Spain & Portugal, Barbara Segall, Princeton Architectural Press, 1999. This slender and handsomely packaged paperback is an edition in the Garden Lover's series. Each edition is filled with color photographs and is written by a noted garden expert. Segall, the author of this guide, is a renowned horticulturist and garden writer. She presents a historical survey of Iberia's gardens and highlights more than one hundred of the most beautiful. Gardens in Northern Spain that are featured include Misión Botánica de Lourizán, Pazo de Mariñán, Pazo de Oca, Parque Quiñones de León, Pazo de Santa Cruz de Rivadulla, Hostal de los Reyes Católicos, Pazo and Monasterio de San Lorenzo de Trasouto, Pazo de Soutomaior (all in Galicia); La Finca Puente San Miguel (Cantabria); and Parque Natural del Señorío de Bértiz (Basque Country). Thorough practical details for visiting gardens that are open to the public are provided, as well as maps. I have perused this and a few other editions (Italy and France in particular) in the series with great success, and I've found each to be useful and at the same time a nice memory book of some of the most pleasant places on earth. *Esencial.*

Design and Decorating

Spanish Style, Suzanne Slesin, Stafford Cliff, and Daniel Rozensztroch, photographs by Gilles de Chabaneix, foreword by Paloma Picasso, special essay contributed by Manuel Canovas, Clarkson Potter, 1990. This edition was the eighth to be published in the highly acclaimed Style Library. (Others include *French Style, Japanese Style,* and *Greek Style.*) Though Northern Spain is not featured at all (the authors seem to have focused on every part of the country—including the Balearic Islands—except Northern Spain, La Rioja, and most of Castilla y León), it's still a great resource for the architectural, design, and decorating details that are uniquely Spanish. More than seven hundred beautiful photos illustrate a variety of images of Spain and interiors of private homes and palaces, both traditional and modern. An eight-page *catalogo* at the back features a list of festivals and traditions and glossaries for Spanish architecture and design and food and drink. Of the books in this category, this is the best.

I have been unable to find a book exclusively devoted to the shops and markets of Spain, but *The Fearless Shopper: How to Get the Best Deals on the Planet* (Kathy Borrus, Travelers' Tales, San Francisco, 2000) is an excellent resource, and Spain is covered in the western Europe chapter. (The only places singled out are Madrid, Toledo, Barcelona, Seville, and the Balearic Islands.) Borrus is a former assistant director, merchandise manager, and buyer for the Smithsonian Institution Museum shops. She has a knack for recognizing a good value and offers great advice in the chapters entitled "Bargaining 101" and "Advanced Bargaining," which may not be especially useful for Northern Spain, where bargaining is less prevalent than elsewhere, but is still worth reading. Shipping items home and online shopping are addressed. Borrus also provides a size and comparison chart and a nineteen-page list of resources and references. This book is not just for travelers. My favorite chapter might be "Fair Trade," in which she quotes someone as saying, "When you buy a product, you're endorsing a way of doing business." *Esencial*.

Anthologies, Journals, and Other Good Things

Dobles, Avid Press, New Paltz, NY. *Dobles* (doubles) is a card and dice game from the Basque region of Spain; this is one of several editions in the Classic Pub Games series, a brilliant and fun line of games packaged in small boxes about the size of index cards—perfect for travelers. The creators note that the games in this series are from their favorite watering holes on four different continents. "We are proud to present them to our friends here at home, and have forced ourselves to consume a lot of memorable local brews in the fulfillment of this endeavor." The description of *dobles* begins with, "it's a rare, stormy winter night in San Sebastián, Spain, and the *tasca* (tavern) is crowded. The patrons are lively and the local vino is rich and heady. Excited cries of '*dobles*' fill the air." I admit I've never seen anyone in San Sebastián playing *dobles,* but perhaps I just don't frequent the right bars . . . no matter: this is a great little game, good for playing on countertops of bars, on long train or bus rides, at the airport while waiting to board, or in your home during cocktail hour.

Mediterraneo (On the Backroads) is a line of truly unique and beautiful desk calendars, notecards, and postcards that evoke aspects and images of the Mediterranean that I've never seen elsewhere. "Products that capture a sense of place" is the company's motto, and I absolutely *love* these goods. If you are passionate about the Mediterranean (I presume you are or you wouldn't be reading this book), I think you will, too. In addition to the pan-Mediterraneo line, there are individual lines featuring Tuscany and Provence as well as gorgeous travel documentaries and a compact disk entitled *Mosaic,* featuring solo guitarist Cole McBride. (McBride's music combines classical, Spanish, and original compositions; he absorbed the music of Asia, Africa, and the Middle East and studied flamenco guitar in Seville.) The founders of Mediterraneo, Kate Ryan and James O'Mara, have traveled extensively around the Mediterranean, and I feel we are kindred spirits, even though we've never met (yet). Upcoming lines to look for will highlight Andalusia, Sicily, Capri, the Amalfi coast, Rome, and Venice. I hope the O'Mara and Ryan team never tire of sharing their views and sensibilities with us. I had a difficult time finding my Mediterraneo calendar in stores and had to order it by mail from Amazon.com. You may prefer to contact the company directly by viewing its website (www.onthebackroads.com) or phoning 800-711-3224 (or 604-925-8330 in Vancouver, British Columbia).

Seaside Interiors, Diane Dorrans Saeks, edited by Angelika Taschen, Taschen, 2000. None of these to-die-for interiors are in Northern Spain, but who cares? This entire book—one in the Interiors series—is gorgeous and particularly irresistible (Spain is represented by three magnificent properties on the Costa Brava, Ibiza, and Majorca).

Traveler's Journal (Peter Pauper Press), *Voyages* (Chronicle Books), *Souvenirs de Voyage: A Traveler's Keepsake Book* (Chronicle Books), and the *Lonely Planet Travel Journal* are my current favorite travel diaries. The first two are spiral-bound, which I like because the pages lie flat. The *Traveler's Journal* features five clear plastic sleeves at the back for ticket stubs, photos, receipts, and the like (a brilliant idea). *Voyages*—a bigger journal, measuring about 8½ by 11 inches—features a blue elastic band that wraps around the book from top to bottom (not quite as good as plastic sleeves, but the band does help to keep loose stuff inside). The very *best* part about the *Voyages* journal, however, is the large envelope at the very back, which allows one to put all sorts of important papers inside, *including* one's passport and credit cards. *Souvenirs de Voyage* is both an invitation to travelers to begin collecting their own travel mementos (and eventually begin making travel collages) as well as an actual journal, with both lined and blank pages and glassine envelopes throughout (the best part, and the single thing that sets this journal apart from others). I have found this diary inspiring and practical, though it is a bit feminine looking, so guys may pass on it. The *Lonely Planet Travel Journal* is entirely different by being rather sleek looking, with a black faux-leather cover measuring approximately 4 by 4 inches. Pages are lined on one side and blank on the reverse (a feature I particularly like), and at the back of the book is a ton of essentials: twelve pages of maps of the world, calendars for a range of years, address pages (useful for sending postcards), useful websites, clothing and footwear sizes, international dialing codes, metric/imperial conversions, a time zone conversion wheel (very nifty), and a pocket inside the back cover for all the loose ephemera one accumulates.

Additional Credits

Informaciones Prácticas: Marie Louise Graff, *Culture Shock! Spain*, Graphic Arts Center Publishing, Portland, Oregon, 2001.

Las Noticias Cotidianas–El Quiosco: Manuel Canovas in *Spanish Style* by Suzanne Slesin, Stafford Cliff, and Daniel Rozensztrock, Clarkson Potter/Publishers, 1990; Ernest Hemingway, *For Whom the Bell Tolls*, Scribner, 1940.

Galicia: James Michener, *Iberia: Spanish Travels and Reflections*, Random House, 1968. Gabriel García Márquez, "Watching the Rain in Galicia," in *Travelers' Tales: Spain,* edited by Lucy McCauley, Travelers' Tales Inc., 1995.

Asturias y Cantabria: H. V. Morton, *A Stranger in Spain*, Dodd, Mead & Co., 1955. Dana Facaros and Michael Pauls, *Cadogan Guide: Northern Spain*, Cadogan Books, London, 2001.

El País Vasco: Mark Kurlansky, *The Basque History of the World*, Walker & Company, 1999.

Navarra y La Rioja: John Crow, *Spain: The Root and the Flower*, Harper & Row, 1963. *Fodor's UpClose: Spain*, Fodor's Travel Publications, 2001.

¡Buen Provecho!: Penelope Casas, *¡Delicioso! The Regional Cooking of Spain*, Alfred A. Knopf, 1996. Beth Nelson, *Postcards from the Basque Country: A Journey of Enchantment and Imagination*, Stewart, Tabori & Chang, 1999.

Mis Favoritos: Dana Facaros and Michael Pauls, *Cadogan Guide: Northern Spain*, Cadogan Books, London, 2001.

Barrie Kerper takes you through the culture, history, and landscapes of some of the world's most popular travel destinations in these other books from her **Collected Traveler** series.

Paris
0-609-80444-8
$16.00 paper
(Canada: $24.00)

Morocco
0-609-80859-1
$16.00 paper
(Canada: $24.00)

Provence
0-609-80678-5
$16.00 paper
(Canada: $24.00)

Central Italy
0-609-80443-X
$16.00 paper
(Canada: $24.00)

Venice
0-609-80858-3
$17.00 paper
(Canada: $26.00)